Lecture Notes in Computer Science

Advances

T0230248

Lecture Notes in Computer Science 796

Edited by G. Goos and J. Hartmanis

Advisory Board: W. Brauer D. Gries J. Stoer

Wolfgang Gentzsch · Uwe Harms (Eds.)

High-Performance Computing and Networking

International Conference and Exhibition
Munich, Germany, April 18-21, 1994
Proceedings
Volume I: Applications

Springer-Verlag
Berlin Heidelberg New York
London Paris Tokyo
Hong Kong Barcelona
Budapest

Wolfgang Gentzsch   Uwe Harms (Eds.)

High-Performance Computing and Networking

International Conference and Exhibition
Munich, Germany, April 18-20, 1994
Proceedings
Volume I: Applications

Springer-Verlag

Berlin Heidelberg New York
London Paris Tokyo
Hong Kong Barcelona
Budapest

Series Editors

Gerhard Goos
Universität Karlsruhe
Postfach 69 80
Vincenz-Priessnitz-Straße 1
D-76131 Karlsruhe, Germany

Juris Hartmanis
Cornell University
Department of Computer Science
4130 Upson Hall
Ithaca, NY 14853, USA

Volume Editors

Wolfgang Gentzsch
FH Regensburg and GENIAS Software GmbH
Erzgebirgstraße 2, D-93073 Neutraubling, Germany

Uwe Harms
Harms Supercomputing Consulting
Bunsenstraße 5, D-81735 München, Germany

CR Subject Classification (1991): C.2-4, D, F.2, G.1, H.2, J.1-2, J.6, K.6

ISBN 3-540-57980-X Springer-Verlag Berlin Heidelberg New York
ISBN 0-387-57980-X Springer-Verlag New York Berlin Heidelberg

© Springer-Verlag Berlin Heidelberg 1994
Printed in Germany

Typesetting: Camera-ready by author
SPIN: 10132095   45/3140-543210 - Printed on acid-free paper

Preface

High-Performance Computing and Networking (HPCN) is driven by several initiatives in Europe, the United States, and Japan. In Europe several groups, the Rubbia Advisory Committee, the European Industry Initiative, the Teraflops Initiative, and others encouraged the Commission of the European Communities (CEC) to start an HPCN programme. They recognized the economic, scientific, and social importance of the HPCN technology for Europe.

Members of these groups started the first HPCN conference last year in Amsterdam. The other player in this field was Supercomputing Europe, an annual exhibition and conference, that was founded by Royal Dutch Fairs in 1989.

Due to the personal engagement of Bob Hertzberger, University Amsterdam, Dorte Olesen, University Copenhagen, Peter Linnenbank, Royal Dutch Fairs, and others, we succeeded in combining important European HPCN activities to organize the HPCN Europe 1994 in Munich.

The HPCN Foundation is responsible for the Conference and the Technology Demonstrators Display. The Exhibition and the Vendors Session is organized by Royal Dutch Fairs. The Organizing Committee's intention is that HPCN Europe becomes a sister of the well-known American supercomputer events.

This new start inspired many HPCN experts in Europe. More than 60 specialists decided to take an active role in the Advisory Board and in the Programme Committee, to look for interesting contributions in this field. They enthusiastically broadened the base for HPCN in Europe.

As a result of this activity, more than 220 contributions from all over the world have been submitted, and the Programme Committee selected 140 papers and 40 posters. Over 20 well-known experts from Europe and the United States have agreed to present an invited lecture, demonstrating the advantages of using high-performance computers in their industrial and research application fields, including the keynote speakers, Horst Forster, CEC, Geoffrey Fox, NPAC, and David Williams, CERN.

Many different application areas, such as engineering, environmental sciences, material sciences, computational chemistry, electrical CAD, high-energy physics, astrophysics, neural networks and parallel databases are covered in the conference. In the context of real applications, subjects like languages, programming environments, algorithms, compilers, data parallel structures, monitoring, debugging, and benchmarking of parallel systems are discussed as well.

This event would not have been possible without the broad and personal support and the invaluable suggestions and contributions of the members of the Programme Committee and the Advisory Board. In addition, we would like to thank the referees in the Programme Committee, who spared no effort in evaluating so many papers, in a very short time over Christmas.

Many thanks to our sponsors, the CEC and the Royal Dutch Fairs, for their financial support of HPCN Europe 1994; without this support it would have been impossible to start such a considerable initiative. Also, we highly appreciate the personal efforts of Monika Grobecker and Anschi Kögler, who managed the conference secretariat and prepared these proceedings, and Hans-Georg Paap, who decoded and uncompressed nearly 100 Mbytes of papers. Finally, we are pleased to thank the staff from Springer-Verlag for publishing these proceedings just in time.

March 1994   On behalf of the Advisory Board
                                              and the Programme Committee
                                              Wolfgang Gentzsch and Uwe Harms

Committees

Organizing Committee

Chairman: Wolfgang Gentzsch	FH Regensburg
Co-Chair: Bob Hertzberger	University Amsterdam
Co-Chair: Dorte Olesen	University Copenhagen
Local Organizer: Uwe Harms	Munich
Demo-Display: Ad Emmen	SARA Amsterdam
Exhibition: Peter Linnenbank	Royal Dutch Fairs Utrecht

Programme Committee

A. Bachem	University of Cologne
T. Bemmerl	RWTH Aachen
A. Bode	Technical University of Munich
H. Burkhart	University of Basel
E. Clementi	University of Strasbourg and CRS4
I. Duff	RAL-CERC Chilton and CERFACS
A. Emmen	SARA, European Watch
W. Gentzsch	FH Regensburg
U. Harms	Supercomputing Consulting Munich
J. Häuser	FH Braunschweig
B. Hertzberger	University of Amsterdam
A. Hey	University of Southampton
G. Hoffmann	ECMWF Reading
F. Hoßfeld	KFA Jülich Research Center
S. Jähnichen	GMD FIRST Berlin
W. Jalby	University of Versailles
E. Krause	RWTH Aachen
C. Lazou	HiPerCom-Consultants London
G. Meurant	CEA Villeneuve-St-Georges
J. Murphy	British Aerospace Bristol
D. Olesen	University of Copenhagen
R. Perrott	University of Belfast
A. Reuter	University of Stuttgart
D. Roose	KU Leuven
U. Trottenberg	GMD St. Augustin
C. Upstill	PAC Southampton
A. van der Steen	ACCU Utrecht
H. van der Vorst	University of Utrecht
J. Volkert	University of Linz
E. Zapata	University of Malaga

Advisory Board

Contents

6. Computational Chemistry

7. Material Sciences

8. Weather Simulations

9. Environmental Applications and Climate

12. Database Applications

Contents of Volume II

15. HPCN Computer Centers Aspects

16. Performance Evaluation and Benchmarking

17. Numerical Algorithms for Engineering

18. Domain Decomposition in Engineering

19. Parallel Programming Environments

20. Load Balancing and Performance Optimization

21. Monitoring, Debugging, and Fault Tolerance

22. Programming Languages in HPC

23. Compilers and Data Parallel Structures

24. Architectural Aspects

25. Late Papers

Information Processing and Opportunities for HPCC Use in Industry

Geoffrey Fox and Kim Mills
Northeast Parallel Architectures Center
Syracuse University
111 College Place, Syracuse, NY 13244-41000
gcf@npac.syr.edu   kim@npac.syr.edu

1 Introduction

The U.S. National HPCC effort, represented by a set of approximately fifty Grand Challenge problems, is largely focused on issues of scientific simulation [1]. In addition to advancing the mission of the federal agencies sponsoring this program, and the state of science in the field of physics, biology, and chemistry, and related fields such as atmospheric science, one can view the HPCC initiative as an effort to speed the process of technological innovation. Hardware systems are now relatively mature, and the HPCC program has successfully accelerated the development of new software technologies such as parallel compilers, scientific libraries, system software, and programming tools. HPCC has matured into a proven technology [2], but its success is mainly limited to applications in the research laboratory. Industry, and society more generally, have not yet adopted HPCC as a mainstream technology. Both technical and social obstacles limit industries' use of HPCC. The scientific community has focused on high performance levels, while industry places much more importance on reliability and ease of use. Perceived risk by industry executives of adopting "exotic" HPCC technologies, a general recommendation not to put "mission-critical" industry applications on HPCC systems, and pressure to maximize short term or end of the quarter earnings [3] are examples of the obstacles to HPCC application development in industry. In many industrial applications, the porting of many millions of lines of existing code from sequential to parallel platforms is an insurmountable difficulty.

We use the term industry applications of HPCC to represent broad application of these technologies in diverse sectors such as manufacturing and health care, as well as education, consumer, and entertainment markets, since it is industry that is most likely to deliver technologies in these areas.   Aside from issues such as performance vs. reliability, or ease of use, which are essential to the success of HPCC technologies in industry, there is a larger more pervasive issue holding back adoption of HPCC. We believe the most important opportunity for HPCC technologies lies in information processing and not simulation applications. This conclusion is based on our interaction with industry over the past three years which we summarize in the form of a survey and describe in section 3 below. The importance of information processing applications in industry is becoming a central issue in many national HPCC meetings such as the industry panel discussions at the Pittsburgh HPCC Workshop [4], the first conference on Commercial Applications of Parallel Processing Systems [3], the National Information Infrastructure workshops at Supercomputing '93 [5], and the industry/HPCC consortia meetings [6]. This issue is now clearly understood with the 1994 HPCC federal plan [24] emphasizing simulation in the so called Grand Challenge but Information intensive applications and the NII (National Information Infrastructure) in a new set of National Challenges.

For HPCC to deliver on its promise, it must be widely adopted and used in industry, and for this to happen, HPCC research and development must be more strongly integrated with the needs of industry. Over the past three years, the U.S. National HPCC effort has emphasized basic research or production of new knowledge, again largely in applications of scientific simulation. Policy experts point out that U.S. government stimulation of technical innovation has been most successful in space and defense, but is largely unsuccessful in civilian applications [7]. Research results alone are not useful to industry. Closely coordinated linkages are needed between a number of different groups which we believe must include: HPCC vendors; industry, government, and university research institutions; and potential HPCC technology consumers such as manufacturers, school districts, or software companies developing products for homes and small businesses. We do not elaborate on this process here but have designed InfoMall, our outreach program for delivering HPCC technologies to industry, in a set of steps to link researchers, vendors, small businesses, system integrators, and consumers [8,9].

This paper describes a classification of industry applications carried out over the past three years as part of our New York State funded industry outreach program [10]. We define four classes of applications based on types of information processing applications: information "production" or simulation; information analysis or data mining; information access and dissemination; and information integration or decision support.

We conclude that a core set of HPCC technologies---parallel architectures, software, and networks--- combined with wide range of enabling technologies from partial differential equation solvers and mesh generators, to video compression and parallel databases, will form the basis of the National Information Infrastructure of the future. While scientific simulation will continue to be essential, information dissemination and analysis applications will become the most important near term, and information integration applications will become the most important long term industry applications of HPCC technologies.

2 Trends in Information Technologies and Applications

Access to information, and the ability to organize and integrate information is playing an increasingly important role in education, business, world affairs, and society in general. This trend will result in applications such as global networks of 800 telephone numbers, instantaneous credit card verification systems, extremely large real-time databases, sophisticated scientific simulations in the classroom, decision support in the global economic war, early warning of political instabilities, and integration of Medicaid databases to streamline processes and uncover inefficiencies.

The success of the HPCC Grand Challenge program, which is focused almost entirely on scientific simulation, is built upon HPCC enabling technologies such as message passing libraries, high performance compilers, parallel operating systems, and numerical optimization software. Information processing applications will require development and integration of new HPCC enabling technologies such as parallel databases, high-speed networks, metacomputer integration software, multimedia support, and compression technology (Table 1).

Table 1: Core Enabling HPCC Technologies Information Analysis, Access, Integration

1. Parallel (Relational) Database e.g. Oracle 7.0
2. Object database
3. High Speed Networks
4. Multilevel Mass Storage
5. Integration Software ("glue")
6. Integration of Parallel and Distributed Computing
7. Multimedia Support
   Video Browsing
   Image Content
   Full Text Search
   Real time I/O (disk ---> network)
8. ATM Network Protocols and Management
9. Compression
10. Parallel Rendering
11. Linkage Analysis (between records of database)
12. Sorting (large databases)
13. Collaboration Services
    Multi user video conferencing
    Electronic whiteboards, etc.

Table 1: Core Enabling HPCC Technologies Information Analysis, Access, Integration (continued)

14. Security and Privacy
15. Usage and Charging Algorithms
16. Televirtuality
    The world as a metacomputer
    Naming
17. Human-Computer Interfaces
    Mosaic
18. Image Processing
    Terrain Rendering
    Kodak Photo-CD
19. Geographical Information Systems
    Spatial databases

Information based industries are rapidly expanding, growing two and a half times faster than the goods economy. Raw materials and labor now account for less than 25% of the cost of goods sold, while the cost of knowledge and information based services contributes to more than 50% of the costs of goods sold for *manufacturing* companies [11]. A competitive advantage will most certainly be captured by industries that can take advantage of HPCC technologies.

These trends in information, and observations about the role of information technologies in a range of applications prompted us to re-examine our initial industry survey of opportunities for HPCC in industry. This survey grouped industrial applications into 18 general areas, including for example computational fluid dynamics, electromagnetic simulation, particle transport problems, transaction processing, command and control and information processing, financial modeling, graphics, and flight simulation. For each application area, we defined example problems, and summarize the nature of parallelism inherent to the problem, and match this to appropriate machine architectures and software models [10]. Although a number of information processing applications were included, our initial survey strongly reflected the emphasis on simulation problems in the HPCC community, a trend which continues to the present day. In [10] we made the observation that information processing applications are the most important opportunity for HPCC application development in industry. We now define our industry survey of HPCC applications according to four types of information processing applications.

3 Classification of Industry Applications

We begin with a very broad definition of information, including both CNN Headline news, and insights gotten from new computational physics models. We define four classes of industry applications of HPCC based on information. These categories, listed in Table 2 HPCC Applications in Information Processing, include: information "production" or simulation; information analysis or "data mining"; information access and dissemination, and information integration. For each class, we outline example applications, and characterize the parallelism present in the problem and the natural hardware/software architectures for supporting the problem.

3.1 Information Production

Information "production" or simulation is currently the main focus of the national HPCC community. Computational fluid dynamics, structural analysis, and electromagnetic simulation are examples of simulation problems with relatively large federal research programs funded by U.S. agencies such as the National Aeronautics and Space Administration, and the Department of Energy. These applications have advanced the development of sophisticated parallel software technologies such as finite element, and finite difference partial differential equation solvers, and turbulence and mesh generators. A difficulty with this application, in terms of HPCC development in industry, is that many industries that use simulation technologies such as the aerospace industry, are in a period of contraction rather than growth. This makes transfer of new technology to industry extremely difficult. Simulation applications in industries experiencing growth, and therefore more amenable to funding new technological approaches, include mortgage pricing and stock option pricing in the financial industry, and systems simulations in defense (SIMNET), education (such as personal computer game SIMCITY), and multimedia/virtual reality in the entertainment industry.

3.2 Information Analysis

Information analysis or "data mining" concerns the extraction of information from typically very large databases. A well established example is the petroleum industry, where oil extraction is based on analysis of terabytes of seismic data. Newer examples include extracting patterns of fraud or inefficiencies in health care, securities, and credit card transaction records, or extracting customer preferences from purchase data. For these information analysis applications, the owners of the database often consider the data itself as their real resource, and are concerned with ways to maximize access to the database, structuring information in ways that create meaning, and developing strategies for fast response to unique customer requests or new products [12]. Market segmentation is an information analysis application aimed at tailoring traditional mass marketing approaches down to the level of the individual, producing "mass customization" for products ranging from banking services, news media, and retail consumer products.

Table 2.1: HPCC Industrial Applications: Simulation or Information Production

Item	Application Area and Examples	Problem Comments	Problem Architecture	Machine and Software
1	Computational Fluid Dynamics	PDE, FEM Turbulence Mesh Generation	Loosely Synchronous Adaptive Mesh is Asynchronous	SIMD, MIMD for irregular, adaptive HPF(+) Unclear for adaptive irregular mesh
2	Structural Dynamics	PDE, FEM Dominated by Vendor Codes (e.g. NASTRAN)	Loosely Synchronous mesh as in 1	MIMD as Complex geometry HPF(+)
3	•Electromagnetic Simulation •Antenna Design •Stealth Vehicles •Noise in high frequency circuits	PDE Moment method (matrix inversion) dominates	Synchronous	SIMD HPF
	•Mobile Phones	Later FEM, FD?	Loosely Synchronous	SIMD, MIMD, HPF(+)
4	Scheduling •Manufacturing •Transportation (Dairy delivery to military deployment) •University Classes •Airline Scheduling of crew, planes in static or dynamic (midwest snowstorm) cases	Expert systems and/or Neural Networks, Simulated Annealing Linear Programming (hard sparse matrix)	Asynchronous Synchronous Loosely Synchronous	MIMD (unclear speedup) Asyncsoft SIMD HPF MIMD
5	Environmental Modeling - Earth/Ocean/ Atmospheric Simulation	PDE, FD, FEM Sensitivity to data	Loosely Synchronous	SIMD, MIMD for irregular, adaptive HPF(+) Unclear for adaptive irregular mesh

PDE	Partial Differential Equation
FEM	Finite Element Method
FD	Finite Difference
ED	Event Driven Simulation
TS	Time Stepped Simulation
VR	Virtual Reality
HPF	High Performance Fortran [16]
HPF+	Natural Extensions of HPF [17]
MPF	Fortran plus message passing for loosely synchronous software
Asyncsoft	Parallel Software System for (particular) class of asynchronous problems
CFD	Computational Fluid Dynamics

Note on Language: HPF, MPF are illustrative for Fortran: one can use parallel C, C++ or any similar extensions of data parallel or message passing languages

Table 2.1: HPCC Industrial Applications: Simulation or Information Production (continued):

Item	Application Area and Examples	Problem Comments	Problem Architecture	Machine and Software
6	Environmental Modeling - Complex systems e.g. lead concentration in blood	Empirical models Monte Carlo and Histograms	Embarrassingly Parallel plus global reductions	Some SIMD MIMD more natural
7	Basic Chemistry •Chemical Potentials •Elemental Reaction Dynamics	Calculate Matrix elements ___ Matrix eigenvalue Multiplication, inversion	Embarrassingly Parallel ___ Synchronous	MIMD (maybe SIMD) HPF
8	Molecular Dynamics	Particle Dynamics with irregular cutoff forces Fast Multipole methods Mix of PDE and Particles in PIC	Loosely Synchronous	HPF(+) or MPF for fast multipole
9	Economic Modeling •Real Time Optimization •Mortgage backed securities •Option Pricing	Individual (Monte Carlo) Full simulations of portfolios	Synchronous, Embarrassingly parallel Metaproblems	SIMD, HPF MIMD, SIMD Integration software
10	Network Simulations	Sparse matrices; Zero structure defined by network connectivity	Loosely Synchronous	MIMD MPF

PDE	Partial Differential Equation
FEM	Finite Element Method
FD	Finite Difference
ED	Event Driven Simulation
TS	Time Stepped Simulation
VR	Virtual Reality
HPF	High Performance Fortran [16]
HPF+	Natural Extensions of HPF [17]
MPF	Fortran plus message passing for loosely synchronous software
Asyncsoft	Parallel Software System for (particular) class of asynchronous problems
CFD	Computational Fluid Dynamics

Note on Language: HPF, MPF are illustrative for Fortran: one can use parallel C, C++ or any similar extensions of data parallel or message passing languages

Table 2.1: HPCC Industrial Applications: Simulation or Information Production (continued):

Item	Application Area and Examples	Problem Comments	Problem Architecture	Machine and Software
11	Particle Transport Problems	Monte Carlo methods as in neutron transport for explosion Simulations	Embarrassingly Parallel (Asynchronous)	MIMD HPF
12	Graphics (rendering) Hollywood Virtual Reality	Several operational Parallel Ray Tracers Distributed model hard	Embarrassingly Parallel (Asynchronous)	MIMD HPF Asyncsoft for distributed database
13	Integrated Complex Systems Simulations •Defense (SIMNET, Flight Simulators) •Education (SIMCITY) •Multimedia/VR in Entertainment •Multiuser virtual worlds •Chemical & Nuclear Plants	Event driven (ED) and Time Stepped (TS) Simulations. Virtual Reality Interfaces. Database backends. Interactive	Metaproblem Fully asynchronous if ED Loosely Synchronous for TS	Timewarp or other ED Asyncsoft HPF(+) Integration Software Database

PDE	Partial Differential Equation
FEM	Finite Element Method
FD	Finite Difference
ED	Event Driven Simulation
TS	Time Stepped Simulation
VR	Virtual Reality
HPF	High Performance Fortran [16]
HPF+	Natural Extensions of HPF [17]
MPF	Fortran plus message passing for loosely synchronous software
Asyncsoft	Parallel Software System for (particular) class of asynchronous problems
CFD	Computational Fluid Dynamics

Note on Language: HPF, MPF are illustrative for Fortran: one can use parallel C, C++ or any similar extensions of data parallel or message passing languages

Table 2.2: HPCC Industrial Applications: Information Analysis - "Data Mining"

Item	Application Area and Examples	Problem Comments	Problem Architecture	Machine and Software
14	Seismic and Environmental data analysis	No oil in NY State. Parallel Computer already important	Embarrassingly parallel as in many "event" analysis problems (high energy physics, astronomy, etc.)	SIMD, maybe MIMD needed HPF
15	•Image Processing •Medical Instruments •EOS (Mission to Planet Earth) •Defense Surveillance •Computer Vision	Commercial Applications of Defense Technology. Component of many Information Integration Applications e.g. Computer Vision in Robotics	Metaproblem Synchronous (low level) Loosely Synchronous (medium level) Asynchronous (expert system)	Metacomputer SIMD (low level) MIMD (medium/high level) HPF(+) Software Integration Asyncsoft Database
16	•Health Fraud Inefficiency •Securities Fraud •Credit Card Fraud	Linkage Analysis of database records for correlations	Synchronous if records "identical" otherwise Loosely Synchronous	SIMD MIMD
17	Market Segmentation	Sort and Classify records to determine customer preference by region (city --> house)	Loosely Synchronous	Aspects could be SIMD MIMD better for sorting?

PDE	Partial Differential Equation
FEM	Finite Element Method
FD	Finite Difference
ED	Event Driven Simulation
TS	Time Stepped Simulation
VR	Virtual Reality
HPF	High Performance Fortran [16]
HPF+	Natural Extensions of HPF [17]
MPF	Fortran plus message passing for loosely synchronous software
Asyncsoft	Parallel Software System for (particular) class of asynchronous problems
CFD	Computational Fluid Dynamics

Note on Language: HPF, MPF are illustrative for Fortran: one can use parallel C, C++ or any similar extensions of data parallel or message passing languages

Table 2.3: HPCC Industrial Applications: Information Access and Dissemination:
InfoVision - Information, Video, Imagery and Simulation on Demand

Item	Application Area and Examples	Problem Comments	Problem Architecture	Machine and Software
18	Transaction Processing •ATM (automatic teller machine)	Database-most transactions short. As add "value" this becomes Information Integration	Embarrassingly Parallel	MIMD Database
19	Collaboratory •Telemedicine	Research Center or doctor(s) - patient interaction without regard to physical location	Asynchronous	High Speed Network
20	Text on Demand •Digital (existing) libraries •ERIC Education database, •United Nations - Worldwide newspapers	Multimedia database Full text search	Embarrassingly Parallel	MIMD Database
21	Video on Demand •Movies, News (CNN Newsource & Newsroom), •Current cable, •United Nations - Policy Support	Multimedia Database Interactive VCR, Video Browsing, Link of video and text database	Embarrassingly Parallel	MIMD Database Compression (SIMD) Video Editing Software
22	Imagery on Demand Kodak GIODE •"clip art" on demand •Medical images •Satelite images	Multimedia database Image Understanding for Content searching and (terrain) medical feature identification	Metaproblem Embarrassingly Parallel plus Loosely Synchronous Image Understanding	MIMD but much SIMD image analysis
23	Simulation on Demand •Education, Tourism, City planning, •Defense mission planning	Multimedia map database Generalized flight simulator Geographical Information System	Synchronous terrain rendering with Asynchronous Hypermedia	SIMD terrain engine (parallel rendering) MIMD database

Table 2.4: HPCC Industrial Applications: Information Integration

	These involve combinations of Information Production, Analysis and Access thus need software and machine architecture issues given for these "subproblems" • Systems of Systems
24	Command and Control • Battle Management, Command, Control, Communication, Intelligence and Surveillance (BMC^{3}IS) • Military Decision Support
25	SIMNET - Military Simulation with computers and people in the loop
26	Business decision support
27	Political decision support United Nationals uses video and multilingual newspaper (Maxwell School at Syracuse University)
28	Robotics
29	Electronic banking
30	Electronic shopping
31	Agile Manufacturing - Multidisciplinary Design - Concurrent Engineering •MADIC Industrial Consortium

3.3 Information Access and Dissemination

Information access and dissemination covers a wide range of applications for which we define four important categories---database information, video, imagery, and simulation on demand. These categories of information type form the basis of our InfoVision program (section 4.1 below).

Information access and dissemination includes text on demand or document retrieval from educational clearinghouses by school teachers, and accessing the world's news media and government reports by political analysts to predict political instabilities. Three dimensional geographic information systems linked with multimedia map databases are a form of simulation on demand, and could be used to deliver educational, tourism, or city planning information to students, the public, or government officials. Video on demand will soon become a large, new commercial market. Information access and dissemination applications are enabled by the National Information Infrastructure, which in the near future will link compute servers, and distributed databases over high-speed network links to the home and office settop box (soon to become a powerful PC). We believe that information access and dissemination will become the most important near term industry application of HPCC. Industry shake-ups, and billion dollar scale investments by the telecommunication and software industry in information sources, initially focused on capturing entertainment markets such as movie libraries and video games, serve to illustrate this opportunity.

The InfoVision activities are "new" applications and do not require porting of existing software. Thus HPCC technologies will not face some of the social and technical problems seen in other areas. The cost-performance advantage of parallel computing should dominate purchase decisions in these naturally parallel applications.

3.4 Information Integration

Information integration combines information production, analysis, and access in a system of systems. One might view information integration as the dual-use equivalent of command, control, communications, and intelligence for business, manufacturing, and the consumer. By analogy to the aviation term "flying by wire," where the pilot is not flying a plane but an informational representative of the plane, the business leader or home shopper might "manage by wire" [14] or use decision support technologies to manage, optimize, and make tradeoffs between informational representatives of complex manufacturing processes or a global consumer market. Information integration represents the largest long term market for HPCC technologies.

4 Information Processing Applications: InfoVision, MADIC, and Electrical Power Networks

We expect information processing applications to become the important opportunity for HPCC in industry. In this section, we describe three application projects that NPAC is currently developing. InfoVision is a set of projects concerning information on demand technologies and applications. MADIC is a multidisciplinary analysis and design industry consortium for developing pre-competitive HPCC software. Transient stability analysis in power networks is an NPAC project to optimize the distribution of power in an electrical transmission system.

4.1 InfoVision

HPCC will play a pervasive role in the information-rich world of the future. HPCC hardware will implement both the networks and the enormous information repositories that will function as servers on the National Information Infrastructure (NII). We term this NII server role as InfoVision, for Information, Video, Imagery and Simulation On demand. Alternately, we can think of InfoVision as high performance multimedia, scalable HPCC algorithms and software used to manage the network packets, and implement new applications running on InfoVision servers.

Dedicated gigabit links between supercomputers will be only one use of the NII. In addition, the NII will support many millions of "personalized" ten megabit/sec streams (this is approximate bandwidth needed to support transport of compressed video) supplying information on demand. InfoVision servers for video on demand will be classical parallel computers---whether clusters of workstations or integrated MPP's. We will have distributed clients with intelligent set top boxes and gigaflop video games in every home, school and business. But we will need production InfoVision servers in large data centers. HPCC techniques will be needed for the necessary hierarchical data storage, browsing, knowledge agents, text and video image content identification, and compression algorithms. (See Table 1) The HPCC community needs to examine message passing standards and see that they not only span all homogeneous parallel machines but also the InfoVision metacomputer (100 million clients demanding real-time response from some 10,000 InfoVision superservers).

InfoVision is an InfoMall project which involves state-of-the-art demonstrations on NYNET, a regional ATM-based gigabit network in New York State, of distributed interactive intelligent information systems. InfoVision is a set of dual-use distributed multimedia projects which prototype near term civilian and military applications of HPCC. We believe that the demonstrations are rich enough to explore most of the essential issues for HPDC information systems---now called National Challenges---which will be implemented on the NII in the near future. These demonstrations need various key enabling technologies, and InfoVision supports the InfoTech (the technology development and software capitalization component of InfoMall) activities needed to develop, test and evaluate these technologies. These technologies include multimedia database, transport protocols, network interoperability, architecture and management, collaboration, compression, security and privacy, graphics rendering, video browsing, image content and full text search techniques, distributed heterogeneous computing environments, user interfaces, and virtual reality. (Table 1)

Several InfoMall partners are needed to form the virtual organizations to both implement the demonstrations with component technologies and system integration as well as to explore the InfoTech activities needed by and opened up by the demonstrations. The partners include Abrams Gentile Entertainment Inc., Columbia University, Cornell University, Digital Equipment Corporation, Eastman Kodak, IBM, Maspar, NYNEX, Oracle, the U.S. Air Force Rome Laboratory, Ultra Inc., and Syracuse University. At Syracuse University, we have involved several organizations including NPAC, Electrical and Computer Engineering (ECE), Computer Applications and Software Engineering (CASE) Center, Computer and Information Science (CIS), the School of Information Studies (IST), the Newhouse School of Communications, the School of Education, and the Maxwell School of Citizenship and Public Affairs.

As part of our InfoVision program, we are currently developing a focused set of application demonstrations which include simulation (using weather simulations and 3D terrain modeling of New York State), text (using full text databases from the Maxwell School and the AskERIC educational resource in IST), imagery (using Kodak's GIODE PhotoCD technology), and video (using real-time educational news clips from CNN as one possible initial example database) on demand. We are using these demonstrations to develop the necessary component technologies, perform the overall system integration, then test and evaluate these information on demand technologies [13].

4.2 MADIC

The Multidisciplinary Analysis and Design Industrial Consortium (MADIC) project addresses applications of high-performance computing and communications technologies to the analysis and design of large-scale, complex products, such as aircraft and automobiles. Complex systems typically require consideration of multiple engineering and scientific disciplines, including fluid dynamics, structural dynamics, heat transfer, combustion, and manufacturing consideration. HPCC technologies are expected to provide a new generation of design tools that make use of large-scale, high-resolution simulations executing simultaneously in a distributed, heterogeneous computing environment. Outreach to large industrial firms was initiated in December 1991. Interested firms organized MADIC in March 1992.

MADIC members collaborate on projects of mutual interest, with teams of members formed to address specific projects. Current projects include evaluation of NASA software for use by industry. Current industrial members of MADIC include: Boeing, Ford Motors, General Electric Aircraft Engines, General Electric Corporate Research & Development, General Motors, Grumman, Lockheed, McDonnell-Douglas, Northrup, Rockwell, United Technologies Research Center, and Vought.

Current industrial practice typically requires 12-18 months to develop new designs for large-scale, complex products, such as aircraft and automobiles. Global competitive pressures demand reductions in time-to-market as well as improved design quality for dual-use (commercial and military) applications. This project is intended to reduce significantly the time required to develop new designs of large-scale systems, while simultaneously improving the quality and reducing the cost of new products.

MADIC provides a mechanism for aerospace and automobile manufacturers to address current challenges in the analysis and design of complex products. MADIC operations are coordinated through the Center for Research in Parallel Computation (CRPC), which has its headquarters at Rice University and also includes the Northeast Parallel Architectures Center (NPAC) at Syracuse University. MADIC firms pay an annual membership fee, which provides primary funding for an Executive Director and support staff. A representative of each member firm sits on a Board of Directors, which provides oversight and coordination. MADIC members form teams to address specific projects, consistent with the objectives of the consortium. Meetings and workshops are arranged at least quarterly. MADIC projects are intended to develop, validate and deploy an integrated analysis and design environment operating on a heterogeneous network that includes workstations, vector supercomputers and massively-parallel processors. A proposal for the entire United States Multidisciplinary Analysis and Design Environments (USMADE) was prepared but rejected in the recent Technology Reinvestment Program. USMADE includes modules for geometry definition, grid generation, physical simulation (fluid dynamics, structural dynamics, electromagnetics), process simulation (manufacturing, maintenance), optimization and visualization. Work on selected aspects relevant to the USMADE project is currently underway with funding from other sources. NASA is funding a project to evaluate physical simulation software for use in industrial applications. In this project, industry teams are applying selected NASA codes to problems of current interest, including wings, wing-body interactions, nozzle flows, internal flows (turbines and compressors) and flexible wings. As part of this project, NPAC researchers are evaluating the suitability of the NASA codes to be implemented in High-Performance Fortran. CRPC researchers at Rice University are evaluating the use of the automatic differentiation system ADIFOR.

4.3 Transient Stability Analysis for Power Systems

One major NPAC project involves the utility industry, where we are working with Niagara Mohawk Power Corporation on simulations of their electrical transmission system [18,23]. This can be done in real time using modern parallel machines with around 64 nodes. We are creating prototype software that Niagara Mohawk will evaluate. Future steps involve the utility industry research consortium EPRI, other utilities and the companies that currently build the sequential power grid software now used by electrical utilities. This application is straightforward to parallelize as it involves forming a matrix (with embarrassingly parallel matrix element generation) followed by a sparse matrix solve [19,20,23]. The latter uses a direct method on a roughly 10000X10000 matrix. Developing an efficient parallel sparse matrix solver is the most difficult problem for this application [19,20,21,22,23]. Utilities must balance the cost of producing power against the cost of failures. Thus an accurate simulation of transient stability analysis---the response of the network to a disturbance---allows better cost---security tradeoffs and hence cheaper power. Power is very expensive and even modest savings from real-time simulation would warrant purchase of HPCC supercomputers by the utilities.

5 Summary and Conclusions

The National Information Infrastructure of the future will be built upon core HPCC technologies such as parallel architectures, software, and high-speed networks. In addition to the key enabling technologies associated with high-performance scientific computing, such as image processing algorithms and linear algebra libraries, information processing applications will require development and integration of new, enabling HPCC technologies such as collaboration services, and multimedia databases. These new technologies will find application in information industries such as home entertainment and agile manufacturing.

While simulation will remain an important HPCC application, the real opportunity for developing significant industrial applications of HPCC technologies lies in information processing. Information industries such as home shopping, electronic banking, distance education, and televirtuality are growing at a much faster rate than the product industries such as aerospace, or other manufactured goods. The current focus on scientific simulation in the national HPCC community must change in response to this trend.

Based on our survey of industrial applications of HPCC compiled over the past three years, we described four classes of information processing---production, analysis, access and distribution, and integration. We concluded that information analysis (e.g., data mining credit card holders' purchase patterns) is the most important near term opportunity, and information integration (e.g., decision support in the global economic war) is the most important long term opportunity for HPCC applications in industry.

6 References

[1] Grand Challenges 1993: High Performance Computing and Communications, The FY 1993 US Research and Development Program, Walter Massey, Chair. A Report by the Committee on Physical, Mathematical, and Engineering Sciences, Federal Coordinating Council for Science, Engineering, and Technology Committee, Office of Science and Technology Policy, 1993. (68 p.)

[2] G. Fox., P. Messina, and R. Williams. Parallel Computing Works!. Morgan Kaufmann, San Mateo, CA. 1994.

[3] Commercial Applications in Parallel Processing (CAPPS). Microelectronics and Computer Technology Corporation. Austin, Texas. October 19-20, 1993.

[4] Workshop on Grand Challenge Applications and Software Technology. May 4-6, 1993. Industry Panel Workshop. Hyatt Regency Hotel, Pittsburgh, PA.

[5] Supercomputing '93. National Information Infrastructure Testbed Panel. Portland, Oregon. November 15-19, 1993. IEEE Computer Society Press, Los Alamitos, CA.

[6] RCI North American Annual Member Executive Conferences on Technology Transfer. RCI, Ltd. Worldwide Headquarters, 1301 East 79th Street, Suite 200, Minneapolis, MN 55425.

[7] T. Pinelli, R. Barclay, A. Bishop, and J. Kennedy. Information Technology and Aerospace Knowledge Diffusion. electronic networking: research, applications and policy. 2:2 31-50. 1992.

[8] G. Fox, E. Bogucz, D. Jones, K. Mills, and M. Podgorny. InfoMall Program Plan: A Scalable Organization for the Development of HPCC Software and Systems. SCCS--531. (Available from NPAC, Syracuse University, Syracuse NY 13210-4100). 1993.

[9] K. Mills and G. Fox. InfoMall: An Innovative Strategy for High-Performance Computing and Communications Applications Development. to be published in electronic networking: research, applications and policy. 1994.

[10] G. C. Fox. Parallel Computing in Industry: An Initial Survey. in proceedings Fifth Australian Supercomputing Conference. World Congress Center. Melbourne, Australia. SCCS--302, Center for Research on Parallel Computation-TR92219. (Available from NPAC, Syracuse University, Syracuse NY 13210-4100). 1992.

[11] N. Johnson. The Nature of Information. in The Knowledge Economy. The Nature of Information in the 21st Century. Institute for Information Studies. 1993-1994.

[12] B. Ives and M. McKeown. The Promise of a New World Information Order. in The Knowledge Economy. The Nature of Information in the 21st Century. Institute for Information Studies. 1993-1994.

[13] G. Fox, S. Hariri, R. Chen, K. Mills, M. Podgorny. InfoVision--Information, Video, Imagery, and Simulation On Demand. SCCS--575. (Available from NPAC, Syracuse University, Syracuse NY 13210-4100). 1993.

[14] S. Haeckel and R. Nolan. The Role of Technology in an Information Age. in The Knowledge Economy. The Nature of Information in the 21st Century. Institute for Information Studies. 1993-1994.

[15] D. Koester, S. Ranka, and G. Fox. Power Systems Transient Stability - A Grand Computing Challenge. SCCS--549. (Available from NPAC, Syracuse University, Syracuse NY 13210-4100). 1992.

[16] High Performance Fortran Forum, (1993). High performance Fortran language specification, High Performance Fortran Forum, May 3, 1993, Version 1.0. 184 pp. HPFF92a. Copyright Rice University, Houston, Texas. (Available by anonymous ftp at minerva/npac.syr.edu HPFF/hpf-v10-final.ps)

[17] Alok Choudhary, Geoffrey Fox, Seema Hiranandani, Ken Kennedy, Chuck Koelbel, Sanjay Ranka and Joel Saltz, A Classification of Irregular Loosely Synchronous Problems and Their Support in Scalable Parallel Software Systems, in Proceedings from Darpa Software Technology Conference, 1992, pp. 138--149. Syracuse University Technical Report SCCS-255, June, 1991.

[18] A.J. Wood and B.F. Wollenberg, Power Generation, Operation and Control, (Wiley, New York, 1984).

[19] IEEE Committee Report, Parallel Processing in Power Systems Computations, IEEE Transactions on Power Systems, 7(2), 629, (1992).

[20] David Koester, Sanjay Ranka, and Geoffrey Fox, Power Systems Transient Stability - A Grand Computing Challenge, NPAC technical report SCCS-549 (1992).

[21] David Koester, Sanjay Ranka, and Geoffrey Fox, Parallel LU Factorization of Block-Diagonal-Bordered Sparse Matrices. NPAC technical report SCCS-550 (1993).

[22] David Koester, Sanjay Ranka, and Geoffrey Fox, Parallel Block-Diagonal-Bordered Sparse Linear Solvers for Electrical Power System Applications, Proceedings of the Scalable Parallel Libraries Conference, Mississippi State University, October 1993. NPAC technical report SCCS-552.

[23] G. Fox, P. Coddington, A. Choudhary, S. Hariri, M. Nilan, and S. Ranka, High Performance Computing and Parallel Processing in the Utility Industry, Final report for Phase 1 of project for Niagara Mohawk Power Corporation, NPAC internal technical report SCCSI-542.

[24] 1994 Federal High Performance Computing Program.

Information Superhighways –
Does Europe Need Them,
Can Europe Build Them?

David.O.Williams
Computing & Networks Division
European Laboratory for Particle Physics (CERN)
1211 Geneva 23
Switzerland
(E.mail: David.O.Williams@cern.ch)

February 1994

A keynote talk at the HPCN Europe 1994 conference, Munich, April 1994

I was in a Printing-house in Hell, and saw the method in which knowledge is transmitted from generation to generation. – *William Blake, The Marriage of Heaven and Hell.*

1 What is an Information Superhighway?

When one reads in the International Herald Tribune (February 3, 1994) of a company set up in Beijing to create a Chinese information superhighway, it is clearly time to think about what we are doing in Europe. However, one must first establish whether an Information Superhighway is anything more than a buzzword or a gimmick.

It is certainly more than a buzzword. Over the last two years it has become clear that networking is coming of age, and is in the process of escaping from the small world of academia and research into the big brash world of commerce and business. This is because it offers economic opportunities, including cheap access to valuable information. Also, for the first time, teleconferencing over a universal network is starting to offer an alternative to the expensive and polluting transport of people to meetings.

The Internet, which I am using here very loosely to mean the interconnected set of all the world's networks, has been growing phenomenally in recent years. From its origins in the research community in the 1970s (ARPAnet etc.) it has spread via high-tech research companies, and then through tentative use by the general business and commerical worlds. For at least the last two years the concept of the Internet, somewhat generalised, and with its name evolved to the Information Superhighway, has been seen in the USA as a straight commercial opportunity to make money. Some European companies are now starting to wonder if they are missing out on what is happening in this field.

The present Internet now spans the world and has a blend of commercial and academic users. With a local area network and a medium speed connection (say 1 Mbit/s) a user with a workstation or high-end personal computer can today access remarkable quantities of information including drawings and images as well as text in multiple fonts. Even with low speed modem connections (typically 9.6 Kbit/s) anybody with a personal computer can access fantastic quantities of text information either on the (TCP/IP) Internet [1] or on commercial services such as CompuServe. The latter has in fact grown from a pure text bulletin board system to become a supplier of several useful services which are billed via the subscriber's credit card on a monthly basis.

The fastest growing information service on the Internet today is the WorldWideWeb [2] which originated at CERN for the particle physics research community, but which is now in use at thousands of sites around the world. It offers simple and consistent access to a multitude of information stored on Web servers all around the world and, above all, without requiring the user to log on to those distant information servers. In a few seconds one can find colour images from the repaired Hubble Space Telescope, a paper on the proof of Fermat's last theorem, or information from the Deutches Klimarechenzentrum in Hamburg. During the preparation of this paper, one of my colleagues used the Web to consult economic data which is publically available from the Central Intelligence Agency (CIA)

Fact Book. Web users are largely unaware of where the information they see is stored and how it reaches their screen. It should also be noted that although what the Web accesses is technically described as "data", it can in fact be any kind of information which can be visualised on a screen. Use of the Web grew by more than 300,000% during 1993. CERN is proud of the Web, but of course it is only a beginning. The Web cannot deliver moving pictures or sound yet, but this can only be a matter of time.

Thus the network can now give access to stored information in a way which, to some of its users, seems as revolutionary as the invention of the printing press. Technology is also close to the market which will allow access to human beings across the network as well: from the primitive mechanisms of electronic mail and conferences using a single text font, we are moving on to the era of multi-media electronic mail and desktop video-conferencing. Both of these technologies have been running as advanced pilot services on the Internet for some time, and one can expect them to emerge as fully interworking multi-vendor products in the near future.

However, even among the academics who already have access to multi-media electronic mail and desktop conferencing, these tools are surprisingly little used. They have not yet become a way of life like plain text electronic mail. In Europe at least, there is no mystery about the reason for this: we do not have enough bandwidth, because bandwidth is too expensive.

Let us for a moment investigate the consequences of assuming that cabling and bandwidth are free. The Internet would probably expand to provide universal service in the style of the telephone network, with several megabits per second into every home and several hundred megabits per second into and out of every enterprise. What could be done with that capacity? The most uninteresting new service (at least to me personally) is the one most widely discussed in the press, namely "video on demand." In this case a magic box attached to every television allows the customer to select and pay for any video which he or she can find in the menus offered by entertainment companies. This is so obviously possible that major contracts were signed last year between entertainment companies, cable TV companies, and systems houses to put such systems into the mass market in the USA. In this case the cabling and bandwidth *are* effectively free, since the cable TV companies have already installed them.

However, cable TV is normally a one-way (outbound from server to client) service. Only a few bauds are necessary to send back the customer's menu selections to the video server, and most cable TV systems allow for this. If we assume that the multi-megabit connections to the home are duplex connections, then every home computer (including the ones built into the television, the washing machine, the heating system, etc.) could have high speed Internet access. With this, homes, schools, businesses, and so on can use *interactive* services which are much more sophisticated than video on demand. As with all revolutionary technologies it is impossible to predict today the use that society will make tomorrow of access to an information superhighway. Just for fun, here are some possibilities for use of the superhighway from your house one Saturday morning:

- Retrieve a copy of your 1990 holiday video tapes from an archive server.
- Inspect a hotel room in Oslo, Florence or San Francisco before booking it.
- Book your seats for La Scala after inspecting the view of the stage that they provide.
- Listen to *Der Spiegel* for the third week of 1991, automatically translated into the language of your choice.

If bandwidth were free, and given how little computing power now costs, none of the above would be unrealistic in an affluent society. But is this idea of an information superhighway just a gimmick? The only answer to this is that the telephone and the car were certainly regarded as gimmicks when invented, and we know what they have done for society. An information superhighway could even begin to undo some of the damage done by the car.

2 Does Europe Need Them?

The title of this section begs the question of whether there should be one information superhighway, or many. In fact, as we have many roads, but one road network, it is probably a meaningless distinction: all information networks should be interconnected although some of them will be better or more expensive to use than others.

It has been common practice for many research scientists to use computer networks on a daily or hourly basis for many years. In recent years this way of collaborating with colleagues has become common throughout the academic community and also inside most major international companies (not only those in the computer business). Within the last two years the Internet has spread into the public domain, with schools, local and national governments (including the White House), and the media (including the BBC World Service) announcing their electronic mail addresses. By early 1994 it became common to encounter references to the Internet in the press or on radio or television.

However, most of this spectacular growth has concerned electronic mail at relatively low speeds, and with strong limitations on such things as accented characters or non-Latin alphabets (which is a very valid source of cultural concern outside the American- or English-speaking world). As mentioned above, modern network technology can do much more than treat simple text, and there will be strong opporunities for other cultures to benefit from the opportunities that are becoming available. Furthermore, scientific or engineering resources can be shared over continental distances. As computing power becomes progressively cheaper, the critical resource to be shared is no longer processor power but mass storage, or rather the contents of the mass store. Every industry or scientific discipline can provide examples. In high energy particle physics research, a grand challenge of the next decade will be the collaborative design of massive and enormously complex detectors for experiments at the Large Hadron Collider planned at CERN for the early years of the next century. Hundreds of engineers and physicists in many countries must collaborate in these design efforts. Unless they can share a design and simulation database containing millions of items, which is constantly up to date, the design will be wrong. Instant high speed network access is not a luxury for them; it is a basic necessity. So it will be for any Europe-wide scientific or engineering collaboration.

It is not by chance that the White House is on the Internet. Both Vice-President Gore and President Clinton have recognised the vital importance of computer networking for high-technology industry. In Europe, we are still years behind the USA in the political understanding of this issue and therefore in any relevant action, despite some progress in work and studies sponsored by the European Commission [3].

I have given elsewhere [4] a number of reasons why Europe, and European industry in particular, must not be left further behind in this race to benefit from high speed networks. Even without extending the network into every home, how can industry function efficiently on a European scale without a network? How can BMW and Rover efficiently share automobile design documents without linking their computer systems at top speed? How can Italian farmers benefit in good time from weather forecasts computed in England? How can aerospace designers share their simulations between workers in different countries? The original HPCN report [5] suggested that such issues may have a significant effect on GNP growth.

Europe has had a hard struggle to maintain the competitivity of its traditional manufacturing industries and it remains weak in many high technology industries. These areas are the ones that can benefit most from high performance, low delay networking to optimise their technical collaboration across the continent. Even if Europe does not succeed in creating an indigenous distributed computing industry, it would be suicidal for the rest of industry not to make the most of this technology.

It is less clear whether Europe should rush into the business of video on demand and the other potential mass-market information highway services. This is in a sense a social and political question before it is an economic one. The desirability of these services is not debated in the USA because the First Amendment to the Constitution makes it impossible to stop them anyway. In Europe this matter is not so clear and one can expect information services for the public to be treated like the broadcast media. We can expect extensive and continuing political debate about pornography, violence, parental guidance, local language content, etc. This was surely prefigured by a recent case in which the Canton of Vaud successfully prosecuted the Director-General of the Swiss PTT over his responsibilities in the provision of pornographic services over the public telephone system.

Nevertheless, an information superhighway which extended into every affluent home in Europe would certainly prove to be an economic motor of some importance. If one assumes that 50 million homes each spent 1000 ECUs per year on such services, the turnover would be 50 billion ECUs, close to half the GDP of Switzerland, and over 11% of the world telecommunications market of 430 billion ECUs [6].

3 Can Europe Build Them?

In the USA, the political will to create a national information superhighway clearly grew out of the long-term networking programme in the research community whose best known results were the ARPANET and the NSFnet.

Today we hear from our American colleagues of plans to upgrade the NSFnet infrastructure from 45 Mbit/s to 155 Mbit/s or even 622 Mbit/s. In Europe, the best continent-wide Internet service we have, EuropaNet [7], operates a 2 Mbit/s backbone and the fastest international pilot so far, BETEL [8], ran at 34 Mbit/s. We clearly lag behind the Americans.

In [4] I gave a list of the barriers to progress in European telematics, and none of them are technical. Many of the issues are economic and political: regulations, tariffs, lack of international competition, conservatism, and lack of political focus. There is also the lack of a solid European scientific computing industry, and hence the lack of the industry-academia collaboration which has been so productive in the USA.

Of course not all the hardware and software technology needed to build an information superhighway exists today, but certainly enough exists to show that there is essentially no technology problem. However, there is one big problem with many of today's Internet services, namely the lack of accounting and billing. Access to most networks forming part of the Internet is normally funded on a global basis by an employer, and most of the services available via the Internet remain free of charge to their individual users. In order for the Internet to evolve fully into the public Information Superhighway, improved accounting and billing facilities will be needed. This will surely not prevent the provision of a whole set of very valuable, but essentially free-of-charge, services being make available for various communities, co-existing with fully commercial services.

Our thoughts about the cost of network services are still too strongly influenced by the idea that bandwidth is a scarce, and therefore expensive, resource. The transmission capacity of optical fibre is already several Gbit/s and wave-division multiplexing will allow more if needed [9]. The ITU has already standardised 9.6 Gbit/s transmission. Even a modest unshielded twisted pair cable of good quality can carry at least 100 Mbit/s over 100 metres, more than enough for distribution quality HDTV. It is beyond the scope of this paper to attempt a full economic analysis, but clearly the investment in cable plant is far greater than that in transmission equipment and switches, and must be written off over much longer periods. With the advent of optical amplifiers in long distance fibres, only the equipment at each end of the fibre will need to be upgraded to increase the bandwidth. It is not obvious why the cost of supplying megabits of data service to each user over a modern cabling infrastructure should be significantly greater than that of Plain Old Telephone Service. The Ethernet connection to my office certainly cost less to install than the telephone.

What this means is that once a decent cable infrastructure (shared fibre for long distances, individual twisted pair or fibre for short distances) is in place, the actual bandwidth consumed by each user is unimportant within reasonable limits of several Mbit/s per user. This will make particularly good sense in an ATM world [10] with properly implemented "available bit rate" services, where each simultaneous transaction will be given a fair share of the currently available bandwidth. When the average load increases, the network providers will have to increase trunk and switch capacity as necessary, but in the future this will rarely involve laying new fibre trunks. As on packet-switching networks or on a public road, this approach will lead to worse response times at busy times of day.

In most countries one pays a fixed fee for road use, usually one that increases with the size of the vehicle. One is frequently required to pay a supplementary toll to use some especially expensive infrastructure such as bridges, tunnels or even, in some countries, the motorways. And, if you return with a load of goods, you will have paid the supplier for them. Thus one could expect to pay a fixed fee for network access, but one that increases with the peak bandwidth available. One could expect to pay a supplementary toll for guaranteed response time, and of course to pay a service provider for the information accessed. However, a road system is only of economic value if its cost to its users is small compared to the value of the goods transported: we expect the cost of driving to the shopping centre to be at most a few percent of our expenditure in the supermarket. In the same way, one should expect the cost of network access to a service to be a small fraction of the cost of the service.

I believe that Europe would benefit by defining tariffing principles where bandwidth is essentially free of charge, but where the suppliers of the network infrastructure are paid on the basis of connectivity (perhaps with premium rates for guaranteed response time), and the suppliers of services are paid by the end user on the basis of the use that is made of their services. Some such fundamental change is needed if Europe is to get out of the current deadlock, where growth in the market for high speed services is completely blocked by tariffs often ten times higher than those in the USA.

Achieving such a change is a political question. The monopoly environment is still too much with us, especially for international connections, and it is effectively stifling any major change in tariff structures. The attempts of the European Commission and of European governments to liberalise telematics regulations have been influenced too strongly by advice from representatives of monopoly or quasi-monopoly suppliers. Users, who will need these tools to remain competitive and to ensure Europe's future economic growth, need to speak out more strongly about their requirements, and, above all, to explain them unambiguously to the polictickians.

In Europe we have the knowledge and skills to build as many information superhighways as we want or need, but it is scarcely worth making serious proposals until the political and economic deadlock over tariffs has been broken by much more open competition.

Acknowledgements:

It is a pleasure to acknowledge many stimulating discussions with my colleagues during the preparation of this paper.

References

1. C.Malamud, Exploring the Internet - a Technical Travelogue, Prentice-Hall, 1992.

2. T.J. Berners-Lee, R. Cailliau, J-F Groff, B. Pollermann, World-Wide Web: The Information Universe, Electronic Networking 2, 52-58 (1992).

3. B. Oakley (ed.), Telematics programme - Mid Term Review Report, Commission of the European Communities, DG XIII, Brussels, July 1993.

4. D.O.Williams, B.E.Carpenter, Data Networking for the European Academic and Research Community: Is It Important?, Electronic Networking, 2, 56-65 (1992).

5. Report of the High Performance Computing and Networking Advisory Committee (Chairman: C.Rubbia), Commission of the European Communities, DG XIII, Brussels, October 1992.

6. Etudes Telecom, 49, 19 (February 1994).

7. S.M. Nielsen, EuropaNet - Contemporary High Speed Networking, Computer Networks and ISDN Systems, 25, S25-S34 (1993).

8. O.H.Martin, Broadband Exchange over Trans-European Links (BETEL), Proc. SMDS Conference, Amsterdam, November 1993.

9. P.E.Green, An All-Optical Computer Network: Lessons Learned, IEEE Network, March 1992, 56-60 (1992).

10. M. De Prycker, Asynchronous Transfer Mode: Solution for Broadband ISDN, Horwood, 1991.

Simulation of Metal Forming Processes with Respect to MPP-Systems

M. Hillmann, J. Weiher

INPRO
Innovationsgesellschaft für fortgeschrittene Produktionssysteme
in der Fahrzeugindustrie mbH
Nürnberger Str. 68/69, 10787 Berlin, Germany
E-Mail: hillmann@inpro.de
weiher@inpro.de

Abstract. This paper describes the activities of INPRO in the field of metal forming simulation. INPRO, as a subsidiary of Daimler-Benz AG, Volkswagen AG, Krupp Hoesch Stahl AG, Hoechst AG, Siemens AG and Voest-Alpine Stahl Ges. mbH. is concerned with advanced manufacturing technology innovations.

A short description of different approaches to sheet metal simulation is given. At INPRO the special purpose program INDEED (INovative DEEp Drawing) has been developed. Although INDEED is highly optimized for well established hardware-platforms, industrial demands require a further reduction of CPU-time.

The announcement of MPP-Systems rises the hope to dramatically speed up the numerical simulation. At present, INPRO investigates how much benefit could be obtained by using MPP-Systems for the simulation of forming processes. The question arises, how much redesign and development of new algorithms are necessary to obtain a reasonable gain of performance.

1 Introduction

Metal forming processes have a substantial meaning in industrial production. There exist various kinds of metal forming processes:
- deep drawing
- forging
- rolling
- extrusion
   ...

The automotive industry is one of the most important branches who benefits from advanced metal forming techniques. In this field the deep drawing process, by which most of the car's inner and outer pannels are produced, is of substantial interest. Sophisticated experience have been gathered over the years and for a long period tool designers have been working on base of their personal experience and trial and error methods exclusively. The growing complexity of the parts and shorter model cycle times lead to a permanently increasing pressure in tool developing.

	in million DM
Conventionell press	2,0 - 4,0
Transfer pressing street	35,0 - 44,0
Deep drawing tool for one outer panel	0,3 - 0,4
Deep drawing tools for one car model	80 - 150
Investment in a pressing plant for a production of 1000 cars/day	500 - 800

Fig. 1 Investment in a pressing plant (source: Mercedes-Benz, 1991)

Considering the extrem high costs which arises in stamping plants, see Fig. 1, it appears naturally that tool designer are demanding for efficient deep drawing simulation programs to support their work. Several major car manufacturers have started to apply simulation programs in industrial environments in the stage of tool design, see Fig. 2.

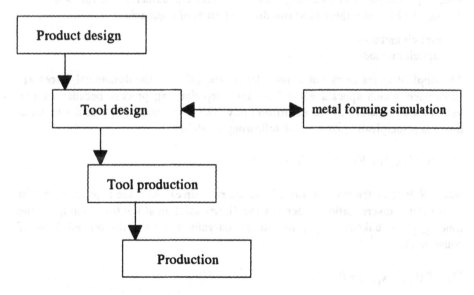

Fig. 2 Use of metal forming simulation

One of the main problems of these programs are huge computational costs, especially for high quality simulation programs, so that at present less parts are simulated than should be. Massively Parallel Processor (MPP) Systems rise the hope to significantly decrease the computational costs but there is still a lot of work to do until benefits can be obtained for industrial applications.

In this paper we focus our interest to sheet metal forming simulation. Problems arising in the simulation of other metal forming processes are quite similar.

2 Deep Drawing Simulation

In recent years large efforts have been spent to develop efficient sheet metal forming simulation programs because of the high benefits mentioned above.

At the beginning scientists concentrated on problems in physical modelling like constitutive and friction laws. But soon it turned out, that the simulation of elasto-plastic processes including contact and friction inequalities lead to very high computational costs. For this reason people considered in the 1970´s and the early 1980´s only two dimensional and rotation symmetrical problems. The step from two dimensional to three dimensional problems lead to a dramatical increase of computational costs. Both, the improving of simulation programs and the permanent increase of computational power made it possible to consider three dimensional problems.

The international conference on sheet metal forming simulation in Zürich 1991 [1] has shown that several Finite Element programs are able to simulate the deep drawing process of a 3D production part, most of them with reasonable results. In the meantime several major car manufacturers have installed deep drawing simulation programs. Beside this success there are still several unsolved problems with respect to physical modelling, CAD interfaces and numerical performance.

Among the FE codes there exist two different kinds of approaches:

- implicit methods
- explicit methods.

The implicit codes carry out a quasistatical analysis, i.e. the dynamical forces are suppressed which appears natural for the deep drawing process because of low velocities and masses of the deformed body. The displacement $x(t)$ of the blank at time t is principically given by the following equation:

(1) $R\,(\dot{x}, x, t) + F\,(x, t) + P\,(t) = 0$

where R denotes the friction force, F the internal forces and P the external load. For a given time discretization x_i denotes the discret solution at the time step t_i. At the time t_{i+1} the unknown x_{i+1} has to be determined by the discretized form of equation (1):

(2) $T\,(x_{i+1}, x_i,...) = 0$

where T denotes an operator depending on the choice of the discretization. The nonlinear implicit equation (2) has to be solved iteratively. Most of the codes use (modified) Newton techniques:

(3) $\quad x_{i+1}^{k+1} = x_{i+1}^{k} - DT(x_{i+1}^{k},...)^{-1} \, T(x_{i+1}^{k},...)$

where DT is the derivative of T with respect to x_{i+1}. Using this implicit method two major problems occur:

- Newton´s method is only locally convergent and especially near singularities (buckling or wrinkling) convergence problems may appear.
- The factorization of DT needs a lot of CPU time and memory.

If explicit codes are used, the dynamical forces may not be suppressed. The following equation has to be solved:

(4) $\quad M\ddot{x} + C\dot{x} + R(\dot{x}, x, t) + F(x, t) + P(t) = 0$

where M describes the mass distribution and C the damping of the system. At time step t_{i+1} the displacement x_{i+1} is determined by the recursive instruction:

(5) $\quad x_{i+1} = T(x_i, x_{i-1},...)$

where T depends on the choice of the discretization of (4).

Obviously there is no iteration necessary to obtain the solution at time t_{i+1} and accordingly there are no problems with matrix invertation or divergence at a given time step. On the other hand explicit methods have to satisfy stability criteria which lead to an upper bound for the time step of a given problem with a given discretization in space. For a typical deep drawing example these stability criteria lead to very small time steps and consequently to very high CPU times. An artificial increasing of the velocity or mass of the blank allows to use larger time steps. Of course this is a change of the underlying physical model and therefore it is not desired.

At present there is a lot of discussion which kind of integration procedure is more appropriate for deep drawing simulation, but for the near future it seems that both methods will have a significance and will be supported by industrial users.

Beside the classical implicit and explicit codes there are other programs based on simplified physical and geometrical modelling in order to reduce CPU costs dramatically. These codes are sometimes used for first rough estimations of the drawability of a part.

3 The Implicit Simulation Program INDEED

INDEED, a special purpose finite element program for sheet metal forming simulation has been developed at INPRO since 1986, [2]. The aim was to develop a program system by which the deep drawing process could be simulated as realistically as possible. Even spring back behavior and failure like wrinkling and necking should be predictable. At present INDEED is installed in several departments of INPRO's shareholders.

The main features of INDEED are:

- 3D total lagrange formulation
- quasistatic implicit integration
- elasto-plastic anisotropical constitutive laws
- contact detection between deformable and rigid bodies
- modified Coulomb's friction law.

To obtain reasonable computational costs INDEED is highly vectorized and uses optimized sparse matrix techniques for the linear solvers.

If we set

(6) $\quad G(\dot{x}, x, t) := R(\dot{x}, x, t) + F(x, t) + P(t)$

(7) $\quad \dot{x}_{i+1} = \Delta x_{i+1} / \Delta t \ , \quad \Delta x_{i+1} = x_{i+1} - x_i$

equation (2) has the following form:

(8) $\quad G(\Delta x_{i+1} / \Delta t, x_i + \Delta x_{i+1}, t_{i+1}) = 0$

in which Δx_{i+1} is the unknown. The Newton iteration (3) can be written as follows:

(9) $\quad \Delta x_{i+1}^{k+1} = \Delta x_{i+1}^{k} - D_x G(\ldots)^{-1} G(\ldots)$

where $D_x G$ and G are evaluated at the last approximation of x_{i+1}.

This iteration is carried out until equation (8) is satisfied with a given tolerance. Because of convergence problems the matrix $D_x G$ is replaced by modified matrices and line search techniques are applied.

Beside satisfying this equilibrium equation there are additional contact conditions:

- there may not be any penetration between nodes of the deformable bodies and the rigid bodies
- nodes of the deformable bodies which are in contact with a rigid body must have pressure forces.

Every time the equilibrium equation is satisfied, the contact conditions are verified and nodes are tied to or separated from the surface of a rigid die if it is necessary.

In Fig. 3 the principal course of a time step of INDEED is shown. There the following phases occur:

- Assembly phase: Provide the matrix $D_x G$
- Solving phase: Factorization of $D_x G$, forward and backward substitution
- Recovery phase: Provide the vector G
- Contact search: Verify the contact conditions.

These four phases cover all essentially work that has to be done in a time step.

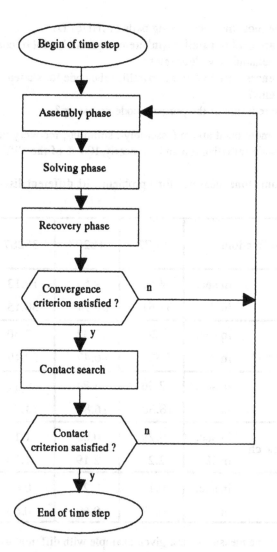

Fig. 3 Flow chart of a time step

4 Strategies of Parallelization

The fairly good and accepted results obtained with INDEED lead to the demand of making these results faster available. INDEED is well optimized for classical vector computers and high end workstations, so it appears natural to consider parallel architectures to further reduce the CPU time requirements.

In order to parallelize a code like INDEED the following questions arise:

- Which are the most time consuming parts of INDEED?
- Which parts are hard to parallize (inherent sequential, a lot of communication)
- Which parts demand new algorithms?
- Which differences arise in order to parallize the code for shared- or distributed memory systems?
- Is a complete redesign of the program code necessary?

The four phases mentioned above (assembly-. solution-, recovery phase and contact search) cover beside initialization and I/O nearly 100 % of the CPU time needed for a simulation.

Fig. 4 shows some time measures for a problem with different discretizations.

Degrees of freedom		9072	18207	35287	71407
Assembly	in sec.	4.83	9.67	19.13	40.11
	in %	37.61	33.74	30.15	26.06
Solution (direct solver)	in sec.	5.26	13.32	33.30	91.62
	in %	40.96	46.47	52.49	59.52
Recovery	in sec.	2.36	4.84	9.48	19.08
	in %	18.38	16.88	14.94	12.39
Contact search	in sec.	0.29	0.63	1.13	2.30
	in %	2.25	2.19	1.78	1.49
Rest	in sec.	0.1	0.2	0.4	0.8
	in %	0.77	0.69	0.63	0.51

Fig. 4 Time measures for a given example with different discretization

If we examine the four phases considering Fig. 4 we can gain the following results: First we see that the linear solver is the only part, which grows higher than linear with the problem size. Therefore the linear solver plays a dominating role for the big examples one want to solve on MPP-Systems. Secondly a closer examination of the parts show that assembly phase, recovery phase and contact search are local to approximately 95 %, 98 % and 99 %, respectively, because they work on element or node level. As a consequence the work to be done here is relatively "easy" to parallize. In opposition to this the solution phase is at a first glance hard to parallize, if direct solvers (with a lot of communication on the global matrix) have to be used.

These facts lead to the conclusion, that, if we want to keep the algorithms as they are, we first have to solve the "solver problem". Otherwise we have to look for different techniques, which do not require the use of direct solvers. This could include a wider redesign with the need of providing different algorithms for different computer architectures. We would like to avoid this because of the resulting increase of software maintenance.

Three groups of linear equation solvers can be distinguished:

1. direct
2. iterative

and

3. domain decompostion methods.

4.1 Direct Solver

Direct solvers lead to the solution of a linear system of equation after a predictable number of steps. An efficient implementation of parallel solvers distribute not only the data but also the work on them most equally with a minimum of communication. Usually, before starting the factorization some optimization on the data has to be performed in order to reduce and calculate the fill-in (see Duff et. al. [3]). These routines also have a tremendous impact on the parallel performance of the solver. Therefore the implementation of direct solvers has to cover the following five steps:

I) Data optimization:
1. preordering (minimizing fill-in, optimizing parallelity)
2. symbolic factorization (calculation fill-in)
3. data distribution

II) Solving the system of equations:
4. numerical factorization
5. forward and backward substitution

For distributed memory systems it is of main importance that the underlying data structure for all these five steps remains the same in order to avoid communication-intensiv reordering and performance decreases. For shared memory computers with about 8 processors C. W. Yang provided a very efficient multifrontal - Cholesky solver including all the steps mentioned above [4].

At NCSA, Illinois, M. Heath and P. Raghavan developed for the first time a multifrontal - Cholesky solver (with nested dissection ordering in a common data structure) for all five steps [5]. The implementation was realized on an Intel iPSC/860.

No wonder that the leading MPP vendors plan to implement this solver on

-   CRAY T3D
-   Intel PARAGON
-   KSR KSR-1 / KSR-2
-   Thinking Machines CM-5.

4.2 Iterative Solver

Iterative solvers are not so difficult to parallize, because they mainly depend on matrix vector multiplications which are easy to parallize.

But the often ill-conditioned problems in forming processes lead to very ill-conditioned matrices, so that even modern iterative methods like GMRES, BCG, QMR, CGS, Bi-CGSTAB, TFQMR or CGNR run into so badly convergence problems, that they can not be used for these industrial applications (see for example A. Peters [6], and the references herein).

Nevertheless we will observe this interesting field of research and we expect in the next future first positive results - which simply means for us: convergence of an iterative method with our kind of matrices.

4.3 Domain Decomposition methods

Domain decomposition methods split the global problem into local problems, which can be solved directly on different processors in parallel without communication between them. To achieve the global solution these results are used for an iteration with "little" communication. It can be shown that this iteration has a better convergence behaviour than a global matrix iteration but we still have to gain more experience with these promising methods to decide, if we can apply them for our kind of problems.

We want to close this chapter with a final remark on an often quoted "argument" against MPP-Systems.

This argument known as "Amdahl's Law" gives a theoretical speed up of a code depending on the parallizable part of the program. Amdahls's Law is formulated independendly of the size of the problem to be solved and therefore it seems to lead to the conclusion, that systems with more than - say - 32 CPU's can only be used efficiently, if the parallizable part of a program is about 99 %. From an other point of view we can find a discussion of Amdahl's Law in Gustafson et. al. [7]. The authors find some "counter examples" of Amdahl's Law, if they simply make it dependent on the size of the problem to be solved (No one wants to solve a small problem on a system with thousands of processors.). There we can also find the observation that the parallizable part of many codes grows with the problem size.

5 Soft- and Hardware Demands

For the use of MPP-Systems in industrial environments at least the following demands have to be fullfilled:

- the systems have to run stable
- it should be possible to checkpoint jobs for maintenance
- on MPP-Systems it should be possible to remove single processors without shuting down the whole system

From the point of view of a software developer for industrial applications the following demands arise:

- For the sake of portability a standardized programming model should be implemented on different parallel platforms.
- The development, care and software support of one (!) code from a workstation to a supercomputer should be possible, beside some hardware specific implementation of a few routines.
- Mathematical librarys should include direct sparse matrix solvers.

References

1. FE-Simulation of 3D Sheet Metal Forming Processes in Automotive Industry, Zürich, 1991, VDI Berichte 894

2. M. Hillmann et al.: "Mathematical Modelling and Numerical Simulation of Sheet Metal Forming Process with INDEED". 6. Internationaler Kongreß BERECHNUNG IM AUTOMOBILBAU, Würzburg, 1992, VDI Berichte 1007

3. I. Duff, A. Erisman, J. Reid: Direct Methods for Sparse Matrices, Oxford, 1986

4. C. Yang: A vector/parallel Implementation of the multifrontal method for sparse symmetric definite linear systems on the Cray Y-MP, Cray Research, 1991

5. M. Heath, P. Raghavan: Distributed Solution of sparse linear systems, Tech. Report UIUCDCS-R-93-1793, University of Illinois, Urbana, 1993

6 A. Peters: Nonsymmetric CG-like Schemes and the Finite Element Solution of the Advection-Dispersion Equation, Int. J. Numerical Methods in Fluids, 1993, Vol. 17, pp. 955-974

7. J. Gustafson, G. Montry, R. Benner: Development of Parallel Methods for a 1024-Processor Hypercube, SIAM J. Sci. and Stat. Comput. Vol. 9, No. 4, July 1988, pp. 609-636

High Image Quality Rendering
on Scalable Parallel Systems

Rolf Herken*

mental images GmbH & Co. KG
Rankestraße 9, 10789 Berlin, Germany

Extended Abstract. The term 'interactive rendering' is commonly associated with the special purpose rendering hardware of current high-end graphics workstations. But although the quality of the images produced by these systems has increased at an astonishing rate over the last few years, the correct simulation of optical phenomena, most notably of global illumination, remains to be outside their reach. Tricks like reflection mapping can be used to produce the illusion of global illumination, but they compromise the physical correctness of the image and thus fail in applications where this is required, such as optical quality control of free-form surfaces in CAD or lighting design in architecture. Furthermore, special purpose hardware systems do not provide the degree of programmability required for high-end computer animation image quality and complexity.

Currently, the commercial rendering systems modelling the widest range of optical phenomena are software based. They support a wide variety of surface representations, most notably trimmed free-form surfaces, and can process procedural shaders which are defined by the user in a special purpose shading language or as C language code fragments that are dynamically compiled and linked to the rendering software. All of these systems operate essentially in batch mode.

The performance of software based rendering systems on today's most powerful workstations is still between three to five orders of magnitude less than that required for real-time interactive work. The rendering of a single image in high-end computer animation production or in an industrial application such as the design of car bodies can take hours or even days on conventional machines for the typical size of the databases involved.

If we define the term 'interactive' to mean that the response time of the system approaches the average response time of the user to create a new situation which requires a recomputation it becomes evident that the current state of the art either compromises image quality or interactive performance.

It is argued that the simultaneous requirements of interactivity and very high image quality suggest the implementation of the rendering software component on truly scalable, distributed memory parallel computers.

This raises a number of implementation problems, in particular with respect to the algorithms and data structures that provide scalable performance on such computer architectures. The main issue is the effective use of distributed memory in the presence of adaptive acceleration techniques that produce irregular memory access patterns. A further requirement dictated by an intended interactive use of the rendering software is the ability to incrementally update the distributed database.

Since it is very likely that scalable parallel computer architectures will provide the dominant basis for large-scale computing in the near future, the development of such rendering software is of great industrial relevance. It can be seen as a first step towards high image quality virtual reality systems.

---

* The author can be reached via e–mail at rolf@mental.de

Parallel Processing in
High Integrity Aircraft Engine Control

S H Duncan, P L Gordon, E J Zaluska[1]
S I Edwards[2]

[1] Parallel Applications Centre, Southampton SO16 7NP, UK
[2] Lucas Electronics, York Road, Birmingham B28 8LN, UK

Abstract. There is a significant and pressing need for greater computing power in aircraft engine digital control systems. Unlike many other
application areas, safety-critical systems can not readily benefit from recent advances in microprocessor technology because of their requirement
for certified, reliable hardware. Parallel processing offers an alternative
solution to the requirement for increased computing power which enables
systems to be built from certified, medium-performance components.
This paper reports the results of a collaborative study by PAC and Lucas Electronics into the use of parallel computing in an aircraft engine
control application. Two key issues; performance and certification, are
identified. A prototype software tool set is described which enables the
parallelisation of sequential control programs written in the LUCOL[3]
high-integrity control language. Results from the parallelisation of an
existing LUCOL engine control program are presented.

1 Introduction

Persistent demand for increased performance and efficiency from aircraft engines
is driving the development of the gas turbine to new levels of sophistication. The
complexity of the controllers required for the new generation of engines now
threatens to outstrip the capability of the microprocessor platforms currently
employed in these systems. Although recent advances in RISC technology have
led to huge increases in the power of individual processors, the potential for the
use of these processors in engine controllers is severely limited by the requirements for high integrity. In particular nondeterministic processor features such
as memory caches are not acceptable in these applications.

The driving factor in the development of digital engine controllers is the
need to make engines more fuel efficient, more reliable and less polluting. Three
approaches can be taken to meet these requirements. Firstly, more advanced
control algorithms can be implemented to provide more precise control. Secondly, additional functionality can be added to existing controllers to perform
on-line health monitoring tasks. Thirdly, performance gains may be obtained by
executing existing algorithms at a faster iteration rate. Each of these options
requires significant increases in computing power: it has been estimated that the

---

[3] LUCOL is a trademark of Lucas Industries PLC

computing requirements for digital engine controls are currently doubling every two to four years.

Parallel architectures have a potential advantage in this application area because they can be built from relatively low-performance, certified components. The design cost and certification risks can therefore be lower for parallel hardware than for newly-developed sequential hardware of comparable performance.

Another benefit offered by parallel architectures is the ability to scale the hardware performance to the required level. It typically becomes increasingly difficult during the development of a controller to maintain the specified performance as new features are added. The ability to add extra processing units to provide incremental performance gains would be a valuable asset to the control systems designer, since it would often allow a great deal of optimisation and redesign effort to be avoided.

Two results must first be demonstrated before parallel architectures can be adopted as a core technology in engine control:

1. **certification** - it must be demonstrated that parallel applications may be developed within the strict software integrity specifications currently enforced for sequential programming languages
2. **performance** - it must be shown that the potential performance of the parallel architecture can actually be achieved on parallel control programs developed to the above specifications

There is relatively little published work relating to the use of parallel processing in high integrity control. Considerable research has been carried out into the use of parallel processing for control but this has not been within the constraints of a certifiable system. Thompson and Fleming[2] looked at the issues of using parallel processing for fault-tolerant gas turbine engine control but concluded that at the time the overheads of parallel processing made it unsuitable for real-time control and that it was unlikely to be acceptable to the certification authorities. Shaffer[3] considered the performance of parallel processing for jet engine control with a graph-based parallelisation technique, but did not consider the certification issues. De Oliveira and Fleming[4] considered the factored state variable description (FSVD) as an alternative method of extracting parallelism from control codes, but again this was only in the context of performance improvement.

The need for fault-tolerant hardware in high-integrity control systems has been studied by several authors (for example, FTMP [5]). Most of these studies have resulted in parallel architectures which can be quickly and reliably reconfigured after a hardware or software failure. A common problem underlying these architectures is that the additional software complexity necessary to control these functions detracts from the performance of the system. For this reason, we have restricted the scope of our study to the improvement of processing performance, with the assumption that the parallel platform can be incorporated into a fault-tolerant multi-lane architecture in much the same way as today's sequential controllers.

The typical approach to parallelisation of control software has in the past been to examine the control algorithm and look for inherent parallelism, concentrating on the most computationally intense parts of the code. This is unsuitable for general application since it tends to produce solutions which are highly dependent on the structure of the particular application. In addition, this approach requires the control system designer to have substantial parallel computing expertise. The approach taken in the work presented in this paper is intended to be more generic, with emphasis placed on software tools which aid the designer to parallelise an existing sequential control program.

The following sections of this paper describe a set of software tools which aid the parallelisation of existing sequential control codes written in the LUCOL[1] high-integrity control language. The parallelisation of a LUCOL code for a gas turbine engine controller is then described, and conclusions are drawn on the suitability of the method for incorporation into a certified development process for producing new parallel control codes.

2 Parallelisation

There are two operations which comprise the parallelisation of a real-time application: *partitioning*, where the application is decomposed into a set of parallel tasks which may be grouped together for allocation to separate processors and *scheduling*, where an ordered list of tasks is generated for each processor such that the performance of the system is maximised according to some measure.

The number of possible ways in which a program may be partitioned for parallel processing is related exponentially to the size of the program. It is therefore very difficult to partition a large program manually and be sure of the best performance. A representation is required which describes the internal structure of the program (the dependency relations between the statements) in a form which can be manipulated by a machine. A synchronous data flow (SDF) graph is such a representation.

A SDF graph (Figure 1) is a collection of nodes (representing processing tasks), connected by directed arcs (representing variables). Each node has a precedence level which determines its execution point in the sequential program. An acyclic SDF graph, in which all connections between a node and other nodes of lower precedence have the same direction, can be transformed into a multiprocessor schedule in which nodes are executed on separate processors[6].

The parallel partitioning and scheduling of algorithms which have SDF graph representations is a well-studied problem; such algorithms occur commonly in signal processing and control. SDF algorithms may be classed as block-type or stream-type depending on their mode of execution[7]. A stream-type algorithm is invoked repeatedly on a continuous stream of data, a block-type algorithm is executed once on a static data set. Performance criteria differ for the two types of algorithm: a block-type algorithm (such as a control program) is likely to be judged by its execution time or latency, whilst for stream-type algorithms the output data rate or throughput is usually more important than the execu-

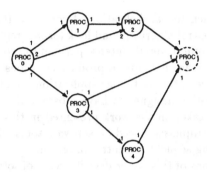

Fig. 1. Typical simple SDF graph

tion time for a particular data sample. The efficient parallelisation of block and stream-type algorithms also differs and is driven by the performance criteria.

For this work we have considered the parallelisation of block-type SDF algorithms. The requirements for certification have meant that a synchronised message-passing distributed-memory model has been adopted for the parallel architecture. This means that the variable space for each processor is completely independent from the others and that data can only be exchanged by agreement which enforces each processor to adhere to its static communications schedule and thus retain deterministic behaviour. This architecture also ensures that if one processor fails the others can be alerted by timeouts at the communication points.

The transformation from a SDF graph representation onto a synchronised message-passing parallel system is straightforward - at worst a synchronised communication is required for each data dependency (arc) which crosses the processor boundary. Figure 2 shows how the SDF graph in figure 1 could be scheduled onto two processors (also see figure 4).

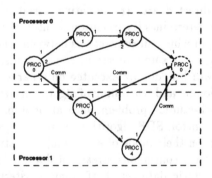

Fig. 2. SDF graph transformation to two processors

3   Parallelisation Tools

Present Lucas engine control codes are written in LUCOL, a specialised control language developed by Lucas for programming high-integrity control systems. LUCOL is a translated language which consists of a set of control-specific subroutines or *modules*, each of which has been coded and validated separately for the target processor. The restricted functionality LUCOL provides compared to a conventional high-level language is typical of control languages and is aimed at producing guaranteed behaviour.

A source code analyser has been developed which converts a standard LUCOL program into a SDF graph representation from which it may then be parallelised. The program consists of three functional stages: a lexical analyser, a parser and a dependency analyser. The lexical analyser and parser act together to transform a LUCOL program from a text file into a token-based data structure which can be manipulated by the dependency analyser. The dependency analyser uses symbol and statement table data to construct and display information about the LUCOL program.

The input program is first partitioned into *grains* to provide conveniently-sized conceptual units and to encapsulate the limited nondeterminism possible in the form of IF and CASE statements - this is essential to enable the execution path through the code to be traced statically and to ensure all nodes in the SDF graph will exist under all conditions. A precedence list is created by tracing the execution of the grains, whose entries correspond to the nodes of the SDF graph. Each grain also has an execution time associated with it stored in the precedence list and this is calculated from a database of worst-case execution times for each LUCOL module. Each grain is searched for external symbol references which are resolved by scanning backwards through the precedence list. A communications matrix (Figure 3) is then generated which shows the number of communications required between the nodes of the SDF graph.

```
                         receiver
                         0  1  2  3  4

          sender

             0           0  1  2  1  0
             1           0  0  1  0  0
             2           1  0  0  0  0
             3           1  0  0  0  1
             4           1  0  0  0  0
```

Fig. 3. Communications matrix

The precedence list and the communications matrix together contain sufficient information to construct the SDF graph and create a parallel schedule for the application.

A graphical scheduling tool has been developed which allows a user to manipulate the SDF representation of a program and place nodes of the graph on parallel processors interactively. The tool only allows the user to create schedules whose functional behaviour is identical to that of the sequential program. An estimate of the speedup obtained from the schedule is also displayed interactively. This is calculated by comparing the sum of all the execution times in the precedence list (the sequential execution time) with the highest of the sums of the execution times for the grains and the idle time between the grains currently allocated to each processor.

The scheduler forces the user to insert synchronisation points in the schedule to enable the communication of data dependencies as shown in the communications matrix. Communications are grouped together at synchronisation points to minimise the number of points required. The scheduler utilises a user-definable model of the communications hardware to reassess the estimated speedup to include the communications time for a given target platform.

An example schedule is shown in Figure 4 with the idle time represented in grey and the communications time in black.

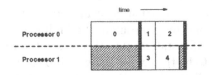

Fig. 4. Parallel schedule

The scheduler generates a separate LUCOL program for each processor in the system with the synchronised communications implemented using just two new LUCOL modules.

For development purposes a source-to-source translator has been developed which translates the output from the scheduler into an intermediate language for compilation on a parallel development platform using commercially-available compilers.

4 Application to Engine Control Code

The LUCOL analysis and scheduling tools have been applied to the parallelisation of a control code for a small commercial gas turbine engine.

The engine control code was developed by engineers at Lucas as part of a separate technology demonstrator project. It contains about 2000 LUCOL statements, and no consideration was made at the time of its development for parallel execution. An engine simulator, also written in LUCOL, is used to test the original engine control code and verify that the parallel version is functionally equivalent under test conditions.

The control code has been parallelised using the tools and executed on a network of Inmos transputers[8]. Closed-loop control has been achieved by running the engine simulator on a separate processor and modelling the sensor/actuator interface using the interprocessor communications. The dynamic behaviour of the closed-loop system has been validated against actual test data supplied by Lucas.

Performance results show that the measured execution time for the parallel schedule is in excellent agreement with the execution time predicted by the scheduler - the measured iteration time on two transputers using link communications is reduced by a factor of 1.18 compared to the scheduler predicted improvement of 1.19 (when scheduled using *typical* execution times for test purposes). Using an improved communications hardware model the scheduler predicts that the *worst-case* iteration rate can be reduced by a factor of 1.5 for a two-processor decomposition.

Note that to meet certification requirements the execution times used to estimate speedup must be *absolute worst-case* to guarantee that under all conditions the code will take no longer than this time to execute. This means the schedule generated is designed to be efficient for the worst-case execution of the code and under normal (measurable) conditions does not represent the optimum schedule.

5 Discussion

The acceptance of parallel processing technology into the high-integrity control industry can only happen gradually. This industry is necessarily conservative because human lives depend on the reliability of control systems. For this reason the approach adopted in this work has been to introduce one new concept at a time.

Initially the performance from parallel processing was demonstrated on a hardware architecture which could be implemented from existing engine control computer technology and using an existing control code. The LUCOL language was used as the basis with the only new constructs providing communications support. By parallelising a fully-functional existing code the (higher-level) fault-tolerance mechanisms have been automatically retained.

All of these considerations will make our results more acceptable to the industry.

To reap the full potential benefit from parallel processing, other issues including the use of active reconfiguration for fault-tolerance, the use of special purpose parallel processors, the use of an alternative language with in-built support for parallel processing etc. will all have to be addressed.

The methods and tools developed will gradually enable parallel control codes to be produced from the outset without the need for a sequential controller as a starting point.

More importantly than all this, however, is the need to demonstrate the certification of a parallel system. This can only happen by certifying a real system with the assistance of the certification authorities. Currently further work in this field is underway to assess the suitability of the Inmos transputer as a possible future parallel engine control processor and to build a potentially certifiable parallel engine control system.

6 Conclusions

This work has demonstrated the two results of certification and performance laid out as prerequisites for the use of parallel technology in high integrity controls. Firstly, the development of a set of tools which enforce constraints on the manipulation of a sequential code ensures that a certifiable code will not have its functional behaviour modified by the parallelisation process. Secondly, the speedup figures presented show that useful performance gains are attainable.

It is now the intention to validate the work further by parallelisation of a commercially significant control code onto parallel hardware suitable for replacing an existing engine control system and then to control a real engine.

If this validation is successful, then within 5 years from now the first parallel engine control systems could be flying.

References

1. Bradbury, M. E.: LUCOL programming manual. Lucas York Road (August 1991)
2. Thompson, H. A., Fleming, P. J.: Fault-tolerant transputer-based controller configurations for gas-turbine engines. IEE Proc. D **137** (July 1990) 253–260
3. Shaffer, P. L.: Multiprocessor implementation of real-time control for a turbojet engine. IEEE Cont. Sys. **10** (June 1990) 38–42
4. De Oliveira, M. C. F., Fleming, P/ J.: Digital controller for parallel processing architectures. Int. J Cont. **v56 n6** (1991) 1413–1437
5. Hopkins, A. L., Smith, T. B., Lala, J. H.: FTMP: a highly reliable fault-tolerant multiprocessor for aircraft. IEEE Proc. **v66 n10** (October 1978) 1221–1239
6. Lee, E. A., Messerschmitt, D. G.: Static scheduling of synchronous data flow programs for digital signal processing. IEEE Trans. Comp. **vC-36 n1** (January 1987) 24–35
7. Konstantinides, K., Kaneshiro, R. T., Tani, J. R.: Task allocation and scheduling models for multiprocessor digital signal processing. IEEE Trans. ASSP **v38 n12** (December 1990) 2151–2161
8. Inmos: The transputer databook (third edition). SGS-Thomson Microelectronics (1992)

An Embedded Solution Using High Performance Computing for Cost Effective On-Line Real-Time Monitoring of Industrial Processes

Daniel García; Francisco Suarez; Manuel García
Universidad de Oviedo, Campus de Viesques 33204 Gijón Spain

Enrique Lasso; Rafael Guzman
Tgi SA, Plaza Marques de Salamanca 3 y 4, 5ª Planta 28006 Madrid Spain

Trevor Carden; David Watson; Chic McGregor
Parsys Ltd, Boundary House, Boston Road, W7 2QE London U.K.

Faustino Obeso; Manuel Tarrio
Ensidesa SA, Industrial Automation Division Apartado 93 33080 Avilés Spain

Gianni Rota; Franco Cocola; Fiorella Degli
Etnoteam Spa, Via Adelaide Bono Carioli 20127 Milano Italy

Abstract. This paper deals with the Esprit Project named ESCORT, within the High Performance Computing (HPC) area. The paper starts with an introduction to the project and the objectives. Following, the technical context of work and the justification of the project are commented. After that, a brief description of the project is given. Within the description, the development approach, functional analysis, product tree, physical architecture and the demonstrator to be built are all commented. Finally, the benefits of the project, including economic and social impacts are shown.

1 Introduction

The ESCORT project is devoted to overcome the technological risks involved in the integration of general purpose MPP platforms in industrial plants and critical processes, designing and developing the necessary subsystems (interfaces to high-speed field-buses, for example), tools and methods to allow its reliable integration as very high-performance embedded systems. To evaluate the performance of the new system and its reliable integration in production lines, a prototype demonstrator will be developed and integrated in a hot rolling mill (steel industry).

At the end of the project, about two years of additional work will be required to reach a fully industrial product. All partners will exploit the results of ESCORT project and it will be mainly marketed through PCI, an European Economic Interest Group and the largest MPP vendor in Europe.

2 Objectives of Escort

The main goal is the obtention of a well proved, hard+soft platform to develop embedded MPP applications of broad industrial applicability. This includes the evaluation of available methodologies and tools for developing applications in real-time on distributed memory MIMD machines in order to establish the proper ones to develop embedded MPP applications. Another goal is the design of a flexible real-time monitoring system for manufacturing plants to allow in-advance detection and control of defects inserted in manufactured products due to the erosion and imperfections of the production machinery. The system will be applied for monitoring the influence in flat products of roller eccentricities in rolling mills.

3 Technical Context of Work

Last decade can be regarded as the basic research phase in MPP. Systems based on a wide variety of architectures and programming models were developed. Nowadays, the research follows two main lines:

- Development of new MPP architectures based on new faster processors and their associated environments for development of applications (operating systems and compilers).
- Utilization of developed hardware/software MPP platforms in high added-value applications.

Suitability of transputer-based MPPs to develop a wide range of embedded systems is basically due to the easy scalability of these architectures and their high performance/cost ratio. However, the integration of MPPs in industrial environments requires the development of interfaces for acquiring field signals in order to integrate them in industrial plants as stand-alone embedded systems. Summarizing, the technical context of ESCORT project is double:

- The European MPP technology based on transputers.
- The market of sophisticated high added-value industrial applications.

4 Justification of Escort Development

In the area of Massive Parallel Processing, the most important platforms are promoted by enterprises from USA o Japan. In the European Community there are platforms implemented using European technology, such as transputer processors. This project is strongly oriented to promote the European MPP platforms in industrial embedded applications. ESCORT will cover the gaps that avoid the integration of MPPs in industry. Besides, it will demonstrate that embedded MPP systems can work in critical environments with full reliability and operating in uninterrupted mode.

5 Description of the Project

5.1 Development Approach

The integration of general purpose MPP platforms in industrial plants is limited for the lack of interfaces with field-buses to retrieve industrial process signals. Other gap is the High-level software to handling signals and dynamic models in real-time over parallel hardware. These facts lead to the product tree of ESCORT system. The following task is the design and development of the architecture and subsystems used to build the HPC embedded system. The subsystems are integrated verifying the performances of the whole system. Later, the prototype is integrated in an industrial environment, verifying that it solves the requirements and problems of the selected industrial demonstrator, checking its reliability too. Finally the guide-lines about the extension of applicability of embedded MPPs to other industrial problems are obtained, making an initial assessment to the exploitation of project results.

5.2 Functional Analysis

The functions to be carried out by the items of the architecture described above, are the following ones:

- *Signal acquisition:* The field signals are acquired using intelligent capturers, which convert the analogical signals to a digital format and send them through a field-bus.

- *Detection of defects in production machinery:* An I/O processor included in the MPP must obtain the signals from the bus and distribute them between the high speed processors dedicated to signal treatment and modelling. This processors must supply the results of signal analysis to other processors to carry out the detection of the influence of production machinery defects over the manufactured products. The communication processor sends information to the process computer about the defects detected in the machinery and receive the actualized physical model of the production line.

- *Information for predictive maintenance and model handling:* A workstation maintains a mathematical model, which includes the geometry of the production line, the dimensions and data of all production machinery installed. This information is contained in a set of data bases, which are actualized through the production computer and/or the graphic intelligent terminals. This information is combined with the data of the products processed in order to predict in-advance the work conditions and the useful life of the tools/actuators/etc in the machinery.

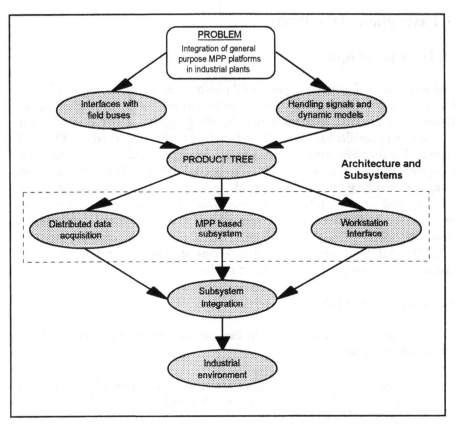

Fig. 1. Development approach of ESCORT project

5.3 Physical Architecture

Figure 2 shows the three level architecture of this system:

- A set of an intelligent capturers of analogical and digital signals, which communicate in digital format with a MPP for signal processing, using one or more field buses.

- The MPP will carry out the mathematical modelling of these field signals and then, doing an intelligent comparison of these models with the actualized model of the process, it will detect the influence level of the defects of the machines in the quality of manufactured products.

- The information about the defects is sent to a general-purpose workstation whose main tasks are the implementation of the on-line strategy for handling production models and accomplish the predictive maintenance of the production machinery.

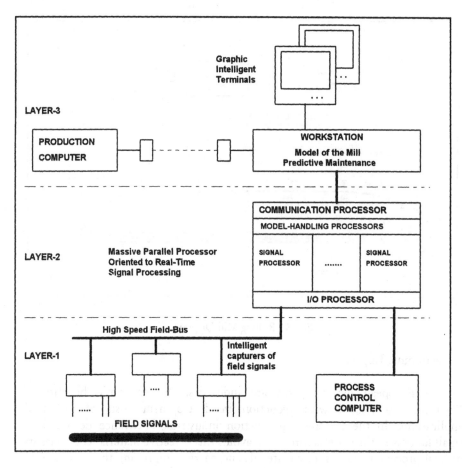

Fig. 2. Three level layered architecture of the system

5.4 Demonstrator

To evaluate the performance of the new system a demonstrator will be developed and integrated in a rolling mill of ENSIDESA. Figure 3 shows a simplified diagram of the demonstrator and its connection with the process. The main objective of the demonstrator is detecting the rollers which introduce thickness defects in laminated products. For that, ESCORT system reads signals (pressure, speed) of each roller in the mill and, carrying out a frequency analysis of these signals and thickness profiles for each coil manufactured in the mill, the raising of periodic defects with characteristic frequencies can be checked.

6 Benefits of the Project

ESCORT benefits are strongly related to information and production industries (economic benefits) and the workers of production industries (social benefits).

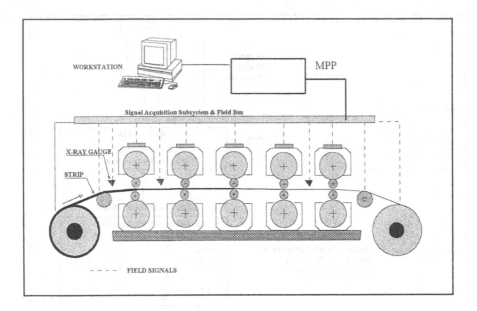

Fig. 3. Rolling Mill Diagram

6.1 Economic Impact

In the European hardware/software industries, the economic benefits of ESCORT are related with reduction in development costs of industrial applications. In the European production industries, in-advance detection of small failures in the material processed avoids this defective material continues its normal processing, saving raw materials and energy, improving the productivity and increasing the efficiency of installations.

6.2 Social Impact

This project affects significantly the work of personnel in the high-speed continuous production lines.

Without ESCORT, the quality control is carried out measuring the quality of products after their manufacturing. After that, the operator tries to search a-posteriori the causes of failures in the quality.

With ESCORT, the operators have an on-line support decision system, to monitor constantly the influence of imperfections in rollers over the manufactured products. The operators concentrate their efforts in predicting a-priori the problems which can originate products out of quality specifications.

EUROPORT - ESPRIT European Porting Projects

Adrian Colbrook

Smith System Engineering Limited, Surrey Research Park
Guildford, Surrey GU2 5YP, UK

Max Lemke

Smith System Engineering Limited, 53 Avenue des Arts, B-1040
Bruxelles

Hermann Mierendorff, Klaus Stüben, Clemens-August Thole,
Owen Thomas
Gesellschaft für Mathematik und Datenverarbeitung mbH,
D-53757 Sankt Augustin

Abstract. The primary objective of the European ESPRIT projects EUROPORT-1 and EUROPORT-2 is to increase the awareness and confidence in parallel high performance computing (HPC) platforms for commercial and industrial applications. This objective will be achieved by porting several large serial commercial and in-house codes to parallel architectures in a manner which will ensure that they have significant industrial impact within the two year time frame. Each of the two EUROPORT projects consists of a management institution and several porting consortia. This paper presents the objectives and structure of EUROPORT.

1   Introduction

At present, the situation regarding industrial applications of high performance parallel computing is unsatisfactory. On one hand robust and reliable hardware is available on the market today but on the other hand application software is largely either not available or not of commercial quality. As long as the major standard codes which are relevant for industrial product development are not available on parallel systems in a well validated form and supported by professional and experienced software vendors, the parallel computing market will stay small. As a consequence, the enormous potential offered by distributed memory parallel computing as opposed to today's state of the art vector parallel high performance computing or parallel shared memory systems for industrial research and commercial applications would not be utilised. The EUROPORT projects, which have a two year timeframe, started in January 1994 and aim to improve this situation.

2 Objectives

The primary objective of the EUROPORT projects is to increase awareness and confidence in parallel high performance computing (HPC) platforms for commercial and industrial applications. This objective will be achieved by porting several large serial commercial and in-house codes to parallel architectures in a manner which will ensure that they have significant industrial impact within the two year timeframe.

Target platforms are distributed memory computers as well as clusters of workstations. The major focus is on achieving high parallel efficiency on a portable basis; fine-tuning for specific hardware is not part of the project. The programming paradigms used in order to achieve portability are PARMACS and PVM. The emerging MPI standard will be used if implementations become available in time.

The ports of the application codes onto parallel architectures are being performed so that the resulting codes meet as many of the following requirements as possible:

- stability and supportability in a practical working environment,
- scalability between small and large machines,
- portability between different parallel architectures,
- functionality equivalent to the original serial code,
- efficiency on the parallel target architectures,
- performance improvements, if compared to traditional architectures,
- good price / performance ratio for systems,
- capability to run larger problems than on traditional architectures.

Systematic benchmarking will be performed on industrially relevant test cases: industrial impact is guaranteed by involving end-users in all benchmarking activities. Finally, in order to achieve increased awareness, major emphasis will be put on information dissemination.

3 General structure

The EUROPORT activity is structured into two clusters (EUROPORT-1 and EUROPORT-2), each consisting of a management organisation and several porting consortia. The management will co-ordinate the project, monitor and review the individual porting and benchmarking activities and disseminate the results. Each porting consortium consists of at least a code owner, a parallelisation expert and an end-user.

- EUROPORT-1 is managed by GMD and includes 9 porting consortia in the areas of computational fluid dynamics (CFD) and computational material dynamics (CMD). Four commercial CMD, three commercial CFD and three proprietary in-house codes of wide industrial use or impact have been selected. In addition, links to two other running ESPRIT projects (one in each of the above areas) have been established.

- EUROPORT-2 is managed by Smith System Engineering and consists of 10 porting consortia from a wide range of distinct application areas: computational chemistry (6 codes), databases, oil reservoir simulation, computational electromagnetics (2 codes), radiotherapy, earth observation, drug design and visualisation. Fifteen codes are being ported.

Clustering the porting activities into larger projects promotes synergy and consistency between ports. It also reduces effort and avoids the replication of tasks. This is especially important for providing services and effective information dissemination. Co-ordinating these are major tasks for the two EUROPORT management teams. Other important tasks are managing financial and contractual aspects of the project, monitoring and reviewing the individual ports as well as guiding and auditing benchmarking.

External service providers will contribute other skills and resources that are not internally available to the individual porting consortia and the management. Examples of services are:

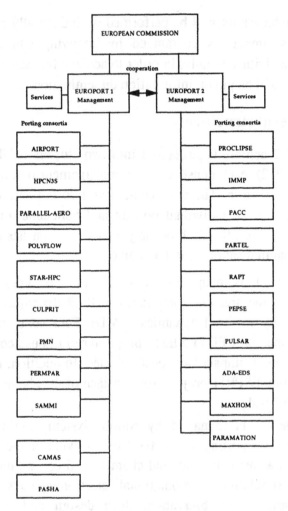

Figure 1: Structure of EUROPORT

- benchmarking services (e.g. hardware platforms including skilled support staff),
- expertise-based services (e.g. parallelisation expertise, platform-specific advice, arbitration advice),
- product-based services (e.g. access to development environments),
- dissemination services (e.g. conference organisation, press releases).

The structure of EUROPORT is shown in Figure 1.

4   Application Codes

EUROPORT has targeted a number of economically important application areas that are most likely to benefit from parallelisation (see above), and from these have been selected a few representative codes. The codes are primarily commercial codes with a large user base. In addition, some application codes, which are still under development and have just started to build their user base, but which still represent significant recent developments, are supported. In some areas, in-house codes are also important and a few of these have been selected. EUROPORT not only covers a range of application areas but also codes which have a variety of market dynamics, from in-house, through niche markets to general purpose.

EUROPORT-1 ports:

- AIRPORT (Aerospatiale, ARA, University of Greenwich, Intel Germany, GENIAS, CLE) is concerned with the port of two important fluid dynamics in-house codes (CEL3GR, SAUNA) that are mainly used for simulation in the aerospace industry. The parallelised codes will be validated and evaluated for several 3D configurations (e.g. wing-body combinations). Euler as well as Navier-Stokes computations will be investigated.

- HPCN3S (EDF, SIMULOG, INRIA, CERFACS, SIMULOG, CISE, von Karman Institut, Institut Francais du Petrol) is concerned with the port of the commercial fluid dynamics package N3S for the solution of compressible and incompressible fluid-flow problems. End-users will validate and evaluate the results through application specific industrial test cases.

- PARALLEL-AERO (EPFL, KTH, CERFACS, Aerospatiale, University of Stuttgart, CIRA, INPT-ENSEEIHT, Saab) is concerned with the port of a recently developed Navier-Stokes aerodynamic program (NSMB). Porting will be to five different parallel architectures, on a portable basis, including workstation clusters. There will be a number of industrial demonstrations, ranging from simple benchmarks to complete aircraft configurations.

- POLYFLOW (POLYFLOW, SOLVAY, Universite Catholique de Louvain) is concerned with the port of the commercial POLYFLOW code, which is used to simulate processes for which flows of viscous liquids play a dominant role. Heterogeneous workstation networks are the primary target architecture. One important end-user, a customer of POLYFLOW, will evaluate the results by running scaleable and realistic test cases.

- STAR-HPC (Computational Dynamics, Pallas, CRFIAT, Ford Motor Company, ICI C & P, Mercedes Benz) is concerned with the port of the commercial fluid dynamics STAR-CD code. The parallel code will be evaluated by four existing large customers of the current version from the automotive and chemical industries.

- CULPRIT (Transvalor, CEMEF, Liverpool University, PARSYS, Rolls-Royce) is concerned with the port of the three dimensional forging modelling package, FORGE3. The parallelisation approach will be based on existing Distributed Data Libraries from Liverpool University. The resulting parallel code will be validated and evaluated with a variety of data from the aero-engine industry.

- PMN (MacNeal Schwendler, BMW, Debis, CASA, PAC University of Southampton) is concerned with the port parts of the well-known MSC-Nastran finite element package. Validation and evaluation will be with a variety of data from the automotive and aerospace industry.

- PERMPAR (INTES, CESCA, IRCN, Bureau Veritas) is concerned with the port of a subset of the well known finite element PERMAS code. The code has a large industrial user base. The project will make use of the HYPERKIT tool for the basic handling of data structures and scheduling. The parallel code will be evaluated by two existing large customers of the current version from ship construction industry.

- SAMMI (SAMTECH, University of Liege, SNECMA) is concerned with the port of the SAMCEF finite element package. The code has a large industrial user base. The parallelised code will be validated and evaluated with a variety of data from the aero-engine industry. The aim is to solve large problems with up to 10^5 - 10^6 degrees of freedom.

- CAMAS-Link (ESI, Audi, BMW): As part of the CAMAS Esprit project, large parts of the crash simulation code PAM-CRASH are being ported. The purpose of the EUROPORT link is the extension of this work to allow a full frontal crash: the basis for benchmarks of the industrial partners.

- PASHA-Link (Cham): The well-known CFD code PHOENICS is being ported onto parallel architectures as part of the Esprit project PASHA. The EUROPORT-Link will provide a portable version available for benchmarking on various architectures.

EUROPORT-2 ports

- PROCLIPSE (Intera, EPCC University of Edinburgh, AGIP, Statoil): A portable, scaleable parallel version of a widely used application code, Eclipse 100, will be developed. The code is used in the petroleum industry for black oil reservoir simulation. The use of parallel processing will enable larger simulations to be conducted (improving accuracy) together with reductions in execution time (reducing costs) compared with the vector parallel systems currently used. Realistic reservoir test cases from the end-users will be chosen for the benchmarking and evaluation of the parallel code.

- IMMP (SERC Daresbury Laboratory, Free University of Amsterdam, University of Erlangen, ICI, Zeneca, Oxford Molecular): Three computational chemistry codes will be ported: GAMESS-UK (ab-initio quantum chemistry), ADF (density functional theory) and VAMP (semi-empirical molecular orbital theory). The use of parallel processing will enable many molecular modelling computations in the chemical and the pharmaceutical industries to become interactive rather than batch oriented thereby reducing development costs. Benchmarking will include geometry and transition state optimisations in the study of chemical reaction processes supplied by the industrial end-users.

- PACC (CRS4, Bayer, ENEA, Unilever, PAC University of Southampton, GMD, University of Karlsruhe, University of Groningen, University of Zürich OCI, ETH Zürich): Three computational chemistry codes will be ported: GROMOS (molecular dynamics), MNDO (semi-empirical quantum chemistry) and TURBOMOLE (ab-initio quantum chemistry). The use of parallel processing will enable many molecular modelling computations in the chemical and the pharmaceutical industries to become interactive rather than batch thereby reducing development costs. Benchmarking and evaluation of the ports will include typical problems occurring in current industrial research, e.g. elucidation of phenomena concerning physi- and chemisorption, and simulation of micro- and mesoscopic phenomena.

- PARTEL (Oxford Parallel, Vector Fields, Nederlandse Philips Bedriven, University of Genova): The aim is to convert the computational electromagnetic codes, TOSCA and ELEKTRA, so that they will run efficiently on a range of parallel processing systems from networked workstations to shared memory multiprocessors. The use of parallel processing will enable larger simulations to be conducted (improving accuracy) together with reductions in execution time (reducing costs) compared with the systems currently used.

- RAPT (Systems and Management, PAC University of Southampton, Ospedali Galliera): The general aim is to build a high performance system for determining the best treatment plans in radio therapy. This will involve the migration of the Monte-Carlo code EGS4 onto a parallel platform and the realisation of software packages which build the 3D representation the patient and enable visualisation of the resulting effects of the various radiation treatment. The use of parallel processing will enable visualisation to be carried out cost-effectively. Only vector parallel systems are currently capable of such calculations within the acceptable time limit and these systems are too expensive to be widely available to hospitals.

- PEPSE (British Aerospace, FEGS, CERFACS, University of Bradford): An electromagnetic problem solving environment will be parallelised, which consists of the Field Analysis Modeller and a three dimensional finite difference time domain solver of Maxwell equations, THREDE. The use of parallel processing will address the main areas where the lack of computational power seriously limits the size of problems that can currently be modelled on vector parallel systems.

- PULSAR (Elsag Bailey, Scot Conseil, NA Software, Liverpool University): This project aims to produce a scaleable parallel and highly portable version of the satellite radar processing and image understanding programs developed by two of the partners. The proposed work falls into two parts, the analysis of radar data and the visualisation of the results. The computational requirements of the algorithms are heavy and current processors, typically workstation-based, provide an inadequate response to deal with the high volumes of data involved. The advent of fully commercial highly parallel computing systems has, however, made it possible to provide adequate power for real-time SAR processing at economic cost.

- ADA-EDS (ICL, Software AG, City of Nottingham): It is proposed to migrate the ADABAS database to the European Declarative System (EDS) parallel platform designed specifically for the large scale commercial corporate market. The technical issues which would need to be resolved concern scaleable performance, reliability and the provision of an integrated single image of the system. The use of parallel processing will enable transaction per second (tps) rates to be achieved that are significantly higher than may be achieved on mainframe systems. In addition, the relative cost of each tps will be much lower than on mainframe systems.

- MAXHOM (EMBL, E Merck, Parsytec Computer): The aim is to implement, optimise and benchmark a protein database search code running on the most advanced parallel computers. This would be achieved by porting the multiple sequence alignment program MAXHOM. The goal of this project is a significant performance improvement such that scanning a complete database using the most sensitive search technique can be done interactively.

- PARAMATION (Perihelion, Cambridge Animation, Siriol Productions): It is proposed to port the cartoon animation ANIMO onto a parallel environment thereby demonstrating the advantages of parallel implementations to the entire visualisation and graphics industries. This will be achieved demonstrating a speed-up of at least a factor of four on the interactive painting operations on each multiprocessor personal computer, and a speed up of at least a factor of five on ten workstations off-line rendering the animation to film, HDTV or videotape.

Communication Requirements in Parallel Crashworthiness Simulation

G.Lonsdale [*], J. Clinckemaillie [⊕], S. Vlachoutsis [⊕]
and J. Dubois [⊕]

[*] ESI GmbH	[⊕] ESI SA
Frankfurter Str. 13-15	20 Rue Saarinen
65760 Eschborn	Silic 270
Germany	94578 Rungis-Cedex
	France

Abstract. This paper deals with the design and implementation of communications strategies for the migration to distributed-memory, MIMD machines of an industrial crashworthiness simulation program, PAM-CRASH, using message-passing. A summary of the algorithmic features and parallelization approach is followed by a discussion of options to minimize overheads introduced by the need for global communication. Implementation issues will be specific to the portable message-passing interfaces PARMACS and PVM, together with future possibilities offered by the MPI standard.

1. Introduction

The effective exploitation by industrial applications of the new generation of parallel High Performance Computing systems based on distributed-memory, MIMD architectures requires a significant porting effort since automatic parallelization tools or parallel language variants (for example, High Performance Fortran) are still at a relatively early stage of development. In order to achieve high efficiency and applicability over a wide range of platforms, the parallel programming paradigm of choice for fully unstructured (finite element) applications currently remains the message-passing paradigm. This paper deals with the design and implementation of communications strategies for the migration of an industrial crashworthiness simulation program, PAM-CRASH, using message-passing.

The features of the core-code, used in the CAMAS Project (see below), affecting its parallelization will be summarized and an overview of the parallelized time-marching algorithm will be given. Particular attention will be paid to the global communication requirements arising in the contact-impact calculations and possibilities for the reduction of the resulting communication overhead. Implementation issues will be specific to the portable message-passing interfaces PARMACS and PVM, together with future possibilities offered by the MPI standard. Results will be presented for the PVM implementation with the basic time-marching scheme.

This work reported on here was performed within the ESPRIT III Project CAMAS (Computer Aided Migration of Applications System). The central objective of this project is the construction of a workbench, an interactive experimentation platform, which will guide the engineer to the best suited parallelization strategy and programming interface for his application, given a specified parallel machine. A major part of this project is the migration of a core of the PAM-CRASH program: this migration being used to provide both input to the workbench design and definition and for validation of the workbench. This core-code migration will be extended to allow for full front car-crash simulations benchmarked for industrially relevant models as a supporting activity to the ESPRIT Europort-1 action.

2. Summary of the Parallelized Core-Code

PAM-CRASH is a Finite-Element Program specialized for solving the highly nonlinear dynamic problems arising in crashworthiness simulation. It uses an explicit time-marching scheme with unstructured meshes comprising mechanical elements which model the behaviour of the structure under consideration: beams, shells, solids and trusses. Quantities to be calculated by the program are either defined on the elements or at the nodal points defining the elements. The basic CAMAS Core Code is representative of the full code in that it maintains the compututational scheme and data structures employed, but restricts the element type to shell elements and includes only one form of contact algorithm (the general requirement for a contact-impact algorithm is described below).

The parallelization of the time-marching scheme with the unstructured shell-element meshes via domain partitioning was described in [1] and only the salient features affecting the communications requirements will be repeated here. In addition, we will consider the inclusion of contact calculations and the communications overheads which they imply. The question of obtaining a partitioning of the mesh is not addressed here - the PAM-CRASH Core Code makes use of a partitioning tool from the CAMAS Workbench - DDT - which is briefly described in [1].

A central-difference scheme is employed for the explicit time-marching at nodal points: given accelerations the central-differencing in time allows the calculation of velocities and displacements. The accelerations are calculated from the forces produced by the velocities and displacements from the previous time-step. These force calculations are performed *element-wise* and comprise over 80% of the computational cost of the simulation. Thus, partitioning is performed element-wise with sub-domain boundaries along element boundaries. The parallelized calculation is organised such that updating of nodal interface points is achieved by two uni-directional communications. An additional communication requirement of the time-marching scheme as described above, is the need for the calculation of a stable time-step based on the *globally* smallest element. Thus, a global reduction operation is also required.

The force calculations include the calculation of penalty forces arising from a contact-impact algorithm. This algorithm will also involve non-local communication due to the necessity for (possibly global) proximity and penetration searches:

Haug *et. al.* [2] give a detailed description of algorithms for contact-impact, we will concentrate here on a specific form, single-surface self-contact, whereby originally separated regions of the structure come into contact with each other due to the structural deformations occurring in the simulation. The contact algorithm has two stages. Firstly, a proximity check between nodes and non-connected elements. The proximity search having been performed, actual node-element penetration can be determined and can be corrected by, for example, the calculation of penalty forces.

Since the partitioning for the remaining calculations allows a near 100% parallel execution of computational tasks, a reasonable approach to parallelise the contact algorithm is to maintain the partitioning and to introduce communication of non-local data to allow the proximity searches to be performed locally. The simplest way of fulfilling this aim would be to provide *each* process with a copy of the full set of elements involved in the contact calculations. For problems where the full domain is prescribed as being eligible for contact to take place - this is not always the case in practice, indeed some applications optimize performance by specifying a significantly restricted set of elements, *a priori*, for the contact calculations - this would imply an all-to-all communication of the full set of unknowns held locally on each process. What is clearly needed to reduce the volume of communication is a filtering of the elements to be included in each local proximity search, based on current spatial locations. This will involve the global communication (all-to-all) of spatial information, but will then require a less extensive point-to-point communication of larger data sections. Such a scheme, using bounding boxes as spatial information, has been proposed by Malone & Johnson [3], and a similar strategy has been recently implemented in the PAM-CRASH core code.

3. Communications Constructs

3.1 Interface Communication

Since the finite element meshes used are unstructured, the interface communication steps (for updating nodal interface points) are: (a) controlled using run-time defined mailing lists, (b) employ asynchronous sends and receives. While some architectures would benefit from synchronous, blocking send & receive's, the organisational overhead would be prohibitive for an unstructured mesh application. The construction currently employed is the most straightforward, from the application point-of-view, but also reflects options which have been available in common, portable programming interfaces. Suppose a process needs to send information to *nsnd* 'neighbouring' (here to be understood as geometrical neighbours) processes and receive information from *nrcv* neigbouring processes. The process first performs *nsnd* locally-blocking, asynchronous sends, followed by *nrcv* blocking receives. This assumes that the mailing system provides sufficient buffering of messages !

An alternative to the above, and one which has not previously been available, would be to first issue *nrcv* non-blocking receives (with either *nrcv* independent user-defined buffers or receipt directly into the user's work-space) followed by *nsnd* locally-blocking sends.

3.2 Constructs for Contact

In Section 2., two possibilities for enabling proximity searches to be performed locally were described: an all-to-all communication of full sets of local process elements involved in contact calculations; an all-to-all communication of spatial information, followed by unique point-to-point communications.

The first option is likely only to be effective when a relatively small subset of elements has been pre-defined to be active for contact calculations. In this case, this subset of elements is most likely to be partitioned over a subset of the processes. Hence, the communication requirement is for an all-to-all communication within the process sub-set.

The second option may also be applicable to a subset of processors, but may just as well be applied when all processes are involved. In addition, the mailing of the spatial information implies the processing of that information and the construction of corresponding mailing lists. For this case, an efficient implementation would make use of a special process-topology, for example, a ring or binary-tree, to perform the communication of the spatial information. This topology would be quite different from that indicated by the connectivity of the sub-domains for the interface communication; i.e. the possibility to address differing process-topologies, with the guarantee of optimized process-processor mapping, is to be desired.

4. Exploitation of Portable Interfaces

The current PAM-CRASH Core Code has been implemented using two widely available, portable programming interfaces: PARMACS (Version 5.1), PVM (Version 2.4). For details of these interfaces, the reader is referred to references [4], [5] respectively. This section reports on features from these interfaces which have been employed and looks ahead to possibilities provided by the forthcoming message-passing standard, MPI.

For both programming interfaces the asynchronous locally-blocking send & blocking receive interface communication was used, as described in Section 3.1. Global communication for the time-step calculations was implemented differently for the two interfaces. The PARMACS interface provides information on a global tree structure, and the reduction operation was constructed using this structure. Although PVM 2.4 includes a broadcast facility, it does not include an all-to-one gather. Thus, the reduction operation was performed by performing all-to-one sends, followed by a broadcast - this option would clearly give lower performance for large processor numbers.

With the intention of portability over a range of architectures, PARMACS' provision of process-processor mapping is to be considered as a major advantage: the communication performance of some architectures is not independent of the distance betweeen processors. The mailing list construction for the sub-domain interface communication is exactly the correct basis for the general graph mapping in PARMACS.

As stated in Section 3, the sub-domain interface communication employed is, while a logically straightforward approach, very much influenced by the restricted point-to-point communication options within such programming interfaces as PARMACS 5.1 & PVM 2.4. The options within the MPI interface are much more extensive. The alternative communication strategy discussed in Section 3 would be feasible in MPI, in particular the avoidance of multiple receive buffers by making use of a MPI_TYPE_INDEXED derived datatype. In addition, full support is given for the global reduction operations arising. For the communications constructs related to the contact calculations, MPI allows global communication to be restricted to user-defined groups of processes and allows multiple topologies to be defined and exploited.

5. Results

In order to investigate the communications overheads for the basic time-marching scheme, i.e. excluding contact calculations, an extremely simple test example was chosen: a rectangle of shell-elements with strip-wise partitioning. This allows both performance patterns and costs to be modelled in an uncomplicated fashion. All results here are for the PVM implementation.

Table 1 shows the overheads due to the interface communications ("Interface") and the time-step calculations ("Reduce") for an FDDI-network of Hewlett-Packard 9000/735 workstations using a 10×500 (i.e. an extremely coarse) mesh, given as percentages of the total elapsed time for 1000 time-steps. Apart from the significantly improved performance of the vsnd-vrcv option over the standard snd-rcv (the former avoids communication via the PVM-daemon), Table 1 highlights the fact that the time-step naturally acts as a synchronization point thus giving overheads for interface updates and the reduction operation of the same magnitude.

Number of	snd-rcv			vsnd-vrcv		
Processes	Interface	Reduce	Total	Interface	Reduce	Total
2	32.0	3.3	34.6	2.1	1.7	3.5
3	29.9	32.6	35.1	2.4	3.7	5.9
4	42.7	44.7	47.5	3.6	4.9	7.6
5	42.9	46.3	49.4	4.6	6.8	10.1
6	47.6	50.2	53.8	6.1	9.3	13.1

Table 1. Max. & Min. Overheads as Percentage of Total Elasped Time

Figure 1 shows the speed-ups obtained on networks of IBM workstations and on the IBM 9076-SP1 with 2 interconnects, for a full simulation of the test example on a 50×500 mesh. The workstations were IBM RS/6000-560 with 16 Mbit/s Token Ring and Serial Optical Channnel Converter interconnects. The 9076-SP1 used 10 Mbit/s Ethernet and the High Performance Switch interconnects. PVM implementations were PVM 2.4 and the IBM specific PVM/6000.

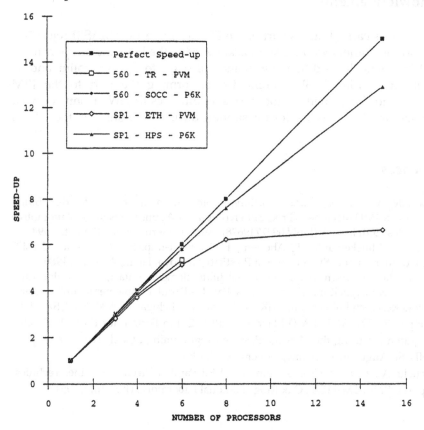

Fig. 1 Performances for a 50×500 mesh

The results in Figure 1 illustrate that the communications constructs are effective for a range of possible communication interconnects at lower processor numbers, and that the tightly-couple machine shows good performance behaviour, with a speed-up of 12.9 on 15 processors; taking a 50×1000 mesh a speed-up of 13.3 on 15 processors is achieved.

6. Conclusions

The parallelization of the PAM-CRASH Core Code and the corresponding communications requirements has been described, together with implementation possibilities for the exploitation of portable programming interfaces. Performance results on machines with powerful processors but relatively low processor numbers have been shown which support the choice of communications strategies. Future work will concentrate on scalability aspects and the behaviour of the communications constructs for contact calculations.

Acknowledgements

This work was carried out as part of the ESPRIT Project CAMAS (Project No. 6756) and the authors would like to acknowledge the help and support of all Project Partners. In addition our thanks also go to: M. Briscolini and F. Valentini from IBM ECSEC, Rome for performing the port to the IBM platforms and for providing the corresponding results; W. Höhn, Convex Computer GmbH, Frankfurt for his support during the testing on the HP735 network.

References

1. Lonsdale, G., *et. al.*, "Crashworthiness Simulation migration to distributed memory, MIMD machines", Proc. Supercomputing Applications in the Automotive Industries, 26th ISATA (ISBN 0947719628), Aachen, Germany, 13-17 Sept., 1993
2. Haug, E., Clinckemaillie, J., Aberlenc, F., "Contact-Impact Problems for Crash", Second International Symposium of Plasticity, Nagoya, Japan, Aug. 4-5, 1989
3. Malone, J.G., Johnson, N.L., "A parallel finite element contact/impact algorithm for nonlinear explicit transient analysis: Part II - Parallel Implementation", General Motors Research Publication GMR-7479, Warren, Michigan 48090-9055, USA, 1991
4. Hempel, R.; The ANL/GMD Macros (PARMACS) in Fortran for Portable Parallel Programming using the Message Passing Programming Model, Technical Report, GMD, St. Augustin, Germany, November 27, 1991
5. Beguelin,A., *et. al.*; A Users's Guide to PVM: Parallel Virtual Machine, Technical Report ORNL/TM-11826, Oak Ridge National Laboratory, USA, July, 1991

PAFEC–FE
A Commercial Parallel Finite Element Package

Ian Boston, Mike Surridge, Colin Upstill

Parallel Applications Centre, Southampton SO16 7NP, UK

Abstract: We present a parallel implementation of PAFEC–FE, one of Europe's leading commercial finite element analysis codes. An important aspect of this work was that the parallel code should retain the full functionally of the sequential code and employ compatible user interfaces. This paper outlines the method of parallelization used, and presents performance figures for a number of dynamics test cases.

1. Introduction.

As the design and development process of many products becomes more rigourous, many users of Finite Element codes are requiring higher levels of detail and accuracy. The factors of safety that were once employed to reduce the cost of the design process can no longer be applied, as the performance pressures of the final products increases.

For example, if the factors of safety can be lowered in the design of a new aircraft component then the overall mass of the aircraft can be reduced. This will have obvious benefits in the improved fuel efficiency of load carrying capacity of the final aircraft. The aircraft manufacturer cannot however sacrifice the safety of the aircraft in order to achieve this improved efficiency, and so the use of more detailed analysis of the components becomes necessary. Highly detailed analysis of components is expensive, and may ultimately not be possible within the design cycle using traditional computing technology. This is leading many producers of Finite Element codes to consider porting to parallel platforms.

PAFEC–FE is a commercial finite element code that has been in existence for many years. The code is not only capable of analysing structural problems but will also analyse many other type of problem including acoustics, magnetics and thermal problems.

The PAFEC–FE code has now been ported by the Parallel Applications Centre to the Intel iPSC/860 as a generic code that could simply be ported to other platforms. The test cases that have been run show considerable performance advantages and will allow the end user a far greater flexibility with the scheduling of many categories of jobs. The certain sections of the code have been rewritten to provide substantial parallel speed-up, whilst retaining all of the serial features of the code. The core solver algorithm used by PAFEC–FE has been retained in a parallel form, allowing the continued use of many of the features that in the past have made the code a successful product. This paper describes the alternatives for parallelization that were available to us during the development of this code on a parallel platform. It also presents performance results of the final code.

2. Domain decomposition.

2.1. Parallel elimination.

The method of domain decomposition is a standard parallel approach where the application data can be associated with a spatial domain, within which the computational algorithms act locally. The region to be analysed is decomposed into many smaller sub–domains, each of which is handled by a separate processor. Other processors must be consulted only when dealing with the edges of the sub–domain, so that the amount of inter–processor communication is often quite small (depending on the range of interaction required by the algorithm). Where suitable, domain decomposition gives high parallel efficiency, and the number of processors can be increased in proportion to model size, allowing very large computational problems to be tackled.

In the case of structural analysis, degrees of freedom are spatially distributed, and their coupling is initially local. The model structure can be divided into sub–domains along element boundaries, giving rise to a set of substructures whose boundary degrees of freedom are "shared" with their neighbours. All interior degrees of freedom can be eliminated in parallel without any interaction between processors. In doing so, each processor will accumulate modifications to the equations for the boundary degrees of freedom, and these must be combined before those degrees of freedom can be eliminated, possibly also in parallel. This procedure is illustrated for a four processor run in Figure 1.

2.2. Parallel back substitution.

Back substitution must then be carried out to obtain values for the degrees of freedom in reverse order from the elimination order. This elimination ordering is now a branched tree rather than a single list, and back substitution for parallel branches of this tree may be carried out in parallel.

The root processor initiates back substitution in the final boundary region, and communicates the solved terms to the contributing processors. This allows them to compute the unknown values in the previous boundary regions, and so on. In this way the back substitution activity propagates back up the reduction tree of Figure 1.

2.3. Expected performance.

The primary advantage of this approach is that the communication overheads will be small, as only data relevant to the boundary regions is communicated. The principal disadvantage is that during the first phase (elimination of interior degrees of freedom), the number of active degrees of freedom undergoing elimination (the front size) for each processor will grow to the size of the boundary of its sub–domain. This will clearly be larger than the maximum front size encountered in sequential (single domain) solution, by a factor of 2 in the case of Figure 1. Subsequently, the front size will grow even larger, although by then the number of degrees of freedom left to be eliminated will be small.

The computational complexity of the reduction algorithm is proportional to the square of the front size. The increase in the latter renders this approach unattractive,

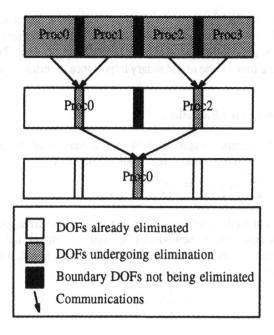

Figure 1. Parallel elimination using domain decomposition

since the amount of computation in the parallel code may be many times that of the sequential code. A further drawback is the increased memory requirement, which will force paging of data in and out of core for smaller models, imposing a further performance overhead.

These drawbacks obviously make the case for a domain decomposition method weaker. While judicious decomposition and subsequent frontal ordering will minimise the increase in computational effort, it was decided after further analysis that this method was not a suitable technique for the parallelization of this code.

3. Parallel Gaussian elimination.

3.1. Overview.

The core solver uses a standard technique of Gaussian elimination to reduce the set of system equations to a list of back substitution information. An alternative to domain decomposition is therefore to introduce a parallel Gaussian elimination method into the core solver. This low level approach does not affect the high level structure of the code, and can be made transparent to the user, who will be aware only that the performance of the code has been improved.

This approach involves parallelization of the forward elimination procedure only, leaving the back substitution to be carried out sequentially as before. Earlier profiling exercises showed that forward elimination dominates the execution time. The back substitution operations were found to be of secondary importance in terms of processor usage.

3.2. Column–parallel Gaussian elimination.

The starting point for this approach is a standard parallel version of the Gaussian elimination procedure for solving systems of equations of the form

$$\sum A_{ij} x_j = b_i \tag{1}$$

The Gaussian elimination method reduces the matrix A_{ij} to upper triangular form, whereupon a simple back substitution method can be used to compute the x_j. The reduction works by selecting each row in turn from equation (1), and modifying subsequent rows according to

$$A_{ij} = A_{ij} - \frac{A_{ik}}{A_{kk}} A_{kj} \tag{2}$$

$$b_i = b_i - \frac{A_{ik}}{A_{kk}} b_k \tag{3}$$

using the fact that the solution x_j is in not changed by replacing an equation (row) by a linear combination of itself and any other equation (row).

The simplest version of this algorithm involves distribution of the matrix A_{ij} by column across the processors. For each pivot row, operations from (2) – (3) must be carried out in many columns, and these can be done in parallel, at the cost of broadcasting a single (pivot) column to all processors.

It is clearly possible to distribute the matrix in other ways to carry out operations (2) – (3) in parallel just as efficiently. The choice of a particular distribution is usually driven by the partial pivoting method in use, or by the known structure of the matrix A_{ij}. The column parallel distribution is ideally suited to dense, non–symmetric matrices and pivoting within a column, in which the pivot row is selected by finding the largest element A_{ij} in the column being eliminated. This column is precisely the data which must be broadcast for a column–wise distribution, so that pivoting does not introduce further communication overheads.

3.3. Row–parallel Gaussian elimination.

Static finite element analysis methods codes deal not with dense, non–symmetric matrices, but with a sparse system matrix S_{ij} that is symmetrical about the diagonal. Furthermore, the PAFEC–FE code (and many other finite element codes) use a frontal solution method, in which the system matrix is generated row by row from a series of contributions, and rows are eliminated as they become complete. By using this approach, finite element codes avoid having to store the entire stiffness matrix, but work with a smaller "window" which can be held entirely within core in many cases. These factors render the simple column–parallel approach unsuitable, and have led us to opt for a row parallel Gaussian elimination, in which the data is distributed by row across the processors.

A further complication is introduced by the fact that the pivoting method used in PAFEC–FE involves selecting the (complete) row with the largest leading diagonal term. In fact, the leading diagonal values are used for other purposes than pivoting, so it was decided to retain them on a single processor (the root), which would carry out all the non–parallelized operations. The right hand side values are also dealt with by the root processor.

The symmetry of the system matrix can be preserved by writing the reduction procedure (2) – (3) for the system matrix as

$$S_{ij} = S_{ij} - S_{kl}S_{kj} \tag{4}$$

With this formulation, only the lower triangle of the matrix need be stored, as the upper triangle can at every stage be determined by symmetry. This also has implications for the parallel implementation, as will be described below.

To summarize, the particular features of the PAFEC–FE reduction algorithm have led us to adopt a row parallel distribution of data and computation for gaussian elimination. The root processor carries out all the operations except the elimination of stiffness rows, which is the only part of the code to be parallelized in the first instance. A set of node processors perform the elimination in parallel, apart from the leading diagonal matrix elements, which are handled by the root processor, which uses their values for pivoting. For this method of computational decomposition, it is necessary for all the processors to receive a copy of the pivot row (scaled so that the leading diagonal term is 1), and this must be communicated between them. The root processor also handles the right hand side values, and stores these along with the pivot row for later use in back substitution.

Initial implementations of the method gave poor performance, achieving speed–up that was barely improving as the number of processors used was increased. It was known that the computational grain size per communication for this algorithm can be rather small, and that performance on the iPSC/860 may be limited by the communications overheads incurred in broadcasting the pivot row to all processors. These overheads increase with the number of processors, so if these were the cause of the poor performance, further deterioration would be found as the number of processors is increased. In fact, the opposite trend was noticed, showing that the raw communications performance was not the problem. The poor performance was therefore believed to be due to sequential bottle–necks (especially on the root processor), and load imbalances.

It is clear that provided the rows of the stiffness matrix are allocated to processors in a sensible fashion, there can be little load imbalance between the node processors. The load balancing issues relate to the amount of work performed by the root processor relative to the nodes. If the root processor has too little work then that processor will be under–utilized, although this will be of little consequence for large enough networks. A more serious problem arises if the root has too much to do, because then all the nodes will have to wait, and the system will be limited by this bottle–neck.

The behaviour of the parallel code was investigated in detail to determine whether such a bottle–neck had arisen. The root processor performs little or no elimination, but it also has to generate the backing store and merge in the next element while the node processors are completing the elimination of the current degree of freedom. As expected, it was found by detailed profiling that these operations were taking too much time, with the most serious bottle–neck being in the writing of the back substitution information to disk. A simple calculation showed that the problem was not due to the output bandwidth of the raw disk, but rather to the time spent waiting for each output statement to be serviced.

This problem was alleviated by using a feature of the parallel machine, which allows data to be written asynchronously to disk. This is done by copying the data from the PAFEC–FE store in to a workspace, and issuing a system call for this data to be written to disk. The system call then operates in the background on a separate I/O processor, and the node processor may perform useful work whilst it is being carried out. When the workspace is required again for another write, a further system call is used to prevent its use until the previous data has been safely written out. It was found that by using several such buffers in rotation to write the back substitution information, the time spent waiting for disk access was reduced over 100 fold. The elimination of this disk access bottle-neck provided significant gains in performance and efficiency.

3.4. Parallel Dynamics

3.4.1   Overview

Inspection of the methods used in PAFEC–FE for dynamic and modal analysis revealed that the most significant computational step involves a similar reduction of a set of system equations containing not only stiffness terms, but also mass, damping and coupling terms. A reduced set of equations is obtained and then solved by various methods, depending on the type of analysis required.

This analysis led us to adopt a similar approach for parallel dynamics to that used to parallelize statics analysis. This is done in two stages :

i)   Parallelization of the (partial) reduction stage, using the same approach as for the statics case;

ii)   Retrieval of the reduced equations, for final analysis on the root processor.

These two steps are described in more detail below.

3.4.2   Reduction of the system equations

Dynamics analysis in the PAFEC–FE code is carried out using a lumped mass model containing a small number of degrees of freedom. This is derived from the full model by reducing out most of the degrees of freedom in a manner analogous to the Gaussian elimination procedure used for statics analysis, leaving behind a set of *master* degrees of freedom which form the reduced model. The main difference between the static and dynamic reduction procedures is that whilst the former involves only stiffness terms, the latter must also deal with mass and damping terms.

Detailed examination of the code reveals that the representation of the dynamics equations in PAFEC–FE is similar to the representation of the statics equations. The stiffness, mass and damping terms are stored as separate matrices in lower triangle form, with only a frontal window being held in memory during reduction. This is carried out by modifying the stiffness, mass and damping matrices within the frontal window only. The master degrees of freedom are often selected automatically as those with a high stiffness to mass ratio, by modifying the pivot selection procedure so that the best candidates are never selected for elimination. For this reason the serial scheme of reducing the stiffness, mass and damping terms for a single degree of freedom at a time has to be retained, and the parallel code could not be allowed to treat these terms separately.

It was therefore decided that all these matrices should be distributed by striping the rows across a set of worker processors, where the reduction procedure can be carried out in parallel, just as in the statics code. The parallel reduction of stiffness terms for each degree of freedom uses the same code as for the statics case, but the treatment of mass and stiffness terms required some extension of the parallel worker processes to incorporate the modification methods for these terms, taken from the sequential PAFEC–FE code.

Just as in the parallel static reduction method, it is necessary to collect together the pivot row of each matrix and distribute it to all the processors, where it is used to modify all other rows in the frontal window in parallel. Because the mass and damping terms from the pivot row are identical before and after the reduction of a stiffness terms, it has been possible to rearrange the detailed implementation so that the pivot data for mass and damping terms can be appended to the stiffness information. This means we need only a single communication call per reduction step, which is more efficient than three calls, each dealing with part of the data.

3.4.3   Retrieval of the reduced equations

When the reduction procedure has been completed, one is left with a number of un–reduced master degrees of freedom, whose stiffness, mass and damping data is distributed across the processors. The next phase is to collect this data onto the root processor for further processing.

Rather than just sending the outstanding freedoms to the root processor, the data is communicated to all processors in the network, including the root. Although at present all further analysis is carried out sequentially by the root, it should be possible to parallelize some of these operations in future, exploiting the fact that all processors have access to the reduced system of master degrees of freedom.

A side effect of implementing the collection procedure for dynamics analysis is to allow the parallel reduction method to be used to solve problems where the user deliberately leaves some degrees of freedom unsolved for later treatment. This has allowed the parallel code to handle sub–structuring, reactions, restarts, and other features which were not supported by the original prototype parallel statics code.

This version of the code has provided satisfactory performance for the reduction procedure, exceeding ten–fold speed–up for models which will run in–core sequentially on a single processor of the iPSC/860 machine. It is possible to introduce further optimisations into the code (by making more use of asynchronous file access, for example), but this has not been done, and will now be deferred whilst more important developments are carried forward.

4. Parallel Performance Results

4.1. Validation

During the development of the method described in Section 3, continuous evaluation of the performance of the method was conducted. Before any performance data could be gathered on the problem a number of validation phases had to be passed. Although these were inspection only tests in the initial phases of the development, the techniques used were stringent.

With the earliest parallel implementations, only small models were analysed. One of these models was a flat two dimensional plate with a front size of 30 degrees of freedom and 238 degrees of freedom in total. Although this model is tiny, it has allowed us to compare every pivot row produced in parallel with each corresponding row in serial. For a model of this size, the verified code produced byte identical back–substitution files, indicating that the parallel code is not only producing identical parallel solutions, but also that the rounding errors are identical.

To test the code more thoroughly a number of three dimensional models were generated with front sizes up to 2034 degrees of freedom. For models of this size, binary comparisons of the parallel and serial back substitution files files were impractical, since round off errors would cause least significant bit changes in the back substitution information. Instead, random nodes were selected from the output files and compared. In general up to 10 nodes throughout the model were compared before the version of the code was accepted as accurate. The impact of the parallel code on methods outside the reduction routine has been tested by passing 120 test cases, supplied by PAFEC Ltd through the code. The test cases are designed to validate all the methods used in the code, for operation and accuracy. Four of these test cases failed, but the parallel code was deemed to have passed initial validation since the failed test cases used optimised elimination techniques for very small models and models run out of core.

4.2. Dynamics Performance Analysis

Performance analysis of the code was performed by timing the elimination of two test jobs, against the elimination time of a serial run. The results of these measurements on the Intel iPSC/860 machine are expressed in terms of parallel speed–up $S(P)$. The sequential run time was found using the sequential version of the code on a single i860 processor, and the ratio of this to the parallel run–times for 2 or more processors is given in Table 1

No of Processors	Front size = 360	Front size = 774
1	1.00	1.00

2	1.40	1.40
4	3.33	3.94
8	5.00	7.59
16	6.52	11.80

Table 1 Parallel speed–up for the reduction phase in modal analysis.

These results are most easily analysed by plotting speed–up and parallel efficiency $S(P)/P$ against the number of processors P (Figure 2.).

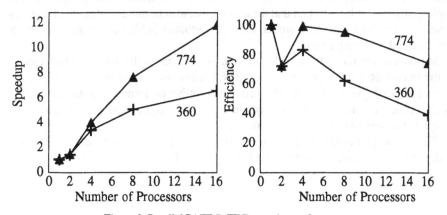

Figure 2. Parallel PAFEC–FE Dynamics performance

From these graphs it is apparent that the two processor implementation is not particularly efficient. This is to be expected, as there is only one worker processor carrying out the reduction, so the only performance improvement to be expected over the sequential code arises from overlapping this and other parts of the code (such as I/O).

For more than two processors, we see that the parallel dynamics code performs reasonably well for the larger of the two test models. Speed–up of nearly 12 over 16 processors will provide a useful reduction in the run time for this phase of the computation.

5. Conclusions

The two approaches for parallelization of the PAFEC–FE identified by code analysis have been investigated.

The drawbacks of the domain decomposition method have been confirmed by experiments using the PAFEC–FE sub–structuring facility. This method is of limited effectiveness, and could only succeed for small processor networks with a low performance interconnect. At present, small workstation clusters may fall into this category.

The alternative low level parallelization of the reduction procedure has proven much more satisfactory. The method has been implemented and validated, and the results agree with those produced by the original PAFEC–FE code. This method is entirely transparent to the user, the only observable difference between parallel and sequential codes being in the speed of reduction.

Performance testing has shown parallel speed up for all sizes of models, with the best results being obtained for large models (with over 1000 degrees of freedom on the solution front). This is entirely satisfactory, since small problems which run in minutes sequentially do not need dramatic improvements in execution speed. Larger models which require hours or days to solve will run much faster through this parallel implementation. It is important that the user be able to determine how many processors should be used for a particular model, and a performance prediction program has been implemented for this purpose.

Memory usage across the parallel machine is efficient, so that models which cannot be run in core on a single processor can fit within core once the data has been divided up amongst multiple processors. This provides a further performance advantage for the parallel code, so that a model which would take over 2 days on a single processor was completed in less than 1.5 hours on 16 processors!

The low level method that has been adopted has been shown to be applicable to all of the primary solution techniques used in PAFEC–FE.

Solving Large-Scale Nonnormal Eigenproblems in the Aeronautical Industry Using Parallel BLAS

M.Bennani[1], T. Braconnier[2] and J.C. Dunyach[3]

[1] ENSIAS, BP 713, Agdal Rabat, Maroc.
[2] CERFACS-ERIN, 42 av. G. Coriolis, 31057 Toulouse cedex.
[3] Aerospatiale Avions, A/DET/AP, 316 Route de Bayonne, 31060 Toulouse Cedex.

Abstract. We consider a large-scale nonnormal eigenvalue problem that occurs in flutter analysis. Matrices arising in such problems are usually sparse, of large order, and highly nonnormal. We use the incomplete Arnoldi method associated with the Tchebycheff acceleration in order to compute a subset of the eigenvalues and their associated eigenvectors. This method has been parallelized using BLAS kernels and has been tested on various vector and parallel machines.
This work has been conducted at CERFACS in cooperation with the Aerospatiale Avions (Structural research and development department).

1 Description of the problem

Most of the large-scale nonnormal eigenproblems that arise in research or engineering fields like mechanics or aerodynamics are related to the stability analysis of a physical system. A large-scale problem is considered that occurs in structural mechanics combined with aerodynamics: the flutter phenomenon. Flutter is a dynamic instability that can occur in structures in motion, subject to aerodynamic loading. It is a self-induced vibrational motion initiated by a source of energy external to the structure. For a wing, it occurs when a torsional vibration is in phase with the flexion motion. This coupling may occur during particular flight conditions (dependent on the speed of the plane, the air density ...). This is the type of phenomenon that aircraft designers seek to eliminate as much as possible. Much of their work is concerned with ensuring stability of airplanes at all times, speeds and altitude ranges.

The modelling of the flutter phenomenon for an airplane in flight under the influence of unsteady aerodynamic loads leads to a differential equation in time, which is then discretized by a finite-element method. The general formulation of the matrix equation using generalized coordinates $\xi(t)$ is :

$$[M]\{\ddot{\xi}(t)\} + [C]\{\dot{\xi}(t)\} + [K]\{\xi(t)\} = \{Q(t)\} \quad (1),$$

where $[M]$, $[K]$ and $[C]$ are the generalized mass, stiffness and damping matrices and $\{Q(t)\}$ the generalized airforce vector in the time domain.
After the finite-element discretization, equation (1) becomes

$$M\ddot{X} + KX = B\dot{X}, \quad \text{see [11]}$$

where M is the mass matrix and K is the structural stiffness matrix arising from the finite-element discretization of the plane. K is sparse, symmetric, strongly positive definite and thus invertible. B is nonsymmetric and nonnormal [5]. The size of all these matrices is N.

¿From the industrial point of view, K and M are well defined and B is an estimation of the aerodynamical contribution at the nodes of the structure. The nonnormality of the problem is given by B. The computation of the critical modes of this physical system yields a quadratic nonnormal eigenproblem which can be classically transformed into the standard form $Ax = \lambda x$, where $A \in \mathcal{M}_{n \times n}(\mathbb{R})$ and $n = 2N$, $x \in \mathbb{C}^n$, with $x = x_0 e^{i\omega t}$ and $\lambda = -\omega^2 \in \mathbb{C}$ (see [8]). A is nonsymmetric and nonnormal ; its order may reach 5×10^5. The critical modes of interest for this system are described by complex eigenvalues whose imaginary parts lie in a frequency range chosen by the engineer.

2 Numerical difficulties of the problem

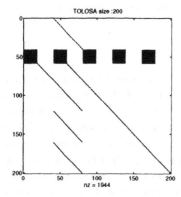

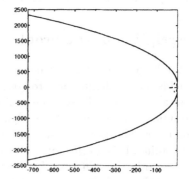

Fig. 1. Pattern of the Tolosa matrix of order 200.

Fig. 2. Spectrum of the Tolosa matrix of order 2.10^3.

The set of matrices obtained from the physical problem is called Tolosa ([2, 10]). As explained in the previous section, the matrices come from a finite-element modelisation and their order can reach values up to 10^5. For such large eigenproblems, we must adopt a **sparse** storage of the matrices. We only store the nonzero entries of the matrix. Figure 1 shows the pattern of the Tolosa matrix of order 200. When we increase the order of the matrix, the number of blocks (say 5) and their sizes (say 18) remain constant; only the diagonals before and after the blocks increase. Figure 2 shows the spectrum of the Tolosa matrix of size 2.10^3 computed by the QR algorithm which is our reference algorithm. The following remarks can be made :

1. when the order of the matrix increases, many eigenvalues can become close or multiple and defective,
2. generally, physical problems which yield such spectra (of "parabolic shape") are known to be unstable,
3. the real parts of the eigenvalues are negative and only the eigenvalues having the largest imaginary parts are interesting from a physical point of view. Hence, we will only calculate a subset ($\sim$ 30) of the eigenvalues.

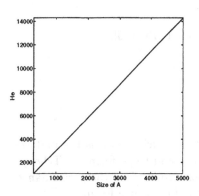

Fig. 3. He versus n.

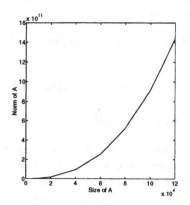

Fig. 4. $\|A\|_F$ versus n.

We can see in Figure 3 that the Tolosa matrices become highly nonnormal when the order n increases. The Henrici number He is the normalized relative measure of the departure of normality. When it is large, the iterative method used can present a bad convergence (see [7]). When He increases, so does $\|A\|$ as shown in Figure 4. To take into account large values of $\|A\|$, we have based our stopping criteria on the backward errors associated with the problem $Ax = \mu x$ (see [4]) :

$$\max_{i=1...r} \frac{\|Ax_i - \mu_i x_i\|_2}{\|A\|_F \|x_i\|_2} = \max_{i=1...r} \eta_{d_i}.$$

3 Choice of the algorithm

The problem is to determine a subset of the r eigenvalues of A with largest imaginary parts and their corresponding eigenvectors, with an eigensolver which takes into account the sparsity of the Tolosa matrix, and which is stable, robust and backward stable on highly nonnormal matrices. For these reasons, we have chosen the iterative **incomplete Arnoldi method**, associated with the **Tchebycheff acceleration** (see [14, 3, 6]). Some remarks can be made about this algorithm :

1. it is based on the QR algorithm on the projected matrix $H = V^*AV$, into the Krylov subspace V of size $m \ll n$ (Eispack routine),

2. The building of the Krylov subspace and the Tchebycheff acceleration steps are the most time consuming part of the algorithm. We use extensively BLAS routines of levels 1 and 2 to obtain the maximum efficiency (these routines are optimized for the target machines),

3. this algorithm is more vectorial than parallel, but since the order of the problem is large ($n \gg 1000$), automatic loop parallelization gives good results,

4. the stopping criteria are based on backward errors,

5. we use a new ellipse determination ; this ellipse is not optimal but is obtained much faster than in the algorithm used in the earlier versions of the code ([13, 14, 3]).

More details about this algorithm can be found in [1, 15, 3, 6].

4 Costs of the computation

4.1 Time computation cost

The algorithm requires, from the user, the routine which performs the matrix-vector product (used to build the Krylov subspace and to perform the Tchebycheff acceleration). This routine must be optimized to increase the performance of the algorithm. In this case, we store the matrix in a sparse form.

The use of the QR algorithm may not be feasible for problems of very large order because it leads to prohibitive CPU time and storage requirements. For these reasons, the choice of the order m of the Hessenberg matrix is crucial for the performance of the method. Another crucial parameter of the method is the choice of k : the degree of the Tchebycheff polynomial. The last computation which costs a significant amount of CPU time is the computation of $\|A\|_F$ used for the stopping criterion. A recommended alternative to avoid this cost is to use an estimation of this value (see [12]).

4.2 Memory cost

Once again, the order m of the Hessenberg matrix H rules the performance of the algorithm. We must store the Krylov basis V (V is of order $n \times m$) to compute the associated eigenvectors of the wanted eigenvalues (recall that if y_i is solution of $H y_i = \mu_i y_i$, then we have $A x_i = \mu_i x_i$ with $x_i = V y_i$). This storage can alternatively be replaced by storing on a disk file the columns of V. On the other hand, the storage of the Tolosa matrix A is optimal and its sparsity is totally exploited. For a Tolosa matrix of order 2.10^3, the computation of 20 eigenvalues leads to a storage of ~ 4 Mwords if we store in memory the full Krylov basis V.

5 Performance of the algorithm

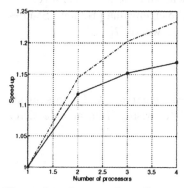

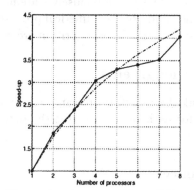

Fig. 5. Speed-up on Cray $C90$.   **Fig. 6.** Speed-up on Alliant $FX80$.

To test the parallel efficiency of the code, we have computed the 4 eigenvalues having the largest imaginary part of the Tolosa matrix of size $n = 10^4$ using the following parameters : $m = 200$ and $k = 400$. This computation has been made on an Alliant $FX80$ with 8 processors (Figure 6) and on a Cray $C90$ with 4 processors (Figure 5). On this figures, solid line corresponds to the effective speed-up and the dashed line to the theorical one. The theorical speed-up is computed according to the Amdhal law (see [9]) : $S_{th} = \frac{p}{f+(1-f)p}$, where

- p is the number of processors,
- f is the percentage of the time spent in parallel routines using one processor.

We have used for the value of f the percentage of time spent in BLAS routines. We can see that the effective speed-up is very close to the theorical one. This proves that our code has a very good parallel efficiency, mainly because it relies upon parallel BLAS for most of the time consuming kernels. For this particular Tolosa matrix of order 10^4, we computed 4 eigenvalues in 830 seconds on an Alliant $FX80$ (with 8 processors) and in 30 seconds on a CRAY $C90$ (with 4 processors). From an industrial point of view, such computations are still expensive but feasible.

6 Conclusions

The incomplete Arnoldi method associated with the Tchebycheff acceleration is one of the most robust algorithm for solving very large eigenproblems. Moreover, our experimentations showed that it can be efficiently parallelized using BLAS kernels and that its CPU and memory requirements are acceptable, even for large matrices.

In the future, new aircraft optimization challenges will require to handle more and more characteristics such as dynamic behaviour with control laws, elastoacoustic coupling and so on... Such large industrial problems modelling physical phenomena are likely to be more and more difficult to compute. In most cases, the numerical results in themselves are not sufficient and should be conforted by a thorough study of the numerical properties of the eigenvalue problem. Studies on the robustness of this algorithm are reported elsewhere [7]

Acknowledgments

We thank the Structural research and development department of Aerospatiale Avions for its help in providing the industrial data arising from aeroelasticity problems.

References

1. W.E. Arnoldi. The principle of minimized iterations in the solution of the matrix eigenvalue problem. *Quart. Appl. Math.*, 9(1):17–29, 1951.
2. Z. Bai. A collection of test matrices for the large scale nonsymmetric eigenvalue problem. Technical report, University of Kentucky, 1993.
3. M. Bennani. *A propos de la stabilité de la résolution d'équations sur ordinateurs.* Ph. D. dissertation, Institut National Polytechnique de Toulouse, December 1991.
4. M. Bennani and T. Braconnier. Stopping criteria for eigensolvers, November 1993. Submitted to Jour. Num. Lin. Alg. Appl.
5. C. Bes and J. Locatelli. Structural optimisation at aerospatiale aircraft. In *A.I.A.A. Structural Dynamics and Materials Conference*, pages 2619–2624, April 1992.
6. T. Braconnier. The Arnoldi-Tchebycheff algorithm for solving large nonsymmetric eigenproblems. Tech. Rep. TR/PA/93/25, CERFACS, 1993.
7. T. Braconnier, F. Chatelin and J.C. Dunyach. Highly Nonnormal Eigenproblems in the Aeronautical Industry, January 1994. Submitted to Japan Jour. of Indus. Appl. Math.
8. F. Chatelin. *Eigenvalues of matrices.* Wiley, Chichester, 1993. Enlarged Translation.
9. M. J. Daydé and I. S. Duff. Use of level 3 BLAS in LU factorization in a multiprocessing environment on three vector multiprocessors, the ALLIANT FX/80, the CRAY-2, and the IBM 3090/VF. *Int. J. of Supercomputer Applics.*, 5:92–110, 1991.
10. I.S. Duff, R.G. Grimes, and J.G. Lewis. User's Guide for the Harwell-Boeing Sparse Matrix Collection. Technical Report TR-PA-92-86, CERFACS, August 1992.
11. C.R. Freberg and E.N. Kemler. *Aircraft Vibration and Flutter.* Wiley, New-York, 1944.
12. W. W. Hager. Condition estimates. *SIAM J. Sci. Stat. Comput.*, 5:311–316, 1984.
13. D. Ho, F. Chatelin, and M. Bennani. Arnoldi-Chebychev method for large scale nonsymmetric matrices. *RAIRO Math. Modell. Num. Anal.*, 24:53–65, 1990.
14. Y. Saad. Chebyshev acceleration techniques for solving nonsymmetric eigenvalue problems. *Math. Comp.*, 42(166):567–588, 1984.
15. Y. Saad. *Numerical Methods for Large Eigenvalue Problems.* Algorithms and Architectures for Advanced Scientific Computing. Manchester University Press, Manchester, U.K., 1992.

Supercomputing on a Workstation Cluster: A Parallelized Lattice-Gas Solver for Transient Navier-Stokes-Flow

M. Krafczyk [1], E. Rank
Lehrstuhl NMI, FB Bauwesen, August-Schmidt-Str. 8
Tel.: ++49 231 755 2093, fax: ++49 231 755 2532,
kraft@busch.bauwesen.uni-dortmund.de
University of Dortmund, D-44221 Dortmund, Germany

Abstract

The last decade has seen the development of Lattice-Gas (LG) schemes as a complementary if not alternative method for the simulation of moderate Reynolds-Number Navier-Stokes-Flow. After a short introduction we present a detailed discussion of implementation features for a specific 2D-LG algorithm, which runs in parallel on a workstation-cluster, discuss simulation results and maximum CPU performances. Finally, we attempt to point out present problems and perspectives of these algorithms on virtual parallel machines.

1 Introduction

During the last 10 years Computational Fluid Dynamics has made tremendous progress in simulating more and more complex flow problems. Numerous publications and conferences indicate the continuously increasing interest not only in the academic but also in the industrial world (e.g. [2]).

Nearly all CFD-methods can be considered as discretization methods for partial differential equations, such as finite difference, finite volume, finite element, spectral or boundary integral element methods. Virtually unrecognized by the scientific mainstream in CFD during the last decade, a completely different approach to flow simulation has been developed in Computational Physics. The basic idea of *Lattice-Gas Solvers* (LGS) goes back to the Cellular Automaton (CA) concept of John von Neumann [6]. A CA is a dynamic system represented by a grid of arbitrary dimension. The state of the system is represented by the discrete states of all of its gridpoints. Dynamic development of the state of a gridpoint is a function of the states of a (predefined) local neighbourhood and its own present state. The mapping of a present state to a subsequent state is

---

[1] The work of the first author was supported by SIEMENS AG, Corporate Research and Development

defined by time independent, predefined rules covering the whole phase space of a neighbourhood. The phase space of a single grid point is usually taken to be very small, eventually binary. Such a class of systems is known to show arbitrarily complex behaviour and to simulate a variety of natural phenomena, provided that an adequate definition of rules is given. As the rules can be applied to the gridpoints simultaneously, CA algorithms are inherently parallelizable, an advantage that might gain significant importance in future.

2   Description

We present simulations using a particular member of a special class of CA, the so-called Lattice-Gases. An extensive bibliography about this topic can be found e.g. in [1], a detailed description of our implementation is given in [5]. LGS use objects ('cells') being extremely simple compared to finite boxes or finite elements. The state of a cell is usually described by only a few bits to represent the existence of particles. These states are subject to simple logical operations defining collision and motion of particles on the grid. Frisch, Hasslacher and Pomeau showed [4], that under certain limitations and for special classes of lattices in such systems large ensembles of particles mimic fluid flow described by the incompressible Navier-Stokes equations. LGS are *explicit* time stepping procedures; *no equation systems* have to be solved. As there is only strictly local interaction between cells, LGS are *inherently parallel*, being suitable to coarse grain as well as to fine grain parallelization. They are very promising for *dynamic* flow phenomena, multi component flow and flow through geometrically very complex structures (e.g. porous media). The outmost challenge would be to construct appropriate hardware to handle the logical operations needed in an LG code in a hardwired manner. Attempts in this direction are under way [7], but usually one has neither special hardware nor a supercomputer on hand. Our simulations showed that there is an alternative at least to midrange supercomputers: A cluster of workstations connected by standard ethernet and a Parallelizing Software Environment (e.g. EXPRESS, PVM) which allows to construct a virtual machine with enormously increased memory and CPU power for our LGS.

3   Results

Figure 1 sketches the Host-Node algorithm for the LG-simulation of moderate Reynolds number flow for one and two flow components. The implementation was done on a workstation cluster of HP 9000/715/50 machines using the EX-PRESS parallel environment [3]. It turned out that due to the inherent structure of lattice gases it is possible to reduce the communication between computing nodes in a way that allows an efficiency of about 85 % using thirty machines. This leads to a maximum nominal performance of about one Gflops in our system. A collection of EXPRESS routines effectively hides the virtual parallel machine from the user by means of automatic domain decompositioning. As a numerical example we present simulation results of dynamic one- and two component flows. Fig. 2 shows a non-stationary grooved channel flow dynamics at $Re \simeq 375$, fig. 3 shows coupled diffusion-flow effects between miscible flows at $Re \simeq 100$.

4   Discussion and Conclusions

The development of LG methods as simulation tools has just begun. Yet it is not clear, how important this class of algorithms will become in the next years. The efficiency of future flow simulations depends apart from other problems on how effectively an algorithm can be mapped onto existing hardware. As future high performance hardware will surely be massively parallel, LG methods seem to offer at least a valuable extension to classical discretization methods, which are often hard to parallelize. The possibility to construct a virtual parallel machine from a workstation cluster using appropriate parallelizing software offers a low cost alternative for high performance simulations in this area.

References

[1] *Bibliography for NATO Workshops on LG-Methods*, Physica D 47 (1991) p. 299-337

[2] CH. HIRSCH ET AL. *Proceedings of the first European CFD Conference*, 7.-11.9.92, Brussels

[3] EXPRESS REFERENCE MANUAL, *ParaSoft Coorporation*

[4] U. FRISCH, B. HASSLACHER AND Y. POMEAU: 'Lattice-Gas automata for the Navier-Stokes equation' in Phys. Rev. Lett. 56 (1986) p. 1505

[5] M. KRAFCZYK, E. RANK   *A Parallelized Lattice-Gas Solver for Transient Navier-Stokes-Flow: Implementation and Simulation Results* submitted to Int. Journal for Num. Methods in Eng. (1993)

[6] J. VON NEUMANN in *Theory of Self-Reproducing Automata*, Univ. of Illinois press 1966

[7] C.M. TEIXEIRA, private communication

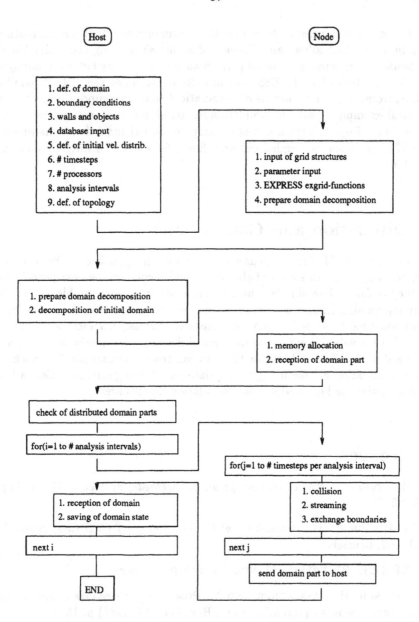

Figure 1: Parallelisation scheme of an LGS implemented as a Host-Node-model

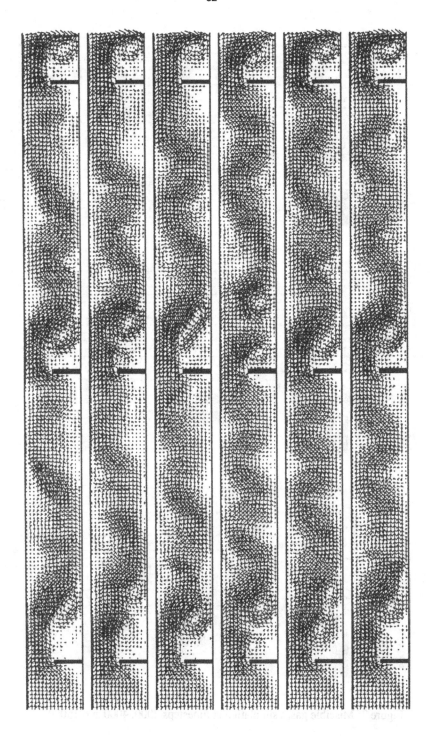

Figure 2: Timeseries of the dynamics of a grooved channel over 25000 timesteps

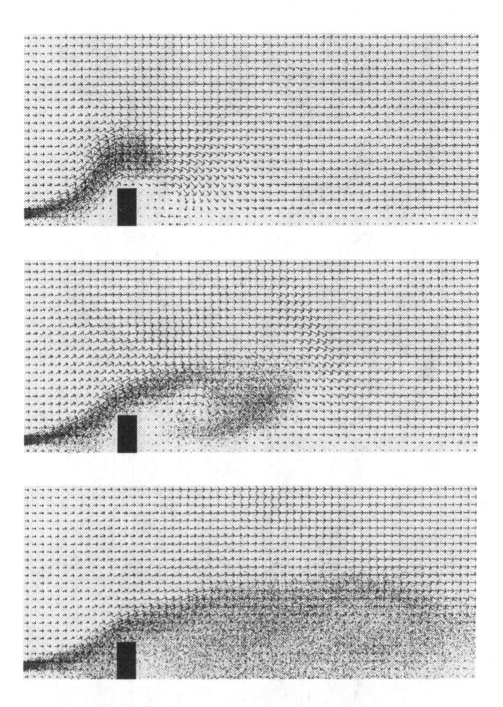

Figure 3: Miscible gases simulation at timesteps 2000, 4000 and 15000

Parallel Techniques for
Large-Scale Nonlinear Network Optimization [1]

Lucio Grandinetti, Francesca Guerriero, Roberto Musmanno

Dipartimento di Elettronica, Informatica e Sistemistica,
Università della Calabria, 87036 - Rende (CS) - Italy

Abstract. In this paper the technical aspects concerning an efficient implementation of parallel methods for solving large-scale network flow optimization problems are discussed. In particular, the attention will be focused to the evaluation of the numerical performance of different synchronous implementations of the relaxation method on shared-memory multiprocessor system. This method is particularly suited for high-performance computing and is applicable for solving problems with millions of variables which arise in several applications.

Keywords. Large scale nonlinear network optimization, relaxation method, complementary slackness, coloring, shared memory multiprocessor.

1 Introduction

The problem treated here can be formally described as follows.

Given a directed network $G = \{N, A\}$, where $N = \{i \mid i = 1, 2, ..., n\}$ is the set of nodes and $A = \{(i,j) \mid i, j \in N\}$ is the set of arcs, the goal is:

$$minimize \quad \sum_{(i,j) \in A} c_{ij}(x_{ij}) \tag{1}$$

s.t.

$$\sum_{j:(i,j) \in A} x_{ij} - \sum_{j:(j,i) \in A} x_{ji} = b_i \quad , \forall i \in N \tag{2}$$

$$l_{ij} \leq x_{ij} \leq u_{ij} \quad , \forall (i,j) \in A , \tag{3}$$

where x_{ij} is the flow on the arc (i,j), $c_{ij} : A \longrightarrow \Re$ is a strictly convex cost function of one variable assumed to be differentiable, b_i is the supply at node i, l_{ij}, u_{ij} are respectively the lower and upper bound for x_{ij} on the arc (i,j); therefore, (2) e (3) specify conservation of flow constraints and capacity constraints.

We assume that the problem (1)-(3) is feasible, that is:

$$\sum_{i \in N} b_i = 0 . \tag{4}$$

This means that there exists a unique optimal solution, given the hypothesis on the cost functions c_{ij} and the fact that the region defined by the constraints (2)-(3) forms a compact set.

---

[1] This research work was partially supported by the National Research Council of Italy, within the special project "Sistemi Informatici e Calcolo Parallelo", under CNR contract No. 93.01606.PF69.

Attaching a vector of lagrangian multipliers $\pi \in \Re^n$ to the equality constraints (2), we obtain the following lagrangian function:

$$L(x,\pi) = \sum_{(i,j)\in\mathcal{A}} c_{ij}(x_{ij}) + \sum_{i\in N}\pi_i\left(\sum_{\{j:(j,i)\in\mathcal{A}\}} x_{ji} - \sum_{\{j:(i,j)\in\mathcal{A}\}} x_{ij} + b_i\right)$$

$$= \sum_{(i,j)\in\mathcal{A}} (c_{ij}(x_{ij}) + (\pi_j - \pi_i)x_{ij}) + \sum_{i\in N}\pi_i b_i . \tag{5}$$

Assigned $\pi \in \Re^n$, the value of the dual function $q(\pi)$ could be obtained by minimizing $L(x,\pi)$ over all flow distribution x which satisfies the lower and upper bounds. Therefore, the dual (D) of (P) can be formulated as follows:

$$maximize \quad q(\pi) \tag{6}$$
$$\pi \in \Re^n ,$$

where

$$q(\pi) = \min_{l_{ij}\le x_{ij}\le u_{ij}} L(x,\pi) = \sum_{(i,j)\in\mathcal{A}} q_{ij}(\pi_i - \pi_j) + \sum_{i\in N}\pi_i b_i , \tag{7}$$

and

$$q_{ij}(\pi_i - \pi_j) = \min_{l_{ij}\le x_{ij}\le u_{ij}} c_{ij}(x_{ij}) - (\pi_i - \pi_j)x_{ij} . \tag{8}$$

A pair (x,π) is optimal respectively for the primal and the dual problem if and only if the complementary slackness conditions are satisfied.

Furthermore, if we consider the partial derivatives of the dual function q with respect to the i-th price π_i, we obtain that $\dfrac{\partial q(\pi)}{\partial \pi_i}$ corresponds to the surplus of the node i associated with the unique flow distribution x for which the pair (x, π) satisfies the complementary slackness conditions.

Differentiability and convexity of q play a crucial role for the definition of iterative methods for solving (6), since, starting from a generic estimate of the dual solution we can improve the dual function along a direction defined by a single component π_i of π. The greatest improvements along the coordinate direction π_i corresponds to $\dfrac{\partial q(\pi)}{\partial \pi_i} = 0$, that is, when the surplus $g_i = 0$.

The computational model of an iteration k of an algorithm for maximizing $q(\pi)$ is the following:

1. Assigned $\pi^{(k)}$ e computed $x^{(k)}$ by means of complementary slackness, choose a node $i\in N$ such that $|g_i^{(k)}| > \varepsilon$, where ε is a tolerance parameter defined by the user; if such node does not exist, stop, $x^{(k)}$ is optimal.

2. Compute $\pi^{(k+1)}$ such that $\pi_j^{(k+1)} = \pi_j^{(k)}$, $\forall\, j \neq i$, with $\pi_i^{(k+1)}$ chosen in such a way $q(\pi)$ could be improved along the i-th coordinate.

3. Determine $x^{(k+1)}$, that is $x_{ij}^{(k+1)} = x_{ij}^{(k)}$ e $x_{ji}^{(k+1)} = x_{ji}^{(k)}$, if the node j is not adjacent to i, whereas for adjacent nodes j, $x_{ij}^{(k+1)}$ is chosen in such a

way the complementary slackness conditions are satisfied:

$$\frac{\partial c_{ij}(x_{ij})}{\partial x_{ij}}\bigg|_{x_{ij}=x_{ij}^{(k+1)}} = \pi_i^{(k+1)} - \pi_j^{(k+1)}.$$

4. Compute the surplus $g_j^{(k+1)}$ for j=i and for all nodes j adjacent to i according to the flow distribution $x^{(k+1)}$.

The asymptotic convergence of the method can be proven ([1]), starting from any estimate π of the solution π^*.

2 The Parallel Synchronous Algorithm

The above iterative scheme suggests various parallel implementations based on the possibility of executing concurrently one or more steps of the algorithm.

The idea considered in this paper is that, since the optimality condition could be violated for more nodes, if p indicates the number of processors available, at each iteration k, at the most of p nodes for which $|g_i^{(k)}| > \varepsilon$ could be detected and the price of such nodes updated (in the sequential case a unique component of π is modified per iteration).

The updating procedure of π_i implies that the price π_j for each node j adjacent to j remains unchanged. For this reason in a parallel synchronous version of the method the price of adjacent nodes could not be updated simultaneously. This introduces the *coloring* of the network graph $(N, \mathcal{A})$ that is the partitioning $\{N_i\}$, i = 1, ..., ξ of the set N such that:

$$\forall \, k, l \in N_i \quad (k,l), (l,k) \notin \mathcal{A}, \quad \forall \, N_i.$$

The same color is assigned to each node $j \in N_i$, whereas adjacent nodes could not have the same color. A more detailed description of the method with the related convergence properties can be found in [1], whereas the first computational experiments are being done by Chajakis and Zenios [2] on a shared-memory multiprocessor and by Zenios and Mulvey [3] on a distributed-memory SIMD system (CM-2).

In this paper we focusize some numerical aspects of the relaxation algorithm on shared-memory parallel architectures, with the aim to emphasize the effectiveness of the synchronous approach especially applied to large-scale transportation problems, based on a dynamic allocation of the nodes to processors, on the basis of which each node is scheduled to a different processor at the beginning of each iteration.

The general scheme of the parallel algorithm is depicted in Fig. 1. The figure shows the synchronization point at the end of the surplus updating procedure. We observe that, even though at each iteration we never select adjacent nodes, we may contemporarily update the surplus of a node j, as shown in Fig. 2. In this case we need a mutual exclusion access to the shared memory location of the surplus. This means that processor i could locally determine the variation $\Delta x_{ij} = x_{ij}^{(k+1)} - x_{ij}^{(k)}$ of the flow along the arc (i,j) and update the surplus $g_j = g_j + \Delta x_{ij}$, by using a lock. When all processors complete this procedure, we will obtain $g_j^{(k+1)} = g_j$.

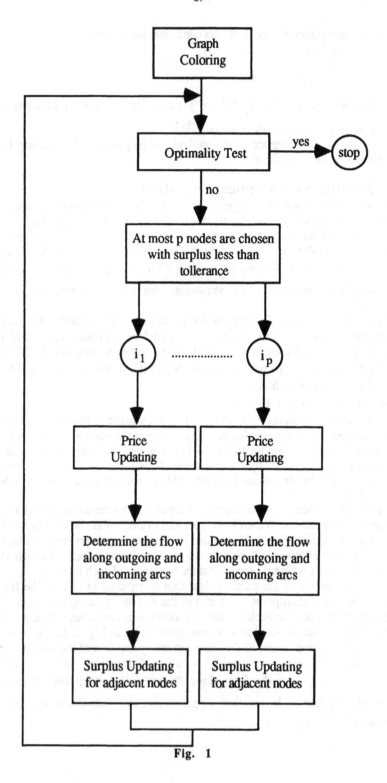

Fig. 1

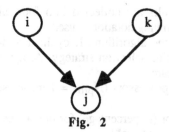

Fig. 2

Several variations of the procedure for selecting nodes at each iteration could be considered. In this paper two different extreme strategies are investigated:

a) cyclical node selection; the nodes are chosen in a cyclical order, by starting from the node selected at the previous iteration;

b) largest surplus selection; at each iteration, for each color ξ, the candidate nodes are the p nodes which correspond to the largest surplus, the sum of which is $S\xi$; the selected node are chosen among the candidates by determining the color $\xi^*=\arg\max_{\xi}\{S\xi\}$.

For each selected node i, the procedure for calculating the price π_i at k-th iteration could be implemented according to one of the following ideas:

a) maximization of q with respect to π_i ;

b) updating of π_i, by the relation: $\pi_i^{(k+1)}= \pi_i^{(k)}+ \delta$.

According to the first possibility, we have implemented an efficient procedure, on the basis of which the price $\pi_i^{(k+1)}$ is determined in such a way $g_i^{(k+1)}= 0$ (in the sequel we refer to this procedure as *exact line search*). In the second case with use a similar approach proposed in [2] (*approximate line search*). For a more detailed description of both the approaches, we remind to [4] .

3 Computational Experiments

Computational experiments have been carried out with the aim to conduct an accurate comparative analysis among versions of the algorithm which use different computational strategies for updating the dual prices and for scheduling the nodes to be processed. In particular, a consistent set of hard-to-solve test problems were considered. The dimension of the problems is reported in the next table. The cost function $c_{ij}, \forall\ (i,j)\in \mathcal{A}$, is a quadratic-type. The problems have been generated by using the public domain software named Netgen [5].

Test	Nodes	Sources	Sinks	Arcs	Colors
1	250	125	125	12500	28
2	500	250	250	50000	50
3	250	125	125	25000	89
4	500	250	250	100000	170

Tab. 1. List of test problems

We use an Alliant FX/80, a shared memory multiprocessor system with 8 processors, each of them characterized by a peak performance of 23 Mflops and a core memory of 64 Mbytes. The compiler used is the FX/Fortran 4.2.40.

The computational results are collected into four tables, one for each test problem, for which the following notation is used.

V   = version of the algorithm; 1: cyclical node selection strategy; 2: largest surplus selection strategy; A: approximate line search; E: exact line search;

N_{proc} = number of processors (N_{proc} = 1 means sequential version of the method);

E   = relative error (in percentage) for the last estimate of the solution; E is defined as $\dfrac{|f^* - q^*|}{q^*}$, where f^* e q^* represent respectively the value of the primal and dual function for the last estimate of the solution;

N_{it} = number of iterates, defined as the sum of iterates computed by each processor;

T   = CPU time (in seconds).

S_p = speed-up advantage of the parallel algorithm, compared to the sequential version.

The tolerance ε is set to $\varepsilon = 10^{-3} \eta$, where $\eta = \dfrac{\sum\limits_{i \in \mathcal{N}} b_i}{2m}$. The parameter η is a scaling which takes into account the difference between the demand and supply, which may substantially vary for each node;

We observe that all the versions converged to a solution which satisfies the tolerance criterion.

In the sequential case, V1E and V2E show the lower execution time. This means that the procedure for maximizing the dual function along the i-th coordinate seems to be more convenient than the approximate procedure for updating the price π_i. The benefit is more evident in the case of denser graphs (test problems 3 and 4). A similar behavior could be explained by the efficiency of the exact line search implemented (the computational workload per node is proportional to the logarithm of the node degree).

As far as the node selection strategy is considered, the results show a fruitful progress obtained by selecting nodes with the largest surplus.

In the parallel case, we generally obtained a substantial reduction of the execution time for the versions with four processors. In several cases the values of speed-up achieved is larger than the theoretical upper limit (e.g., 4) which could be obtained by considering a local parallelism, that is, by executing simultaneously the operations for updating the price, flow and surplus for a unique node per iteration. Also in the parallel case, for determining the price vector, the exact line search is more preferable than the updating procedure.

A further remark deals with the performance obtained by using eight processors instead of four (there is not evident progress). It is mainly due to the high density of the test problems used. This reduces the possibility of selecting, at each iteration, a number of nodes close to p, that ensures that maximum level of parallelism. The evidence is represented by the number of colors needed (for test problem 4 the number of colors used is approximately 34% of the number of nodes). Furthermore, numerical experiments carried out on sparse graphs have shown that the availability of eight processors is extremely convenient.

V	N_{proc}	E	N_{it}	T	S_p
V1A	1	1.04E-2	3287	234.98	-
	4	2.92E-2	6251	31.11	7.55
	8	3.60E-2	12400	73.89	3.18
V1E	1	9.00E-2	747	76.33	-
	4	3.95E-2	955	17.72	4.30
	8	4.00E-2	1097	15.13	5.05
V2A	1	7.82E-2	2713	123.46	-
	4	1.87E-2	4147	18.10	6.82
	8	2.12E-2	3922	13.13	9.40
V2E	1	0.11E+0	682	70.13	-
V2E	4	4.11E-2	1082	22.22	3.16
V2E	8	5.60E-2	990	11.82	5.93

Tab. 2. Numerical results for test problem 1

V	N_{proc}	E	N_{it}	T	S_p
V1A	1	0.44E+0	9711	1658.87	-
	4	0.44E+0	17225	192.28	8.62
	8	0.44E+0	28090	254.55	6.51
V1E	1	0.46E+0	1561	534.20	-
	4	0.45E+0	1944	76.79	6.96
	8	0.45E+0	1987	56.10	9.52
V2A	1	0.43E+0	7671	1126.57	-
	4	0.45E+0	13590	140.30	8.03
	8	0.44E+0	12700	87.12	12.93
V2E	1	0.43E+0	1285	428.84	-
	4	0.44E+0	2364	92.24	4.65
	8	0.44E+0	2173	52.03	8.24

Tab. 3. Numerical results for test problem 2

V	N_{proc}	E	N_{it}	T	S_p
V1A	1	0.32E+0	4642	1237.55	-
	4	0.36E+0	32513	792.07	1.56
	8	0.35E+0	49674	850.48	1.45
V1E	1	0.16E+0	721	236.39	-
	4	0.26E+0	1915	187.15	1.26
	8	0.31E+0	1457	101.43	2.33
V2A	1	0.47E+0	4160	579.52	-
	4	0.38E+0	6086	72.27	8.01
	8	0.38E+0	5734	61.83	9.37
V2E	1	0.53E+0	635	207.48	-
	4	0.49E+0	854	43.97	4.71
	8	0.49E+0	775	35.88	5.78

Tab. 4. Numerical results for test problem 3

V	N_{proc}	E	N_{it}	T	S_p
V1A	1	2.75E-3	14477	15306.24	-
	4	1.36E-3	173178	9093.33	1.68
	8	6.97E-4	383981	11264.69	1.35
V1E	1	6.96E-3	1446	1695.59	-
	4	3.36E-3	7607	1578.94	1.07
	8	3.23E-3	11133	1064.42	1.59
V2A	1	1.13E-3	11444	2975.90	-
	4	1.57E-3	16846	395.90	7.52
	8	1.23E-3	16265	355.73	8.36
V2E	1	2.68E-3	1236	1454.65	-
	4	1.37E-3	1734	189.85	7.66
	8	1.52E-3	1647	157.53	9.23

Tab. 5. Numerical results for test problem 4

4 Acknowledgment

We would like to acknowledge the director and the staff of CERFACS, Toulouse, France, for the fruitful possibility to use the Alliant FX/80 for obtaining our computational results.

5 References

[1] Bertsekas D.P. and Tsitsiklis J.N., *Parallel and Distributed Computation (Numerical Methods)*, Prentice-Hall, Englewood Cliffs, New Jersey, 1989.

[2] Chajakis E.D. and Zenios A.S., Synchronous and Asinchronous Impementations of Relaxation Algorithms for Nonlinear Network Optimization, *Parallel Computing*, (17), 873-894, 1991.

[3] Zenios S.A. and Mulvey J.M., A Distributed Algorithm for Convex Network Optimization Problems, *Parallel Computing* (6), 43-56, 1988.

[4] F. Guerriero and R. Musmanno, Un algoritmo parallelo iterativo per il problema di flusso a costo minimo non lineare, Technical Report C.N.R. no. 1/164 - Progetto Finalizzato "Sistemi Informatici e Calcolo Parallelo", Sottoprogetto 1: "Calcolo Scientifico per Grandi Sistemi", 1993.

[5] Klingman D., Napier A. and Stutz J., NETGEN - A Program for Generating Large Scale (Un)Capacitede Assignment, Transportation and Minimum Cost Flow Network Problems, *Management Science* (20), 814-822, 1974.

EXPERIENCES CONCERNING THE PARALLELIZATION OF THE FINITE ELEMENT CODE SMART

Astrid Watermann and Jürgen Altes

Institute for Safety Research and Reactor Technology
Research Center Jülich, 52425 Jülich, Germany

Convection dominated flows are calculated by the SMART code using the finite element method. In this way it is possible to get an approximation of the solution for the system of differential equations, given by the equations for continuity and heat transfer and the Navier-Stokes-equations. Computing times for problems of practical interest, which are often nonlinear, are very long, so a reduction can be achieved using massive parallel supercomputers, i.e. the Intel/Paragon at Research Center Jülich.

SMART is a FORTRAN code with nearly 300 000 statements. The parallel version can be described as follows:

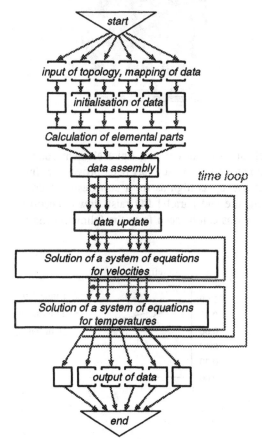

Before starting the real application some preprocessing of the topological and numerical data must be done. In this step we integrate the domaindecomposition, so every node can start the SMART calculation on his own subdomain. After reading the topological description, using parallel input, every node performs different routines, depending on the elements, which are used to discretize the subdomain. Following computations can be done in parallel without any communication. Assembly of the global system matrix, however, needs communication in order to update data which couple the split domains.

Calculation of the system of equations is done using a conjugate gradient and a Cholesky method.

Example: Rayleigh-Bénard-Convection
We regard water in a rectangular vessel which is heated from below. After reaching the critical Rayleigh number a convective flow is induced by buoyancy. A problem time of 400 s is calculated, using timesteps of 2 s, before a steady state is reached.

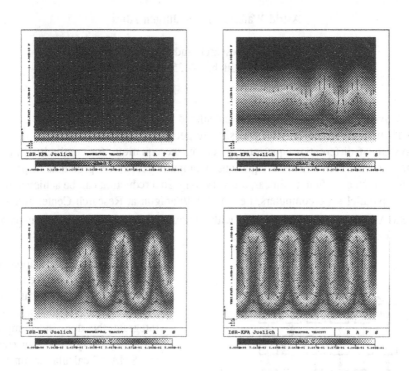

Experience:
Our investigations concern the parallelization of an existing finite element code in order to get a fast version of a well-known system, which has been proven by time. Therefore it is not possible to get an efficiency as high as for a new designed code, especially problems concerning datastructure and parallel I/O raise down speed-up. However, up to now results are satisfactory as can be seen from the following charts.

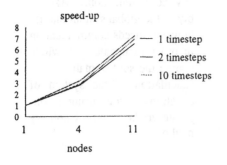

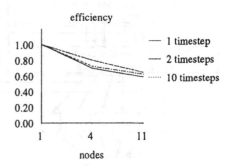

Elektrosmog & Electromagnetic CAD

Dr. Wilfried Daehn
SICAN F&E Betriebsgesellschaft mbH
Garbsener Landstraße 10
30419 Hannover

Abtract. Microelectronics has penetrated all areas of public life. This penetration has resulted in an increased exposure of man and machines to electromagnetic fields that are produced by other electronic equipment and which are summarized under the term electrosmog. On the other hands the progress in microelectronics has also born supercomputers with throughput in the range of several GFLOPS and Megabytes of main memory. They are the hardware basis for finite difference time domain an other space grid solvers for Maxwell's equations. Government regulations concerning electromagnetic compatibility and the public's increased awareness of electrosmog have emerged a new interest in the computation of electromagnetic fields and their impact on human life.

1. Introduction

Human beings have been exposed to electromagnetic fields from the very beginning. Thunderstorms and lightnings have always been combined with high electrostatic fields and instantaneous discharges. Electromagnetic fields may have a direct and an indirect impact on human life. A Lightning that hits a person causes direct injuries whereas malfunctions of machines under the influence of undesired electromagnetic fields have a mainly indirect impact.

The sources of electromagnetic fields can be categorized by the obtainable field strength and the wave lengths. Table 1 gives an overview.

High voltage power lines produce the strongest fields. The wave length is however very large. Radio and TV stations are among the second biggest sources of electromagnetic fields. The wavelengths are in the range from 0.5 to 3.5 meters. Mobile telephones are a relatively new source of electrosmog. They exhibit the smallest power but the highest frequencies. The wave length is in the range from 15 to 30 cm.

Despite of their small power mobile telephones have caused severe malfunctions of technical equipment. In Norway the engine of a small car always stopped when the telephone was used inside the car /1/. This happened no matter whether the driver was called or whether he wanted to use the telephone himself. In London the stage manipulator of the Adelphi theater showed an unpredictable behavior whenever a mobile telephone was used outside the theater /2/.

Table 1: Sources of Elektrosmog

Nr.	source	field	power	frequency	wave length
1.	Power Line (380 kV)	5.5 V/m, 11 mT		50 Hz	6000 km
2.a	Radio Station NDR 2		80 kW	87.6 MHz	3.4 m
2.b	TV-Station ARD		>50 kW	203,25 MHz	1,5 m
2.3	TV-Station ZDF		250 - 500 kW	543.25 MHz	0.55 m
3	Cellular Tele-phone		2 - 3 W	1 - 2 GHz	15 - 30 cm

Micro wave ovens are another type of electromagnetic source. Inside oven the dissipated power is used to heat the food. This gives rise to the question whether electromagnetic fields in general might heat the human body and in an undesired way and destroy its proteins.

In the following section we will address the equations that govern the propagation of waves and their penetration into matter. A space grid method is presented that allows the calculation of electromagnetic field on a supercomputer. Section 3 addresses shielding and resonance inside cars. The last section addresses computer simulation of the penetration of electromagnetic field into the human body.

2. Electromagnetic Field Equations

The propagation of electromagnetic fields is governed by the set of partial differential equations knows as Maxwell's equations/3/.

$$\nabla \times \vec{E} = -\frac{d\vec{B}}{dt}$$

$$\nabla \times \vec{H} = \frac{d\vec{D}}{dt} + \vec{\imath}$$

These equations are complemented by three equations that govern the effect of matter. For simple linear and isotropic matter the relations is as follows.

$$\vec{D} = \varepsilon \bullet \vec{E}$$

$$\vec{\imath} = \sigma \bullet \vec{E}$$

$$\vec{B} = \mu \bullet \vec{H}$$

By discretization of time and space a finite difference time domain formulation /4/ is obtained allowing the calculation of electromagnetic fields on a parallel vector computer.

3. Shielding of electromagnetic field inside cars

For a long time cars have been considered as nearly perfect shields protecting passengers from lightnings and other external electromagnetic fields. While this is still true for static or slowly changing electromagnetic fields the situation is completely different when waves with a high frequency are incident on the car. The cabin acts as a resonator. Excitation of resonant modes is done through the windows of the car. As the size of the windows is about the same as the wave length of incident waves the fields are strongly coupled. This is the reason why mobile telephones may be used inside a car witout an additional antenna. Figure 1 shows the vertical component of the electric field inside the empty car. The frequency is 600 MHz.

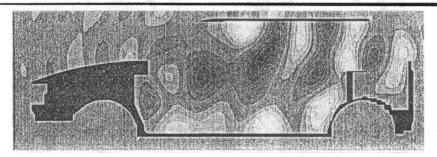

Fig. 1: Resulting field of a TEM-wave with f=600 MHz incident on a car (vertical component)

The electric field has its maximum at the usual location of the driver. Resonant modes are not only excited by incident waves. Mobile telephones used inside the car are further sources of resonances inside the cabin. Hence the recommendation of manufacturers to connect the telephone station to an outside antenna when using the mobile telephone inside the car.

4. Penetration of electromagnetic fields into the human body

The effect of electromagnetic fields has been investigated since the beginning of this century. In 1911 Dunlap /5/ reported flicker phenomena at the periphery of the visual field of persons that were exposed to a high magnetic field (B > 2 mT) with a low frequency (<50Hz). While this effect of the field is reversible an other well known effect is irreversible. Organic material that is exposed to microwaves is heated. This effect forms the basis of the micro wave oven. As a secondary effect of the exposure proteins are destroyed by the heat as soon as the temperature exceeds 41 degrees celsius. Until now most regulation concerning the maximum exposure of man to electromagnetic fields are based on the assumption that heating occurs homogeneously distributed over the whole body. While this assumption might be true for low frequency field the validity has to be doubted when the frequency exceeds 1GHz. The wavelength inside the body are smaller than the body's dimensions. In particular for micro wave frequencies the propagation of waves in lossless media is governed by the laws of geometric optic. Therefor focussing of waves, even inside the body is possible. Figure 2 shows in principle the case for a wave incident on the human head.

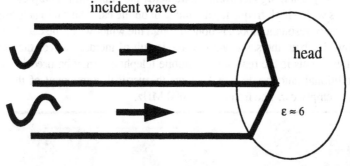

Fig. 2: Focussing of electromagnetic waves by dielectric bodies

Table 2 lists the values of permittivity and conductivity for relevant materials.

A realistic structural model of the human head is currently under development.

Table 2: permittivity and conductivity of organic substances

material	ε	σ
skin	40	1.5
fat	7	0.8
bones	6	0.8
eyes	50	8
brain	7	0.8

Literature

/1/   "Call a Corsa", FOCUS, 7.6.1993.

/2/   "Musicalstart geplatz - Mobiltelefon als Störenfried", dpa, 12.6.1993.

/3/   J.C. Maxwell, "A Treatise on Electricity and Magnetism", Prentice Hall, 1869.

/4/   A. Taflove, "Computational Electrodynamic", Artech House, 1993.

/5/   K. Dunlap, "Visual Sensations from the Alternating Magnetic Field", Science, Vol. XXXIII. No. 837, pp. 68 - 71, 1911.

THREE-DIMENSIONAL SIMULATION OF SEMICONDUCTOR DEVICES

Wilfried Klix [1], Ralf Dittmann [1], Roland Stenzel [2]

[1] Technische Universität Dresden
Institut für Grundlagen der Elektrotechnik/Elektronik
Mommsenstr. 13
D-01062 Dresden

[2] Hochschule für Technik und Wirtschaft Dresden
Fachbereich Elektrotechnik
Friedrich-List-Platz 1
D-01069 Dresden

Abstract. In this paper we will present methods for the simulation of semiconductor devices. The basic physical model, extended for the simulation of hetero junction devices is discussed. To get an acceptable CPU time, vectorization and parallelization is used in the numerical solution methods. For a demonstration of some possibilities of the simulation program, we have simulated an HBT and an IPG-FET.

1. Introduction

Rapidly rising development costs for new technologies and simultaneously the demand for shorter development times for semiconductor devices needs the use of simulation tools for the internal electronic behaviour and the fabrication process (process simulation). Novel devices with significant three-dimensional effects and the shrinkage of device features require a use of 3D-simulation methods. The objectives of device simulation are:

- Calculation of device characteristics before the technological realization,
- Optimization of technology dependent device parameters,
- Understanding of internal electronic processes,
- Determination of internal electronic quantities, which are not or very difficult measurable,
- Determination of equivalent circuit parameters of the devices.

We will limit our discussion to a simulation method based on the numerical solution of the so-called basic semiconductor equations, especially to the program SIMBA, which is part of a simulation system for process and device simulation, developed at the Dresden University of Technology and the HTW Dresden, see Fig. 1.

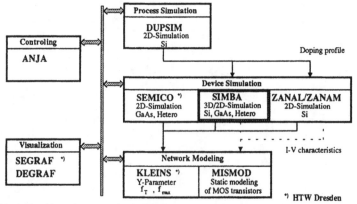

Fig.1: Device and process simulation system

2. Physical models

Using the electrostatic potential φ, the hole density p and the electron density n as the vector of unknowns, the basic semiconductor equations can be written as follows.
Poisson equation:

$$\text{div}(\varepsilon \cdot \text{grad } \varphi) = -e\left(p - n + N_D^+ - N_A^-\right) , \tag{1}$$

continuity equations for hole and electron current density:

$$\text{div } \vec{J}_p = -e \cdot \left(R - G + \frac{\partial p}{\partial t}\right) , \qquad \text{div } \vec{J}_n = e \cdot \left(R - G + \frac{\partial n}{\partial t}\right) , \tag{2,3}$$

and the corresponding transport equations:

$$\vec{J}_p = -e \cdot \mu_p \cdot \left(p \cdot \text{grad}(\varphi - \Theta_p) + U_T \cdot \text{grad } p\right), \quad \vec{J}_n = -e \cdot \mu_n \cdot \left(n \cdot \text{grad}(\varphi + \Theta_n) - U_T \cdot \text{grad } n\right) . \tag{4,5}$$

The Band Parameters Θ_p and Θ_n in (4,5) are included to modify the carrier transport with respect hetero junctions [1]. Besides of silicon devices it is also possible to simulate semiconductor devices, consisting of GaAs, InP, SiGe, other compounded semiconductors like $Al_x Ga_{1-x} As$, $In_x Ga_{1-x} As_y P_{1-y}$, or any combination of them. The carrier mobilities μ_p, resp. μ_n, arising in (4,5) are depending on the total impurity density, temperature and the electrical field strength [2], [3], [12]. Also for the recombination and generation rates R and G in (2,3) a large variety of models is used (Shockley/Read/Hall recombination, Auger recombination, avalanche and alpha-particle generation [3], [12]). These models and the use of technological relevant model parameters does influence the simulation results highly. For the simulation of the thermal behaviour, the heat flow equation can be used in addition to the above mentioned equations:

$$\text{div }(\lambda \cdot \text{grad } T) = -H , \tag{6}$$

whereas the heat generation rate H in (6) depends on the current densities $\vec{J}$ and the electrical field strength $\vec{E}$ and the heat conductivity λ is a non-linear function of the temperature.

3. Numerical methods and results
3.1. Boundary conditions, Discretization and solution methods

The boundary conditions are Dirichlet conditions (ohmic and Schottky contacts for the semiconductor equations and thermal contacts for the heat flow equation), Neumann conditions (oxide boundary or thermal insulation, resp.) and mixed conditions (MOS contacts or the model for thermal radiation, resp.).
The semiconductor equations and the heat flow equation will be discretized by using an orthogonal, noneqidistant grid and applying a box method. Non planar surfaces can be considered. This regular grid leads to an also regular 7 diagonal banded matrix. For typical examples the number of equations is between some 10.000 and more then 100.000 equations.
The discretized equations (1-5) can be solved as one large non-linear system of equations, the simultaneous algorithm, usually realized by Newton's method. Supplying a good initial guess, this method has good convergence behaviour in the case of strongly non-linear generation effects (avalanche generation) and if high current densities occur. At low current densities

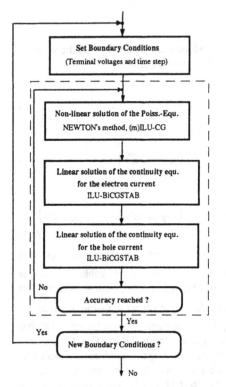

Figure 2: Modified GUMMEL algorithm in SIMBA

(backward biased pn-junctions) accuracy problems are possible. This method is often used in 2D simulation programs (SEMICO, ZANAL, see fig. 1).

Another solution method is the decoupling of the semiconductor equations, the so-called successive solution method, or Gummel's algorithm [4]. By neglecting the nonlinearity of the recombination and generation rates R, G in (2,3) during one iteration step, the continuity equations can be solved as a linear system of equations. This method shows a good convergence behaviour in the case of low current densities, even with a bad initial guess, but for high current densities and non-linear generation effects the computational effort increases drastically. The algorithm can be extended by additional equations, like heat flow equation, or relations for the energy and momentum of the charge carriers.

In the program SIMBA a modification of Gummel's algorithm is used, see fig. 2. The hole and electron density is assumed to be dependend on the electrostatic potential. In this case the discretization of the Poisson equation leads to a non-linear system of equations. Simulating real semiconductor problems (high current densities in MOS or bipolar devices, complicated structures like IGBT's) ill conditioned systems occur, especially for the discretized continuity equations. The solution of these linear systems must be stable and nevertheless fast. For the solution of the linearized Poisson and heat flow equation a CG-solver [5] combined with a modified ILU preconditioner (Gustaffson [6]) is preferred and for the continuity equations an ILUBiCGSTAB- [8] or ILUBCG-solver [7].

The solution of the linear systems of equations is the most time consuming part of the simulation. For typical problems it takes more then 90 % of the CPU time. Ways to reduces this effort are vectorization and parallelization (depending on used machines).

3.2. Vectorization

All of the CG solution algorithms for the linear systems of equations mainly consist of matrix vector products, dot products, vector updates, evaluation of the stopping criterion and the solution of triangular systems in the preconditioner. All these parts without the solution of the triangular systems are easy to vectorize. By solving the triangular systems, each of them consists of 3 diagonals, the outer diagonals can be handled with a vector processor. Only the execution of linear reccurrencies at the inner diagonal must be done in scalar mode if no modification of the algorithm is applied. For a typical problem (MOS transistor) the CPU time distribution of the whole ILUCG algorithm [5] and the ILU preconditioner does illustrate this problem, see fig. 3. With this method we have reached an overall speedup (scalar / vectorized) of about 2 on an IBM3090/VF.

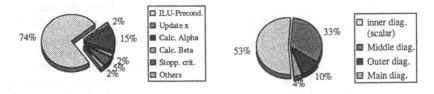

Figure 3: CPU-Time distribution for the ILUCG-algorithm (left) and the ILU-Preconditioner (right)

Several attempts where made to get a fully vectorized version of the solution method (reordering of unknowns in a chessboard manner, diagonal ordering, Neumann truncation, [9],[10],[11]). None of them was satisfactory, only the diagonal ordering (for 3D case called "hyperplane method") seems to be a help to overcome this "bottleneck" on several vector computers. There are further considerations necessary.

3.3. Parallelization

The following considerations are limited to the parallelization on computers with a small number of processors and distributed memory or workstation clusters. Investigations on a computer with shared memory where made earlier (on a IBM3090E/VF multiprocessor, CMS operating system) without advantages for every day problems in device simulation because of the multi-user activity in a central computer center and the operating system.

Considering the parallelization of the entire solution cycle it seems to be good to minimize the number of synchronization points and the effort for data exchange. This leads to the demand for a so-called coarse grain granularity. An other aim is to have a good load balance resulting in similar time consuming parts for the processors.

The coarsest grain granularity can be achieved by solving several bias points (contact voltages or time steps) in parallel. This approach is only for a few problems useful. The computational effort for different bias points usually differ extremely for most of the semiconductor devices. The result would be a bad load balance and the opportunity of extrapolation for initial guesses for a new bias point would be reduced. For a lot of devices not all bias points can be calculated starting at the same point.

An other way is to solve independent or nearly independent equations in parallel. If the recombination and generation rates R, G in (2,3) would be calculated before the solution of the continuity equations, they can be considered as independent and solved in parallel. The computational results and convergence behaviour for the original algorithm (fig. 2) and this "parallized" method are similar. If parallelism is introduced into the solution of linear systems it is possible to achieve a good load balancing, but there are a lot of synchronization points necessary for the calculation of one bias point. We used instead of the traditional ILU decomposition a twisted factorization [11] for the preconditioner. For a one-dimensional problem the matrix coming from a discretized partial differential equation is tridiagonal and can be easy factored in a twisted manner. The decomposition and the back substitutions can be calculated almost entirely in parallel on two processors. For the two-dimensional case the matrix can be considered as a block tridiagonal matrix with diagonal matrices as elements at the off-diagonals and tridiagonal matrices as elements at the main diagonal and can be carried out in parallel on four processors. This consideration can be extended to the 3D case for eight processors as shown in Figure 4.

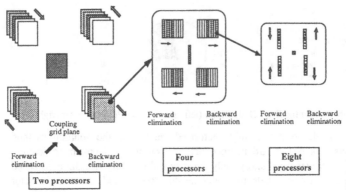

Using the parallized Gummel algorithm and the twisted factorization for the three-dimensional case the simulation can be done on 16 processors in parallel.

Fig. 4: Elimination scheme for the twisted factorization

4. Simulation results
4.1. Heterojunction bipolar transistor (HBT)

HBTs have received great interest for application to high-speed and high-frequency devices. To achieve higher cut-off frequencies we carried out an optmization of base and collector doping and thickness. Fig. 5 shows the device cross section of the AlGaAs/GaAs-HBT [13]. The dynamic simulations yielded maximum cut-off frequencies at $V_{DS} = 2$ V, $V_{GS} = 1.65$ V. The results in Fig. 6 show the influence of base doping on the cut-off frequencies. With increasing base doping the base bulk resistance decreases and f_{max} rises slightly. On the other hand an increasing base doping causes a decrease of current gain and carrier mobilities and a rise of junction capacitances. Therefore the transit frequency f_T goes down. The increasing base thickness causes first of all a rise of base transit time and consequently a decrease of the transit frequency. f_{max} is nearly independent on the base thickness because of the compensation of the base transit time increasing by the reduction of base bulk resistance with increasing base thickness.

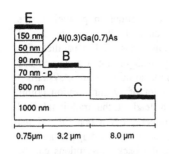

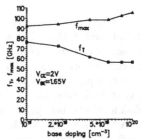

Fig. 5: Cross section of the HBT

Fig. 6: Cut-off frequencies versus base doping

4.2. In-plane-gated field effect transistor (IPG-FET)

A first concept of an IPG-FET was reported by A., D. Wieck and K. Ploog [14]. We carried out 3D-simulation to obtain design rules for this device [12],[13]. Fig. 7 shows a view of the half device used for the simulation with the isolation barrier (shaded region) between the gate electrode (left) and the 1D current channel (right). The 2DEG of a MODFET layer sequence is separated into four electrode regions and a quasi one-dimensional (1D) current channel. The functional principle of the device is fully three dimensional. The layered MODFET structure used for the simulation consists of a modulation-doped $Al_{0.25}Ga_{0.75}As/GaAs$ heterostructure with a 2DEG pseudomorphic $In_{0.21}Ga_{0.79}As$ quantum well layer. The obtained output characteristics is shown in Fig. 8. A complete depletion achieved at $V_{GS} = -7.4$ V. The corresponding transconductance is about 18 µS.

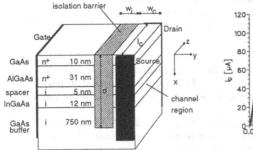
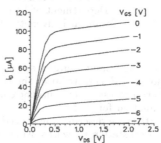

Fig. 8: Cross section of the IPG-FET   Fig. 9: Output characteristic

5.   Conclusions

We have presented methods for the simulation of semiconductor devices. During the solution process very ill conditioned systems of linear equations occur. From all the tested solution algorithms, especially the ILUBiCGSTAB algorithm seems to be the best candidate. The very time consuming problem of 3D-simulation can be accelerated not only by main frames with vector processors, but also with workstation clusters with a mentioning speedup. As an example for novel semiconductor devices, an HBT and an IPG-FET was simulated.

6.   References

[1]   Sutherland, J., E., Hauser, J., R.: IEEE Trans. on ED - 24 (1977), pp. 363-372.
[2]   Chaughey, D., M., Thomas, R., E.: Proc. IEEE 1967, Vol 55, pp. 2192-2193.
[3]   Selberherr, S.: Analysis and Simulation of Semiconductor Devices, Springer-Verlag, Wien, New York, 1984, ISBN 3-211-81800-6.
[4]   Gummel, H., K.: IEEE Trans. on ED - 11 (1964), pp. 455-465.
[5]   Meijerink, J., A., van der Vorst, H., A., SIAM J. Math. of Comp. 1977, Vol. 31, No. 137, pp. 148-162.
[6]   Gustafsson, I.: BIT 18 (1978), pp. 142-156.
[7]   Fletcher, R.: in G. A. Watson, ed., Proc. of the Dundee Biennal Conference on Numerical Analysis 1974, pp. 73-89, University of Dundee, Scotland, Springer-Verlag, New York 1975.
[8]   Driessen, M., van der Vorst, H., A.: Simulation of Semiconductor Devices and Processes, Vol. 4, ed. by W. Fichtner et. al., Zurich, Sept. 1991, pp. 56-54.
[9]   Traar, K., P., Stiftinger, M., Heinrichsberger, O., Selberherr, S.: Proc. of the 1991 International Conference on Supercomputers, June 17-21, 1991 Cologne, pp. 154-162.
[10]   van der Vorst, H., A.: SIAM J. Sci. Stat. Comp., Vol. 3, No. 3, Sept. 1982, pp. 350-356.
[11]   van der Vorst, H., A.: Parallel Computing, 5 (1987), pp. 45-54.
[12]   Stenzel, R., Klix, W.: Proc. of the 2. IEEE International Workshop on Discrete Time Domain Modelling of Electromagnetic Fields and Networks, Berlin, October 28 and 29, 1993.
[13]   Stenzel, R., Leier, H.: GME-Fachbericht 11, VDE-Verlag, 1993, pp.259 - 264
[14]   Wieck , A., D., Ploog, K.: Appl. Phys. Lett. 56 (1990), pp. 928 - 930

A Distributed Automatic Test Pattern Generation System *

Peter A. KRAUSS

Institute of Electronic Design Automation
Department of Electrical Engineering
Technical University of Munich, Germany

Abstract. The fault parallel approach to the automatic test pattern generation (ATPG) distributes the target faults to be processed in parallel. Every processor performs the complete test pattern generation and fault simulation for its faults.

In this article we describe our procedures to gain nearly linear speedup on large workstation networks using suitable methods for fault distribution, dynamic load balancing, and fault tolerance. Experimental results validate the efficiency of our approach.

1 Introduction

An electric circuit with memory elements is a binary coded finite state machine (FSM), termed *sequential* circuit. Due to a production fault the behavior of the circuit might be changed, resulting in a different FSM. If the verification of the equivalence of both FSMs succeeds, the fault is not testable due to some circuit redundancies. Otherwise, a test has been found to detect this fault. The logic values of the circuit input connectors are the test patterns, to be used in their specific order as *test sequences*.

The problem of ATPG has been pointed out to be NP-complete [1], even for combinational circuits without memory elements. Although ATPG can be performed in several ways, for sequential circuits a deterministic test pattern generator combined with a fault simulator has proven to be most efficient. Nevertheless, for large sequential circuits the computation may last several days, sometimes even weeks. Therefore, methods to parallelize ATPG have been a major research topic since a few years [1, 2, 3, 4].

The next section presents our approach to an efficient fault parallel ATPG running on large workstation networks. The achieved results are discussed in Section 3. In the last section we conclude our article.

2 Fault Parallelism

Among the different possibilities to parallelize the ATPG process, the fault parallelism distributes the target fault list to available processors for executing test pattern generation in parallel. The order how the faults are distributed influences in a very sensitive way the overall performance. With a growing number of processors, in order to achieve a high speedup it is obligatory to maintain a good load balancing and to consider the constraints of fault dependency.

* This research is supported by the DFG (Deutsche Forschungsgemeinschaft) within the project SFB 0342 (Tools and Methods for Utilizing Parallel Computers)

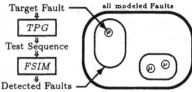

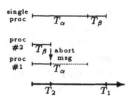

Fig. 1. Fault Dependency   **Fig. 2.** Abort Message

Figure 1 illustrates the concept of fault dependency. For target fault φ, the test pattern generator *TPG* may have produced test sequence t_φ. The fault simulator *FSIM* uses t_φ to determine other faults which are additionally detected by this test sequence. Fault simulation consumes considerably less computation time than test pattern generation. Therefore, the overall ATPG process is significantly accelerated.

Two faults which can be detected by the same test sequence are called dependent on each other. If one processor works on fault μ, while a second processor finds a test sequence for a different fault ν which also detects μ, the computation time spent on fault μ is wasted. Hence, dependent faults should not be distributed to different processors at the same time.

The concatenation of two test sequences results in a new test sequence. If test sequence t_μ detects fault μ and test sequence t_ν fault ν, then the concatenated test sequence $t_\mu t_\nu$ detects both faults. It is theoretically impossible to extract any independent faults from sequential circuits due to the fact that the concatenation of all test sequences covers all faults. In practice, we consider only test sequences with limited length. Now it is possible to determine sets of mutually independent faults. Akers et al. have proposed the *test counting* algorithm [5] which analyzes combinational circuits and determines certain pairs of faults that can't be detected by the same test pattern. We have extended test counting to sequential circuits. Together with methods derived from [6] it forms a heuristic which recognizes the constraints of fault dependency. A more detailed explanation is beyond the scope of this article.

The management of the target fault list can be done either by the processors themselves or by a central control processor. In the *distributed self-management* approach the target fault list is initially divided among the working processors, named *workers*. If a worker finishes its assignment and becomes idle, it sends a request to non-idle workers for a part of their unprocessed fault list.

The number of messages sent between the processors will increase considerably as the run nears completion caused by the shrinking size of the fault lists. This can be avoided by partitioning the lists only to a given granularity [6]. Still, to reduce duplicated work arising from fault dependency, the processors have to synchronize their fault lists by broadcasting the detected faults to each other, producing significant communication overhead.

These drawbacks are avoided using a *central control management*. The communication model of this approach is based on a star topology. The central control processor, named *controller*, keeps the whole target fault list. An idle worker requests a new job from the controller. Now the controller has the possibility to select the faults to be processed next according to the criteria fault dependency, estimated computation time, and selected job size.

The result sent back to the controller is either the generated test sequence together with faults detected by this test sequence, or this fault is reported untestable. A third possible reply is that the search was aborted because of exceeding some resource limits.

The fault dependency criteria has been already discussed. Concerning the job size, assigning only one single fault to each processor at a time reduces the possibility that this fault is covered by a test sequence generated by a second processor. The additional communication overhead is negligible, because the computation time for each fault is much higher than the communication time, starting with moderately large circuits.

With the central control management approach, the amount of communication is much less than with the distributed self-management, because now each worker exchanges messages only with the controller, whereas before each worker had to communicate with each other worker.

The search for test sequences is based on a branch and bound backtracking. For different faults it needs different computation time. It is not possible to exactly calculate this time in advance, but an estimation is done by using some heuristics. However, the time spent for computation may also vary because of some load from other processes on the same processor. Also, using networks of heterogeneous workstations results in different computation times.

This shows that static fault partitioning methods are not feasible. The chosen approach of distributing faults to requesting workers automatically leads to a dynamic load balancing. Here, step by step each worker only gets the amount of faults that it can handle in equal time as the other workers. The method of distributing only single faults yields a large number of jobs. This results in a parallelism fine-grained enough for an excellent load balancing.

If the fault dependency constraints leave any degrees of freedom, the estimation of the computation time is used to distribute faults with a supposedly long computation time first. This reduces the occurrence of straggling workers. The combination of considering fault dependency and using estimated computation time leads to our *fault ordering heuristic*.

While distributing faults the controller uses the fault ordering heuristic explained before. It may sometimes fail, i.e., some faults are covered by a test sequence reported back from a worker while they are assigned to another worker. As the controller knows which fault is currently assigned to which worker, it sends immediately an abort message to the respective worker to reduce further wasting of computation time.

Sometimes the abort messages can cause a superlinear speedup. We will explain this with help of Fig. 2, which shows the times needed to generate test sequences for faults α and β in a single and in a double processor configuration. We suppose, that time T_α to process fault α is considerably longer than time T_β for processing fault β, and that the test sequence generated for β covers α.

The single processor configuration is shown in the upper part of Fig. 2. Because β was processed after α the time spent for processing α is unrecoverably wasted, the ATPG needs the time $T_1 = T_\alpha + T_\beta$. But in the double processor configuration shown in the lower part, the controller sends an abort message after having received the result from processor #2. By doing so, the ATPG only needs $T_2 = T_\beta$. The resulting speedup $S = \frac{T_1}{T_2} = 1 + \frac{T_\alpha}{T_\beta}$ is superlinear due to $T_\alpha > T_\beta$.

Within large networks of workstations the probability of a processor failure

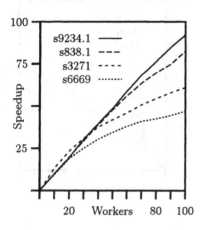

Fig. 3. Some Speedups

Circuit	ass.Flts.	T_1	T_{100}	Spup
s208.1	206	262.84 s	5.38 s	48.86
s382	307	1068.69 s	38.68 s	27.63
s386	213	233.20 s	5.48 s	42.55
s400	388	205.57 s	2.92 s	70.40
s420.1	440	985.48 s	16.11 s	61.17
s444	404	1717.90 s	67.38 s	25.50
s499	539	320.37 s	5.50 s	58.25
s526	514	1599.05 s	34.31 s	46.61
s526n	525	1394.84 s	21.35 s	65.33
s635	666	589.78 s	7.51 s	78.53
s820	658	2947.09 s	35.22 s	83.68
s832	694	3303.93 s	42.76 s	77.27
s838.1	895	2178.20 s	26.47 s	82.29
s1196	359	100.50 s	4.66 s	21.57
s1238	428	177.15 s	13.32 s	13.30
s1269	850	514.34 s	6.33 s	81.25
s1423	1375	2456.51 s	28.66 s	85.71
s1488	499	5991.60 s	75.87 s	78.97
s1494	515	6566.43 s	87.47 s	75.07
s3271	478	3445.68 s	56.62 s	60.86
s3330	1020	1656.77 s	24.05 s	68.89
s3384	772	777.15 s	19.25 s	40.37
s5378	1650	7478.15 s	81.53 s	91.72
s6669	1092	1568.46 s	33.48 s	46.85
s9234.1	3565	26699.47 s	290.41 s	91.94

Fig. 4. Results

grows. This implies the need for fault tolerance, which is also covered by the concept of requesting workers. If a worker fails, it will neither block other workers nor the controller. While other workers will continue to work, the task given to the failed worker will be reassigned to another worker later on. Hence, nothing is lost by the failure of some workers. The controller terminates the ATPG process after having a result for each fault of its list.

3 Results

Our fault parallel ATPG runs on large networks of heterogeneous workstations and on some special parallel machines, using the *p4 programming system* [7]. The results presented here were achieved on a network of 100 Hewlett-Packard 9000/720 workstations with the ISCAS '89 benchmark circuits [8].

We measure the speedup as the usual ratio T_1/T_N, with T_1 being the wall-clock time needed by the parallel algorithm running on one worker, and T_N the time needed by N workers.

The ATPG process running on only one worker needs over 7 hours for circuit s9234.1, whereas 100 workers complete this task in less than 5 minutes, resulting in a speedup of 92. For other moderately large circuits we also achieve speedup values of up to 90, presented in Fig. 3. Figure 4 summarizes measured values from our experiments with 100 workers. Only circuits with more than 200 assigned faults are shown. A number of assigned faults per worker which is too low prevents the stabilization of a good dynamic load balancing. ATPG for circuits with only a few faults is better accomplished on smaller networks. For 100 workers, Fig. 5 displays for each circuit the average number of assigned faults per worker and the achieved speedup. It illustrates that one condition for obtaining a good speedup (e.g. of at least 75) are at least five assigned faults per worker. But also short computation time of test pattern generation and fault simulation reduces the obtainable speedup due to an increasing ratio of communication to computation time.

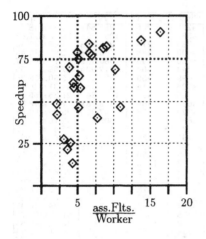

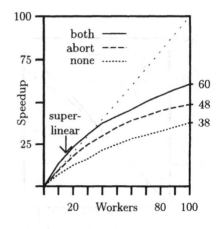

Fig. 5. Speedup versus assigned faults   **Fig. 6.** Fault ordering and abort messages

Circuits with low speedup values can be divided into three groups:

1. too few assigned faults (s208.1, s382, s386, ...),
2. a too short computation time (s1196, s1238, ...), and
3. failing of the fault ordering heuristic (s3384, s6669, ...).

Whereas the speedup of the first and second group stagnates starting from a certain number of workers due to invariant circuit characteristics, the speedup of the third group could be improved by a better fault ordering.

The improvement achieved by combining the fault ordering heuristic with the abort messages is demonstrated in Fig. 6. Again using circuit s3271 it shows:

- the speedup curve of the fault parallel ATPG obtained from an early development stage without any additional features (dotted),
- the curve with using abort messages only (dashed), and
- the curve with using both abort messages and fault ordering heuristic (solid).

The combination of fault ordering heuristic and abort messages has improved the speedup value for this circuit from 38 to 60 at 100 workers. A further effect observable in Fig. 6 is a superlinear speedup for up to 30 workers, as explained in Section 2.

The achieved load balancing of a typical test pattern generation session is shown in Fig. 7. Here, for circuit s3271 the test patterns were produced by 10 workers in parallel. The time needed for treating one fault is the vertical bar between two tics. The controller is shown on the left side. It is only active during the time when workers report their results and request new faults. Due to the coarse time resolution it is impossible to see the interaction between controller and workers. Figure 8, a zoomed in view of Fig. 7, obviously shows that the controller has a lot of idle time. Therefore, it can react quickly to a worker requiring attention. The worker only waits briefly until it gets its next task. Even if more than one worker requires attention at nearly the same time the delay is negligible. Although the diagram displays a session with only 10 workers, the mentioned advantages hold for 100 workers and more. An excellent load balancing is the result of our proposed methods.

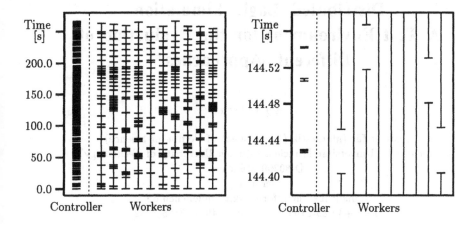

Fig. 7. ATPG with 10 workers   **Fig. 8.** Zoomed in view of Figure 7

4 Conclusion

In this article we have presented our approach to fault parallelism. We achieved nearly linear speedup on a network with 100 workstations. The size of this network is an order of magnitude larger than used so far for fault parallel ATPG. The main characteristics of our approach are a new fault ordering heuristic, an efficient dynamic load balancing, and a necessary fault tolerance.

References

1. R. H. Klenke, R. D. Williams, and J. H. Aylor, "Parallel–Processing Techniques for Automatic Test Pattern Generation," *IEEE Computer*, pp. 71–84, 1992.
2. B. Ramkumar and P. Banerjee, "Portable Parallel Test Generation for Sequential Circuits," in *Proceedings IEEE/ACM International Conference on Computer–Aided Design*, pp. 220–223, 1992.
3. P. Agrawal, V. D. Agrawal, and J. Villoldo, "Sequential Circuit Test Generation on a Distributed System," in *Proceedings IEEE/ACM Design Automation Conference*, pp. 107–111, 1993.
4. P. A. Krauss and K. J. Antreich, *Application of Fault Parallelism to the Automatic Test Pattern Generation for Sequential Circuits*, vol. Parallel Computer Architectures: Theory, Hardware, Software, Applications of *Lecture Notes in Computer Science No. 732*, pp. 234–245. Springer–Verlag, 1993.
5. S. B. Akers and B. Krishnamurthy, "Test Counting: A Tool for VLSI Testing," *IEEE Design & Test of Computers*, pp. 58–73, 1989.
6. S. Patil and P. Banerjee, "Fault Partitioning Issues in an Integrated Parallel Test Generation / Fault Simulation Environment," in *Proceedings IEEE International Test Conference*, pp. 718–726, 1989.
7. R. Butler and E. Lusk, "User's Guide to the p4 Parallel Programming System," Tech. Rep. ANL-92/17, Argonne National Laboratory, Mathematics and Computer Science Division, 1992.
8. F. Brglez, D. Bryan, and K. Kozminski, "Combinational Profiles of Sequential Benchmark Circuits," in *Proceedings IEEE International Symposium on Circuits and Systems*, pp. 1929–1934, 1989.

Distributed Logic Simulation
A Test Environment for the Evaluation of
Different Approaches *

Peter Luksch

Institut für Informatik (Department of Computer Science)
Technische Universität München (Munich University of Technology)
D-80290 München
Germany
e-mail: luksch@informatik.tu-muenchen.de
Tel.: +49-89-2105-8164; Fax: +49-89-2105-8232

Abstract. A portable and flexible testbed is presented that enables an unbiased comparison of different methods for DDES. The great variety of algorithms that have been proposed up to now is subdivided into a small number of fundamentally different approaches. Criteria for the classification are the distribution of functions and data structures and the way processes are synchronized. Based on this classification, four methods have been selected and applied to a gate level logic simulator.

1 Classification of Approaches to DDES

Distributed discrete event simulation (DDES) approaches can be classified according to the following criteria:

Distribution of functions and data structures onto processes. In the function partitioning approach, the simulation algorithm itself is composed into subtasks which are implemented as processes that process the stream of events in a pipelined fashion. In the model partitioning approach, the sequential simulator is replicated and complemented by communication and synchronization components.

Process synchronization. The model partitioning approach can be further subdivided according to the type of synchronization used to coordinate the processes. In the centralized approach, simulators are synchronized by a global simulation time while in the decentralized approach each simulator has a local clock which is advanced according to a synchronization protocol. A simulator may only process an event e with execution time t_e safely, if it can be sure that it will not receive no more events with execution times before t_e.

There are two different solutions to the synchronization problem described above. In the **conservative** approach, no event is processed before the process can make sure that no earlier events can arrive. The optimistic approach proceeds

---

* This work has been partially funded by the DFG ("Deutsche Forschungsgemeinschaft", German science foundation) under contract No. SFB 342, TP A1.

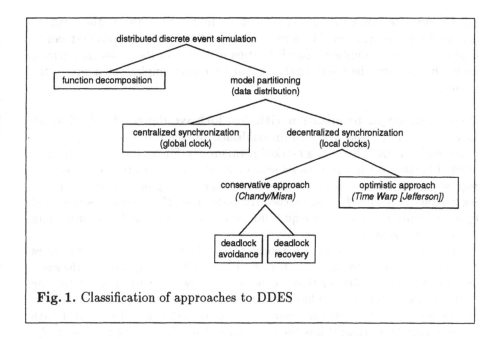

Fig. 1. Classification of approaches to DDES

without waiting for events to arrive making the optimistic assumption that no event will arrive "out of order". A potential error is detected if an event in the local past arrives, i.e. with execution time before the current local simulation time. Then, part of the computation done so far is invalid and has to be undone. **Deadlock** may occur in the conservative approach if there is a cycle of simulators each waiting for its predecessor to send an event message. Conservative protocols can be subdivided into two subclasses: deadlock avoidance and deadlock recovery. In the first case, the protocol avoids deadlocks by null messages or by time requests. The second subclass, deadlock recovery, allows deadlocks to occur and therefore has to detect deadlock and recover from it.

In contrast to the conservative approach, the optimistic approach (*Time Warp*) is guaranteed to be free of deadlock. Figure 1 illustrates the classification presented in this section.

2 A Testbed for DDES

The core of the testbed is a gate level logic simulator. This application of DDES was chosen because gate level simulation has become an indispensable tool in VLSI design an requires large amounts of computational power if complex systems are simulated.

The testbed has been implemented based on a machine-independent message passing library [2]. Thus it is portable within the whole class of distributed memory multiprocessors. By applying a representative selection of parallelization methods to the same simulator, different approaches to distributed simulation can be evaluated in a uniform environment. In addition, the testbed can be extended very easily. It provides a comprehensive library of functions that can be used to implement additional parallelization methods. In the following sections, we briefly describe the parallelizations that have been implemented within the testbed.

Conservative Synchronization with deadlock avoidance. Deadlock avoidance uses a time request algorithm published by Bain and Scott [1] to prevent simulators from becoming blocked permanently. Each time a simulator gets blocked because it can't process its next event at (simulated) time t^*, it sends a request to all predecessors that prevent it from proceeding in its simulation, asking whether they already have reached simulated time t^*. A request is answered by a 'yes' reply as soon as the requesting process can be assured that processing its next event is save.

A cycle of processes waiting for each other is detected if a simulator receives two or more requests for the same time t^* that have been originated by the same process. All but the first of these requests are answered with 'ryes' indicating to the requester that a cycle has been encountered. A 'yes' reply is sent for the first request if the requester can safely process its next event. If any event with a time stamp lower than t^* has been sent on a channel following an 'ryes' reply, a 'no' reply is sent for the very first request, because such an event could cause an event earlier than t^* to be received by the requesting simulator.

The requesting simulator may continue its simulation if it has received 'yes' or 'ryes' replies for all of its requests. If any 'no' replies have been received, the simulator remains blocked and has to issue requests once again.

Conservative Synchronization with Deadlock Recovery. Our implementation of deadlock recovery detects deadlocks using Mattern's vector method [5]. A circulating control message contains a vector that records the difference between the number sent and received messages for each simulator. In addition, for each process there is a flag indicating whether its simulation is blocked. For all simulators that are blocked, the message contains their next event time. Each process that receives the message updates it before passing it on. There is a deadlock if all the vector components are zero and if all simulators are marked as blocked. To recover from deadlock, the process having detected it determines the minimum of the next event times in the control message and tells all simulators with less or equal next event times to continue. In addition to the circulating control message a parallel version of the vector method has been implemented. It performs slightly better for more than eight processes.

Time Warp. In Time Warp [3] a simulator is never blocked. Simulation is allowed to proceed under the optimistic assumption of all external input signals being valid all the time. A possible error is detected if a *straggler* arrives, i.e. an event message with a time stamp that lies in the past with respect to the current local simulation time. Then, part of the computation done so far is potentially invalid and therefore has to be undone. Local events are undone by

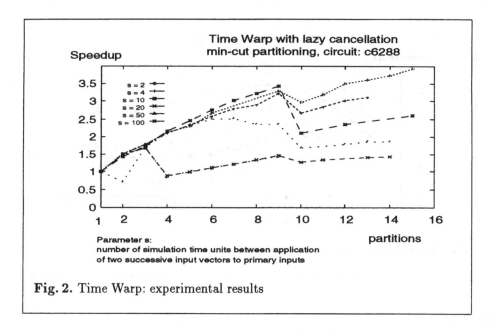

Fig. 2. Time Warp: experimental results

restoring a previously saved state; sent event messages are canceled by sending anti-messages. Our Time Warp parallel simulator [4] implements an incremental state saving policy which uses the event list as the data structure where signal values are stored.

Both aggressive and lazy cancellation are available as options. As an extension to the basic Time Warp protocol, re-simulation of a time interval has been optimized by saving element evaluations whenever possible. This optimization reduces the cost of rollbacks especially for models containing elements that are computationally complex to evaluate, e.g. software models of microprocessors.

3 Experimental Results

Run-time measurements have been carried out on the iPSC/2 and iPSC/860 distributed memory multiprocessors using the ISCAS benchmark circuits as workloads. The maximum available configuration were 16 processors. The benchmarks are circuits from industry whose function, however, is not known in detail. Therefore, randomly generated sequences of input vectors have been applied to them for our run-time measurements.

Function partitioning couldn't achieve significant speedup due to the implementation platform's high communication latency. For the replicated worker parallelizations, maximum speedup factors of about half the number of processors engaged in the simulation have been been observed. However, performance strongly depends on the circuit being simulated and even on the stimuli applied to it. Figures 2 and 3 show some examples from our runtime measurements.

Based on the measurements done so far, none of the three synchronization

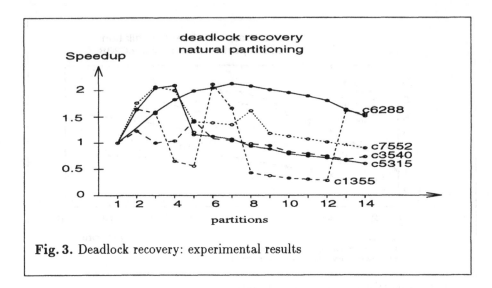

Fig. 3. Deadlock recovery: experimental results

protocols can be clearly favored. We have used two static partitioning methods: natural partitioning which assigns elements to partitions in the order in which they appear in the net list and min-cost partitioning which is a generalization of Fiduccia/Mattheyses' min-cut heuristic [6]. Runtime results were similar for both methods. Despite the fact that both methods generate equally sized partitions, computational load has been found to be distributed very unevenly among the processes. The total number of evaluations has been observed to vary by several orders of magnitude from element to element. In addition, the center of activity "migrates" throughout the simulation.

From the observed load imbalances we conclude that static partitioning based on circuit topology alone is not sufficient to distribute computational load evenly among the processors. Therefore, our implementation of min-cost partitioning allows elements and signals to be weighted individually to account for different activity rates. Estimates for activity rates can easily be obtained from a previous run at no extra cost, since, during the design process, usually an almost identical simulation is executed several times in a sequence.

In addition to static partitioning, we have implemented a dynamic load balancing mechanism as an option in the Time Warp parallel simulator. Load is measured from periodic snapshots of local simulation times (LVT's) which are taken for GVT computation. A simulator whose LVT is lagging behind the other processes' LVT's in a certain number of subsequent snapshots is considered to be heavily loaded. If LVT's differ by more than a threshold value, the circuit is re-partitioned: the most heavily loaded simulator moves elements out of its partition into that of a lightly loaded simulator, i.e. one whose LVT is far ahead of the others. Our measurement have shown that dynamic re-partitioning results in a more balanced progress of LVT's.

4 Conclusion and Future Work.

In our measurements, the stimuli applied to primary inputs had a strong impact on performance. Unfortunately, the functions of the ISCAS benchmark circuits is not known so that it is difficult to decide whether a given sequence of input vectors results in typical operating conditions. Therefore, a program for converting circuit descriptions has been written that allows us to enlarge our set of benchmarks with a number of large circuits designed previously on a commercial CAE system in our laboratory. Comparing results obtained from simulations of these systems using stimuli "that make sense" with those obtained from the ISCAS benchmarks will help to find out how activity distribution in different types of circuits affects parallel simulation behavior.

Other topics of future research will be a detailed analysis of the optimizations implemented in the existing parallel versions of the simulator, investigation of further parallelization methods, and consideration of new target architectures. We will also investigate to what extend results obtained from our study of parallelizing logic simulation can be generalized for other types of discrete simulation applications. As a first step into this direction, we have just begun to parallelize a commercially used discrete event simulation package which has originally been designed for simulation of production processes but in our group is used to model shared virtual memory computer architectures.

References

1. W. Bain and D. Scott. An algorithm for time synchronisation in distributed discrete event simulation. In *Distributed Simulation*, 1988.
2. T. Bemmerl, A. Bode, T. Ludwig, and S. Tritscher. MMK - Multiprocessor Multitasking Kernel (User's Guide and User's Reference Manual). SFB-Bericht 342/26/90 A, Technische Universität München, Institut für Informatik, Aug. 1990.
3. D. Jefferson. Virtual Time. *ACM Transactions on Programming Languages and Systems*, 7(3):404–425, July 1985.
4. P. Luksch and H. Weitlich. Time Warp Parallel Logic Simulation on a Distributed Memory Multiprocessor. In *Modelling and Simulation ESM 93, Proceedings of the 1993 European Simulation Multiconference*, pages 585–589, Lyon, June 1993. SCS.
5. F. Mattern. *Verteilte Basisalgorithmen*, volume 226 of *Informatik-Fachberichte*. Springer-Verlag, Berlin, 1989.
6. G. Vijayan. Min-Cost Partitioning on a Tree Structure and Applications. In *26th ACM/IEEE Design Automation Conference*, pages 771–774, 1989.

Modelling hierarchy as guideline for parallel simulation

Axel Hunger
Frank Müller

Universität -GH- Duisburg
Fachbereich 9 / Datenverarbeitung
Bismarckstraße 81
47057 Duisburg

1. Abstract

With this paper, a strategy is explained which allows to map the hierarchy of a model onto a network of parallel computing nodes for simulation purposes. It is shown that exploiting hierarchy can support the solution of many computational tasks, especially the devide and conquer approach of partitioning a given problem before solving it. Demonstrated results were gained in the field of logic and fault simulation of digital circuits; the parallel computer used is a transputer net with 40 nodes. The developed approach shows general strategies for a broad class of applications in discret event simulation.

2. Hierarchical Modelling

This principal is explained by way of the design of digital circuits. All CAD tools provide the user with some basic primitives, out of which he can construct a first set of subdevices (e.g. adder, multiplexer, and decoder may be constructed using basic gates). In a second step, more complex modules will be constructed, e.g. an arithmetic unit consisting of several adders and multiplexers. The designer takes advantage in the high degree of equality of the instances in the sense that he constructs each module only once, on the next higher level of design he will only refer to the memorized design of subcircuits, i.e. he uses the subcircuit in many instances. Most CAD tools flatten such a hierarchical design and work on a representation which describes all instances in the same detailed way every time the subcircuit is used.

Due to the fact, that such flattened descriptions of large designs are workloads difficult to handle sometimes even for powerful workstations, the simulator TESI (TEst and SImulation) has been developed. Exceptional feature of this simulator is that the hierarchy of the design is not only used for model description but also during run time of the simulator. For his porpuse, a substructure of a circuit which is used in multiple areas of the model is stored only once; only a reference to its unique definiton is stored at the places where the substructure is used. This fact results in very compact internal data structures. As a consequence, the required space for working memory as well as CPU time for loading and storing the net list are dramatically reduced /1/.

3. Parallel simulation

The technique descibed above has been developed for an ordanary sequential simulator. In addition, it turned out that it can be exploited as a basic strategy for parallel simulation. Reasons are:

- The simulation of a large circuit can easily be broken into the simulation of substructures given by design hierarchy. No time consuming cutting algorithms has to be used to create artifical subcircuits.

- Due to the fact that many substructures are identical (i.e. instances of the some basic type), the number of different substructures is significantly smaller than the number of sub-structures of similar sizes gained from a cutting algorithm. Therefore this partitioning will map on a net with fewer computing nodes.

- Due to the very compact internal data structures of these models it is possible to load many different instances (sometimes the entire model) on each and every computing node of the parallel computing net. As a consequence mechanisms can be constructed which allow easy and fast load ballancing when the simulation of some instances requires significantly more or less computing time than the average of all nodes of the net.

Based on these considerations a parallel version of the simulator TESI has been implemented on a transputer net with 40 nodes. The described devide and conquer method revealed to be efficient although frequent communication between nodes is obviously the drawback of this approach. Alternative experiments using different strategies (e.g. partitioning of the fault list) showed that hierarchy can be used as a reasonable way of problem partitioning. Together with the advantages in memory requirement and load time it is especially worthwhile to use it for the simulation of large circuits /2/.

4. Outlook

The poster explains the strategies sketched above in more detail, and gives figures of merit of some experiments.

/1/ Hunger, A.,   Acceleration of simulation time by hierarchical modelling.
Papathanasiou, A.   In: Silvester, P.P.: Software Applications in Elelectrical Engineering, Computational Mechanics Publications, Southampton, 1993

/2/ Müller, F.   Methodische Analyse der digitalen Fehlersimulation als Grundlage für die Entwicklung effizienter Parallelisierungs-ansätze.
Als Dissertation eingereicht beim Fachbereich Elektro-technik der Universität-GH-Duisburg, 1993.

Large implicit finite element simulations of time-dependent incompressible flows on scalable parallel systems

H. Daniels[1], A. Peters[1] and O. Bergen[2], C. Forkel[2]

[1] ISAM, IBM Scientific Center, Vangerowstr. 18, 69115 Heidelberg
[2] IWW, RWTH Aachen, Mies-van-der-Rohe-Str.1, 52056 Aachen

Abstract. An efficient numerical scheme to solve the time-dependent incompressible Navier-Stokes equations was implemented for vector-super-computers [2] and distributed parallel systems [4]. The approximate 'projection 2' method [7] allows the decoupled solution of the components of the momentum equation and the continuity equation. Element level divergence free finite elements and irregular meshes approximate arbitrary geometries. Time-dependent boundary conditions on curved surfaces are possible. The *parallel version* of the code uses a parallel data structure as in domain decomposition. The implicit systems of equations are assembled for submeshes on distributed processors and all data and matrices are always kept local. Iterative conjugate gradient methods solve the implicit systems of equations for the intire computational domain, while they work on the local data and employ block preconditioning on the submeshes. The method always obtains *exactly* the sequential solution while it does the works on parallel processors. The parallel version allows high spatial resolution because the feasible problem size grows linearly with the amount of distributed memory.

1 NAVIER-STOKES EQUATIONS

We solve the time-dependent incompressible Navier-Stokes equations for the primitive variables velocity ($\mathbf{u} = (u, v, w)^T$) and kinematic pressure ($P = p/\rho_0$) in a bounded domain Ω:

$$\frac{\partial \mathbf{u}}{\partial t} + \mathbf{u} \cdot \nabla \mathbf{u} = -\nabla P + \nu \nabla^2 \mathbf{u} + \mathbf{f}, \tag{1}$$

$$\nabla \cdot \mathbf{u} = 0 \qquad \text{in } \Omega. \tag{2}$$

with boundary conditions (BC's): (Dirichlet) on Γ_1 and natural 'pseudo traction' (Neumann) on Γ_2:

$$\mathbf{u} = \mathbf{w} \qquad \text{on } \Gamma_1 \tag{3}$$

$$-P + \nu \frac{\partial u_n}{\partial n} = F_n \text{ and } \nu \frac{\partial u_\tau}{\partial n} = F_\tau \quad \text{on } \Gamma_2. \tag{4}$$

Here $\Gamma_1 \cap \Gamma_2 = \partial\Omega$ is the boundary of Ω. n represents the outward normal direction ($u_n = \mathbf{u} \cdot \mathbf{n}$), τ is the corresponding tangential direction ($u_\tau = \mathbf{u} \cdot \tau$)

and F_n and F_τ are the normal and tangential components of specified boundary traction. Initial conditions for the velocities:

$$\mathbf{u}(x_i, 0) = \mathbf{u}_0(x_i) \text{ in } \Omega \tag{5}$$

are required. These must fulfill the continuity equation and the normal boundary conditions on Γ_1 in order that a solution exists:

$$\nabla \cdot \mathbf{u}_0 = 0 \qquad \text{in } \Omega \tag{6}$$

$$\mathbf{n} \cdot \mathbf{u}_0 = \mathbf{n} \cdot \mathbf{w}(x_i, 0) \qquad \text{on } \Gamma_1. \tag{7}$$

Should $\Gamma_1 = \partial\Omega$ (velocities specified on the intire boundary), the global mass conservation is another solvability constraint.

2 FINITE ELEMENTS AND PROJECTION

Our code [2] uses Q1-P0 finite elements in three-dimensional space and weighted finite differences in time to approximate the solution of the continuous Navier-Stokes equations within a finite space-time domain $(\bar{\Omega}, \bar{T})$ with a finite discrete number of linearly independent approximation functions $(\phi_i, \psi_i) \in \bar{\Omega}$ and a finite discrete number of time steps $(\Delta t) \in \bar{T}$. In semi-discrete notation (finite elements in space, continous in time) we then have for (1) and (2):

$$\mathbf{M}\dot{\mathbf{u}}_i + (\mathbf{D} + \mathbf{V})\mathbf{u}_i = -\mathbf{C}_i\mathbf{P} + \mathbf{f}_i \,, i = 1, 2, 3 \tag{8}$$

$$\mathbf{C}_i^T\mathbf{u}_i = \mathbf{g} \qquad \text{in } \bar{\Omega}. \tag{9}$$

Gresho [7] proposed the 'projection 2' time integration algorithm for (8) and (9). Daniels [2] implemented the first 3D version of the method. We use consistent mass in the momentum equations. It produces much better phase speed accuracy than lumped mass. We use lumped mass for the pressure mass matrix, because its inverse is required. Nevertheless, the method is 2nd order accurate [3], [12]. Combined with conjugate gradient like schemes [10] it reaches high efficiency (chapter 3). The discrete algorithm is:

0) Given $\mathbf{u}_{i0}$ with $\mathbf{C}_i^T\mathbf{u}_{i0} = \mathbf{g}_0$ and $\mathbf{P}_0$:
1) Solve (p.e. with trapezoidal rule) the three momentum equations for one component of the intermediate velocity vector $\tilde{\mathbf{u}}$ with $\tilde{\mathbf{u}}_0 = \mathbf{u}_0$ at a time:

$$\left[\frac{2}{\Delta t}\mathbf{M} + \mathbf{D} + \mathbf{V}\right]\tilde{\mathbf{u}}_i = \left[\frac{2}{\Delta t}\mathbf{M} - \mathbf{D} - \mathbf{V}\right]\tilde{\mathbf{u}}_{i0} - \tag{10}$$

$$\mathbf{MM}_{Li}^{-1}\left(2\mathbf{C}_i\mathbf{P}_0 - \tilde{\mathbf{f}}_i - \mathbf{f}_{i0}\right) \,, i = 1, 2, 3 \text{ in } \bar{\Omega},$$

The boundary conditions for (10) are the Navier-Stokes boundary conditions. While (10) and (11) to (13) below decouple easily in carthesian coordinate notation, the method becomes much more involved when normal and tangential boundary conditions on curved surfaces must be specified. For a thorough discussion on discrete boundary condtions and details on the implementation see [2].

2) Project $\tilde{\mathbf{u}}$ to the subspace of discretely divergence-free velocities $\mathbf{v}$:

$$\begin{bmatrix} \mathbf{M}_x & 0 & 0 & \mathbf{C}_x \\ 0 & \mathbf{M}_y & 0 & \mathbf{C}_y \\ 0 & 0 & \mathbf{M}_z & \mathbf{C}_z \\ \mathbf{C}_x & \mathbf{C}_y & \mathbf{C}_z & 0 \end{bmatrix} \cdot \begin{bmatrix} \mathbf{v}_x \\ \mathbf{v}_y \\ \mathbf{v}_z \\ \varphi \end{bmatrix} = \begin{bmatrix} \mathbf{M}_x \tilde{\mathbf{u}}_x \\ \mathbf{M}_y \tilde{\mathbf{u}}_y \\ \mathbf{M}_z \tilde{\mathbf{u}}_z \\ 0 \end{bmatrix} \quad \text{in } \bar{\Omega}, \tag{11}$$

where the indices x, y, z on the mass matrices mean the Dirichlet BC's have already been built into the system. Using lumped mass (11) can be reduced to the Shur complement for φ and (11) can be decomposed into four sequential equations:

$$\left[\mathbf{C}_x^T \mathbf{M}_{Lx}^{-1} \mathbf{C}_x + \mathbf{C}_y^T \mathbf{M}_{Ly}^{-1} \mathbf{C}_y + \mathbf{C}_z^T \mathbf{M}_{Lz}^{-1} \mathbf{C}_z \right] \varphi = \mathbf{C}_x^T \tilde{\mathbf{u}}_x + \mathbf{C}_y^T \tilde{\mathbf{u}}_y + \mathbf{C}_z^T \tilde{\mathbf{u}}_z \tag{12}$$

$$\mathbf{v}_x = \tilde{\mathbf{u}}_x - \mathbf{M}_{Lx}^{-1} \mathbf{C}_x \varphi, \ \mathbf{v}_y = \tilde{\mathbf{u}}_y - \mathbf{M}_{Ly}^{-1} \mathbf{C}_y \varphi, \ \mathbf{v}_z = \tilde{\mathbf{u}}_z - \mathbf{M}_{Lz}^{-1} \mathbf{C}_z \varphi \tag{13}$$

The pressure-like variable φ (12) is obtained from the implicit equation (12). The divergence free velocities $\mathbf{v}_i$ result from the explicit updates (13).

3) Extrapolate $\mathbf{P}$ from a Taylor series expansion as:

$$\mathbf{P} = \mathbf{P}_0 + 2\varphi/\Delta t \quad \text{in } \bar{\Omega}. \tag{14}$$

4) Report $\mathbf{v}$ and $\mathbf{P}$, then advance the time $t = t_0 + \Delta t$ and set $\mathbf{P}_0 = \mathbf{P}, \mathbf{u}_0 = \mathbf{v}$ in Ω and go to step 1).

3 PARALLEL RESULTS

The current parallel implementation uses a host-node programming model and the public domain message passing library PVM [6]. The parallel data model partitions the computational domain into subdomains. The data of each subdomain is assigned to individual copies of the node program, which is very similar to the serial program for one (vector) processor. Communication between processors occurs inside of the preconditioned parallel conjugate gradient (CG-like) iterative solvers. The parallel solvers achieve exactly the same result as in the case of a serial computation in each CG iteration. Interface vectors (data) and partial scalar products are exchanged between processors in each CG iteration in order to retrieve the sequential algorithm and behavior for the complete computational domain, while the work is done in parallel on distributed processors as proposed by [?], [9] and [8]. For details on the implementation we have [4].

The method is *not* the classical domain decomposition. Parallel computations with our code have exactly the same stability and accuracy behavior as serial computations. The data partitioning is similar to domain decomposition and block preconditioning of the iterative solvers can be done on the submeshes with ILU for large problems (more than 250,000 unknowns per processor) and even direct sparse matrix solvers for medium size problems [11].

A number of calculations with 30,000 up to 750,000 three-dimensional finite elements and 130,000 up to 3,200,000 unknowns per time step were performed on an 8-way cluster of IBM RS/6000 and an 8-processor IBM 9076 SP1. The results indicate that

- the proposed data parallel method scales almost linearly (as expected) with the availability of distributed memory and very large problems become feasible. However,
- the efficiency, expressed as (CPU time)/(elapsed time), depends on the volume to surface ratio of the (unstructured) geometrical subdomains.

We now begin to use the Parallel Environment communication library. We expect a communication speedup on the SP1 of more than an order of magnitude compared to the public domain PVM version. This will bring the costs for an implicit simulation with **1,000,000** unstructured 3D finite elements (5,000,000 unknowns) down to 2-3 minutes per time step on an 8-processor SP1 for a well conditioned problem.

3.1 Benchmark for a drinking water reservoir

As a real research application, we select a project, which is studied at the Institut für Wasserbau of the RWTH Aachen. They use the serial vectorized version of the PASTIS-3D code [2] to simulate a flow and contaminant transport problem in a drinking water reservoir [1]. We have made benchmarks of the problem on an IBM POWERparallel System 9076 SP1 with the parallel version of the code. In order to allow comparisons with other supercomputers, which have less memory than the SP1, we selected an option of the code, which needs little memory, but requires substantially more operations per time step than the fastest options (see [2] for details).

The computational domain is the inlet basin of the Möhnetalsperre, a major drinking water reservoir in Germany. The model area has a wild (natural) three-dimensioanl shape and dimensions of (Length/Width/Depth) of (2,500 m/ 50 - 500 m/ 0.30 m - 20.0 m). Figure 1 shows a plot of the surface of the finite element mesh, which consists of 241,557 finite elements and 282,286 nodes. On each node there are 4 unknowns (u,v,w,T) and in each element there is 1 unknown (P). In the figure only 20% of the surface elements have been displayed to retain visibility. In a first attempt to model the three-dimensional flow field and recalculate a tracer transport experiment, which was conducted in the reservoir in 1982, an algebraic turbulence model was used. Details about it, the boundary conditions, time steps and results can be found in [1].

For the benchmark on the SP1 we partioned the mesh to 3,4,6,7 and 8 processors and obtained the results for elapsed time (wall clock time) per time step (dt) and CPU time per time step as shown in the following table.

no. processors (nP)	3	4	6	7	8
elaped/dt [s]	516	510	352	214	208
max. CPU/dt [s]	484	468	310	248	241
efficiency [%]	98.3	93.3	88.3	85.6	87.4
max no. elements/P	82,911	62,167	41,543	37,232	32,856
min no. elements/P	78,616	57,207	38,276	32,928	28,936

The table contains the average elapsed time per time step in [s], which was measured for the case, when the parallel diagonally scaled conjugate gradient solver was asked to solve the system of equations to a final residuum (L2-norm of Ax-b) $< 10^{-8}$. This required 38 DCG-iterations each for u,v,w and T and 200 DCG-iterations for the pressure P in the average. The listed CPU times are those, which were measured for the partition with the most finite elements. Load balancing cannot be perfect for a totally unstructured mesh, of course, and some partitions required a little less operations (and CPU time) per time step. The table shows, that inspite of the very low bandwidth of the public domain PVM 2.4 message passing library and the many DCG iterations (352 in the average per time step) the parallel efficiencies (max CPU / elapsed) are very good for this problem. A reason is the lengthy geometry of the basin. This leads to small interfaces between adjacent submeshes when we devide the mesh into strips.

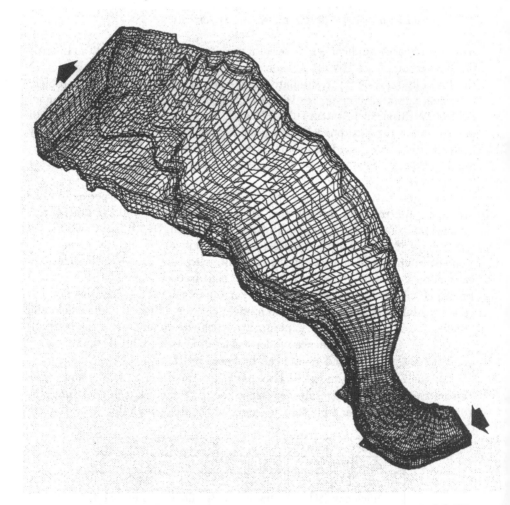

Fig.1: Surface of 3D finite element mesh for drinking water reservoir [1]. The mesh has been coarsened to 20% of the real density for clarity of the figure.

References

1. Bergen, O., *Numerische Simulation der Strömung und des Transports wasserlöslicher Stoffe in Seen und Talsperren am Beispiel des Vorbeckens der Möhnetalsperre*, Diplomarbeit, Inst. f. Wasserbau, RWTH Aachen, Aachen, Juli 1993.

2. Daniels, H., *PASTIS-3D Finite Element Projection Algorithm Solver for Transient Incompressible Flow Simulations - Implementation Aspects and User's Manual*, **UCRL-MA-111833**, Lawrence Livermore National Laborarory, Livermore, CA, August 1992.

3. Daniels, H., *PASTIS-3D - A new generation finite element solver for the incompressible Navier-Stokes equations*, VIII Int. Conf. Finite Elements in Fluids, Barcelona, Spain, **Vol.1**, Pineridge Press, 1993, 101-110.

4. Daniels, H. and A. Peters, *Solving Large Incompressible Time-Dependent Flow Problems on Scalable Parallel Systems*, prep. for Int. J. Num. Meth. Fluids, IBM TR **75.94**, 1994.

5. Dryja, M., *A finite element capacitance method for elliptic problems on regions partitioned into subdomains*, Numer. Math., **44**, 1984, 153-168.

6. Geist, A., A. Beguelin, J. Dongarra, W. Jiang, R. Manchek and V. Sunderam, *PVM 3 User's Guide and Manual*, Report No. **ORNL/TM-12187** , Eng. Phys. and Math. Div., ORNL, Oak Ridge, TN, 1993

7. Gresho, P.M., *On the theory of semi-implicit projection methods for viscous incompressible flow and its implementation via a finite element method that also introduces a nearly-consistent mass matrix, Part 1: Theory*, Int. J. Num. Meth. in Fluids, **11**, 1990, 587-620.

8. Haase, G. and U. Langer, *Parallelisierung und Vorkonditionierung des CG-Verfahrens durch Gebietszerlegung*, Num. Algebra auf Transputersystemen, Teubner, 1993.

9. Keyes, D.E. and W.D. Gropp, *A comparison of domain decompositions techniques for elliptic partial differential equations and their parallel implementation*, SIAM J. SCI. STAT. COMPUT., **8**, No. 2, 1987, 166-202.

10. Peters, A., *Non-symmetric CG-like schemes and the finite element solution of the advection-dispersion equation*, Int. J. Num. Meth. Fluids, **17**, 1993, 955-974.

11. Schmidt, P., *Vorkonditioniertes paralleles Verfahren der konjugierten Gradienten für elliptische Differentialgleichungen* , Thesis, Prakt. Math., Karlsruhe Univ., IBM, 1993.

12. Shin, J., *On Error Estimates of Some Higher Order Projection and Penalty-Projection Methods for Navier-Stokes Equations* , Report No. **A1190**, Dept. of Math., Penn State, submitted to Numerische Mathematik, Oct. 1991.

Parallel Simulation of Reacting Flows Using Detailed Chemistry

Dominique Thévenin[1,2], Frank Behrendt[1], Ulrich Maas[1] and Jürgen Warnatz[1]

[1] Institut für Technische Verbrennung, Stuttgart University, Pfaffenwaldring 12, D-70550 Stuttgart, Germany
[2] Interdisziplinäres Zentrum für Wissenschaftliches Rechnen, Heidelberg University, Im Neuenheimer Feld 368, D-69120 Heidelberg, Germany

1 Introduction

The numerical simulation of turbulent reacting flows remains up to now a very difficult and expensive task. In simple configurations that do not involve any geometrical complexity, the two-dimensional computation of laminar non-reacting flows has become an easy job. But as soon as chemical reactions are considered, the complexity increases tremendously. In supplement to the classical four variables (density, x- and y-components of velocity, total energy), hundreds of reactive species have to be computed and stored at each time-step [1]. Moreover, the time-scales introduced by the reactive processes are very disparate, and the smallest of these time-scales generally determine the maximal acceptable time-step for the computation. This results in a strong limitation of the time-step as well as in a very stiff set of partial differential equations [2].

Considering turbulent configurations leads also to a dramatic change in the problem complexity. Even if simple turbulence models like the k-ϵ one can sometimes give results accurate enough for industrial purposes, the fundamental study of the interaction between turbulence and chemical reaction can only be undertaken using very detailed models. Indeed, only Direct Numerical Simulation (DNS), Large-Eddy Simulation, and Probability Density Functions (PDF) methods can be considered to be accurate enough. In the case of DNS, which we will consider for the rest of this work, all spatial and temporal scales that are physically significant must be solved numerically [3]. This results in very small grid spacings, and therefore leads to a very large number of grid points, or to a limitation of the size of the computational domain. Moreover, while many reactive flow configurations can be studied with two-dimensional simulations, this is definitely not the case in general when turbulence is considered. The cost of DNS computations is so high that the aim of DNS is presently more to help developing and tuning simpler turbulence models than to be used directly for large simulations. But even in this reduced frame, a critical size must be reached in order to get results relevant enough to interest turbulence modellers.

Trying to estimate the cost of a "complete" computation, namely a three-dimensional DNS computation with hundred reactive species leads to a clear conclusion : such a computation cannot be done reasonably on classical vector supercomputers. On the other hand, the very quick development of parallel supercomputers gives to think that such simulations could probably become possible in the next few years. This provides the motivation for the development of a parallel DNS code with detailed models for the reactive and diffusive processes [4]. In a first step, this code is only two-dimensional, as present computing power is still limited. But the extension of the developed code to a three-dimensional frame is straightforward, and will be decided as soon as the needed node speed and memory becomes available.

2 Development of the Sequential Code

In order to do DNS computations, it is necessary to get a very high accuracy in space and time, because no numerical dissipation is allowed, and all spatial and temporal scales must be solved with the smallest possible error [3]. We therefore implemented sixth-order spectral-like centered spatial derivatives [5] and a fourth-order explicit Runge-Kutta time solver [6]. The decision to employ a fully explicit time-integration to solve the reactive Navier-Stokes equations [7] relies on three considerations :

1. The obtained parallel efficiency is high, as will be shown in Sect.4, and this without any major programming difficulty
2. Previous tests did not prove the interest of using implicit methods, the obtained gain in time-step being compensated by the increased cost of one iteration for such a high-order (typically at least fourth) implicit method
3. The time-step of the computation is generally limited by the reactive processes when considering flows with chemical reactions. A newly developed reduction procedure ([8],[9]) removes the stiffest time-scales introduced by the chemistry while keeping a high accuracy for the reaction terms, leading to an efficient explicit integration with relatively large time-steps

The time-step of the computation is controlled by three different limiting conditions, a Courant-Friedrichs-Lewy (CFL) stability criterion, a Fourier stability criterion, and an accuracy control obtained through timestep-doubling with the Runge-Kutta procedure [6]. Using the reduction procedure described above for the chemical terms, the time-step is generally limited by the CFL criterion.

Previous works proved the necessity of using carefully tuned boundary conditions when employing DNS methods in order to avoid any production of computational noise at the boundaries, and to let the disturbing acoustic waves leave the computational domain. We therefore implemented an extended version of the Navier-Stokes Characteristic Boundary Conditions (NSCBC) [10] that takes into account the presence of reacting species in the system [11]. Excellent results have been obtained up to now with this method in various configurations.

In order to reduce the amound of needed grid points while keeping a high spatial resolution, an adaptive gridding procedure is also implemented in the code. The regridding decision is based on a classical mesh-function equidistribution in both directions [12]. This procedure can offer substantial gains in memory and run-time to a small cost in terms of lower accuracy. As the node memory remains quite limited on present parallel architectures, this static adaptive gridding constitutes often at present time the only possibility to tackle problems with large computational domains at an acceptable run-time memory expense.

The reactive processes are modeled with detailed sets of Arrhenius coefficients describing the different possible reactive paths [13]. Accurate polynomial approximations of all needed thermodynamical parameters are gathered in a database and used throughout the computation. A detailed modeling of the transport properties (with Soret effect) is also included in the computation in order to reproduce accurately diffusion-limited processes.

3 Parallelization Procedure

The parallelization of the code relies on a classical regular domain-decomposition in two dimensions, which is considered as the best way when using an explicit time-integration [14]. Great care was given to make sure that a multiprocessor computation produces *exactly* the same result as a monoprocessor one. It was observed that debugging the code is in practice impossible when this condition is not fulfilled.

Portability remains at present time one major problem of parallel computing. Different Multiple-Instruction Multiple-Data (MIMD) architectures generally offer uncompatible message-passing and processor control possibilities. Though some "standards" (e.g. PVM) begin to be implemented on virtually all major parallel computers, there is generally a non-negligible overhead when using these modules instead of the local native message-passing libraries. In order to achieve an easy portability, the reactive flow solver is in our code completely separated from the library of subroutines controlling the parallel work. This means that, in order to implement the code on another kind of MIMD computer, only a few lines responsible for actual message-passing or processor initialization (typically less than 100 lines of code) have to be adapted to the currently considered architecture. These changes are afterwards automatically done through editor macros, i.e. the user only gives the identification of the desired architecture, let the macro modify the code, and compiles the output on the parallel computer. Thanks to this easy portability, the code has been employed on a variety of architectures listed in Table 1.

Table 1. Employed parallel computers

Abbreviation	Architecture	Node	Size	Communication
ParSC	Parsytec Supercluster	T805	128	native async.
InPar	Intel Paragon XP/S 5	i860 XP Risc	72	native async.
T3Demu	T3D emulator on YMP	Cray YMP node	8	PVM3
RiscPVM	IBM Risc network	RISC 6000/550	6	PVM3

We always use asynchronous message-passing in order to spare run-time through overlapping of computation and communication, though the obtained gain over synchronous communication is small. The optimal processor configuration used for the computation is automatically determined knowing how many nodes are available by minimizing the length of the processor boundaries (and therefore the amount of inter-processor communication).

The first tests on these different architectures proved that a control of the load on each node is a necessity. This is explained by two reasons :

1. The adaptive gridding causes numerous point additions and deletions. This generally quickly results in large differences in the amount of grid points on different nodes, leading to a very poor load balance (and efficiency)
2. On workstation networks (and computers with shared nodes), the work of other users cannot be foreseen. Some kind of work redistribution when one node suddenly becomes heavily loaded is therefore needed to preserve the computational efficiency

Considering these two points, a dynamic load balancing procedure was introduced in the code. It relies on the measurement of the real time needed by each node to proceed with one integration step. When large enough discrepancies appear between the processors, a grid-point redistribution between neighbouring nodes takes place, with the aim of evening the load. We show in Fig.1 a comparison of the maximal relative load imbalance between all processors with and without dynamic load balancing. Implementing this procedure clearly leads to a much better load distribution. Of course, it leads also to substantial gains in the needed computing time (39% reduction in the example shown), and in the parallel efficiency.

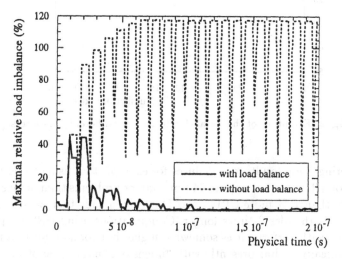

Fig. 1. Effect of dynamic load balancing for a typical computation (InPar with 8 nodes)

4 Parallel Efficiency of the Code

Having developed this parallel solver, we decide to test the obtained efficiency on different parallel architectures. As the aim of parallel computations in the field of reactive fluid dynamics is much more to tackle bigger problems than to solve the same problems as today in a shorter time, we are mainly interested in the efficiencies obtained for a test *scaling with the number of nodes*. We model the ignition of a H_2-air diffusion flame, taken as a typical combustion configuration, using a chemical scheme with 9 reactive species and 38 chemical reactions. When increasing the number of nodes, we increase accordingly the size of the computational domain in order to keep the initial number of grid points per node constant. We always use adaptive gridding. This results in a slight variation of the number of grid points per node at the end of the computation (i.e., after adaptive regridding), but this difference does not change much the obtained efficiencies and corresponds anyway to what is observed in physically interesting configurations. Results obtained on the parallel architectures listed in Table 1 are shown in Fig.2.

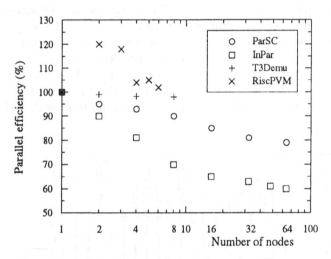

Fig. 2. Evolution of the parallel efficiency for different computers

Considering these results, one deduces for example that using 64 nodes of an Intel Paragon allows us to compute 64 times larger problems than on one processor with less than 70% more CPU-time. This corresponds to a two-dimensional domain with both sides 8 times longer. Computations using DNS on powerful workstations (with performances somewhat higher but comparable to a Paragon node) are typically dealing presently with dimensions on the order of a few square millimeters [15]. Gains obtained with parallel computing can therefore already authorize two-dimensional computations with dimensions of a few square centimeters, which approaches the typical size of combustion chambers. Using more nodes or more powerful nodes should relatively soon allow three-dimensional computations with each dimension as long as 1 to 10 cm, which corresponds to sizes of practical interest for industrial as well as research purposes.

5 Conclusion

We described in this paper the development of a parallel Direct Numerical Simulation code designed to solve the reactive Navier-Stokes equations with accurate models for the reactive and transport properties. We proved that the fully explicit time-integration leads to high parallel efficiencies, provided a dynamic load balancing procedure is used. First combustion applications concerning flame stability and flame structure are presently underway.

References

1. Kee, R.J., Miller, J.A., Evans, G.H. and Dixon-Lewis G. : A computational model of the structure and extinction of strained, opposed flow, premixed methane-air flames. 22nd Symp. (Int.) Comb. (1988) 1479-1494
2. Oran, E.S. and Boris, J.P. : Numerical simulation of reactive flows. Elsevier (1987)
3. Reynolds, W.C. : The potential and limitations of direct and large eddy simulations. Lecture Notes in Physics **357**, Springer Verlag (1990) 313-343
4. Thévenin, D., Behrendt, F., Maas, U. and Warnatz, J. : Parallel direct simulation of two-dimensional flows with detailed chemistry. Proc. 5th Int. Conf. on Numerical Combustion, Garmisch-Partenkirchen, Germany (1993) 121
5. Lele, S.K. : Compact finite differences schemes with spectral-like resolution. J. Comp. Phys. **103** (1992) 16-42
6. Press, W.H., Flannery, B.P., Teukolsky, S.A. and Vetterling, W.T. : Numerical recipes. Cambridge University Press (1989)
7. Williams, F.A. : Combustion theory. Benjamin/Cummings Publishing Company (1985)
8. Maas, U. and Pope, S.B. : Simplifying chemical kinetics : intrinsic low-dimensional manifolds in composition space. Combust. Flame **88** (1992) 239-264
9. Schmidt, D., Maas, U. and Warnatz, J. : Simplifying chemical kinetics for the simulation of hypersonic flows using intrinsic low-dimensional manifolds. Proc. 5th Int. Symp. on Computational Fluid Mechanics, Sendai, Japan (1993) 81-86
10. Poinsot, T.J. and Lele, S.K. : Boundary conditions for direct simulations of compressible viscous flows. J. Comp. Phys. **101** (1992) 104-129
11. Baum, M., Poinsot, T. and Thévenin, D. : Accurate boundary conditions for multicomponent reactive flows. submitted J. Comp. Phys.
12. Maas, U. and Warnatz, J. : Simulation of chemically reacting flows in two-dimensional geometries. Impact Comput. Sci. Eng. 1 (1989) 394-420
13. Maas, U. and Warnatz, J. : Ignition processes in hydrogen-oxygen mixtures. Combust. Flame **74** (1988) 53-69
14. Gropp, D.W. and Smith, E.B. : Computational fluid dynamics on parallel processors. Computers & Fluids **18**, 3 (1990) 289-304
15. Thévenin, D. : Dynamique de l'allumage de flammes de diffusion dans des écoulements cisaillés. Thèse de Doctorat, Ecole Centrale Paris ECP92-042 (1992)

Unstructured Computational Fluid Dynamics on Massively-Parallel SIMD-Systems

Stefan Haberhauer
E-Mail: shaberha@hermes.informatik.uni-stuttgart.de

Abstract. This article reports of a scheme for the solution of the time-dependent two-dimensional Euler-equations with strong shocks using Roe's Approximate Riemann-Solver. This scheme reproduces strong shocks accurately though it is just first-order accurate in space. The computational domain is an unstructured grid, which allows calculation around complex geometries but at the expense of a complex hierarchical data structure with relations between points, sides and elements. Although this approach is more computationally intensive than finite difference schemes, it offers the advantages of being robust and producing a sharp resolution of shocks, where other schemes (especially those with artificial viscousity or the FTC concept) tend to smear.

The target machine was the MasPar MP-1216 of the IPVR[1] of the University of Stuttgart, which is a SIMD computer with 16k processor elements. The implementation was done in MasPar Fortran (MPF, MasPar's Fortran 90 subset).

1   Overview

This article focuses on the solution of the two-dimensional Euler-Equations on unstructured grids using a massively-parallel computer with a SIMD-architecture. After a short introduction in the governing equations, the mapping of the data-structure onto this special kind of hardware is explained in detail. Finally, an example is shown with performance measurement data.

2   Governing Equations

The motion of fluid is assumed to be described by the time-dependent Euler equations which express the conservation of mass, momentum and energy for a compressible, inviscid nonconducting adiabatic fluid following the ideal-gas assumption.

The conservation form of the two-dimensional time-dependent Euler equations can be written as

$$\frac{\partial}{\partial t}\int_{\Omega} U dV + \oint_{\partial\Omega} \vec{F}\vec{n}ds = 0 \qquad\qquad \text{(equ. 1)}$$

where

$$U = \begin{bmatrix} \rho \\ \rho u \\ \rho v \\ e \end{bmatrix} \qquad\qquad \text{(equ. 2)}$$

is the vector of the conservative variables of state and

---

1. Institut für parallele und verteilte Höchstleistungsrechner

$$\vec{F} \cdot \vec{n} = q \begin{bmatrix} \rho \\ \rho u \\ \rho v \\ e+p \end{bmatrix} + p \begin{bmatrix} 0 \\ n_x \\ n_y \\ 0 \end{bmatrix} \qquad \text{(equ. 3)}$$

gives the flux components over the element-interfaces. The introduction of the equation of state for an ideal gas leads to

$$e = \frac{p}{\gamma - 1} + \frac{\rho}{2} (u^2 + v^2) \qquad \text{(equ. 4)}$$

In the equations following abbreviations are introduced:

ρ is the density
p is the pressure
u and v are the Cartesian components of velocity and $q = \sqrt{u^2 + v^2}$
e is the total energy per unit volume
γ is the ratio of specific heats c_p/c_v and is set to 1.4 for air
n_x and n_y are the Cartesian components of the exterior surface unit normal

3 Spatial Discretization

Calculation of the new states is done using Roe's Approximate Riemann Solver [Roe 1981], which is based on a linearized formulation of the Euler equations [Hirsch 1990]. Because the focus of this paper is the implementation and not the numerical scheme, the interested reader should consult the references for explanation.

4 Time Integration

Time integration is done explicitly using simple forward differencing

$$U_i^{(n+1)} = U_i^{(n)} - \frac{\Delta t}{V_i} (\sum_{sides} F_{LR}S) \qquad \text{(equ. 5)}$$

where S is the length of the side.

5 MasPar MP-1216 Architecture

5.1 Hardware

The MasPar MP–1216 of IPVR consists of a front_end-computer (FE), in this case an Unix-workstation DECstation 5000 and a data_parallel_unit (DPU), which represents the original SIMD part. The FE does job control and networking while the DPU is used exclusively for working in parallel on numerical data at runtime. Peak-performance is given with 550 MFLOPS(64bit) and 1200 MFLOPS(32bit). The DPU could be subdivided into three logical parts: the array control_unit (ACU), the processor array with up to 16k (16384) processor-elements (PE) and the communication networks (figure 1). There is no global address space but each PE has its local data memory (PMEM) of 16kByte (distributed memory machine). It is used exclusively for data storage, because the instruction stream is processed by the scalar ACU. If any PE needs data from another PE these data has to be exchanged using a communication operation. There are two different networks for this data exchange: x–net for regular patterns and global_router for random-access. Scalar data is stored and processed on FE and may be transported to the DPU via the VME-bus before combining with data located in the PMEM..

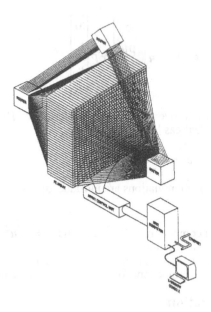

Figure 1 MasPar MP-1216 architecture

Communication between PEs

Inter-processor communication is very important because of the distributed data memory. The implemented algorithm needs multiple data exchange using indirect addresses. This kind of communication uses the three stage global router network. In a MP-1216 there are 1024 PE–clusters with 16 PEs each. Every cluster has exactly one input and one output channel to the global router. If more than one PE in a certain cluster participates in communication in the same direction, this communication pattern is resolved sequentially. Figure 2 shows an example for a conflict-situation: clusters 1 to 3 are assumed to send data via the global router connection to cluster 4. All target PEs are located on the same cluster, so this pattern is resolved sequentially and requires four communication cycles.

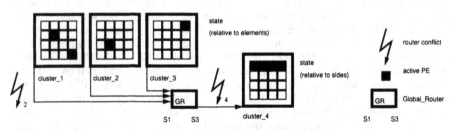

Figure 2 Router conflicts

5.2 Operating System

MasPar's FE (a DECstation 5000) operates Ultrix, DEC's Unix. Some extensions allow controlling the resources of the DPU.

5.3   Programming Environment

The implementation was done in MPF, MasPar's Fortran'90 subset. MPF allows writing machine-independent programs which could be run on machines of different vendors. Another benefit of MPF is the ability of handling arrays with more elements than PEs in the DPU, as the virtualization is done completely by the compiler. Compiler options are available to the application programmer to control the mapping of the arrays for optimizing.

The communication is also transparent to the programmer. Using indirect addresses, all inter-processor-communication is done via the global router. In the MPF code this kind of data access appears as an one dimensional integer array, called index vector. Scalar data is allocated in FE's memory and has to be transmitted to the DPU if used together with array constructs.

6   Porting Algorithm Onto MP-1216

The solver consists of the iteration loop with the following four logical steps:

(1) Assigning the variables of state (u^n) of the elements separated by the sides to the side's PEs.

(2) Calculation of fluxes over the sides assuming each element interface separates two different constant values of the variables of state and using Roe's Approximate Riemann Solver

(3) Summation of the fluxes for all sides of each element

(4) Calculation of the new state (u^{n+1}) in each element (time integration)

To show the flexibility of the data structure and the strategy of mapping to the processors, we will assume the following grid as an example data set and map it to a PE-Array with 4x4=16 PEs. There is no restriction made on the maximal number of sides of each element, the order of data relation is not stipulated. In the left part figure 3 shows the grid consisting of three elements, nine sides and seven points. The input-data can be subdivided into four blocks: the block of nodes, the block of sides, the block of elements and the block of element-sides. Data of each block is mapped to the processor-array using the compiler-option `cmpf map...(ALLBITS[,PMEM]`. Now we will have a look at the iteration steps and the resulting communication patterns.

(1) The vector u with the conservative variables of state is stored with regard to elements. This is a communication step and after its execution the data of the two seperated elements is located on the same PE. Figure 3 gives an example. The PE containing the data of a side (S8) gets the data of the two separated elements. To archive this, the internal numbers of the two elements (stored in the data set of S8) are used for indirect addressing.

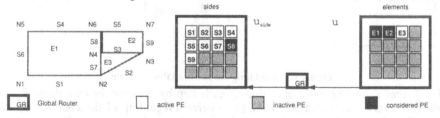

Figure 3 Assigning variables of state of the two separated elements to the PE of the side

(2) Calculating fluxes happens in parallel without inter-processor-communication on the PE-Array because the data is stored locally in PMEM. Some single data is sloshed from FE to the DPU. In this step most of the floating point operations are performed.

There are two different flux routines: one for the inner sides (S3, S7, S8) and one for the boundary-fluxes (S1, S2, S4, S5, S9).

Figure 4 Flux calculation

(3) The next step consists of summing up the fluxes over all sides for each element. Because of the the one-dimensional index-vectors used for indirect addressing in MPF there's an outer loop doing summation sequentially over element/sides, but parallel for all elements. Because there is no explicit order in the input data, we have to introduce the variable orientierung. All inner sides separate exactly two elements. Flux is calculated in step (2) from the first to the second element, so the flux of the first element is negative (it leaves the element) and though orientierung=-1 and for the other element orientierung=+1. In this step most inter-processor-communication happens.

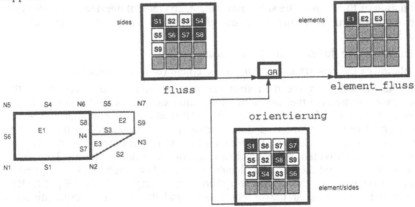

Figure 5 Summation of element-fluxes

(4) After summing up fluxes for each element the new variables of state can be calculated locally (time integration) either with a simple forward differencing scheme or with the four stage Runge-Kutta scheme.

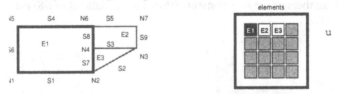

Figure 6 Calculating the new variables of state

The figures show one basic operation of each step by drawing the considered PE(s) black. In every step is data-parallism: (1) is parallel regarding all sides and sequential regarding the two elements. (2) is parallel regarding sides. (3) is parallel regarding elements and sequential regarding the sides of each element and (4) is parallel regarding elements. Some communication is done at step (1) but mostly at step (3). This is performed via the global router, because of the unstructured communication patterns.

7 Example: Transsonical flow over NACA 0012-airfoil

The example shows the flow over a NACA 0012-airfoil at an angle of attack of 0° at a speed of $318 \; \frac{m}{s}$. For this case the flow will be symmetrical, so just the upper half is calculated.

7.1 Grid geometry

For the ease of grid generation a rather simple structured grid is chosen for this example. It doesn't really need the full flexibility of the program, but it has got an amount of data which justifies the use of a massively-parallel computer.

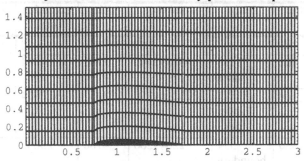

Figure 7 Computational domain and NACA 0012-airfoil
(the figure shows only every 20th grid line)

Grid parameters are listed in table 3. The number of inner sides and elements with variable state are chosen near to n*16k, where n is an integer. The geometric shape is equal to a structured grid of 192 * 83 elements.

Nodes		16704
Sides	Total	33129
	Inner	32575
	Boundary	554
Elements	Total	16426
	Variable state	16254
	Fixed state	172

Table 3 Parameters of the grid

7.2 Numerical Results

Figure 13 shows the Iso-Mach-areas. Covered values reach from Ma=0.36 to Ma=1.11 with a ΔMa=0.06 between them. In the airfoil's back is the strong shock.

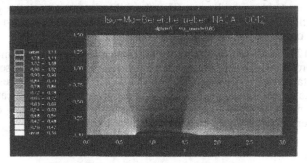

Figure 8 Numerical results: Iso-Mach-areas

7.3 Performance results

Table 4 shows the operations count and performance results achieved for the second example (the airfoil). Sustained performance depends obviously on local disposal of data on the PEs (subroutins flux, flux_roe, flux_rand, zeitintegral). In subroutine flux_rand there are too few boundary sides, so data covers only 3,4 % of the PE-array. In subroutine fluxintegral the fluxes are summed up for each element, so data has to be transmitted via the global router, which is quite time consuming. Routine fluxintegral contains only 4,6 % of the floating-point operations, but consumes 30,2 % of execution time of the iteration loop.

step	subroutine	factor	total ops	ticks	execution time	performance (64bit)
			$[+^a]$	[ticks^b]	[s]	[MFLOPS]
2	flux	33129 sides	481695660	2701	5.4024	42.16
1&2	flux_roe	32575 inner sides	23232164250	33133	66.2664	165.76
1&2	flux_rand	554 boundary sides	22049200	4180	8.3602	1.25
3	fluxintegral	65704 element-sides	1159018560	18682	37.3644	14.67
4	zeitintegral^c	16426 elements	1872728260	2892	5.784	153.09
	total		2.676766E 10	61588	123.1774	102.75^d

a. all operations are weighted relative to execution time needed for an add
b. measured with profiling-tool mpprof, 1 tick = 2 ms
c. timeintegration
d. sustained performance of the iteration kernel is about 18.7% of the Peak-Performancebecause
- Peak-Performance is timed for operations on data stored in the local registers not for data stored in PMEM
- of the communication overhead for indirect addressing

Table 4 Performance results of the iteration loop (1000 iteration cycles)

8 Conclusion

Roe's Approximate Riemann Solver has been implemented for the time-dependent Euler-equations on unstructured grids. No explicit restriction was introduced for the maximal number of sides per element. This flexibility in geometry has a great impact on communication, because data locality is not determined at compile-time and can not be used for optimizing the communication pattern.

MasPar's MP-1216 suits best for problems with a great amount of data, mapped to the PE-array and processed locally. The algorithm described in this report uses a complex hierarchical data structure. This forces a substantial use of indirect addressing, which is performed via global router connections for inter-processor communication. So it is shown that the machine is not limited to process regular data structures, even though the sustained performance would be quite better, naturally.

References

[Blank 1990]   Blank, Tom
                  „The MasPar MP-1 Architecture"
                  published in: *Proceedings of IEEE Compcon Spring 1990*
                  IEEE Computer Society Press Reprint, Los Alamitos, 1990

[Frink 1990]   Frink, Neal T.
                  „Upwind Scheme for Solving the Euler Equations on
                  Unstructured Tetrahedral Meshes"
                  in *AIAA Journal*, Vol. 30, Nr. 1, p. 70-77
                  Januar 1992

[Haberhauer 1993] Haberhauer, Stefan
                  „Massiv–parallele Lösung der instationären 2D-
                  Euler–Gleichungen auf unstrukturierten Gittern mit dem
                  approximierenden Gleichungslöser nach Roe"
                  Diplomarbeit / Interner Bericht Nr. 78
                  Rechenzentrum der Universität Stuttgart
                  Mai 1993

[Hirsch 1990]   Hirsch, Charles
                  „Numerical Computation of Internal and External Flows"
                  Vol.1 & 2
                  John Wiley & Sons, 1990

[Long 1991]   Long, Lyle N., Khan M.M.S. & Sharp, H. Thomas
                  „Massively Parallel Three-Dimensional Euler/Navier-
                  Stokes Method"
                  in *AIAA Journal*, Vol. 29, Nr. 5 p. 70-77
                  Mai1991

[Nickolls 1990]   Nickolls, John R.
                  „The Design of the MasPar MP-1: a Cost Effective Massively
                  Parallel Computer"
                  published in: *Proceedings of IEEE Compcon Spring 1990*
                  IEEE Computer Society Press Reprint, Los Alamitos, 1990

[Prechelt 1992]   Prechelt, Lutz
                  „Measurements of MasPar MP–1216A Communication
                  Operations"
                  Draft Technical Report Dxx/93
                  Institut für Programmstrukturen und Datenorganisation
                  Fakultät für Informatik / Universität Karlsruhe
                  November 1992

[Roe 1981]   Roe, Philip L.
                  „Approximate Riemann solvers, parameter vectors and
                  difference schemes"
                  in *Journal on Computational Physics*, **43**, p. 357-372
                  März 1981

[Roe 1986]   Roe, Philip L.
                  „Discrete models for the numerical analysis of time-dependent
                  multidimensional gas dynamics"
                  in *Journal on Computational Physics*, **63**, p. 458-476
                  Mai 1985

An Advanced Parallel Multiblock Code for the Solution of 2D Flow-Fields

C. de Nicola[1], G. De Pietro[2], M. Giuliani[1]

[1] Gasdynamics Institute, University of Naples, P.le Tecchio, Naples, Italy
[2] IRSIP, National Research Council of Italy, Via P. Castellino 111, Naples, Italy

Abstract. In this paper an advanced parallel multiblock code for the solution of 2D transonic inviscid flows is presented. Some optimization techniques were applied to obtain satisfying performances on parallel machines. The results confirm the effectiveness of the proposed approaches.

1 Introduction

It is well-known that Computational Fluid Dynamics represents one of the application fields in which there is great demand for computing power. Recently, many efforts were made for using parallel computers to solve CFD problems in order to verify the effectiveness and suitability of such architectures, especially when real world problems have to be faced. For this aim, a lot of work has been made in porting existing codes on parallel architectures; however, the parallel versions often suffer for several limitations because of difficulty to put together all the facilities that the sequential versions offer (e.g. convergence accelerators, local grid refinement techniques, etc).

In this paper a very complete and advanced CFD code, developed for MIMD parallel architectures, is presented. Several techniques have been applied to obtain an efficient parallel implementation, especially when different convergence accelerators are simultaneously used. Nowadays, this code is used by local aerospace industries and research centers.

2 Code Description

A code for the analysis of transonic inviscid flows, described by Euler's equations [1], has been developed. A Multiblock technique is adopted by which the computational domain is subdivided into subdomains called "blocks" according to the geometry complexity and to the flow field; in fact this technique offers many facilities that allow an accurate description of flows around complex configurations by using locally structured but globally unstructured grids. Because of the block decomposition, apart from the physical conditions at the boundaries of the computational domain, further conditions at interfaces between blocks have to be imposed. Moreover, in a typical multiblock code

- different blocks contain different number of nodes;

- different mathematical models can be assigned in different blocks;
- the solution differently evolves in each block owing to Fluid Dynamics non-linearities (shock waves, chemical reactions, viscosity).

It should be observed that all these features have a strong impact for an efficient parallel implementation.

Steady solutions can be obtained through a time marching procedure called Time Dependent Procedure (TDP) and the space derivatives are executed according to a central finite volume scheme [1] on a structured grid.

The speed of convergence of TDP can be increased by several techniques such as Multistage Time Stepping (MTS), Local Time Stepping, Residual Averaging and Enthalpy Damping [1] which do not involve problems for parallel implementation if multiblock algorithms with frozen interface conditions are used [2].

A remarkable acceleration for the integration process is based on techniques that use more than one computational grid, such as Multilevel or Multigrid. In other words, Nested Iteration (Multilevel) consists in calculating an initial solution guess by performing a fixed number of iterations on coarser grids, thus quickly obtaining a satisfactory level of convergence, especially for the global aerodynamic coefficients [3]. Multigrid techniques increase the convergence rate by attenuating the low- frequence components of the residual calculating it on coarser grids [4]. In fact it is well-known that the low-frequence components of the error are generally responsible for the loss of efficiency in iterative process [5]. Multigrid and Multiblock techniques can be coupled in two different ways:

- Horizontal: at a fixed grid level of multigrid cycle, calculation is performed for all blocks.
- Vertical: a computational cycle is independently completed in each block.

The horizontal algorithm needs to update the interface conditions at each level of the multigrid cycles after the calculation has been completed for all blocks. On the other hand, the vertical algorithm freezes the interface conditions during the calculation of multigrid cycles and update them just at the end of each cycle for all grid levels. Numerical results [3] have shown that the horizontal algorithm is more effective (see fig.(1)) but, as regards the parallel implementation, vertical algorithm can be more efficient.

Finally it should be pointed out that the proposed methods can be applied for the solutions of more complex models, such as the description of 3D viscous flows.

3   Parallel Implementation

In general, the main causes of inefficiency in using parallel architectures are an uneven load-balancing and the communication overheads.

With reference to our specific application, the Multiblock technique can generate load balancing problems because the size and \ or computation of blocks can widely differ; so we have properly to assign blocks to processors. For this

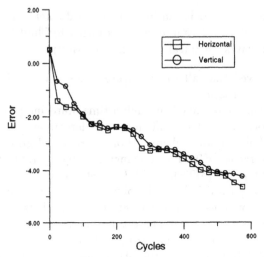

Fig. 1. Convergence history.

aim, a preprocessor has been designed. It is able to find an optimal mapping of the blocks on the processors, which, after information about the block size, is available.

This preprocessor is based on the FFD heuristic used to solve the bin-packing problem [6]. At first the block indexes are arranged in a non decreasing ordered list according to the estimated computational load then, a block load map is built by creating a correspondence among blocks indexes, B_i, and processor indexes, P_j, as it is shown in fig.(2). We should consider that this technique fits well whenever the number of blocks is greater than the number of available processors, which is the typical situation for real applications.

Even if the present version of the code supports only static load balancing, the adopted technique can be profitably used for solving dynamic load balancing problems (e.g. whenever the computational load of some block changes owing to adaptive local grid refinement).

The communication overheads is mainly related to the introduction of convergence accelerators. In particular, using Nested Iterations, at each time iteration, data need to be exchanged between processors containing adjacent block interfaces; concerning the iterations performed on coarser grids, the time spent for interprocessor communication can represent a considerable part compared to the computation time. However, in real applications, only the 15 - 20% of the total number of iterations are performed on coarse grids; so the impact of the Nested Iteration technique on the overall performance is not crucial.

More attention must be paid in the application of Multigrid technique which usually is a severe test for distributed memory systems. As we explained before, for Multiblock methods different boundary condition updating strategies can be adopted for the Multigrid cycle. If the horizontal strategy is used, the updating is performed at each grid level, both in the descending and in the ascending phases. In this case, say L the number of grid levels for a V cycle, $2*L-1$ communication for each block boundary needs. In order to reduce the number of communication, it has been chosen to update boundary condition one time at the beginning of each cycle (vertical strategy), so reducing the number of communication for cycle to one. However, as already shown in fig.(1), in this case the number of cycles for obtaining the same solution accuracy increases. That means we save computational time if the following inequality holds:

$$(N_v - N_h)\, T_v < N_h * T_c * 2(L-1) \tag{1}$$

where N_v and N_h are, respectively, the number of cycles by applying the vertical and horizontal strategy, T_v is the time spent for one cycle using the vertical strategy and T_c is the communication time spent to exchange information with all the block boundaries.

The following technique has been adopted to minimize further communication overheads: the calculation related to the ascending phase of the multigrid cycle has been subdivided into two steps. In the first one, the new values related to the block boundary cells are calculated, while the calculation of the values of the remaining points (the block "core") is demanded to the second step. Communication is performed between these two computational steps, so allowing to overlap the data transmission time with the computing time of the "core" (see fig.(3)).

The code was written in Fortran 77 in addition to PVM 2.4 routines for interprocessor communication [7]; in order to meet the goal of overlapping computation and communication, non-blocking communication primitives have been used.

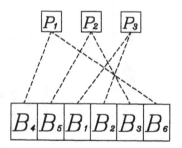

Fig. 2. Example of block assignement.

4   Results

Numerical test have been performed on Convex C210 MPP0 with a cluster of 4 HP730 nodes. A NACA 0012 airfoil has been employed as test case with a 320x64 grid, which has been decomposed according to different multiblock topologies.

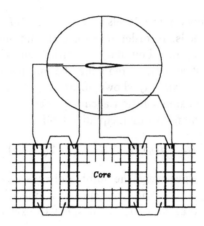

Fig. 3. Boundary cells exchange.

In figure (4) the speedup and the efficiency for a grid composed by 4 equal sized blocks (80x64) are presented; the results obtained by using different acceleration techniques are shown. We must consider that the simultaneous use of all the accelerators (full multigrid) represents the worst case from the parallel point of view; however, even in this case there is higher efficiency.

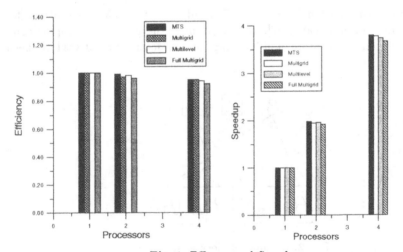

Fig. 4. Effiency and Speedup.

In order to verify the effectiveness of the load balancing algorithm further tests have been performed on a grid having 10 blocks of different sizes; the blocks size has been chosen so as to realize a perfect load balancing. In figure (5) comparisons between executions with and without load preprocessing are given; in the first case, the preprocessor is able to assign the same workload to each processor, while in the second one the blocks are assigned to processors according to their topological order (i.e. each processor contains only adjacent blocks). In this last one, two processors have a twice computational load compared to the other processors; that means, say T_{opt} the computing time with a perfect load balancing, a $T_{opt}/3$ time increase is expected. Note that results show performance improvements of some 33% when load preprocessor is used, according to the estimated values.

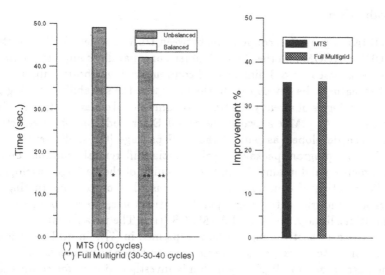

Fig. 5. Computing time and Performance improvement.

References

1. Jameson A.: Numerical Solutions of the Euler Equations for Compressible Inviscid Fluids, MAE Report 1643, 1985
2. de Nicola C., De Pietro G., Paparone L.: Evaluation of Different Approaches to Parallel Processing for CFD, Proc. Parallel CFD 92, New Brunswick, New Jersey 1992, North-Holland
3. Giuliani M.: Solution of the Euler Equations for Flows around Airfoils through Advanced Techniques for Acceleration of Convergence, Degree Thesis, University of Naples, 1993, Advisors: C. de Nicola, G. De Pietro, L. Paparone
4. Jameson A.: Solution of the Euler Equations for two Dimensional Transonic Flows by a Multigrid Method, Applied Math. and Computations, 13, 1985
5. Briggs W. L.: A Multigrid Tutorial, SIAM, Philadelphia,1987
6. Mayr E. W.: Theoretical Aspects of Parallel Computation VLSI and PARALLEL COMPUTATION, R. Suaya and G., Birtwistle Eds, Morgan Kaufmann, 1990
7. Geist G. A.: Network-Based Concurrent Computing on the PVM, Concurrency, Practice and Experience, Vol.4, 1992

Parallel multigrid results for Euler equations and grid partitioning into a large number of blocks.

C.W. Oosterlee, H. Ritzdorf, A. Schüller, B. Steckel

Gesellschaft für Mathematik und Datenverarbeitung,
P.O. Box 1316, 53731 St. Augustin.

1. Introduction

In the POPINDA project, a cooperation between DLR, Dornier, DASA, Deutsche Airbus, IBM, ORCOM and the GMD, 3 dimensional parallel compressible Navier-Stokes solvers, based on a 3 dimensional communications library will, amongst many other features, be developed. In the first stage the suitability of using parallelization strategies of already existing two dimensional codes for the 3D solvers is investigated. At GMD a two dimensional Euler code for block-structured grids has been developed as part of the LiSS package [6]. LiSS, developed in the eighties, is a program package to solve partial differential equations on general two-dimensional domains. From the beginning of the package development the parallel solution of equations has been focussed upon by constructing efficient parallel multigrid methods and parallelization tools, like a two-dimensional communications library, based on PARMACS ([1]). The parallelization strategy adopted is the grid partitioning method (explained in [7]). In grid partitioning the grid is split into blocks, which are mapped to different processes. The quality of the parallelized multigrid algorithm is investigated here for compressible Euler equations. A flow problem around an airfoil is taken and the domain is split into many blocks (up to 256). When a grid is split into many blocks, which are all smoothed simultaneously multigrid looses its h-independent convergence. In ([5]) this was observed and treatments to overcome this problem were given for the incompressible Navier-Stokes equations. We investigate these treatments for compressible equations solved for first order accuracy and with defect correction for second order accuracy for grid partitionings into very many blocks. Furthermore, the multigrid code is tested on several parallel machines, like the IBM SP1 with 10 nodes, the CM5 with 64 nodes and a cluster of workstations containing 17 nodes. Solution times for grid partitionings up to 32 blocks are presented.

2. The discretization of the Euler equations

The 2D compressible Euler equations are commonly written in their differential form as follows

$$\frac{\partial}{\partial x}\begin{bmatrix} \rho u \\ \rho u^2 + p \\ \rho uv \\ (E+p)u \end{bmatrix} + \frac{\partial}{\partial y}\begin{bmatrix} \rho v \\ \rho uv \\ \rho v^2 + p \\ (E+p)v \end{bmatrix} = 0$$

$$p = (\gamma - 1)(E - \frac{1}{2}\rho(u^2 + v^2)), \tag{1}$$

ρ is the density, u and v the two Cartesian velocity components, E the total energy, p the pressure, and γ (assumed to be constant) is the ratio of the specific heats at constant pressure and constant volume.

The vertex-centered finite volume discretization adopted is not described here. It is based on the cell-centered discretization described in [4] and [8]. With the Godunov upwind approach the solution of an arisen 1D Riemann problem is found with the approximate Riemann solver proposed by Osher. With defect correction second order accuracy is obtained by iterating with the first order discretized operator and by correcting the right-hand-side with a second order operator. Multigrid with defect correction starts on the coarsest grid (FMG). After the finest grid has been reached one additional FAS cycle is made, before defect correction starts. Only on the finest grid the right-hand-side is corrected. The second order scheme used is van Leer's κ-scheme. Details on discretization and boundary conditions for LiSS as well as some trans- and supersonic channel flow calculations are presented in [2].

3. Parallel multigrid

The parallel multigrid algorithm consists of a host and a node program. The host program takes care for the organization of in- and output, creates node processes, mails initial data to node processes and receives calculated results, like residuals. These tasks are taken care for by PARMACS-based ([1]) routines of the 2-D Communications Library. In the node program the calculation takes place, also the communication between nodes is taken care for. Grid partitioning, the technique to distribute parts of a domain to different processes, is explained for example in [7]. Along the interior block boundaries, an overlap region is placed, and all operations in multigrid, restriction, prolongation and smoothing can be performed in parallel. Keeping values in overlap regions up-to-date requires communication between nodes. A first order discretization requires an overlap of one line of cells in order to achieve accuracy, while for the second order the stencil for evaluation of the right-hand-side grows and an overlap of two cells is needed for accuracy. In [5] with 32 blocks a similar convergence factor was obtained as for single block with an extra internal boundary relaxation after each smoothing sweep and with an extra update of the overlap region, when smoothing along lines in the first direction of the alternating method was finished. This strategy is investigated here for 2D Euler equations with Coupled Damped Alternating Line-Gauss-Seidel (DALGS) per block as smoother in a multigrid F-cycle. A problem exists in grid coarsening. At a certain stage on a coarse level every process contains the minimal number of grid points. However, when the domain is split into many blocks this coarse level does not need to be the global coarsest grid. With an agglomeration strategy ([3]) grids can be coarsened further leaving some processors idle and re-mapping the busy processors to an optimal configuration with little communication time. Here an agglomeration strategy is not yet implemented; all processors contain a minimal number of grid points per block on the coarsest grid level. When a 257×65-grid is split into 256 equal sized 9×9 blocks three multigrid levels remain with a one cell overlap.

4. Results

The computational domain around a NACA0012 airfoil is a C-grid consisting of 257×65 cells. The popular transonic testcase presented here is: Mach number $M_\infty = 0.85$ and angle of attack $\alpha = 1°$ with a strong lee-side shock and a less strong wind-side shock (see Figure 1).

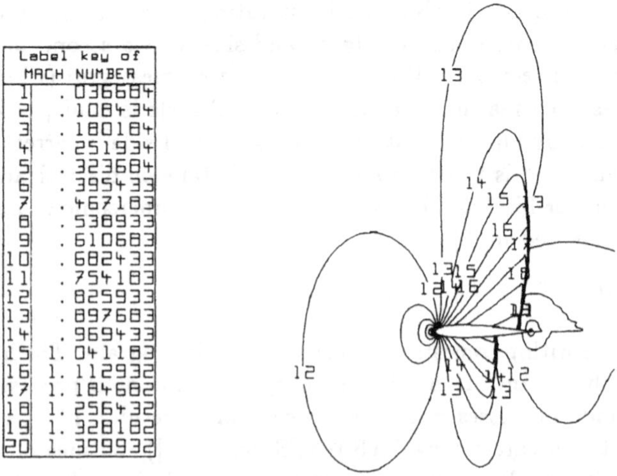

Label key of MACH NUMBER	
1	.036684
2	.108434
3	.180184
4	.251934
5	.323684
6	.395433
7	.467183
8	.538933
9	.610683
10	.682433
11	.754183
12	.825933
13	.897683
14	.969433
15	1.041183
16	1.112932
17	1.184682
18	1.256432
19	1.328182
20	1.399932

Figure 1: Mach number distribution for flow around an airfoil, $M_\infty = 0.85, \alpha = 1°$.

First order discretization. First, for all splittings the influence of an additional update of the overlap region and/or an extra interior boundary relaxation on the convergence factor is investigated for the first order discretization. The details of the nonlinear multigrid algorithm are: FAS F-cycle with nested iteration and 1 pre- and 1 post-smoothing (=F(1,1)) is used. Underrelaxation ω for DALGS depended on the number of blocks into which the grid was partitioned. This is probably due to the absence of an agglomeration strategy. For 1 to 16 block splittings $\omega = 0.8$ resulted in satisfactory convergence, for 64 blocks $\omega = 0.7$; for 256 blocks $\omega = 0.45$ was best. In Figure 2 the convergence of the 1 block and the 16 block cases with and without an additional update of the overlap and with and without an extra interior boundary relaxation sweep are compared. It can be seen that with one additional boundary relaxation every smoothing step on interior block boundaries and with an extra update of overlap the multigrid convergence is not much affected by grid partitioning. In Figure 3 the convergence of several block splittings with both additional update and interior boundary relaxation is presented versus single block in one diagram. Up to 64 blocks (with 17×17 points per block) the convergence behaviour is similar to the single block behaviour, as is underrelaxation factor ω. For 256 blocks convergence slows down, due to smaller underrelaxation that necessarily needs to be used.

Also the performance of the algorithm is investigated on a cluster of 17 work-

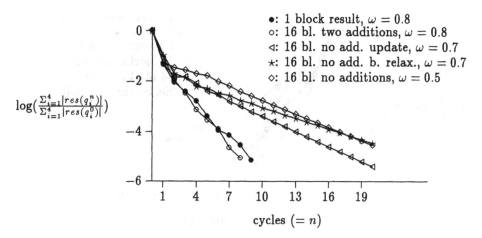

Figure 2: *F(1,1)-cycles with DALGS relaxations; 16 block results compared.*

stations, on IBM SP1 with 10 nodes and on CM5 Connection Machine with 64 nodes. Due to the implementation consisting of a host and a node program, it is necessary to use one node as host. Therefore, the maximal number of blocks is taken to be 32 on the CM5. For all splittings the same algorithm is investigated: 5 F(1,1) cycles with two additions, started with nested iteration are performed. Figure 4 shows solution times for several splittings on different computers.

Defect correction. For defect correction similar investigations are performed. As second order convergence criterium convergence of the lift coefficient (c_L) is taken. With an overlap region of two cells the finest partitioning is taken to be the 64 block case, resulting in three multigrid levels. F(2,1) is used for this splitting, for single block, 4, 8 and 16 block splittings F(1,1) is taken. In Figure 5 it can be seen that the convergence of c_L is still fast when the domain is split into many blocks (again with one extra boundary relaxation and an extra update).

5. Conclusions

The convergence behaviour of multigrid is investigated for compressible Euler equations discretized on a block-structured grid, partitioned into many blocks. It is found that with one additional boundary relaxation and an extra update of the overlap region multigrid convergence is not much affected by grid partitioning for many splittings investigated. For a splitting into very many blocks (256) with little points per block on the finest level satisfactory convergence can still be obtained with a smaller underrelaxation, but level-independency is impaired without an agglomeration strategy. For defect correction with the second order accurate κ-scheme an overlap of two cells is needed in order to reach the required accuracy. The lift coefficient, the criterium for defect correction convergence, converges almost independent of the number of blocks, with again both additions. Solution times obtained on different parallel computers show a promising performance on IBM SP1.

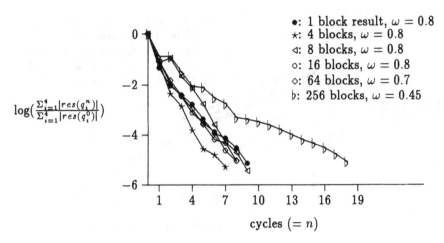

Figure 3: *F(1,1)-cycles with DALGS relaxations; several block results with extra interior boundary relaxation and update of the overlap during smoothing.*

References

[1] L. Bomans, R. Hempel, D. Roose, The Argonne/GMD macros in Fortran for portable parallel programming and their implementation on the Intel iPSC/2. *Parallel Comp.* **15**, 119–132 (1990).

[2] J. Canu, J. Linden, *Multigrid solution of 2D Euler equations: A comparison of Osher's and Dick's flux difference splitting schemes.* GMD Arbeitspapiere 693, GMD St. Augustin, Germany (1992).

[3] R. Hempel, A. Schüller, *Experiments with parallel multigrid algorithms using the SUPRENUM communications subroutine library.* GMD Arbeitspapiere 141, GMD St. Augustin, Germany (1988).

[4] B. Koren, Defect correction and multigrid for an efficient and accurate computation of airfoil flows. *J. Comp. Phys.* **77**, 183–206 (1988).

[5] G. Lonsdale, A. Schüller, Multigrid efficiency for complex flow simulations on distributed memory machines. *Parallel Comp.* **19**, 23–32 (1993).

[6] G. Lonsdale, H. Ritzdorf, K. Stüben, *The LiSS package.* GMD Arbeitspapier 745, GMD St. Augustin, Germany (1993).

[7] O.A. McBryan, P.O. Frederickson, J. Linden, A. Schüller, K. Solchenbach, K. Stüben, C.A. Thole, U. Trottenberg, Multigrid methods on parallel computers - a survey of recent developments. *Impact Comp. Science and Eng.* **3**, 1–75 (1991).

[8] S.P. Spekreijse, *Multigrid solution of the steady Euler equations,* CWI Tract 46 (1988).

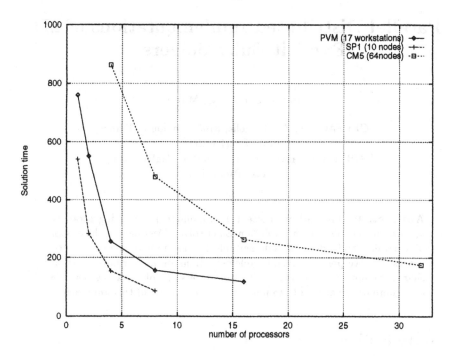

Figure 4: *Solution times for different partitionings on different machines.*

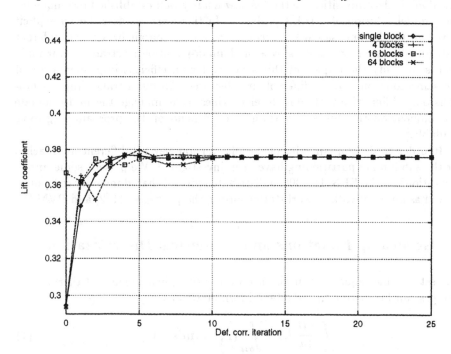

Figure 5: The convergence of the lift coefficient c_L for a flow around an airfoil when the domain is split into 1, 4, 16 and 64 equal sized blocks.

Parallel Distributed Implementations of 2D Explicit Euler Solvers *

L. Giraud[1] and G. M. Manzini[2]

[1] CERFACS, 42 Av. Coriolis, 31057 Toulouse, France,
giraud@cerfacs.fr
[2] CRS4, via Nazario Sauro 10, 09100 Cagliari, Italy,
manzini@crs4.it

Abstract. In this work we present a subdomain partitioning strategy applied to an explicit high-resolution Euler solver. We describe the design of a parallel multi-domain code suitable for distributed memory multi-processors. We present several implementations on a distributed virtual shared memory computer as well as on a network of workstations. We give computational results to illustrate the efficiency of this approach.

1 Introduction

The domain decomposition method is now a fairly well-established technique for the parallel solution of P.D.E.s problems. In this work we describe an explicit solver for the bidimensional Euler equations and its parallelization on different distributed memory computers by a subdomain-partitioning strategy. Our main goal is to study the impact of this strategy for an efficient implementation of the same code on several different architectures. All our parallel implementations only differ within the low level routines, that manage the multi-domain environment on the different machines and depend on the programming tools available.

In order to develop an efficient parallel version, several different approaches for the subdomain partitioning have been investigated. We present some implementations on the BBN TC2000, a distributed virtual shared memory computer, as well as on a network of workstations using the packages P4 [2] and PVM [1].

2 Governing Equations and Numerical Discretization

The set of Euler equations in absence of diffusive phenomena and thermal exchanges can be written in the integral formulation as :

$$\int_\Omega \frac{\partial U}{\partial t} d\Omega + \oint_{\partial \Omega} (F,G) \cdot \mathbf{n} ds = 0 \,, \tag{1}$$

---

* This work has been carried out with the financial support of CERFACS and partially with the financial contribution of the Sardinia Regional Authorities.

where Ω is an arbitrary domain of integration defined by a closed curve $\partial\Omega$, and **n** is the outward normal vector to this curve. The conservative variables and the fluxes are given by :

$$
U = \begin{pmatrix} \rho \\ \rho u \\ \rho v \\ \rho E \end{pmatrix} \qquad
F(U) = \begin{pmatrix} \rho u \\ \rho u^2 + p \\ \rho uv \\ \rho u H \end{pmatrix} \qquad
G(U) = \begin{pmatrix} \rho v \\ \rho uv \\ \rho v^2 + p \\ \rho v H \end{pmatrix}.
$$

In the above formulae, ρ is the density, ρu and ρv are the two components of the momentum, ρE is the energy, p is the pressure and H is the dynamic enthalpy. This last variable is related to the other quantities by $H = E + \frac{p}{\rho}$. Assuming the gas is calorically perfect and polytropic, pressure is related to the other variables by $E = \frac{p}{\gamma-1} + \frac{1}{2}(u^2 + v^2)$ where γ is the ratio of specific heats and takes for air the value of 1.4.

The Equations 1 are discretized on a structured quadrilateral mesh using a conservative shock-capturing high-order accurate Godunov-type scheme in a cell-centered finite-volume formulation. High-order accuracy is achieved by using a TVD-MUSCL or an ENO reconstruction both on conservative and characteristic variables. Fluxes estimation can be computed by three different Riemann solvers : the approximate one by Roe [8], the iterative one by Gottlieb and Groth [5] and the HLLE approximate one developed by Einfeldt [3]. The time-stepping is given by an explicit 2nd or 3rd order TVD Runge-Kutta scheme.

3 An Unsteady Compressible Test Case : the Double Mach Reflection

To show the ability of the code to capture shocks and contact discontinuities in two-dimensional compressible flows we consider the double Mach reflection of a shock wave on a $40°$ ramp. A detailed description of the parameters of the calculation and of the physical phenomena can be found in [6], [4]. In Figure 1 we report the results of a numerical simulation on a 200×100 grid using the 2nd order ENO scheme on the conservative variables in space, the exact iterative Riemann solver and the 2nd order TVD Runge-Kutta scheme by Shu in time. The first ten iterations of this calculation has been taken as a test case to evaluate the performance of the different parallel implementations reported in Section 4.2.

The sequential performance of some implemented schemes are displayed in Table 1. The times displayed in this table show that the 2nd order ENO scheme used in conjunction with the exact Riemann solver is poorly vectorizable. On the Convex, which is a vector computer, the speed up produced by the vectorization is 1.94, due to the implemented reconstruction technique and the exact Riemann solver which are essentially scalar. However, this technique is highly accurate for CFD computations and efficient parallel implementations can be considered.

Fig. 1. Double Mach Reflection : domain of integration and computed solution

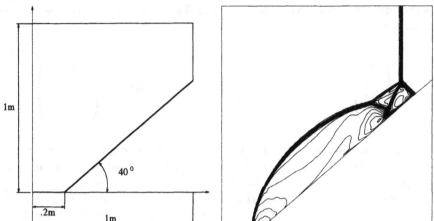

Table 1. CPU time (μsec) of the different numerical schemes per cell per time-step on a 200 $\times$ 100 grid

Numerical Scheme	IBM RS6000 mod. 550	Convex C220 without vectorization	Convex C220 with vectorization
2nd Ord. ENO (Cons) + Exact Riemann Solver	534.85	1315.90	677.55
2nd Ord. ENO (Char) + Exact Riemann Solver	713.45	1890.70	945.55
3rd Ord. MUSCL (Cons) + Exact Riemann Solver	527.45	1075.20	476.70

4 Parallel distributed implementations

The explicit numerical schemes considered in Section 2 have a natural parallelism. From the point of view of a parallel implementation, we consider an implementation suitable for distributed memory computers based on a decomposition of the physical domain into subdomains assigned to different processors. That is an alternative to a more standard but also more strongly machine dependent loop-level tuning of the code convenient for shared memory computers.

The update of the flow variables of a cell in the mesh requires the knowledge of the flow variables in a local region around the cell in consideration. This is immediately clear when the MUSCL or the ENO reconstruction/interpolation methods are implemented, because they require a wide stencil of neighbouring cells. For any cell close to an internal boundary, shared by two adjacent subdomains, a portion of this stencil falls outside the subdomain in a neighbouring one and requires interprocessor communication. The size of the regions of any subdomain needed by the neighbouring processors is a function of the order of the reconstruction and are referred to as the overlapping data areas. The multidomain environment developed for any of our parallel implementations works in the following way :

- each processor takes the values on the overlapping data areas in the neighbouring domains which it needs for its update;
- each processor performs a complete update of its domain, which means it computes the reconstruction, it solves all the Riemann problems and does one time step for each cell;
- each processor makes available to its neighbours the updated values in the overlapping areas.

4.1 The computing environments

The results presented in Section 4.2 have been observed on different target computers : a BBN TC2000, a distributed virtual shared memory computer, and a network of IBM RS/6000 workstations interconnected by Ethernet. The BBN TC2000 is a MIMD distributed memory computer that exhibits features of both shared and distributed memory architectures. The nodes communicate through a high performance switch (the butterfly switch). It can provide a transparent access by each processor to all locations in memory, whether local to a processor or remote on another processor.

The implementation of the first and the last step of the algorithm described above depends on the target multiprocessor : a simple copy from local to global data structures on distributed virtual shared systems, the use of some P4 or PVM message passing routines for distributed implementations.

4.2 Experimental Results

The performance shown in Table 2 corresponds to the first ten iterations of the simulation described in Figure 1 using 64-bits double precision. The number in the second column represents the elapsed time T_1 for a stand alone execution of the single domain version (the most efficient sequential version of the code). In the remaining columns, the number of domains corresponding to the number of processors involved in the computation is varied. We display the speedup for the parallel experiments. The speedup is given by : $SU_p = \dfrac{T_1}{T_p}$ where T_p is the elapsed time for a stand alone execution on p processors.

In Table 2 it can be seen, that on the network of workstations the performance of the PVM implementation is always worse than the P4 one. The inefficiencies were found to be mainly caused by both the PVM architecture and the Aix operating system, which is not very efficient performing context switches and semaphores handling as mentioned in [7]. On the BBN, since the CPU is slower and the communication network faster, the performance in term of speedup is better. The curves depicted in Figure 2 show the effect of the granularity of the parallel tasks on the performance. Lastly, the experiments with P4 illustrate the portability of the codes developed using such packages, as the results displayed in Table 2 correspond exactly to the same code performed on the different platforms, BBN and IBM workstations.

Table 2. Performance of the distributed implementations on a 200 × 100 grid

Computer	# domains					
	1	2	4	8	16	20
BBN Fortran	429.00	1.98	3.91	7.61	13.70	16.14
P4 BBN	429.00	1.99	3.83	7.67	13.98	16.76
P4 RS/6000	140.54	1.92	3.73	7.11	-	-
PVM RS/6000	140.54	1.83	3.39	5.54	-	-

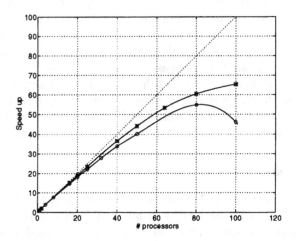

Fig. 2. Speed up on a 128 nodes BBN TC2000; o : 200 × 100 mesh * : 400 × 200 mesh

For all our experiments, two different strategies have been explored for decomposing the global mesh in subdomains : box-partitioning and slice-partitioning. It can be noted that for a fixed number of subdomains, box-partitioning minimizes the amount of communicated data while slice-partitioning minimizes the number of messages exchanged between the processors. Especially, on the BBN box-partitioning yields better performance by minimizing the amount of exchanged data, while, slice-partitioning yields better performance on the network of workstations, by minimizing the number of exchanged messages, due to the high latency time to access Ethernet. For a detailed discussion about these partitioning effects as well as for implementation details we refer to [4].

5 Concluding Remarks

This experience shows that for some applications of CFD based on explicit time-advancing schemes, a domain decomposition approach can result in a very good strategy to efficiently parallelize a code.

On the BBN, the parallelism provided by the explicit scheme is efficiently exploited since the observed speedups are around 65 on 100 nodes for a medium size (400×200) mesh, since in this case each processor only works on a 40×20 subgrid. TVD and ENO high-order shock-capturing methods generally require enough computation to provide us with a good ratio between communication and computation. This feature can be directly exploited for efficient implementations on networks of workstations. In this case, we observed a speedup greater than seven on eight workstations with very low traffic on the local area network. Of course, an increase in traffic would have a negative impact on the performance due to a bad balance between communication and computation time because of Ethernet contention.

Lastly, the parallel versions of our code is easily portable on most of the MIMD multiprocessors and heterogeneous networks of computers currently available, as well as on the future MPP, as the Cray T3D, due to application of standard public domain message-passing packages like P4 and PVM.

Acknowledgments : We would like to thank the Lawrence Livermore National Lab for having provided us with an access to the 128 nodes BBN TC2000. It allowed us to complete our experiments and evaluate the scalability of the developed code.

References

[1] A. Beguelin, J. Dongara, A. Geist, R. Manchek, and V. Sunderam. A user's guide to PVM Parallel Virtual Machine. Technical Report ORNL/TM-11826, Oak Ridge National Laboratory, Tennessee 37831, 1992.

[2] R. Butler and E. Lusk. User's guide to the P4 Parallel Programming System. Mathematics and Computer Science Division, Argonne National Laboratory, 1992.

[3] B. Einfeldt, C. D.Muntz, P. L. Roe, and B. Sjogreen. On godunov-type methods near low densities. *Journal of Computational Physics*, 92:273–295, 1991.

[4] L. Giraud and G.M. Manzini. Parallel implementations of a multidomain explicit high-order accurate Euler solver. Technical Report TR/CFD-PA/93/49, CERFACS, Toulouse, France, 1993.

[5] J. J. Gottlieb and C. P. T. Groth. Assesment of Riemann solvers for unsteady one-dimensional inviscid flows of perfect gases. *Journal of Computational Physics*, 78:437–458, 1988.

[6] P. A. Jacobs. Single-block Navier-Stokes integrator. Technical Report ICASE Interim Report 18, ICASE, 1991.

[7] G. Richelli. The PVMe user guide aix 3.2 version. Technical Report ECSEC, Italy, 1992.

[8] P. L. Roe. Approximate Riemann solvers, parameter vectors, and difference schemes. *Journal of Computational Physics*, 43:357–372, 1981.

A Parallel Multiblock Euler/Navier-Stokes Solver on a Cluster of Workstations using PVM

Emmanuel Issman[1], Gérard Degrez[1] and Johan De Keyser[2]

[1] Von Karman Institute for Fluid Dynamics, CFD Group, Rhode-St-Genèse, Belgium
[2] Katholiek Universiteit Leuven, Dept. of Computer Science, Belgium

Abstract. An adaptive 2D multiblock Euler/Navier-Stokes solver has been parallelised using the LOCO software library which performs automatic load-balancing at run-time by an appropriate distribution of the blocks onto the processors of the parallel computer. We describe our experience in porting the solver onto a Unix workstation cluster environment equipped with the Parallel Virtual Machine communication software.

1 Introduction

A 2D finite-volume multiblock solver for computation of viscous compressible flows has been developed containing first and second order spatial discretizations and explicit solution techniques. The solver has been designed so that any configuration of blocks is possible and that gridlines in adjacent blocks do not need to be continuous along the block boundaries [1] . Adaptive refinement has been incorporated based on several refinement criteria [2] (e.g. entropy, pressure and Mach-number gradients). When a block is refined, it is split into four blocks, each of which contains about the same number of grid cells as the original unrefined block.

The code has been parallelized using the LOCO software library [3] which was originally written for the message passing system running on iPSC hypercubes. It has been extended to support the PVM communication primitives [4] and the multiblock code can be ported now on any cluster of homogeneous workstations.

We describe in Sect.2 the LOCO library. Details related to PVM implementation are discussed in Sect.3 and performance figures are derived in Sect.4. Section 5 presents issues related to PVM communication capabilities and Sect.6 draws the conclusion.

2 The LOCO Library

The LOCO library supports the *SPMD* (*Single Program, Multiple Data*) or *data parallel* programming model based on the distribution of the problem's data set among the processors. The problem of *load-balancing* consists of the partitioning of the grid into blocks and the subsequent mapping of these blocks onto the processors in a way which aims at minimizing the total execution time of the parallel program. In such a distribution scheme, all processors have approximately the same amount of work and the number and length of the data exchanges are limited. LOCO incorporates several load-balancing techniques such as recursive bisection, branch and bound and evolution algorithms [5].

The LOCO library provides a programming interface which allows to specify data parallel program and perfoms automatically the data exchange communication. In this approach, the parallel execution of the program is broken down into elementary *phases*. Given the graph that represents the interconnection of the blocks, LOCO may perform the following actions during the execution of a single phase:

- computing a new work distribution:
  1. gathering information about the estimated calculation and communication costs
  2. computing the distribution scheme according to a load-balancing algorithm
  3. broadcasting the scheme to all processors and physically transferring the data partitions to processors to which they have been newly assigned
- sending and receiving all data exchange messages
- applying a specified operation in parallel to all processors (which is now guaranteed to be load-balanced)

LOCO does not make use of dynamic process management routines. The number of processes remains unchanged throughout the entire program's execution, avoiding the need of primitives for starting or killing processes.

3 PVM Implementation

3.1 Process configuration

According to the SPMD programming model, the parallel program consists of a number of identical process instances. Since there is no primitive in PVM which allows to obtain the number of parallel processes which have been started under Unix (and which may have or not yet contacted the PVM daemon), a specific program *pvmload* has been designed taking as run-time argument the number of parallel processes to be started on the PVM network. Immediately after starting the processes, the *pvmload* program sends the number of processes and their PVM task identification numbers to each of them. When the application processes first access the LOCO environment, they will read this message and therefore be properly initialized. Thereafter, all LOCO processes join one PVM process group which remains unique throughout program execution. This group may be used for specifying for example barrier synchronization.

3.2 Machine Architecture

LOCO can in conjunction with the PVM communication primitives distinguish between two abstract parallel computer topologies: either a fully connected or a hypercube topology (in which case the number of processors is limited to a power of two) and can accordingly use specific load-balancing algorithms. Both topologies can be chosen independently from the actual hardware. For the specific case of a hypercube topology, global operations as well as most load-balancing algorithms used by LOCO may be implemented more efficiently.

3.3 Input/Output

A process which is started from the Unix shell prompt has three i/o streams: an input, output and an error output stream from/to the shell it was started on and which may be redirected. However, a process which is started using **pvm_spawn** has no input stream associated with it, and both its output and error output stream are merged into one stream written either onto the shell or onto a pvm logfile (**pvml.userid**) which is truncated when a specified limit-size is exceeded. In order to avoid these limitations, both LOCO and the multiblock application read from and write to files which are opened by process 0. All other processes receive their input and write their output through messages via process 0.

4 Multiblock Performance

Testing has been made on a cluster of 4 DEC Alpha AXP3100/400 workstations, each equipped with 128 Mb internal memory. A second order Van Leer Mach isoline plot of a 84-block scramjet testcase (with about 32000 finite volumes) is shown in Fig.1. Blocks have non-uniform sizes varying from 10×15 to 35×15. Tests have been performed with $P = 1, 2, ..., 32$ processes on the 4-processor cluster with the following communication options: FDDI interconnection hardware between the processors, the **PvmDirectRoute** direct process-to-process socket interconnection and we avoided XDR-encoding (**PvmDataRaw** option).

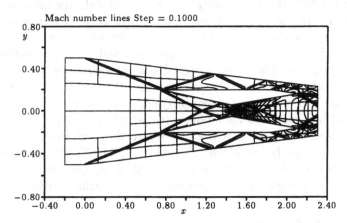

Fig. 1. Mach isoline plot for the scramjet testcase, 2nd order Van Leer solution, supersonic inflow at Mach $M_\infty = 3.6$, total temperature $T_0 = 300K$ and total pressure $p_0 = 100,000Pa$

The *effectivity* α of a parallel computation is defined as the fraction of time spent in the actual computations:

$$\alpha(P, N) = \frac{\sum_{u_i \in \mathcal{U}} t_i^{\text{calc}}}{P \cdot T(P, N)} \qquad (1)$$

where $\mathcal{U}$ denotes the set of N blocks, T the parallel execution time for one iteration, and t_i^{calc} the calculation time for block u_i.

The *scheduling overhead* σ is defined as the fraction of time spent by LOCO in managing blocks and in scheduling calculation and communication operations. The *measured calculation load-balance* is defined as

$$\lambda(P, N) = \frac{\sum_{u_i \in \mathcal{U}} t_i^{\text{calc}}}{P \cdot \max_{q \in \mathcal{Q}}\{\sum_{u_i \in \mathcal{U}(q)} t_i^{\text{calc}}\}} \qquad (2)$$

where $\mathcal{Q}$ represents the set of processes, and $\mathcal{U}(q)$ the set of blocks assigned to processor q. Experiments show that cost estimates provided by the multiblock code to the mapping algorithm in LOCO are fairly accurate, and that the mapping is of good quality, so that a good balance is achieved when N/P is large enough. This is confirmed in Table 1 where the achieved load is almost perfect until it falls off swiftly beyond $P = 16$. As the scheduling overhead σ and the load imbalance $1 - \lambda$ are very small, parallel performance losses are mainly due to the communication overhead. Measuring the communication overhead is not straightforward and one distinguishes three kinds of overhead:

- t_i^{pack}, the overhead encurred by the application following packing and unpacking application data related to the block borders into and out of data exchange messages
- t_i^{prim}, the time spent in the communication primitives, essentially the message startup-time
- ν, the *message transfer delay* due to the traveling time needed for messages to reach their destination

Only the two first kinds of overhead can be directly measured by the *communication overhead* μ defined as

$$\mu(P, N) = \frac{\sum_{u_i \in \mathcal{U}}(t_i^{\text{pack}} + t_i^{\text{prim}})}{P \cdot T(P, N)} \qquad (3)$$

The delay ν can only be estimated as it cannot be separated from the idle time due to the load imbalance (this idle time representing a fraction α/λ out of the total execution time) and the scheduling overhead σ. The message transfer delay ν is then estimated as:

$$\nu = 1 - \mu - \sigma - \frac{\alpha}{\lambda} \qquad (4)$$

Table 1 shows how the time per iteration T drops as the number of processes increases, until the load imbalance and an increased communication overhead (as a $P-$processor machine is simulated on a 4-processor cluster) start to dominate.

Effectivities for $P = 2, 4$ appear reasonable. It can be seen that the communication overhead μ is about constant as t_i^{pack} and the main part of t_i^{prim} are independant of the number of processes involved. As load imbalance and communication overhead dominate for larger number of processes, μ becomes a smaller fraction of the total time.

Table 1 displays as well the *parallel efficiency* of the code:

$$\varepsilon(P, N) = \frac{T(1, N)}{P \cdot T(P, N)} \tag{5}$$

which compares the time needed to run on P processors the single-processor execution time. Efficiencies for $P > 4$ refer to a simulation of a P-processor machine on the 4-processor cluster.

Table 1. Performance for the 84-block scramjet computation, FDDI hardware, process-to-process socket interconnection, no XDR-encoding, on 4 DEC Alpha workstations

P	λ	μ	α	$T(ms)$	$\varepsilon(\%)$
1	100.0	6	92	1189	100
2	98.8	15	81	685	86.8
4	95.6	18	78	350	84.8
8	90.4	16	77	183	(81.2)
16	76	9	36	191	(38.9)
32	55	1	9	2789	(0.01)

5 PVM Communication

The effect of the underlying communication hard- and software on the communication performance has been investigated. At the level of the communication hardware, tests were performed with TCP/IP Ethernet vs. FDDI interconnection. At the level of the Unix inter-process-communication, we compared the

Table 2. Communication startup time and transfer time: (1) Reference, (2) XDR-encoding, (3) Daemon-routing, (4) Ethernet

	(1)		(2)		(3)		(4)	
P	μ	ν	μ	ν	μ	ν	μ	ν
1	6	0	6	0	6	0	6	0
2	15	2	18	1	16	2	14	4
4	18	2	19	1	20	0	16	3

use of direct process-to-process connections (**PvmRouteDirect** option) vs. connection through the PVM daemon (**PvmDontRoute** option) , two times slower but limiting the number of sockets to be used. Finally, the effect of XDR format conversion which would be needed in a heterogeneous workstation cluster has been tested by comparing the **PvmDataRaw** vs **PvmDataDefault** communication modes, the first of which avoiding XDR encoding. Results are listed in Table 2 showing only slight variations between the different options.

6   Conclusions

Experiments with the code on a cluster of workstations with a few processors but with a large physical and virtual memory allows to compute solutions in greater details than previously feasible with single-processor machines. Moreover, such an environment leads to a simple and efficient load-balancing technique. As the number of processors is small and the number of blocks is large, a good calculation load-balance can be achieved. The relatively slow communication performance becomes therefore less important as:

- there are less processors
- the problem size per processor is larger
- the proper communication hard- and software options are used

A good solution of the communication problem by an appropriate mapping technique remains a key factor to achieve good parallel performance. The LOCO library provides the necessary support to achieve both load-balance and minimal communication overhead.

7   Acknowledgments

The research on the DEC Alpha AXP3100/400 workstations was supported by a grant from Digital Equipment Corporation.

References

1. C. Mensink: A 2D Parallel Multiblock Method for Viscous and Inviscid Compressible Flows. Ph.D. Thesis (1992), Von Karman Institute for Fluid Dynamics
2. K. Lust, Johan De Keyser and D. Roose: A Parallel Multiblock Euler/Navier-Stokes Code with Adaptive Refinement and Run-Time Load Balancing. Report TW 187, Dept of Computer Science, K.U.Leuven
3. J. De Keyser: LOCO: a library supporting data parallelism on MIMD computers. Report TW 185, Dept of Computer Science, K.U.Leuven
4. V. S. Sunderam. PVM: A framework for parallel distributed computing. Concurrency: Practice and Experience, **2(1)** 1-16 (1990)
5. J. De Keyser and D. Roose: Load-balancing data-parallel programs on distributed memory computers. Report TW 162, Dept of Computer Science, K.U.Leuven

Parallelization of a 3D multi-block Navier-Stokes flow solver on a distributed memory MIMD machine

G. van Beek * , J.P. Geschiere ** and A.R. Sukul ***

1 Introduction.

Within the frame work of the ISNaS (Information System for Navier-Stokes flow solving) project [1] a three-dimensional multi-block multi-zone compressible Navier-Stokes flow solver has been developed by NLR and University of Twente [2]. With this solver called SOLEQS it is possible to calculate flows around multi-element airfoil geometries with extended flaps and slats, based on the Reynolds Averaged Navier-Stokes equations and semi- empirical turbulence models. The performance of present day supercomputers is sufficient for this solver.

Computational Fluid Dynamics which is aimed to support Computer Aided Engineering (CAE) of aircraft in industry has to produce accurate aerodynamic results for a wide range of flow conditions. The modeling of turbulence is the central theme for this. The turbulence calculations in future may well replace the semi-empirical data and models which are widely used at present. Both Large Eddy Simulations (LES) and Direct Numerical Simulations (DNS) in future have to provide more insight into turbulence characteristics and phenomena. They are subjects of research by aerodynamicists.

The supercomputers that are based on a limited number of vector processors, may still be considered as the most powerful machines for large problems like CFD simulations. The computations which are to be done for CFD problems on the basis of LES and DNS, however, grow beyond the capacities of the present computers. Therefore, in order to be able to cope with the demands with respect to CFD of aerodynamicists in research and engineers in industry, high performance parallel computing is becoming necessary more and more.

2 SOLEQS, a 3D multi-block compressible flow solver

The flow solver SOLEQS, consisting of 120,000 lines of code, has been developed on architecture and construction principles that support maintainability,

* National Aerospace Laboratory NLR, Informatics Division, P.O. Box 90502, 1006 BM Amsterdam, The Netherlands
** Leiden University, Department of Computer Science, High Performance Computing Division, P.O. Box 9512, 2300 RA Leiden, The Netherlands
*** Vrije Universiteit Amsterdam, Department of Computer Science and Mathematics, De Boelelaan 1081a, 1081 HV Amsterdam, The Netherlands

testability and adaptability. The development was done in a structured way by decomposing the development and production process and by decomposing the functions to be realized by the flow solver.

Decomposing the development and production process appeared to be essential in the strategy for the required interdisciplinary development of CFD systems to enable quality control and quality assurance [3]. Decomposing the functions (extract topology, define variables, define equations, solve equations) is necessary to enable the solver to conserve different methods, to add new models and algorithms easily, and to conserve and exchange information with external processes like grid generation and post-processing.

The decompositions facilitate the application of design control and process control that is required by the industry standard ISO 9001. This standard is applied by the Informatics Division of NLR for the development of information systems. The division has an ISO 9001 certificate.

The multi-block concept which was adopted when designing SOLEQS has initially been applied in order to be able to select different physical models for different parts of the computational domain (the blocks). Implementation choices are the Euler, the laminar Navier-Stokes and the turbulent Navier-Stokes models [2].

In order to improve its performance, at first vectorization has been optimized for SOLEQS on the NEC SX-3 [4]. For an 8-blocks grid with about 35,000 points this resulted into a gain of both CPU time and performance of about 50% compared to the non-optimized version. After this, developments were directed towards parallelization of the flow solver.

3   Parallelization Techniques and Parallel Computer Architectures

The multi-block concept of SOLEQS is extremely suitable for parallel algorithms as it bears a "natural" parallelism in it. The parallelization of SOLEQS is based on this multi-block concept [5] and consists of:

- distribution over the processors of the blocks that possibly have different characteristics. Block characteristics concern a.o. the physical model which is applied and the size of the block;
- execution of the calculations of each block on the processor to which it was assigned;
- communication between processors is required to exchange data that are necessary to determine the flow status on common block boundaries of blocks that are assigned to different processors.

Architectures of parallel machines may be classified in several ways. First, the parallel architectures may be classified according to the classes SIMD (Single Instruction Multiple Data) and MIMD (Multiple Instruction Multiple Data). When the multi-block concept is used as basis for the parallelization of SOLEQS,

SIMD machines cannot be used because this type of parallel computer architecture does not offer the flexibility to handle blocks with different characteristics efficiently. Furthermore, within the class of MIMD machines, Distributed Memory (DM) and Shared Memory (SM) may be distinguished.

When comparing SM and DM machines, DM machines are relatively fast in performing huge amounts of computations at a processor because the access of each processor to its private memory is relatively fast. On the other side, interprocessor communication at DM machines is relatively slow. As a parallel version of SOLEQS, based on the multi-block concept as described above, is an application for which communication time is a relatively small part of the total execution time, DM machines may be advantageous.

The DM MIMD platform which NLR uses to parallelize SOLEQS in the pre-commercial phase is a cluster of one host and three nodes of IBM RISC/6000 workstations (models 220 and 370). This platform was chosen for two reasons. First, DM MIMD machines are still a topic of much development. Therefore NLR has chosen to start its parallelization efforts on a not too expensive system in order to minimize investment risks. Second, clusters of workstations may be a good alternative for smaller industrial companies that want to have better performance but cannot afford to buy high performance computers.

4 Parallelization of SOLEQS by Message Passing

In figure 1 a schematic overview of the sequence of processes which takes place in SOLEQS is given. Especially the computationally most intensive part of the solver is paid much attention to in this scheme. There are two processes in this scheme in which data between neighboring blocks (i.e. blocks in the computational domain which have grid points in common) have to be interchanged. These processes are the averaging of the flow field and the application of global boundary conditions. If neighboring blocks were assigned to different processors, communication between these processors must take place. This communication is the main difference between the sequential and the parallel version of SOLEQS.

The handling of the communication between different processors is done by applying the public domain message passing tool PVM (Parallel Virtual Machine). With this tool the sending and receiving of the messages (packages of data) between the processors can be organized. For the parallelization of SOLEQS version 3.2.6 of PVM has been used.

The second pass of SOLEQS (see figure 1) is the computationally most intensive part of the solver. It is in this part of the solver where the parallelization is applied. The communication of data between neighboring blocks that are on different processors requires synchronization of the processes, involved in a communication. In figure 2 the computational scheme of a message passing-based parallel version of SOLEQS is given. During every iteration there are two synchronization moments between those neighboring blocks that are not assigned to the same processor.

The performance gain which has been reached by the parallelization effort is often expressed in a speed-up factor. As it is the user's main interest to obtain the results faster, the wall clock time is the basis for the definition of the speed-up factor. The speed-up factor for a p processor system is defined in the following way:

$$S_p = \frac{\text{wall clock time of fastest sequential implementation of SOLEQS}[1]}{\text{wall clock time of parallel implementation of SOLEQS on p processors}}$$

5 Load Balancing

The speed-up which can be reached is highly dependent of the distribution of the workload over the processors. In order to get an optimal speed-up, the workloads of the processors should be balanced. NLR has developed a preprocessing program to generate a distribution of the tasks (in this case: the blocks) over the processors which finds an optimal speed-up by constructing a distribution of blocks that satisfies this requirement best [6]. This preprocessor performs static load balancing.

Balancing the workload is an optimization problem. The workload of a processor is defined as the total execution time plus the total communication time, needed to execute the tasks which have been assigned to that specific processor. As the wall clock time is a measure which depends on the hardly predictable parameter that specifies the amount of activities on the system, it is modeled by the workload as defined above.

The processor to which the largest workload has been assigned is decisive for the wall clock time of the whole system. Thus, the maximal workload of a processor must be minimized in order to get the minimal wall clock time and thus to get the highest speed-up. So, the objective of the preprocessor is: Find the distribution of blocks for which $min_{all\ possible\ solutions}(max_{1 \leq p \leq P} WL(p))$ is reached (P is the number of processors, $WL(p)$ is the workload of processor p).

In order to be able to calculate the optimal distribution of blocks over the processors before execution starts, accurate estimates of the execution and communication time per block must be made. Especially the determination of the execution times is a difficult process.

So far, NLR has developed two solutions for this problem. The first solution is developing a function which depends on the four most important parameters that determine the execution time of a block. These parameters are: number of gridpoints, number of iterations, physical model and time- stepping algorithm (Runge-Kutta 3 or 5). It may be evident that this function is approximately linearly dependent of the first two parameters. Based on experiments, estimations for the influence of the other parameters on the execution time have been made.

The second solution for the determination of the execution time is:

---

[1] On the cluster of IBM workstations (operating system AIX 3.2.5) the fastest sequential version of SOLEQS is obtained with the -O compiler option. O stands for optimization.

- first, perform one sequential iteration (timestep) of SOLEQS on the fastest processor of the system and measure the execution time of each block;
- if necessary, scale the execution times of the blocks for the other processors (only necessary if processors have different speed);
- determine the optimal block distribution, based on the measured times;
- distribute the blocks over the processors according to the optimal distribution;
- perform the other iterations of SOLEQS in parallel.

The optimization problem is solved by applying a branch-and-bound method. This method is set up to search through the whole space of possible solutions. At every partial solution of the problem it decides whether this partial solution will possibly lead to a better solution than the one found so far. If not, this branch of the search tree will be skipped.

6 Initial results

The release of a first working parallel version of SOLEQS on the cluster of RISC/6000 workstations was in January 1994. A testcase was selected which consists of a twelve blocks grid for a single airfoil geometry. The grid consists of about 35,000 grid points. In the inner blocks (the blocks adjacent to the airfoil) the laminar Navier-Stokes model is applied, whereas in the outer blocks the Euler model is applied. The speed-up factors on the cluster for this testcase are given in table 1.

number of processors	speedup factor
2	1.78
3	2.32

Table 1. Speedup factors for the twelve blocks testcase

testcase	theoretically best solution	optimal solution by preprocessor	deviation
12 blocks grid	654.0 s	682.2 s	4.3 %
37 blocks grid	836.6 s	858.0 s	2.6 %

Table 2. Load balancing results

As these results are very preliminary, more results with respect to other testcases are necessary to draw conclusions about the performance of this parallel version.

Moreover, results with respect to the load balancing preprocessor are available. A number of testcases has been used to test the performance of the preprocessor [6]. Some results are given in table 2.

In table 2 the theoretically best maximum workload and the maximum workload of the optimal distribution, found by the preprocessor, are given. In the last column, the deviation is given of the found solution from the theoretically optimal solution.

With respect to the sequential version on the SX-3, the performance on the SX-3 will still be about 6-8 times better than the parallel version of SOLEQS on the cluster with three nodes.

SOLEQS

    Start-up phase

    First pass

    Second pass

        FOR each iteration

            save the old flow status in all blocks

            calculate the time-steps in all blocks

            advance the flow-status in all blocks

            average the flow-status on the boundaries of all blocks

            apply the local boundary conditions in all blocks

            apply the global boundary conditions in all blocks

            apply the local boundary conditions in all blocks

            calculate the contribution to aerodynamic coefficients for the current iteration of each block

            calculate the residuals in the domain, for all blocks

      ENDFOR

    Close-down

Fig. 1. Scheme of sequential SOLEQS.

FOR EACH processor i
PAR DO

    Start-up phase
        Read data from local secondary memory and initialize data
        with respect to $LBLOCKS(i)$

    First pass
        Read data from local secondary memory and initialize data
        with respect to $LBLOCKS(i)$

    Second pass

        FOR each iteration

            FOR EACH block B in $LBLOCKS(i)$
                save old flow-status in B
                calculate time-step in B
                advance flow-status in B
                send average-variables from B to neighboring blocks
                receive average-variables from neighboring blocks
            ENDFOR

            receive average-variables which have not arrived yet

            FOR EACH block B in $LBLOCKS(i)$
                average flow-status on the boundaries of B
                apply local boundary conditions on B
                send dummy-variables from B to neighboring blocks
                receive dummy-variables from neighboring blocks
            ENDFOR

            receive dummy-variables which have not arrived yet

            FOR EACH block B in $LBLOCKS(i)$
                apply global boundary conditions on B
                apply local boundary conditions on B
            ENDFOR

            send and receive convergence results

        ENDFOR

    Close-down

ENDPARDO

Fig. 2. Scheme of parallel SOLEQS

Acknowledgment

In this paper, results of previous work on vectorization by P.A. van Mourik (NLR) was used. We thank her for her contribution.

References

1. M. E. S. Vogels, W. Loeve, *Development of ISNaS, an information system for flow simulation in design*, In Proceedings of CAPE89, Tokyo (1989), North Holland.
2. M. E. S. Vogels, *Information System for flow simulation based on the Navier-Stokes equations (ISNaS), Detailed Design of a multi block Navier-Stokes solver for compressible flow*, NLR CR 92418 L (1992).
3. W. Loeve, *Engineering of systems for application of scientific computing in industry*, Proceedings of the IFIP WG2, WG 5.3 and CATE TF Workshop "Manufacturing in the era of concurrent engineering", Tel Aviv, 1992, Elsevier (1992).
4. P.A. van Mourik, *Vectorization of a multi-block Navier-Stokes solver*, NLR TP 93082 L, National Aerospace Laboratory NLR, Amsterdam, 1993
5. J. P. Geschiere, *A large grain parallel Navier-Stokes solver, Phase 6 of PARASOL: Data-decomposition for a distributed memory MIMD machine*, NLR TR 93456 L, National Aerospace Laboratory NLR Amsterdam, 1993
6. A.R. Sukul, *Design of a load balancing preprocessor*, NLR TR 93463 L, National Aerospace Laboratory NLR Amsterdam, 1993 (to be published)

Porting of a Three-Dimensional Navier-Stokes Solver to a Range of Parallel Computers and a Network of Workstations

Isabelle d'Ast

CERFACS, 42 av. Gustave Coriolis, F-31057 Toulouse Cedex
and MATRA MARCONI SPACE, 31, rue des Cosmonautes,
F-31077 Toulouse Cedex, France

Abstract. Present research and development in aerospace science disclose the strong need for more computing power and not least memory. Traditional super vector computers more and more reach physical limitations and are increasingly expensive. A different approach to obtain more computing power and storage has been the development of multiprocessors systems with powerful RISC processors.

The aim of this work is the parallelization of an industrial three-dimensional Navier-Stokes program with the object to achieve an efficiency of at least 0.8 on a distributed memory computer with more than 64 processors.

1 Description of the Industrial Code NSFLEX

NSFLEX is a finite-volume program that solves the three-dimensional compressible unsteady Navier-Stokes equations. In order to evaluate the inviscid fluxes a Riemann problem is solved at the finite-volume faces. A third order accurate local characteristic flux extrapolation scheme (MUSCL type flux difference splitting) is utilized using Van Albada type sensors. At very strong shocks a hyper diffusive modified Steger-Warming flux is used. The viscous fluxes are constructed with central differences. The unfactored implicit equations are solved by a red-black point Gauss-Seidel relaxation technique. For a more detailed description of the NSFLEX code we refer to [4] and [5].

2 Parallel Hardware and Software

Two types of parallel machines are explored: shared memory computers where each processor has access to the entire memory and distributed memory machines where the processors do not share the physical memory, but have their own private memory (which implies data exchanges between the processors). The shared memory computers are the ALLIANT FX/80 (eight processors with 188 MFlops of theoretical peak performance) and the CRAY-2 (four processors and two GFlops). The distributed memory machines are the BBN TC2000 (30 processors and 300 MFlops), the iPSC/860 (128 processors and seven GFlops) and an IBM RS/6000 network consisting of eight workstations (33 MFlops each).

3 Characteristics of the Parallel Code

In order to parallelize the code, the structure of the initial solution algorithm has been changed. In the original version, the blocks solve sequentially a linear system each, which implies that at the internal interfaces the solution belongs to the same time step. In the parallel version, this structure can not be maintained since each block treats its domain simultaneously and thus does not know the solution of the same time level in the other blocks. Hence, at each time step, the boundary update has to be effected before executing the solver part.

Concerning the data structure, the dimensions of the variables describing the mesh and the physical quantities are reduced to the size of the largest domain used by a processor in all the principal subroutines. For the shared memory program, the main program keeps the data of the whole domain (while the subroutines work only with the reduced dimensions). It executes the pre-processing phase consisting of the initialization of the variables, the solver part and the post-processing step containing essentially the interpolation of the physical flow quantities from the cell centers to the mesh nodes. The distributed memory code, executed totally separately on each processor, knows only the reduced variables. The pre-processing and post-processing steps, that use the variables on the whole domain are executed sequentially.

The subroutines necessary for the update of the block overlapping interfaces slightly differ for the two versions. On shared memory computers, the update of the overlapped interfaces is effected sequentially by a simple copy, while for distributed memory computers, the message passing allows these updates between the processors. It is implemented using the Intel primitives on the iPSC/860, P4 on the BBN TC2000 and PVM on the RS/6000 network. The so-called 'distribute and collect' message passing strategy is applied which means that in a first stage all messages are sent out by all processors and collected in a second stage. An other strategy is the 'pre-scheduled message exchange', which, however, has been shown to be less efficient than the former strategy [1].

4 Numerical Results

4.1 Description of the Test Case

The test case for the parallelization of the present program is the hypersonic flow around a double-ellipsoid. The flow is characterized by the free-stream Mach number $M_\infty = 8.15$ and an angle of attack of $\alpha = 30°$ which corresponds to a standard workshop test case [2]. Both explicit and implicit calculations are performed. The fine grid contains a total of 76440 nodes. The coarse grid is obtained by taking away every second grid line which results in 12768 nodes. The grid is partitioning into 72 blocks with four layers containing 18 blocks each For details on the grid partitioning we refer to [3].

4.2   Physical Results

The parallel code resolves well the significant flow features for this configuration (a strong detached bow shock ahead of the nose and a secondary shock at the "canopy"). The Mach number contours at the symmetry plane and at the axial cut near x = 0 obtained after 1500 iterations on 32 iPSC/860 processors are presented in Figure 1. The same convergence rate as for the sequential version is obtained.

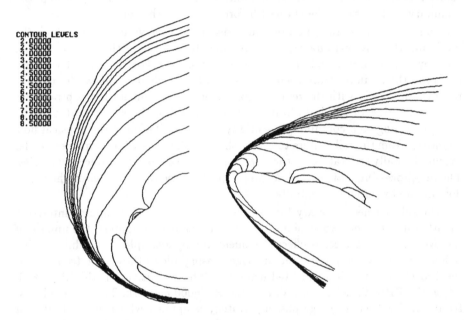

Fig. 1. Mach number contours in cross-section plane at x=0m and in symmetry plane.

4.3   Parallel Performance

On the CRAY-2, the best efficiency (0.84 on four processors) is obtained for the implicit run on the fine mesh (see Figure 2). This corresponds to the maximal computational load per processor. On the ALLIANT FX/80, it is not the fine mesh that does give the best results, which is due to the cache faults resulting from a coarse grid parallelism exploited on a big amount of data.

For our investigations on the BBN TC2000 (used as a distributed memory machine), the message passing is managed by the P4 software. The best performance is obtained for the implicit calculations on the fine grid (see Figure 3). Moreover, a phenomena of super-linearity (the efficiency is greater than one) appears which is explained by too many page faults causing disk swaps. Thus, the execution on one processor decreases the sequential performance and results

174

in a relatively better parallel performance. The data communication appears to be well handled by the P4 software since it is not too costly as seen in Figure 3.

On the iPSC/860, no tests were undertaken in a single node mode due to the memory limitation of 16 MB. However, in order to measure the parallel performance, the sequential elapsed time has been estimated by summing the computation time on each processor of the smallest hypercube still able to perform the test. The fine mesh test case in combination with the implicit solver yields the best efficiency results: up to 0.88 on the fine mesh on 64 processors and up to 0.70 on the coarse mesh as the Figure 4 shows it. Though the percentage of the communication increases with the number of processors it still remains low (two percent for the implicit calculations on the fine mesh with 64 processors, see Figure 4). It is smaller for the implicit calculations since the computational part is more significant than the message exchange.

On the RS/6000 network, message passing is handled by the PVM software. For the evaluation of the efficiency, the program has been executed on one node which is feasible due to a virtual memory management. However, page faults are caused by the real memory size. The decrease of the efficiency for the calculations on the fine mesh are due to page faults and cache misses (see Figure 5). The Ethernet network does not provide fast communication due to the small debit of the link and the high latency to access to the network during a data transfer. But, improved efficiencies are achieved with the SOC ('Serial Optical Channel').

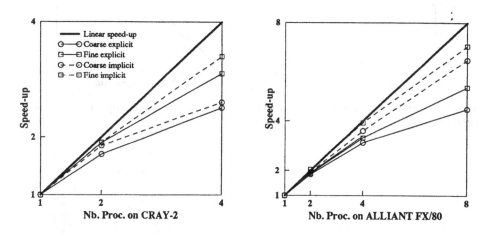

Fig. 2. Speed-up on shared memory computers: the CRAY-2 and the ALLIANT FX/80

5 Conclusions

The implementation of the industrial three-dimensional Navier-Stokes flow solver NSFLEX on parallel computers of different architectures appears to be very efficient: while the parallel version preserves the same convergence rate as the

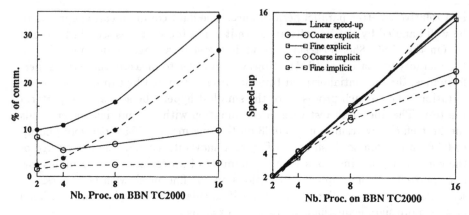

Fig. 3. Communication time and speed-up on a virtual shared memory computer: the BBN TC2000

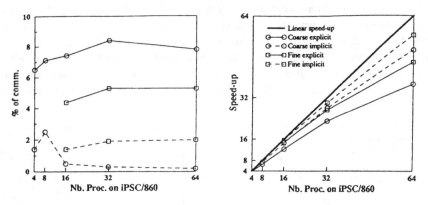

Fig. 4. Communication time and speed-up on a distributed memory machine: the iPSC860

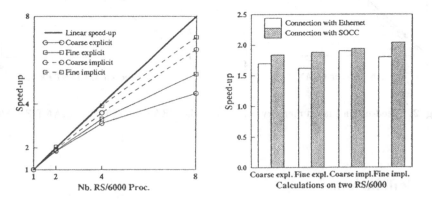

Fig. 5. Speed-up on a RS/6000 Network and comparison between Ethernet and SOC links

sequential version, the former executes up to 3.4 times faster on all four processors of a CRAY-2 and up to 56 times faster on 64 i860 processors (for the implicit solver and on the fine mesh case).

The parallel implementation of the code on shared memory multi-processors requires only a few changes of the original sequential version. The shared parallelization basically contains concurrent calls of the subroutines involved in the flow calculations. These concurrent calls are implemented using directives provided by the compilers on the CRAY-2 and the ALLIANT FX/80.

The distributed memory parallel version, however, necessitates more important modifications. The implementation of the message passing routines requires special attention in order to run the parallel code efficiently. The efficiency increases by reducing the data exchanges between the processors and, at the same time, with growing amount of local private computations. But, distributed memory computers present two main interests: not only the computation power is increased by adding nodes but also the amount of available memory.

On both the shared memory and the distributed memory computers, the best efficiency has been achieved for the implicit calculations on the fine mesh (for which the maximum computational load of the processors is achieved) with exception of the ALLIANT FX/80 where the coarse grain parallelism on large amount of data causes many cache faults.

The RS/6000 network is efficient under the following conditions: the debit of the link is sufficiently high, the network is not overloaded and the workstations are powerful in terms of both execution time and memory size.

Finally, a helpful way of parallelizing a computer program on distributed memory computers is the implementation on machines like the BBN TC2000. This architecture provides both shared and distributed memory facilities as well as a powerful parallel debugger. This allows the progressive programming of the parallelization tools which facilitates the step from the shared to the distributed version.

References

1. Mensink, C.; Corbett, P.; Deconink, H.: Parallelization of 2d Euler/Navier-Stokes multiblock codes. Technical report, Von Karman Institute, 1992.
2. Workshop on *Hypersonic Flows for Reentry Problems*, I.N.R.I.A. and GAMNI-SMAI (Organ.), Antibes/France, January 1990 (Part I) and April 1991 (Part II).
3. Paap, H.G.: Parallelization of 2d and 3d grid generation. Technical report, GENIAS Software GmbH, Neutraubling, 1993.
4. Schmatz, M.A.: Three-dimensional viscous flow simulations using an implicit relaxation scheme. Kordulla, W. (ed.): *Numerical simulation of compressible viscous-flow aerodynamics*. NNFM Vol. 22, Vieweg, 1988, pp. 226-242.
5. Schmatz, M.A.: *Hypersonic three-dimensional Navier-Stokes calculations for equilibrium air*. AIAA-paper 89-2183, 1989.

Lattice gas automata and molecular dynamics on a network of computers

K. Boryczko[1], M. Bubak[1], J. Kitowski[1,2], J. Mościński[1,2]
and R. Słota[1]

[1] Instytut Informatyki, AGH, al. Mickiewicza 30, 30-059 Kraków, Poland
[2] A.C.K. CYFRONET, ul. Nawojki 11, 30-950 Kraków, Poland

Abstract. Parallel algorithms and programs for lattice gas automata and molecular dynamics for fluid flow simulation were developed and investigated using PVM, Express, Network Linda and p4 on a network of workstations and a CONVEX C3210.

1 Introduction

We have developed and investigated parallel algorithms for lattice gas automata (LGA) and molecular dynamics (MD) for the study of hydrodynamic phenomena at microscopic level [1]. Geometric decomposition of the problem was applied. The following software for distributed parallel processing was used: PVM [2], Parasoft Express [3], p4 [4] and Network Linda [5]. The experiments were performed during the standard load of the computers; especially CONVEX C3210 (C2) was heavily used. Besides C3210, the following workstations connected via Ethernet were used: SUN SPARCstation SLC (SLC), SUN SPARCserver 470 (S470), SUN SPARCstation 2 (SS2), SUN SPARCstation IPX (IPX), IBM RS/6000-320 (RS6) and HP Apollo 9000/720 (HP9).

2 LGA on networked workstations

LGA FHP model with the full set of 76 particle collision rules was used. The evolution of the lattice consist of the absorption, collision, injection and free particle streaming. At the beginning of the simulation the lattice is divided along $y-$ axis into several domains with equal number of lattice sites and each domain is assigned to a different process (computer network node). After each timestep border rows of domains are transmitted between neighbours. The averaging is accomplished on each node separately.

The aim of load-balancing (LB) is to obtain the same wall-clock time on each node of the computer network. As the cpu time of calculation per one timestep and one lattice site, is independent of number of sites in a lattice, LB can be realised by changing the number of rows of the lattice assigned to computing nodes.

3 Distributed MD simulation

Interactions between the particles are the short-range 12/6 Lennard–Jones. The computational box is a long cylinder with periodic boundary conditions along its axis (z) only. The integer cutoff number n_C is introduced, where n_C is the number of neighbours interacting with a given particle. Particles in the cylinder are sorted due to their z coordinates and the index vector is set up on return to original particle indices.

For distributed computing domain decomposition is proposed. The box is divided along z direction into loosely coupled domains allocated on different computers. The following elements are calculated independently: interparticle interactions, interactions between the particles and the wall of the computational box, solution of the equations of motion, physical quantities and sorting. The communication is needed only for particles moving from one domain to another (according to the motion or load-balancing), for interparticle forces calculations at the boundaries of the domains and for sending partial global results from each domain to evaluate global quantities of the whole box. Criterion for the LB is to get the same execution *wall-clock* time on each node.

4 Results

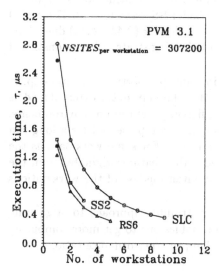

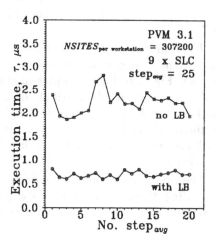

Fig. 1. Execution time of LGA for different homogenous clusters of workstations

Fig. 2. Load-balancing for LGA on SLC network

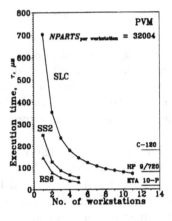

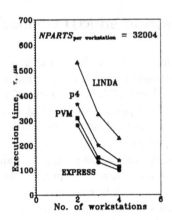

Fig. 3. Execution time of MD program for different homogenous clusters of workstations

Fig. 4. Comparison of environments using MD program; to SLC (host) – S470, SS2, SS2 were added

For LGA, the dependence of execution time per one timestep and one lattice site, τ, on the number of workstations for different homogenous clusters of RS6, SS2 and SLC is shown in Fig. 1. The filled marks represent τ (cpu time) for our best sequential LGA program. As the speedup was close to the perfect one we have used the serial fraction [7] as a metric of parallelization. For isolated clusters serial fraction $f = f_k \times k$ (k - number of computing nodes), remains almost constant ($0.23 - 0.29$ for SLC, $0.30 - 0.33$ for RS6, and $0.45 - 0.47$ for SS2) whereas for loaded SLC cluster it has irregular behavior ($2.43 - 4.42$) due to the changing load. Efficiency of elaborated load-balancing strategy is demonstrated in Fig. 2.

The comparison of MD program execution time per particle and timestep, τ, for different homogeneous clusters under PVM, isolated from the external load, is shown in Fig. 3. In Fig. 4 τ is presented for different programming environments. In Fig. 5 τ and particle distribution on computers are presented for a long run on the network of computers with S470 as a host. For some workstations the maximum allowed distribution was attained – this feature originates from the small system memory (HP9) or from the simultaneous use of the workstations for other jobs (SS2).

The experiments show the efficiency of distributed approach to large scale computing. Using the network of computers enables one to get more computing power and more system memory at reasonable price/performance ratio.

Acknowledgments

The authors gratefully acknowledge Mr. W. Alda and M. Pogoda for the assistance during the computer experiments. This research was partially supported by KBN grants PB 8 S503 0(21, 22) 05 and PB 2 P302073 05.

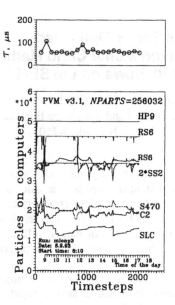

Fig. 5. Execution wall-clock time, τ, and particle distribution between 8 processing nodes. Standard load. PVM v3.1.

References

1. Mareschal, M., and Holian, B.L., eds.: Microscopic simulations of complex hydrodynamic phenomena. NATO ASI Series, Series B: Physics VOL.292, Plenum Press, New York and London, 1992
2. Geist, A. Beguelin, A., Dongarra, J., Jiang, W., Manchek, R., and Sunderam, V.: PVM 3.0 A users' guide and reference manual. ORNL/TM–12187, USA February, 1993
3. Express v3.0 Operational Manual. *ParaSoft* Corp., Pasadena, 1990
4. Butler, R., and Lusk, E.: User's guide to the p4 programming system. Argonne National Laboratory, ANL-92/17, October 1992
5. Carriero, N.J., and Gelernter, D.H.: Linda in context. Communications of the ACM, **32** (1989) 444-458
6. Kitowski, J., and Mościński, J.: Microcomputers against Supercomputers ? – On the geometric partition of the computational box for vectorized MD algorithms. Mol. Simul., **8** (1992) 305-319
7. Karp, A.H., Flatt, P.H.: Measuring parallel processor performance. Communications of the ACM, **33** (1990) 539-543

Parallel Scalar Optimized Direct Simulation Monte Carlo Method for Rarefied Flows on the SP-1

Stefan Dietrich; Iain Boyd
Sibley School of Mechanical and Aerospace Engineering,
Cornell University, Ithaca, NY 14853-7501, USA.

Introduction

The "Direct Simulation Monte Carlo (DSMC)" method [1], which models the gas at the microscopic level, has become a standard tool for the calculation of rarefied gas flows. But even in continuum flows, whenever microscopic effects influence the flow behavior, the DSMC method can be usefully applied for verification of continuum methods based on the Navier-Stokes equations. Since the DSMC method requires large numbers of particles under those conditions, tremendous computational power is necessary.

In order to achieve higher performance, recently, efficient implementations of the DSMC algorithms were oriented towards the use of supercomputers [2,3]. To make use of the vector registers, sublists of particles have to be built for which similar calculations have to be performed. This leads to an uneconomical usage of these computers. Scalar processors, for example as used in todays workstations, are therefore much better suited for the DSMC method. However, they do not reach the same performance level as vector processors. On the other hand, they are inexpensive and many may be connected together yielding a parallel computer system. IBM's SP-1 is such a parallel computer system. A maximum of 64 RS6000 workstations are connected via a "High Performance Switch" for fast communication between them.

Scalar Optimization and Parallelization

To achieve an overall high efficiency on a parallel computer system, the node program has to be optimized first. Scientific software used today was mostly written under the assumption that each element of an array can be accessed in the same time. This was true on most supercomputers, but it is no longer true on workstations. There, a fast cache memory is used as data buffer between the relatively slow, but inexpensive, main memory and the processor. Data, which reside in the cache, can be accessed about 10 times faster than data which has to be fetched from main memory. Simply transferring codes written for supercomputers will therefore result in poor performance often an order of magnitude lower than the peak performance of the machine. In particular, implementations of the DSMC method often make extensive use of indirect addressing resulting in a scattered access of memory elements. This can be avoided if an appropriate data structure increasing the data locality is used [4]. Further performance improvements can be achieved if the superscalar feature of the RS6000 processor, which allows execution of a fixed-point, a floating-point and a branch construct at the same time, is taken into account when writing the program.

Parallelization of the DSMC algorithm requires again to increase locality of data, now at the workstation level. Any access of data on a different node has to be avoided. Although the "High Performance Switch" delivers sufficient communication speed, the access of elements on different nodes is several orders of magnitude slower than the access of data on the same node. For the DSMC method this problem can be solved by using an appropriate algorithm for the particle motion[3].

Performance

Main emphasis in the current research has been to achieve a general purpose code, naturally decreasing performance by a certain degree, but improving the versatility of the code. The developed "MONACO" software system runs either on a single workstations, on parallel workstation clusters and even on vector-supercomputers. Although flexible load balancing is still under development, first results in Fig. 1 show that on the SP-1, performance equivalent to a Cray C90 is reached using only eight processors. Highest parallel efficiency is reached with 16 processors and using more than 28 processors requires better load balancing to avoid the current existence of a communication bottleneck.

Conclusions

Simply transferring codes originally developed for a supercomputer to a cache based workstation architecture will generally result in poor performance. Better data locality is required for good cache management which can generally only be achieved by rewriting the code using a different data structure. Data locality at a higher level is also required if a distributed memory parallel computer is used. A change in the DSMC algorithm is then required.

Acknowledgments

Funds provided by DFG and Cornell Theory Center who also supplied use of the SP-1. Thanks to Adolfy Hoisie for helpful discussions on optimization for the RS6000 workstations.

References

[1] Bird, G. A., *Molecular Gas Dynamics*, Clarendon Press, Oxford, 1976.
[2] Boyd, I. D.: *Vectorization of a Monte Carlo Simulation Scheme for Nonequilibrium Gas Dynamics*, J. Comp. Phys. 96, 1991
[3] Dietrich, S.: *An Efficient Computation of Particle Movement in 3-d DSMC Calculations on Structured Body-Fitted Grids*, Proc. of the 17th RGD-Symp., 1990
[4] Dietrich, S.; Boyd, I. D.: *A Scalar Optimized Parallel Implementation of the DSMC Method*, AIAA 94-0355, Reno, 1994.

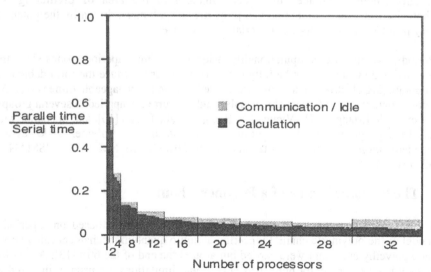

Fig. 1:Timing result of the MONACO software on the SP-1.

Modern Quantum Mechanical Techniques
and
Computations on the Electronic Structure of Polymers

J. M.André, B. Champagne, J. Delhalle, J.G. Fripiat, D.H. Mosley
Laboratoire de Chimie Théorique Appliquée
Facultés Universitaires Notre-Dame de la Paix
61 rue de Bruxelles
B-5000 Namur, BELGIUM

Abstract: Some aspects of ab initio computations on the electronic structure of polymers are discussed. The periodic model of the polymer chain is introduced, together with the principles of LCAO band structure calculations of polymers. Emphasis is given to the computational difficulties encountered, to particular aspects of the implementation of the Namur PLH program, and to the calculation of the longitudinal polarizability of polymers. Finally, attention is drawn to some possible practical applications of the computational modelling of polymers.

1 Introduction

Since the first pioneering theoretical works in the sixties on LCAO techniques in polymer quantum chemistry [1-6] the field has known a rapid development. More recently, many advances have been made into the area of predicting the photoelectron, electrical and optical properties of polymers, driven by the potential they possess for use in organic material-based devices.

Periodic systems are computationally easier to treat than aperiodic ones since the translational symmetry can be fully exploited in order to reduce the formidable task of computing electronic states of an extended system to manageable dimensions. Ab initio programs for polymers are available and are currently applied in several groups, for example Erlangen [7] , Vienna [8], Budapest [9] , Torino [10], and in Namur with our PLH program [11]. It is illuminating to note that all polymer packages use standard "molecular" strategies taken from the IBMOL, KGNMOL, GAUSSIAN or other series.

2 The Periodic Model of a Polymer Chain

The standard quantum mechanical treatment of polymers is based on a periodic model of the polymeric chain. Pioneering ab initio quantum mechanical calculations on a polyethylene chain were carried out around the end of the 60's [13]. A detailed review has been recently published [14]. Some limitations are usually imposed in standard quantum chemical polymeric calculations. A first limitation is that we usually consider an isolated chain. In practice, the chain is never isolated but exists in a liquid or solid-state environment. A second limitation is that the chain is taken to be infinite and perfectly stereoregular. Considering the chain as infinite is not a severe limitation since polymers can have very large molecular weights; in the case of conventional polymers such as polyethylene or polypropylene, molecular weights in the range of 10^5-10^6 Dalton are attainable. The model also neglects chain end effects and the importance of such effects has yet to be studied in detail. The crudest assumption of all is that of the perfect stereoregularity of the linear chain. However, this does allow the translational symmetry to be taken into account and enables the application of concepts encountered in condensed matter physics in order to provide a rather complete description of the electronic structure of polymers.

3 Principles of LCAO Band Structure Calculations on Polymers

The condensed matter physicist makes full use of the translational symmetry of the lattice and uses the language of Brillouin zones introduced in the classical work by Bloch in 1928. In this context, the so-called Bloch functions (molecular orbitals for an infinite one-dimensional (1D) chain) are eigenfunctions of a translation operator and as such are expressed in terms of a wave number, k, defined in the reciprocal space.

From a conceptual point of view, it appears that polymer quantum chemistry is an ideal field for co-operation between condensed matter physicists and molecular quantum chemists. A common interpretation exists in the discussions concerning orbital energies, orbital symmetry, and gross charges by chemists, and solid-state physicists who use terms less familiar to the chemist such as the first Brillouin zone, the dependence of "wave function" (in fact the monoelectronic wave function is called an orbital by the chemist) with respect to wave vector k, Fermi surfaces, Fermi contours, and density of states.

However, polymer quantum chemistry is not, strictly speaking, one-dimensional physics. It must be emphasized that even if we deal with 1D periodic systems, the orbitals are truly 3D, so that polymer quantum chemistry is not a reduction of solid-state physics to a single dimension space. In the strictly 1D physics, the systems are periodic in one dimension and have 1D wavefunctions. The three-dimensionality of the basic Bloch orbitals renders important theorems applicable to purely 1D systems invalid. A typical example is that of the presence of extrema in energy bands which should only occur at the center and the edges of the Brillouin zone in a strictly 1D system. For polymers, even in simple cases such as the linear zig-zag polyethylene chain, some extrema of the energy bands are encountered at arbitrary positions in the first Brillouin zone which are not high symmetry points [12].

Considering practical applications, it is clear from the previous discussion that the numerical procedure must combine equations from molecular quantum chemistry and solid-state physics. In molecular quantum chemistry, a molecular orbital is expanded in terms of basis functions; secular systems of equations and determinants are solved, the eigenvalues of which are the orbital energies. From the LCAO coefficients, charges and bond orders (projection of the density matrices onto the limited basis used) are calculated. In polymer quantum chemistry, the orbitals, the systems of equations, and the determinants are no longer real but have imaginary components. In our definition of the problem, assuming the translational symmetry of the polymer through a repeated unit cell, means that in our treatment we can exploit the lattice periodicity and introduce lattice sums which then need to be evaluated by adequate procedures. The key problem is obtaining the exact numerical value or an approximate value of the various matrix elements over the basis functions. Fortunately, it is known from the form of the AO's that in the case of non-metallic systems these matrix elements should decrease exponentially with the distance between their orbital centers and thus give rise to a convergency of the lattice sums appearing in the secular systems and in the secular determinant. It is to be noted that through taking the one-dimensional periodicity into account the dimensions of the matrix equations to be solved are equal to the number of atomic orbitals per unit cell, the effect of the infinite lattice being included in the formally infinite but naturally convergent sums.

The discussion so far has demonstrated that in a general way a polymer can be considered as a large molecule. Bearing this in mind, it is likely that the usual methods of quantum chemistry can be used to investigate the electronic structure of polymers. Indeed, the well-known approximations of molecular quantum chemistry can be introduced into the formalism of polymeric orbitals (e.g., the use of contracted Gaussian orbitals [14]). LCAO-based *ab initio* calculations require the definition of a atomic basis set of size N and imply the calculation of integrals or matrix elements between the N basis functions of the basis set. For atoms, all the basis functions are centered on the same location and the integrals are said to be one-centered. For large molecules and/or large basis sets, a huge number of integrals has to be calculated, which constitutes the bottleneck of first principles *ab initio* SCF-MO-LCAO calculations on large oligomeric systems. In the infinite regular polymeric chain as in the molecular or oligomeric cases, nonempirical methods are dependent on the fourth power of the number of orbitals considered. If N_C is the number of cells for which all the overlap and Fock elements are greater than a given threshold (e.g., 10^{-6} au) and N is the size of the basis set in a unit cell, we have to calculate $N_C N(N+1)/2$ Fock integrals and overlap terms. The repulsion operator due to its two-electron character gives rise to much more complex matrices. In usual schemes, these matrices (of number N_c^3) contain $N^2(N+1)^2/8$ integrals as a first approximation. As a consequence, the time-limiting step of an *ab initio* method has a roughly $N_c^3 N^4/8$ dependence.

Thus, the application of *ab initio* methods to the study of the electronic structure of medium- and large-size molecules requires substantial computational resources. The situation is exaggerated when considering polymers of chemical or biological importance. Therefore, it is evident that for the *ab initio* study of polymeric systems interest should be directed towards the development of efficient programs, specifically designed for polymers and requiring less computing time than the programs which already exist. In our code this has been achieved by implementing, into a general system, fast techniques for evaluating integrals over Gaussian-type functions, efficient methods of computing long-range electrostatic effects and the explicit use of helical symmetry. In general, this has been achieved through the adoption of a methodology which is more "polymer-minded" than "molecular-minded". This approach is summarized in section 5.

4 Calculation of the Longitudinal Polarizability of Polymers

In recent years, there has been major and intense research activity in the field of materials which exhibit high linear and nonlinear responses. Organic systems are of particular interest due to their stability, their high laser damage threshold and the almost boundless potential of organic synthesis. High electric susceptibilities are greatly dependent upon the nature of the electron delocalization and it is important to find the molecular structures which yield the highest possible responses because, amongst other advantages, a smaller electric field will be required to achieve the desired effect. The domain is ideal for the application of quantum chemistry in molecular engineering to provide the most promising materials through the investigation into the structural requirements and the provision of reliable predictions of the electronic properties. With such a vast range of candidate systems, the pursuit of theoretical studies is economically prudent and the knowledge acquired can be applied subsequently to help steer synthetic research towards materials which possess the most potential.

The methods of calculation of (hyper)polarizibilities of infinite systems cannot be considered as a trivial extension of those used for molecular systems. At present, only a few studies have been devoted to obtaining the asymptotic value of the polarizability per unit cell directly. Two methods are currently used; the first one is based on a perturbation approach. It is sometimes called the S.O.S. (Summation-Over-States) method or an uncoupled Hartree-Fock scheme [16-20]. The method does suffer from a serious drawback in that it corresponds to an uncoupled scheme, neglecting the reorganizational effects induced on the application of a field. Recently, a coupled scheme has been developed in the framework of the random phase approximation (RPA) formalism [21,22]. To date, the results obtained from this approach on model systems have been encouraging, although considerable effort is required in the development of efficient algorithms to minimize the substantial computational cost before the technique can become more widely applicable. Both methods have the advantage that they provide insight into the origin of optical properties through the analysis of the polarizability in terms of the topology of the contributing bands. They are integral part of our PLH code [11].

5 Particular Aspects of Computer Implementation

The PLH package, developed in our labratory, computes the band structure and longitudinal polarizability per unit cell of regular and helical polymers exploiting the one-dimensional translational symmetry. The package is designed on a modular basis with each module performing a well defined task, that is: input of geometry of the unit cell and atomic basis sets; calculation of one-electron integrals; calculation of two-electron integrals; SCF iterations, printing of energy bands and short population analysis; and calculation of the longitudinal uncoupled Hartree-Fock polarizability.

Additional interfaces exist to graphics programs to enable the visualization of the unit cell and of the resulting band structure and density of states.

A particular feature of the Namur PLH code is the way in which it treats long-range Coulombic interactions. In a short-range region, all Coulomb and exchange contributions are evaluated exactly. Secondly, over an intermediate range, only the Coulomb terms are evaluated exactly. Beyond this range, the interactions are computed rapidly using a multipolar expansion technique. Further aspects of the code, such as the use of the permutational symmetry of the two-electron integral indices, the Fock matrix formation, aids to convergence of the SCF procedure, and computation of the density of states, are discussed in detail in [11].

6 Conclusions

Many applications of the quantum theory applied to the electronic structure of polymers can be found in the literature. For the sake of simplicity, we refer to some review papers which describe the present state-of-the art of quantum chemical calculations on stereoregular polymers [23,24].
In a book devoted to lecture notes in computer science, it is worth reminding the numerous fields of electronics to which the organic solid state and its theoretical analysis described in the two parts of this paper could contribute:
-   organic metals ↔ electronic components, plastic batteries,
-   electro-optics and nonlinear optical phenomena ↔ frequency
    doublers,modulators, integrated optics, optical computers,
or other timely fields for an active research as:
-   solid-state reactions ↔ chemical sensors,
-   solid-state photochemical reactions ↔ optical information storage,
-   piezoelectric or ferroelectric phenomena ↔ transducers (electret
    microphones),
-   organic photoconductors or semiconductors ↔ photocopiers, solar
    cells,
-   organic superconductors ↔ Josephson junctions, computer logic
    gates, high-field magnets, generator, motors,
-   liquid crystals ↔ electronic displays,
-   ferromagnetism ↔ magnetic recording, magneto-optic recording.
The PLH code is available through the METECC initiative.

7 Acknowledgments

D.H.M. thanks the Services de la Programmation de la Politique Scientifique (SPPS) for his grant received in the framework of the ELSAM (Electronic Large Scale Computational System for Advanced Materials) project, part of the Belgian National Program of Impulsion in Information Technology. B.C. thanks the Belgian National Fund for Scientific Research (FNRS) for his Senior Research Assistant position. This work has benefited from the financial support of the Belgian National Interuniversity Research Program on "Sciences of Interfacial and Mesoscopic Structures" (PAI/IUAP No. P3-049). The authors gratefully acknowledge the financial support of the FNRS-

FRFC, the "Loterie Nationale" for the convention No. 9.4593.92, and the FNRS within the framework of the "Action d'impulsion à la recherche fondamentale" of the Belgian Ministry of Science under the convention D.4511.93.

References

1. J. Ladik, Acta Phys. Hung., **18**, 173 (1965)
2. J. Ladik, Acta Phys. Hung., **18**, 185 (1965)
3. J.M. André, L. Gouverneur and G. Leroy, Int. J. Quantum Chem., **1**, 427 (1967)
4. J.M. André, L. Gouverneur and G. Leroy, Int. J. Quantum Chem., **1**, 451 (1967)
5. G. Del Re, J. Ladik and G. Biczo, Phys. Rev., **155**, 997 (1967)
6. J.M. André, J. Chem. Phys., **50**, 1536 (1969)
7. S. Suhai and J. Ladik, Solid State Commun., **22**, 227 (1977)
8. A. Karpfen, Int. J. Quantum Chem., **19**, 1297 (1981)
9. M. Kertesz, Acta Phys. Acad. Sci. Hung., **41**, 127 (1976)
10. C. Pisani, R. Dovesi and C. Roetti, Hartree-Fock Treatment of Crystalline Systems, SpringerVerlag, Berlin (1988)
11. J.M. André, D.H. Mosley, B. Champagne, J. Delhalle, J.G. Fripiat, J.L. Brédas, D.J. Vanderveken and D.P. Vercauteren, in: Methods and Techniques in Computational Chemistry : METECC-94, Volume B : Medium Size Systems, E. Clementi (ed.),p 423, STEF, Cagliari (1993)
12. J.M. André, Int. J. Quantum Chem., **S24**, 65 (1990)
13. J.M. André and G. Leroy, Chem. Phys. Lett., **5**, 71 (1970)
14. B. Champagne, J.G. Fripiat and J.M. André, Physicalia Mag., **14**, 123 (1992)
15. S.F. Boys, Proc. Roy. Soc., **A200**, 542 (1950)
16. C. Barbier, J. Delhalle and J.M. André, in: Nonlinear Optical Properties of Polymers, A.J. Heeger, J. Orenstein and D.R. Ulrich (Eds.),p.239, Materials Research Society, Pittsburgh (1988)
17. C. Barbier, J. Delhalle and J.M. André, J. Mol. Struct. (Theochem), **188**, 299 (1989)
18. J.M. André, B. Champagne, in: Organic Molecules for Nonlinear Optics and Photonics, J. Messier, F. Kazjar, and P. Prasad (eds.), Kluwer Academic Publishers (1991), pp. 1
19. B. Champagne and J.M. André, Int. J. Quantum Chem., **42**, 1009 (1992)
20. B. Champagne, D.H. Mosley, J.G. Fripiat and J.M. André, SPIE Vol.1775, Nonlinear Optical Properties of Organic Materials V, 236 (1992)
21. B. Champagne, D.H. Mosley, J.G. Fripiat and J.M. André, Int. J. Quantum Chem., **46**, 1 (1993)
22. B. Champagne, D.H. Mosley and J.M. André, Int. J. Quantum Chem., **S27**, 667 (1993)
23. J.M. André, J. Delhalle and J.L. Brédas, Quantum Chemistry Aided Design of Organic Polymers, World Scientific (1991)
24. J.M. André and J. Delhalle, Quantum chemistry aided molecular engineering of polymeric materials for optoelectronics, Chem. Rev., **91**, 843 (1991)

Object Oriented Simulation Software
for Drug Design

Robert Bywater[1], Wouter Joosen[2], Stijn Bijnens[2], Pierre Verbaeten[2], Thomas
Larsen[3] and John Perram[3]

[1] Novo Nordisk A/S, Novo Alle, DK-2880 Bagsvaerd, Denmark
[2] K.U.Leuven, Dept. of Comp. Sc., Celestijnenlaan 200A, B-3001 Leuven, Belgium
[3] LCAM Odense, Forskerparken 10, DK-5230 Odense, Denmark

Abstract. In this paper, we report on the design and implementation
of a parallel object-oriented implementation of a protein simulation application, which is the heart of a drug design software package, to be
exploited at Novo Nordisk Research Labs on a large cluster of workstations.

The application is implemented in C++ on top of the XENOOPS environment, which offers location independent object invocation at the
application programming interface. Thus the software is truly object-
oriented – as opposed to C++ combined with low level message passing
primitives.

We evaluate the productivity of software developers in this application
and illustrate the role of the object-oriented environment and methodology. We compare different versions of the simulator, as different decompositions have been realised (resulting in various degrees of concurrency).
Our paper reveals many positive experiences as a result of this (still ongoing) R&D effort. The conclusion includes a recommendation to exploit
modern software engineering techniques to develop HPCN software.

1   Introduction

Computational techniques give the drug designer the possibility of directly simulating the structure and dynamics of large molecules. These include not only the
drug molecules themselves, but increasingly, the focus is on the target molecules,
receptors, to which these drugs bind. A complete description of such a system requires the simulation to cope with anything up to 50000 atoms. Moreover, these
simulations have to proceed over time periods long enough to obtain meaningful
results. Conventional molecular dynamics software running on serial computers can not cope with calculations of this magnitude. Thus, in common with
all advanced pharmaceutical companies, Novo Nordisk has a set of computational biology and chemistry problems which cannot adequately be addressed
with currently available software and hardware platforms. This paper reports
on the development of end user oriented simulation software, that encapsulates
state-of-the-art algorithms and that is engineered to ensure maintenance and
portability over a range of architectures.

The protein simulation package we develop mainly consists of a molecular dynamics simulator and a graphical user interface, that enables real time and post mortem visualisation, as well as an advanced molecule editor to feed the simulation. The focus of this paper is of course on the molecular dynamics (MD) simulation, as it requires high performance computing capabilities.

This paper is structured as follows. Section two covers a high level description of the MD simulator and the various algorithms that constitute its functionality. Section three discusses the design of the parallel MD simulator. Here we justify the use of *object parallelism*, a paradigm which allows us to combine data decomposition and functional (algorithmic) parallelism in a flexible and elegant way. Object parallelism is offered by the XENOOPS[2] environment, which offers location independent object invocation at the language level[4]. Section four discusses the implementation, and highlights the relatively short development time. Section five evaluates the current prototype, which is used to simulate polymers of varying chain length to tune the "reference" implementation (running on a network of DEC/alphas). This evaluation covers performance issues, comparing different levels of concurrency, portability issues and manpower effectiveness achieved within this project. The conclusion will also discuss the future of this application, discussing its potential for the Novo Nordisk Research Labs and its technical evolution. The latter includes the realisation of dynamic load balancing.

2 Application Domain

Particle simulations are used to observe the macroscopic behaviour of a physical system by simulating that system at the microscopic level. The physical system is then considered as a large collection of particles (e.g. atoms, molecules, electrons and nuclei...). One specific class of such simulations is molecular dynamics.

The fundamental aim of molecular dynamics is to predict the behaviour of condensed matter from a knowledge of the forces acting between the component atoms. This is done by numerically solving the Newtonian equations of motion to obtain the time evolution of the molecular trajectories.

A protein molecule can be thought of as a complex flexible mechanical system subject to a number of forces between parts of itself and the environment. For each type of force, specific force calculation algorithms have been developed by application domain experts. We summarise the forces below as we will rely on their properties in the sequel of this paper.

1. **Short ranged forces**: In fact, this category contains short ranged repulsions between atoms, medium ranged dispersion forces between atoms not bonded to each other, three body forces arising from the bending of chemical bonds and four body forces due to torsion of two parts of a molecule about the bond joining them.

---

[4] In fact, XENOOPS extends C++ for aspects related to concurrency and distribution.

Short ranged forces are best known in the parallel computing area, as they are caused by interaction between particles which are close to one another, thus locality is high and parallelisation becomes easy. Notice that earlier efforts in the parallelisation of MD simulators mainly concentrate on short range force calculations. This type of problem poses no load balancing problems. The challenge to acquire a load equilibrium is much higher when the other forces – mentioned below – are incorporated in the simulation model.

2. **Forces of constraint**: A complex molecule consists of a collection of atoms connected together by chemical bonds which constrain the distances between the connected atoms. In some circumstances, bond angles can also be constrained in a similar way.

   Constraint dynamics is a set of mathematical techniques which reduce the problem of simulating complicated mechanical systems to a set of standard numerical algorithms. Two mathematical formalisms have been applied to describe the forces of constraint in a complex molecule, i.e. the Lagrangian formalism and the Hamiltonian formalism. In our current prototype, we focus on the latter model. When applying the Hamiltonian approach, each molecule will be treated for the forces of constraint by solving a set of linear equations whose size is proportional to the number of atoms in the molecule. The parallelisation of such algorithms is well understood (conjugate gradient, LU decomposition etc.).

3. **Electrostatic forces**: These forces are caused by the interaction between charge distributions. Electrostatic forces between pairs of particles are proportional to $\frac{1}{r^2}$ and thus exist between a pair of particles with a relatively long distance. Therefore, the intermolecular forces in most molecular systems of interest are dominated by the electrostatic forces between molecular charge distributions. Simulation in periodic boundary conditions need special techniques to remove artifacts introduced by surface effects in electrostatics [1].

4. **Thermostatic forces**: These forces adapt the simulation to different environments. The thermostatic forces arise from the desirability of computing the trajectories at constant average temperature, rather than at constant total energy which would be the case for a conservative mechanical system. The thermostatic forces thus express the coupling of the system to an external energy source.

The calculation of all the forces is the major part in the computation of our application. A differential equation solver has to calculate velocities and position of particles each time all the forces on the particles have been obtained.

3 Design of a Parallel Simulator

The XENOOPS application programming interface supports the object-oriented development of simulation software with concurrent semantics and distribution transparency.

XENOOPS offers a framework to develop simulation software using the concept of *object parallelism*. Object parallelism can be easily characterised by the idea that the total work, to be performed by the simulation, must be decomposed into active objects called *work units* that operate concurrently in the simulation software. Work units have to be scheduled according to a policy that respects the semantics of the application; each time a work unit has been scheduled, a part of the work associated with it is performed.

Thus the development of the simulation software starts from the identification of key abstractions: work units. Various alternatives can be identified.

1. In a traditional approach, a work unit encapsulates all the particles in a geometrical fraction of the physical system. This simulation corresponds to a data decomposition (*data parallel*) approach[5]. This way all the force calculations on the encapsulated particles and the computation of new positions of these particles are treated by the same work unit.

2. On the other hand, when different work units operate in the same geometrical fraction, but perform different force calculations[6], we have *algorithmic* parallelism.

3. Various possibilities exist in which data parallelism and algorithmic parallelism are combined: the geometrical space will be decomposed in many fractions, and each fraction in its turn will correspond to different work units, representing one specific work abstraction. One possibility we mention here is the model in which for a given geometrical fraction, we identify five work unit types: one to calculate the positions of work units, and one work unit type per force calculation mentioned above.

We have chosen for the latter approach for various reasons.

1. Units dealing with different force calculations or with the position calculation can be developed and tested separately[7]. This improves the fundamental quality of the software and reduces the overall development time.

2. For each of the work abstractions, encapsulated in different work unit subtypes, one can choose for the most appropriate discretisation for each specific algorithm. Consequently, when work units of different types interact[8], conversions must occur between the corresponding discretisations.

3. The application is developed with a maximal degree of logical concurrency[9]. Of course, in practice, for a specific simulation type, one has to find out whether this higher degree of concurrency outperforms the overhead that is

---

[5] When allocating one work unit per node, one builds an SPMD program.

[6] Notice that these can occur concurrently.

[7] In fact different algorithm experts are dealing with these work units.

[8] This typically occurs between the position calculation and each of the force calculation units.

[9] The constraint forces are calculated using the Hamiltonian formalism[4]; domain experts will notice that in that case, also constraint forces can be computed concurrently.

the result of the extra interaction between work units with a different work abstraction (cfr. the conversions mentioned above).

It is clear that this benefit may turn out to cause disadvantages when it comes to a performance evaluation. This is not the case: the optimal parallel implementation can be derived from the initial implementation by building new work abstractions that combine the basic ones from our first implementation. The reader can intuitively see that this combining[10] can be automated as source code transformations, whereas the opposite transformation (i.e. functional decomposition by source code transformation) is not realistic.

The strength of our design is that we have chosen for a fine grain decomposition into functional units[11], but at the same time remain able to derive coarser grained concurrency by applying source code transformations. In conclusion, the concurrent program can be customised to specific target hardware.

4 Implementation

As mentioned above, our initial implementation starts from a functional decomposition in which the different types of force calculations, as well as the calculation of particles' positions, are treated as concurrent units of work.

We clarify our implementation – and thus the benefits of our design – by summarising the major characteristics (functionality, discretisation and dependency) of the work units in one of our prototypes, which excludes the electrostatic and thermostatic forces. This application is of sufficient complexity to illustrate the essentials of the overall development.

- Work units for short range forces: for the calculation of short-range forces, we have chosen the well known linked-cell method. The linked-cell method converts the continuos problem of finding all particle-pair within some given distance, i.e. not separated to further away from each other than some distance r_{cutoff}, into an equivalent grid-problem. This is done by dividing the simulation-box into equal-sized volumes, represented by a list of particles. Finding all particles-pairs within r_{cutoff} may now be performed by iteratively scanning each volume, and checking the particles in these with particles from neighbour-volumes. A volume X is considered a neighbour-volume of a given volume Y if the distance between X and Y is small enough. This distance is defined as the smallest distance between a pair of particles which belong to X and Y respectively.

    We have decomposed the linked-cell method into a set of work units each holding a continuous set of volumes. These work-units interact to update shared state.

---

[10] with the technique of multiple inheritance

[11] Recall that this decomposition is orthogonal to the data decomposition in the physical system being simulated.

- Work units for constraint dynamics: Our constraint-systems are described by a number of Euclidean-distances between pairs of particles. These are either given as a fixed bound-length or as a fixed bound-angle between particle p_1, p_2 and p_3 (with resulting distance between particle p_1 and p_3 as constant). Such system therefore quite natural leads to a graph-representation, where the set of vertices represent the set of particles, while the set of edges represent bound-lengths. Notice that the representation of this graph is encapsulated in a data-structure with the following components:

  a list containing all edges,

  a set of particles,

  information, specific for the Hamiltonian formalism.

- Work units for position calculations: To perform the low-level differential equation solution (i.e. mapping current positions, momentas, time-derivatives of positions and momentas into new positions and momentas) the super-class "DESolver" was defined. A sub-class "DESolverRK2" was derived to provide the popular Runge-Kutta second order scheme. Other DE solvers may be derived in the future.

  Essential for the position calculation work units is that they interact both with constraint dynamics work units and with short range force work units. Therefore, they encapsulate both volume-based and graph-representation-based discretisations.

5 Evaluation

Program Development

The object-oriented approach clearly leads to a man power effective development of new codes. The first prototype of our simulation system – as outlined in section 4 – has been implemented in 4 man months time. This system includes, apart from the functionality described above, I/O functionality that produces not only formatted output of particles' positions and velocities, but that also calculates pressure and pairwise correlation properties of the simulated system. We believe the production time of this highly modular code is more than encouraging, given the fact that the preliminary training of the programmer involved took about 4 months as well.

Performance Issues

Molecular dynamics simulations have been realised on MIMD architectures, because a large part of the calculations expose enough locality to successfully apply a data decomposition based parallelisation. There is no doubt one can obtain successful parallelisations for this kind of application.

As our prototype is developed on a network of workstations (DEC/alphas), interconnected by a standard Ethernet, the performance results from this system are not relevant so far.

One interesting issue to evaluate is whether different versions with varying degree of logical concurrency perform differently. We have built different versions of the simulator by combining work units that originally encapsulated just one force calculation. It turns out that the performance penalty for *extra concurrency* within one processor which is not exploited by the hardware, goes up to 25% of the total execution time. We need further and extensive experimentation to study this phenomena, but as we announced, compile time combination of functional entities that map on the same geometrical area of the simulated system will be an important issue in order to combine the benefits of a modular development process with optimal performance.

Portability

Finally, we mention the portability issue. It is clear that our application has a maximal portability potential because the application programming interface completely hides the architecture of the underlying system. XENOOPS currently runs on top of OSF/1 and Solaris. An advanced application writer still can tune the run time system to achieve maximal performance on a specific platform. This issue is beyond the scope of this paper. For the interested reader, see [3].

6   Conclusion and Future Work

With this paper, we report on our experience in the development of an object-oriented parallel application in the high performance computing area. The object-oriented methodology enables a high productivity of a development team; it is a firm basis for portability purposes.

The key target is to tackle the issue of protein simulations. An example of the studies that are planned are the simulation of two proteins of roughly the same size, but having a different aminoacid composition. In this case, there will inevitably be considerable differences in the patterns of interatomic interactions within the two proteins. The pattern of forces is different, and so force calculations will be decomposed differently in the simulation of these two protein molecules. Such examples will underline the need for load balancing. Initially then, the emphasis will be on studying protein molecules of similar size (but with different aminoacid composition) in order to address this subject.

Further work will include the study of larger proteins, their interactions with solvent, lipid, and, of greatest importance, the ligands that bind to the target protein. A later embodiment of the MD program will enable the prediction of binding constants for these ligands, and, given a sufficient throughput of calculations, ligands can effectively be screened for activity in this way. Ligands which possess suitable binding characteristics now become serious candidates ("lead compounds") for drug development, which is carried forward by the established techniques of medicinal chemistry. But this initial screening and selection process represents a tremendous saving of time and effort in the process of drug design.

Of ever increasing importance is the need to eliminate side effects for drugs, and here again, it will become possible to carry out "negative screening" of drugs against receptor molecules (insofar as their structures are available or can be calculated) that one wishes the drug *not* to bind to.

The simulation work described above poses a set of massive calculation problems, that can only be solved by use of massively parallel devices or clusters of high-performance workstations. Such applications require exactly the kind of advanced software that is the subject of the present work. It is only within the context of object-oriented software engineering, and in particular within the concept of *object parallelism*, that we can address this problem satisfactorily. Our future developments will accelerate the simulator as we are currently adding dynamic load balancing software to the current version. A key issue here is the fact that we achieve this without modifying the application specific code in the actual implementation.

References

1. S.W. de Leeuw, J.W. Perram, and E.R. Smith. Simulation of electrostatic systems in periodic boundary conditions. i lattice sums and dielectric constants. *Proc. Roy. Soc.*, 27:A373, 1980.
2. Wouter Joosen, Stijn Bijnens, and Pierre Verbaeten. Massively Parallel Programming Using Object Parallelism. In *Working Conference on Massively Parallel Programming Models*. IEEE, September 1993.
3. Wouter Joosen Stijn Bijnens and Pierre Verbaeten. A Reflective Invocation Scheme to realise Advanced Object Management. In M. Riveill R. Guerraoui, O. Nierstrasz, editor, *Object-Based Distributed Programming*, volume 791, pages 142–154. Springer Verlag, 1994.
4. J.W. Perram S.W. de Leeuw and H.G. Petersen. Hamilton's Equations for Constrained Dynamical Systems. *J. Stat. Phys.*, 61:1203–1222, 1990.

Mapping Strategies for
Sequential Sequence Comparison Algorithms
on LAN-Based Message Passing Architectures

Oswaldo Trelles-Salazar (1), Emilio L. Zapata (1)
and José-María Carazo (1,2)

(1) Department of Computer Architecture, University of Malaga, Spain and
(2) BioComputing Unit, Centro Nacional de Biotecnología (CSIC),
Univ.Autónoma, 28049 Madrid, Spain, e-mail: carazo@Samba.cnb.uam.es.

Abstract. In this work we discuss possible strategies for mapping sequential sequence comparison algorithms onto LAN-based message passing computer architectures. The software-integration tool used is the public-domain PVM 3.1 system. We present two possible mapping strategies, one centered around a file server using Guided Self Scheduling and the other based on socket to socket communications. We will show how communication latency and overall data-passing load is significantly reduced, as well as dynamic load balancing and fault tolerant capabilities are achieved. The mapping methodology used in this study can scale well from simple workstation clusters to far more complex general message-passing architectures.

Introduction

As a case study of problems in the biological sequence analysis field on LAN-based architectures, we have addressed the one of sequential sequence comparison. That is, given a query-sequence, search a large database in order to find information on this sequence by a one to one comparison with the rest of the sequences in the data base. In this work we have worked around the well known Smith-Waterman (Smith and Waterman, 1981) and FASTA (Pearson and Lipman, 1988) algorithms, although any sequential comparison method could in fact be used.

A number of approaches to parallel computing of biological sequences have been presented, starting with the pioneering work of Coulson et al. (1987) on on the ICL-DAP massive parallel computer; Deshpande et al. (1991) presented a work on the parallelization of the process of searching biological sequence databases on hypercube computers. On a completely different architecture, Jones (1992) discussed parallelization issues when using the Connection Machine 2 computer. On workstations networks, Barton (1991) introduced this topic in the molecular biology field also studying the sequence analysis problem using what we will refer to as a "file oriented approach (File-O)". A similar computational platform was later used by Miller et al. (1992) when addressing the topic of genetic linkage. At the level of software tools on these different architectures, the parallel programming language known as Lynda was compared to the use of machine-specific calls on the study case of a hypercube computer and a network of workstations by Miller at el. (1992). Still more recently, Pearson et al. (Pearson, personal communication) have worked on the generalization of the mapping strategy that they first used for hypercubes onto a cluster of workstations using a file oriented approach.

In this work we will propose two strategies for the parallelization of sequential sequence comparison algorithms, the first one using a file server and a guided self scheduling (GSS) scheme (Polychonospoulos, 1989), and the other one that is fully based on data transmission through sockets. The software integration tool that we will use is the public domain PVM, "Parallel Virtual Machine", system (Sunderam, 1990 : PVM version 3.1). We will discuss strategies for minimizing transmission overhead as well as for optimizing the execution control of the process, allowing for a fault-tolerant implementation and machine independence.

Algorithm

As far as the Smith and Waterman algorithm is concerned, the ratio between local computations and inter-workstation communications is quite high, and there are no problems in obtaining an efficient algorithmic parallelization. However, the situation is quite different for FASTP, since the local computational load is much lighter and communication factors may affect the whole process. Also, considering that workstations are becoming more powerful, the parallelization of FASTP on present day workstations may cast light on the problem of parallelizing the Smith and Waterman algorithm in next generation workstations. In the following we will show only results on FASTP, since this is the "worst case" from the point of view of parallelism due to the relatively few computations required per given sequence.

Implementation

Mapping strategies: Socket-oriented approach (Sock-O)

The basic and simple idea of our Sock-O approach is, essentially, that the client sends to each server the actual sequences to be processed through the sockets, the servers process these sequences and, finally, the client assembles the results. However, and as we will show, a very careful design of the client-server strategy has to be achieved in order for this approach to be really efficient.

On the maximization of the effective system bandwidth, and considering that the most obvious limitation of our virtual parallel computer is the reduced bandwidth of a typical Local Area Network, we started by measuring the effective bandwidth available for mapping our application. Figure 1 shows the effective bandwidth obtained in a Ethernet-LAN based cluster of seven HP-720's and one HP-705 when the client (a HP-720's) broadcasts a message of a fixed length to the seven other servers without waiting for any answer from them. It is clear that for the transmission to be effective the message length should be in the order of 4K for this computer platform. Also, in this situation in which there is processing neither on the client nor on the servers and where servers do not report back anything to the client, the effective bandwidth is in the order of 700 KB. Obviously, as we really map our application on this system and each server has to answer back to the client and the client itself has to do some processing, the effective data bandwidth will be reduced.

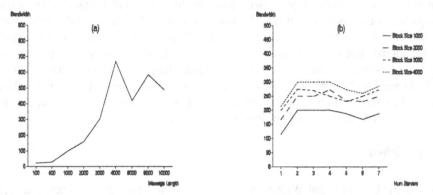

Fig.1. Effective data bandwidth for our Sock-O approach. (a) Bandwidth in Kb versus the message block size in bytes for a process involving transmissions with no further processing. (b) Bandwidth in Kb versus number of servers for our implementation of FASTP, involving communications from client to servers and back from servers to client, plus processing at client and servers.

Translating these results to our protein sequence comparison application, in which the average sequence length is of 361 aa, it is clear that transmission of individual sequences over the LAN would be very inefficient. We therefore devised an strategy that translated the problem of transmitting sequences into the one of transmitting blocks of sequences. A block of sequences is defined as a client assembled block of data containing the maximum number of sequences such that the total length of the block is less than or equal to 4K (for those special cases in which the sequence length is larger than 4K, a block is defined as one sequence transmitted over chunks of 4K). Conversely, servers also group their answers into blocks, each one containing the results of the processing of the sequences in the incoming block.

For an effective Dynamic Load Balance to be implemented, special considerations has to be given to the potential heterogeneity of the processing power across the virtual parallel computer have to be considered. The heterogeneity arises both from the difference in absolute computing power among the platforms integrated in the virtual parallel computer and from the fact that any given computer can be effectively disconnected or used for local calculations, resulting in a temporal dependency of the performance of that specific machine that is being used locally. Furthermore, the computing time that FASTP needs to calculate a similarity score on a given sequence depends on the sequence itself , both on its length and on its similarity to the (constant) query sequence.

It is clear that the mapping strategy should allocate more work to the effectively faster processors, bearing in mind that an element availability, and so its response time, may change during process execution. That is, the load must be distributed in a dynamic way, based on the information provided by the servers on the status of the different tasks allocated to them.

The goal of Dynamic Load Balance was achieved by making the client send a new block of sequences to a server only upon reception of a response block from that server. This strategy had a caveat, however, since it forces the server to remain inactive while receiving a new block of sequences from the client. We then introduced a buffering strategy in our block-based communication scheme, such that the client sent to servers more than just the next block of sequences to be analyzed, in such a way that servers never remained inactive after completition of a given block of data because another block was already awaiting in their communication buffer. The number of buffered blocks may depend on the system, specially as a function of the total bandwidth of the parallel computer. In our case a small value of one or two blocks was sufficient to allow servers not to remain inactive upon completition of a block. It is interesting to note that the overhead incurred by the client in the control of all the above processes is not very high, since the client CPU load remained in all cases around 5-20%.

That all these design considerations indeed resulted in a parallel implementation that used reasonably well the available communication bandwidth is shown in Fig.1.b. As a reference point, we comment that a direct Sock-O approach with neither grouping no buffering resulted in an effective bandwidth almost an order of magnitude lower. It is very important to notice that this effective bandwidth does not degrade when the number of servers increases, indicating that the proposed approach scales well with the number of processors.

Mapping strategies: File-oriented approach (File-O)

We will start by briefly presenting the parallelization strategy first proposed by Jones, 1991, then for Deshpande et al., 1991, for hypercube topologies, and latter adapted by Pearson to a cluster of workstation (Pearson, personal communication) when addressing the problem of sequential sequence comparison in parallel architectures. After this introduction our modifications to this approach will be presented.

In essence, the central idea is that the client process controls the server's dataflow by providing them with pointers to specific records to files. On reception of these pointers, servers access concurrently a central file system and directly read the information from the file system. In the original hypercube study of Deshpande et al., the file system was a dedicated piece of hardware designed to support concurrent file access from the different nodes of the hypercube, while in the cluster version the LAN file server, mounted on NFS, was actually used.

In this work we have enhanced this File-O procedure in two ways: Firstly, servers always report to client grouping their results into blocks (each NR sequences processed) and, secondly, a Guided Self Schedule (GSS) scheme has been followed to dynamically control the workload. In summary, when the client sends a message to the server it stores the number of sequences within the block. The server begin processing, sending a result message to the client every NR sequences. The client then decreases the server sequence counter and if the value so obtained is less than a certain base level, it sends a new block to prevent the server being starved of data.

Prior to a well-tuned implementation of this method is the identification of the effective system bandwidth for this File-O strategy. In Figure 2 we analyze the effective data bandwidth of the network as a function of the data block size to be read by each server from the central file system. Clearly, for the method to be effective the block size should be at least of the order of 50KB, with an average of about 140 protein sequences each, since smaller block sizes results in small and unstable effective bandwidths. In this way sequences were read by the servers in relatively large blocks and, in turn, servers returned their results to the client all grouped in one single block

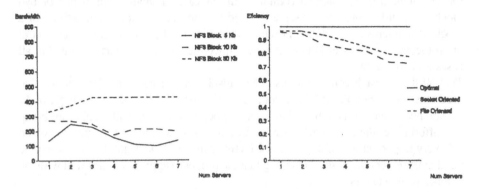

Fig 2. Effective bandwidth in Kbytes versus the number of servers as a function of the data block size in a File-O approach.

Fig 3. Performance comparison between the Sock-O approach and the (modified) File-O approach versus number of servers.

With respect to the second and more important modification, that is the introduction of a GSS scheme to dynamically control the work load, the basic idea is to "guide" the processors on the amount of work they read from the file server in such a way that they require larger amounts of data at the beginning than they do at the end. In this way all processors will end calculations almost at the same time.

Performance results.

In Figure 3 we show the relative performance of our modified version of the File-O approach using data block sizes of 50KB compared to the new Sock-O method in terms of Efficiency. As can be seen from this Figure, the measures of performance are very similar.

Discussion

Considering that the client processors in the Sock-O approach had a computational load of only about 20%, and that GSS is a very good load balancing mechanism in our File-O approach, we would expect both methods to scale well to larger size networks of workstations.

Considering the potential heterogeneity of a network of workstations, as well as the possible algorithmic dependencies between the computing time and the specific composition of the sequences to be analyzed, a very careful analysis of how the work load is distributed among the different processors as a function of time is mandatory. Our Sock-O approach clearly provides a simple and direct way to balance any changing situation through the sending of relatively small blocks. On the other hand, the load balancing in the File-O approach in not that fine, since it requires block sizes of an order the magnitude larger, but the introducction of GSS assures that all servers keep continuously working and that all of them end at about the same time.

Both Sock-O and File-O approach are implemented in such a way that client transmissions stop upon detection of a partial system failure (both, server process failure or server machine failure). The recovery strategy we devised is very simple and powerful : The Client process calculates the few extra lost sequences when all servers finish their parallel jobs.

The portability of our approaches may be expected to be very good since the three main parameter of the method (data block size, the grouping of answers from the servers, and the buffering strategy) can be tuned to the specific characteristics of the system in terms of the effective data communication bandwidth and the computer power of the nodes. Our Sock-O approach also, is independent on the presence of special I/O hardware in the parallel system.

References

1. Barton, G. (1991), Scanning protein sequence data banks using a distributed processing network, CABIOS, **7**(1), 85-88.
2. Coulson,A., Collins,J. and Lyall,A. (1987), Protein and nucleic-acid sequence database searching:a suitable case for parallel processing, The Comp.Journal,**30**(5),420-424.
3. Deshpande, A.S., Richards, D.S. and Pearson, W.R. (1991),A platform for biological sequence comparison on parallel computers, CABIOS, **7**(2), 237-247.
4. Jones, R. (1992),, Sequence pattern matching on a massively parallel computer, CABIOS, **8**(4), 377-383.
5. Pearson, W.R. and Lipman, D.J.(1988), Improved tools for biological sequence comparison, Proc. Nat. Acad. Sci. USA, **85**, 2444-2448.
6. Miller, P.L., Nadkarni, P.M. and Pearson, W. (1992a), Comparing machine-independent versus machine-specific parallelization of a software platform for biological sequence comparison, CABIOS, **8**(2), 167-175.
7. Miller, P.L., Nadkarni, P.M. and Bercovitz, P.A. (1992b), Harnessing networked workstations as a powerful parallel computer,CABIOS, **8**(2), 141-147.
8. Polychonospoulos, C.D. (1989), Static and dynamic loop scheduling, in Parallel programming and compilers, Kluwer Academic Publishers.
9. Sunderam, V.S. (1990), PVM: A framework for parallel distributed computing, Concurrence, Practice and Experience, **2**(4), 315-339.

Parallel computing in Quantum Chemistry - message passing and beyond for a general ab initio program system

Hans Lischka and Holger Dachsel
Institut für Theoretische Chemie und Strahlenchemie, University of Vienna, Austria
Ron Shepard
Argonne National Laboratory, Argonne, Illinois
and
Robert J. Harrison
Pacific Northwest Laboratory, Richland, Washington

1. Introduction

One of the most prominent aims in Computational Chemistry is the modeling of chemical reactions and the prediction of molecular properties. Quantum chemical methods are used for the calculation of molecular structures, spectra, reaction energy profiles and many other interesting quantities. Nowadays, the accuracy of the theoretical calculations can compete to an increasing extent with the experimental one. Therefore, theoretical methods have become a very useful tool for the solution of many realistic chemical questions. The just described capabilities are not only of pure academic interest. Quantum chemical methods are also well established in the research laboratories of the chemical industry. There, they are used successfully for many routine applications. However, what is much more important, they provide a detailed source of information which helps in a better understanding of chemical processes - a knowledge which is crucial for a directed development of new classes of chemical compounds and materials. All of the computational methods used are extremely time consuming and rely heavily on the availablity of sufficient computer power. Parallel computing is the only way to open new dimensions in the field of the computer simulation of molecules.

A great variety of quantum chemical methods exist ranging from the standard Hartree-Fock theory to sophisticated electron correlation approaches. From a computational point of view all these methods require rather lengthy and complicated program codes (ten thousands to several hundreds of thousands of lines) and have to handle a large amount of data to be stored on external devices. In the simplest case, the Hartree-Fock (SCF) method, "direct" algorithms have eliminated the I/O and storage bottleneck and have opened the way to parallel implementations. For post-Hartree-Fock methods the situation is much more complicated as will be demonstrated below. Therefore, most of the previous attempts in parallelizing quantum chemical ab initio programs concentrated on SCF methods.

Starting with the pioneering work by Clementi and coworkers on "loosely coupled array of processors (LCAP)" [1] several investigations on the parallelization of SCF programs have been reported [2-11]. In addition, electron correlation methods based on Møller-Plesset Second Order Perturbation Theory [12], Coupled-Cluster theory [13,14] and full CI [15,16] have been considered as well. For reviews on the use massively parallel computers in Quantum Chemistry see e.g. [17,18].

Our investigations presented here are a continuation of our previous work [19] on the the parallelization of the COLUMBUS program system [20,21]. The COLUMBUS program is based on the multireference single- and double-excitation configuration interaction (MRSDCI) approach, is very well portable and runs on a large variety of computers including numerous Unix-based workstations, VAX/VMS minicomputers, IBM mainframes and Cray supercomputers.

2. Quantum Chemical Methods

In the configuration interaction method (see e.g. [22]) the Ritz variation principle is used to solve the molecular Schrödinger equation

$$H\Psi = E\Psi \tag{1}$$

where H is the Hamiltonian operator describing the molecular system, Ψ is a many-electron wave function and E is the molecular energy. Expansion of Ψ into a linear combination of configuration state functions (CSFs)

$$\Psi = \sum_i c_i \Psi_i . \tag{2}$$

and application of the variation principle leads to the following matrix eigenvalue problem

$$\mathbf{Hc} = \tilde{E}\mathbf{c}. \tag{3}$$

$\mathbf{H}$ is the matrix representation of the Hamiltonian H in the basis of the CSFs, the vector $\mathbf{c}$ collects the coefficients c_i of Eq. (1) and $\tilde{E}$ is an approximation to the exact energy E. The many-electron functions Ψ_i are constructed from one-elctron functions (molecular orbitals, MOs) Φ_j according to the Pauli principle. The MOs in turn are expanded into a fixed basis χ_k (atomic orbitals, AOs) as

$$\Phi_j = \sum_k d_{kj}\chi_k . \tag{4}$$

The actual choice of CSFs and basis sets has a long tradition in Quantum Chemistry and need not be discussed here. In MRCI wave functions, the dimension of the matrix eigenvalue problem in Eq. (3) can easily reach hundreds of thousands or several millions. Because of the properties of the Hamiltonian operator the Hamiltonian matrix $\mathbf{H}$ is sparse. Without going into details, the following main steps have to be executed: calculation of one- and two-electron integrals in the atomic orbital (AO) basis, calculation of molecular orbitals (MOs) by means of a SCF or MCSCF procedure, transformation of the AO integrals to the MO basis and solution of the aforementioned eigenvalue problem. The last step is the most complicated and in many cases also by far the most time consuming one. For this reason we concentrated on it even though it is clear that, finally, all the aforementioned computational steps have to be parallelized.

In most cases one is only interested in a few of the lowest eigenvalues and eigenvectors in Eq. (3). They are usually obtained by a subspace expansion into a set of trial vectors according to Davidson [23]. In this method the eigenvector $\mathbf{c}$ is approximated by a vector $\mathbf{u}$ which is expanded into a linear combination of correction vectors $\mathbf{v}_i$

$$\mathbf{u} = \sum_{i=1}^{N} \alpha_i \mathbf{v}_i \tag{5}$$

N is the dimension of the subspace and the expansion coefficients α_i are determined from the small eigenvalue problem $\overline{\mathbf{H}}\alpha = \overline{\mathbf{E}}\alpha$ where $\overline{H}_{ij} = \mathbf{v}_i'\mathbf{H}\mathbf{v}_j$. From the residuum $\mathbf{r} = (\mathbf{H} - \overline{E})\mathbf{u}$ a new expansion vector $\mathbf{v}_{N+1}$ is computed (for details see [23]) and an improved approximation $\mathbf{u}$ according to (5) is determined. This iteration scheme is completed until a certain convergence limit is reached. The most time consuming step is the calculation of the matrix-vector product

$$\mathbf{w}_i = \mathbf{H}\mathbf{v}_i. \tag{6}$$

Because of the aforementioned sparsity of the matrix $\mathbf{H}$ the Hamiltonian matrix times vector product in Eq. (6) can be split into a series of dense matrix operations in such a way that $\mathbf{H}$ is never constructed explicitly (direct CI). The dense matrices are, however, of the dimension of the MO basis only (i.e. up to a few hundred at most). We use dense-matrix product kernels (e.g. BLAS(3) routines [24]) which have proven to be very efficient on vector and scalar pipelined computers. In this way efficiency and portability are achieved to a very large degree. The computational step shown in Eq. (6) is not only important in terms of CPU time but also because large amounts of data (two-electron integrals) have to be processed and because the whole logic of the computation of the respective contributions to $\mathbf{H}$ (formula tape) has to be done here.

3. Parallel algorithm

3.1. General considerations

Our strategy for parallelization was strongly guided by portability considerations. We wanted to have a program system which should work efficiently on shared memory and on distributed memory machines including workstation clusters as well. From the aforementioned small size of the dense matrices an attempt to parallelize at this matrix level was not very attractive. After analyzing various choices we decided for coarse grain parallelization at the topmost level in our program [19]. In order to do this, $\mathbf{v}$ and $\mathbf{w}$ are split into segments. The multiplication of the symmetric matrix $\mathbf{H}$ times the vector $\mathbf{v}$ (Eq. (6)) was originally written in our sequential program as loops over segments pairs in the following way:

```
DO SEG1 = 1 , NSEG
    READ vSEG1 , wSEG1
    DO SEG2 = 1 , SEG1
        READ vSEG2 , wSEG2
        UPDATE wSEG1 , wSEG2      ! Contributions from HSEG1,SEG2
                                   and HSEG2,SEG1 Hamiltonian blocks
        WRITE wSEG2
    ENDDO
    WRITE wSEG1
ENDDO
```

The actual work - not shown in this scheme - is done in the routine UPDATE. Also not shown is the handling of the case SEG1 = SEG2 and various other special cases. In the parallel program the same loop structure as in the sequential case is used. To each process work for updating one segment pair is passed at a time and load balancing is used to distribute the work evenly over all processes. The advantage of this scheme is that the routine UPDATE which comprises most of the total program code remains completely intact. Thus, we can still use the optimized dense matrix multiplication routines and it will be straightforward to make use of any further improvements which will be made in the sequential program. For this scheme message passing is adequate and straightforward to implement. The actual implementation is performed via the portable programming toolkit TCGMSG developed by one of us (RJH) [25]. TCGMSG supplies a set of Fortran and C callable library routines by which message passing can be introduced into the application program code. A Single Program Multiple Data approach is used.

3.2. First implementations

In our first implementation [19] only the sparse matrix vector vector product of Eq. (6) was parallelized. The vector v was kept on disk as one single file shared by all processes. Local copies of the update vector w were held for each process and were added up via a global sum operation after completion of the loop over all segment pairs. The Davidson step was not parallelized at all. This version was installed on a variety of parallel computers like the Alliant FX/2800, the CRAY Y-MP, the Convex C2 and the Intel iPSC/860. The program worked very well on the Alliant, CRAY and Convex. E.g., on a dedicated 8 processor CRAY Y-MP roughly one GFLOP per wall clock second was achieved. On the iPSC/860 a serious degradation in performance was observed already with 7 processors due to the slow data transfer rate to and from disk.

In any case, we could show that our overall approach of defining tasks by segmenting the v and w vectors was successful. Thus, in the next step efforts were made to reduce the I/O while changing the basic outline of the program as little as possible. This goal was achieved by introducing two features: a) the concept of a local virtual disk and b) by developing a data compression scheme for the v and w vectors. The virtual disk gave us a flexible tool to store files in the local central memory of each processor. By means of the data compression the size of the v and w vectors were reduced by factors of four to five. Obviously, best results could be achieved when all data could be kept in core.

This second program version was tested on the Intel Touchstone Delta and and the IBM SP1. Now, the performance was very good for up to about 32 processors. Almost 100% efficiency could be achieved for the H·v step. However, we still had the bottleneck to distribute the v vector for each iteration to all processors and to perform a global sum for w at the end of each iteration. Also, the Davidson iteration was still not performed in parallel. From our experience gained so far it was clear that we needed more flexibility in the data organization. For larger calculations we could not keep identical copies of all files in the memory of each processor as would have been necessary for an optimal calculation. What we needed was the possibility to distribute the contents of a file globally over the memory of all processors and to allow all compute processes asynchronous access to these data. Again, as it has already been stressed above, portability was a crucial requirement for such software tools.

3.3. Global arrays

The global-array tools [26] which we were using can be characterized in the following way: these tools support one-sided access to data structures (here limited to one- and two-dimensional arrays) in the spirit of shared memory. With some effort this can be done portably, and in return for this investment we gain a much easier programming environment, speeding code development and improving extensibility and maintainability. We also gain a significant performance enhancement from increased asynchrony of execution of processes. The tools efficiently support both task and data parallelism.

By means of the global-array tools all major files (**v** and **w**, two-electron integrals) were now stored as a single copy. In particular, reading of the **v** vector and accumulating the contributions to the **w** vector could be done asynchronously by the different processes as needed. No overall distribution step at the beginning of an iteration and no collection of results at the end of each iteration is necessary anymore. It was also straightforward to parallelize the Davidson procedure.

3.4. Benchmark calculations

At present, the program works on the Intel Touchstone Delta and on the IBM SP1. Benchmark tests (see below) were taken on the Delta, those on the SP1 will follow shortly. As test example we used a C_{2v}-$pVTZ$ calculation on the CH_3 molecule as given in full detail in Ref. [19]. The dimension of the CI expansion is 624 334 CSFs. The number of segments was held constant at 24 giving 481 segment pairs (including subdivisions of certain pair types) in total. Calculations with up to 112 processors were performed.

In Fig. 1 for one typical iteration the speedup with the number of processors is shown and compared to the theoretical value.

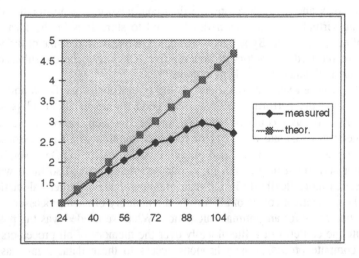

The results are very satisfactory up to about 64 processors and then start to deteriorate. Beginning with 96 processors there is no increase in the speedup anymore. The main reason for this retardation is the fact that the load balancing mechanism is not so efficient anymory because only a few segment pairs are available for each processor. Moreover, also other events which were not relevant before now increase in relative importance.

4. Conclusions and outlook

We regard it as a great success that we can run the CI section of the COLUMBUS program system - which incorporates all the complexity of the MRSDCI method - efficiently on a distributed memory system like the Delta. Investigations on the SP1 machine are in progress. Our next main step will be the introduction of a "double direct" approach which avoids the storage and sorting of the 3- and 4-external two-electron integrals. A sequential, AO driven code is already available [27]. We are confident that with this new features included we will be able to run our program efficiently on several hundred processors.

Acknowledgments

This work was performed under the auspices of the Austrian "Fonds zur Förderung der wissenschaftlichen Forschung", project nr. P9032 and the High Performance Computing and Communication Program of the Office of Scientific Computing, U.S. Department of Energy. The calculations on the Intel Touchstone Delta were performed at the CCSF at Caltech, those on the IBM SP1 at the ACRF of the Argonne National Laboratory. We are grateful for the competent support of our work by these computer centers.

References

1　E. Clementi, in *Modern Techniques in Computational Chemistry*, chap. 1, E. Clementi, Ed., Escom Science Publishers, 1990; D. Folsom, in *Modern Techniques in Computational Chemistry*, chap. 27, E. Clementi, Ed., Escom Science Publishers, 1990

2　M. Dupuis and J. D. Watts, Theor. Chim. Acta **71** (1987) 91

3　R. J. Harrison and R. A. Kendall, Theor. Chim. Acta **79** (1991) 337

4　H. P. Lüthi, J. E. Mertz, M. W. Feyereisen and J. E. Almlöf, J. Comp. Chem. **13** (1992) 160

5　S. Kindermann, E. Michel and P. Otto, J. Comp. Chem. **13** (1992) 414

6　M. W. Feyereisen, R. A. Kendall, J. Nichols, D. Dame and J. T. Golab, J. Comp. Chem. **14** (1993) 818

7　S. Brode, H. Horn, M. Ehrig, D. Moldrup, J. E. Rice and R. Ahlrichs, J. Comp. Chem. **14** (1993) 1142

8　M. W. Schmidt, K. K. Baldridge, J. A. Boatz, S. T. Elbert, M. S. Gordon, J. H. Jensen, S. Koseki, N. Matsunaga, K. A. Nguyen, S. Su, T. L. Windus, M. Dupuis and J. A. Montgomery, Jr., J. Comp. Chem. **14** (1993) 1347

9　M. E. Colvin, C. L. Janssen, R. A. Whiteside and C. H. Tong, Theor. Chim. Acta **84** (1993) 301

10　L. G. M. Petterson and T. Faxen, Theor. Chim. Acta **85** (1993) 345

11　A. Burkhardt, U. Wedig and H. G. v. Schnering, Theor. Chim. Acta **86** (1993) 497

12　J. D. Watts and M. Dupuis, J. Comp. Chemistry **9** (1988) 158

13 A. P. Rendell, T. J. Lee and R. Lindh, Chem. Phys. Lett. **194** (1992) 84

14 A. P. Rendell, M. F. Guest, R. A. Kendall. J. Comp. Chem. **14** (1993) 1429

15 R. J. Harrison and E. A. Stahlberg, J. Parallel and Distributed Computing (1992)

16 G. L. Bendazzoli and S. Evangelisti, J. Chem. Phys. **98** (1993) 3141

17 M. E. Colvin, R. A. Whiteside and H. F. Schaefer III in *Methods in Computational Chemistry*, vol. 3, S. Wilson, Ed., Plenum, N.Y., p. 167

18 R. A. Kendall, Int. J. Quantum Chem. **S27** (1993) 769

19 M. Schüler, T. Kovar, H. Lischka, R. Shepard and R. J. Harrison, Theor. Chim. Acta **84** (1993) 489

20 H. Lischka, R. Shepard, F. Brown, and I. Shavitt, Int. J. Quantum Chem. **S15** (1981) 91

21 R. Shepard, I. Shavitt, R. M. Pitzer, D. C. Comeau, M. Pepper, H. Lischka, P. G. Szalay, R. Ahlrichs, F. B. Brown, J. G. Zhao, Int. J. Quantum Chem. **S22** (1988) 149

22 I. Shavitt, in *Modern Theoretical Chemistry*, vol. 3, H. F. Schaefer III, Ed., Plenum 1977, p. 189

23 E. R. Davidson, J Comp Phys **17** (1975) 84

24 a) J. J. Dongarra, J. DuCroz, S. Hammerling and R. Hanson, ACM Trans. on Math. Soft. **14** (1988) 1
    b) J. J. Dongarra, J. DuCroz, I. Duff and S. Hammerling, ACM Trans. on Math. Soft. **16** (1990) 1

25 R. J. Harrison, Intern. J. Quantum Chem. **40** (1991) 847

26 R. J. Harrison, Theor. Chim. Acta **84** (1993) 363 and unpublished further work

27 T. Kovar and H. Lischka, unpublished results

Solving Dynamic and Quantum Chemical Problems with the Help of Concurrent Processors

P.BLECKMANN and F.H. WALTER
Universität Dortmund, Fachbereich Chemie, D–44221 Dortmund
e–Mail: uch001 at unidozr.hrz.uni–dortmund.de

Introduction

In this paper we consider algorithms in which computations are to be performed on particle–particle interactions in molecules, in solid phases and in molecules adsorbed on metal surfaces. The calculations must be carried out for all possible pairs of objects in a data base. The transputer system (Fig. 2) has been employed in the simulation of the molecular geometries of all the 12 isomers of dichlorohexane.

Description

Molecular dynamics calculations require algorithms which deal with short–range interactions between all possible pairs of atoms (van der Waals interactions). When the intermolecular force law has long–range components (Coulombic components) we take into account all the pairs of atoms in the unit cells. Thus, long range interactions involving more than a few thousand atoms (in quantum mechanical terms: electron–electron, electron–nucleus, and nucleus–nucleus interactions) provide a challenge for even the fastest computers.

A unit cell with n atoms, which can be either separate or bonded in clusters, is capable of 3n lattice vibrations. Three of these will be the acoustic branches and will have zero frequency when the wave vector is equal to zero. In the external mode approach, one views the unit cell as containing m rigidly bound molecules with their external branches (3m–3) corresponding to the translation vibrations and the remaining 3m to the rotational vibrations (librations). Three translations must be assigned to the free translations of the unit cell.

The degrees of freedom in which the different atoms of the molecule(s) move relative to each other are referred to as the internal vibrations. The treatment of the lattice vibrations by use of the GF–matrix method is described in the literature [1,2]. In order to calculate the internal vibrations of the molecules as well as the external lattice vibrations in the crystal, we used a calculation model which takes into account interactions between molecular and lattice vibrations [3]. We have therefore introduced flexible vibrating molecules coupled to their neighbours by intermolecular atom–atom forces [1]. In this way, a three–dimensional macromolecule is formed, the basic element of which is the crystal unit cell.

The potential function used for this model in normal mode calculations contains force constants corresponding to an intramolecular component ΔV_{mol} and to an intermolecular component ΔV_{latt}:

$$\Delta V = \Delta V_{mol} + \Delta V_{latt} \tag{1}$$

The intermolecular component of the potential function was calculated from the Buckingham–type potential function

$$V = Ar^{-6} + B \cdot \exp(-\alpha r) \tag{2}$$

for all the intermolecular atom–atom bonds. The values of A, B and α can be taken from Kitaigorodskii et al. [4] and Deprez [5].

If we denote the number of atoms (particles) in the unit cell by N_p, the total potential of a system of atoms which interact via a pair potential $\Phi(y_i, y_j)$ is given by

$$2V = \sum_{i=1}^{N_p} \sum_{j=1}^{N_p} \Phi(y_i, y_j) \tag{3}$$

By choosing an appropriate basis co–ordinate column vector y and the transposed row vector ỹ and setting up the kinetic energy matrix $\mathbf{G_y}$ and the force constant matrix $\mathbf{F_y}$ defined by

$$2T = \tilde{y} \ \mathbf{G_y}^{-1} \ \dot{y} \tag{4}$$

$$2V = \tilde{y} \ \mathbf{F_y}^{-1} \ y \tag{5}$$

we obtain

$$\tilde{y} \ \mathbf{F_y}^{-1} \ y = \sum_{i=1}^{N_p} \sum_{j=1}^{N_p} \Phi(y_i, y_j) \tag{6}$$

The expression $G_y \cdot F_y$ is diagonalized by the transformation $y = L_y \cdot Q$ (with L_y being the normal mode matrix and Q the normal coordinate matrix).

$$\tilde{L}_y \; G_y \; F_y \; L_y = \Lambda \tag{7}$$

The a–th diagonal element λ_a of Λ is the a–th frequency parameter. The a–th normal frequency ν_a is given by

$$\lambda_a = 4\pi^2 c^2 \nu_a^2 \tag{8}$$

The a–th normal coordinate Q_a is given by

$$Q_a = A_a \cdot \sin(2\pi c \nu_a t + \delta) \tag{9}$$

A_a is the amplitude, c the velocity of light.

In our contribution we present the basic communication strategy by outlining the method for calculating the vibrational potential energy of a system of particles that interact via pair potentials.

To solve this problem we use a very simple interconnection topology which is able to evaluate the total potential energy by solving all the pair potentials. For this purpose we connect n processors in a ring. We first have to distribute all the particles in the molecule or in the unit cell (in the case of solid phases) among the n processors. Every particle (atom or molecule) "visits" all the processors in the ring by taking n–1 steps in either a clockwise or counterclockwise direction. The point crucial to the practicality of this method is that the communications and the calculations of the pair potentials can be done concurrently.

Parallel Analysis

Problems of this type involving long–range and short–range forces appear to be particularly suitable for parallel processing [6]. We first have to distribute all the particles in the unit cell between the processors. That means, if there are n_p particles, and n_{proc} of them are stored in a processor, then that processor must obtain the attributes (Cartesian coordinates, masses, charges etc.) of the other $n_p - n_{proc}$ particles and compute $n_{proc} \cdot n_p$ pairwise interactions.

The time required for the calculation is:

$$t_{cal} = n_{proc} \cdot n_p \cdot t_{pair} \tag{10}$$

where t_{pair} is the time needed to compute the interaction of a pair of atoms. In order to evaluate all of the pairs of atoms, these pairs must meet in some processor at some time in the calculation. In this manner every particle must visit every processor and, while there, its interactions with all the particles in that processor must be tallied.

To solve this problem the processors are arranged in a ring. Then we divide the total number of particles into N equal parts and assign these to the N processors (Fig.1a) so that every particle can visit all the processors in the ring by taking $N - 1$ steps in either a clockwise or a counterclockwise direction (Fig.1b). Thus the N equal parts of different particles, pt_1 through pt_N, can visit the same N processors.

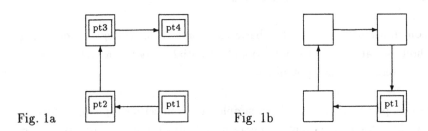

Fig. 1a   Fig. 1b

Performing a Task On a Transputer Cluster

In general, solving a problem on a transputer cluster is independent of the cluster's configuration. The transputer station which we use consists of 16 processors (type T800), the host processor and the graphic processor. The configuration can be seen as a combination of a pipe — which begins with the TBX host processor and ends with the VG1280 graphics processor — and four rings, each of them holding four processors (Fig.2; one of the rings is emphasized.).

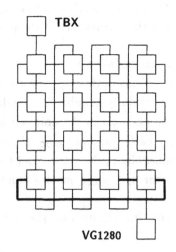

Fig. 2

A transputer cluster configuration is written down in the 'resource map', which does not need to be altered by the user.

The total parallel program is called a 'task force'; it consists of separate units, the 'tasks'. The way tasks interact within a task force is described in a CDL[1]–script [7].

While the CDL–script obtains a general description of the task force communication, the tasks themselves have to be equipped with special read/write commands to perform the data transfer. These are the POSIX read/write commands. The programming language generally used for writing a task is C, but the use of FORTRAN is also possible.

Parallel Analysis: Performance

The data flow scheme of the parallel decomposition can be seen in Fig.3 . One master task controls the four–membered worker ring, sending the four parts of the input data file to the workers and, after finishing the calculations, the master task receives the results. It also executes the I/O from and to the host computer. Data channel numbering always starts with '0'. The even numbers represent read and odd numbers write channels.

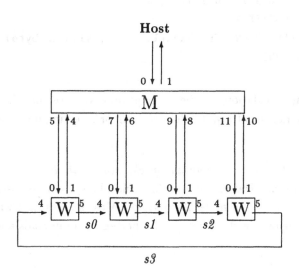

Fig. 3

The CDL–script belonging to that task force looks like this ('♯' is the beginning of a comment, '<>' is the symbol for a bidirectional communication):

---

[1] Component Distribution Language

♯ COMPONENT DECLARATION: DATA STREAMS
component worker[0] {stream , , , , <|{s3}, >|{s0} ;}
component worker[1] {stream , , , , <|{s0}, >|{s1} ;}
component worker[2] {stream , , , , <|{s1}, >|{s2} ;}
component worker[3] {stream , , , , <|{s2}, >|{s3} ;}

♯ TASK FORCE DEFINITION
master (,[k<4] <> worker{k})

Each of the four processors calculates equation (3). The worker program — written in FORTRAN here — performs the calculation for the *NPU* particles 'belonging' to the processor *u* and the *NPV* particles of the part which *u* has actually received:

```
     DO 10 K=1,4
        CALL POS READ(channel, array, size in byte)
        DO 20 I=1,NPU
          DO 20 J=1,NPV
            C a l c u l a t i o n
  20        CONTINUE
        CALL POS WRITE(channel, array, size in byte)
  10 CONTINUE
```

Because the calculations on the different processors require the same amount of time, no worker has to wait before sending or receiving information.

Parallel Applications of Quantum–mechanical Methods
Quantum–mechanical calculations for molecular systems are used to study problems in chemistry and molecular physics. Most studies deal with electron density phenomena, the structure and properties of compounds and dynamical behaviour.

Initially an apprximate molecular geometry is calculated using a well–established molecular modelling method. In a further step the results (Cartesian coordinates of the atoms in the molecule) are fitted to the exact geometry with the help of standard quantum–mechanical methods [8–11]. We have parallelized this step using our parallel processing system (Fig. 2). It has been employed in the simulation of the geometries of all the 12 isomers of dichlorohexane (Table).

Speed–ups of various combinations (from 2 to 12) of different dichlorohexane isomers (Table) have been obtained (Fig. 4a,b). The same version of the quantum chemical AMPAC–program–package runs on all the processors (from 2 to 12).

Table	1	1,1–Dichlorohexane	42.77	min.
	2	1,2–Dichlorohexane	26.69	"
	3	1,3–Dichlorohexane	33.85	"
	4	1,4–Dichlorohexane	29.89	"
	5	1,5–Dichlorohexane	26.92	"
	6	1,6–Dichlorohexane	21.78	"
	7	2,2–Dichlorohexane	13.01	"
	8	2,3–Dichlorohexane	27.81	"
	9	2,4–Dichlorohexane	34.56	"
	10	2,5–Dichlorohexane	38.82	"
	11	3,3–Dichlorohexane	19.61	"
	12	3,4–Dichlorohexane	25.12	"

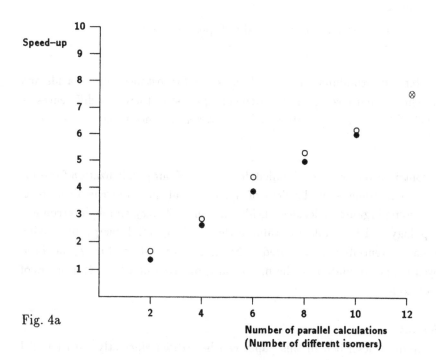

Fig. 4a

Number of parallel calculations
(Number of different isomers)

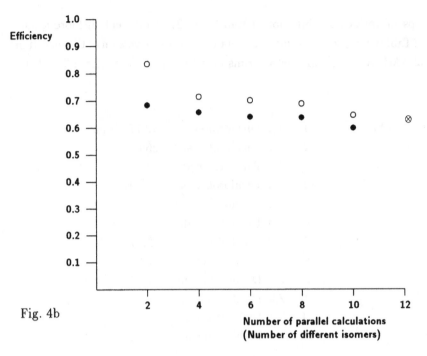

Fig. 4b

Number of parallel calculations
(Number of different isomers)

Fig. 4   Parallel calculation of several dichlorohexane isomers: speed–up and
efficiency.
O best   ● worst results;   ⊗ all (12) possible isomers.

Other interesting combinations of molecules are, for instance, amino acids and
heterocyclic aromatic compounds. Depending on size, there are differences of
up to 2000% between the shortest and longest performance time.

Results
In this contribution we give a detailed description of our parallelization for some
exemplary experiments in the field of dynamic and quantum chemical treatments of some organic molecules (dichlorohexane). A very simple interconnection topology which is able to evaluate the total potential energy by solving
all the pair potentials is represented. The transputer system (Fig. 2) has been
employed in the simulation of the molecular geometries of all the 12 isomers of
dichlorohexane.

Conclusions
The techniques described in this paper can be treated efficiently with parallel
computers and can be applied to any problem that requires the treatment of
every pair of objects in a molecule or in a unit cell. We have found that the

applications of these algorithms to problems involving short– and long–range forces is extremely efficient. This is quite surprising, since the calculations are very communication–intensive. The communication topology is extremely simple. Communications take place concurrently around a ring of processors.

Literature

[1] P.Bleckmann, B.Schrader, *Ber. Bunsenges. Phys. Chem.* **75**, 1279 (1971)

[2] T.Shimanouchi *et al.*, *J. Chem. Phys.* **35**, 1597 (1961)

[3] P.Bleckmann, M. Thibud, *J. Raman Spec.* **12**, 105 (1982)

[4] A.I.Kitaigorodskii, Molekularni kristali, (Nauka, Moskva, 1971)

[5] G.Deprez, Thesis, University of Lille (1969)

[6] G.Fox et al., *"Solving problems on concurrent processors"*, Prentice–Hall, 1st Ed. 1988, p.155 f.

[7] *"The CDL Guide"*, Distributed Software Ltd., 1990.

[8] R.C.Bingham, M.J.S.Dewar, D.H.Lo, *J. Am. Chem. Soc.* **97**, (1975)

[9] M.J.S.Dewar, W.Thiel, *J. Am. Chem. Soc.* **99**, 4899, (1977)

[10] M.J.S.Dewar, E.G.Zoebisch, E.F.Healy, *J. Am. Chem. Soc.* **107**, 3902, (1985)

[11] T.Clark, *A Handbook of Computational Chemistry*, J.Wiley& Sons, New York, 1st Ed. 1985

Intelligent Software: The OpenMol Program

Geerd H F Diercksen
Max-Planck-Institut für Astrophysik
Karl-Schwarzschild-Strasse 1
D-85740 Garching bei München, Germany
e-mail: ghd@mpa-garching.mpg.de

Intelligent software is the answer to the growing complexity of large packages, used in Quantum Chemistry and other fields, and leads to a program which is easy to use, flexible and open to evolutionary development.

Abstract:

The case is argued that the rigorous use of expert systems and abstract data types for quantum chemical calculations can lead to a more open, more flexible program, which is easier for a novice to use but also, through the possibility of rapid-prototyping and symbolic manipulation, for an expert to exploit as an important working tool. The ideas behind this program are, however, quite general and apply equally to many other scientific areas where experience and different numerical techniques have to be combined in a flexible way to produce useful results.

Introduction

In principle, Quantum Chemistry offers the chemist, whether in academia or industry, an independent method of investigating molecular structure, properties and processes. It has the advantage over experimental techniques that it can handle short-lived, or chemically impossible, species as easily as stable molecules, and excited states, or transition states, as well as ground states. Using it, a wide variety of properties, electrical, magnetic, nuclear, spectroscopic or thermal can be calculated. This versatility ensures that many chemists, who have no wish to follow the details of how its results are obtained, may be interested in using it. In practice, for all properties, it is necessary first to calculate, or at least to postulate, a molecular wavefunction and, since the wavefunction is always of limited accuracy, the derived results are also limited in accuracy. The accuracy problem becomes progressively more serious as the number of electrons in the molecule increases. The uncritical use of the program to produce results for various properties can then lead to false conclusions. This justifies our emphasis on estimating the accuracy of results.

OpenMol

OpenMol [1] is an integrated program for electronic structure and property calculations on molecules. User guidance, the evaluation and interpretation of results and computer based learning are the three unique features of OpenMol that distinguish it from all other programs in the field. The concept of OpenMol is based on the fundamental ideas of two software concepts, the rule based expert system and the abstract data type model. These together lead to the syntheses of knowledge engineering and numerical data processing and give birth to the idea of *intelligent software* The rigorous use of these concepts has lead to a more flexible program, which is easier for a novice to use but also, through the possibility of rapid prototyping and symbolic manipulation, for an expert to exploit as an important working tool. abstract data types are at the core of object-oriented technology, allowing for flexibility but preserving the efficiency of numerical operations.

The abstract data types of the OpenMol program have been chosen so that the program will have a shell structure. There is a kernel of abstract data types representing the results of quantum mechanical methods. This kernel is surrounded by a shell of abstract data types, called the kernel interface. The operations in the kernel will only access instances of abstract data types in the kernel interface. The kernel interface is surrounded by a shell of abstract data types defining and integrating software resources initially external to OpenMol, like the knowledge systems, data bases, other user programs, graphical systems, and the user interface. This three level structure of the OpenMol numerical software has important advantages. The kernel operations, by interfacing with the outer shell only via the kernel interface, are kept independent of the details of the external world. This very much simplifies the porting of the kernel to other hard- and software environments.

The use of the abstract data types allows the calculation to be divided into two layers. At the upper layer all decisions are taken and all results made available. At the lower level all the details needed for the computer to perform the calculation are provided in subroutines which correspond to the operations of the upper level. This division means that the upper level is machine-independent and the lower level is more readily portable than are most packages. This move to the rigorous use of two levels of abstraction in the software constitutes a *revolution in quantum chemistry packages* which will lead to more useful and more transparent programs.

The solution of any problem in computational chemistry divides naturally into four phases which are largely independent and consecutive. In the first, the definition phase, the goal of the calculation must be defined as precisely as possible. This will require the specification of the molecular system, the property and the accuracy needed to establish or reject the theoretical hypothesis. Then, in the strategy phase, the major decisions in the calculation, such as selecting the form of the trial wavefunction and determining the input data required to compute the property, must be taken. To find the strategy to achieve the goal requires the exercise of considerable judgement bearing on the previous experience of such calculations. The process can even be iterative. For example, if the initial goal cannot be reached using the available resources, some modified goal may be substituted. The third phase is the numerical calculation itself. Nowadays, with computer networks, this involves both the efficient use of the resources available and the preparation of the calculation using independent operations optimised to suit the characteristics of the distributed computer system. The interpretation phase may provide useful correlations between various properties. It must, through its evaluation of the accuracy attained, determine whether the goal of the entire effort has, or has not, been achieved.

OpenMol follows these four phases in its structure. Through its expert systems it seeks to provide knowledgeable advice on all the choices required. However, the expert user remains free to strike out in a new direction both globally by defining a new goal and in detail through modifications to the choices. It is noted that the first three phases are independent of one another so that, for example, alternative strategies for the calculation can be explored using the expert system without the need to have a specific molecule in mind and without the need to proceed to numerical calculations. *The object of a calculation should not be simply to produce numbers but to provide insight into nature and our theories about it.* Thus an important aspect of the OpenMol program is the critical assessment of the quality of the results which it will provide.

The effective calculation of a molecular property requires access to information of various types. In OpenMol the need for several different knowledge bases has been identified which provide the expert help so that the decisions about the calculation are efficiently made and produce results that meet the expectations of the user. Among these knowledge bases are those concerning molecular geometry, computational methods, operating and computing resources, interpretation and accuracy of results. These are not wholly independent but cross-referencing between them is likely to be limited. A common theme is accuracy and *feedback* on this topic, especially between the original goals and the final results, is considered vital to the success of the program.

Within recent years chemical and pharmaceutical industry have successfully applied quantum chemical methods to assist in the search for new chemical substances with special technological or pharmaceutical characteristics. The motivation for the use of theoretical methods has been to reduce costs by guiding the search for new substances and by reducing the number of substances that finally have to be studied experimentally. As the costs for developing one new drug range between 10 and 25 million ECU such savings may become substantial. Industry has employed for these studies commercially available software. The correct and efficient use of this software requires expert knowledge and, usually, a special training in the use of the programs. OpenMol, through expert guidance and the evaluation and interpretation of results, will be easy for a novice to use but also, through the possibility of rapid-prototyping and symbolic manipulation, for an expert to exploit as an important working tool. Therefore OpenMol is a more cost effective tool for applying quantum chemical methods than available so far and and makes these studies affordable for large and small industry alike. In addition, it can serve as depository for company owned knowledge and experience and for training new employes in the use of these techniques.

The broad structure of OpenMol has been established, many numerical modules have been designed and implemented following the conventional life-cycle for software development and are now under extensive beta testing:

Conclusions

We have tried to demonstrate that the use of expert systems, with their facilities for the storing and processing of knowledge can remedy some of the problems now being experienced in providing the novice user with a program which can give him realistic results for a property of interest with an evaluation of their accuracy and significance. This is achieved without depriving the more expert user of a rapid prototyping tool with which to test out his own theoretical ideas about the molecules being considered, about the form of calculation, about the properties, or about the evaluation of some special feature of the results. The expert system provides a knowledge environment for the entire calculation which is goal driven instead of procedure driven. This is a flexible and efficient method of producing and using the software .

The device of the abstract data type has allowed the calculation to be divided into two layers. The user, whether novice or expert, will normally see only the upper layer where all decisions are taken and all results made available. At the lower level all the details needed for the computer to perform the calculation will be provided in subroutines which correspond to the operations of the upper level. This division means that the upper level is machine-independent and the lower level is more readily portable than are most packages. We believe that this move to the rigorous use of two levels of abstraction in the software constitutes a revolution in quantum chemistry packages which will lead to more useful and more transparent programs.

The expert system also gives an open framework which encourages further evolutionary developments. Alternative procedures to perform numerical operations can be substituted without difficulty. Procedures to calculate new properties can be added freely. The systematic use of symbolic computing is possible. The complications of porting the package to another computer will be easier to resolve since all the upper level of operating is computer independent.

References

[1] GHF Diercksen and GG Hall. Intelligent Software: The OpenMol Program, Computers in Physics, 1994, and references therein.

Parallel Molecular Dynamics Simulation of Commercial Surfactants

Eamonn O'Toole, Mike Surridge and Colin Upstill

Parallel Applications Centre
2 Venture Road
Southampton
SO16 7NP
UK

Extended Abstract

The Parallel Applications Centre has been working in collaboration with Unilever Research in Port Sunlight and the University of Southampton Department of Chemistry to develop a set of tools which will enable a chemist to investigate the properties of surfactant layers using the molecular dynamics simulation technique. Surfactant layers are commonly encountered in consumer chemical products such as fabric softeners, detergents, etc., in which Unilever has a strong commercial interest. At present, active ingredients for such products are developed by synthesizing and testing molecules from a very large class of candidates whose properties are only broadly understood. Success as a fabric softener (say) is difficult to quantify, so the test procedures often involve collecting subjective opinions directly from consumers, an expensive and time consuming process.

The immediate objective of the project is to support research into the detailed properties of surfactant molecules, refining the requirements for candidate molecules. A longer term objective is to use molecular dynamics simulation to screen molecules prior to synthesis, reducing the amount of consumer testing required in product development.

The systems of interest are not simple. Typical products consist of mixtures of surfactants, electrolytes, other active ingredients and water. They often act at poorly characterised interfaces such as fabrics and cell membranes. Modelling such systems requires the handling of charged particles and flexible long chain molecules. The properties and simulation conditions of interest require new algorithm development and combinations of techniques never applied before. Finally, extraction of bulk properties requires the simulation of relatively long intervals of around a 1 nanosecond. Since each simulation time-step represents a few femtoseconds, it is necessary to run the simulation for least 105 to 106 steps, making this an industrial 'Grand Challenge' problem. Only parallel computing can provide the performance required to solve these problems in sufficient detail within reasonable timescales.

As an initial task the collaboration is directed towards the simulation of a cationic surfactant. The approach taken is to develop a code which will simulate the target molecule and a range of related molecules. The target molecule is dimethyl-distearyl ammonium chloride. The molecule consists of a nitrogen atom bonded to two methyl and two 18 unit hydrocarbon chains. The nitrogen is positively charged and consequently requires a counter ion which in the case of this simulation is a chloride ion. In order to perform molecular dynamics a potential model must be formulated which models the atomic interactions within and between the molecules. The potential model used allows for bending of bond angles and rotation of groups about bonds, for repulsion-dispersion between unconnected atoms, and for electrostatic interactions between charged atoms.

As a starting configuration the molecules are ordered in a monolayer or bilayer in the xy plane with periodic boundary conditions applied in the x and y coordinate directions. The z-direction is bounded by the cotton surface, which is represented using a surface potential. Each unit cell contains typically 64 to 256 molecules. At present, all runs (including test runs) are allowed to proceed for 100,000 equilibration steps (in which the temperature is held constant), and then for 100,000 'production' steps at constant energy. Trajectory files are created during this latter stage which form the basis for subsequent analysis of bulk properties. The configuration set up and subsequent analysis operations use codes which have been integrated into the Biosym package, with which the users of the code are already familiar.

All the simulation code is original to the collaboration. A major objective is portability between as wide a range of machines and architectures as possible. To enable this a modular approach has been taken, in which dependencies on particular machines are restricted to a small number of routines. By combining this approach with adherence to the FORTRAN 77 standard (plus limited use of common extensions), a highly portable code has been produced. The code can be ported between different parallel systems by modifying the architecture-dependent routines only. This has allowed the code to be run successfully on the Intel iPSC/860 machine (under the NX/2 parallel operating system), an IBM SP1 machine, on workstation clusters under PVM, and on serial machines. The core computational routines have been designed for efficient execution on vector machines, so the code should perform well on traditional vector supercomputers, although this has not yet been necessary.

While deciding on the parallel implementation most appropriate for our purposes, an important consideration was that connectivity information is required during the calculation of the potentials. We believed that this was significant enough to dictate that any parallel decomposition of the data structure should not break up individual molecules. The system sizes that can reasonably be simulated with currently available computing power are small enough for an individual molecule to extend over a significant proportion of the simulation domain. The standard geometric decomposition approach would therefore have split individual molecules between processors. This fact, along with the problem of handing the long range electrostatic interactions, led us to seek an alternative parallel approach.

A more straight forward 'brute-force' parallelisation of the code was eventually selected. Each processor is assigned a set of molecules and is responsible for the calculation of the dihedral, valence and surface potential interactions, and the integration of the equations of motion, for these molecules. Whilst these are being computed, global communications are carried out to support calculation of repulsion-dispersion and long-range electrostatic interactions.

To date the code has been timed on an Intel iPSC/860, an IBM SP1 and a range of workstations. All results were obtained from the same simulation code, recompiled where necessary, and show that significant performance benefits can be gained with this code by using a parallel machine. Parallel efficiency remains respectably high up to 32 processors, even though the number of molecules per processor becomes quite small. For systems of over 256 molecules it should be possible to use MPP systems with more than 100 processors.

The total run-time for a typical production run of 100,000 steps with 64 molecules on a 32 processor parallel machine is less than 24 hours, which would be adequate for routine use in a product development environment. The time for a 256 molecule run is of order 1 week, which is adequate for research purposes. None of the workstations available today can meet these targets for overall run-time.

Inevitably, as computing power increases, ever more sophisticated simulations will be attempted. Parallel high-performance computing technology allows any desired degree of sophistication to be achieved around 2 years before it is attainable with sequential processing technology. Our work shows that it is possible to create software to exploit this advantage for commercially significant systems.

Computer Simulations of Molecular Collision Processes

J. Schulte

*National Superconductiong Cyclotron Laboratory, Michigan State University,
East Lansing, Michigan 48824, USA*

G. Seifert

*Institut für Theoretische Physik, Technische Universität Dresden,
D-01069 Dresden, Germany*

Abstract. A method for molecular dynamics (MD) simulations of molecular collision processes on the basis of the Density-Functional-Theory within the Local Density Approximation (DFT-LDA) and LCAO representation is presented. The consideration of the collision statistics is realized employing parallel computer techniques. The results of simulations for carbon cluster deuterium collisions are given

Molecular dynamics simulations are very powerful to get more insight into the dynamics of collision processes. Simulations of such processes have been succesfully performed using empirical interaction potentials. More recently the combination of the Density-Functional-Theory within the Local Density Approximation (DFT-LDA) with Molecular Dynamics (MD) has been realized. A simplified LCAO-DFT-LDA scheme, which enables us to consider the electronic states in the calculation of the forces on the atoms, was developed and applied to simulations of molecular collisions. For more details on the method and its application see refs. [1] and [3], respectively. The authors demonstrate the extension of such calculations by considering the statistics of molecular collision processes. The relatively small computational effort of the LCAO-DFT-LDA method allows to consider statistics in the collision process, and in this way to calculate reaction cross sections and reaction rates of collisions of clusters or large molecules by (Monte Carlo) integration over impact parameters, averaging over different relative orientations of the collision partners, consideration of internal energies, and calculations at different collision energies [4].

The realization of the collision statistics is ideally suited for parallel computing. The different trajectories or sets of trajectories can run parallel on different processors of a parallel computer. The simulations presented here, have been carried out on a multiple instruction multiple data (MIMD) parallel super computer (nCUBE2), where sets of trajectories run parallel on sets of processors. Special use of nCUBE processor optimized basic linear algebra subroutines has been made. Employing a hypercube of 64 processors the calculations on nCUBE have been approximately twice as fast as runs on a CRAY-YMP. With this approach the CPU-time of the program scales nearly linearly with the number of the processors, i.e., a gain of an additional factor of two can be achieved by switching from 64 processors to 128 processors.

The computational model proposed here may be viewed as a hybrid between an *ab initio* molecular dynamics based on DFT and the use of purely empirical potentials. It has the advantage over the latter of overcoming the transferability problem. The computational effort of this approach is less than that of a full *ab initio* MD calculation, and in this way it is possible to run several thousand trajectories parallel on parallel computers with rather limited average memory per processor.

As an example for the application of the method, we have chosen the reaction of carbon clusters with hydrogen (resp. deuterium). The reactivity of carbon clusters is of great interest for chemistry of astrochemical environments as well as combustion processes for example. As special cases we have investigated the reactions of C_2 and C_{60} (Buckminsterfullerene - Bf) with D_2.

The simulations were realized by calculating sets of MD trajectories, and then considering the statistics. At every single trajectory the collision partners were set at a center of mass distance of 10 *atu*, and then the system was allowed to propagate over a time period of 100,000 atu ($\sim 2.5ps$). In order to avoid collision orientation correlations the clusters were randomly rotated through Euler's angles about their internal axes. In the present simulations we did not consider rotational or vibrational excitations in the initial state of the colliding systems. The maximum impact parameter b_m has been determined by the convergence-test of the reaction probability versus the impact parameter [4]. In order to achieve convergence in the reaction probabilities more than 10^3 trajectories have been calculated in this way. A time step of 10 *atu* (1 *atu* = $2.4 \cdot 10^{-17} sec$) has been proofed to guarantee the conservation of energy over the entire period (some 10^{-12} sec) of a trajectory. The MD equations of motion for the atoms:

$$M_k \ddot{\vec{R}}_k = -\partial E / \partial \vec{R}_k$$

are integrated using the Verlet algorithm [2]. As to a detailed description see [6].

For the reaction of C_2 with D_2 there are two different possible reaction channels:

$$C_2 + D_2 \longrightarrow C_2 D_2 \tag{a}$$

and

$$C_2 + D_2 \longrightarrow C_2 D + D \tag{b}$$

Other reactions (e.g. $C_2 + D_2 \longrightarrow 2CD$) are strongly endothermic. The formation of an acetylene-like structure (a) is energetically clearly favoured over the incomplete addition of D_2 (b). Our simulation of the reaction dynamics shows too that the energetically favoured product is preferred. At the collision energy of 1 eV no dissociation of C_2 was found, and elastic scattering processes dominate ($\approx$ 80% of the total number of trajectories). The calculated integrated cross section σ_r as a function of the impact parameter b is shown in Fig. 1.

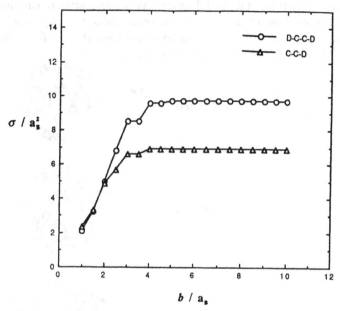

Fig. 1: Integrated reaction cross section σ of the $C_2 + D_2$ collision at 1 eV as function of the maximum impact parameter b_m. (σ in a_B^2, $1a_B = 0.529\text{Å}$)

The cross section shows convergence at about $5a_B$. The largest "reactive" impact parameter is a somewhat larger than the simple geometrical estimate ($R(C_2) + R(D_2) \approx 3.8a_B$, R is the bond length). In our simulations we did not find the formation of a transition complex ($C = CD_2$), as discussed in the literature [7]. The reaction of D_2 with C_2 is better characterized by the simultaneous $D - D$ bond breaking and $C - D$ bond formation, and either the scattering of the second D atom (forming $C_2D + D$) or directing the second D atom to the other carbon atom (forming C_2D_2). Our simulations show a remarkable larger reaction cross section for the collision of $C_2^+ + D_2$ compared to the $C_2 + D_2$ collision.

In the $C_2^+ + D_2$ collision the formation of C_2D dominates clearly over the formation of C_2D_2. The calculated reaction rate constant of $CC - D$ formation ($6.3 \times 10^{-10} cm^3 s^{-1}$) is much larger than for the formation of $D - CC - D$ ($5.2 \times 10^{-11} cm^3 s^{-1}$). These values are in qualitative agreement with the experimental findings by Mc Elvany et al. [7] for collisions of small charged carbon clusters with D_2. Energetically the formation of an acetylene-like complex, however, should still dominate. Thus, the reason for this behaviour may be viewed as a dynamical effect, which is difficult to observe in ordinary minimum reaction path calculations. In our simulations the formation of long living products (life times $> 10^{-12} sec$) are predicted, but no "transition complexes" (life times $< 10^{-13} sec$) are observed.

The highly symmetric C_{60} fullerene is a very stable cluster [9], but not an inert molecule. For instance, hydrogen can easily react with C_{60} up to a $C_{60}H_{36}$ [10]. We performed simulations of $C_{60} + D_2$ collisions to learn more about the mechanism of these reactions. Of special interest is the formation of endohedral complexes, i.e., the capture of an atom or molecule inside the C_{60} cage. The formation of such endohedral $X@C_{60}$ complexes has been studied for $X = He$ in experiments [11, 12, 13] and theoretically in [14].

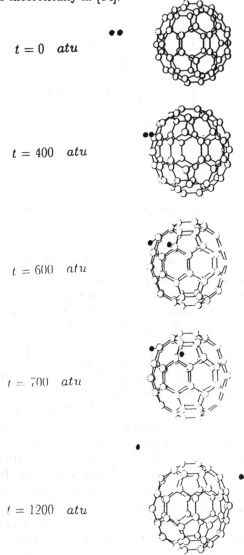

$t = 0 \quad atu$

$t = 400 \quad atu$

$t = 600 \quad atu$

$t = 700 \quad atu$

$t = 1200 \quad atu$

Fig. 2: Time evolution of one trajectory of a $D_2 - C_{60}$ collision at 40 eV. Time in atomic time units (1 $atu = 2.4 \times 10^{-17}$ sec). The deuterium atoms are marked by filled circles.

The time evolution of a single trajectory for a $D_2 - C_{60}$ collision at 40 eV (centre of mass - c.m.) collision energy is plotted in Fig. 2.

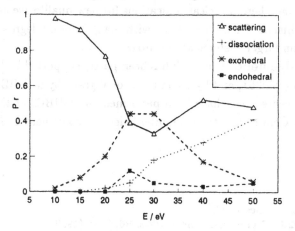

Fig. 3: Reaction probabilities (P_r) of the $C_{60} + D_2$ collision as a function of the collision energy. $P_r = N_r/N$, where N_r is the number of "reactive" trajectories of the corresponding reaction channel, and N the total number of trajectories, respectively.

The reaction probabilities were calculated for the collisions of D_2 with C_{60} considering the statistics in a similar way as described above for the $C_2 - D_2$ collisions. The calculated reaction probabilities as a function of the c.m. collision energy are plotted in Fig. 3. At low collision energies only elastic scattering of the D_2 molecules is observed. As a further reaction channel the formation of exohedral $D - C_{60}$ complexes has been observed. With increasing energy the occurance of such events increases, where elastic scattering decreases. Besides these reaction channels dissociation of D_2 occurs, where both D atoms are scattered. The probability of this reaction channel increases nearly monotonically with increasing energy, whereas the probability of the formation of exohedral $D - C_{60}$ complexes reaches a maximum between 20 eV and 30 eV collision energy. We have found also a nonzero probability for the formation of endohedral $D@C_{60}$ complexes with a distinct maximum at 25 eV collision energy. This means, there seems to be an "window of energy" for the capture of D inside C_{60}. However, the analysis of the "reaction products" shows that for all of the endohedral $D@C_{60}$ complexes, no D atom is found at a central position of the C_{60} cage. The D atoms are "trapped" at the "bonding shell" inside the C_{60} cage. Furthermore, in our simulations no $D_2@C_{60}$ complexes have been found.

We have presented a new scheme for handling molecular collision processes on the basis of an approximate DFT-LDA method combined with molecular dynamics (MD), and considering collision statistics employing parallel computer techniques. The method was applied to the reaction of C_2 and C_{60} (Bf) with D_2, and the simulations give new insights into the mechanism of these reactions.

The results clearly show the importance of the dynamics in the understanding of reactions. The advantage of the method is that it can be easily applied to rather large systems, and there are clear indications for new qualitative aspects in the dynamics of collisions for large systems with many internal degrees of freedom. Investigations on larger systems are in progress.

Acknowledgement. This work has been partly supported by NATO under Grant No. CRG 930351, and by a computational grant by nCUBE. Part of the calculations presented here have been performed on nCUBE2 at the San Diego Supercomputer Center, and the Computer Science Department at Texas A & M University.

References

[1] Seifert G. and Jones R. O.:
Z. Phys. **D20**, 77 (1991), J. Chem. Phys. **96**, 7564 (1992)

[2] Verlet L.:
Phys. Rev. **159** , 98 (1967)

[3] Seifert, G. and Schmidt, R.:
New J. Chem.**16** , 1145 (1992)

[4] Schulte,J., Lucchese, R.R. and Marlow, W.H.:
J. Chem. Phys. **99** (2), 1178 (1993)

[5] Schmidt, R., Seifert G. and Lutz, H.O.:
Physics Letters **A158**, 231 (1991)

[6] Seifert G. and Schulte, J.:
Physics Letters , (submitted for publication)

[7] McElvany, S.W., Dunlap, B.I. and O'Keefe, A.:
J. Chem. Phys. **86**, 715 (1987)

[8] Schulte,J., Lucchese, R.R. and Marlow, W.H.:
Proc. of the Mater. Res. Soc. **206**, 189 (1991)

[9] Krätzschmer, W., Lamb, L.D., Fostiropoulos, K. and Huffman, D.R.:
Nature **347**, 354 (1990)

[10] Haufler, R.E., Conceicao, J., Chibante, L.P.F., Chai, Y.,Byrne, N.E., Flanangan, S., Haley, M.M., O'Brien, S.C., Pan, C., Xiao, Z., Billups, W.E., Cinfolini, M.A., Hauge, R.H., Margrave, J.L., Wilson, L.J., Curl, R.F. and Smalley, R.E.:
J. Chem. Phys. **94**, 8634 (1990)

[11] Weiske, T., Hrusak, J., Böhme, D.K. and Schwarz, H.:
Chem. Phys. Lett. **186**, 459 (1991)

[12] Wan, Z., Christian, J.F., Anderson, S.L. :
J. Chem. Phys. **96**, 3344 (1992)

[13] Campbell, E.E.B., Ehlich, R., Hielscher, A., Frazao, J.M.A. and Hertel, I.V.:
Z. Phys. **D23**, 1 (1992)

[14] Ehlich, R., Campbell, E.E.B., Knospe, O. and Schmidt, R.:
Z. Phys. **D28**, 153 (1993)

Parallel Processing for Generating Large Molecular Databases

Hartmut Braun, Margret Assfalg, Klaus Weymann

Pharma Research New Technologies

F. Hoffmann - La Roche Ltd, Basel

Tom Harvey

Avalon Computer Systems, Santa Barbara, CA

1 Introduction

The MIQ (Molecular Identity Query) system is an in-house tool developed at Roche that allows the research chemist to gain quick access to 10 million substances from Chemical Abstracts Service (CAS) and Beilstein. This unique tool is a key element of our corporate research chemistry.

The key problem in developing the MIQ system was to find a way of loading the large (4 GB) structure database in reasonable time (less than 10 days for 1 load) and with moderate hardware and software investment (by using the existing VAX-4200).

We have successfully reached this goal by linking an array of 8 parallel processors to the VAX. Our solution was designed and implemented in cooperation with Avalon.

2 Key Problem

The core of MIQ is a 4-GB database containing 10 million chemical substances. The source data, provided by Chemical Abstracts Service and Beilstein, are merged into an integrated system.

Given a VAX-4200 (5 vups), the bottleneck in generating the large database is the cpu-bound property calculation that has to be executed for every molecule. On the average, the property calculation requires 2-3 sec elapsed time per molecule, which adds up to almost a year for a single database load. Clearly, this approach is prohibitive. We needed an effective compute power of 150 vups to load the database in 10 days.

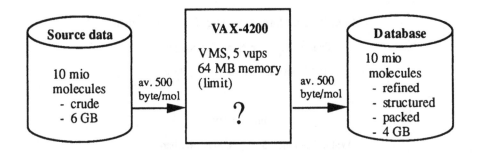

Fig. 1. The bottleneck on the VAX-4200 is the cpu-bound molecular property calculation, 3 sec /molecule

3 Solution

The method of choice for the solution is parallel processing.

Our parallel processing system consists of a VAX-4200 (VMS, 64 MB, 5 vups, Q-Bus) to which an array of 8 Avalon AP30 RISC processors is linked via a Q-Bus extender. Each AP30 has 4 MB of local memory and delivers 30 mips of compute power.

The processor node reads the input data from shared memory on the VAX, performs the calculation for 1 molecule, and writes the result data back to VAX memory. The same program (executable) runs on all AP30 processors. No disk I/O is done by the accelerators.

The parallel processing controller synchronizes the parallel tasks. It also reads the source data from disk and writes the result data into the database on disk, 500 bytes per molecule on the average. Multiple buffering in shared memory is used for the data transfer between the controller and the AP30s.

The code that calculates the molecular properties is very difficult to parallelize. The algorithms perform mainly logical operations on molecules; the amount of vector operations is insignificant. Hence, the lowest level of straightforward problem separation is the molecular level. We found that the SPMD (Single Program Multiple Data) architecture offers the simplest and most efficient solution.

As expected, the bottleneck in the database load process turns to disk I/O when stepping from 1 to 8 workers. The processor array delivers the results faster than the VAX-4200 can store the result data and provide new input data.

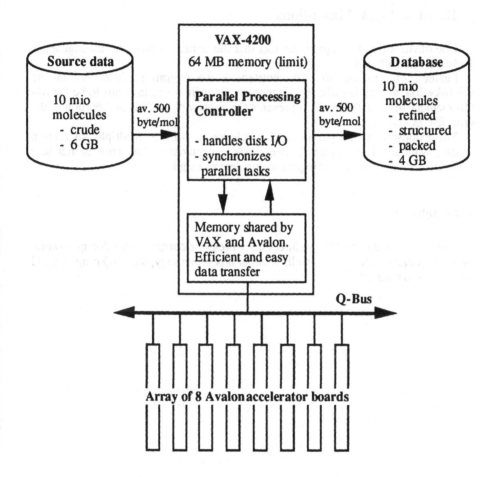

Fig. 2. The VAX/Avalon parallel processing architecture

4 Advantages

Our VAX/Avalon SPMD implementation is applicable to many compute-intensive problems that can be separated into individual tasks on the molecular level. The solution is cost-effective, powerful, and of manageable complexity.

Due to the very high VAX/VMS compatibility of the Avalon system (compiler, linker, runtime library) it provides an efficient development environment. Identical source code is used for the VAX and for the Avalon boards. The resulting identical functionalities allow us to load the structure database either sequentially on the VAX (with a small number of molecules), sequentially using 1 Avalon worker, or in parallel using 2 to 8 workers.

5 Disadvantages, Limitations

One obvious disadvantage is the fact that the system consists of heterogeneous hardware and software.

Further, due to the disk I/O bottleneck the overall performance of the VAX/Avalon system is difficult to improve. The main obstacle seems to be the 64-MB memory limit on the VAX. It prevents the transfer of a substantial portion of the slow disk I/O into fast memory.

The extension of the parallelization scheme to MIMD (Multiple Instruction stream, Multiple Data stream), which one can envisage for more demanding molecular calculations, would require a complete redesign.

6 Conclusion

The VAX/Avalon SPMD architecture serves our current needs for generating large molecular databases very well. Without this technology, the MIQ project could not have been realized.

Applications of Parallel Constraint Logic Programming to Molecular Biology and Genetics.

Dominic A. Clark, Christopher Rawlings and Jack Shirazi

Biomedical Informatics Unit, Imperial Cancer Research Fund

1 Overview

Many scientific problems in molecular biology and genetics can be viewed as an attempt to find consistent solutions from a large, though finite, hypothesis space which simultaneously maximally satisfies constraints arising from data and domain theories. In EP 6708 APPLAUSE, we are tackling two challenging problems from molecular biology using the ElipSys parallel constraint logic programming (CLP) system[1].

2 Protein Topology Prediction

Proteins mediate most biological activities and understanding the role and function of proteins in the control of cell growth is an important part of contemporary cancer research. Protein topology is a level of structural organization based on spatial adjacency and orientation relations between secondary structures. A topological prediction can be used to identify similar proteins of known structure and can provide a low resolution working hypothesis to guide experimental investigation. In protein topology prediction there are many types of mutually constraining data and theories of protein structural organisation that need to be integrated in order to identify a single consistent prediction (or predictions) from a large combinatorial search space. Traditional computational approaches have been based on the 'generate and test' paradigm. We have demonstrated the benefits of a new approach which uses the CLP 'constrain and generate' paradigm as embodied in ElipSys[2]. Here, constraints are used for a priori pruning of the hypothesis space while parallelism enhances search efficiency. Initial results show orders of magnitude improvement in performance over other approaches. This significantly extends the range and complexity of scientific problems that can be addressed.

3 Genetic Map Construction

Genetic maps provide a long range view of the genome by locating markers either inferred by genetic analysis (the inheritance patterns of genes) or by physical methods such as hybridization fingerprinting (HF)[3]. An important outcome of

HF is to establish ordered libraries of cloned DNA sequences covering entire chromosomes. These can be used to "home in" on sections of a chromosome or particular genes. The computational problem is to determine the most complete and consistent ordered clone map from the pattern of hybridizations found between cloned DNA samples bound in arrays onto nylon filters which are exposed to sets of radioactive probes (short fragments of DNA).

The data analysis is affected by a number of problems, including: random noise (from experimental methods), artefacts arising from clones containing more than one distinct parts of the genome and clones with internal deletions and probes containing repeated elements. Furthermore, there is a general requirement for consistency with maps generated by other techniques and related experimental datasets. We have developed a program, CME[4], for generating probe maps from HF data. CLP features are used to integrate pre-existing mapping information (partial probe orders from cytogenetic maps and local physical maps) into the global map generation process, while parallelism enhances search. Scaling results showed that each constraint reduced processing time by an order of magnitude. Furthermore, near linear speed-ups were achieved through parallelism. Using 55 probes from Chromosome 2 of the yeast Schizosaccharomyces pombe, CME could generate maps as well as (and sometimes better) than other methods.

4 Discussion

Many parallel CLP features (consistency methods, cost minimization and finite domains) directly contribute to the improved performance and functionality that we have obtained. For both our applications we have demonstrated good performance in areas where existing techniques prove computationally inefficient or provide only partial solutions. Whereas many problems still remain, a number of existing computational bottlenecks have now been addressed.

References

1. Veron, A, Schuerman, K, Reeve, M. and Li, L-L. (1993) How and Why in the ElipSys OR-parallel CLP System. In Bode, A, Reeve, M. and Wolf, G. (eds) PARLE '93, Lecture Notes in Computer Science, 694, Springer-Verlag, Heidelberg. pp 291-304
2. Clark, D. A, Rawlings, C. J, Shirazi, J, et al. (1993) Solving Large Combinatorial Problems in Molecular Biology Using the ElipSys Parallel Constraint Logic Programming System. The Computer Journal, 36(8), 690-701.
3. Lehrach, H., Drmanac, R., Hoheisel, J. et al. (1990) "Hybridization Fingerprinting in Genome Mapping and Sequencing" In: Genome Analysis - Genetic and Physical Mapping, Vol 1, Eds. Davies, K.E. and Tilghman, S, Cold Spring Harbour Laboratory Press, 39-81
4. Clark, D. A, Rawlings, C. J, Doursenot, S. and Veron, A. (1994) Genetic Mapping with Constraints, Proceedings 2nd International conference on the Practical Application of Prolog (Ed) Sterling, L, forthcoming.

Simulating Biological Evolution on a Parallel Computer *

Uwe Tangen[1] and Helmut Weberpals[2]

[1] Max-Planck-Institut für biophysikalische Chemie, Am Fassberg, D-37077 Göttingen and Institut für Molekulare Biotechnologie, Beutenbergstr. 11, D-07745 Jena, Germany
[2] Technische Informatik II, TU Hamburg–Harburg, Harburger Schlosstrasse 20, D-21071 Hamburg, Germany

Abstract. *Evolution* or the question of the origin of life belongs to the most challenging research projects currently undertaken. One of the main topics in theoretical research is to develop an understanding of evolving systems from simple to complex life forms. A complex program (50000 lines of code, 400 subroutines) simulating such evolutionary systems has been parallelized for the multiprocessor KSR1 manufactured by Kendall Square Research. The parallelization allows for the creation of multiple threads per processor and thus particularly suits an XPRAM model of parallel computation.

1 Introduction

There are several attempts to tackle the question of the origin of life, cf. [2, 3, 4, 5, 6, 7]. The theoretical framework underlying our research is the theory of *quasi-species* by Manfred Eigen [1]. This theory exhibits fundamental limits to the capability to accumulate information. For example, each processing of information is subject to errors as long as information processing in real evolutionary systems is concerned. In a population which evolves by replicating its individuals, only a certain amount of information can be gained or stabilized over time. The main objective of our work is to find a *bridging model* between this theory, developed for molecular evolutionary scenarios and information processing known in the realm of computer science. While the notion of information used in evolution theory means a description to process something, the notion used in computer science is strongly coupled with functionality. We investigate organizational structures developing and evolving in a population of entities on a molecular biological level.

2 Model of simulation

The *model* investigated in this paper takes a population of individuals situated in three-dimensional Euclidian space; time proceeds in discrete steps. The

---

* Financial support by the Max–Planck–Gesellschaft, Institut für Molekulare Biotechnologie, Jena, and the Deutsche Forschungsgemeinschaft is gratefully acknowledged.

individuals act as information carriers in the sense that each is given the capability to store a program in its memory. This memory is copied by replication of each individual subject to errors, which act on the level of bits. A program consists of elements, some of which are operators that perform certain functions, for example, the allocation of energy. Individuals communicate via links, which are built up from a further operator in the program of each individual. Individuals to be processed are selected randomly; offspring is put in a certain spatial neighbourhood of the processed individuals.

The resulting dynamics of the system, though highly stochastic, abounds of *evolving structures*. The simulation of these extremely difficult dynamics requires an enormous *time* as well as *space complexity* which calls for a parallel computer.

3 Parallel implementation

The program has been parallelized for the *multiprocessor* KSR1 manufactured by Kendall Square Research [9]. The parallelization crucially depends on the CREW PRAM capability of the shared virtual memory system of the KSR1. In particular, the program exploits the light weighted *locking* mechanism of cache lines for synchronization. The high stochasticity of the dynamics imposes a *fine grained parallelism*. The appropriate means therefore is to parallelize on the level of MACH *threads*, the deepest level possible. Locking was done such that each thread (*virtual processor*) waiting for some resources suspends itself until it will be called by its predecessor. This feature allows for the creation of multiple threads per processor and thus particularly suits an XPRAM model of parallel computation [10]. These locking procedures have been incorporated into a memory management package developed to ensure data integrity and fast storage and retrieval of the complete data set during a simulation run.

Evolving structures within the population are reflected in the formation of clusters in space which grow and decline rapidly. Algorithmically, the problem of handling this clustering is solved using an *index–tree* [8], which allows for a quick storage and retrieval of entities inhomogeneously situated in n–dimensional space. The index–tree is constructed recursively. The left picture in Fig. 1 shows an example of dividing the x–y–plane into subplanes. The division starts with two positions P_1 and P_2. A new hyperplane e_1 is created perpendicular to the middle of the line connecting P_1 and P_2. Correspondingly, a new element in the index–tree is built in as sketched in the right hand part of Fig. 1. This element contains the description of this new hyperplane. To introduce a new individual P_3, the algorithm descends the tree to the left if the actual dividing hyperplane lies to the right of P_3 or to the right in the opposite case. Reaching the bottom of the tree a new hyperplane, in our example plane e_2, will be created. The retrieval of individuals is done in the same way. This algorithm yields an $\mathcal{O}(N \log N)$ access to each individual. Because of the high dynamics in the simulation this tree is not always balanced. While the depth of the *balanced* tree accounts to about 30 levels experience shows that there are about 40 to 60 levels needed in the simulation.

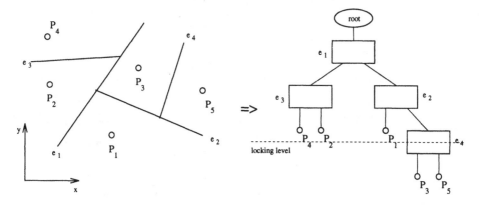

Fig. 1. Construction of the index–tree in the x–y–plane.

Initialize subroutine and set node pointer at the root of the index tree.		
Execute as long as the node pointer is not equal zero.		
Status of the actual node?		
This node has two successor nodes.	This node is a parent of a leave.	Nothing available.
Calculate the projection of the target coordinate along the normal vector of the hyperplain stored in the actual node. Decide whether the target coordinate is situated to the left or right of the hyperplain.	Decouple old leave. Calculate a new hyperplain and append the nodes of the two hyperspheres. Cconnect one of the nodes with the old leave. Append new leave to the other node.	This node is not used. The new leave can be appended without changing the tree structure.
One step down in the hierarchie on the correct side of the hyperplain.	Next node pointer is set to zero.	
Mark all visited nodes with the current time.		

Fig. 2. Introducing a new individual into the index–tree.

In a parallel implementation the access to individuals becomes a serious problem because congestion arises near the root of the tree. The idea to solve this problem is simply to resort to the CREW capability of the KSR operating system. The levels near the root will exists as copies for each thread and the tree is then locked at deeper levels. Thus, statistically, the threads will not disturb each other. Another problem arises, because in the case of deleting parts of the tree the locking algorithm becomes inconsistent, since deleting a hyperplane in the tree the level above must be locked. On the other hand, other threads do not know that they should look for locked data structures at a level above the general locking level. If they look one level ahead, they have to look at every level above, because the tree is not always complete down to the general locking level.

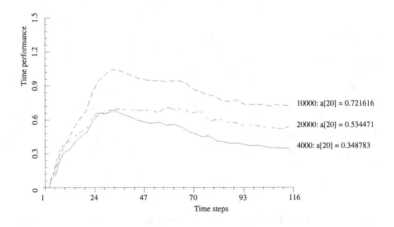

Fig. 3. The *efficiency* over time (floating average of the last 20 time steps) of three runs on 128 processors for various sizes of the population: 4000, 10000, and 20000 individuals.

Since looking ahead necessitates locking always, the same congestion problem arises again. To solve this dilemma, deleting of hyperplanes above the general locking level is forbidden. In Fig. 2, the algorithm to introduce a new individual into the index–tree is shown. This *parallel* implementation of the index–tree has rendered a very stable and fast storage of spatially inhomogeneously distributed entities. Locking levels of about 35 proved to be adequate.

4   Results and Conclusions

After initial problems with the KSR1 operating system, the program turned out to run very well; *96 hours in a run with a 16 processor set could be achieved.* KSR arranged to do scalability tests on a 128 processor machine in the United States. Fig. 3 shows the *efficiency* over time of a run on 128 processors for various sizes of the population. In this simulation, 217 threads were running in parallel. While a population size of 4000 individuals is too small for an efficient parallelization on 128 processors, a population size of 20000 individuals yields too heavy a traffic in cache–handling and therefore a saturation in the communication lines between processors; under these circumstances a population size of 10000 individuals proved adequate. The effect of too small a population size becomes also apparent in Fig. 4, which contrasts three runs on different processor sets. When a population of a 4000 individuals is simulated, the efficiency using the 128 processor run fell drastically compared to the runs using 16 or 64 processors. This effect is due to the increased rate of interactions per thread,

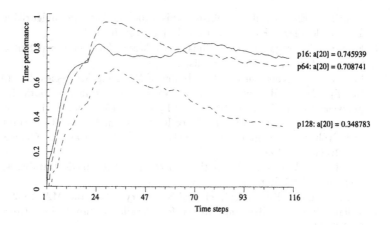

Fig. 4. The *efficiency* over time (floating average of the last 20 time steps) of three runs with a population size of 4000 individuals using 16, 64 and 128 processors per run.

which runs into the latency catastrophe.

Shared virtual memory turns out to be a good approximation to the *Parallel Random Access Machine* endowed with the *Concurrent Read* and *Exclusive Write* capability. This feature allows for the creation of multiple threads per processor and for the migration of both threads and data between processors, which lies at the heart of our parallelization.

One of the major benefits in parallelizing biological population simulations arises from the possibility of using real time simulations. Unfortunately, this conflicts with the goal of achieving a high efficiency of the parallelization. Typically, the population size is restricted via a certain amount of resource usable in the simulation. If the population size becomes large enough to allow for highly efficient runs, the available resources eventually will not be used entirely and the population starts to grow forever. This, of course, cannot be handled by real computers and thus, the population size has to be restricted by the number of individuals (cf. the notion of *constant overall organization* in [1]). Therefore, the simulations reside in a mixture phase of sequential and parallel processing.

References

1. Eigen M.: Selforganization of Matter and the Evolution of Biological Macromolecules. Naturwissenschaften, **58**:465–523, 1971.
2. McCaskill J. S.: Polymer Chemistry on Tape: A Computational Model for Emergent Genetics. Max–Planck–Society, 1991 Report.

3. Thürk M.: Ein Modell zur Selbstorganisation von Automatenalgorithmen zum Studium molekularer Evolution. Diss. Universität Jena, 1993.
4. Fontana W.: Algorithmic Chemistry: A Model for Functional Self-Organization. Santa Fe Institute, 1990 Unpublished.
5. Lindgren K.: Evolution in a Population of Mutating Strategies. Nordita, **22**, 1990.
6. Boerlijst M. C., Hogeweg P.: Spiral Wave Structure in Pre-Biotic Evolution: Hypercycles Stable Against Parasites. Physica D, **48**:17–28, 1991.
7. Rasmussen S., Knudsen C., Feldberg R., Hinsholm M.: The Coreworld: Emergence and Evolution of Cooperative Structures in a Computational Chemistry. Physica D, **42**:111–134, 1990.
8. Six H.-W., Widmayer P.: Spatial Searching in Geometric Databases. Universität Karlsruhe, 1987 Report.
9. Kendall Square Research, Technical Summary. Waltham, MA, 1992.
10. Valiant L. G.: A Bridging Model for Parallel Computation. Commun. ACM, **33**:103–111, 1990.

Supercomputing in Polymer Research

Kurt Kremer
IFF
Forschungszentrum Jülich
D-53425 Jülich
Germany

ABSTRACT. The paper discusses some current methods to simulate polymeric systems. It covers both neutral and charged polymers.

1. Introduction

For many problems in modern technology but also for daily life polymeric materials play a rather crucial role. Polymers, namely chain molecules consisting of many repeat units, are the basis for a huge variety of materials ranging from simple shopping bags to high tech polymer glasses and to biological systems. The most prominent biological polymer of course is the DNA. One significant and very distinct aspect compared to all other materials is the fact that the conformational entropy of the long flexible chains plays a crucial role for many macroscopic physical properties. This entropic part of the chain free energy gives rise to a huge variety of interesting and important phenomena, but also makes detailed analytical theories often extremely difficult to handle.

For most practical applications polymer materials are either polymer melts, which are (partially) frozen into a glassy state (disordered melt of coils, such as a bowl of very long molecular spaghetti), or polymer networks, such as gels or rubber. For networks the (usually) melt of disordered polymer coils is crosslinked, e. g. via vulcanization. Most biological polymers, but also an increasing number of synthetic systems, contain either strong dipolar units along the chain or are even charged. This adds additional complications, however many of these polymers are soluble in water. It is one of the important future problems to replace the often toxic organic solvents by water or less toxic liquids.

In the longer run one would like to deduce the macroscopic physical properties both quantitatively and qualitatively from the chemical structure of the individual monomers. Today this is not possible, and there is still a far way to go. The reason comes from two aspects. One is the importance of the conformational degrees of freedom. The number of accessible states grows exponentially with the number of repeat units, monomers, leading to a finite conformational entropy per monomer. The second is the huge variety of different chemical species, which makes it just impossible to cover all polymers in e.g. an extensive quantum chemistry investigation. For computer simulations an additional complication comes from time scales, rangeing from $10^{-13} sec$ of the oscillation time of local chemical bonds to hours or days for macroscopic relaxation.

The huge variety of different polymers can easily be illustrated. Typical examples of monomers which are connected to chains (of N repeat units), are

PE	$(CH_2)_N$	polyethylene
PDMS	$(Si(CH_3)_2O)_N$	polydimethylsiloxane
PS	$(CH_2(CH(C_6H_5)))_N$	polystyrene
BPAPC	$(C_6H_4C(CH_3)_2C_6H_4CO_3)_N$	bisphenyl A polycarbonate
NaPSS	$(CH_2(CH(C_6H_4SO_3^-Na^+)))_N$	sulfonated polystyrene

These are just five examples ranging from the most simple case of PE to the technically very important but more complicated BPAPC, which is used e. g. for compact discs. The last one is a so called strongly charged flexibe polyelectrolyte. NaPSS is water soluble and dissociates Na^+ ions into the water. At a very first glance it is tempting and would be very interesting to perform a full scale MD (molecular dynamics) simulation, which includes all the chemical details. A valid question, however, is to what extent this can be done or is it necessary at all? The short list of monomers illustrates that there are just far too many different polymers that can be chemically synthesized. Thus one would be restricted to the study of a very few model systems. However, even then it is not always clear how to determine the force fields properly. In many cases they are not very well known. In particular the complicated interchain or polymer-solvent interactions are only poorly understood at present.

Thus today it is not possible to perform such a simulation properly. Even if one were able to overcome such difficulties the situation would have improved only marginally, if at all. The reason lies in the huge variation of the relevant time and length scales, as Fig. 1 illustrates for the most simple polymer available. The typical times range from 10^{-13} s for

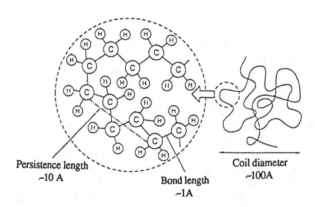

Fig. 1. A sketch of the different length scales in polymer problems for the simple example of polyethylene [1, 2]

local oscillations, requiring MD timesteps of about 10^{-14} s, up to seconds or hours for the diffusion time of a chain and to much longer times for collective phenomena or relaxation near the glass transition. A time of the order of the chain diffusion time is needed to relax the chain conformations. In a similar way we have to deal with length scale variations that range from 1 Å to several hundreds of Å's. For a reasonably sized system, no computer will cover this range of $\mathcal{O}(10^{14})$ timesteps. Even semi-detailed models would require too much time. The reptation study which will be discussed later took altogether around 1000h of cpu time (Cray YMP, optimized linked cell code) [3–5]. A similar study, which would cover roughly the same effective chain lengths and a similar time scale, employing Roe's PE model [6, 7], a unified atom model where the H-atoms are incorporated into a then havier effective carbon atom, with a C-C spring constant reduced by a factor of 7, would have taken several hundreds of thousand hours of cpu time on a Cray YMP [8, 2]. It is easy to imagine the requirements of e. g. the PE model with "full" atomistic details or even more ineteresting polymers such as BPAPC. It is just a prohibitively large amount of CPU time required even for the now coming massively parallel systems. From that point of view one could stop and turn to different but simpler problems. However despite these tremendous complications the situation is better than the analysis suggests. To what extent and for what kind of problems do we really need the chemical details? Fig. 1 gives a caricature of the various relevant length scales. It also illustrates universality. For properties, which are governed by length scales larger than a few Kuhn lengths (the stiffness length) their general behaviour becomes independent of the local chemistry. For example in the limit of long chains of N monomers the mean squared end-to-end distance $\langle R^2(N) \rangle = AN^{2\nu}$. ν is a universal exponent, which is 0.588 in a good-solvent and 0.5 in the melt for neutral chains. The chemical details are hidden in the prefactor A. This suggests a somewhat better situation, namely for most questions of interest one can confine the simulation to the simplest and for computational purposes the fastest models. In many cases one just needs the monomer-monomer excluded volume and the chain connectivity. These models are often called coarse-grained models. Later on, of course one faces the problem of "mapping properties back to a given chemical system". Though these prefactors only quantitatively shift the reasults, they are in most cases the more relevant parameters for a specific technical application. This problem will be mentioned at various places.

In the following only methods, which are also useful for investigation of dynamics will be discussed. I however mention already here, that they only should be used if no faster scheme is available.

2. Polymer simulations: general considerations

Typically, there are three classes of models used for computer simulations of coarse grained models of polymers The simplest model, and most widely used one, is the simple self-avoiding walk (SAW) on a lattice [9]. Each lattice point can be occupied only once. It is trivial to introduce nearest-neighbour energies and other generalizations. The second model system would be the direct generalization for continuous space, the pearl necklace model. The chain consists of hard spheres of diameter σ_0 and a fixed bond length ℓ_0. The third variant is mainly used in MD simulations. The monomers consist of point particles which interact with, in most cases, a purely repulsive Lennard Jones interaction. For the bonded nearest-neighbours along the chain an additional spring potential is added which together with the Lennard Jones repulsion determines the bond length ℓ. Sometimes combinations of these models are used. The purpose of a simulation is to generate statistically independent conformations or to follow the time evolution of a given global configuration. The most natural ansatz would be to simply perform a MD simulation, where Newton's equations of motion

$$d^2\mathbf{r}_i/dt^2 = -\nabla V_i(\{\mathbf{r}_i\}) \tag{1}$$

are solved numerically. $\mathbf{r}_i$ is the position of monomer i, and V_i is the potential from the interaction with all the other monomers. However, this direct approach cannot be used for isolated chains. The reason lies in the structural properties of the chains. A linear polymer without excluded volume interactions has the structure of a random walk [10]. Its dynamics can be described by eigenmodes, Rouse modes, which decouple [11]. Thus solving eqn (1) exactly without excluded volume would never equilibrate the chain. In the case of a SAW, the Rouse modes are no longer eigenmodes of the chain. However, the deviations come mainly from the long range contacts (monomers which are far apart along the chain) which still obey the excluded volume constraint if they approach each other in space. However, the chains are fractal objects with a fractal dimension $d_f = 1/\nu$. For long chains the density decays with a power law. Consequently, the necessary long range interactions, which cause the swelling of the chains, are very infrequent. Thus the natural MD approach can only be used for a chain interacting directly with solvent, other chains or for chains with long range interaction potentials. To avoid this problem one has to couple the chains to a stochastic process. This can typically be done using the Monte Carlo method. Another technique, for use in conjunction

TABLE I

An illustration of the timescales in polymer simulations compared to simple liquids.

	Liquid	Polymer melt	Charged Polymer
particles	N_{TOT}	N_{TOT}	N_{TOT}
density	ρ_0	ρ_0	ρ_0
cpu time per timestep	$\propto N_{TOT}$	$\propto N_{TOT}$	$\propto N_{TOT}^2$
motion distance to equilibrate	$\propto \rho_0^{-1/d} \propto N_{TOT}^0$	$\propto \langle R^2(N)\rangle^{1/2} \propto N^{1/2}$	$\propto \langle R^2(N)\rangle^{1/2} \propto N^{1/2\ldots1}$
physical relaxation time	$\tau \propto N_{TOT}^0$	$\tau_N \propto N^{2\ldots3.4}$	$\tau_N \propto N^{2\ldots3.4}$
		(varies with chain length)	(varies with chain length)
CPU time	$T \propto N_{TOT}$	$T \propto N_{TOT} \cdot N^{2\ldots3.4}$	$T \propto N_{TOT}^2 \cdot N^{2\ldots3.4}$

with the MD method, would be to introduce local stochastic jumps. This would result in a so-called dynamic MC simulation. Such local changes follow the characteristic Langevin dynamics of the chains. These *local move algorithms* should, however, be avoided whenever possible. To illustrate this, let us compare a simple liquid or a lattice gas, a polymer melt of the same density and total number of particles and system of charged chains. A timestep for MD is explicit in the algorithm, while for MC it can be taken as one attempted move per particle of the system. Of course, the comparison does not hold for critical phenomena within the liquid; there critical slowing down also significantly increases the cpu-time requirements. The exponent N^x, $x = 2\ldots3.4$ can actually be interpreted as a dynamical exponent for the critical slowing down [11]. (In the language of critical phenomena the inverse chain length corresponds to $(T-T_c)/T_c$. Thus the relaxation time follows $((T-T_c)/T_c)^z$ with $2 \leq z \leq 3.4$.) This causes significant problems since typical N values of interest in most cases start at around 50 to 100. For charged systems, there are better algorithms available than the simple $N_{(TOT)}^2$ summation of the Coulomb energy. However up to now the limitations from the chain relaxation time confines the system size to a region, where these methods are not yet applicable. Thus there is one important rule that should be taken into account before starting a polymer simulation: if possible, avoid algorithms with slow physical dynamics. However for the following, I will only discuss applications, where it is necessary or useful to use such methods. A more general dicussion can be found in [12].

3. Simulations of polymer dynamics

If one wants information about dynamics, which covers the time range of up to the order of the chain relaxation time, one has to follow the slow physical path. There are many tricks to vectorize or simplify the algorithms, but these only manipulate the prefactors of the power laws shown in Table I. It is certainly tempting to avoid this problem, but all attempts to do so necessarily include a model of dynamics which is far beyond the molecular basis. Thus any simulation which does not start from these basic principles is, in the context of dynamics, extremely questionable, unless one can show the compatibility of the model with experiment [9, 1, 13, 8]. Even so, this does not prove the underlying model to be valid.

Thus we are faced with the problem of a naturally very slow process forced to extremely simple models. The direct and conceptually simple method of studying dynamics is the molecular dynamics approach. This method is very versatile and has great potential. In most cases, however, it is more time consuming than the stochastic Monte Carlo methods. Direct Langevin dynamics (Brownian Dynamics) is usually even more time consuming and will not be discussed here.

Firstly, let us consider dynamical Monte Carlo methods. Since MC is a stochastic method, it does not have an intrinsic natural time-scale. In addition, as an aside, there are deep problems of principle if one wants to study hydrodynamics with dynamical MC methods. For the properties of melts and for model dynamics in more dilute systems, the so called free draining limit, this is not included and not needed. To test the applicability of a method we have to find a basic model for dynamics. This model is the so called Rouse model [11]. This is still the only model on a "molecular level", which can be solved analytically. The Rouse model treats the dynamics of a harmonic random walk in the overdamped limit. All the complicated interchain and intrachain interactions are summarized in the viscous background and the heat bath. Thus, we totally disregard excluded volume and topology constraints beyond the plain chain connectivity. This model can easily be solved analytically. With r_i being the position of the ith monomer, the Rouse equation of motion is written as

$$\zeta dr_i/dt = -k(2r_i - r_{i+1} - r_{i-1}) + f_i(t) . \tag{2}$$

ζ is the monomeric friction constant, k the bond spring constant and $f_i(t)$ the heat bath with $\langle f_i \rangle = 0$. ζ and $f_i(t)$ are coupled via the fluctuation dissipation theorem $\langle f_i(t)f_i(0) \rangle = 2d\zeta k_B T \delta(t)\delta_{ij}$. Thus the resulting deviation from free diffusion is only due to the connectivity of the chain. Within this model the eigenmodes decay exponentially, $\langle x_p(t)x_p(0) \rangle / \langle x_p^2 \rangle = \exp(-t/\tau_p)$, $\tau_p \propto N^2/p^2$, resulting in an overall chain diffusion constant

$$D = k_B T/\zeta N \tag{3}$$

for the whole chain. This simple model describes the dynamics of polymer melts of short chains rather well. All the complicated chain-chain interactions seem to be represented reasonably by a heat bath and a frictional background.

This model now gives a basis for the dynamic interpretation of stochastic algorithms. Besides the standard requirements for MC procedures (detailed balance etc.) we need the following property [9]: any algorithm with stochastic or artificial dynamics must have local moves and must yield Rouse dynamics for random walks in order to be valid to study the dynamics of polymer chains. If we use the heat bath picture, then, at any time, each monomer is affected equally on average by the random force and the heat bath. Therefore it is natural to define a MC timestep as one attempted move per monomer of the whole system. This defines up to a prefactor the physical time unit τ_0. The prefactor is adjusted in direct comparison to experiment. Such simple lattice algorithms however have the disadvantage that they are mostly restricted to rather low densities. Conformations can block each other and one faces precursors of the glass transition in a region, where one does not expect them from typical experiments. A way out to avoid these problems to some extend and still stick to the computationally very efficient lattice models, is the so called *Bond fluctuation algorithm* of Carmesin and Kremer [14, 15]. This very effective algorithm combines the ideas from the standard lattice MC methods with the notation that the one should allow the bond angle and even the bond length to vary.

Fig. 2 illustrates the method $d = 3$. Each monomer consists of 2^d lattice sites. In addition to the excluded volume interaction, the bond length l is restricted to a maximum extension to avoid bond crossing. On the square lattice, one has the constraint that $1 < l < \sqrt{16}$. For $d = 3$, the situation is slightly more complicated. In this case a set of 108 different bonds are allowed [17, 18, 16]. Since each monomer occupies 2^d sites, but every jump only requires 2^{d-1} empty sites, the method works effectively at high densities. It also suffers less from the nonergodicity problems due to blocked conformations than the standard methods do. For the 3-d study of the dynamics of polymer melts[16] densities as large as 0.5 were used, although higher densities are also possible. Such a density corresponds to a much higher effective density than for the same number of occupied sites using the standard lattice models. An optimized vector program gave approximately 1.7×10^6 attempted moves per second for one processor on the Cray YMP [17, 18] for the same density. At high density or for long range interactions the *Molecular dynamics* method is an interesting alternative. The simulations using the MD

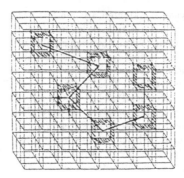

Fig. 2. An illustration of the bond fluctuation model for a 3-d linear polymer [16]. Typical elementary moves are indicated.

method, which are discussed here, employ the bead-spring model [19], where each monomer is weakly coupled to a heat bath. Each polymer chain consists of N monomers of mass m connected by an anharmonic spring. The monomers interact through a shifted Lennard-Jones potential given by

$$
v^0(r) = \begin{cases} 4\epsilon\left[\left(\frac{\sigma}{r}\right)^{12} - \left(\frac{\sigma}{r}\right)^6 - \left(\frac{\sigma}{r_c}\right)^{12} + \left(\frac{\sigma}{r_c}\right)^6\right] & r \le r_c \\ 0 & r > r_c \end{cases} \tag{4}
$$

where r_c is the interaction cutoff. For the polymer melts, we choose $r_c = 2^{1/6}\sigma$ so that the interaction is purely repulsive. For monomers which are connected we add an additional attractive interaction potential of the form [20]

$$
v^{\text{bond}}(r) = \begin{cases} -0.5kR_0^2\ln\left[1 - \left(\frac{r}{R_0}\right)^2\right] & r \le R_0 \\ \infty & r > R_0 \end{cases} . \tag{5}
$$

For melts the parameters $k = 30\epsilon/\sigma^2$ and $R_0 = 1.5\sigma$ are chosen to be the same as in [19].

Denoting the total potential of monomer i by V_i, the equation of motion for monomer i is given by

$$
m\frac{d^2\mathbf{r}_i}{dt^2} = -\nabla V_i - \Gamma\frac{d\mathbf{r}_i}{dt} + \mathbf{W}_i(t) . \tag{6}
$$

Here Γ is the bead friction which acts to couple the monomers to the heat bath. $\mathbf{W}_i(t)$ describes the random force acting on each bead. It can be written as a Gaussian white noise with $\langle\mathbf{W}_i(t)\cdot\mathbf{W}_j(t')\rangle = \delta_{ij}\delta(t-t')6k_BT\Gamma$, where T is the temperature and k_B is the Boltzmann constant. This approach is necessary in order to stabilize the runs. MD runs for polymers typically exceed the stability limits of a microcanonical simulation. We have used $\Gamma = 0.5\tau^{-1}$ and $k_BT = 1.0\epsilon$ in most cases and $m = 1$[3–5]. The equations of motion are solved using a Verlet algorithm with a timestep $\Delta t = 0.01\tau$ in typical Lennard Jones units. The program can be vectorized for a Cray supercomputer following the procedure described by Grest et al. [21] except that an additional interaction between monomers which are connected was added. The cpu time per step increased approximately linearly with N. On the Cray YMP at Jülich our program runs at a speed of $140000/(MN)$ time steps per second where M is the number of chains of N monomers in the melt. In a recent improvement of the way the Verlet table is set up and the forces are calculated an additional speed up, for this case, of a factor of two was reached[22]. Tests using the parallelization on a Cray YMP8/832 gave a speedup of 6 for 8 processors and 40000 particles, compared to a theoretical speedup of 6.9 for the linked cell code[23]. For the present problems the C90 turns out to be again faster by a factor of 1.7 compared to the YMP. First tests of a parallel version, which ran on a Cray T3D will be presented at the meeting.

In most cases MC is more effective, however more limited. For a more general discussion see [8]. In the following I discuss shortly two applications. The first is a study of the reptation dynamics in polymer melts, where both Monte Carlo and MD was used. The second is an investigation of a polyelectrolyte solution, where for the first time the counterions, which make the system neutral are explicitly taken into account.

4. Reptation in Polymer Melts

The dynamics of polymer melts is observed experimentally to change from an apparent Rouse-like behaviour to a dramatically slower dynamics for chains exceeding the characteristic length N_e. There are several theoretical models which try to explain this behaviour. However, only the reptation concept of Edwards and de Gennes [11] and variants of this approach take the non-crossing of the chains explicitly into account. It is the only one, which at least qualitatively, can account for a wide variety of different experimental results, such as neutron spin echo scattering, diffusion and viscosity. While it cannot explain all experimental data it does remarkably well, particularly considering its conceptual simplicity. For short chains the topological constraints do not play an important role. The dynamics is reasonably well described by the Rouse model. This experimental and numerical observation is surprising and still not understood. For longer chains, exceeding a characteristic entanglement length N_e, one observes a dramatic slowing down to $D \propto N^{-2}$ and the vsicosity $\eta \propto N^{3.4}$. The idea of the reptation model is that the topological constraints of each chain, as imposed by the surrounding, cause a motion along the polymers own coarse-grained contour. The diameter of the tube, in which the chain is constrained, is the diameter of a subchain of length N_e, namely $d_T \propto N_e^{1/2}$. The chains follow the Rouse relaxation up to the time $\tau_e \propto N_e^2$. For longer times the constraints are supposed to become dominant and the chain moves along its own contour. In order to leave the tube, the chain has to diffuse along the tube a distance of the order of its own contour length, $d_T N/N_e$. This gives $D \propto N^{-2}$ and $\eta \propto N^3$. The difference between the predicted and the measured exponent for η is still not completely understood.

One way to characterize the transition from Rouse to reptation is to investigate the diffusion constant $D(N)$,

$$D(N) = \frac{k_B T}{N\zeta}, \quad N < N_e \tag{7}$$

$$D(N) \propto N^{-2}, \quad N \gg N_e. \tag{8}$$

Here ζ is the monomeric friction coefficient. In order to be able to make a significant contribution by simulation, the data must be capable of covering this crossover. Following eqns (7) and (8), $D(N)N$ should define a plateau for small N, giving the monomeric friction or mobility. To compare results from different simulations and also experiment, a plot of $D(N)/D_{Rouse}(N)$ versus N/N_e or M/M_e respectively should give one universal curve since N_e is thought to be the only characteristic length of the crossover. Here $D_{Rouse} = k_B T/\zeta N$ and M_e is the experimental entanglement mass. This mapping is important for our understanding, since experiment and simulation use different methods to estimate M_e or N_e. The scaling of the different data onto one curve, Fig. 3, shows, that for both cases the same length scale is used[8, 3–5, 16]. The MD [3–5] simulations were performed at a density of $\rho = 0.85\sigma^{-3}$ and the MC simulations at two different volume fractions $\phi = 0.4, 0.5$. The experimental data are NMR measurements of Pearson et al. [24] for PE.

Finally for our discussion of the dense systems, let us ask to what extent can one follow the motion of the monomers along the contour of the chains. For the chain lengths available

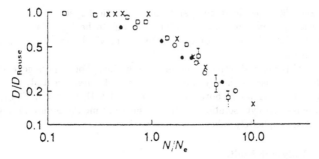

Fig. 3. The diffusion constant normalized to the Rouse diffusion constant for MD data and MC data at two different densities and for PE, as a function of N/N_e, from [16].

we have to restrict ourselves to the primitive chain. For the original chain of $N = 200$ from our MD data the tube diameter d_T is only $(N/N_e)^{1/2} \approx 2.4$ times smaller than the mean end-to-end distance of the chain itself. To improve this we [3–5] constructed a primitive chain using

$$\mathbf{R}_1 = \frac{1}{N_e} \sum_{i=1}^{N_e} \mathbf{r}_i; \, \mathbf{R}_2 = \frac{1}{N_e} \sum_{i=3}^{N_e+2} \mathbf{r}_i \ldots \tag{9}$$

The primitive chain (PC) feels the constraints of the tube much more strongly. From $g_1(t)$, now evaluated for the PC, we find a tube diameter $d_{T,PC} \approx 5\sigma$. If we now simply plot conformations of the PC, separated by a constant time increment, we can directly observe the confinement into the tube. Fig. 4 gives plot of 20 conformations spaced 1200τ apart for a total elapsed time of 24000τ (about $13\tau_e$) for $N = 200$. For this time we expect an inner monomer of the PC to travel a distance of $(3g_1(\tau_{max}))^{1/2} \approx 13\sigma$ compared to the tube diameter $d_t \approx (3g_1(\tau_e))^{1/2} = 5\sigma$ if the chains did not reptate [3–5]. The figure clearly shows the confinement of the chain to a tube. Visualizing the reptation concept qualitatively gives a profound picture of the underlying physical mechanism. More detailed investigations support

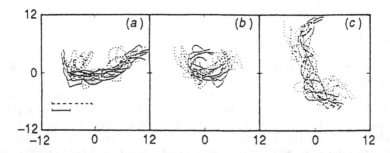

Fig. 4. Plot of the conformations of the PC of a chain of $N = 200$ from MD simulations. The two bars indicate the estimated tube diameter and the estimated motion distance from isotropic motion [3–5].

the impression, which one gets from Fig. 4. Note that the data do not agree with the mode coupling approach of Schweizer [25] since the motion is anisotropic. The data now can be used to directly predict time and length scales for experimental tests. For details see [26].

5. Polyelectrolytes

Polyelectrolytes remain one of the most mysterious states of condensed matter. This is in great contrast to the well developed theory of neutral polymer solutions [10,27,28]. Experimentally bulk properties like the osmotic pressure and the viscosity are well known, but an understanding of the microscopic origin is lacking. This ignorance is especially critical since, for example, one of the prototypical polyelectrolytes is DNA. The lack of progress is in part due to the unfortunate situation in which theory is best done in one regime (dilute) and experiment is best done in another regime (semidilute). In such a situation simulations can be very helpful to bridge this gap. For this case it actually turns out, that MD is a very efficient method to simulate the chains, mainly because of the correlated motion of the charged monomers and the solvated counterions. Here I want only show the example of the form factor of a given chain as a function of polymer and thus charge content in the system. The counterions are explicitly taken into account and the electrostatic interaction is summed using the Ewald sum in a spherical approximation. This can be done, since the Wigner Seitz cell of a body centered cubic crystal was used as simulation box. Experimentally this form factor is almost impossible to obtain, since not only the chains, but also the counterions and the solvent itself scatters. A way out would be neutron scattering, however in order to cover the dilute solution limit, the concentrations become too low. The figure shows the crossover from an almost

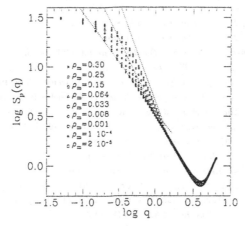

Fig. 5. Form factor of a single polyelectrolyte chain of N=64 charged monomers as a funtion of monomer density. The behavior changes from an almost stretched conformation to the high density random walk structure. [28,27].

stretched chain, $S(k) \propto k^{-1}$, to the random walk limit, $S(k) \propto k^{-2}$, at high densities. An especially interesting and also important aspect is, that at high k already for very low densities a significant local roughness of the chain is observable. This is in contrast to the usual semiflexible chain approach.

6. Conclusions

The present very short overview should give a first introduction to the possibilities and complications of polymer simulations. Compared to the extremely large simulations of e. g. Ising models, used to obtain critical exponents to an accuracy of more than 3 digits, the computer simulations of polymers are just in their infancy. The reason is in the huge number of intrinsic degrees of freedom and the slow relaxation. Nevertheless, there has been significant progress over the last years, which is due to improved models and algorithms and to improved hardware. Currently the advent of massively parallel computers, with individual nodes which have the computational power of a modern workstation, will enable significant progress in many new areas. This can, however, only be achieved if the close contact with analytical theory *and* is maintained.

Acknowledgements

The work described here was supported by the Deutsche Forschungsgemeinschaft (DFG) and a NATO travel grant. For the polymer melts (MD) and solutions cpu time was granted by the German Supercomputer Centre, HLRZ in Jülich. The work described here was performed in a pleasant and close collaboration with K. Binder, B. Dünweg, G.S. Grest, J. Batoulis, I. Carmesin, H.P. Wittmann, W. Paul, D.W. Heermann, E.R. Duering, M. Stevens and R. Everaers.

References

[1] K. BINDER, J. Bicerano, New York, Basel, Hong Kong, 1992.

[2] K. KREMER and G. S. GREST, in *Computer simulations of polymers*, edited by R. J. ROE, Prentice Hall, Englewood Cliffs NJ, 1991.

[3] K. KREMER and G. S. GREST, *J. Chem. Phys.* **92**, 5057 (1990).

[4] K. KREMER and G. S. GREST, *J. Chem. Phys.* **94**, 4103 (1991), erratum.

[5] K. KREMER and I. CARMESIN, *Phys. Rev. Lett.* **61**, 566 (1990).

[6] D. RIGBY and R. J. ROE, *J. Chem. Phys.* **87**, 7285 (1987).

[7] D. RIGBY and R. J. ROE, *J. Chem. Phys.* **89**, 5280 (1988).

[8] K. KREMER and G. S. GREST, *J. Chem. Soc. Faraday Trans.* **88**, 1707 (1992).

[9] K. KREMER and K. BINDER, *Comput. Phys. Rep.* **7**, 259 (1988).

[10] P. G. DE GENNES, *Scaling concepts in polymer physics*, Cornell University Press, Ithaca, NY, 1979.

[11] M. S. DOI and S. F. EDWARDS, *Theory of Polymer Dynamics*, Clarendon Press, Oxford, 1986.

[12] K. K. IN, *Computer simulations in chemical physics*, Kluwer Academic Publishers, 1993.

[13] H. MARK and B. ERMAN, *Elastomeric Polymer Networks*, Prentice Hall, Englewood Cliffs NJ, 1992.

[14] I. CARMESIN and K. KREMER, *Macromolecules* **21**, 2819 (1988).

[15] I. CARMESIN and K. KREMER, *J. Phys., Paris* **51**, 1567 (1990).

[16] W. PAUL, K. BINDER, D. W. HEERMANN, and K. KREMER, *J. Phys., Paris* **37**, II1 (1991).

[17] H. P. WITTMANN and K. KREMER, *Comput. Phys. Commun.* **61**, 309 (1990).

[18] H. P. WITTMANN and K. KREMER, *Comput. Phys. Commun.* **71**, 343 (1992), erratum.

[19] G. S. GREST and K. KREMER, *Phys. Rev. A* **33**, 3628 (1986).

[20] R. B. BIRD, R. C. ARMSTRONG, and O. HASSAGER, *Dynamics of Polymeric Liquids*, J. Wiley NY, 1971.

[21] G. S. GREST, B. DÜNWEG, and K. KREMER, *Comput. Phys. Commun.* **55**, 269 (1989).

[22] R. EVERAERS and K. KREMER, *Comp. Phys. Comm.* **xx**, xxx (1994).

[23] N. ATTIG and K. KREMER, (1994), in preparation.

[24] D. S. PEARSON, G. V. STRATE, E. VON MEERWALL, and F. C. SCHILLING, *Macromolecules* **20**, 1133 (1987).

[25] K. S. SCHWEIZER, *J. Chem. Phys.* **91**, 5802 (1989).

[26] K. KREMER and G. S. GREST, in *Computer simulations in polymer physics*, edited by K. BINDER, Oxford Univ. Press, 1994.

[27] B. DUENWEG, M. J. STEVENS, and I. K. KREMER, in *Computer simulations in polymer physics*, edited by K. BINDER, Oxford Univ. Press, 1994.

[28] M. J. STEVENS and K. KREMER, *Macromolecules* **26**, 4717 (1993).

Parallel Finite Element Algorithms Applied to Polymer Flow

R. Keunings, R. Aggarwal, P. Henriksen, D. Vanderstraeten, and O. Zone

Centre for Systems Engineering and Applied Mechanics (CESAME),
Université Catholique de Louvain, B-1348 Louvain-la-Neuve, Belgium

Abstract. Parallel finite element algorithms are proposed for the solution of physical problems described by means of non-linear partial differential or integro-differential equations of mixed type, using unstructured computational meshes. Typical applications include the flow of viscoelastic fluids and of fiber-reinforced polymer melts. A generic parallel approach to the assembly and solution of the finite element equation sets is described, together with the associated load balancing and mesh partitioning tools. Finally, the proposed algorithms are evaluated in the simulation of viscoelastic flows, performed on various distributed memory MIMD parallel computers such as the INTEL iPSC/860 hypercube, the CONVEX Meta Series, and a heterogeneous network of workstations.

1 Review of Research Objectives

Much progress has been made over the last decade towards the realistic computer modeling of materials engineering processes. For example, the particular field of polymer matrix composites has benefitted greatly from advances in general polymer flow computations [1, 2], as well as in process-specific simulation tools [3]. Demands in computer resources are enormous in these fields, and the efficient exploitation of parallel computers is of particular interest. The continuum-mechanical description of materials engineering processes leads to non-linear sets of partial differential or integro-differential equations of mixed type (elliptic/hyperbolic), for which appropriate finite element discretization principles must be designed. The linearized discretized equations take the form of a large algebraic system whose matrix is sparse, but does not possess the properties of symmetry and positive-definiteness that are met in simpler physical problems (e.g. linear elasticity and Stokes flow). As a result, parallel approaches to the solution of these equations, based on Conjugate-Gradient-like iterative schemes [4, 5] are unlikely to be successful.

The objective of our work is to develop a generic approach to parallel finite element calculations on Multiple Instruction Multiple Data (MIMD) computers, with local, distributed memory or virtual, shared memory. Target applications are physical problems solved with unstructured computational meshes that lead to general, sparse system matrices (i.e. non-symmetric and indefinite).

In a series of publications, we have addressed the following topics:

– *Parallel, element-by-element evaluation and assembly of the finite element equations:* This apparently "embarrassingly-parallel" problem is in fact quite difficult in some applications (i.e. flow of integral viscoelastic fluids) where the compute load in each element cannot be predicted *a priori*, is spatially-heterogeneous, and can change during the course of the non-linear iterative process. We have proposed a dynamic load balancing scheme to handle this difficulty [6, 7], as well as a natural, "work-on-demand" allocation procedure particularly appropriate for heterogeneous networks of workstations [8].

– *Parallel solution of general finite element equation sets by means of a direct, frontal method:* The proposed algorithm is based on the domain decomposition paradigm. It uses the frontal method in each subdomain and a divide-and-conquer parallel treatment of the interface problem [9, 10]. Let P be the number of available processors. First, the finite element mesh is decomposed in P subdomains. At the beginning of the calculations, each processor is allocated the elements of a subdomain. All processors then perform in parallel the sequential frontal method within their subdomain. At the end of this local elimination step, each processor holds an active system which corresponds to the nodes located at the interface with neighbor subdomains. A communication phase is then needed to assemble the interface contributions and to solve the interface problem. We can view this phase as the traversal of a binary tree where the arcs represent a communication at each level, and the leaves correspond to the different processors. The parallel processing of the interface problem involves two traversals of the tree. First, the tree is traversed from the leaves to the root. At each level, half of the active processors send in parallel their interface system to a neighbor processor, after which they become idle; the receiving processors assemble in parallel the neighbor contributions with their own, and eliminate the common interface variables by means of Gaussian elimination. This procedure is repeated until the "root" processor is reached. The second traversal goes from the root to the leaves. It consists of a backsubstitution followed by the communication of the computed values of the interface variables. A processor having performed the elimination of an interface variable during the first traversal computes this variable by backsubstitution. When the interface problem has been solved, the processors perform in parallel the backsubstitution of their internal variables.
The way the interface system is communicated, assembled, and solved is a key issue as far as parallel efficiency is concerned. In order to maximize parallel efficiency, we compute an *interface processing tree* in such a way that the maximum number of interface variables is eliminated at the lowest possible level of the tree.

– *Automatic partitioning of unstructured computational meshes:* The efficiency of the above parallel direct solver depends on the quality of the decomposition of the finite element meshes. A good decomposition should ensure an equal and minimum computational load within the subdomains, and it should have an interface size as small as possible. We have developed a mesh partitioning strategy that involves two steps [11, 12, 13]: the use of a *direct partitioning* scheme to provide an initial partition (e.g. Recursive Graph Bisection), followed by an *optimization step* based on graph theory and using combinatorial non-deterministic heuristics (e.g. Simulated Annealing). The optimization techniques are based on the following principle: elements located along the interface are randomly selected and transferred to a neighboring subdomain with some probability. Transfers that increase the quality of the decomposition are always accepted, while transfers that decrease it are accepted with a probability inversely proportional to the loss of quality. The quality of the decomposition is estimated by a cost function that takes into account the total interface size and the load imbalance:

$$Cost = \alpha I + (1 - \alpha) \sum_{k=1}^{P} (N_k - N_{best,k})^2,$$

where I is the interface size, N_k (resp. $N_{best,k}$) is the number (resp. the optimal number) of elements in subdomain k, and α is a penalty parameter. Since the parallel solver uses a frontal method in each subdomain, we model the load in subdomain k by

$$Load_k = N_{best,k} \times Front_k^{max} \times Front_k^{mean},$$

where $Front_k^{max}$ and $Front_k^{mean}$ represent the maximum and the mean frontal widths, respectively. The a priori-unknown values of the $N_{best,k}$'s are computed during the optimization process such that $Load_k$ is as small as possible and is independent of k. This implies a series of element renumbering phases within each subdomains, which are performed by means of the heuristics developed in [14].

– *Tools for easing software development on message-passing parallel machines:* Altough these particular developments were not intended when we started the project, it quickly turned out that available software tools for message-passing computers remain too rudimentary to allow easy cross-platform portability. We have thus developed a software library based on PVM [15] that eases program development and addresses some of the most pressing needs of "message-passing" programmers. It has allowed us to port the proposed parallel algorithms on a variety of platforms (INTEL, CONVEX, heterogeneous networks of workstations) [16].

A review of the above developments is given in [17]. Illustrative results are reported in the next section.

2 Illustrative Results

We report in Table 1 parallel speedup results obtained on the INTEL iPSC/860 hypercube for the stick–slip flow of a particular integral viscoelastic fluid [6].

P	2	4	8	16	32	64	128
Speedup	2	3.7	6.6	13.0	24.7	46.5	78.7

Table 1. Parallel speedup for the stick–slip flow of an integral viscoelastic fluid [6].

This problem involves the parallel calculation and assembly of the finite element equations followed by a short, sequential solution phase. The results of Table 1 are quite satisfactory in view of the fact that they have been produced with a simple task allocation strategy that has no *a priori* knowledge of the workload within each element. Improved results have been reported in [7] using an *adaptative* allocation scheme that uses measured workload data from previous non-linear iterations to redistribute the elements to the processors during the iterative process, if deemed necessary. Similar results have been obtained on a heterogeneous network of workstations, using a *work-on-demand* allocation procedure [8].

Decomposition results for a variety of 2D and 3D meshes with a number of subdomains ranging between 2 and 64 are reported in [11, 13]. We show in Fig. 1b

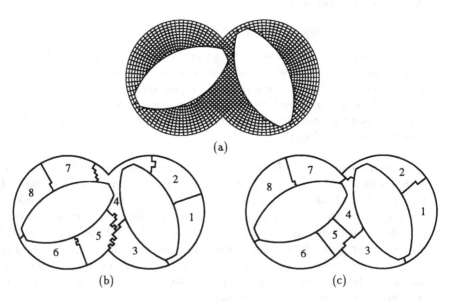

Fig. 1. Typical example. The mesh (a) is decomposed in 8 subdomains with a direct RGB scheme (b) and then optimized by means of a SA scheme (c).

a decomposition in 8 subdomains generated in the first step of the automatic partitioning method. We have used the Recursive Graph Bisection technique (RGB). Fig. 1c shows the decomposition obtained by the second step, wherein the initial partition is optimized by means of a Simulated Annealing scheme (SA). We can observe that the number of interface nodes has been reduced by 25%. Moreover, the maximum load $Load_k$ over the subdomains has been reduced by a factor 2. We also observe that the interface is much smoother. This can be of crucial importance to finite element techniques that use a Lagrange multiplier treatment of the interface conditions. Table 2 gives the number of interface nodes and the reduction afforded by the optimizer SA, compared to a direct RGB scheme for the mesh of Fig. 1a. For the entire set of problems tested [11], the reduction in the number of interface nodes ranges between 20% and 50%.

P	Number of interface nodes					
	2		4		8	
RGB	40		56		103	
SA	26	35%	36	36%	77	25%

Table 2. Number of interface nodes and percentage reduction between a direct algorithm (RGB) and an optimizer (SA) that includes a series of element renumbering steps (mesh of Fig. 1a).

P	Max. frontal width (380 for P=1)					
	2		4		8	
RGB	432	+14%	557	+47%	487	+28%
SA	352	- 7%	363	- 4%	346	- 9%

Table 3. Maximum frontal width and percentage difference compared to the mono-domain frontal width for the direct (RGB) and the optimization (SA) decomposition techniques (mesh of Fig. 1a).

Table 3 shows the maximum frontal widths over the subdomains obtained with the renumbering scheme. They are compared to the frontal width of 380 for the mono-domain mesh (26082 variables). The interface variables cannot be eliminated and increase therefore the frontal width. We observe though that the maximum frontal width can be *smaller* than the mono-domain value for some optimized decompositions.

The positive impact of the optimized decompositions on the efficiency of the proposed direct parallel solver is illustrated in Table 4, where we list speedup data measured on a CONVEX Meta Series for the flow of a particular differential viscoelastic fluid in the geometry of Fig. 1.

Table 4 gives the observed speedup relative to the *mono-domain* sequential run, for the decompositions of the mesh of Fig. 1 obtained with a direct method (RGB) and with an optimizer (SA). The increase in speedup with the optimizer compared to the direct method is caused by the decrease of the frontal width and of the interface size. Since we measure parallel speedup with respect to the

259

P	2	4	8
RGB	1.66	2.48	3.77
SA	2.63	3.76	11.81

Table 4. Parallel speedup relative to the *mono-domain* sequential time obtained for the mesh of Fig. 1a. The decompositions are computed with a direct algorithm (RGB) and an optimizer (SA).

sequential run on the *mono-domain* mesh, superlinear speedup can be obtained when the maximum frontal width within the subdomains is lower than that of the mono-domain mesh, and when a good load balance is achieved. When superlinear speedup happens, an improved *sequential* algorithm is readily available. Indeed, it suffices to run the parallel code on a single processor, which is possible in the PVM environment of the CONVEX Meta Series [10].

Use of the proposed parallel solver in very large-scale simulations is underway.

3 Conclusions

The results reviewed in the present paper demonstrate the benefits gained by parallel computing in the simulations of complex materials engineering processes. Most of the proposed methodology is now sufficiently developed to allow large-scale simulations that would be unfeasible to conduct on sequential computers. The automatic decomposition techniques developed in our work can be applied to grid-oriented problems in general, whether they be based on finite elements, finite volumes, finite differences or spectral elements. Finally, while the proposed direct parallel solver performs very well in moderate-size simulations, further work is needed towards hybrid direct-iterative schemes to allow for large-scale problems. We have started work in that direction following an approach similar to the Dual Schur Complement technique developed for elliptic problems [18].

Acknowledgements

This work is supported by the European Commission (*BRITE/EURAM* programme), the Belgian *Services de Programmation de la Politique Scientifique* (*Interuniversity Attraction Poles* programme), and the Belgian *Région Wallonne* (*FIRST* programme). The Ph.D. work of Denis Vanderstraeten is supported by the *Fonds National de la Recherche Scientifique* of the Belgian State. Access to the CONVEX Meta Series has been granted by the UCL in the framework of the *GPU Calcul Intensif* project.

References

1. M.J. Crochet, "Numerical Simulation of Viscoelastic Flow: A Review", in *Rubber Chemistry and Technology, Amer. Chem. Soc.*, 62, pp. 426–455 (1989)

2. R. Keunings, "Simulation of Viscoelastic Fluid Flow", in *Fundamentals of Computer Modeling for Polymer Processing*, C. L. Tucker III (Ed.), Carl Hanser Verlag, pp. 402–470 (1989)

3. K.T. O'Brien (Ed.), *Computer Modeling for Extrusion and Other Continuous Polymer Processes*, Carl Hanser Verlag (1992)

4. C. Farhat, "Which Parallel Finite Element Algorithm for Which Architecture and Which Problem?", *Eng. Comp.*, 7, pp. 186–195 (1990)

5. P.E. Bjordstad and O.B. Wildlund, " Iterative Methods for Solving Elliptic Problems on Regions Partitionned into Substructures", *SIAM J. Num. An.*, 23, pp 1097–1120 (1986)

6. R. Aggarwal, R. Keunings, and F.X. Roux, "Numerical Simulation of Polymer Flows: A Parallel Computing Approach", Proc. 6th *SIAM Conf. on Parallel Processing for Scientific Computing*, R.F. Sincovec et al. (Eds), SIAM, pp 79–82 (1993)

7. R. Aggarwal, R. Keunings, and F.X. Roux, "Simulation of the Flow of Integral Viscoelastic Fluids on a Distributed Memory Parallel Computer", *J. of Rheology*, accepted, in press (1994)

8. P. Henriksen and R. Keunings, "Parallel Computation of the Flow of Integral Viscoelastic Fluids on a Heterogeneous Network of Workstations", *Int. J. Num. Meth. in Fluids*, accepted, in press (1994)

9. O. Zone and R. Keunings, "Direct Solution of Two-Dimensional Finite Element Equations on Distributed Memory Parallel Computers", in *High Performance Computing II*, M. Durand and F. El Dabaghi (Eds.), North-Holland, pp. 333–344 (1991)

10. O. Zone, D. Vanderstraeten, P. Henriksen, and R. Keunings, "A Parallel Direct Solver for Implicit Finite Element Problems Based on Automatic Domain Decomposition", to appear in Proc. of the *EUROSIM Conf. on Massively Parallel Processing*, J.C. Zuidervaart and L. Dekker (Eds.) (1994)

11. D. Vanderstraeten and R. Keunings, "Optimized Partitioning of Unstructured Finite Element Meshes", *Internat. J. Numer. Meth. Engrg.*, accepted, in press (1993)

12. D. Vanderstraeten, O. Zone, R. Keunings, and L. Wolsey, "Non-deterministic Heuristics for Automatic Domain Decomposition in Direct Finite Element Calculations", *Proc. 6th SIAM Conf. on Parallel Processing for Scientific Computing*, pp. 929–932 (1993)

13. D. Vanderstraeten, R. Keunings, and C. Farhat, "Optimization of Mesh Partitions and Impact on Parallel CFD", in *Proc. Parallel CFD'93*, A. Ecer et al. (Eds.), accepted, in press (1994)

14. C.C. de Souza, R. Keunings, L.A. Wolsey, O. Zone, "A New Approach to Minimising the Frontwidth in Finite Element Calculations", *Comput Methods Appl. Mech. Engrg.*, accepted, in press (1994)

15. J. Dongarra, G.A. Geist, R. Manchek, and V.S Sunderam, "Integrated PVM Framework Supports Heterogeneous Network Computing", *Computers in Physics*, 7(2) (1993)

16. P. Henriksen and R. Keunings, "Development Environment for Parallel Programs Based upon PVM", to appear in *Proc. Int. HP Users Conf.*, accepted, in press (1994)

17. R. Keunings, "Parallel Finite Element Algorithms Applied to Computational Rheology", *Computers and Chemical Engng.*, accepted, in press (1994)

18. R. Aggarwal, F.X. Roux, and R. Keunings, "Iterative Methods for the Integral Viscoelastic Equations on Parallel Computers", in *Proc. Parallel CFD'93*, P. Leca (Ed.), accepted, in press (1994)

Performance of a molecular–dynamics algorithm on Connection Machines CM-200 and CM-5

Ole Holm Nielsen[1,2]

[1] UNI•C (Danish Computer Center for Research and Education), Bldg. 304, DTH, DK-2800 Lyngby, Denmark, and
[2] Center for Atomic–scale Materials Physics, Physics Department, Bldg. 307, DTH, DK-2800 Lyngby, Denmark.

Abstract. This paper describes briefly our projects which involve Molecular Dynamics simulations carried out on Connection Machine CM-200 and CM-5 supercomputers. The algorithms are discussed, and the implementation on data–parallel computers is described. Performance measurements obtained on CM-200 and CM-5 are reported.

1 The molecular–dynamics problem and the algorithm

Molecular Dynamics (MD) simulations of atomic or molecular microscopic systems are very important in several fields of science, such as solid–state physics and biochemistry, and the more general N–body problem occurs also in astrophysics, fluid dynamics, and other fields. The present projects at Center for Atomic–scale Materials Physics of the Technical University of Denmark, in collaboration with UNI•C, deal with the materials–physics properties of "large" solid–state systems, consisting of from 10.000 to 1 million atoms, or as large as the computer capacity makes practical. This is in contrast to MD studies performed on traditional computers (workstations), which would typically be at least an order of magnitude smaller.

These systems are "large" from the atomistic viewpoint normally taken in solid–state physics, but small on a macroscopic scale. Our aim is to bridge the gap between microscopic and macroscopic physics by studying the "mesoscopic" size domain in between, thereby learning what impact microscopic properties rooted in quantum mechanics has on physics at the macroscopic, or classical, scale.

The basis of all MD studies is a theoretical model of the interactions between the constituent atoms. In the present work, which deals with metallic systems (for example, copper or aluminium), a comprehensive theoretical framework has been built up, leading to an *Effective Medium Theory*[1] for atomic interactions. In this theory, charge density "tails" from neighboring atoms are accumulated, and a non-linear functional is used to derive the interatomic forces. Owing to the physical properties of metals, these interactions have a short range of 4–5 atomic diameters.

Such short range interactions dictate the types of algorithms chosen for MD simulations: Only well localized interactions need to be taken into account, in contrast to other systems requiring global interactions. Hence MD algorithms must be considered which allow for efficient access to atomic data in localized regions of space.

The algorithm chosen is based upon a decomposition of the physical system into identical cells laid out on a regular 3–dimensional grid. Thus the algorithm only needs to consider data that reside in nearby cells on the grid. This is naturally reflected in the implementation on distributed–memory data–parallel computers such as the Connection Machines.

The relevant data for our MD simulations are the atoms' types (atomic number in the periodic table), coordinates and momenta. Each cell in the grid holds an array of such data in "slots"; a slot may hold the data for 0 or 1 atoms.

In order for a cell to access the data in neighboring cells, regular communication of data is used (so–called "NEWS" communication, in Connection Machine terminology). Using a pair of communication paths in local 3x3x3 or 5x5x5 subgrids, all relevant information from the neighborhood of the cell is accumulated. The forces are then evaluated, and finally the equations of motion are integrated by the Verlet algorithm.

Due to the grid–based nature of the algorithm, an atom will likely migrate from one grid–cell (corresponding to a physical or virtual processor) to another. Such updates are carried out after each timestep, communicating emigrating atoms' data as described above. When only few atoms are emigrating, or when reading data from disk, another updating algorithm is used based upon copying from and to the grid using a linear–list layout of the data.

The MD problem is inherently parallel, since all atoms in the systems can evaluate their forces independently of all other atoms, once the data from neighboring cells have been made available. Hence, the code implemented is for all practical purposes 100% parallel. The only global communication of data necessary is when global averages have to be made, such as for calculating the total energy of the system.

Another interesting feature of the present code is that the atom–atom interactions are relatively complicated since a single interaction requires about 160 floating–point operations (FLOPs). This is in contrast to the simpler "Lennard–Jones" potentials, which require of the order of 10 FLOPs per interaction. Hence our problem will have a much higher computation/communication ratio than the Lennard–Jones problem, making it more amenable to efficient implementation on parallel computers.

Several physics projects are in progress based upon simulations with this MD algorithm. Firstly, we have studied the details of the melting process in small metal clusters (diameters of the order of 100 Å), which differs in interesting ways from the melting of macroscopic materials.[2] Simulations were mainly with two sizes of clusters containing about 17000 and 178000 atoms of copper. Secondly, we have studied the dynamics of cracks and dislocations in crystalline metals, obtaining new information about Peierls' stress, the dislocation velocities, the parameters governing the emission of a dislocation, and the structure and energy of the dislocation core.

2 Performance measurements on the CM-200

Our MD code, which has been running in production mode for over 2 years, was run for the purpose of obtaining timing measurements on the CM-200 at UNI•C using the CM–Fortran compiler (CMF) release 1.2. Preliminary experiences with CMF release 2.1.1 shows no improvements over the older release for our code. The table below gives the timings of both "elapsed" and "busy" times, which are both of interest in order to estimate the effectiveness of the code on the CM-200.

The "busy" time counts the number of seconds where the CM-200 hardware was busy executing user instructions, whereas the "elapsed" time includes also the time when the CM-200 was idle waiting for the Sun UNIX frontend to issue CM-200 instructions. The "elapsed" minus "busy" times should be as close to zero as possible; if this is not the case, it is a signature that the Sun computer was busy doing other tasks, mainly operations on scalar data not involving the CM-200, but possibly also disk I/O and time spent on other users' processes. As is seen in the table, there is very little wasted idle time in the present code, which is effectively 100% parallel. The timings were obtained with the CM-200 in "production mode", i.e., with *Time–sharing* running up to 6 simultaneous jobs.

The rows of the table indicate the timings for *10 MD timesteps*, for a system with approximately 178.000 atoms, of the following parts of the code: **Atomic forces kernel** is the all–dominating computational kernel, where all interactions between pairs of atoms are computed. This timing only refers to local floating–point operations, and no communication is taking place in this part of the code. **Kernel: communication** represents the inter–processor communication within the CM-200, when data are exchanged between neighboring processors using the CSHIFT Fortran–90 intrinsic function (or the pshift library function). **Atomic rearrangement** is carried out after every time step for those atoms that have to be reassigned to new computational processors. **Front–end disk I/O** is the time it takes to transfer data from the CM-200 to the Sun UNIX hard disk; here one could have chosen to exploit the fast parallel disk array of the CM-200, but since the disk I/O takes only a very limited time, this was never deemed necessary.

The last column labeled "MFLOPS" is derived by counting the number of floating–point operations of the code sections, ignoring all front–end scalar operations as well as any work carried out outside of the computational kernel (i.e., the number given is a lower bound on the actual MFLOPS count). The *Total* MFLOPS is derived from the total timings, subtracting however the disk I/O part which in production runs is done much more rarely than in this test, as discussed above. Also, if the I/O became a bottleneck, it would be natural to use the parallel disk array (DataVault) of the Connection Machine in stead of the UNIX disks.

Part of the code	CM–elapsed (secs)	CM–busy (secs)	MFLOPS
Atomic forces kernel (CMF)	721.3	713.0	880
Kernel: communication	40.4	40.2	≈ 0
Atomic rearrangement	50.3	41.9	≈ 0
Front–end disk I/O	45.3	40.4	-
Total	858.0	835.8	789

The next table corresponds to the case where the "Atomic forces kernel" was hand-tuned using CM-200 PEAC assembler for controlling the Weitek floating–point chips. In this code a single Fortran module containing the atomic forces kernel was rewritten, taking the compiler–generated PEAC assembler code and rearranging it for optimum performance.

Part of the code	CM–elapsed (secs)	CM–busy (secs)	MFLOPS
Atomic forces kernel (PEAC)	587.1	578.5	1085
Kernel: communication	42.8	40.6	≈ 0
Atomic rearrangement	63.0	42.0	≈ 0
Front–end disk I/O	44.5	40.7	-
Total	739.4	702.0	949

Counting the number of floating–point operations in the PEAC code, and the number of machine clock cycles, the MFLOPS rate is calculated to be above 1200 MFLOPS on the UNI•C machine. Any memory operations and max or min operations do not contribute to the MFLOPS rate, but nevertheless do consume a substantial number of machine cycles. The measured performance including all overheads due to the front–end etc. (see table) is 1085 MFLOPS, which is 42% of the machine's theoretical peak performance. The code's overall performance is 949 MFLOPS. This is an excellent result, since all possible performance has been utilized in the PEAC assembler code.

3 Performance measurements on the CM-5

The code was ported to the CM-5 in a matter of minutes. One bug in the CMF version 2.0 beta compiler was detected and a 1-line workaround was made. The resulting source code runs in identical forms on both CM-200 and CM-5. It should be noted that the CMF compiler has been improved since these benchmarks were run, so it is possible that better performance would be obtained with one of the newer releases of the compiler.

For the same problem as reported in the preceding section, the following performance was obtained with an untuned CM–Fortran code on a small, 32–node CM-5 (often considered roughly equivalent to an 8k CM-200 such as the one at UNI•C):

Part of the code	CM–elapsed (secs)	CM–busy (secs)	MFLOPS
Atomic forces kernel (CMF 2.0)	779.9	774.8	810
Kernel: communication	62.0	59.4	≈ 0
Atomic rearrangement	45.4	44.0	≈ 0
Front–end disk I/O	66.7	35.6	-
Total	954.3	914.0	714

The elapsed time for I/O is excessively long on this particular UNIX system, because the disks were network-mounted via NFS. This is a problem in configuring the I/O system of the front–end, rather than a problem related to the CM-5 computer. A more finely tuned installation would not suffer from such problems. Also, the Scalable Disk Array (SDA) could be used instead for parallel I/O.

The atomic forces kernel was again hand-tuned using the CDPEAC assembler for the CM-5 Vector Units. It was obvious from this coding experience that the Vector Units of the CM-5 have been designed in a much more complete way than the (older) Weitek CPUs in the CM-200. Most useful was the large set of 128 registers, the ability to load constant numbers immediately into registers, single–cycle memory loads, and generally fewer clock cycles per vector operation. The fact that CDPEAC is coded in C with macros makes it much easier to write and to interpret than the CM-200 PEAC assembler.

Part of the code	CM–elapsed (secs)	CM–busy (secs)	MFLOPS
Atomic forces kernel (CDPEAC)	275.8	275.8	2275
Kernel: communication	61.7	59.8	≈ 0
Atomic rearrangement	48.5	45.4	≈ 0
Front–end disk I/O	147.0	32.3	-
Total	533.3	413.6	1647

It is seen that the atomic forces kernel is now much faster than for the code generated by the CMF 2.0 beta compiler. This is mainly because the programmer can allocate registers and perform memory loads and stores more intelligently than this version of the compiler. Also, the entire outer loop over the parallel sections of the array was integrated into a single tight loop, allowing for much better performance. Again, we believe that the current implementation of the algorithm is very close to the peak performance that can be achieved on the CM-5. The 32–node CM-5 has a theoretical peak performance of 4096 MFLOPS, when all operations can be made as chained multiply–add operations. Since only a small part of our problem involves multiply–add, our problem should expect to achieve not much more than 2000 MFLOPS, and in fact we achieve 56% of the peak performance within the kernel. The elapsed time for I/O for this CM-5 benchmark is much too long, as was noted in the above benchmark as well.

4 Conclusion

A production code for Molecular Dynamics simulations was implemented on Connection Machine CM-200, and ported painlessly to CM-5. This code has been used heavily in scientific work at the Technical University of Denmark. The CM-200 code obtains an excellent overall performance (including all overheads and input/output) of 789 MFLOPS on the 8k CM-200 at UNI•C, or 31% of the theoretical peak performance of this machine. This shows that it is indeed possible to obtain very high performance on this parallel machine.

The CM-5 execution of the same code is even more efficient than the CM-200 one, after the main computational kernel has been hand–tuned in CDPEAC assembler for the CM-5 Vector Units. The overall performance of the code (including all overheads and input/output) is 1647 MFLOPS on a 32–node CM-5, which is an excellent supercomputer performance level. It corresponds to 40% of the CM-5 theoretical peak performance. The computational kernel performs slightly over 1 floating–point operation per clock cycle overall, which shows that this type of parallel computer is very well suited for this MD algorithm.

It is found that the Connection Machine compilers, libraries and run–time system are so stable that serious scientific production runs can be made, without undue effort being spent on working around system–related problems or compiler deficiencies.

These performances notwithstanding, one should note that algorithmic improvements may lead to even better performing parallel codes in the future.

5 Acknowledgments

The MD code was ported from the CM-200 to the CM-5 installation at *Institut de Physique du Globe de Paris* (IPGP), who kindly provided time for the benchmarks. The CM-5 computational kernel was rewritten in CDPEAC by Malcolm Brown of Thinking Machines Corp.

References

1. K. W. Jacobsen, J. K. Nørskov, and M. J. Puska, Phys. Rev. B **35**, 7423 (1987); K. W. Jacobsen, Comments Cond. Mat. Phys. **14**, 129 (1988).
2. O. H. Nielsen, J. P. Sethna, P. Stoltze, K. W. Jacobsen and J. K. Nørskov, *Melting a copper cluster: Critical droplet theory*, Europhysics Letters, in press.

Parallel Molecular Dynamics Simulations of Liquid and Amorphous Metals

Ulrich K. Rößler and Helmar Teichler

Institut für Metallphysik der Universität Göttingen
Hospitalstr. 3/7, D-37073 Göttingen, Germany
and SFB 345

Abstract. We report about molecular dynamics simulations on a virtually shared-memory parallel computer (KSR1-32). Applications comprise massive runs of several nanoseconds simulation-time with models using nearest-neighbour pair-interactions in the study of the dynamics close to the glass transition, and modelling of the atomistic structure of amorphous and liquid metals, using more involved interaction-potentials. Satisfactory parallelization, optimized to small sample sizes, may be achieved in both types of simulations.

1. Introduction

Atomistic simulations have become a valuable tool in material science and condensed matter physics. Molecular dynamics (MD) is especially powerful as it models the time evolution of a many-particle system by trajectories of the particles in phase space. The simulation is performed by a direct numerical integration of the system's equation of motion. This allows a detailed understanding of dynamics and structure at an atomistic level. Here we give a report about MD-simulations of amorphous and liquid metals. Modelling of such systems is of particular interest as supercooled liquids and glasses are marked by specific (slow) dynamics or relaxations, the features of which should be linked to their disordered structure. Progress in the understanding of these phenomena depends on the development of high-speed computers.

2. Models

We may specify the requirements of our simulations by three "inputs", namely timescale, system-size and interactions.

The timescale of the phenomena under study is given by the distinction between a glass, where effectively all dynamics affecting the structure is frozen, and a liquid, which show a continuous flow of the particles. Our simulations show, that a carefully quenched metallic computer-glass (cooling rate $1.5 \cdot 10^{12}\,\mathrm{Ks}^{-1}$) may be identified as glass only after 1-2 nanoseconds of simulation time[1, 2], by the vanishing slope of the mean square displacements (MSD) $\Delta(t)$ of the atoms. When using a typical timestep of $2 \cdot 10^{-15}$ s, the integration requires at least

10^6 timesteps. The onset of the dynamics (or glass transition) in the supercooled liquid is consequently ruled by this timescale. At temperatures above this frozen state, in the supercooled liquid, we find at times distinct steps in $\Delta(t)$. These steps mark highly cooperative processes in the amorphous matrix, where groups of atoms change places in rings or cascades [1, 2] (Fig.1).

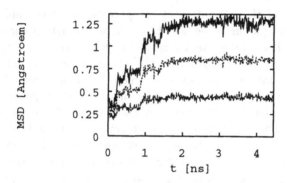

Fig. 1. Time evolution of the mean square displacements $\Delta(t)$ per atom in a MD-simulation of a−$Ni_{50}Zr_{50}$. Glass temperature is here between 825 and 850K. Data are taken from Ref.[2].

Structural information derived from experiments on metallic glasses is mainly given by pair correlation functions measured for a few neighbour distances, generally in the range of 10Å. Moreover, glasses and liquids seem to be rather homogeneous down to similar length scales. Therefore, useful results may be already drawn from simulations of about 1000 atoms.

The crucial point in MD-simulations are the interaction potentials of the atoms. Generally, bonding in metals is of short range only. Simple models are often restricted to next-neighbour pair interactions with ranges of about 4Å. In these models an atom has bonds with less than 20 neighbours. There isn't yet a rigorous method in modelling the forces between atoms but advances in the electron theory of condensed matter result in more involved interaction models; these include many-body interactions leading to forces which depend on the surrounding of the bond or forces connected with bond angle distorsions. A survey of this field may be found in Ref.[3]. In the case of transition metals, of special interest to us, the importance of interactions beyond pair-potentials is well established by theoretical and experimental arguments [4].

Summarizing this section we may say that the computational expense is given either by very long simulation times and/or by complicated interaction models.

In view of the long simulation times needed it is consequently prohibitive to use large models.

3. Methods

The settings of the last section characterize the structure of the MD-program.

Its framework is given by a fifth order Gear-predictor-corrector algorithm to integrate the equation of motion [5].

Vital feature of the evaluation of the potential energies and forces is the maintenance of neighbour tables which list the atoms actually interacting with a distinct atom. These tables are calculated with a radius $r_{cut} + \delta$, where r_{cut} is the range of the interactions. Updating these tables after 10-20 integration steps is sufficient depending on temperature or mobility of the atoms. In simulations with short ranged interactions this method yields already a speedup of one order of magnitude compared to MD-methods updating the list of actually existing interactions at each step. Based on this structure additional routines perform the regulation of temperature pressure or volume and similar tasks.

This program is used for rather different systems with regard to interaction potentials, (binary) alloy compositions, and the diagnostics employed. Parallelization must therefore be easily adjustable to different applications demanding a general scheme rather than an optimization to a special simulation.

Unfortunately adjustement to the parallel-machine at hand is inevitable. The following outline of the KSR1-32's architecture doesn't imply any preference for this machine; it's simply the parallel computer we currently use. The KSR1-32 machine is a distributed-memory parallel computer providing a single global address space. The "allcache" memory system of the KSR1 is realized as the collection of local memories of the individual processor nodes. The local memories act as large caches to hold data referenced frequently by their processors. A reference to an address not available in the local memory cache will be satisfied by transfering a subpage containing the required datum to the requesting node. These updates are performed by the search engine of the KSR1, which holds directories about the physical locations of global addresses and uses a hierarchy of one way rings for communication among the nodes. Up to 32 processors can be connected to a lowest level ring, and up to 34 such rings can be combined in a higher level. There are only 32 processors in the KSR1 at our site, of which at most 16 can be used at a time by a single user.

In view of the coarse granularity of the KSR1-machine the load-balance of the processors is the crucial point about parallization. Parallelization of the MD-program is achieved in a simple way: we assign groups of atoms to processors which perform all computations related to these atoms. In the case of simple tasks, as the application of the integration algorithms, the amount of work related with one atom is equal for all atoms. This is different in the case of the computation of the neighbour-tables or of the forces. In the case of pair-interactions this is tantamount to the calculation of the entries in the upper (or lower) triangle of a matrix. A satisfactory load balance is consequently guaranteed by assignment of *two* sections of atoms to one processor with low and high column numbers of this matrix, respectively.

In the case of three-body interactions the calculation of the forces outweighs the other tasks by far and it suffices to optimize this task. Here we use a dynamic assignment of the atoms to the processors during a prologue to the MD-run which automatically finds a convenient division of the enumeration of atoms.

In view of the global visibility of data in the address space, a distinct processor may easily acquire copies of data from concurrent processors. But writing data should be restricted as far as possible to private data since this means invalidating all copies of that data item in the set of processors. This is important when evaluating the forces which is done first by each processor in a private array Each processor calculates for his set of atoms the forces exerted by atoms with higher column number in the matrix of partial forces. At the end of these calculations the partial forces of all atoms acting on a given atom are added by the processor in charge of this atom. We may improve performance additionally by taking into account the correlation between the spatial distribution of the atoms in the MD-cell and their assignment to processors. This can be done by a simple decomposition of the MD-cell in sub-cells and a permutation in the enumeration of the atoms. In the liquid state where continuous rearrangement of the atoms takes place both optimization schemes may be updated in due time to guarantee load balance between the processors, and data locality.

4. Results

Here we report a choice of performance data of typical MD-runs. The first pertains to a simulation of amorphous $Ni_{50}Zr_{50}$ using hybrid next-neighbour pair-interactions, the shapes of which are infered from electron-theory, while the analytic representation is given by Weber-Stillinger potentials [6]. The sample size of this runs is 648 atoms only. Performance data are displayed in Fig.2.

The decomposition of the computation-time in different tasks shows that the explicit communication overhead, **Replica**, involved with the setting-up and summation of the partial forces in each processor is the main reason in the downgrading of efficiency with increasing number of processors. Using 16 processors 14 % of computation time is used here. Monitoring communication activity between the processors reveals that more than 60% of this time is spent on passing data. Poor efficiency of the tasks denoted **Integrator** which handle in parallel the vectors of position or velocity of the atoms is mainly caused by too short iteration counts when using more than 6 processors. This prevents efficient pipelining of floating-point-operations. In fully optimized runs on 16 processors we achieve an efficiency of 0.57 for runs on 16 processors and the MD-step takes only 0.035s averaged over 1000 steps.

The second example is a computationally more demanding simulation of $Fe_{50}Zr_{50}$ based on an electron-theoretical model [9] with particular long ranges of the pair-interactions (7-8 Å). We make use here of the *Multiple-Time-Step-*

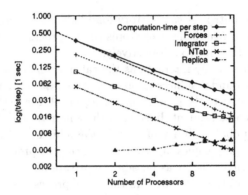

Fig. 2. MD-simulation of a$-Ni_{50}Zr_{50}$ (648 atoms at 800K): Variation of total computation-time per MD-step with number of processors and decomposition of computation-tasks in main tasks. The dashed line with slope -1 indicates ideal performance. **Forces** represents evaluation of the potential and forces, **Integrator** denotes the application of the Gear-predictor-corrector-algorithm plus *all* other parallelized tasks with equal computational expense per atom, and **NTab** denotes the renewing of the neighbour-tables. **Replica** indicates the total time spent on setting-up and collecting the replica of the array of forces in the concurrent processors.

(MTS) method [7], i.e. we divide the forces on an atom. The forces exerted by its nearest-neighbours are evaluated at each MD-step Δt. The forces due to more distant atoms are evaluated at invervals of n · Δt, and extrapolated by a Taylor-series expansion in between. As this extrapolation steps may be done by each processor without additional communication overhead the MTS-method is especially suited for parallel machines [8]. In our example we achieve an efficiency of 0.84 (0.91) on 16 processors in simulations with 648 (5184) atoms, with 0.59 s (4.78 s) per MD-step.

Both examples document optimized runs where local clusters of atoms in the MD-box were assigned to each processor. This improves in general the efficiency in runs with 16 processors by 0.05 compared to runs where the atoms are randomly assigned to the processors.

In a simulation of liquid transition metals based on a first-principle model with 2- and 3-body forces[10] we reach an efficiency of 0.84 on 16 processors (1024 atoms of liquid Mo). This is yet another class of simulation as compared to pair-potential models. The model requires summation of potential contributions of triples of atoms. One MD-timestep costs here 1.9s computation time. The optimization to improve the data locality yields an improvement by 0.04 in the efficiency of 16 processors. Dynamic load balance as described in the last section yields another improvement by 0.04.

5. Discussion

The program (avoiding the splitted summation of forces on several processors) can be directly ported to one processor runs or workstations. Vectorizing this program proved to be rather difficult as the small sample sizes and (in general) short interaction radii make loop iteration counts too short. We took advantage of this structure of our models by the introduction of neighbour tables. But this prevents simple vectorizing as the calculation of the forces on an atom results in indirect array references. The small sample size affects as well the performance of the parallelized program, yet we reach in a variety of cases satisfactory speed-up. The dynamic assignment of atoms to processors proved to be a suitable method to improve performance in a more involved model. This relies on computationally cheap hard-ware clocks measuring performance of the single processors. Future optimizations should take into account the communication overhead of the processors to improve dynamically the assignment of atoms to processors. This will be especially important when simulating larger samples In principle the neighbour tables contain all information to organize efficiently an asynchronous transfer of data-items. Moreover in view of the long simulation-times there seems enough time to optimize the performance in the first 100 or so integration steps by gathering information about the run-time behaviour. This might as well improve portability of the MD-code to other parallel machines with different networks and local memories.

6. Conclusion

The MD-program presented here is a general tool for real applications in condensed matter physics or material science. By relatively simple means satisfactory parallelization on a virtually shared-memory parallel computer may be achieved for rather different models and small sample sizes. The single address space provides the advantage that the dynamic variables of the MD-simulations are globally visible. Reading these data in parallel is simple, and still computationally cheap. Thus in the present implementation, the parallel evaluation of diagnostics as single-particle time-correlations or pair-correlations may be added easily.

Acknowledgment

Support by the DFG to the parallel computing project and perpetual help and advice by the GWD Göttingen are gratefully acknowledged. We wish to thank Prof.O.Haan for his proposal to write this paper and his kind help in doing so.

References

1. H.Sieber: unpublished, Diplomawork, University Göttingen, 1992
2. B.Kiefer: unpublished, Diplomawork, University Göttingen, 1994
3. R.M. Nieminen, M.J. Puska (eds.): "Many-atom interactions in solids" Springer, Berlin [etc.] 1990
4. J.A.Moriarty: Phys.Rev.B 38 (1988) 3188
5. C.W.Gear: "Numerical Initial Value Problems in Ordinary Differential Equations" Prentice-Hall, Englewood Cliffs, N.J. 1971
6. H.Teichler: phys.stat.sol.(b) 172 (1992) 325
7. A.Ahmad and L.Cohen: J.Comput.Phys. 12 (1973) 389; W.B.Streett and D.J.Tildesley: Mol.Phys. 35 (1978) 635
8. A.Nakano, P.Vashishta and R.K.Kalia: Comput.Phys.Commun. 77 (1993) 303
9. Ch.Hausleitner and J.Hafner: Phys.Rev.B 45 (1992) 115,118
10. J.A.Moriarty: Phys.Rev.B 42 (1990) 1609

COMPUTATIONAL MATERIALS SCIENCE FROM FIRST PRINCIPLES

D. Hohl

Institut für Festkörperforschung,
Forschungszentrum Jülich GmbH,
D–52425 Jülich, Germany

Abstract. We review recent developments in atomistic computer simulations of matter incorporating both quantum and classical statistical mechanical elements. These methods treat the electronic and geometric structure of solids, liquids and molecules on an equal footing and require no a priori knowledge (i.e. they are based on "first principles", the basic laws of quantum and classical physics, not on experimental information). They borrow elements from quantum chemistry and solid state electron theories on one side and classical mechanics on the other. Such unified approach leads to more reliable computer-based predictions of materials properties over traditional simulation methods but requires substantial supercomputing resources. We present two typical applications in chemistry (nanoscale clusters of the element phosphorus) and solid state physics (the element hydrogen at extremely high compression).

1   Introduction

The numerical calculation of structure and properties of matter has taken a very steep upwards development with the availability of usable digital computers starting in the 1950s. Two separate landmark developments had an enormous impact on what became today's "computational materials science": (i) Molecular Dynamics (MD) [1], the numerical solution of the classical equations of motion of an N-particle system with finite difference methods. MD can perform the task of computing macroscopic quantities based on microscopic simulations and providing a direct view into the microscopic world of complex systems. (ii) Modern first principles ("ab initio"), i.e. quantum-mechanics based, methods from solid state physics [2] and chemistry for the numerical solution of the problem of n electrons interacting with one another and with N nuclei. Both fields suffer from a set of characteristic drawbacks when viewed in isolation:

– MD can treat large numbers of particles (up to 10^7 atoms) at finite temperatures but relies on an a priori qualitative and quantitative knowledge of the interaction between the particles. Although this approach has provided much important qualitative insight into the structure and dynamics of, e.g., liquids and polymers, it often fails when covalent chemical bonding comes into play and when specific materials properties rather than universal ones are sought.

- First principles solid state physics and quantum chemistry methods can treat complex chemical bonds with high precision, and with no input other than the type of atoms in the material. These methods, however, were long confined to point-by-point calculations for small numbers of particles (10-30) because of the high computational demand.

In this paper, we review an important development unifying MD (Sec. 2) with first principles methods (Sec. 3) proposed by *Car* and *Parrinello* 1985 [3]. We describe the "*ab initio* Molecular Dynamics" method (Sec. 4), give an account of the computational machinery and demands, and present two representative applications (Sec. 5).

2 Molecular Dynamics

In MD one follows the "trajectory" $\Gamma(t)$ of a system of N particles (atoms, molecules etc.), i.e. the evolution in time of the particle velocities and positions $\{\dot{\mathbf{R}}_I(t)\}, \{\mathbf{R}_I(t)\}$. $\mathbf{R}_I(t)$ denotes the coordinates of particle I in space. Basic statistical theory teaches that quantities $\langle A \rangle_{\text{time}}$ computed as time averages over the trajectories correspond to physical "observables". Except for a small number of unrealistic model systems like the "ideal gas", the trajectories $\Gamma(t)$ of the particles cannot be calculated analytically, and one has to resort to numerical methods to solve the equations of motion (EOM)

$$\mathbf{F}_I(t) = M_I \ddot{\mathbf{R}}_I(t) = -\nabla_{\mathbf{R}_I} U(\{\mathbf{R}_I(t)\}) \tag{1}$$

$\mathbf{F}_I(t)$ is the force (vector) acting on particle I with mass M_I at time t and $U(\{\mathbf{R}_I(t)\})$ the (scalar) potential energy of the particles at t, i.e. the sum of interaction energies between all particles at this instant. Eq. 1 is a system of $3N$ coupled ordinary, nonlinear, 2nd order differential equations, and must be solved iteratively by discretization in the independent time variable t, symbolically $t = 0 \rightarrow t + \Delta t \rightarrow t + 2\Delta t \rightarrow ... \rightarrow t_{end}$. Eq. 1 is also an initial value problem where one starts from some set of initial conditions $\{\mathbf{R}_I(t = 0)\}, \{\mathbf{R}_I(t = 0)\}$. The most obvious algorithm to use is also the most widely used, the so-called (forth-order) Verlet algorithm

$$R(t + \Delta t) = 2R(t) - R(t - \Delta t) + \frac{\Delta t^2}{M} F(t) \tag{2}$$

It becomes clear immediately that even with the largest computing resources one needs to confine oneself to modeling a relatively modest number of interacting particles over a finite period of time t_{end}. Most MD simulations proceed by filling microscopically small boxes ("MD unit cells") with anywhere from 50 to 10^7 particles and following their motion for 10^3–10^7 time steps Δt. These are still minute periods of "real" time (picosecond to nanosecond range), and one basic difficulty of MD simulations is that even on the fastest available computers physics happens in extreme slow motion ($\sim 10^{15}$ times slower than reality).

It is somewhat less obvious that the feasibility of the calculation hinges on the ease with which the interaction energy $U(\{\mathbf{R}_I(t)\})$ can be computed since this has to be done in every step of the calculation. For that reason, simple pairwise additive short-range interactions of the type $U(\{\mathbf{R}_I\}) = \sum_{I<J} u(|\mathbf{R}_I - \mathbf{R}_J|)$ are most widely used. This type of potential is a good representation for a few interesting systems (e.g. interacting rare-gas atoms) but generally fails when covalent chemical bonds play an important role. The basic reason is that chemical interactions are *not* pairwise additive but are instead governed by the complex electronic structure of the participating atoms. All attempt to model the—fundamentally quantum mechanical—chemical many-body forces between atoms with parametrized models for $U(\{\mathbf{R}_I\})$ have so far been unsuccessful. For lack of knowledge, one has to solve the full quantum mechanical Schrödinger equation

$$\mathcal{H}\Psi(\{\mathbf{R}_I(t)\}), \{\mathbf{r}_i\}) = U(\{\mathbf{R}_I(t)\})\Psi(\{\mathbf{R}_I(t)\}), \{\mathbf{r}_i\}) \tag{3}$$

with n electrons i in space positions $\mathbf{r}_1...\mathbf{r}_i...\mathbf{r}_n$. $\mathcal{H}$ is the total quantum-mechanical energy ("Hamiltonian") operator. Incorporating those additional electronic degrees of freedom increases the computational demand vastly, and we will now describe various approximations to the full Schrödinger equation simplifying the solution greatly.

3   First-principles Methods

All powerful first-principles methods that target realistic chemical systems of appreciable size use a "mean-field" approach as underlying approximation to solve Eq. 3. One imagines all n electrons moving independently of one another in a mean potential field $V(\mathbf{r})$ of all the other electrons. This *Ansatz* initially shifts the difficulty from calculating the complicated total $3n$-dimensional wavefunction $\Psi(\{\mathbf{r}_i\})$ in Eq. 3 to calculating a complicated function $V(\mathbf{r})$ of only 3 space coordinates x, y, z and solving a set of n coupled 2nd order partial differential (Schrödinger-like) equations

$$\mathcal{H}_{\text{el}}\psi_i(\mathbf{r}) = (-\frac{1}{2}\nabla^2 + V(\mathbf{r}))\,\psi_i(\mathbf{r}) = \epsilon_i\psi_i(\mathbf{r}) \tag{4}$$

where $\mathcal{H}_{\text{el}}$ is now a one-electron Hamiltonian operator. The one-electron wavefunctions are expanded in a set of M basis functions $\phi_m(\mathbf{r})$, and the set of differential equations (4) becomes a matrix eigenvalue problem with eigenvalues ϵ_i and eigenvectors $\mathbf{c}_i$ (vector length M)

$$\psi_i(\mathbf{r}) = \sum_{m=1}^{M} c_{i,m}\phi_m(\mathbf{r}) \tag{5}$$

$$\sum_m h_{km}\,c_{j,m} = \epsilon_j\,c_{j,k} \tag{6}$$

The total energy of the system U can be calculated once the lowest n one-electron eigenvalues ϵ_i and eigenvectors $\mathbf{c}_i$ are known. Computationally, the solution of the eigenvalue problem (6) can become very demanding: (i) It is a "pseudo" eigenvalue problem (the matrix elements $h_{km} = \langle \phi_k(\mathbf{r})|\mathcal{H}_{el}|\phi_m(\mathbf{r})\rangle$ depend on the eigenvectors because the mean potential field $V(\mathbf{r})$ does) requiring iterative solution to self-consistency. (ii) The dimension of the matrix depends on how well the basis functions $\phi_m(\mathbf{r})$ can represent the distribution of electrons in the subtance under investigation. Unfortunately, spatially well-localized "chemical" basis functions often lead to *small* matrix dimension $M=100$–1000 but an awkward evaluation of the integrals h_{km}. Functional forms for the $\phi_m(\mathbf{r})$ that offer easy evaluation of the matrix elements tend to require *very large* $M=10^3$–10^6.

4 Density Functional Theory and Molecular Dynamics

The goal of traditional quantum-chemical methods is to use the eigenfunctions $\psi_i(\mathbf{r})$ computed with the general procedure just outlined to again approximate the total wavefunction $\Psi(\{\mathbf{r}_i\})$ and compute the corresponding energies U. The ensuing Hartree-Fock (one-determinant) and configuration interaction (CI, multi-determinant) methods are plagued with high computational effort and unfavorable scaling with system size ($\geq N^4$, depending on the particular method). The solution of Eq. 3 becomes very demanding already for *one single* set of atomic positions $\{\mathbf{R}_I(t)\}$, and we need to solve it thousands of times along an MD trajectory! Other first-principles methods must be used, and Car and Parrinello (CP, [3]) have recognized that density functional theory (DFT), a well-established method in solid-state and molecular physics [2], can perform the task with high accuracy and moderate computational effort. Their invention of a unified MD-DFT procedure marks one of the most important developments in computational materials science in decades.

DFT, unlike the quantum chemical methods, uses the eigenfunctions $\psi_i(\mathbf{r})$ to construct the total electron density of a system $n(\mathbf{r}) = \sum_{i=1}^n |\psi_i(\mathbf{r})|^2$, a much easier quantity than the multi-dimensional total wavefunction. All ground-state properties of a system of electrons and nuclei can be derived from it [2]. The electron potential $V(\mathbf{r})$ is of a particularly simple form $V(\mathbf{r}) = V_{ext}(\mathbf{r}) + \varphi(\mathbf{r}) + v_{xc}[n(\mathbf{r})]$ when a local approximation to electron exchange and correlation v_{xc} is used (so-called LDA). This is in striking contrast to quantum chemical methods, where the inclusion of electron correlation is possible only at very high cost. $V_{ext}(\mathbf{r})$ is the external electric field from the positively charged nuclei, $\varphi(\mathbf{r})$ the field of the other electrons.

Other important ingredients of the CP method are the use of a large ($M=10^3$–10^6) plane wave basis set for the one-electron eigenfunctions (Eq. 7) in conjunction with pseudopotentials for the electron-ion interaction, iterative matrix eigenvalue algorithms, and the realization that FFT methods can be used to perform the necessary convolutions in reciprocal space as multiplications in real space [4].

$$\psi_i(\mathbf{r}) = \sum_{m=1}^M c_j \mathbf{G}_m \exp(i\mathbf{G}_m\mathbf{r}) \qquad (7)$$

In MD simulations it is crucial that all degrees of freedom move with EOM that are mutually compatible and conserve the sum of all kinetic and potential energy terms. Within the CP scheme this leads to two coupled sets of EOM for the electronic wavefunctions $\psi_i(t)$ and atomic positions $\mathbf{R}_I(t)$

$$\mu\ddot{\psi}_i(\mathbf{r}, t) = -\frac{\delta U_{\text{DFT}}}{\delta\psi_i^*(\mathbf{r}, t)} + \sum_k \Lambda_{ik}(t)\psi_k(\mathbf{r}, t) \tag{8}$$

$$M_I\ddot{\mathbf{R}}_I = -\nabla_{\mathbf{R}_I} U_{\text{DFT}}(\{\mathbf{R}_I(t)\}) \tag{9}$$

These EOM are identical to those in Eq. 1 except that the electronic wavefunctions evolve in time together with the atomic positions, and that now the first-principles DFT expression U_{DFT} appears as the potential energy of the particles. The ψ_i get fictitious "masses" μ and need to be orthogonalized in every time step with the Lagrange multiplier method (Λ_{ik}, second term in Eq. 8).

5 Applications

5.1 Nanoscale Phosphorus Clusters

At the boundary between chemistry and physics, microclusters represent a challenge to atomistic modelling. With the discovery of carbon fullerenes, the interest in these systems extended beyond the quantum chemistry community to touch upon material science. As can be expected on the basis of simple considerations, the cluster size plays a non-trivial role in determining their properties. With increasing number of atoms N, chemical, optical, dynamical and magnetic properties change in a non-monotonic way, and only slowly approach those of bulk systems. *Ab-initio* methods have been particularly useful to describe this evolution, and, for a large class of elements (mainly semiconductors and simple metals), they provide the only reliable model.

We have mainly concentrated on semiconductor clusters in our own work and we will discuss the results for phosphorus clusters P_N representative for other applications. Bulk phosphorus displays a great structural variability characterized by a whole spectrum of chemical and physical properties. Already clusters with only a few atoms present a very large number of isomers, and finding the most stable points of the energy function $U(\{\mathbf{R}_I\})$ is a challenging optimization task. Simulated annealing, a method borrowed from statistical theory, can be used here very efficiently in conjunction with the MD-DFT method. Studies for P_N clusters with $N=2$–11 show many unexpected features [4]. They provide valuable information on different subjects, like reactivity, nucleation, and the relation between different solid phases. Fig. 1 shows how complicated the optimal cluster geometries can become. "Chemical intuition" and point-wise zero-temperature calculations have failed to conceive structures anywhere near the correct one for P_8. They predicted a cube instead!

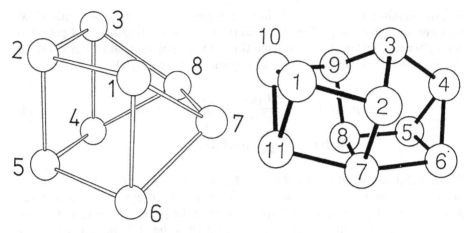

Fig. 1. Structure of the most stable geometries of P_8 and P_{11}

5.2 Hydrogen at Extreme Pressures and Temperatures

Hydrogen, the simplest of all elements, still holds many surprises. On earth, it exists only in the form of H_2 molecules, but under compression it undergoes a number of complex phase transformations. Normally a molecular insulator, physicists have hypothesized for decades if and under what conditions of pressure P and temperature T it might lose its molecular character and/or metallize. Such "atomic hydrogen metal" would be of very fundamental importance to the understanding of matter and, because hydrogen is by far the most ubiquitous element in the universe, would shed new light on a number of astrophysical phenomena. For experimentalists it becomes increasingly difficult to perform reproducible measurements when T and P are raised. The current pressure limit for hydrogen is $\sim$2 Mbar, and no transition to an atomic form of hydrogen could be observed.

For theorists, increasing P and T is not much more than changing an input parameter. We have performed extensive MD-DFT simulations for high-pressure hydrogen with 64 [5] and 128 atoms at P=0.5, 1.5 and 3 Mbar in the temperature range 200–3000 K. It is absolutely essential for a faithful simulation under such extreme conditions to accommodate changes in chemical bonding by incorporating the electrons directly into the simulation. No empirical potential can be expected to have any predictive capability in this regime. The computational effort is very substantial. For a system of 128 atoms, the matrix size (see Sec. 3) is M=5000, the discretization time step (see Sec. 2) is $\Delta t = 5.5 \times 10^{-17}$ s, and one step takes 5 s on a single Cray YMP M94 processor. Several 10000 steps are necessary to "measure" the quantities of interest for each P/T point. Perhaps most surprisingly, we observe that the molecular character is largely retained even at the highest pressure. The H_2 molecules can be observed, however, to line up in "strings", perhaps signaling the onset of atomization (see Fig. 2). Our calculations indicate that atomic hydrogen will remain accessible only to theorists for the foreseeable future.

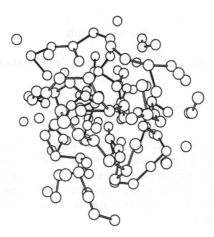

Fig. 2. Snapshot of a configuration from a simulation of 128 hydrogen atoms at 3000 K and 3 Mbar. The disordered "strings" of atoms are apparent.

The scheme just described provides a powerful and reliable framework to simulate a large class of systems. Limitations remain on the size of the systems we can study (100–400 atoms), on the length of the simulation (ps range), and several chemical elements (most notably transition metals and oxygen) are still problematic. These limitations, however, are not fundamental but computational in nature. Algorithm and method development on one side (e.g. new pseudopotentials, basis sets with chemically motivated functional forms [6], linearly scaling methods) and the maturing massively parallel supercomputer technology on the other will advance the field rapidly. The ultimate goal is the capability to perform dynamical calculations for up to 1000 atoms of *any* element in the periodic table.

References

1. B.J. Alder and T.E. Wainwright, J. Chem. Phys. **27**, 1208 (1957).
2. P. Hohenberg and W. Kohn, Phys. Rev. **136**, B864 (1964); W. Kohn and L.J. Sham, Phys. Rev. **140**, A1133 (1965).
3. R. Car and M. Parrinello, Phys. Rev. Lett. **55**, 2471 (1985).
4. R.O. Jones and D. Hohl, J. Chem. Phys. **92**, 6710 (1990); R.O. Jones and G. Seifert, J. Chem. Phys. **96**, 7564 (1992).
5. D. Hohl *et al.*, Phys. Rev. Lett. , 541 (1993).
6. J. Harris and D. Hohl, J. Phys.: Condens. Matter **2**, 5161 (1990); Z. Lin and J. Harris, J. Phys.: Condens. Matter **5**, 1055 (1993).

Automatic Parallelization of a Crystal Growth Simulation Program for Distributed-Memory Systems

Michael Gerndt

Central Institute for Applied Mathematics
Research Centre Jülich
D-52425 Jülich
email: m.gerndt@kfa-juelich.de

Abstract. This article outlines two parallelization tools, i.e. the Vienna Fortran Compilation System and FORGE 90, and discusses their analysis and transformation capabilities in the context of a regular grid application simulating the growth of a silicon crystal. We present performance results obtained on an iPSC/860 for both versions and for a manually parallelized version.

1 Introduction

Parallelization of sequential applications for massively parallel systems is currently performed manually. The programmer first has to rewrite the whole application in the message passing programming model before test runs can be performed to evaluate the parallelization strategy. Manual parallelization can be facilitated by appropriate tools, such as TOP^2 [1] that was developed at KFA and allows the programmer to separate individual subroutines and provides an environment for test runs of the parallel implementation of that subroutine.

Automatic parallelization is supported only by a few tools, e.g. the Vienna Fortran Compilation System (VFCS) [6, 4], the Fortran D environment [3], and FORGE 90, xHPF77 [2]. All these tools are based on the data distribution approach. The user specifies the distribution of arrays to the processors and the parallelization tool adapts the sequential code to the specified distribution. The annotations specifying the data distribution have been standardized as High Performance Fortran (HPF) [5].

In this article we introduce two tools, the VFCS and FORGE 90. We parallelized a regular grid application simulating the melting process of silicon with both tools and also used a hand-coded parallel version developed according to the same parallelization strategy to analyze the effectiveness of the parallelization tools.

2 Crystal Growth Simulation

The Crystal Growth Simulation is an application developed at KFA [7] for the optimization of the silicon production process. For the quality of the silicon

282

crystal a constant convection in the melt is very important. The convection results from the heating, the rotation of the crucible, and the rotation of the crystal. The convection is modeled by a set of partial differential equations and determined by an explicit finite difference scheme. Thus, array references are regular and the application is a good candidate for state-of-the-art parallelization tools.

The simulated crucible has a radius of 3 cm and a height of 4 cm and is discretized into 30 x 90 x 40 elements. This determines the shape of the main arrays to be 32 x 92 x 42 including some additional boundary cells. The boundary cells determine the boundary conditions at the surface of the crucible, e.g. the temperature of the heating, and the values at the inner surface where the crucible is unfolded to give a regular three-dimensional structure. This relation between the crucible and the main arrays is shown in Figure 1.

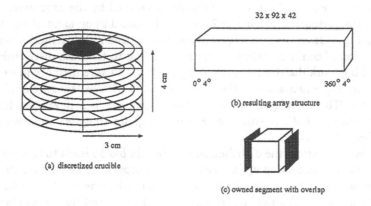

Fig. 1. Application Domain

The algorithm consists of an initialization phase, a time loop, and an output phase. In the time loop for each time step the new temperature, the pressure, and the velocity are computed and the boundary conditions are updated. The most time consuming procedure is the computation of the velocity and the pressure. Here the linear equation system resulting from the partial differential equations is solved by successive overrelaxation.

In this subroutine as well as in the other operations of the time loop mostly stencil operations are performed on the data structures, i.e. to compute an array element only the values of neighboring elements are needed. When updating the boundary conditions some non-local operations are applied, such as copying plane 91 onto plane 1 and plane 2 onto plane 92, thus simulating the closed crucible.

The code is designed such that a simulation can be split into a sequence of program runs. The program generates a continuation data set at the end of a run. In addition, data can be output during the time loop to allow off-line visualization. The I/O operations could not be parallelized by both tools and are only supported in the manual version.

3 Parallelization Strategy

The code is parallelized according to the data partitioning approach. The main arrays are divided into blocks that are assigned to the processors. For the application the HPF BLOCK distribution strategy is optimal. Depending on the number of processors all three dimensions can be partitioned.

The computation for such a distributed array is spread among the processors with respect to data locality. Most systems apply the owner-computes rule, i.e. the owner of an array element computes its new values. Current parallelization tools either strictly apply this rule or individual loops are spread according to the owner of a single array reference in the loop body and assignments to other arrays may be executed for array elements not owned by the processor.

The transformation of Fortran 77 with data distribution annotations to message passing code consists of several steps: interprocedural distribution analysis, computation of communication patterns according to the data distribution and the resulting work distribution, shrinking of arrays to save memory in each processor, and implementation of the communication with as few synchronizations as possible. The techniques applied in these steps are well developed for regular computations but are still in a research stage for irregular applications like finite-element codes.

In this application, the distribution of arrays in blocks leads to two communication patterns: an overlap update and a remote copy. If we assume a distribution in the second dimension, the stencil operations induce access to the boundary elements of the neighboring blocks. Therefore, the left- and rightmost plane have to be sent to the neighboring processors prior to the computation.

The copy operation outlined in the previous section leads to communication between the rightmost and the leftmost processor only if the second dimension is distributed. In all other cases this operation can be executed locally. There is a similar operation to be performed in the first dimension.

4 Vienna Fortran Compilation System

The VFCS developed at the University of Vienna is the successor of the SUPERB system. The input language is Vienna Fortran, a language extension to Fortran 77 providing very flexible data distribution mechanisms.

The system performs an automatic communication analysis which is specifically tailored to overlap communication resulting from stencil operations. The tool computes the overlap areas automatically from the work distribution and the data distribution of right-hand side arrays.

Since the VFCS applies the owner-computes rule, assignments to auxiliary variables in loops are executed by all processors, i.e. scalar variables are replicated. If such an assignment is part of a stencil operation the overlap area cannot be determined precisely. In such situations the user can apply several transformations to interactively optimize the code.

Mask propagation [4] determines, on the basis of dataflow information, in which iterations a processor has to execute such an assignment. If those iterations are unique the information can be used to determine the communication pattern. This transformation is very useful for our application and makes it possible to detect most of the stencil operations.

Since the VFCS is tailored to overlap communication, copy operations in that application cannot be handled efficiently. They lead to an overlap area in each process that consists of the total array. Since this results in a lot of communication and memory overhead only the third dimension of the arrays was distributed. In that dimension no copy operations occur.

In the communication optimization step the communication is vectorized and performed very efficiently. An important missing optimization is the combination of messages updating overlap areas of different arrays. Although the messages are exchanged among the same pair of processors they are not combined to one message.

During the work distribution optimization the loops are transformed such that processors only execute those iterations that contain local computations. This transformation is successful for almost all loops in that program. Only in a few cases the distribution of work is performed on statement level. Individual masks for statements in a loop are generated in the form of logical-ifs because the loop transformation cannot ensure the owner-computes rule. A simple extension of the existing transformation that allows to mask the entire loop based on loop invariant expressions used in the statement-masks would allow to generate efficient code.

The tool automatically shrinks the arrays to an appropriate shape for the local part and the overlap area, i.e. the memory where communicated overlap information is stored. This transformation as well as some other transformations imply that the number of processors and the distribution is fixed at compile-time. The generated code uses very few functions of a runtime library and thus can be optimized manually.

5 FORGE 90

FORGE 90 is a commercial parallelization tool developed by Applied Parallel Research. Similar to the VFCS it is an interactive tool that supports data distributions as the basis for parallelization. The tool currently supports one-dimensional block and cyclic distribution.

In the first step, the user supplies the data distribution. Then the user has to pick individual loops in the program to spread the iterations over the processors. In contrast to the VFCS that strictly applies the owner-computes rule, the generated code may contain remote stores.

The user can explicitly specify a work distribution which gives him much flexibility to optimize data locality. When picking loops the user has to take into account that FORGE 90 will implement communication resulting from the data distribution and the work distribution in the best case before and after the selected loop. Thus messages are vectorized with respect to this loop but more aggressive message vectorization across surrounding sequential loops is not supported.

This enforces that the first dimension of the arrays in our application has to be distributed. The loops are implemented in such a way that the longest loop, i.e. running over the second dimension, is the innermost to allow efficient vectorization on Cray. Manual loop interchange in the entire code is an error-prone operation and communicating values in the inner loops leads to very small messages and a lot of communication overhead.

The loop partitioning step computes information which values have to be communicated in a loop. The information presented is imprecise since it consists of all references to distributed arrays. An analysis whether communication is really necessary is later on performed in the backend. But an experienced user can use the presented information to determine those references that do not need any communication and thus can help the backend to eliminate unnecessary runtime overhead.

Shrinking of arrays can be specified with the data distribution. Since memory for shrinked arrays is allocated dynamically and all references to shrinked arrays are linearized, the performance is not as good as with full-size arrays. Although the difference was within a few percent we used full-size arrays for our performance measurements. Due to these memory allocation strategies the generated code can be executed on any number of processors. It includes a lot of calls to a runtime library and thus manual optimization of the generated code is nearly impossible.

6 Conclusion

Our experiments on the iPSC/860 showed that both tools lead to similar performance if the data distribution was selected with respect to the capabilities of the tools, i.e. distribution of the third dimension for the VFCS and of the first dimension for FORGE 90 [1]. Both tools support only one-dimensional distributions for this application. The one-dimensional hand-coded version is 10 percent faster than the automatically parallelized versions (Table 1).

The HPF BLOCK distribution is not suited if the number of elements in a dimension is not much larger than the number of nodes. For example, the 16-node version of Manual1D can utilize only 14 nodes and the 32-node version 21 nodes. The Vienna Fortran BLOCK strategy distributes the 42 elements in the third dimension more evenly among the processors.

The two-dimensional hand-coded version performed much better due to a lower communication overhead and a better load balance. In future, similar execution times can be expected for the automatically parallelized code if the

---

[1] The FORGE 90 test version was limited to 16 nodes.

processors	FORGE 90	VFCS	Manual1D	Manual2D
1	198	197	176	176
2	120	116	104	100
4	79	82	70	50
8	58	55	54	29
16	41	42	37	17
32	*	39	35	10.5
speedup 16	4.8	4.7	4.8	10.5
speedup 32		5	5	17

Table 1. Execution Times (secs) and Speedup

tools are able to handle multi-dimensional distributions effectively. Extensions of the techniques used in both tools, i.e. the compile-time analysis as well as the code generation strategies for communication and work distribution, would be sufficient for efficient parallelization of that application.

Acknowledgement

We thank K. Wingerath (Institut für Festkörperforschung) for providing access to the application and giving us a lot of background information and R. Dissemond for implementing the manually parallelized version.

References

1. U. Detert, H.M. Gerndt, *TOP² : Tool Suite for Partial Parallelization, Version 2.01, User's Guide*, Forschungszentrum Jülich, Interner Bericht KFA-ZAM-IB-9321, 1993
2. Applied Parallel Research, *FORGE 90, Distributed Memory Parallelizer, User's Guide, Version 8.7, User's Guide*, 1993
3. S. Hiranandani, K. Kennedy, C. Tseng, *Compiler Optimizations for Fortran D on MIMD Distributed-Memory Machines*, Proceedings of the Supercomputing Conference 1991, Albuquerque, 86-100, November 1991
4. M. Gerndt, *Updating Distributed Variables in Local Computations*, Concurrency: Practice and Experience, Vol. 2(3), 171-193, September 1990
5. HPFF, *High Performance Fortran Language Specification*, High Performance Fortran Forum, Version 1.0, Rice University Houston Texas, May 1993
6. H. Zima, P. Brezany, B. Chapman, P. Mehrotra, A. Schwald, *Vienna Fortran - A language Specification Version 1.1*, University of Vienna, ACPC-TR 92-4, March 1992
7. M. Mihelcic, H. Wenzl, K. Wingerath, *Flow in Czochralski Crystal Growth Melts*, Bericht des Forschungszentrums Jülich, No. 2697, ISSN 0366-0885, December 1992

A parallel molecular-dynamics simulation of crystal growth at a cluster of workstations

M.J.P. Nijmeijer[*]

Center for Simulational Physics
University of Georgia
Athens, Georgia 30602
USA

Abstract. To enable a simulation of the growth of crystalline fibers at a cluster of workstations, I developed a parallel molecular-dynamics (MD) algorithm. The structure of the MD algorithm is described briefly, together with its parallelization. Some specific features of our application will be discussed and an illustration of the program performance will be given.

1 Introduction

As an example of how the growing capabilities of computers enable simulations of increasingly realistic systems, a simulation of a crystal growth technique known as "laser heated pedestal growth" (LHPG) [1] is discussed. This growth technique forms a quick and inexpensive way to grow e.g. optical fibers, it works as follows. A rod of feed material is placed vertically in a vacuum-tight chamber where its top is molten by a laser. On top of the rod forms a small pool of liquid feed material in which a seed is dipped. The seed is a small piece of crystal of, usually, feed material, kept at room temperature. While the liquid crystallizes against the seed, forming the fiber, the seed is slowly pulled upwards. The pulling is slow enough for the lower end of the growing fiber to remain dipped in the pool. The liquid keeps crystallizing against it, ensuring the continuation of the fiber growth. In order not to drain the liquid pool, the feed rod is simultaneously pushed upwards to melt new feed material into the pool.

The process of particle melting, their transport through the liquid and recrystallization in the fiber is complex and a better understanding could improve fiber growth conditions. MD is expected to be a suitable simulation technique to study LHPG because it follows the trajectories of all individual particles in time. Such a detailed description requires however a large computational effort because of which nearly all simulations of crystal growth techniques have taken a coarse-grained approach. They represent the particles by a continuum through which particle and heat currents flow with the advantage of being able to study much larger systems but at the price of a loss of detail.

---

[*] current address: Laboratoire de Physique Théorique et Hautes Energies, Bâtiment 211, Université Paris-Sud, 91405 Orsay, France

In a first study [2], D.P. Landau and the present author demonstrated the feasability of a MD simulation of LHPG but performed the simulation in 2 dimensions in order to limit memory requirements and CPU times. Even with those precautions the simulations were rather demanding for the available resources which were mainly IBM Risc/6000 model 550 workstations. They are most streneous at low pulling rates when not only the physical process is slow but also the thickest fibers are produced. The systems became as large as 6000 particles in which case it took approximately 10 hours of CPU time to grow a fiber.

In a next step [3], we decided to improve upon this work, most importantly so by going to 3 dimensions. The resulting increase in system sizes (which now turned out to be as large as 30000 particles) prompted us to carry out the most time consuming calculations in a parallel fashion on our cluster of workstations.

In the next section, the most commonly used MD algorithm is sketched. The parallelization of the algorithm is explained in section 3. Section 4 addresses some aspects of the implementation and the performance.

2 The molecular-dynamics algorithm ...

Molecular dynamics is a simulation technique which calculates the positions and velocities of a set of N particles as a function of the time t. The particle positions and velocities evolve under the influence of the forces which the particles exert on each other according to Newton's equations of motion. Space limits permit me to only summarize the main characteristics of a regular, i.e. serial, MD algorithm [4].

The equations of motion are solved on a grid of timesteps Δt on which the system is propagated from one timestep to the next. The most CPU time consuming step in the propagation to the next timestep is the calculation of the forces $\{\mathbf{F}_i\}_{i=1}^{N}$ on each particle i. In our application the forces are short-ranged two-body forces. The force calculation for such forces is most efficiently carried out with a pair list. This list contains all the particle pairs with an inter-particle distance of less than $r_c + \delta$, where r_c is the maximum range of the two-body forces. The skin length δ is usually small and guarantees that the list contains all interacting particle pairs for a number of timesteps. The pair list has to be recalculated as soon as one particle has moved a distance $\delta/2$ since the last pair list update. The list itself is most efficiently set up with a cell presorting scheme, i.e. the volume in which the particles move is divided into cells such that particles within a distance of $r_c + \delta$ from each other occur only within the same cell or within two neighboring cells. The algorithm has the following structure:

1. Supply a set of initial positions and velocities.
2. Determine which particles are in each cell and construct the pair list.
3. Set the forces $\{\mathbf{F}_i\}$ to zero.
4. Loop over all pairs in the list: if the inter-particle distance of a pair of particles (i, j) in the list is smaller than r_c, calculate the force on i and j due to the $i - j$ interaction and add them to $\mathbf{F}_i$ and $\mathbf{F}_j$ respectively.

5. Calculate all particle positions and velocites at the next timestep with the aid of the forces calculated in step 4.
6. Check whether there is a particle that has moved a distance $\delta/2$ since the last update of the pair list. If so, return to step 2, otherwise, return to step 3.

The program will terminate at step 5 after a sufficient number of timesteps.

Essential for this scheme is the short-ranged nature of the forces, not the restriction to pair interactions. In the presence of e.g. three-body forces one can construct a list of interacting particle triplets with a cell presorting scheme.

3 ...and its parallel implementation

The parallelization of this algorithm is of the "geometric" type, i.e. the volume in which the particles move is divided into subvolumes (not to be confused with the cells), each of which is assigned to a different processor which only updates the positions and velocities of the particles in that subvolume [5]. Special care has to be taken at the boundaries of a subvolume because, firstly, particles near the boundaries will interact with particles in the neighboring processsor subvolume and, secondly, particles can cross subvolume boundaries. For our application, the entire volume is subdivided in a one-dimensional array of subvolumes along the dimension in which the fiber grows (see the figure). The subvolume boundaries slice the fiber perpendicular to its length,

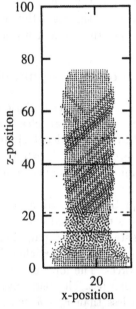

Fig: 2-d projection of a growing fiber. Each dot represents a particle; this configuration is obtained at the end of run 3 of the table. The solid lines give the decomposition of the volume in 3 subvolumes with equal number of particles at the start of run 3. The dashed lines give this for the displayed configuration.

a decomposition which minimizes the number of particles along these boundaries. This one-dimensional decomposition also simplifies the algorithm as each subvolume only has a neigboring subvolume above and below (except for the top and bottom subvolume which have only one neighbor). Consequently, each processor communicates with only 2 other processors, again with the exception of the top and bottom processor (I only consider the main communication needed to do a timestep).

Each processor uses a cell decomposition within its own subvolume which is, besides to construct a pair list, also used in the communication with the neighboring processors. Namely, particles in the lowest layer of cells of a subvolume will, of all the particles in the subvolume below, only interact with those in the upper layer of cells of that subvolume. Each processor thus only needs to receive the positions of the particles in the upper layer of cells of the subvolume below and the positions of the particles in the lower layer of cells of the subvolume above. Once these positions are known to the processor, it can calculate the forces on all the particles in its own subvolume and propagate these particles one timestep further.

Note that this communication of particle positions has to happen each timestep because, after a timestep, the new position of a particle is only known to the processor which handles the subvolume in which the particle is. This need for communication tightly synchronizes the processors: they can not start with a new timestep before each of them has finished the previous one.

All processors refresh their pair list at the same time. This is efficient since, if one processor is updating its pair list, all others will have to wait anyway before the next timestep can be made. After the propagation step, each processor checks whether there is a particle in its subvolume that has moved a distance larger than $\delta/2$ and reports this to the bottom processor (the choice for the bottom processor is arbitrary). If the bottom processor hears from one or more processors that they need to update their pair list, it will tell all processors to do so, otherwise it will tell all of them to continue with the next timestep.

The processors use the set-up of a new pair list to check whether particles have entered or left their subvolume. Namely, particles can have moved no more than a distance $\delta/2$ since the last pair list update. Therefore, the only particles that can have left the subvolume were in the upper or lower layer of cells at the time of the last pair list update. The only particles that can have entered the subvolume were in either of the two neighboring layers of cells. At the time of a pair list update, each processor loops over these particles and checks which of them are currently in its subvolume. Subsequently, it assigns those to the appropriate cells and exchanges particle positions in the cells along the boundaries with the neighboring processors. It can then construct the new pair list. It will handle all particles currently in its subvolume as the ones it has to propagate until it checks again at the next list update. The algorithm for one processor looks as follows:

1. Receive the positions and velocities of the particles that are initially in its assigned subvolume.
2. Divide the subvolume into cells and determine which particles are in each cell.
3. Send particle coordinates in the upper layer of cells to the processor of the subvolume above, send particle coordinates in the lower layer to the processor of the subvolume below and receive the information that those two processors send.
4. Construct the pair list.
5. Calculate the force on each particle in its subvolume as in the steps 3 and 4 of the serial algorithm.

6. Update the positions and velocities as in step 5 of the serial algorithm.
7. The same communication procedure as in step 3, needed to exchange the updated positions.
8. Communicate to bottom processor whether the pair list has to be updated.
9. Hear from the bottom processor whether the pair list has to be updated (this will always be the case if an update request was sent out in the previous step). If not, go to step 5, else continue.
10. Check which particles are currently in its subvolume and go to step 2.

This general scheme has to be supplemented with a number of "special features" to model LHPG which are, however, not in the scope of this paper.

4 Some implementation specifics and program performance

The program ran on a cluster of workstations which can be viewed as a multiple instruction, multiple data (MIMD) parallel machine. The algorithm does not require any shared memory. The communication between the processors ran over an Ethernet network using the communication package PVM (Parallel Virtual Machine). For each processor subvolume in the simulation a process is started which, normally spoken, runs on a separate processor. There is a separate executable code for the very lowest subvolume (which only interacts with the subvolume above) and the very top subvolume (which only interacts with the subvolume below) but the processes for the subvolumes in between run the same code. The lengths of the subvolumes are independent from each other but each subvolume must fit at least one layer of cells. There needs to be a bottom and a top process but there can be any number of middle processes, including none. The simulation is controlled by a "main" process which spawns the subvolume processes and gathers data but does not take an appreciable amount of CPU time and shares a processor with one of the subvolume processes. All simulations were done on a cluster of 3 Risc/6000 350 workstations but test runs on up to 6 processors and 60000 particles proved its broader applicability. There is a wide range of communication loads: data gathering requires approximately 10 MB to be sent to the main process every 1000 timesteps, exchange of particle positions requires roughly 25-100 kB to be exchanged between processors of neigboring subvolumes every timestep, pair list update information requires the communication of 32 B between the bottom processor and all other subvolume processors. The number of subvolumes is an input parameter in the program. Load balancing between them is carried out by the main process which divides the total volume such that each subvolume contains the same number of particles initially. The number of particles in the upper subvolume will grow as the fiber grows but so slowly that the subvolumes need not be changed during a run. The following table illustrates the program performance by a sequence of 4 runs of 40000 timesteps each during which a full fiber was grown. All runs employed one middle process, the 3 workstations were otherwise free of CPU

run	# particles	total CPU	% CPU top	communication time	ratio wall-clock/CPU
1	13088	20.1	34	3.6	0.52
2	17746	23.6	39	2.0	0.47
3	21584	29.2	38	1.8	0.44
4	25489	35.0	37	2.1	0.43

Table 1. Column 1: run number, each run starts where the previous run ended. Column 2: number of particles at the end of the run (run 1 started with 9488 particles). Column 3: Total CPU time of the 3 processors in hours. Column 4: Percentage of the total CPU time used by the top process (the remaining CPU time is almost equally split between the bottom and middle process). Column 5: Communication time, defined as the wall-clock time minus the CPU time of the top process, in hours. Column 6: Wall-clock time divided by total CPU time (ideally, if communication would take no time, this ration is 1/3).

intensive processes. The program speed increases from 12.0×10^3 particle updates per wall clock second in the first run to 17.2×10^3 in the fourth run. The serial program (which is a non-parallel but otherwise identical code) runs approximately $(7.2 \pm 0.2) \times 10^3$ particle updates per wall-clock second for systems of about 20000 particles.

Acknowledgements

The courteous assistence of the University Computing and Networking Services, in particular of A.M. Ferrenberg, has been very helpful. These simulations were initiated and supported by D.P. Landau. C. Bruin proofread the manuscript which was written at the International Center for Theoretical Physics in Trieste (Italy). This research was supported in part by DARPA grant # N00014-90-J-4088 and EC HCM Institutional Grant # ERBCHBGCT920182.

References

1. S.M. Jacobsen, B.M. Tissue and W.M. Yen, J. Phys. Chem. **96**, 1547 (1992).
2. M.J.P. Nijmeijer and D.P. Landau, Computational Materials Sci. **1**, 389 (1993).
3. M.J.P. Nijmeijer and D.P. Landau, to be published.
4. R.W. Hockney and J.W. Eastwood, Computer Simulations using Particles (McGraw-Hill, New York, 1981).
5. M.R.S. Pinches, D.J. Tildesley and W. Smith, Molec. Simulations **6**, 51 (1991).

Simulated Annealing for N-body Systems

J.M. Voogd *, P.M.A. Sloot *, R. v. Dantzig **

* Parallel Scientific Computing and Simulation Group
University of Amsterdam, Kruislaan 403
1098 SJ Amsterdam, The Netherlands
** NIKHEF, PO Box 41882
1009 DB Amsterdam, The Netherlands

Abstract

In this paper we discuss the mapping of the physical problem of 2D crystallization with spherical boundary conditions onto a Simulated Annealing model, and the mapping of this model onto a parallel computer. We discuss some aspects of the finetuning of the simulation code and the overall behaviour, stability and scalability, of our parallel implementation.

1 Introduction

We study crystallization on a closed two dimensional surface. Crystallization with this type of constraints is poorly understood. As a model for such (bio)physically relevant systems we started with particles, e.g. molecules, confined to a spherical surface. Examples of actual systems are buckyballs, viruses and vesicles. There are different types of interaction potentials between the particles for various systems, examples are Lennard-Jones, Coulomb and van der Waals interactions. The mentioned systems are studied by computer experimentation. Powerful new types of computer platforms are nowadays available to the research community and advanced simulation techniques with rather large numbers of particles are now possible.

In this paper we discuss the method of simulation we use in our study on spherical crystallization of N-body systems. To do the suggested computer experiments we need an algorithm adapted to the problem, minimization of the free energy in our system. A well established computational scheme for such problems is Simulated Annealing (SA), a stochastic optimization technique that mimics the essentials of physical annealing. The SA method is discussed in section 2.

The next step is to map the model onto a computer system. For our experiments we use a parallel implementation with a hybrid topology on the Parsytec GCel transputer platform with 512 nodes, installed at the University of Amsterdam. This mapping is discussed in section 3.

One more step to take is finetuning the code in order to reach an efficient implementation. In section 4 we discuss two variants of the SA algorithm and their performance on the parallel machine.

2 Simulated Annealing Applied to Crystallization

Many problems in physics, chemistry and mathematics can be formulated as optimization problems. A vast majority of these involve a search for the absolute minimum of an underlying multidimensional function. Usually, this is far from trivial, since the solution must be attained from a large configuration space, containing many local (candidate) extrema. As a consequence, the computational effort required for solution grows more rapidly than a polynomial function of the problem size, the problem is said to be NP (non-polynomial time) complete. Because it is often impossible to examine all solution candidates, approximation methods are required.

We apply SA to model the behaviour of our system. It is closely related to the physical phenomenon that we are studying. In physical annealing a material is heated to a high temperature, and then allowed to cool slowly. At high temperature the system can explore most of the phase space. During cooling the system will spend more time in minima, from which it can still escape; molecules move relatively freely with respect to one another. If thermal mobility is lost, the molecules search for the lowest energy consistent with the physical constraints.

The SA algorithm for solving combinatorial optimization problems was formulated in 1983 by Kirkpatrick et al.[1]. It is based on a method developed by Metropolis et al.[2] to study the equilibrium properties of large systems of interacting particles at finite temperature. In terms of the crystallization problem at hand the procedure works as follows. First the particles are randomly placed on a spherical surface. The annealing begins by creating a Markov chain of given length at a given temperature. The Markov chain grows by randomly displacing particles and calculating the corresponding change in energy of the system, while deciding on acceptance of the displacement. If the energy of the system is lowered, the step is accepted. If the energy increases, the step is accepted according to an exponential probability, with the temperature as a parameter. At low temperatures these uphill steps are almost never accepted.

After a chain has ended, the temperature is lowered, (see section 4), after which a new chain is started. This process continues until a stop criterion is met, for example when the standard deviation in the final energies of the last ten chains falls below a certain small value. The energy of the system is defined as the energy per particle. This removes dependence of the energy on the number of particles such that the stop criterion can be fixed.

Normally the SA method is applied to combinatorial optimization with discrete perturbation steps. However, in our research we are dealing with particles on a continuous surface and thus we need a continuous algorithm. For our application we have developed the following method to use the SA algorithm on continuous spaces. The displacement of a particle is constructed by generating a random distance and a random direction. The distance is drawn from a Cauchy distribution of a certain width. The Cauchy (rather than a Boltzmann) distribution is used because of the stronger tail, which allows large perturbations to be generated, and makes escapes from local minima more probable. The width of the Cauchy distribution is adaptively changed such that about half of the particle moves are accepted.

Although - in principle - SA "guarantees" finding the global minimum, the time required for the algorithm to converge increases rapidly with increasing number of degrees of freedom and/or local minima. In the crystallization problem we are dealing with a large number of particles and the number of local minima (quasi-stable particle configurations) can also be large. Therefore conventional annealing implementations are of very limited use; more efficient methods need to be investigated. With the new breed of parallel machines and programming paradigms, fast implementations come within reach.

3 Parallel Simulated Annealing on a Transputer System

The desired simulations are extremely computationally intensive. Therefore we investigate the possibility of parallel execution of our solver. We use two parallelization methods at the same time. The first is a parallel scheme for the SA method itself and the second is a functional decomposition of the cost function evaluation, i.e. the calculation of the energy of our N-particle system.

Since the SA method is inherently sequential we can expect that a parallel version needs special mechanisms. A synchronous parallel algorithm that does not mimic sequential annealing is systolic SA, see Aarts et al. 1986[3]. In systolic SA, a Markov chain is assigned to each of the available processors. All chains have equal length. The chains are executed in parallel and during execution, information is transferred from a given chain to its successor. Each Markov chain is divided into a number of sub-chains equal to the number of available processors. The execution of a new chain is started as soon as the first sub-chain of the previous chain is generated. At the start of each new sub-chain there is a choice of continuing with the final configuration from the previous sub-chain or adopting the configuration of the last generated sub-chain from the previous chain calculated in parallel.

In addition to this parallel SA algorithm we exploit the parallelism that can be obtained from an ordinary Monte Carlo algorithm. Here the most time consuming part of the program is the calculation of the energy difference resulting from the perturbations. Since these calculations are independent, we parallelize this part of the program by functional decomposition, see ter Laak et al. 1992[4].

To calculate the energy difference ΔE for a particle displacement we have to calculate two-body potential energies. Since these calculations are independent, we can perform them in parallel. If we connect a processor farm to a processor generating Markov chains, it can assign ΔE calculation jobs to processors in the farm. We use a hybrid implementation, systolic SA with energy calculations in a farm; so we need a farm attached to every processor in the systolic decomposition.

In the systolic annealing scheme, there have to be connections from one processor to an other processor which is calculating the next Markov chain. This simple communication pattern can efficiently be implemented in a ring topology. The communication overhead is small since each processor contains a complete independent database for the optimization problem. Information about the intermediate state is only interchanged at the end of each sub-chain. In order to cut the communication costs of the farm for the energy calculation, we use a tree configuration and let every processor hold a copy of the complete N-particle configuration.

4 Finetuning and Overall Behaviour

In order to reach optimum convergence a problem-dependent finetuning of the cooling strategy and chain length is needed. We have studied two different cooling rules, a fixed rule and an adaptive rule. The fixed rule gives the temperature of chain number k based only on the temperature of chain k-1

$$T_k = \text{coolrate} * T_{k-1} \tag{1}$$

The adaptive rule is based on the principle that the stationary distribution of states of two successive chains should be close to each other. This strategy uses additional information about the previous chain to determine the temperature of the new chain

$$T_k = T_{k-1} * \left(1 + \frac{\ln(1+\delta) * T_{k-1}}{3 * \sigma(T_{k-1})}\right)^{-1} \tag{2}$$

The $\sigma(T_{k-1})$ is the standard deviation in the value of the cost function (free energy) of the previous chain. The parameter δ controls how much the stationary distributions of successive chains may differ, it has a small value (0.1) which is kept constant for the experiments we present here.

The strategies mentioned above are elements of the SA method which are applicable to sequential and parallel implementations. As it turns out, the parallel implementation has some properties that are influenced by the number of processors used in the systolic annealing scheme.

We have done a series of experiments for 20 particles with the systolic annealing code in the hybrid topology. If the fixed cooling rule is applied we observe that the quality of the solution decreases if the number of systolic processors increases. This is because the fraction of configurations, adopted from a previous chain, is very low (a few percent). Thus the configuration of the first sub-chain is the one that is very likely to be the only configuration used by the next Markov chain. Since the length of all sub-chains decrease if the number of processors increases, we observe a decreasing quality of the solution.

If we want to keep the quality of the obtained solutions to be the same for an increasing number of processors, we have to use a larger chain length for higher numbers of processors. The execution time, however will then increase and the speedup gained will be lost.

For the dynamically adjusted cooling we find an opposite tendency. Here we observe that if the sub-chains get shorter (the number of processors increase) the deviation of the cost function in the first sub-chain increases and that thus the temperature for the next chain is only slightly lowered. This means, however, that the number of Markov chains needed is also increasing since the temperature steps are smaller.

In order to give a fair comparison between the two cooling strategies we have looked for the chain lengths that gave the same quality of solutions. For the fixed cooling this means that we have used a larger chain length for higher numbers of processors and for the dynamically adjusted temperature we could use lower chain lengths with increasing number of processors. In figure 1 we give the execution times for both strategies. We can see that the time for the dynamically adjusted temperature increases more rapidly than that of the fixed temperature rule. In the case of fixed cooling rule, this is because of the increased chain length that had to be used. In the dynamically adjusted temperature case this increase in execution time is due to the higher number of Markov chains that had to be generated before a stable configuration is found.

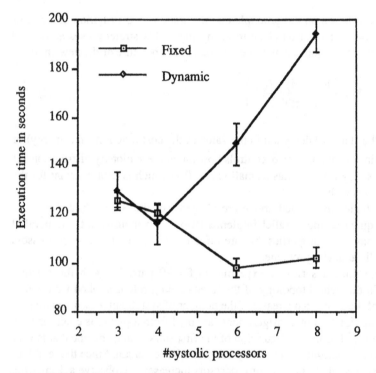

Figure 1) Execution times of the implementations.

In figure 1 we see that the dynamic adjustment has a minimum at 4 systolic processors while the fixed temperature adjustment has its minimum at 6 processors. The execution time that can be achieved is the lowest for the fixed temperature adjustment strategy.

5 Conclusions

The SA algorithm is an inherently sequential scheme. Parallelizing it by the systolic SA method introduces a functional difference with the sequential version. This parallelization has consequences for the accuracy of the iterative processes. We observe that the quality of the solutions tends to be influenced by the number of processors used in the systolic algorithm. For the two used cooling rules we had to optimise chain lengths in order to ensure that the quality of the solutions is independent of the number of processors.

Comparing the obtained results we find that the fixed cooling rule has its minimum in the execution time at a larger number of processors than the dynamic adjustment. Therefore the fixed rule implementation gives shorter execution times.

6 Acknowledgements

The authors wish to thank Prof. D. Frenkel (AMOLF) for fruitful discussions on the physics of the experiments.

The research was funded by the 'Stichting Fundamenteel Onderzoek der Materie' (FOM) under number FI-A-a-3640.

7 References

[1]   S. Kirkpatrick, C.D. Gelatt, Jr., M.P. Vechi, *Optimization by Simulated Annealing*, Science 220, number 4598 (May 1983), pp. 671-680

[2]   N. Metropolis, A.W. Rosenbluth, M.N. Rosenbluth, A.H. Teller and E. Teller, *Equation of State Calculations by Fast Computing Machines*, J. of chem. physics, Volume 21, number 6 (1953), pp. 1087-1092.

[3]   E.H.L. Aarts, F.M.J. de Bont, E.H.A. Habers and P.J.M van Laarhoven, *Parallel implementations of the Statistical Cooling algorithm*, North Holland Integration, the VLSI journal 4 (2986), pp. 209-238

[4]   A. ter Laak, L.O. Hertzberger, P.M.A. Sloot, *NonConvex Continuous Optimization Experiments on a Transputer System*, Transputer Systems - Ongoing Research, ed. A.R. Allen (IOS Press, Amsterdam, 1992) p.251

The Message Passing Version
of ECMWF's Weather Forecast Model

Saulo R. M. Barros*, David Dent, Lars Isaksen,
Guy Robinson, and Fritz G. Wollenweber

European Centre for Medium-Range Weather Forecasts,
Reading, RG2 9AX, UK

Abstract. In this paper we describe the parallelization of ECMWF's
forecast model (IFS), reporting first results and outlining ongoing work.

1 Introduction

The European Centre for Medium-Range Weather Forecasts (ECMWF's) operational model is a global spectral model, run at a current resolution of T213L31
(triangular truncation, 213 waves around a great circle on the globe, 31 atmospheric levels on the vertical) [3]. It employs a grid of more than 4 million points
and is run operationally on a Cray C90/16, consuming about two hours wallclock
time to produce a 10-day forecast.

In this paper we describe how this large Fortran production code has been
developed into a portable parallel benchmark, part of the RAPS collection. The
first step in this process was to develop a portable Fortran-77 code, without the
Cray extentions. This portable code provided the basis for the development of
the message passing benchmark code. Portability of the message passing was
achieved by the use of PARMACS [2].

The SPMD version of ECMWF's spectral model has been designed to enable
the efficient utilization of up to a few thousand parallel processors, at the current
model resolution. Our first version, for which we present results in this paper,
still has limited parallelism. It can efficiently utilize up to about two hundred
processors, the version exploiting extended parallelism is under implementation.

Several points had to be addressed in the design of the parallel code. They
concern the choice of parallelization strategy for the spectral method, the handling of semi-Lagrangian advection and load balancing due to the use of a non-
uniform grid. These questions are adressed in section 2.

The benchmark code has been written with a flexible data layout, so the
degree of parallelism versus vectorization can be chosen easily. The data structure
is also flexible to the extent, that by the setting of some parameters the data
layout in the local memory can be modified to best suit RISC processors or
vector nodes. We discuss this point in section 3.

We conclude the paper with initial results from benchmark runs on Meiko
CS-2 and IBM SP1. They are compared with the performance on ECMWF's
Cray C90 in section 4.

---

* On leave from IME, University of São Paulo, Brazil.

2 Parallelization Aspects

2.1 Transposition

The global dependencies inherent to spectral models create the need for global communication, no matter which data partition is employed. As a basic strategy for the parallelization of the spectral model we have chosen the transposition method, which compares favourably to other approaches, as shown in [1]. A closer look at the dependency patterns in the model shows that in any phase of the algorithm there is just one direction (coordinate) in which the computations are non locally coupled. The two remaining dimensions provide a large amount of parallelism that can be exploited. However, the coupling direction changes from phase to phase of the algorithm. A data transposition between two such phases is used to ensure that coupled data will reside on a single processor during every phase.

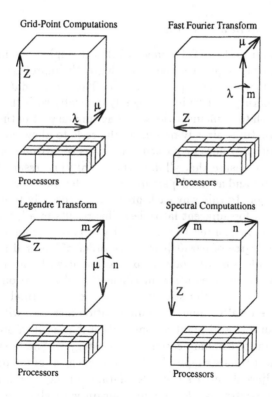

Fig. 1. Schematic representation of the full transposition method

In our current implementation the grid is partitioned among the processors, each one treating a set of some adjacent latitudes. This partition allows all the computations in grid-point space to be carried out in parallel, with no need for communication, except for the semi-Lagrangian part, to be discussed next section. This partition also allows the Fourier transforms to be performed independently. The spectral coefficients are spread among the processors according to their zonal wave-numbers, therefore allowing the Legendre transforms to be computed in parallel with no communication. Between the Legendre and Fourier transforms, these fields are transposed from a decomposition by latitudes to a decomposition by zonal wave numbers and vice-versa, involving a global communication step among the processors (see [1] for details).

We are currently extending the transposition strategy to exploit parallelism in two space dimensions at the same time. For example, the spectral fields will in addition be partitioned over the levels, while grid-point fields will be partitioned in both latitudinal and longitudinal directions. A time step of the algorithm requires six transposition steps. The full strategy is shown in Figure 1, where the necessary transposition steps during the algorithm and the fields distribution are outlined.

2.2 Semi-Lagrangian advection

A second characteristic of ECMWF's model is that it employs a semi-Lagrangian advection [6] in the time-stepping scheme, which greatly improves the overall performance, because longer time steps can be used. This creates data dependencies which are local in nature, but which change dynamically with the winds.

The first approach to implement the semi-Lagrangian part of the model made extensive use of structures already present in the code to allow macrotasking on the Cray C90. Entire latitudes or packed collections of latitudes are exchanged between processors to ensure that all data (potentially) necessary for interpolations at the mid-point and at the departure point of the trajectories are available within every processor. In this way each processor needs only to exchange data with a few processors for adjacent latitudes. This results in a local communication pattern which is well suited to the majority of parallel computers available today and allows a degree of parallelism of the order of hundred processors.

Finer grain parallelism will have to be exploited with the full transposition, increasing the requirements for an efficient implementation of the semi-Lagrangian scheme. A characteristic of the scheme (as normal for grid-point methods) is that the total volume of communication increases with the number of processors. A suitable grid point decomposition is needed in order to reduce the necessary amount of communication. One strategy will be to split the globe into patches of almost square shapes. Such an arrangement of the patches should ensure that only adjacent patches exchange data, reducing overall message traffic. In this way a processor needs to communicate with about six neighbours, while the use of more elongated and narrow patches leads to processors exchanging messages with about twenty neighbours. However, we keep the code design flexible, such that we can also use more elongated patches, which may be advantageous to minimize load inbalances caused by the dynamics of weather patterns.

Due to the dynamic characteristics of the semi-Lagrangian scheme, the locations of departure points change from time-step to time-step. This implies that in order to be on the safe side, one actually exchanges more data than actually needed by the scheme, since it is not possible to know in advance which data will be required. If possible, it would be preferable to only exchange data as required. Any strategy trying to exploit these features will have to be dynamical and will include some overheads. This will be an area where global memory facilities provided by some vendors could turn out to be useful.

2.3 Reduced grid

ECMWF's operational model employs a quasi regular grid for the physics processes and all other grid-point computations, the so called reduced grid [5]. In this grid the number of points per latitude is gradually reduced towards the poles, amounting to about two thirds of the number of grid points of a uniform latitude-longitude at same resolution, but retaining the overall accuracy of the model. However, the use of this grid poses some load balancing problems for the parallel model, since it is then not obvious how to distribute the latitudes in a optimal way (we still require that a processor treats a set of consecutive latitudes, since this reduces the communication in the semi-Lagrangian part of the model). We derived an algorithm which always compute an optimal distribution for the latitudes, minimizing the resulting load inbalance. Even with an optimal distribution there will still remain a certain inbalance. Figure 2 displays this inbalance for the resolutions most used at ECMWF, operationally and for research. With the extended parallelism version this inbalance will be reduced.

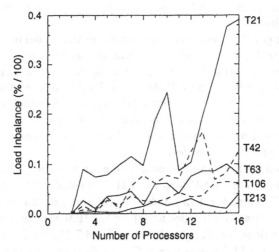

Fig. 2. Load inbalances when using the reduced grid

3 Single node performance

The variations in architecture among the parallel systems available today require some flexibility in the design of a parallel code in order to achieve good performance in very different machines. One of the important aspects is the single node performance. Today we still have machines employing vector nodes, while others have opted for RISC type processors. Achieving good performance on vector machines requires relatively long vectors, while cashe reusage is the most important aspect for RISC type processors.

About 80% of the total computational time in ECMWF's forecast model is spent in the grid point computations. The operational model has been designed to run efficiently on Cray vector computers and therefore uses long vectors in grid point space. This data structure is likely not to suit RISC processors. Therefore, the data layout to be used in grid point computations can be supplied as a parameter at compilation time. This 'vector length' or 'cashe line' parameter can vary between 1 and the number of grid points in a full latitude (or even of some latitudes), and determines the inner dimension in the arrays used in grid point space. Large values lead to longer vectors, while small values should be more adequate to RISC processors. This flexibility in the code is also necessary for the implementation of finer grain parallelism, where the splitting of latitudes is used.

4 Results

We have run our code on several platforms, also demonstrating the portability of the code. We present here results obtained on a Meiko-CS2 and on an IBM-SP1. For the sake of comparison we also present some C-90 results. We point out that we made no effort to optimize the code for any of these machines, and therefore the results should be viewed as preliminary. The portable parallel code is part of the RAPS benchmark suite, and several vendors are in the process of optimizing it for their machines.

The following graphics show the performance of the model on the Meiko and on the IBM. A good parallel efficiency is achieved on both machines, what can be seen by the almost straight lines in Figure 3. Runs on a larger number of processors will be necessary to evaluate the scalability of the model and of the machines. The times correspond to five time steps of the model, run with semi-Lagrangian advection and Physics. Radiation was computed in just one of the five time steps. The Eulerian model was used for the T63 runs on the IBM. All resolutions employed 19 vertical levels.

For comparison we have run the model on a single node of ECMWF's Cray C90. The performance is 169 Mflops for T21 / full grid, 161 Mflops for T21 / reduced grid, 187 Mflops for T42 / reduced grid and 195 Mflops for T42 / full grid. The corresponding results (per node) for the IBM are: 19.5 Mflops for T21 / full grid, 19.2 Mflops for T21 / reduced grid, 18.7 Mflops for T42 / full grid and 18.2 Mflops for T42 / reduced grid. The performance on the Meiko is 14.4 Mflops for the T21 runs.

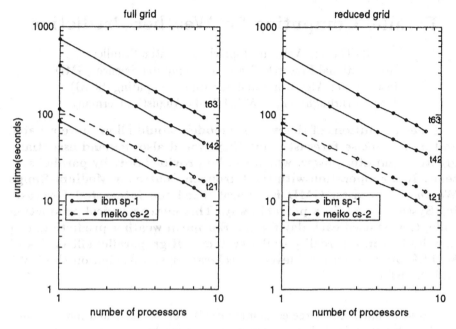

Fig. 3. Times for five time step runs on IBM-SP1 and Meiko-CS2

5 Acknowledgements

This work has been partially funded by the European Comission projects GP-MIMD2 and PPPE. Adrian Simmons and Geerd Hoffman are coordinating the MPP efforts at ECMWF. Ute Gärtel, Wolfgang Joppich and Anton Schüller implemented a simplified parallel version of IFS [4], which as used as a starting point for our implementation. We thank all of them.

References

1. Barros, S. R. M., Kauranne, T.: On the parallelization of global spectral weather models, Parallel Computing (1994), (to appear)
2. Bomans, L., Hempel, R., Roose,D.: The Argonne / GMD macros in fortran for portable parallel programming and their implementation on Intel iPSC/2, Parallel Computing **15** (1990), 119-132.
3. Dent, D., Simmons, A.J.: The ECMWF multi-tasking weather prediction model, Computer Physics Reports **11** (1989), 153-194.
4. Gärtel, U., Joppich, W., Schüller,A: First results with a parallelized 3D Weather prediction code (short communication), Parallel Computing **19** (1993), 1427-1430.
5. Hortal, M., Simmons, A. J.: Use of reduced Gaussian grids in spectral models, Monthly Weather Review **119** (1991),1057-1074.
6. Staniforth, A., Côtè, J.: Semi-Lagrangian integration schemes for atmospheric models - a review, Monthly Weather Review **119** (1991),2206-2223.

Parallel Computing for Weather Prediction

Ute Gärtel, Wolfgang Joppich and Anton Schüller
German National Research Center for Computer Science (GMD)
Institute for Algorithms and Scientific Computing (SCAI)
Schloss Birlinghoven, D–53734 Sankt Augustin, Germany

Finer resolutions of the weather models would allow more reliable and more precise forecasts, but they would also demand essentially greater computer power, which can be provided only by parallel systems. In a cooperation with the European Centre for Medium-Range Weather Forecasts, GMD has parallelized the Integrated Forecasting System (IFS), in a portable way. This meteorological production code, that is used each day for the European weather prediction, can now be run in on 'real' parallel systems. High parallel efficencies of 80-90% and more are achieved on relevant systems, e.g., on the CM5 and the SP1.

BACKGROUND: The large economic benefit from a faster and more reliable weather prediction is obvious. Finer resolutions would allow more reliable and more precise forecasts, but they would also demand essentially greater computer power, which can be provided only by parallel computers. There is no doubt that the degree of parallelism will increase significantly in the next generation of supercomputers. In order to exploit the possibilities of such massively parallel systems, the corresponding software has to be adapted.

THE APPLICATION: The IFS is the operational code of the European Centre for Medium-Range Weather Forecasts (ECMWF). The program is run daily and produces a ten day forecast for Europe. Starting from measured input data, the predictive variables wind, temperature, humidity and pressure are calculated. The numerical model uses a global three-dimensional grid consisting of more than four million points (640 latitudes, 320 longitudes, 31 vertical levels) to compute the unknowns per time step (approximately 1,000 time steps for a ten days period).

THE ALGORITHM: The solution method employed in the IFS is the spectral transform technique using triangular truncation (for more details see [3]). In order to exploit the fact that the spherical harmonics are eigenfunctions of an essential part of the underlying operator, certain parts of the calculations are performed in spectral space. Other computations such as the whole physics are carried out in the grid point space. Altogether, three different discrete function spaces are involved in the calculations: grid point space, Fourier space and spectral space (compare Figure 1).

DIFFICULTIES: The basic parallelization strategy had to be choosen taking into account the narrow time-frame of the project and the complexity of the sequential code. A further side condition was the wish of the ECMWF to avoid program modifications in the numerical kernels of the code whenever possible, resulting in the need to introduce more sophisticated data structures in the parallel version. Problems of the parallelization are caused by the variety of data structures employed in the code. One triangular and two rectangular data spaces are used by the spectral transform method which requires non-trivial mappings of the data to the processes and special considerations for the efficient parallelization and the data structuring in the parallel program. Load balancing issues have to be taken into account.

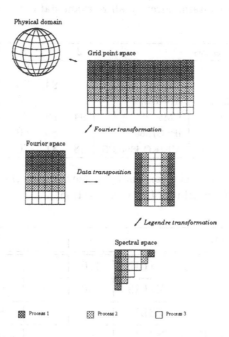

Figure 1: Schematic representation for the partitioning of data in the different data spaces to 3 processes.

THE PARALLELIZATION STRATEGY: A careful analysis showed that the data transposition [1, 5] strategy allowed the fulfilment of all the aforementioned requirements. In particular, it comprises advantageous features with respect to the parallel efficiency as compared with alternative parallelization approaches [1, 4, 7, 8]. This strategy re-distributes the complete data to the processes at various stages of the algorithm such that the arithmetic computations between two consecutive transpositions can be performed without any interprocess communication. This approach is feasible since there are only data dependencies within one coordinate direction, this direction being different within the main algorithmic components. Figure 1 illustrates the chosen mapping strategy.

PORTABILITY: In order to guarantee portability among the variety of different parallel computers currently on the market, the portable PARMACS message passing interface [2] was selected for the parallelization.

NUMERICAL RESULTS: We present results for resolutions ranging from T21L19 to T106L19, where TmLk denotes the truncation number m for the spectral space computations, and k the number of vertical levels employed. In the physical space, this corresponds to resolutions ranging from 64 longitudes × 32 latitudes to 320 longitudes × 160 latitudes and 19 levels in the vertical direction for the full 3D model (resp. 1 level in the 2D case). [1] A more detailed presentation of the parallelization and numerical results can be found in [6].

The first milestone of the project was the parallelization of the 2D model of the IFS, which contains already all relevant data structures and algorithmic

Processors		2	4	8	16	32
Efficiency (in %)	iPSC/2	–	97	97	96	94
	Parsytec GCel	–	94	93	91	84
	nCUBE/2	–	–	90	86	84
	CM5	94	90	87	84	77
	iPSC/860	–	86	80	76	64
	MEIKO i860 CS	88	81	70	60	–

Table 1: Parallel efficiencies for T63L1, achieved with the portable IFS-2D code on different parallel machines (no vectorization).

Processors		1	2	4	8
Efficiency (%)	T21L19	100	94	88	84
	T42L19	100	94	90	81
	T63L19	–	94	89	84
	T84L19	–	–	90	86
	T106L19	–	–	91	87
Time (sec)	T21L19	136.9	73.3	39.0	20.7
	T42L19	588.5	316.4	163.5	105.9
	T63L19	–	729.4	393.2	142.0
	T84L19	–	–	721.7	388.5
	T106L19	–	–	1218.3	636.7

Table 2: Parallel efficiencies and computing times in seconds, on the SP1 (compiler option: -O) for the portable parallel IFS-3D code (no optimization for the RS6000's), ten time steps.

---

[1] The resolution T106L19 was the previous operational model of the ECMWF; today the T213L31 model is standard.

components of the corresponding 3D models. The parallelized IFS-2D runs with high efficiencies on all parallel machines used, compare Table 1 and [5] for further numerical results.

Of course, the 3D code has much higher demands with respect to the system resources. This affects both, memory and performance. Typically, the load module itself requires about 5 MBytes of memory. This explains why some of the machines, on which the parallel 2D code was run, are not suited for the 3D code. Tables 2 and 3 show results obtained with the portable IFS-3D on the SP1 and the CM5 of GMD.

The largest problem we could run on our SP1 (8 nodes, 128 MByte memory each) was T106L19, which corresponds to a resolution which is as twice as coarse as T213L31 that is run operationally today at ECMWF. Efficiencies of more than 80% are obtained. The memory restrictions on our CM5 (32 MByte per node) allowed to solve only resolutions up to T42L19. Here, efficiencies of more than 90% are typically reached.

Processors		1	2	4	8	11	16	22	32
Efficiency (%)	T21L19	–	99	97	96	90	96	–	–
	T42L19	–	–	–	97	93	96	92	93
Time (sec)	T21L19	–	494	254	128	98	65	–	–
	T42L19	–	–	–	526	396	265	203	137

Table 3: Parallel efficiencies and computing times in seconds, on the CM5 (compiler option: -O) for the portable parallel IFS-3D code (no vectorization), ten time steps.

The most striking feature of the parallel performance of the 3D code is that the parallel efficiencies are even higher than in the 2D case. The reason for this is that the computational work increases with the number of levels *and* with the physics computations (which are not included in the 2D model), while the latter does not influence the communication costs. Therefore, the ratio of arithmetic and communication is much better for the parallelization when dealing with the 3D case.

All the results presented above were obtained without any special system–dependent optimization. Main emphasis during the development of the parallel code was laid on the portability of the code, instead.

OPTIMIZATIONS: There is much room left for optimization and tuning of the code according to the features of any specific parallel system. This applies to the implementation of the transposition strategy, the arithmetic components of the parallel code and to system–dependent communication layers. Two examples demonstrate the influence of two different types of optimization for the IBM SP1, the corresponding results being contained in Table 4:

1. One crucial point for the performance of a portable parallel code is the communication. On the SP1 no native PARMACS implementation has been available so far. For the results in the previous section, a PARMACS version built on top of PVM was used. This PVM layer, however, does not use the High Performance Switch of the SP1 efficiently. In order to utilize the system's capabilities, an internal PARMACS interface based directly on the POE of the SP1 has been developed at GMD. An analysis shows that this reduces the time spent in communication up to a factor of three for the IFS–3D, resulting in significantly improved parallel efficiencies and computing times.

2. The portable parallel code still reflects the tuning of the underlying sequential code with respect to a certain vectorization concept. This vectorization concept conflicts in a certain sense with the possible optimization for cache–oriented processors. It optimizes the vector length rather than the cache utilization.

   The most favourite example for this is the special matrix multiply (routine SGEMMX) which is extensively used during the Legendre transforms. This routine is responsible for about 20 % of the whole arithmetic computations. R. Reuter from IBM Heidelberg provided an optimized version for the SP1, which reduces the computing times up to 19 % for T106L19. Similar improvements can be expected for optimizations of other arithmetic routines.

The parallel efficiencies of more than 90 % on 7 processors for the parallel code with the optimized SGEMMX and PARMACS routines promise an excellent performance of large resolutions on a larger number of processors, too.

References

[1] Barros, S.R.M.; Kauranne, T.: *Spectral and multigrid spherical Helmholtz equation solvers on distributed memory parallel computers.* Proceedings of Fourth Workshop on Use of Parallel Processors in Meteorology, 26–30 November 1990, ECMWF, 1–27.

[2] Calkin, R.; Hempel, R.; Hoppe, H.-C.; Wypior, P.: *Portable programming with the PARMACS message passing library.* to appear in Parallel Computing, North–Holland.

[3] Dent, D.; Simmons, A.: *The ECMWF multi-tasking weather prediction model.* Computer Physics Reports 11 (1989) 153–194, North–Holland.

[4] Foster, I.; Gropp, W.; Stevens, R.: *The parallel scalability of the spectral transform method.* Monthly Weather Review 120 (1992) 835–850.

310

[5] Gärtel, U.; Joppich, W.; Schüller, A.: *Parallelizing the ECMWF's weather forecast program: the 2D case.* Parallel Computing 19 (1993), North-Holland.

[6] Gärtel, U.; Joppich, W.; Schüller, A.: *Portable Parallelization of the ECMWF's Weather Forecast Program.* Technical documentation and results. Arbeitspapiere der GMD 920, GMD, St. Augustin, 1994.

[7] Walker, D.W.; Worley, P.H.; Drake, J.B.: *Parallelizing the spectral transform method – part II.* Tech. Rep. ORNL/TM-11855, Oak Ridge National Laboratory, Oak Ridge, 1991.

[8] Worley, P.H.; Drake, J.B.: *Parallelizing the spectral transform method – part I.* Tech. Rep. ORNL/TM-11747, Oak Ridge National Laboratory, Oak Ridge, 1991.

Processors		4			7		
Software		no tuning PVM	no tuning POE	optimized SGEMMX POE	no tuning PVM	no tuning POE	optimized SGEMMX POE
PARMACS on							
Eff.(%)	T42	90	95	96	77	85	85
	T63	89	96	96	84	91	92
	T106	91	96	97	88	95	95
time (sec)	T42	163.5	156.4	139.2	123.2	103.4	92.1
	T63	393.2	357.7	319.6	242.0	218.5	190.3
	T106	1218.3	1156.3	930.5	718.1	657.6	541.4

Table 4: Parallel efficiency and computing times in seconds on the IBM SP1, PARMACS on PVM (Pallas), PARMACS on POE (H. Ritzdorf,GMD); cache optimization for SGEMMX (R. Reuter,IBM); compiler option: -O.

Parallelization of a Mesoscale Model of Atmospheric Circulation — An Object-Oriented Approach

Jens Gerlach, Birgit Kähler
{jens,birgit}@first.gmd.de

German National Corporation for Computer Science
GMD-FIRST, Rudower Chaussee 5, Gebäude 13.7, D-12489 Berlin, Germany

1 Introduction

Mesoscale phenomena describe atmospheric motions with wavelengths of ten or hundreds of kilometers (e.g. the sea-breeze circulation system). They play a significant part in local weather and in dispersion of air pollutants [1].

High resolution mesoscale models demand for high performance computing. Since these models contain a lot of parallelism (mainly data parallelism), it is quite natural to execute them on machines with distributed memory.

Usually, existing codes are "parallelized", i.e. programs that were written without having in mind the demands of a distributed memory architecture, are prepared to run on a parallel machine. In the course of parallelization, a "task" designed for a single computer is decomposed into smaller tasks which are distributed onto several CPUs. If the application is highly data parallel the resulting tasks are able to work in parallel without spending an immoderate amount of time for synchronization or exchange of data between each other.

Often the phase of decomposition is rather hard and results more or less in a complete redesign of the program. We think that these difficulties are caused by improper chosen data structures of the original program. When programs must specifically be structured for parallelization big problems come up with maintaining the different data structures of sequential and parallel versions. Double work is unavoidable.

In this paper we describe how the paradigm of *object-orientation* can be used to design a software system in such a way that it can be composed from smaller sub-systems and does not have to be decomposed in an unnatural complicated manner in order to use its inherent parallelism. We do this in the light of a complex program from the area of mesoscale flow modeling. Our work has been encouraged by the experience we have gained with object-oriented programming at the parallelization of a simple mesoscale circulation model [2].

An object-oriented language must compete with traditional languages in terms of run-time efficiency. In the area of high performance computing Fortran and C are the preferred languages. We have chosen C++ as implementation language, since on the one hand it offers a lot support for data abstraction and object-oriented programming. On the other hand C++ has been designed "to ensure that anything that can be done in C can be done in C++ with no added run-time overhead" [6].

2 Model Foundations

In this section we outline the physical/mathematical foundations of the meso-scale flow model GESIMA. The model has been developed and originally implemented by Kapitza and Eppel [4] at the GKSS Research Center Geesthacht. Here, we focus on these aspects of the model that influence the parallelism of the model.

2.1 Basic Equations

The dynamic frame of GESIMA is based on equations which describe conservation laws for the density ϱ, the velocity $\mathbf{v}$, the pressure p, and the potential temperature Θ in a dry atmosphere.

Pressure, density, and the potential temperature are coupled through the state equation of an ideal gas.

This system describes among others some phenomena which make almost no contributions to the balance of energy of the system (e.g sound waves). Nevertheless sound waves with their high phase velocity force a very small time step in the numerical integration. Therefore it is more efficient to approximate the equations in such a way that on the one hand sound waves are eliminated while on the other hand the balance of energy in the system is ensured.

This is achieved in GESIMA by the so-called anelastic approximation. While doing so the equation of continuity degenerates from a prognostic equation for the mass density ϱ into a diagnostic one for the impulse density $\varrho\mathbf{v}$.

2.2 Numerics

A discretization divides the model domain into a three-dimensional grid of cells. For the discretization of the anelastically approximated system of equations a staggered grid is used so that the discretized impulse density is located in the center of a face of a grid cell while the transported quantities are defined in cell center. This staggered grid prevents a grid separation which occurs at some grid types and difference schemes [4].

The MacCormack difference scheme is used for a numerical integration of the prognostic model equations. It is a predictor-corrector method which is of second order accuracy and belongs to the class of Lax-Wendroff schemes.

From the anelastic approximation follows that the pressure cannot be determined via the state equation of an ideal gas. It has to be determined in such a way that the flux is free of divergence. This leads to a Poisson equation for the pressure which has to be solved in each time step of the numerical integration scheme. A preconditioned conjugate gradient method is used for the iterative solution of this elliptic equation.

In general it can be said, that the algorithms used in the model are highly data parallel and act locally on the grids, i.e. each cell only needs data from its faces or from its neighboring cells. An analogous statement can be made for the faces of cells.

3 Object-oriented Analysis and Design

3.1 Finding Classes

According to Meyer [5] we mean by object-oriented design (OOD)

> the construction of software systems as structured collections of abstract data type implementations.

By an object-oriented analysis (OOA) the outer representatives of the software objects have to be unearthed. These "outer objects" will be described by *classes*, which are abstract data type implementations. Inheritance is used to build class hierarchies.

Candidates for classes can easily be made out in GESIMA. The discretization of the partial differential equations that govern the model foundations divides the model domain into a grid of small cells.

Usually, the various discretized quantities are represented by arrays of a floating-point type, i.e. the global aspects of a grid are emphasized. We have avoided this straightforward solution since arrays present a rather low-level feature.

This can be realized when looking on implementations that are built on such structures. No distinction is made between *what* happens and *where* something happens. Even when there is a algorithm that treats the grid elements completely independent from each other, indices for the involved quantities have to be heavily used. That is both tiresome and error-prone and above all it blurs the different levels within the algorithms.

In our opinion, a more natural representation is the choice of the cells themselves as the base data structure. A discretized quantity is now presented by members of a class Cell. Thus, we do not have many arrays of a floating point type, but rather one array of cells. Such an approach becomes even more evident when irregular grids (as they occur e.g. at finite element discretizations) have to be described, since then there is no direct correspondence to the regularity of an array.

As we have mentioned above a staggered grid is used for the spatial discretization. Thus, cells are not the only interesting objects, but the faces of the cells too. According to the different directions there are three face classes namely XFace, YFace, and ZFace.

3.2 Building Hierarchies of Objects

Local Aspects of the algorithms can be conveniently described in terms of cells and faces. Another important task is to express in which grid elements and in which order a given procedure must be applied. Thus, we have to deal with global coordination of local events.

The class **Area** implements the abstraction of three-dimensional grids of cells and faces. This basic abstraction can be used both by a sequential or parallel program version. In a sequential program a unique **Area** object will be enough. In a parallel program many **Area** objects can be distributed over the parallel machine. The common aspects of a sequential and a parallel program version are described by the class **Area**. The specific demands of sequential and parallel program versions are expressed by introducing new class hierarchies on top of **Area**.

Here we see, that the method of object-oriented design can lead to a more natural system structure. We do not have to decompose a given task, rather we formulate elementary tasks that can easily be composed to more complex ones.

3.3 Details of Implementation

Stroustrup equates "support for data abstraction" with the ability to define and use new types and equates "support for object-oriented programming" with the ability to develop type hierarchies [6] . He assumes that in computations based on classical arithmetic types the "facilities needed for the support of object-oriented programming seem unnecessary".

In this section we shortly outline how we used inheritance to build hierarchies of types. Inheritance has not been used for its own sake. The aim has been the exploitation of the internal symmetries of the algorithms.

Because of the regular grid structure one could expect a spatial isotropic behavior of the algorithms. This is not quite true since on the one hand the gravity enforces another physical behavior in vertical direction than in the horizontal ones. Another reason is the use of boundary-fitted coordinate systems. The algorithms reflect geometrical distorsions. Within the horizontal directions there is almost no different behavior in the x- and the y-direction.

Our design of the class **Cell** and of the classes **XFace**, **YFace**, and **ZFace** supports the exploitations of the internal symmetries. Common aspects within data and methods are united in base classes which saves a lot of similar code. It has to be pointed out that this *internal* reuse of software were much harder to implement if *arrays* were our basic data structures.

A very important aim of our design work is to ensure that an object-oriented way of structuring a large application from the area of flow simulation does not lead to unacceptable performance losses. In C++ so-called **inline** functions allow the implementation of class methods, where internal details of a class can be accessed without any function-call overhead. This is especially useful when a method whose body only contains a few instructions is called inside a loop, which is a typical situation in a numerical application like GESIMA. However, the use of **inline** methods has a repercussion on design, since it sometimes forces the introduction of additional classes within a class hierarchy especially when concepts that are described by different class hierarchies are very closely related (e.g cells and faces).

Figure 1 shows the inheritance graphs of the two class assemblies.

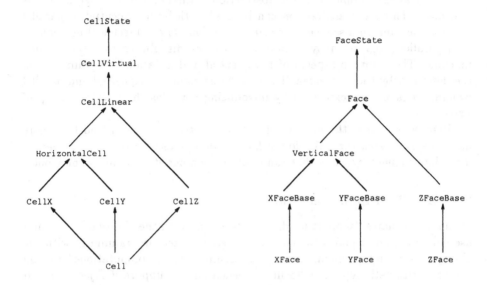

Fig. 1. Inheritance graphs of the cell and face class hierarchies

4   Object-Orientation and High Performance Computing

Nowadays there are several initiatives for high performance extensions of traditional languages (think of High Performance Fortran (HPF) [3] or High Performance C (HPC)). Their aim is to support the development of data parallel programs for distributed memory architectures.

We think that High Performance Computing should not solely focus on runtime efficiency. The often poor structure of existing large applications usually forbids shifting to more flexible and efficient implementations and using new hardware architectures like massively parallel systems.

We see many natural applications for object-orientation especially in the context of parallel programming. As we have shown object granularity is a good candidate for parallel processing. It is much more problem-oriented than parallelism on the process or instruction level. The problems of mapping and parallel execution can easier be solved.

The paradigm of object-orientation provides support for the writing of flexible, extensible and portable software. Therefore we strive for object-oriented programming as a base of high performance computing.

One advantage of C++ is that in contrast to other languages its object-oriented side is extremely lightweight. This and its ability to support several programming styles (consider the large C-subset that allows a smooth transition into the world of object-orientation) make it very attractive to use C++ as a base language for high performance computing.

We consider a shift to object-oriented programming and C++ as a promising project, although we feel that C++ compilers are still in their infancy. There will surely ever be a overhead when features are used that support an abstraction from underlying hardware architecture. However, we think that the benefits of object-oriented programming together with forthcoming massively parallel hardware will clearly outweigh any shortsighted performance consideration.

5 Acknowledgments

We want to express our gratitude to Dr. Eppel and Dr. Kapitza from GKSS-Geesthacht for their encouragement to design GESIMA using the paradigm of object-orientation. Our colleague Steffen Unger has given us invaluable advices when we analyzed the model.

Especially we are bound in gratitude to Wolfgang Schröder-Preikschat, Jörg Nolte and many other members of the PEACE group for the fruitful discussions on object-oriented design and details of the C++ programming language.

Rüdiger Krahl and Steffen Unger have carefully read early manuscripts of the paper.

References

1. **Dutton, J. A.:** *The Ceaseless Wind, An Introduction to the Theory of Atmospheric Motion*, Dover Publications, Mineola, 1986
2. **Gerlach, J., Schmidt, M.:** *Parallele Implementierung von Modellen für die Luftschadstoffanalyse*, Fortschritte der Simulationstechnik, Band 6, Vieweg, Braunschweig, 1993
3. *High Performance Fortran language specification, version 1.0, final*, Technical Report CRPC-TR92225, Center for Research on Parallel Computations, Rice University, Houston Texas
4. **Kapitza, H., Eppel, D. P.:** *The Non-Hydrostatic Mesoscale Model GESIMA. Part I: Dynamical Equations and Tests*, Beiträge zur Physik der Atmosphäre, May 1992; Vol. 65, No. 2; p. 129-146
5. **Meyer, B.:** *Object-oriented Software Construction*, Prentice Hall, 1988
6. **Stroustrup, B.:** *Object-Oriented Programming*, IEEE Software Magazine, May 1988

Parallelization of Scientific Applications: Data Assimilation in Meteorology

Y. Trémolet[1], F.X. Le Dimet[2] and D. Trystram[1]

[1] LMC-IMAG, 46 Av. Félix Viallet, 38031 Grenoble Cedex 1, France
[2] LMC-IMAG, Université Joseph Fourier, BP 53, 38041 Grenoble Cedex 9, France

Abstract. We describe in this paper the parallelization of data assimilation in meteorology. We present two ways of parallelizing this algorithm and report experiments and results.

1 Introduction

In the past few years, an increasing demand for meteorological prediction has emerged, particularly for local and short range prediction (storms, strong precipitations). This prediction is more tough than medium range prediction which has been well developed during the last decades. The physical phenomena are more difficult to modelize, the data to take in account are less regular. From a computational point of view, the data assimilation process is ten to twenty more costly than the effective integration of the model. Since a few years, parallel computers offer new prospects to solve this problem. But, the transition from sequential supercomputers to massively parallel is not easy. It implies to think up new algorithms suited to these new architectures, this needs to combine abilities in parallel computing and data assimilation processes.

This project is included in the working group "ParAppli" from the IMAG Institute. This group was created two years ago in order to help people who are not specialists in parallelism to use efficiently parallel machines. ParAppli proposes monthly meetings where researchers coming from various fields (computer science, numerical analysis, physicists, ...) work together on the implementation of parallel applications. We share methods and parallel numerical libraries and we propose access on most existing parallel machines. Among the numerous applications developed in ParAppli, the most important ones are in astrophysics [4], molecular dynamics and meteorology. This paper is devoted to the parallel implementation of this last problem using PVM [1]. Experiments are currently done on workstation networks, extensions are planed on IBM SP1.

2 The data assimilation problem

The data assimilation problem can be given as follows: how to take account of the meteorological observations which are not simultaneous and not uniform in a numerical model? In practice, it consists in determining the initial condition to minimize the gap between the observations and the numerical result of the model. To solve this problem, we use the following mathematical model of the evolution of the atmosphere [3]:

$$\frac{dX}{dt} = F(X) + B.V \text{ with } X(0) = U$$

where X is the state variable describing the atmosphere after discretization in space, V represents the boundary condition and B is a linear operator.

The discrepancy between the observation and the state of the atmosphere is measured by the cost function J defined by:

$$J(X) = \frac{1}{2} \int_0^T \|C.X - X_{obs}\|^2 dt$$

where X_{obs} represents the observations and C is the operator which allows the transformation of the state space into the space of the observations. We want to minimize this cost function, the truncated Newton method is generaly used to solve this problem with sequential computers.

2.1   The Truncated-Newton method

The Newton method is based on minimizing the approximate function

$$f(x_k + p) = f(x_k) + g(x_k)^t.p + \frac{1}{2}p^t.H(x_k).p$$

The minimum is reached for p verifying

$$\frac{\partial f(x_k + p)}{\partial p} = 0 \qquad \Longrightarrow \qquad g_k + H_k.p = 0$$

The Newton algorithm consists in computing a sequence of steps $\{p_k\}$ and iterates $\{x_k\}$ by iterating the following sequence:

1. Solve $H_k p_k = -g_k$
2. $x_{k+1} = x_k + p_k$

where H_k is the Hessian and g_k the gradient of the cost function at x_k. The idea of the Truncated-Newton method is that when x_k is far away from the solution, we do not need to solve exactly the Newton equation. Thus, we can truncate the conjugate gradient method used to solve the equation of step 1 to a given precision η (see [2] for more details).

We see that we need the values of the gradient vector and the Hessian of the cost function, or more precisely the product of the Hessian by a vector. To obtain these values, we use the adjoint and second order adjoint models.

2.2 Adjoint models

The adjoint model is defined by:

$$\frac{dP}{dt} + \left[\frac{\partial F(X)}{\partial X}\right]^t .P = C^t(CX - X_{obs}) \text{ with } P(T) = 0$$

where P is the adjoint variable of X. It gives the gradient of the cost function (see [3] for extra mathematical details) according to:

$$\begin{cases} \nabla J_U = -P(0) \\ \nabla J_V = B^t.P \end{cases}$$

The second order adjoint model is defined by:

$$\frac{d\hat{P}}{dt} = -\left[\frac{\partial F(X)}{\partial X}\right]^t .\hat{P} - \left[\frac{\partial^2 F(X)}{\partial X^2}\right]^t .P + C^t C \hat{X} \text{ with } \hat{P}(T) = 0$$

The backward integration of this system gives [5]:

$$\begin{cases} \nabla_U^2 J.U' = \hat{P}(0) \\ \nabla_V^2 J.V' = B^t.\hat{P} \end{cases}$$

3 Parallelization of the meteorological model

The model we use is a Shallow-Water model which description can be found in [5]. The discretization used in the implementation of the model is a finite difference in space and time. The scheme is explicit in time and is a five points scheme in space. We parallelize the model by a two dimensional domain decomposition in the North-South and East-West directions. We distribute one subdomain to each processor and the boundary values are sent to the processor which have the adjacent subdomain at each time step. To increase the efficiency of the parallelization, we first compute the values to be sent and then the interior points of the subdomain. The algorithm could be simply described by:

Iterate in parallel until convergence

- *Compute and send to adjacent subdomains the values on the boundaries*
- *Compute the values in the interior of the subdomains*
- *Receive the values of the adjacent subdomains*

By the same method, we also parallelize the tangent linear model, the adjoint model and the second order adjoint model. The aim of this parallelization is to overlap the communication step by the computational step. This allows to obtain a very good efficiency. For instance, with a cluster of IBM RS6000 workstations and using PVM 3.2 [1], we obtain more than 80% of efficiency with 4 machines.

Applying the truncated Newton method using respectively the parallelized adjoint and second order adjoint models to compute g_k and H_k, the efficiency is not as good as it was for the different kinds of model integration because we need several phases of global reduction and broadcast to compute the inner product and the step size in the conjugate gradient. These operations require a lot of communications which lead to a poor efficiency.

The experiments show that a good sequential algorithm used on a parallel machine can be inefficient. Thus, we propose a new algorithm we designed especially for parallel architectures.

4   Parallelization and data assimilation

Regarding to the poor efficiency of the previous method, we now consider a different approach. We consider data assimilation as a way of parallelizing the model and its derivatives. The idea is to use the data assimilation process to adjust the values at the boundaries of the subdomains.

The algorithm consists in an iteration of the data assimilation process on each subdomain with an usual red-black ordering. This assimilation is done on initial and boundary conditions, the starting point for the boundary condition is the result of the assimilation for the adjacent subdomains. Each processor is in charge of one red and one black subdomain in order to minimize the idle time.

The figure 1 shows the observed initial condition (that we want to find), the randomized initial condition (before data assimilation) and the optimized initial condition obtained by the parallel method for a problem of size 16×16. This run was done with 8 steps of the Newton method with 5 steps of conjugate gradient for each iteration, the cost function is divided by 3000. This emphasizes the validity of the algorithm.

The figure 2 shows the evolution of the value of the cost function as a function of the number of Newton iteration. The curve for the parallel method is obtained with 5 iterations of conjugate gradient for each Newton step and 9 subdomains. For the sequential case, two curves are shown for 5 and 20 conjugate gradient iteration. We can see that with the usual algorithm, 5 conjugate gradient iterations are not enough because of the size of the problem (324 000 variables) while in the parallel method, it is enough to solve the Newton equation on each subdomain (36 000 variables). The speed up for a 100×100 problem is as follows:

Number of processors	Number of subdomains	Speed-up
2	4	3.5
8	16	8.9

The parallel algorithm reaches an efficiency greater than 1 and allows us to save computationnal time because the conjugate gradient iterations are faster (they are independent on each subdomain) and because fewer iterations are needed.

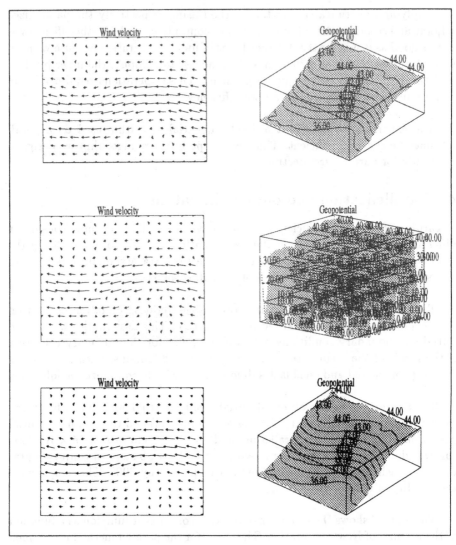

Fig. 1. Observed(top), Randomized(middle) and Optimized(bottom) initial condition

5 Conclusion

We described in this paper the parallelization of a meteorological problem which requires a big amount of data and computations. We showed that the parallelization of such an algorithm is not a straightforward process. It implies of course knowledge in parallel processing but also in the field on application of the code to parallelize. That is the aim of the ParAppli group which gathers computer scientists on one hand, physicians and applied mathematicians on the other hand and which permits such works to advance.

322

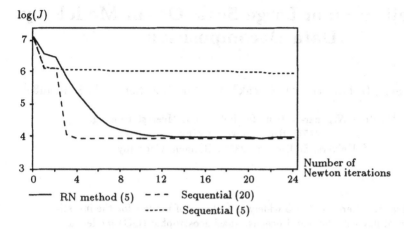

Fig. 2. Cost evolution

The method we have presented can be extended to other applications. We can use it to link subdomains where the model are different. For instance, the meteorological models can be adapted to the relief of the area corresponding to each subdomain (mountains, coast). It can also be used to couple some models: a regional model with a global model or a meteorological model with an oceanographical model.

References

1. A. Geist, A. Beguelin, J. Dongarra, W. Jiang, R. Manchek and V. Sunderam. *PVM 3 user's guide and reference manual*, 1993.
2. Ron S. Dembo and Trond Steihaug. Truncated-Newton algorithms for large-scale unconstrained optimization. *Mathematical Programming*, 26:190–212, 1983.
3. F.X. Le Dimet and O. Talagrand. Variational algorithms for analysis and assimilation of meteorological observations: Theoretical aspects. *Tellus*, 38A:97–110, 1986.
4. L. Colombet, L. Desbat, L. Gautier, F. Ménard, Y. Trémolet and D. Trystram. Industrial and Scientific Applications using PVM. *Parallel CFD'93*.
5. Z. Wang, I. M. Navon, F.X. Le Dimet and X. Zou. The second order adjoint analysis: theory and applications. *Meteorology and atmospheric physics*, 1992.

Parallelization of Large Scale Ocean Models by Data Decomposition

H.-P. Kersken[2], B. Fritzsch[2], O. Schenk[2], W. Hiller[1], J. Behrens[1], E. Krauße[1]

[1] Alfred-Wegener-Institut für Polar- und Meeresforschung,
27515 Bremerhaven, Germany
[2] Universität Bremen, 28334 Bremen, Germany

Abstract. There exist two widely used types of models for the investigation of flows in the world oceans: quasi-geostrophic (QG) models and models based on the primitive equations of motion (PE-models). Starting from existing sequential programs we investigate different strategies for their parallelization. Implementation strategies for the QG-model on a multiprocessor with shared memory and a few nodes are discussed. For the PE-model we describe an implementation on a distributed memory machine with special emphasis on the load balancing issue and communication costs.

1 Introduction

We shall describe the implementation of two oceanographic models for the theoretical investigation of the circulation in the world's oceans on parallel computers: an implementation of a quasi-geostrophic (QG) model on a vector multiprocessor with shared memory and a model based on the primitive equations (PE) of motion on a distributed memory machine. Both are widely used (community models) for ocean modeling and furthermore can be regarded as prototypes for a wide class of finite difference implementations of atmospheric and ocean models. The use of high resolution in regional and global ocean modeling demands for parallel, scalable version of these models. Starting from existing sequential and partially parallelized codes we investigated the efficiency of different parallelization strategies. The aspect of acquiring experience in porting large models to parallel machines as in [6] and [5] was only one issue of our work. Furthermore the parallelized programs are meant to be used as real production codes for oceanographic research. Therefore we focused our attention on the architectures available at our site: a four and three processor Cray YMP-EL, a three processor Cray-YMP with shared memory and a 32 processor KSR1 with distributed memory. In the following we shall describe the two models in more detail and discuss different strategies for data partitioning with respect to load balancing and communication and give some results concerning the obtained performance and speedup.

2 The QG-Model

The quasi-geostrophic model describes the ocean as a fluid consisting of a small number of layers of different density.Usually, due to physical restrictions, three layers are used in large scale simulations. In each layer the horizontal motion is calculated by using an approximation to the Navier-Stokes equation which assumes the motion to be in almost geostrophic equilibrium. Changes in salinity and temperature due to the motion are not taken into account. The model is driven by a wind field at the surface [3]. For each layer a prognostic equation for the streamfunction is obtained. These coupled equations together with appropriate boundary conditions have to be solved in each time step of a numerical simulation where a conservatie finite difference for discretization in space is used. To decouple the equations a transformation into a modal description is performed which yields a set of equations for the transformed streamfunction in each mode which are now couple by their right hand sides only. When stepping forward in time the right hand sides of these equations are calculated by using streamfunction values at previous time steps reducing the system to an uncoupled set of Helmholtz equations. The calculation of the the right hand sides consists of the forcing terms (i. e. the wind stress at the surface), the friction terms (internal and bottom friction) and the advection terms (Jacobians involving the streamfunctions and their derivatives) and eventually applying the transformation into the modal space. Then the solution of the Helmholtz equations is performed in the modal space and the streamfunction is transformed back into the physical space for stepping the model forward in time. Table 1 shows the relative amount of cpu-time spent in different subroutines for calculating the above mentioned terms for a reference test case were we used a multi-grid solver for the solution of the Helmholtz equation with a fixed number of iterations.

On a multiprocessor Cray we first used autotasking for parallelizing the sequential program using only a few directives to help the compiler. For most of the routines satisfactory speedup was obtained. But the multi-grid solver behaved badly, in contrast to earlier experiences on an Alliant FX80 system [2], because it spends some time on the coarser grids where, due to efficiency con-

Table 1. Relative amount of cpu-time spend in the different parts of the program for a three layer test case using a 259×259 grid in each layer and two iterations in the multi-grid solver for the Helmholtz equation.

task	work
right hand side	46%
transformation	12%
time stepping	3%
Helmholtz equations	36%
i/o	3%

Table 2. Times and speedup for the model mentioned above for one time step and different numbers of processors on a four processor Cray YMP-EL[1].

#CPUs	Mflop/s	speedup	remark
1	46	1	vectorization only
2	79	1.7	autotasking for the rhs except friction, transformation and forward stepping; solution of two elliptic problems in parallel and one elliptic problem and calculation of friction terms in parallel
3	122	2.7	solution of the elliptic problems in parallel, autotasking for the remaining part
4	146	3.2	autotasking for the rhs except friction, transformation, and forward stepping; solution of the elliptic problems and calculation of the friction terms in parallel

siderations (no overhead by parallel calls), the calculation is performed by one processor only. In the second approach we used microtasking directives to force the calculation to be performed in parallel for the layers and modes, respectively. This is an appropriate approach for a system with a number of processors which matches the number of layers. It worked perfectly well for the Helmholtz problem, the transformation, and the time stepping part. But we lost some efficiency when calculating the right hand sides because different amounts of work have to be done for the bottom, the top, and the interior layer. The best result was obtained by combining both approaches, taking the best method for each part. A further improvement is obtained by taking into account that for calculating the friction terms values of the streamfunction of the last but one time step are needed which are already available when solving the Helmholtz-equations. If there are more processors than layers an additional processor can be employed to calculate these terms in parallel to the solution of the Helmholtz equations. This gives an additional improvement in efficiency and the additional processor can be used for calculating the remaining part of the right hand side, the transformation and the time stepping part, too. The cpu-times for the most efficient version for different numbers of processors are shown in Table 2. This approach, of course, does not carry over to machines with distributed memory where we have to consider the communication costs which become prohibitively large even for medium sized models. Anyway, for the given resources (a Cray YMP-EL with four processors) this approach seems to be an almost optimal way to exploit the computing power of the system and, as the preliminary results show, can be used with similar efficiency on a four processor Cray C90.

---

[1] On a Cray C90 preliminary results showed a similar speedup while the performance increased by a factor of 12 compared to those listed in the table, i. e. a performance of 1.75Gflop/s is obtained on four processors.

3 PE-Model

The primitive equation models are essentially based on the Navier-Stokes equations [1]. A simplification is introduced by the Boussinesq-approximation and the assumption of hydrostatic equilibrium. This reduces the momentum balance equations to two equations for the horizontal velocity components and the hydrostatic relation. The application of the rigid lid boundary condition (no vertical movement of the surface) allows to split the horizontal velocities into a barotropic and a baroclinic part. The equations are discretized by the finite volume method on a staggered grid. For the baroclinic part an explicit time stepping scheme is used while for the barotropic part a two dimensional Helmholtz-type equation for the streamfunction can be derived which is solved by an SOR algorithm. The SOR method is chosen not for it's (in)efficiency but for it's robustness. Using an explicit integration scheme for this part as well would require very small time steps. Together with the momentum balance equations transport equations for two tracers (salinity and temperature) are solved. Most of the time (ca. 95%) is spent in the routines for the time stepping (the calculation of the development of the baroclinic velocities and the tracers) and the solution of the elliptic problem. They contribute approximately the same portion to the total cpu-time.

The original code was partially (the time stepping part) parallelized for Cray multiprocessor systems [4]. The computational domain was split into slabs extending from east to west and from the top to the bottom of the ocean. In the north-south direction the slabs are bounded by parallels which determine the size of each slab. Each slab is assigned to one processor. The computations in each slab are independent except for points at the slab boundary. When ported to the KSR1, due to it's distributed memory, the question for the communication costs caused by this approach arises. When compared to other possibilities like splitting of the domain into horizontal layers, splitting into slabs bounded by meridians or a splitting into vertical columns of smaller cross-sections the approach described above has the advantage of requiring the smallest amount of communication because only at slab boundaries data have to be shared. Although the version which uses a partitioning into horizontal layers seems to be more attractive because the work is naturally divided into chunks of almost equal size it has the disadvantage of requiring the transfer of the whole layer's data when calculating vertical integrals. The partitioning into slabs along meridians or into columns would require additional communication when calculating Fourier-transforms along parallels for filtering in the high latitude regions. However, for a larger number of processors the column partitioning will be unavoidable to obtain good load balancing. For the elliptic problem a similar splitting is used. But the boundaries of the strips may not coincide with those for the slabs in the time stepping part. The transfer of data which is caused by shifting the boundaries is very small only two arrays of the size of a horizontal grid are used in the solution of the elliptic problem. For a larger number of processors the same remark as above applies.

The load balancing issue has to be tackled already in our implementation

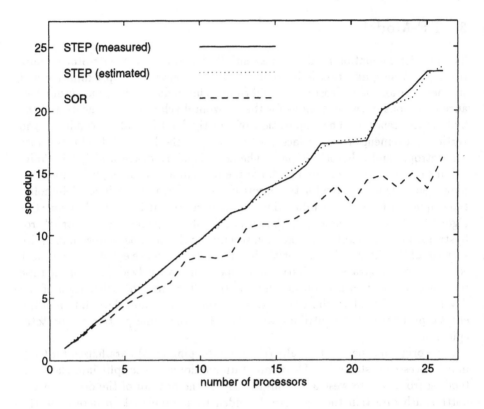

Fig. 1. Speedup for the time stepping part (measured and estimated from the calculated distribution of work load) and for the red-black SOR solver including the treatment of island boundaries for a 1° × .75° world ocean model with 15 vertical layers (360 × 228 × 15 grid points on a KSR1).

for a medium sized parallel machine. For the time stepping part (baroclinic velocities and tracers) the partition into equal sized slabs failed to yield a good load balancing due to the irregular distribution of continents in the world ocean and the restriction of the filtering to the high latitude regions. To partition the work more evenly we estimated the work to be done in a vertical slab with an extension of one point in north-south direction by measuring the cpu-times during a run on a single processor for each of these slabs and used the results to determine the optimal positions of the slab boundaries by a simulated annealing algorithm for the multiprocessor runs. Using the proposed method of partitioning the load balance can not be perfect because the granularity is limited by the work to be done in a one point (north-south direction) wide slab. This is the smallest amount of work to be distributed. It can not be split up further to obtain the same work for each processor. The results (see Fig. 1) show that, for the number of processors we used, this is the limiting factor for the achievable speedup in this part of the program.

For the elliptic problem the grid is split into sub-domains of the same size. The same number of operations are performed at each grid point whether it is in the ocean or on the continents. Therefore this part is perfectly load balanced. An additional problem arises due to internal boundaries caused by islands embedded in the ocean which require a special treatment: A line integral around each island has to be calculated together with the interior points of the ocean. From the parallelization point of view this special treatment induces an additional load balance problem and extra synchronization points. Furthermore it renders the matrix for the elliptic problem nonsymetric which makes the use of a conjugate gradient solver inefficient. Instead the SOR method with red-black ordering is used. Results for the speedup are shown in Fig. 1. Here the speedup is limited by the overhead caused by synchronization and data transfer.

The results shown indicate a good scalability of our approach for the time stepping part although other partitioning techniques have to be used for a larger number of processors. For the elliptic problem other solvers (based on Krylov-subspace or multi-grid methods) may result in faster solution and better speedup. Up to now we did not care for an optimization of the code with respect to the RISC-architecture of the node processors which would primarily require to restructure arrays and eliminate temporary arrays introduced to allow better vectorization. This may result in an increase of the performance of up to a factor of 3.

Acknowledgments

We wish to thank Chresten Wübber for helpful discussions and Rüdiger Wolff from Cray Research for performing the time measurements on the C90. This work was supported by the Bundesministerium für Forschung und Technologie under grant 07 KFT 82/2.

References

1. Bryan, K.: A Numerical Method for the Study of the Circulation of the World Ocean. J. Comp. Phys. 4 (1969) 347–376
2. Hiller, W., Behrens, J.: Parallelisierung von Mehrgitteralgorithmen auf der Alliant FX/80 in H. W. Meuer, Ed., Parallelisierung komplexer Probleme, Springer Verlag, Berlin, (1991) 37–82
3. Holland, W. R.: The role of mesoscale eddies in the general circulation of the ocean–Numerical experiments using a wind-driven quasi-geostrophic model. J. Phys. Oceanography 8 (1978) 363–392
4. Pacanowski, R., Dixon, K., Rosati, A.: The G.F.D.L. Modular Ocean Model Users Guide, GFDL Ocean Group Technical Report #2, (1991,1993)
5. Procassini, R. J., Whitman, S. R., Dannevik, W. P.: Porting a Global Ocean Model onto a Shared-Memory Multiprocessor: Observations and Guidelines. The J. of Supercomuting 7 (1993) 287–321
6. Singh, J. P., Hennessy, J. L.: Finding and Exploiting Parallelism in an Ocean Simulation Program: Experience, Results, and Implications. J. Par. Dist. Comp. 15 (1992) 27–48

Simulation of tidal flows for Southern North Sea and sediment transports for Western Scheldt estuary on parallel computers

Z.W. Song, K.P.P. Pathirana, D. Roose and J. Berlamont
Laboratory of Hydraulics and Department of Computer Science
Catholic University of Leuven
de Croylaan 2, B–3001 Heverlee, Belgium

1. Introduction

Human activities in shelf sea and estuarine areas often lead to undesirable consequences for the environment. Mathematical models are used more and more to study a wide range of flow and transport problems in coastal areas. The mathematical models based on the two–dimensional (2D), depth–averaged shallow water equations are used for describing the hydrodynamics. The output of these models is often used as input for other models (eg. sediment transport models, water quality models). However, computer simulations of large tidal flows and sediment transports are very time–consuming. The computing time is a major limitation to improve the accuracy in both space and time. In order to use fine meshes and small time step sizes, parallel supercomputers must be used. Parallelism can be achieved by partitioning the physical domain into subdomains. Parallelism can also be exploited by running uncoupled hydrodynamic and transport models in parallel. In real world engineering applications, the domain shape is irregular and the boundary conditions are complex. This poses additional difficulties for parallel implementation.

In this study, a parallel implementation of a hydrodynamic and a sediment transport model have been studied in detail. The hydrodynamic model is based on a finite difference discretization of the 2D Shallow Water Equations (SWEs). Various time integration methods for the 2D SWEs ranging from explicit methods via semi–implicit methods to implicit methods have been parallelized. A domain partitioner is developed to insure a good load balance. The hydrodynamic model has been used to simulate the tidal flows in the Southern North Sea and the English Channel. A finite element transport model has been developed. The complete sediment transport model comprises three major sub–models which are related to hydrodynamic, sediment transport and bed level computations. The frontal solution method used in the transport model has been parallelized by adopting a domain decomposition technique. The complete transport model has been applied to the Western Scheldt estuary. Timing results for the two models are presented.

2. Parallelization Aspects

The Hydrodynamic Model

Successful parallel implementation requires that an algorithm suited for the parallel machine is chosen, that a good load balance is achieved and that the extra work due to parallel implementation is minimal. In this study, three commonly used numerical schemes ranging from explicit methods via semi–implicit methods to implicit methods are used to solve the 2D SWEs in parallel. The semi–implicit ADI method has the advantage that the stability condition does not pose severe restrictions on the magnitude of the time–step size in comparison to explicit methods. In comparison to fully implicit methods, the ADI method has the advantage that only tridiagonal systems must be solved and that the memory requirements are limited (similar to memory requirement for explicit methods). Therefore, ADI methods are preferred on sequential computers. On parallel computers, the explicit methods have the advantage of easy implementation and high degree of parallelism. Irregular domains do not pose severe problems. In the ADI method, the difficulty of a parallel implementation arises from the need to solve tridiagonal system alternatingly in X and Y directions. Some parallel tridiagonal system solvers work well on regular domains but not on irregular domains. A fully implicit method is not attractive on sequential computers due to the big sparse system of equations to be solved and the large memory requirements, but on parallel computers it can be considered as an alternative. To parallelize the ADI method, a first approach consists of dividing the domain into strips along one coordinate direction. Then, the Thomas algorithm can only be used in the first half–step. The tridiagonal systems in the other direction are distributed over several processors and parallel methods must be used to solve them in the second half–step [1] [2]. A second approach consists of dividing the domain alternatingly into strips in x- and y-directions for the two half–steps respectively. Then the Thomas algorithm can be used in both half–steps, but an intermediate data transposition is needed. Various communication schemes for the ADI method based on the second approach have been implemented and evaluated. These schemes are the simple collect and redistribute algorithm, the bi–directional tree structure communication algorithm, a simple matrix transposition algorithm and the recursive matrix transposition algorithm [3]. To achieve a good load balance, a domain partitioner using a geometry based recursive bisection algorithm has been developed [4].

The Sediment Transport Model

The finite element method has been used in the transport model to solve the 2D depth–averaged advection–dispersion equation which involves the set–up and solution of large sparse systems. To improve the computational performance, a parallel version of the frontal solver has been developed based on domain decomposition. The computational domain was partitioned into a number of subdomains. The parallel frontal solver consists of three phrases: 1) local elimination of the internal variables; 2) solution of the interface system; 3) computation of the internal variables using the interface solution (back–substitution) [5]. This approach is equivalent to substructuring or the Schur Complement method.

3. Applications

The Hydrodynamic Model

The tidal motions in the Southern North Sea and the English Channel (figure 1) have been simulated with the data obtained from a data base for tidal flow simulation in the model area [6]. The calculations were done on a 61*82 grid. The grid sizes used in both directions were 8953 m and 9266 m. The explicit, implicit and ADI time integration methods have been used, the time step used in the simulation was 200 seconds for the explicit method and 10 minutes

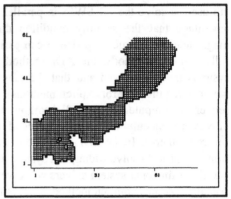

Fig 1: The North Sea

for the ADI and implicit methods. 11 tidal constituents (O1, K1, M2, N2, S2, K2, M4, MS4, MN4, M6 and 2MS6) have been used as open boundary forcing at the west and the north open boundaries. The simulated time was 72 hours. The performance results obtained on the Intel iPSC parallel computer are listed in table (1). Only the results obtained with the best parallel implementation of the ADI method (i.e. Thomas algorithm with simple matrix transposition) is presented in table (1).

Table 1: The total speed up on the model applications.

Tidal flow simulation on the Southern North Sea and the English Channel					
# Procs	1	2	4	8	16
Explicit	0.55	1.08	1.96	3.36	5.12
ADI	0.79	1.44	2.64	4.56	6.72
Implicit	1.00	1.91	3.45	5.71	8.59

The explicit and the implicit methods used in solving the 2D SWEs can be easily parallelized. The irregularity of the domain does not pose severe problems in implementation, and the work load can be fairly balanced by the domain partitioner that we have developed. In both explicit and implicit methods only nearest neighbour communication occurs. The difficulty of implementing an ADI method on a parallel computer lies in the solution of the resulting tridiagonal systems in both x- and y-directions.

One notes that the parallel speed-up for all the three methods is far from linear. For the explicit and implicit methods, the reason is that the problem size is not large enough (only 1431 calculation grid points). The communication cost due to parallelization and the extra sequential work for the subdomain boundary checking caused by the irregularity of the domain have large influence on the total execution time. We expect a better parallel performance when larger problems are solved. However, with the increase of the problem size, the number of iterations needed for convergence in implicit methods also increases. So techniques to improve the convergence rate is an important issue in order to be able to use implicit methods for large scale problems. When Thomas algorithm with data transposition is used within ADI method, a global communication is needed. The low speed–up for the ADI method is the result of the expensive communication cost and it will not change much when the size of the problem changes. Nevertheless, the ADI method based on Thomas algorithm with data transposition is still interesting for real world applications for the following reasons: 1) the total efficiency (taking parallel efficiency and numerical efficiency into account) for this method is acceptable with small number of processors (e.g. less than 16 processors); 2) it can be easily implemented starting from an existing sequential code without too much changes; 3) the irregularity of the domain does not cause severe problems. Iterative techniques can also be used in the ADI method but the number of iterations for calculation to convergence is problem dependent.

The Sediment Transport Model

The transport model has been applied to the Western Scheldt estuary from the Liefkenshoek in Belgium to Vlissingen in the Netherlands, i.e. the mouth of the estuary (figure 2). The total length of the simulated estuary is about 52 km. The finite difference flow model used a regular mesh with a grid size of 200m by 200m while the finite element transport model used an irregular mesh of quadrilateral elements with nine nodes. A bi–linear interpolation function has been used to transform the hydrodynamic parameters from the flow model to the transport

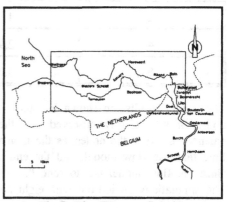

Fig 2: The Western Scheldt

model. Several simulations were performed on the Intel iPSC hypercube with two, four and eight processors [7]. In each simulation, one node was allocated to the flow model and the other nodes were allocated to the transport and the bed models.

Table 2: The execution time (sec) of 10 time–steps for sediment transport simulation in the Western Scheldt.

# Procs	Flow model	Processors used by the transport and the bed models						
	0	1	2	3	4	5	6	7
1	175.1	(Flow model + Transport Model + Bed model)						
2	37.2	138.2	–	–	–	–	–	–
4	37.2	59.6	59.6	59.5	–	–	–	–
8	37.2	35.8	36.0	35.9	35.8	35.8	36.0	36.1

Table 3: The speed–up and the parallel efficiencies for sediment transport simulation.

Number of nodes	Speed–up	Parallel efficiency
1	1.0	100%
2	1.3	63.3%
4	2.9	73.4%
8	4.7	58.8%

The timing results are shown in table 2 and 3. In case of simulation with two nodes, it was clearly observed that the computational load was not properly balanced between the nodes, as the transport models had a much higher execution time than the flow model. At the end of each time step synchronisation occurs since the flow model has to send the hydrodynamic data to the transport model. The simulations carried out with eight nodes showed that the load balance among the processors was optimal and, therefore, idle time of the processor assigned to the flow model was negligible. The speed–up rate of the complete model was 4.7 and the parallel efficiency was 58.8% when compared to the one node case. This parallel efficiency loss was mainly due to the fact that the additional computations to be performed were very large due to the increase in frontal width. In addition, handling of the interface system, including communications, assembly and solution, is still sequential. Note that when a frontal solver is parallelized, an increase of the frontal width is often unavoidable. The parallel performance can be slightly improved by using a parallel algorithm to solve the interface system, in which the communication and assembly of interface matrices are carried out in parallel.

Acknowledgement

We would like to thank A. Krechel, H. Plum and K. Stuben of the GMD, Sankt Augustin, Germany, for providing the parallel tridiagonal solver based on cyclic reduction. We are grateful to Lutgarde Beernaert, Johan De Keyser, Stefan Vandewalle and Hugo Embrechts for sharing their parallel experience with us. Thanks also to Werner Verhoeven for his help concerning the use of the iPSC/2 parallel computer.

References

1   Krechel, A., Plum,H.J. and Stuben,K. *"Parallel solution of tridiagonal linear systems"*, in F.Andre and J.Verjus, eds, Hypercube and distributed computers, Elsevier, pp 49–64, 1989.

2.   Song, Z.W., Yu, C.S., Roose, D. and Berlamont, J. *"Solving the 2D shallow water equations by explicit and ADI methods on a distributed memory parallel computer"*, in Proceedings of Int. Conf. on Applications of Supercomputers in Engineering 3, Bath SPA, UK, pp. 239–252, 1993.

3.   Song, Z.W., Yu,C.S., Roose,D. and Berlamont,J. *"Parallel solutions of the 2D shallow water equations on irregular domains with distributed parallel computers"*, in Proceedings of Int. Conf. on Hydro–Science and Engineering, Washington, DC., 1993.

4.   De Keyser, J. and Roose, D. *"Grid partitioning by inertial recursive bisection"*, Report TW 174, July 1992.

5.   Zone, o and R. Keunings. *"Direct solution of two–dimensional finite element equations on distributed memory parallel computers"*, Proc. of the 2 Symp. on High Performance Computing, Montpellier, France, 1991.

6.   Werner, F.E. and Lynch,D.R. *"Tides in the Southern North Sea and the English Channel: data files and procedure for reference computations"*. Thayer School of Engineering, Dartmouth College, Hanover, USA, 1988.

7.   Pathirana, K.P.P. *"Modelling cohesive sediment transport in estuaries and coastal waters"*, PhD Dissertation, Department of civil engineering, Catholic University of Leuven, Belgium, 1994.

A Sequential-Parallel Approach for Coupling Chemistry and Transport in Groundwater Quality Modelling

Christophe Kervévan, Robert Fabriol, Antonio Guillén, Jean-Pierre Sauty

BRGM (French Geological Survey), BP 6009, F-45060 Orléans cédex 2, France

Abstract. Groundwater quality modelling requires taking into account coupled mechanisms such as chemistry and hydrodynamics, for which numerical treatment is almost always necessary. However, when attempting to simulate natural systems, the computation time on conventional computers limits the use of such calculation codes. A numerical code (CAT//), in which the Transport module and the Chemistry module are successively called at each time step, was developed by the BRGM. We show that such a sequential algorithm is readily adaptable to parallel computing with relatively little programming effort. A test of this code on four different parallel computers showed the required CPU time to be reduced by a factor close to the number of processors available. This approach seems well adapted to modelling coupled phenomena since coupling of major mechanisms can be approximated by a sequential algorithm.

1 Introduction

Risk assessment is an important phase in the design of facilities in which hazardous materials are handled (e.g. waste disposal sites). The migration of pollutants in groundwater must often be evaluated in order to determine environmental impact. Similar predictions are needed when determining preventive or remedial action to be taken in groundwater quality management. The complexity of coupling the physico-chemical mechanisms involved, even if we limit ourselves to chemistry and hydrodynamics, is such that numerical simulation is nearly always required. We deal here with this type of groundwater quality modelling.

A recent analysis of the state-of-the-art [1] identifies three principal methods for coupling chemistry and hydrodynamics: simultaneous solving of **D**ifferential and **A**lgebraic **E**quations (DAE), the **D**irect **S**ubstitution **A**pproach (DSA) and the **S**equential **I**terative **A**pproach (SIA). The CPU time presently required on conventional computers to simulate real systems, while decreasing constantly, still represents the major barrier to such simulations. The running of appropriate codes on parallel architecture machines can radically reduce computation time. One of the advantages of the **S**equential-**P**arallel **A**pproach (SPA) proposed here, directly derived from the SIA, is that it is easily adaptable to parallel computing. We present here the results of parallel computing of a benchmark simulation test run on four parallel computers.

2 The Model Characteristics

The coupled code CAT (Chemistry And Transport), developed by the BRGM, is sequential in nature: the two main subroutines calculating transport and chemistry are totally independent and called sequentially at each time step [2].

The *Transport module* is based on a Random Walk algorithm: the total mass of a chemical element present in the system at a given time step is distributed over a large number (e.g. 100,000) of virtual particles which are moved by advection and dispersion. The new breakdown of the particles in the various volumes of the grid cells of the domain allows us to evaluate new concentrations which are passed to the chemistry subroutine for the next chemical calculation. Displacement of a particle involves both a component corresponding to the real velocity of the fluid (advection) and a random component simulating dispersion. Contrary to finite element or finite difference methods, displacement here is independent of concentrations in the neighbouring cells. This technique requires no particular treatment near the system boundaries. Particle tracking transport is therefore well adapted to parallelization since the displacement of each particle can be calculated with the same algorithm, independent of the others.

Chemistry calculations require working with concentrations. It is therefore necessary to discretize the domain in each space direction.

The *Chemistry subroutine* calculates the distribution of chemical elements between a mobile phase (water) and any number of non-mobile phases (minerals). The chemical system is described by a set of non-linear differential equations (kinetic reactions can be easily taken into account). As opposed to calculations done with classical geochemical codes (EQ3/6, PHREEQE, etc.), here only equations relevant to the specific problem studied are considered. They are written in a quasi-mathematical high-level language and automatically translated into a FORTRAN code using the ALLAN™-NEPTUNIX software package [3]. This software, distributed by CISI Industrie, prevents introduction of coding errors. The chemical model is designed as a cluster of individual submodels, each corresponding to a phase of the system. This allows us to test the submodels individually and thereby to ensure validity and robustness of the global system model.

Chemistry-Transport coupling consists in a sequential call to the Transport and Chemistry modules at each time step. The time step is generally calculated so that the Courant number is lower than or equal to 1. The variables passed from one subroutine to another are chemical element concentrations (H, O, Na, C, etc.) instead of species concentrations (OH^-, H^+, NaOH, etc.). The main advantage of this approach is that it allows us to work with a much lower number of variables.

3 The Sequential Parallel Approach (SPA)

Parallelization is based on the assumption that each cell, at each time step, is a closed chemical system. This means that each chemical calculation can be run on one processor, independently of all the others. Programming the parallelization is therefore simple: it starts before the CALL loop and closes immediately thereafter.

The test can be easily run on various computers although, due to the complexity of the chemistry subroutine, it requires a MIMD computer with powerful processors.

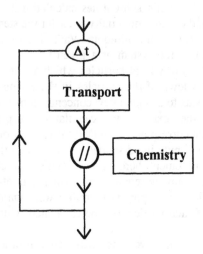

Fig. 1. Principle of the parallelization of the Chemistry routine call

The BRGM submitted a test problem to several parallel computer manufacturers: DEC (farm of Alpha workstations), CRAY (T3D), TMC (CM5), INTEL (Paragon). The numerical code used was CAT//, the parallel version of the code presented above. Parallelizing this code simply involved adding instructions to the compiler so that the Chemistry loop was executed in parallel. The nature of the instructions added depends, of course, on the type of machine used.

The test data were derived from one of the verification exercises proposed in the CHEMVAL CEC Project [4]. The purpose of this exercise was to simulate the permeation of groundwater through a cement (of simplified chemical composition) barrier. The processes involved are reversible precipitation and dissolution, aqueous complexation and 1-D hydrodispersive transport (advection and dispersion). Some of the results of this simulation are presented in figure 2.

The results concerning the total accumulated CPU time spent in the Chemistry loop at the end of the simulation as a function of the number of processors and the type of computer used are given in table 1.

The purpose of this study was to check the feasibility of this parallelization. The above results confirm the interest of such an approach since the increase in computation speed is approximately proportional to the number of processors used. A more complete optimization of the code (parallelization of the Transport module) would, of course, be of great interest for use in real cases. This could be done with relatively little programming effort, due to the particle tracking method used for Transport simulation.

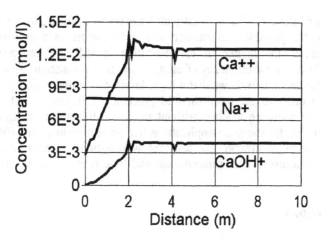

Fig. 2. Concentrations profiles of Na^+, Ca^{++}, $CaOH^+$ along the pathlength at 100 years

DIGITAL	cumulative time spent in the // Loop	relative computation speed / 4000-60
4000-60	2802.0 s	1.0
Alpha 200 Mhz	144.0 s	19.5
Alpha 150 Mhz 1 Node	221.0 s	12.7
Alpha 150 Mhz 2 Nodes	115.0 s	24.4
Alpha 150 Mhz 4 Nodes	56.0 s	50.0
Alpha 150 Mhz 8 Nodes	31.0 s	90.4
INTEL		
Paragon 1 Node	720.0 s	3.9
Paragon 81 Nodes	8.7 s	323.6
TMC		
SPARC II	3608.0 s	0.8
CM5 16 Nodes	101.0 s	27.6
CRAY		
T3D 16 Nodes	12.0 s	234.0

Table 1. Accumulated CPU time spent in the Chemistry loop and computation speed.

On the basis of these results, it is difficult however to evaluate, by a simple linear interpolation, the possible performance of a computation on a massively parallel machine. Indeed, the degree of parallelization is still the key parameter for calculating the potential efficiency of an application as a function of the number of processors. Amdahl's law shows that a high degree of parallelization (at least 99%) is required in order to use more than 20 processors efficiently. Such a degree of parallelization cannot be reached without major modifications in algorithms and coding. Therefore, for the usual applications treated at present by the BRGM in this domain, the farm of around ten powerful workstations appears to be the best compromise in terms of performance, cost and time needed to develop algorithms and codes.

4 Conclusions

The SPA offers some advantages: i) it provides an easy approach for modelling a 3D system with realistic chemistry, ii) the Transport model and the Chemical model are independent, and therefore easier to verify and to develop, iii) parallelizing the code requires relatively little effort. The principle of the parallelization of the Chemistry loop call tested here would, however, be just as applicable if transport was computed by finite element or finite difference. This approach seems well adapted to modelling coupled phenomena where major mechanisms can be calculated sequentially.

Acknowledgements

The development of the coupled code CAT and the conception of its parallelization have been funded by the Research Direction of the BRGM. Tests on parallel computers result from joint contributions of CISI Industrie and four computer manufacturers: CRAY, DEC, INTEL, and TMC.

References

1. Yeh G. T. and V. S. Tripathi: A critical evaluation of recent developments in hydrogeochemical transport models of reactive multichemical components. Water Resour. Res., 25 (1), 93-108 (1989).

2. R. Fabriol, J.P. Sauty and G. Ouzounian: Coupling geochemistry with a particle tracking transport model. J. Contam. Hydrol., 13, 117-129 (1993).

3. R. Fabriol and I. Czernichowski-Lauriol: A new approach to geochemical modelling with an integrated simulator generation system. In: Y. K. Kharaka and A. S. Maaest, Proceedings of the WRI 7 Symposium, Park City, Utah, USA, 13-18 July, 213-216 (1992).

4. D. Read: Chemval Project Report on stages 3 and 4: Testing of coupled chemical transport models. CEC Report n°EUR 13675 EN (1991).

Supporting an oil reservoir simulator in a distributed memory environment*

C. Addison[1], T. Christensen[2], J. Larsen[2], T. Oliver[1] and A. Sunderland[1]

[1] Institute of Advanced Scientific Computation, University of Liverpool, Liverpool, U.K.
[2] Math-Tech ApS, Gentofte, Denmark

One of the objectives of the EUREKA project PARSIM is to develop a distributed memory version of the COSI oil reservoir simulation package. As with most application packages, it is essential that the parallel version of COSI remains as faithful as possible to the original sequential code – the top level of the code must be hardware independent so users can run the same code on different hardware configurations and obtain more or less identical results.

This goal imposes some severe constraints on a key part of the simulator package – the linear equation solver. Parallel versions of both a sparse direct and a sparse iterative solver are required to maintain compatibility. In the following we provide an overview of how we have attempted to provide an integrated support environment for both solvers, what decisions have been made on the basic iterative technique and on the preconditioning to use and how these decisions were made.

1 Background

Oil reservoir simulation is an important tool in the effective exploitation of hydrocarbon reserves in places such as the North Sea, [1]. A typical reservoir is a thin area of porous rock containing fluid – a mixture of oil, water and gas. When an oil well is introduced into this zone of porous rock, and fluid removed, the inherent pressure in the reservoir drops. If care is not taken, the pressure may drop below the point at which the fluid can be brought to the surface even though there are still large quantities of fluid remaining. To maintain the pressure, fluid is injected into the reservoir through injection wells. Given a basic description of an oil reservoir, reservoir simulation attempts to model the properties of the reservoir as fluid is removed and injected over a time period of several years. Typically a reservoir description is given in terms of the porosity and permeability of its constituent rocks, the shape of the reservoir and the initial properties of the oil, water and gas components of the reservoir fluids, The accuracy of such simulations depends highly on the quality of the initial reservoir description, but usually the accuracy is sufficiently good that reservoir simulation plays an important rôle in determining the siting of wells and the production strategy employed to take maximum advantage of a reservoir's resources.

* This work was funded by the U.K.'s Department of Trade and Industry and by the Danish Erhvervsfremmestyrelsen as part of the EUREKA Project EU 638, PARSIM.

The associated system of nonlinear and time dependent partial differential equations typically provide values for the oil pressure and fluid phase saturations of oil, gas and water. As with most problems of this type, the equations are discretised in both time and space. Finite differences or related techniques are often used to define the spatial discretisation. An implicit time stepping scheme is required, for at least the pressure equation, in order to obtain a stable numerical solution with a sufficiently large time step. Therefore at each time step, a system of nonlinear equations must be solved in order to advance to the next time step and this system of nonlinear equations is solved by a Newton-like iteration scheme, which involves the successive solution of systems of linear equations.

2 Data distribution issues in the solver

Given the discretisation employed, the resulting system of linear equations tends to have a seven-banded structure consistent with a finite difference discretisation of a 3-D box. However, while this is often a useful abstraction, the models usually have a more complicated structure because of the presence of well terms and faults, which connect non-adjacent cell blocks together, and because reservoirs are not homogeneous boxes.

This potential irregularity meant that the original COSI developers decided on a direct sparse solver that used a general sparse matrix structure. It uses a dynamic pivot selection strategy, based on a variation of Markowitz pivoting to minimise fill-in while still retaining numerical stability, [2]. A parallel version of this solver was developed for COSI within the ESPRIT Supernode 2 project, [3]. The parallel solver ran on a ring of T800 transputers and has proven relatively effective on moderately sized problems on up to 31 processors.

A key feature of the parallel solver is that it assumes that the matrix rows are distributed across the processors in a cyclic fashion. This is consistent with the approach taken with dense linear equation solvers, but it does create complications when interfacing the parallel solver module to the rest of the COSI package.

At each time step, the matrix to be used in the linear equation solver is formed. The matrix elements for a given cell block depend upon the physical rock properties of the particular area of the reservoir as well as upon the pressure and saturations of fluids present. There is also some influence from neighbouring cells. This matrix formation therefore can be easily parallelised, with little communication required, if the reservoir is partitioned in a block-like fashion among the processors. This partitioning is not at all like that used in the direct solver, so that in going from matrix formation to matrix solution, the matrix has to be redistributed over the processors in a transpose-like operation. At the end of the solver stage, a reverse operation is required to move the solution vector from its cyclic distribution to blocked distribution.

This considerable data movement is less of a concern on newer generation parallel machines with hardware support for communications between arbitrary processors, but it still tends to tell against the direct solver. Another difficulty with the direct solver is that it becomes very expensive in terms of memory and time required because of the additional computation caused by fill-in when the problem size starts to get large. These facts led to the need to develop an effective sparse iterative solver to complement the direct solver.

Therefore, any parallel code developed had to provide distributed data structures appropriate for the matrix set-up and the two different solvers. As can be inferred from the earlier description of the parallel direct solver, the data structures for this solver are particularly complicated. Also, a major practical constraint was that the parallel code "appeared" the same to the user and that the differences between the sequential and parallel versions were kept to the minimum to make maintenance easier.

In order to meet this constraint, all of the required data distributions, and the manipulations between them, are supported under the general umbrella of a distributed data environment that builds upon a set of basic decomposition operations for vectors and matrices over a logical 1-D ring of processors, [4]. In effect, this environment provides a middle layer of software that allows a sequential thread of execution (usually running as a host process) to manipulate distributed sparse objects via a series of procedure calls that invoke parallel operations on the data. Therefore, at the top level, the developer can specify that a matrix-vector multiplication is to be performed with matrix object A and vector object x, and at the parallel end, code to perform the matrix-vector operation with the matrix, vector and the result vector distributed in a certain format is called on each of the worker processors. Ideally this format matches exactly the format in which the objects are currently stored. If not, automatic transformations are performed to move from one format to the other.

3 A parallel iterative solver

As mentioned earlier, there is a sparse iterative solver option available to complement the direct solver. The core of many iterative methods can be implemented efficiently in a parallel setting, so the best method in a sequential setting also tends to be the one to use in a parallel setting.

The standard iterative solver for symmetric systems of linear equations is preconditioned conjugate gradients. Unfortunately, the systems involved here are highly nonsymmetric and related Krylov subspace methods, [5], have had to be considered. Orthomin[3], was the most popular nonsymmetric Krylov-subspace method for earlier generations of reservoir simulators, but the amount of memory and computation required per iteration by Orthomin increases with the number of iterations. There are alternative Krylov methods that require a constant amount of memory and computation per iteration, but these all tend to lack a minimisation property. Examples include the conugate gradient squared (CGS) method, and the stabilised bi-conjugate gradient (Bi-CGstab) method. Recently, Freund and others have developed efficient Krylov-subspace methods

---

[3] Orthomin, CGS and Bi-CGstab are described in [5]

with a quasi-minimisation property and these have considerable attractiveness because of their robustness and relatively low cost per iteration.

In testing carried out on reservoir simulation problems from the Harwell-Boeing test, [6], set as well as on some ill-conditioned linear systems from COSI, the transpose-free quasi-minimal residual method (TFQMR), [7], and CGS method regularly performed as well as or better than other methods, in terms of the number of iterations required to obtain an answer with a particular accuracy. This was particularly true when block-Jacobi or incomplete factorisation preconditioning was employed. Bi-CGstab also tended to perform well, but would occasionally not produce as accurate an answer as the other two methods. In addition, there were a small number of test problems for which the irregular convergence properties of CGS appeared to cause difficulties – the answers were quantitatively inferior to those obtained from TFQMR. Moreover, on our test problems and with our preconditioners, we did not see any benefit from going to a QMR method with look-ahead. When no preconditioning is performed, such methods are more robust, but require the explicit use of A^T, [8]. As a result of this testing, most of our effort has gone into developing a suitable version of TFQMR and this currently is our method of choice.

In addition to selecting the underlying iteration method, an appropriate preconditioner must be selected, (see [5], Chapter 3). Most of the iterative methods under consideration can be implemented effectively in parallel, but the same cannot be said for the preconditioning. It is important that a considerable amount of testing be performed on a single processor in order to ensure that the computation required to form more sophisticated preconditioners (which often do not to parallelise well) is justified for the types of linear systems that will be encountered.

If there are p processors involved in the parallel iterative solution, then a simple preconditioner is defined by performing an LU factorisation on each of the p square matrices on the block diagonal of the matrix. These are usually roughly equal in size and are almost always non-singular. This is a block-Jacobi preconditioner and has almost ideal parallel properties, although good performance does impose some restrictions on p. In addition, block-Jacobi only produces reasonable results provided that the off-block entries in the matrix are not "too" large.

Unfortunately, this is not always the case and more sophisticated preconditioners may be faster. The matrix of interest, A, can always be written as the sum of three matrices: $A = L + D + U$, where D is the block diagonal matrix used in the block-Jacobi preconditioning, L is the strictly lower triangular components not in D and U the strictly upper triangular components not in D. If instead of just D, we use an incomplete block factorisation (or block ILU) preconditioner defined by $(I + LD^{-1})(U + D)$, the number of iterations required for a given tolerance will decrease, possibly by a considerable factor.

Forming triangular factors for the blocks of D can be expensive, so that a variant of simple point-wise ILU may be attractive [5]. Rather than performing a complete LU-factorisation over all (or part) of a matrix, an incomplete factorisation is performed. It is incomplete because only a certain, predetermined, level of fill-in is allowed. This approach provides the user with near total control over the amount of memory required and good results are often obtained from even no-fill ILU. It is a popular technique in a sequential setting. A word of caution, emphasized by test results described below is, however required. Point ILU preconditioners become more expensive if pivoting is required in order to maintain numerical stability, particularly if some intermediate levels of fill are retained. If pivoting is required, but not performed, then the cost per iteration remains low, but the number of iterations can escalate as do the chances of complete failure because the computations become swamped with round-off error.

It is also important to remember that a decrease in the number of iterations does not necessarily mean a decrease in overall time. In a sequential setting, a decrease of nearly a factor of 2 in the number of iterations is required before using the block ILU takes fewer operations than block-Jacobi because each system of equations solved using the block ILU takes about as many operations as solving 2 systems of equations with D alone and performing a matrix-vector multiplication with $(A - D)$. Therefore, the results given in Table 1 include both the time and the number of iterations required to obtain a solution to a system of linear equations with a residual norm smaller than 10^{-6}.

Identifier	Order	Number of entries	Condition number estimate	ILU Time (secs)	ILU Num. iters	Number of blocks	Block ILU Time (secs)	Block ILU Num. iters	Block Time (secs)	Block Num. iters
SHERMAN 1	1000	3750	2.2×10^4	0.3	32	20	0.5	14	0.7	36
SHERMAN 2	1080	23094	1.4×10^{12}	0.3	6	36	0.9	14	1.0	30
SHERMAN 3	5005	20033	6.9×10^{16}	3.9	81	13	9.6	59	13.9	151
SHERMAN 4	1104	3768	7.1×10^3	0.2	24	16	0.7	19	0.9	44
SHERMAN 5	3312	20793	3.9×10^5	1.0	24	16	2.9	20	3.8	47
PORES 2	1224	9613	3.3×10^8	0.5	27	17	7.9	202	11.5	498
COSI 000	4000	38504	1.1×10^{10}	fail	fail	100	2.9	12	4.6	40
COSI 001	4000	20002	7.9×10^7	1.6	32	100	1.1	4	1.6	9
COSI 055	4000	28993	5.8×10^{10}	5.2	94	100	2.6	13	3.4	30
COSI 151	4000	29217	1.2×10^{12}	9.5	175	100	2.8	14	3.6	33
COSI 156	4000	29207	1.1×10^{12}	7.6	141	100	3.0	16	3.9	37
COSI 251	4000	29165	5.1×10^{10}	5.5	100	100	2.5	12	3.2	29

Table 1. Test results of TFQMR using different preconditioners

Three different preconditioners are considered: a no-fill ILU preconditioner that comes as part of the SLAP package, [9], a block ILU method and a block-Jacobi preconditioner. All results were obtained on an IBM RS/6000 Model 250, which uses the new PowerPC 601 processor. The software was written in Fortran. The basic iterative method was TFQMR and the UMFPACK, [10], provided an attractive environment in which to perform the required block factorisations. The first 6 problems are reservoir simulation matrices from the Harwell-Boeing test suite. The final 6 problems arise from the solution of a simple (and small) 3-D test problem in COSI.

There is a marked difference between the Harwell-Boeing problems and the COSI problems in terms of the performance of the simple ILU preconditioner. Simple ILU was not an effective preconditioner for these latter problems and allowing further levels of fill-in did not improve its attractiveness. The dramatic difference in performance on the Pores2 problem probably stems from the facts that large off-block terms were present and that diagonal blocks varied in size. The block ILU preconditioner is the most expensive of the three preconditioners, which is shown by the modest drops in time versus the significant drop in numbers of iterations when compared to the block-Jacobi preconditioner.

The relative attractiveness of the preconditioners reverses when one considers using them in a distributed memory parallel environment. When the matrices are distributed in a block-like fashion among processors, solving systems of equations with the point-ILU or block-ILU preconditioner matrices is nearly a sequential operation; so that the difference in time per application of these two preconditioners versus using block-Jacobi grows as the number of processors. Therefore, if the reported COSI problems are typical, some variation of block-Jacobi appears to be the parallel preconditioner of choice.

References

1. K. Aziz and A. Settari, *Petroleum Reservoir Simulation*, Applied Science Publ., London, England, 1979.
2. N. Houbak, SESYS - A sparse matrix linear equation solver: Users Guide, Rapport nr. 12, Ris/o/ National Laboratory, Technical University of Denmark, June, 1985.
3. J. Larsen and T. Christensen, A parallel sparse matrix solver, *Nordic Transputer Applications*, IOS Press 1991.
4. C. Addison, B. Beattie, N. Brown, R. Cook, B. Stevens, and D. Watson. Distributed objects: sequential objects with parallel performance. In *Proc. Sixth SIAM Conf. Parallel Processing for Sci. Comput.*, 1993.
5. R. Barrett, M. Berry, T. Chan, J. Demmel, J. Donato, J. Dongarra, V. Eijkhout, R. Pozo, C. Romine and H. van der Vorst, *Templates for the Solution of Linear Systems: Building Blocks for Iterative Methods*, SIAM, Philadelphia, 1993.
6. I. S. Duff, R. G. Grimes, and J. G. Lewis. Sparse matrix test problems. *ACM Trans. Math. Software*, 15:1–14, 1989.
7. R. W. Freund. A transpose-free quasi-minimal residual algorithm for non-Hermitian linear systems. *SIAM J. Sci. Statist. Comput.*, 14:470–482, 1993.
8. R. W. Freund, G. H. Golub, and N. M. Nachtigal. Recent advances in Lanczos-based iterative methods for non-symmetric linear systems. Tech. Rept., RIACS, NASA Ames Research Center, Moffat Field, CA, 1992.
9. M. Seager, *A SLAP for the Masses*, Lawrence Livermore Nat. Laboratory Technical Report UCRL-100267, December, 1988.
10. T. A. Davis. User's guide for the unsymmetric-pattern multifrontal package (UMF-PACK). Tech. Rept. TR-93-020, Comput. and Information Sci. Dept., Univ. Florida, Gainsville, 1993.

The Parallelisation of the AEA Probabilistic Safety Assessment Program, MASCOT

H W Yau[1], K A Cliffe[2], J E Sinclair[2] and P J Sumner[2]

[1] Edinburgh Parallel Computing Centre,
James Clerk Maxwell Building, King's Buildings,
Mayfield Road, Edinburgh EH9–3JZ, UK.
[2] Radwaste Disposal Division,
Decommissioning and Waste Management Business,
AEA Technology, 424.4 Harwell, Didcot, Oxfordshire OX11–ORA, UK.

Abstract. The AEA Technology Monte Carlo probabilistic safety assessment program MASCOT has been parallelised using portable library constructs. The serial code ran on a Cray-YMP supercomputer, but is inherently unable to make use of its vector facilities, although it is amenable to a Task-farm approach. Results are presented comparing the parallelised code running on a heterogeneous mix of workstations in Harwell with their Cray-YMP. In addition, good scaling behaviour is demonstrated on a dedicated distributed memory machine.

1 AEA Technology and the EPCC

The work discussed here represents a six months collaborative project between the Radwaste Disposal Division of the Decommissioning and Waste Management Business of AEA Technology, and the Edinburgh Parallel Computing Centre (EPCC). The focus of the effort is the porting to a parallel platform of the Probabilistic Safety Assessment (PSA) code MASCOT, which was developed by AEA Technology under contract to UK Nirex Ltd.

2 MASCOT

MASCOT is a 26,000 lines Fortran 77 program for modelling the consequences of the disposal of radioactive waste in underground repositories [SA93]. In particular, it is able to take account of uncertainties in the model parameters by making a number of Monte Carlo samples in the parameters' probability density functions (PDFs).

The MASCOT program receives a textual description of the disposal system to be modelled, performs the necessary calculations, and outputs the *consequences* as a text file and as a machine-readable dump file for postprocessing by the MASCOT Output Processor (MOP). The system model that MASCOT receives is built up out of a set of submodels, for example representing a source term, transport through geological layers, and release to the biosphere. All the input into a MASCOT run are from a text description file, which is parsed and interpreted using the AEA ASSIST syntax and data structure package [Sin91]. With this, the user is able to specify the choice of submodels, the PDFs for the necessary parameters, and compile mathematical expressions, all through entering a high-level language description of the problem. At present, the submodels available all represent the transport of radionuclides through the groundwater pathway, the dominant mode of transport for these substances. However, the code is designed such that extensions to include other transport mechanisms could readily be included.

Traditionally, the serial code ran on Harwell's Cray-YMP, whilst the intended platform for the parallelised code (pMASCOT) is a network of Silicon Graphics workstations, possibly with a heterogeneous mix of Sun workstations. Each MASCOT run consists of four parts: an initialisation phase for setting up the necessary ASSIST data structures; an input phase where the input file is read in and decoded into a number of *Cases*; a calculation phase involving a loop over the Cases to find the final consequences of the model; and finally an optional averaging calculation over all the consequences. With the latter two phases, a diagnostic text output and a Fortran unformatted dump are written out to external files.

3   Requirements of pMASCOT

The parallelisation is over the calculation loop as described above, and in the average calculations, with the requirement that the outputs from the parallelised code are invariant with respect to the original serial code. In addition, a degree of fault tolerance was considered desirable, whereby a disconnected worker will be timed out and its task re-sent to another worker.

The acceptance criteria demanded by Harwell are the following:

- The textual outputs should be invariant with respect to the serial code's output, and in particular the output from the workers should be presented to the user in a Case-ordered manner.
- The unformatted dump output should also be invariant with respect to the serial code, allowing the postprocessor program MOP to be used unaltered.
- An implementation across a heterogeneous Sun and Silicon Graphics workstation network be demonstrated.
- Fault tolerance to be built into the implementation, and be demonstrated.

4   Implementation of pMASCOT

The basic paradigm for pMASCOT is a Task farm with a Master process acting as the Source for Cases to be computed and Sink for results to be collected, and a set of Worker processes distributed over the available compute resources. The message passing interface used is the EPCC developed 'CHIMP' (Common High-level Interface to Message Passing) [BM92] which, like the recently announced MPI (Message Passing Interface) standard, allows developers to write portable libraries across a variety of platforms. In particular, the EPCC PUL (Parallel Utilities Libraries) utilities: PUL-TF [Tre93] and PUL-GF [Cha93] are used to implement the Task Farm (TF) and the common Global File (GF) access, respectively. Initial development was on a single Sun workstation, with versions quickly developed for a network of workstations, Silicon Graphics workstations, and a 16-node Meiko i860 CS-1.

4.1 The Task Farm

When *p*MASCOT is executed the constituent Master and Worker programs begin by performing their initialisations. In addition the Master reads in an description file of the modelling parameters specified by the user, which is then parsed and placed into the appropriately created data structures via the ASSIST package. Control of the program is then passed over to the PUL-TF Task Farm utility. PUL-TF manages the communications between the Master and the Workers, sending out packets of work to the appropriate Worker, and receiving partial averages computed by each Worker upon the completion of all the Cases. PUL-TF will then remove the completed Worker processes and control of *p*MASCOT will then be handed back to the Master program, in order to perform the remaining operations, largely concerned with the output of statistical averages over the Cases.

One of the requirements of *p*MASCOT was for some form of fault tolerance, such that if a Worker develops an unrecoverable fault this will not require the entire run to be re-executed. The functionality provided by the present version of PUL-TF does not include such a feature, although it is obviously highly desirable if *p*MASCOT is to be used as a production code. As a result the Source, Sink and Worker routines were altered to include a time-out mechanism, whereby the Source re-submits a Case for computation should a Worker take more than a prescribed amount of time to respond with a 'Case-completed' message to the Sink. Obviously, this mechanism cannot recover from a problem on the Master itself, but it has been demonstrated to cope with hardware faults occurring on a Worker.

The nature of the Task Farm paradigm provides a balancing of the loads across the processing nodes. However, we acknowledge that *p*MASCOT makes no allowance for the relative performance of machines in a heterogeneous network, but instead treats each machine as equal. In the worst scenario, this means the final Case may be given to the slowest node when it would be better to wait for a swifter node to complete its current Case.

4.2 The Output Files

The serial MASCOT program produces two files: a text file and an unformatted dump file, both of which should be reproduced as closely as possible by the parallel implementation.

Text outputs occur in three phases: before, during, and after the parallel computations of the Cases. *p*MASCOT writes the contributions from these three phases into separate files, which are then later merged by a postprocessing step. One complication is that the text output from the parallelised phase needed to be sorted into Case-order, and this resulted in an additional field containing the Case number to be attached to each line of text. This field is used to sort the lines in the file, and are removed in the sorted output. The use of PUL-GF functions allow several lines of text to be written out without intrusions from the output of other processes.

Unformatted dumps occur in two phases: before and during the parallel computation of the Cases; as with the text output, these are initially written out to separate files to be postprocess merged. PUL-GF functions are used in the parallel phase, where the Workers all write to the one global file simultaneously, such that the completed file will be Case-ordered. This is possible because the record for each case is the same length, and can be computed in advance.

5   Results

The first two requirements listed in Section 3 were fulfilled by comparing the outputs from the serial and parallel implementations, for a suite of test inputs given by AEA Technology [SRWM93]. Only negligible differences occurred in the output between the two implementations. The third requirement was satisfied when pMASCOT was installed on the AEA Technology network of Silicon Graphics and Sun workstations at Harwell. Finally, tolerance to hardware faults in the network was demonstrated.

In additional to the test suite, another input file was provided which more closely matched a typical production run, and this was used to make the following timing results. Table 1 presents results for a problem with 100 Cases, spread over a variety of machines. The discrepancy between the CPU seconds and the elapsed seconds is due to overhead times (initialisation and reading in the input file), and other users on the systems. The former in particular is responsible for the large discrepancy in the Cray's CPU and elapsed times.

This demonstrates that for a modest number of workstations, a performance comparable to the Cray-YMP can be obtained. However, one should note that the relatively poor performance of the Cray against a single workstations is due to the non vector nature of the MASCOT code, which at present can only properly utilise the scalar capabilities of the Cray machine.

We have also made timings for representative production Cases on an EPCC parallel machine, based on a 16-node Meiko i860 CS-1, and these are shown in Figure 1 ($\diamond$). The communications of this machine is appreciably better than for a typical workstation network, and we can demonstrate a near linear speed-up for 1 to 16 processors, despite non-trivial I/O requirements. If N is the total number of Cases and p is the number of workers, the machine's performance approaches the function $\alpha/p + \kappa$, where α is a constant proportional to the number of Cases, and κ is the time taken to execute the serial part of the parallelised code. For comparison, we have also included the result for the serial MASCOT program on the same problem ($\square$), which gives an indication how much additional start-

Table 1. Timings in seconds for an example production run of 100 Cases on AEA Technology's network of workstations, and comparisons with a run on a Cray-YMP. The platforms are for Silicon Graphics Iris Indigo R4000 and (two) R3000 workstations, Sun SPARC-1 and SPARC-2 workstations, and a time-shared Cray-YMP. The number of Cases given to each machine in the task-farm reflects their relative performance, as revealed in the second timing where the twice as powerful R4000 receives twice as many Cases as the R3000. The third column refers to the CPU seconds spent by each worker in calculations, while the fourth column is the elapsed wall-clock time.

Platform	Number of Cases	CPU Seconds calculating	Elapsed seconds
R4000	100	5559	5665
R4000	67	3779	3972
R3000	33	3883	
R4000	51	2865	3105
R3000(a)	23	3005	
R3000(b)	26	2935	
R4000	46	2570	3058
R3000(a)	23	2724	
R3000(b)	21	2672	
SPARC-2	10	2888	
R4000	45	2452	3270
R3000(a)	21	2647	
R3000(b)	21	2618	
SPARC-2	9	2445	
SPARC-1	5	2939	
Cray-YMP	100	2453	4143

up time is required by the parallel implementation. In order to keep down the percentage time pMASCOT spends on this start-up phase, it would be necessary to increase the number of Cases proportionally to the number of processors.

These timings were obtained by running the Master part of the program concurrently on the same processing node as one of the Workers. However, since non-blocking communications are used by the PUL-TF utility, we can achieve a better single Worker ($p = 1$) performance if the Master is executed on a separate processing node; this is illustrated by the datum point ($\times$) in Figure 1.

References

[BM92]   R A A Bruce and J G Mills. CHIMP Version 1.0 Interface. Technical Report EPCC-KTP-CHIMP-IFACE-1.4, EPCC, 29th of May 1992.

[Cha93] S R Chapple. PUL-GF Prototype user guide. Technical Report EPCC-KTP-PUL-GF-UG-0.1, EPCC, 1st of February 1993.

[SA93]   J E Sinclair and P J Agg. Mascot and MOP programs for Probabilistic Safety Assessment, Part A: overview (Mascot version 3B and MOP version 2E). Technical Report AEA-D&R-0476, AEA Technology Harwell, January 1993.

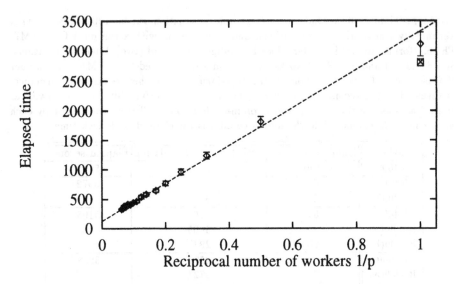

Fig. 1. Elapsed times in seconds (◊) plotted against the reciprocal number of workers, for a 100 Case example production run on a 16-node Meiko i860 CS-1 parallel computer. The results for the parallel implementation is fitted to a $\alpha/p + \kappa$ line ($- - -$) where α (130 ± 10) is a constant proportional to the total number of Cases, p is the number of processors and κ (3200 ± 100) is the serial start-up constant. The least squares linear fit is achieved with a confidence of 86%, using a 5% error on each data point; this shows the parallelised program scales linearly up to 16 processors for the Meiko machine. The Master program is executed concurrently with one of the Workers on the same processing node. For comparison, a datum point (□) is included for the serial program, and another (×) for the 1-Worker plus Master parallel code running on separate nodes.

[Sin91]   J E Sinclair. ASSIST —A package of Fortran routines for handling input under specified syntax rules and for management of data structures. Technical Report AEA-D&R-0106, AEA Technology Harwell, February 1991.

[SRWM93] J E Sinclair, P C Robinson, M J Williams, and K J Morgan. Mascot and MOP programs for Probabilistic Safety Assessment, Part H: Mascot (version 3B) Test library. Technical Report AEA-D&R-0476, AEA Technology Harwell, January 1993.

[Tre93]   S M Trewin. PUL-TF Prototype user guide. Technical Report EPCC-KTP-PUL-TF-UG-1.6, EPCC, 8th of April 1993.

Monte Carlo Simulations of Lattice Gauge Theories on Multiprocessor Systems

Peter Altevogt[1] and Fritz Gutbrod[2]

[1] Institute for Supercomputing and Applied Mathematics (ISAM)
IBM Deutschland Informationssysteme GmbH
Vangerowstr. 18
69115 Heidelberg, Germany
Tel.: 06221–59–4471, altevogt@dhdibm1.bitnet
[2] Deutsches Elektronen–Synchroton DESY
Notkestr. 85
22603 Hamburg, Germany
Tel.: 040–8998–2093 , t00gbd@dhhdesy.bitnet

Abstract. A large scale numerical simulation in the field of lattice gauge theory has been performed, relevant for elementary particle physics. Lattices of size 64×24^3 have been studied on a cluster of IBM RISC System/6000-workstations, on an IBM 9076 SP1 parallel computer with 8 nodes and on other parallel computers. A sustained performance of 30 MFLOPS/node has been reached (without special tuning steps), and a speedup of 7.1 has been found for 8 nodes on the IBM 9076 SP1. Details on the computational aspects are given. We investigate the static quark-antiquark potential up to the distance of 8 lattice spacings for pure $SU(2)$ lattice gauge theory. Numerical simulations are performed in a large range of bare coupling constants. The action is the Wilson action with an asymmetric coupling for timelike plaquettes. The potential is obtained by fitting 'cooled' Wilson loops with up to 3 exponential terms. An interpolation of the potentials by a sum of a perturbative and a linear term shows only approximate scaling in comparison with the symmetric case.

1 Introduction

Computer simulations using Monte Carlo methods[3] are of outstanding importance in physics, but also in other sciences, e.g. in economics[1]. In this paper we will discuss the application of Monte Carlo methods in theoretical physics, more precisely in theoretical high energy physics[2]. Here in general Monte Carlo methods are used to create states of a physical system according to a certain probability distribution (e.g. according to a Boltzmann distribution). These states are then used to measure physical observables of the system.

---

[3] We define Monte Carlo methods as computer simulation methods using random numbers.

Being very demanding concerning CPU time, multiprocessor systems of MIMD-type with distributed memory seem to be the only appropriate computer systems for large Monte Carlo simulations[3]. In general, the use of these computer systems requires an explicit parallelization of the algorithms under consideration and the implementation using e.g. a programming environment for parallel programs.

In the sequel, we will study the implementation of a Monte Carlo simulation of a SU(2) lattice gauge theory on various MIMD systems with distributed memory, e.g. on a workstation cluster, consisting of IBM RISC System/6000 workstations, on an IBM 9076 SP1 multiprocessor system[4] and on other multiprocessor systems.

We will start the next chapter with a discussion of the physics underlying our simulation. Afterwards we describe the implementation of the simulation on multiprocessor systems and present our results.

2 Monte Carlo Simulations in Lattice Gauge Theory

2.1 The Theoretical Basis

The simulation of non-abelian gauge theories on the lattice [4] by Monte Carlo methods is presently the only way to obtain quantitative information on the nonperturbative aspects of these nonlinear theories. Here, Monte Carlo simulations are in effect the evaluation of a path integral,

$$Z = \int DU \, e^{-\beta S[U]}, \tag{1}$$

over millions of variables U (here complex unitary matrices) and of correlation functions

$$< U_{i_1} U_{i_2} ... > = \frac{1}{Z} \int DU \, U_{i_1} U_{i_2} ... e^{-\beta S[U]} \tag{2}$$

We will not give details on the action $S[U]$ here, but will only remark, that the quantity β is a free parameter, which controls the ratio of the lattice spacing a to some physical length. If $\beta \to \infty$, the lattice theory should approach the continuum theory. 'Measuring' on the computer the variation of the ratio of a physical quantity over a β–dependent lattice scale parameter, usually called Λ, provides an indication how well the continuum limit has been approached.

One of the most elementary quantities to be studied is the static potential between quarks and antiquarks in the quenched approximations, i.e. without inclusion of fermion loops. Data on this potential as a function of distance and of the bare coupling constant $g_0^2 = 4/\beta$ have been obtained in the past [5, 6], with slow progress in lattice sizes and β. All previous results are consistent with the picture that the potential at short distances is dominated by the perturbative

---

[4] RISC System/6000 and 9076 SP1 are trademarks of the IBM Corporation

Coulomb potential, modified by logarithmic terms, and that at large distances the potential is linearly increasing [5]. This is what has been expected from the general ideas about quark confinement.

Some quantitative aspects are still unsettled, especially the variation of the potential with β. Most investigations have shown that there is a variation of the coefficient of the linear term (the string tension σ), when expressed in the lattice scale Λ, both in SU(2) and in SU(3). Instead of

$$\sigma/\Lambda^2 = const, \tag{3}$$

one observes an variation of this ratio by about 20 %, if Λ is varied by a factor 2. It is not easy to study this phenomenon systematically by increasing β further and further, because this would require a rapid (exponential) growth of lattice sizes and of computer time. Another tool in a systematic study is a variation of the action $S[U]$. Here we consider an action which has different β's in the space- and in the time-like direction. Physical observables must be invariant -up to scale transformations- under such changes, and this we want to test. The extra factor for timelike contributions, relative to spacelike ones, is taken as $\xi^2 = 1.5$, which leads to a scale factor close to ξ [7]. Two technical difficulties are: First of all, the potential is defined only at a few discrete points of the quark-antiquark separation R. We try to overcome this by using a theoretically motivated inter-polation formula. Secondly, the lattice structure introduces deviations from the continuum limit at small distances, which are not well known. We determine the necessary corrections by a comparison of the continuum expression with the lattice simulation result at very large β, where the nonperturbative contributions are negligible.

2.2 The Computer Simulation

The numerical approximations to the expressions 1 and 2 are obtained from a Markow-chain of configurations $\{U_n\}$, with the probability density $P(\{U\})$

$$P(\{U\}) \sim e^{-\beta S(\{U\})}. \tag{4}$$

These probability densities can be generated by changes of individual U_i (e.g. Metropolis-, heatbath-, or overrelaxation algorithms). One essentially has to calculate the local action, $S(\{U\})$, i.e. only the nearest neighbours of U_i have to be known. For SU(2), a basic local change needs about 470 floating point operations, with 4 words representing one U_i. These numbers are favourable for parallelization in the sense that many floating point operations have to be performed for one datum.

The parallelization of these simulations is done by dividing the four dimensional lattice in sublattices and associating a process (respectively a processor of

---

[5] Empirically, the transition between both regions can be described by simply adding the two contributions

the multiprocessor system) to each of the sublattices[6]. For the calculation of the action, the processors have to communicate the data associated with the boundaries of their sublattices. Since the sublattices are not very large (otherwise the simulation will take too long) the volume of the boundary is roughly equal to that of the interior region (we work in 4 dimensions).

Physical observables $O(\{U\})$ (e.g. of correlation functions, see eq. 2) are calculated as

$$< O(\{U\}) >= \lim_{n \to \infty} \frac{1}{n} \sum_{i=1}^{n} O(\{U_n\}) \tag{5}$$

The calculation of the operators $O(\{U\})$, which are in general nonlocal, requires data from many processors after parallelization. In order to avoid communication of individual SU(2)-matrices, the lattice has been reordered by message passing, which turned out to be quite tedious to program.

The Markow–chains have to be long, since equilibration requires several thousand iterations. Thus the configurations have to be stored on disks, which causes considerable strain on the I/O-system.

2.3   The Data and Results

Lattice sizes of 32^4, $16^3 \times 32$ and $24^3 \times 64$ have been studied. Using the IBM Message Passing Library (MPL) on an IBM 9076 SP1 multiprocessor system with 8 nodes, it took $16\mu sec$ to update one link on a 32^4 lattice[7], which has been divided in 8 lattices of sizes $16^3 \times 32$. This corresponds to a sustained performance of about 30 MFLOPS per processor. The effective bandwidth between two processors (including scatter and gather operations to distribute and collect the data to be sent) has been about 4.1 MB/sec. To update all links of the sublattice, about 1.5 MB of data has to be communicated. The efficiency of the parallelization is about 90%[8].

Simulations have been performed for β in the range from 2.2 to 2.9 in intervals of 0.1. Updating was done by a mixture of heatbath steps to overrelaxation steps in the ratio 1:7. After 10 or 20 sweeps, the spacelike links were cooled in 5 iterations, by replacing the link variables by the normalized sum of spacelike staples. Planar Wilson loops [4] up to size 12×8, extended in the time-direction

---

[6] Using this approach to parallelization, the serial algorithms do hardly need to be modified

[7] This result could probably be improved by about 40% by optimizing the code e.g. to make better use of the floating point unit and to minimize cache misses.

[8] Using a checkerboard structure on the lattice and parallelizing in all 4 space–time directions, each processor has to send one message in each space–time direction (4) for each of the two structures (2) to both of his neighbours (2), resulting in 16 messages. Therefore, the latency of about $200\mu sec$ of the MPL is of minor relevance and the use of other message passing systems with much less latency, like e.g. the MPL/p on the IBM 9076 SP1 with about $30\mu sec$ latency, would only have minor impact on the communication performance.

and in all space directions have been averaged over the lattice and stored for further analysis. Also this 'measuring' section has been fully parallelized.

Between 15.000 and 100.000 iterations have been performed for each value of β on the following computers: on a cluster of IBM RISC System/6000 workstations, an IBM 9076 SP1 multiprocessor system, an Intel iPSC/860 with 32 nodes and an Intel Paragon XP/S with 64 nodes[9]. Portation of code was easy. Runs on different computers at the same values of β are in good agreement with one exception, which is most likely caused by 'freezing' of the configuration due to a β-value too large for the given lattice size.

The potential $V(R)$ is extracted from the cooled Wilson loops by a fit with up to 3 exponentials, and then is corrected for the lattice artifacts. The result is interpolated as a funtion of R, and the string tension σ is determined from the fit. The typical quality of the fit is shown, for the largest values of β, in figure 1,

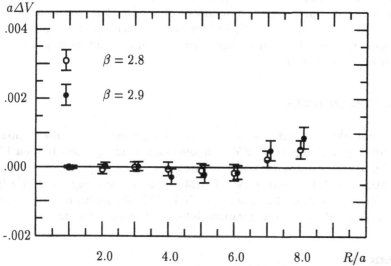

Figure 1: Differences between potential and fit for $\beta = 2.8$ and 2.9

where the difference between the fit and the Monte-Carlo data is plotted. The small errors have to be compared with a variation of the potential in the indicated range of R by about 0.2 units. The accuracy of the data is good enough to determine the string tension at the smallest values of β with an accuracy of about 5 %.

As a preliminary result, we obtain that the ratio σ/Λ^2 seems to be lower by 20 - 30 % as compared to the case with a symmetric action [10].

---

[9] iPSC/860 and Paragon XP/S are trademarks of the Intel Corporation.
[10] The final error analysis will require more information on the lattice artifacts

3 Conclusions

We have assumed that

- at $\beta = 2.8$ the static potential is well described by lattice perturbation theory. This defines the short distance lattice artifacts at this β.
- that these lattice artifacts can be used at smaller β to determine the string tension σ by a fit to the potential, including the Coulomb term.

The statistical analysis of the Monte Carlo data for many β, obtained on several parallel computers, is in very good agreement with the above assumptions. Accurate results on the linear term in the potential have been extracted, which indicate a slight failure of the scaling test.

This simulation of a SU(2) lattice gauge theory demonstrates, how multiprocessor systems of MIMD–type with distributed memory may be applied to a huge class of related problems of computational physics. The overhead for communication is in the order of 10 %, and for ultimate performance, optimization of the algorithms and their implementation is as important as improving the communication bandwidth.

Acknowledgements

We would like to thank several institutes for providing us with computational resources and support: DESY (Zeuthen) for providing access to their IBM 9076 SP1 multiprocessor system, the "Institute for Supercomputing and Applied Mathematics (ISAM)" (Heidelberg) of IBM Germany for using an IBM RISC System/6000 workstation cluster and an IBM 9076 SP1 multiprocessor system and the HLRZ (Jülich) for using various Intel multiprocessor systems.

References

1. Z.Griliches, M.D.Intriligator (eds.), Handbook of Econometric (Elsevier Science Publishers B.V., Amsterdam 1984).
2. M.Creutz (ed.), Quantum Fields on the Computer (World Scientific Publishing Co. Pte. Ltd., Singapore 1992).
3. J.P.Mesirov (ed.), Very Large Scale Computation in the 21st Ce (SIAM, Philadelphia 1991).
4. H.J.Rothe, Lattice Gauge Theories, An Introduction (World Scientific Publishing Co. Pte. Ltd., Singapore 1992).
5. S.P. Booth, A. Hulsebos, A.C. Irving, A. McKerrel, C. Michael, P.S. Spencer and P.W. Stephenson, Nucl. Phys. B394 (1993), 509
6. F. Gutbrod, Z. Phys. C 37, (1987), 143
7. F. Karsch, Nucl. Phys. B205 (1982), 285

The Formation of Galaxies: A Challenge for Supercomputers – a Simple Task for GRAPE ?

Matthias Steinmetz

Max–Planck–Institut für Astrophysik, Postfach 1523, 85740 Garching (FRG)
e-mail: mhs@MPA-Garching.MPG.DE

Abstract. We present numerical simulations of galaxy formation, one of the most challenging problems in computational astrophysics. The key point in such simulations is the efficient solution of the N–body problem. If the gas of a galaxy is treated by means of smoothed particle hydrodynamics (SPH), the hydrodynamic equations can be reduced to a form similar to that of the N–body problem. A straightforward implementation requires a computational effort $\propto N^2$, making it prohibitively expensive to simulate systems larger than 10^5 particles even on the largest available supercomputers.

After a description of the physical and numerical problems, we shortly review the standard numerical methods to tackle these problems and discuss their advantages and drawbacks. We also present a completely different approach to perform such simulations using a workstation in combination with the special purpose hardware GRAPE. After a discussion of the main features of GRAPE, we present a simple implementation of a SPH–N–body code on such a configuration. Comparing results and performance of these two approaches, we show, that with an investment of US $ 50000, the problem can be solved up to 5 times faster than on a CRAY YMP.

1 Introduction

During the last decade one of the most active fields of astrophysics has been the study of the formation of galaxies. It is commonly believed, that up to 95% of the matter of the universe is composed of dark matter, which is probably of non–baryonic origin and interacts mainly via gravitation. According to a widely accepted idea galaxies form by the collapse of gravitationally unstable primordial density fluctuations. The evolution of the gravitationally dominant dark matter is treated by N–body techniques. During the last years, one has begun to add gasdynamics to the simulations to mimic the evolution of the baryons. In some simulations, stars and galaxies are formed out of the collapsing gas, which are again treated by N–body techniques. The grand computational challenge of such simulations is twofold: Firstly, one can show [1], that the gravitational collapse must proceed anisotropically, i.e., three–dimensional simulations are necessary. Secondly, very different length scales are involved, starting from 1 pc ($\approx 3.1\ 10^{13}$ km), which is the size of a typical star forming region, up to several hundred Mpc, a volume which can be considered to be a representative piece of our universe. This range of scales must be compared with the largest simulations feasible nowadays, which are performed on a grid of about 300^3 zones. Besides classical finite–difference methods, a completely different approach to solve the hydrodynamic equations is used in the astrophysical community: *Smoothed Particle Hydrodynamics* (SPH, [2]). Its main advantage is to be a free Lagrangean method. This makes it optimally suited for highly irregular clustered systems like galaxies. Although it is still to prove mathematically that the SPH equations converge to the hydrodynamical fluid equations, a series of test calculations has shown that the quality of SPH results can compete with that of modern finite difference schemes [3], even with suprisingly small particle numbers!

2 Current techniques

The key problem to perform large scale computer simulations of structure formation is an efficient solution of the N-body problem, i.e., the calculation of the acceleration $\frac{d}{dt}\mathbf{v}_i$ of the particle i due to the gravitational interaction with all other particles j of the system:

$$\frac{d\mathbf{v}_i}{dt} = -G \sum_{j \neq i} \frac{m_j}{\left(r_{ij}^2 + s^2\right)^{3/2}} (\mathbf{r}_i - \mathbf{r}_j), \tag{1}$$

with $r_{ij} = |\mathbf{r}_i - \mathbf{r}_j|$. s is the so called softening parameter, which prevents the $1/r^2$ divergence of the force for $r \to 0$ and limits the resolution. Methods which directly solve the system (1) are called *Particle–Particle* (PP) methods [4]. Because gravity is a long range force, the computational effort to determine the force on all N particles grows $\propto N^2$. This makes it prohibitively expensive to perform simulations involving much more than 10^4 particles, even on the fastest available supercomputers. In SPH, the force law is of similar form, it is given by

$$\langle \varrho(\mathbf{r}_i) \rangle = \int d^3r' \varrho(\mathbf{r}')W(\mathbf{r}_i - \mathbf{r}', h) \approx \sum mW(\mathbf{r}_i - \mathbf{r}_i, h)$$

$$\frac{d\mathbf{v}_i}{dt} = \frac{d\mathbf{v}_i}{dt}\bigg|_{\text{grav}} - \sum_j m_j \left(\frac{P_i}{\varrho_i} + \frac{P_j}{\varrho_j} + Q_{ij}\right) \nabla_i W(r_{ij}, h) \tag{2}$$

$$\frac{d\varepsilon_i}{dt} = \sum_j m_j \left(\frac{P_i}{\varrho_i^2} + \frac{1}{2}Q_{ij}\right) (\mathbf{v}_i - \mathbf{v}_j) \cdot \nabla_i W(r_{ij}, h).$$

In this equations, W is the interpolation kernel with a shape similar to a Gaussian. h is the smoothing length. $d\mathbf{v}_i/dt|_{\text{grav}}$ is the gravitational acceleration according to Eq. (1). Besides the particle number, h determines the resolution of the system. The pressure P, the internal energy ε and the density ϱ are related by an equation of state. Q_{ij} is an artificial viscosity introduced to treat shock waves. Note, that as long as the kernel W has compact support, all the corrections of Eqs (2) to Eq. (1) are of short range nature, i.e., the additional computational effort is only $\propto N$.

In the past, several techniques have been developed to circumvent the N^2 behaviour: Particle–mesh methods (PM) do not explicitly solve Eq. (1). Instead, the distribution of particles is assigned to a grid, the mass per zone defining a density. Via Fast Fourier Transform (FFT), Poisson's equation is solved on the grid. The forces are than interpolated to the particle position. The computational effort grows only $\propto N \log M$, where M is the number of zones per dimension. Though PM schemes are very fast, they are only suitable for relatively homogeneous systems. The resolution of a PM calculation is determined by the size of a zone, and even the largest current PM simulations with 500^3 zones and 250^3 particles have only a very limited spatial resolution. One tries to circumvent these problems by the P^3M (= PP PM) technique. Here, the long range forces are calculated via the PM method, but the short range forces exerted by particles in the same or in the neighbouring zones are treated by the PP technique. The main drawback of P^3M is that for highly clumped structures, a large number of particles is placed within a few zones, and the PP part becomes computationally dominant. For very large simulations (200^3) particle numbers exceeding 10^4 per zone are not atypical. The computational effort of P^3M is difficult to estimate: for a homogeneous system it is $\propto N \log M$ as for PM, in the worst case, most of the paricles are located in a few cells, the performance is degraded to the N^2 behaviour of the PP method. Another approach is the tree algorithm [5], [6]. Here, the main idea is to group distant particles together and to approximate the force exerted by this group by that of one particle of the same mass. A tree data structure is used to systematically group particles together. Comparing the extension of the group with its distance to a specific particle, one can determine whether this force approximation is accurate enough, or whether the group has to be split into subgroups, for which the same procedure is applied. The result is, that instead of N only $\propto \log N$ interactions are to be calculated for every particle. Therefore, the computational effort scales like $N \log N$. The performance of tree methods also decreases with increasing clumpiness, although much weaker than P^3M methods. However, the construction of the tree causes some overhead, which may become critical in a multiple timestep scheme, if only the force for a few particles has to be calculated. Finally, tree algorithms are relatively complex and require a lot of memory.

There exist various implementations of SPH and N–body codes on vector computers, but only very few on massively parallel machines (e.g. [7], [8], [9], [10]). Therefore, only very vague statements can be made about their performance. To implement very efficient PP codes on vector or shared memory machines is quite easy, but on a distributed memory machine this task is not unproblematic. For PM and P^3M the FFT part can be handled efficiently. However, the mesh assignment of particles and the force interpolation are difficult to vectorize and involve a lot of indirect addressing. In case of parallel machines it is difficult to achieve a good load balancing for the mesh asignment and interpolation step. The recursive structure of a tree algorithm is difficult to vectorize, a lot of indirect addressing combined with short vector lengths is involved. By area decomposition, it is possible to run a tree code on a distributed memory machine with high performance [7], but major changes to the standard tree code have to be made. The currently largest N-body simulations (260^3) were done with such a code [11]. However, we think it is difficult to get a good load balancing if a multiple time step scheme is used, which is essential for a good performance of a SPH code.

In summary, there exist different techniques to tackle the N-body system with good performance on current supercomputers, although it is difficult to come close to the peak performance. For a good compromise between speed and resolution, P^3M and tree codes are the favourite choices. Simulations involving 300^3 particles are the current limit. In combination with SPH, the respective numbers are much smaller and even the largest simulations involve only a few times 10^5 particles. The main reasons are: (i) The force calculation becomes more expensive. (ii) The particles have an extension, which increases the number of short range force evaluations. (iii) The number of time steps is 10–100 times higher. The resources necessary to perform a typical simulation of the formation of galaxies (timings for a tree code on one CRAY YMP processor) are the following: A 4000 particle N-body simulation (≈ 1000 timesteps) requires 40 min. The same simulation using a two component system of 4000 SPH and 4000 N-body particles (15000 timesteps) requires about 10 h, and a simulation with 4000 SPH, 4000 N-body, and at the end about 25000 star particles (N-body) needs 60 hours. Simulations with 32^3 gas and dark matter particles as performed by [12] have consumed more than 200 CRAY hours. Calculations with a million particles of two or three different species would consume several thousands of CRAY hours. Finally note, that although these calculations may be regarded as grand challenges for future generations of supercomputers, from the physical point of view they still have only a very limited resolution!

3 The GRAPE Project

Up to now, all methods are based on software development. A completely different approach was chosen by Sugimoto and collaborators at the University of Tokyo (for an overview see [13]): The calculation of one force interaction is a combination of a very few specific arithmetic operations: three differences, three squares, one sum, etc. Then, the inter particle forces have to be summed up. Furthermore, many of these operations do not depend on each other and can be done in a pipeline. Since the number of operations to get the total force on one particle is the same for every particle, one can parallelize it with a very good load balancing. Sugimoto et al. have designed a series of special purpose hardware boards GRAPE (GRAvity PipE) to calculate (1). Furthermore, a list of particles within a sphere of a given radius h_i of particle i is returned, too. This is very helpful for an implementation of SPH. The board is connected to a workstation via a VME interface. Libraries allow one to use GRAPE by FORTRAN or C subroutine calls. The prototype GRAPE1 reached 240 Mflops in 1989. Meanwhile there exist two series of boards: the odd numbers (GRAPE1, GRAPE3) are low precision boards (18 bit or $\approx 1\%$ accuracy in the force), which are sufficient for most astrophysical applications. The machines with even numbers (GRAPE2 and GRAPE4) are working with 32 and 64 bit arithmetic and are designed to calculate molecular systems and specific stellar dynamical problems. In GRAPE3, one GRAPE1A board is put into a customized LSI chip. Presently, GRAPE3Af, which consists of 8 such chips, is produced in a small series and is available for about US $ 20000. Its peak performance is 4.8 Gflops. Up to 16 boards can be put together to work in parallel. Up to 1995 the GRAPE4 project should be finished. In GRAPE4, the GRAPE2 board is put into a LSI chip and 1500 of such chips are combined together. This board will reach a performance in the Teraflop regime. Although the flop rate of GRAPE is very impressive, one should keep in mind that PP techniques have a much larger operation count to calculate the force on a particle than the approximative techniques mentioned above. Furthermore, in hydrodynamic simulations, a non–negligible part of the computational time is necessary to calculate the pressure force and the equation of state.

In a series of publications the Tokyo group has shown that it is possible to perform large N–body simulations on such a board with a speed close to its peak performance. Furthermore, a SPH code was implemented. In such a code, the gravitational force and the neighbour list was obtained with GRAPE, the evaluation of the hydrodynamic force and the solution of the equation of state being done on a workstation. A tree code was implemented on GRAPE, too. Again, the force evaluation is done on the board, but the tree construction and the determination of the interaction list has to be done on the host. Thus, a powerful workstation is essential, in order to use a SPH and/or a tree code with GRAPE efficiently. It should also be no serious problem to implement a P^3M on GRAPE: The PM part is done on the host, the PP part on GRAPE.

4 Results

The following comparison holds for a multiple timestep SPH–N–body tree code [3] written and optimized to run on a CRAY. All CPU timings are given for one processor of a CRAY YMP 4/64 (333 Mflops). The timings for GRAPE are obtained on one single GRAPE 3Af board (8 LSI chips, 4.8 Gflops). The host is a SPARC10 clone ($\approx$ 15 Mflops). The unchanged tree code runs about 20 times slower on the SPARC10 than on the CRAY. Using GRAPE the main code structure remains unchanged, only the subroutines for the force calculation and the neighbour list are replaced by the GRAPE routines, i.e., we compare a *tree code* on the CRAY with a *PP code* on GRAPE. To accelerate the computations on the workstation, REAL*4 arithmetic is used whenever possible. Only little effort was spent to optimize the host calculation for the SUN. Comparing N–body simulations one should keep in mind that the N–body system is chaotic. Thus, it is not possible to compare position, velocities and other properties of specific particles, but only the structure and kinematic of the whole system.

To become familiar with GRAPE and to adapt the N–body code required only two days. A 4000 (33000) body simulation requires 40 min (10 h) on the CRAY. The same result was obtained with GRAPE in 9 min (1.7 h). More than

80% of the calculations are done on the board. In both cases, the system ends in a highly clustered state, which is advantageous for GRAPE. In the case of a 64^3 calculation, the CRAY is about two times faster for a moderately clustered system, in the case of a highly clustered system two times slower. The break even point between PP on GRAPE and tree on CRAY is of the order of a few 10^5 particles. The tree code requires 220 MB of memory, the GRAPE only 50 MB (REAL*4), i.e., one can perform the same simulation without any problem on a mid class workstation. Running the same code on two boards gives a speed up of 1.1, 1.5 and 1.9 for 4000, 33000 and 64^3 particles. A multi board version combined with a fast workstation would allow simulations with several million particles within a few days.

In the last paragraph we discussed the performance of GRAPE for a well suited problem. Even more interesting is its performance for more general problems, which only partially exploit the special features of GRAPE. In the CRAY code, the computing time for the SPH part is about 10%, i.e., the problem is computationally dominated by gravitation. In contrast to the previous problem, some changes in the algorithms are necessary before SPH runs efficiently, but the effort for these changes is negligible compared to the effort necessary to run the code on a parallel platform. The resulting code requires about 7 hours for a simulation with 4000 SPH and 4000 dark matter particles. This is about 1.3 times faster than on the CRAY. About 80% of the computations were done on the workstation. Replacing the relatively slow SPARC10 by a faster one, a speedup of a factor 2 or even more should be easily possible. The behaviour should be even better for larger particle numbers, because the performance on GRAPE is limited by the SPH part, which grows $\propto N$, whereas the performance on CRAY is limited by the gravitational force calculation which grows like $N \log N$. Furthermore, judging from our experience the maximum possible simulation on GRAPE will not be limited by the N^2 behaviour of GRAPE for large particle numbers but rather by a shortage of memory and I/O operations on the workstation. Therefore, we believe that it makes no sense to use more than one board for such simulations. In another simulation, we have taken star formation into account, i.e., in gravitationally unstable regions, some mass is removed from the gas particles and put into new collisionless star particles. Consequently, during a simulation the number of N-body particles continuously grows. Typically, 10000–25000 star particles are formed from 4000 gas particles [14]. Because all new particles are located in the densest regions, the degree of clustering increases, which results in a larger computing time on a CRAY (about 60 hours). On GRAPE the computing time is still limited by the hydrodynamic part, which does not depend on the number of star particles. Therefore, the computing time grows only moderately to about 20 hours, i.e., GRAPE is three times faster.

5 Conclusion

We have presented a highly active and interesting field of current astrophysical research, namely structure formation in the universe. We have shown that the scientific progress in this field is tightly coupled to the capabilities of the available supercomputers. As an alternative, a combination of a workstation with the special purpose hardware GRAPE can solve problems of comparable size within a time comparable to that on a supercomputer like a CRAY. The GRAPE hardware is applicable to N–body simulations and SPH hydrodynamical simulations the power of the host being crucial for a good performance in the latter case. A meaningful use of GRAPE requires a problem dominated by the calculation of gravitational forces. The force evaluation on the low precision boards (GRAPE3) is only accurate to $\approx 1\%$. Numerical simulations which demand a higher precision should be run on the high precision boards (GRAPE4). In that case, however, an investment of about US $ 100 000 is necessary to get a similar performance. In summary, the GRAPE hardware is applicable to a whole class of astrophysical problems. It is a very attractive alternative to current supercomputers, at least for problems which are dominated by CPU time rather than by memory.

Acknowledgements: I would like to thank D. Sugimoto for the possibility to use the GRAPE board in Tokyo. I. Hachisu, J. Makino and M. Taiji are gratefully acknowledged for their help during my work on GRAPE. E. Bertschinger, E. Müller, R. Spurzem and S. White are greatfully acknowledged for discussions and suggestions about the different aspects of large scale N–body and hydrodynamical simulations. All CRAY simulations have been performed on the CRAY YMP 4/64 of the Rechenzentrum Garching and all GRAPE calculations on the GRAPE3Af board of the University of Tokyo.

References

1. Zel'dovich, Y.B.: 1970, *Astron. Astrophys.* **5**, 84.
2. Lucy, L.: 1977, *Astron. J.* **82**, 1013.
3. Steinmetz, M., Müller, E.: 1993, *Astron. Astrophys.* **268**, 391.
4. Hockney, R.W., Eastwood, J.W.: 1981, *Computer Simulation Using Particles*, McGraw Hill, New York.
5. Porter, D., 1985: *Ph.D. thesis*, University of California, Berkeley.
6. Barnes, J., Hut, P.: 1986, *Nature* **324**, 446.
7. Salmon, J.K.: 1991, *PhD thesis* Pasadena: Caltech, 1991.
8. Theuns, T.: 1993, *Computer Physics Communication*, **78**, 238.
9. Theuns, T., Rathsack, M.E.: 1993, *Computer Physics Communication* **76**, 141.
10. Ferrell, B., Bertschinger, E.: 1994, *International Journal of Modern Physics C*, in press.
11. Warren, M.S., Zurek, W.H., Quinn, P.J., Salmon, J.K.: 1993, in *181st Meeting of the American Astronomical Society* Phoenix, Arizona.
12. Katz, N., Hernquist, L., Weinberg, D.H.: 1992, *Astrophys. J. (Letters)* **399**, L109.
13. Sugimoto, D.: 1993, *Physics World* **11/1993**, 32.
14. Steinmetz, M., Müller, E.: 1994, *Astron. Astrophys.* **281**, L97.

Parallel magnetohydrodynamics on the CM-5

S. Poedts[1], P.M. Meijer[1], J.P. Goedbloed[1], H.A. van der Vorst[2], and
A. Jakoby[3]

[1] FOM-Institute for Plasmaphysics, P.O.Box 1207, 3430 BE Nieuwegein,
The Netherlands
[2] Mathematics Institute, Universiteit Utrecht, P.O.Box 80010, 3508 TA Utrecht,
The Netherlands
[3] Thinking Machines GmbH, Corneliusstraße 6, D-80469 München, Germany

Abstract. The equations of magnetohydrodynamics (MHD) describe
the interaction of hot ionised gases (plasmas) with magnetic fields. MHD
phenomena basically involve 3D time-dependent structures characterised
by the simultaneous presence of both very fine-scale and global variations
in a complex magnetic field geometry evolving on a number of vastly different time scales. The parallelism (performance and scalability) of the
essential building blocks of MHD codes (FFTs, matrix-vector multiplications, inner products, etc.) is studied on the CM-5.

1 Introduction

The interaction of hot ionised gases (plasmas) with magnetic fields is described
by the equations of *magnetohydrodynamics* (MHD). Plasma is the main state of
matter in the universe and magnetic fields turn out to dominate the dynamical
behaviour of plasmas. Our knowledge of the interaction of magnetic fields with
plasmas has increased substantially due to the research of energy production
from controlled thermonuclear fusion. In turn, this has stimulated the research
of astrophysical plasmas in which magnetic fields turn out to play an even more
important role. MHD phenomena occur e.g. in the solar atmosphere (corona)
where virtually all phenomena which are important in a tokamak (presently the
most promising fusion experiment) return in a modified form. Consequently,
research of MHD from the two points of view of nuclear fusion and astrophysics
has turned out to be an extremely fruitful area.

The MHD equations are *non-linear partial differential equations*, which contain those of gas dynamics and fluid mechanics as a special case (vanishing
magnetic field). In dimensionless form, these equations can be written as:

$$\frac{\partial \rho}{\partial t} = -\nabla \cdot (\rho \mathbf{V}), \tag{1}$$

$$\rho \frac{\partial \mathbf{V}}{\partial t} = -\rho \mathbf{V} \cdot \nabla \mathbf{V} - \nabla p + (\nabla \times \mathbf{B}) \times \mathbf{B}, \tag{2}$$

$$\frac{\partial p}{\partial t} = -\nabla \cdot (p\mathbf{V}) - (\gamma - 1)p \nabla \cdot \mathbf{V} + (\gamma - 1)\eta(\nabla \times \mathbf{B})^2, \tag{3}$$

$$\frac{\partial \mathbf{B}}{\partial t} = \nabla \times (\mathbf{V} \times \mathbf{B}) - \nabla \times (\eta \nabla \times \mathbf{B}), \tag{4}$$

$$\text{and} \quad \nabla \cdot \mathbf{B} = 0. \tag{5}$$

Here ρ, $\mathbf{V}$, p, and $\mathbf{B}$ denote the plasma density, the velocity field, the thermal pressure, and the magnetic field, respectively. The ratio of specific heats, γ, is assumed to be 5/3 and η is the plasma resistivity. The divergence equation, $\nabla \cdot \mathbf{B} = 0$, serves as an initial condition on $\mathbf{B}$. The magnetic field complicates the plasma dynamics considerably and the essential problems in fusion and astrophysical plasma dynamics basically involve 3D time-dependent MHD structures characterised by the simultaneous presence of both very fine-scale and global variations in a complex magnetic field geometry evolving on a number of vastly different time scales. The magnetic Reynolds number R_m, defined as $R_m \equiv l_0 V_0 / \eta$, with l_0 a typical length scale and V_0 a typical speed, is extremely high in both tokamak plasmas and astrophysical plasmas. Therefore, the required spatial and temporal resolutions for realistic computer simulations surpass the limits of present supercomputer power.

2 Linear dynamics: MHD spectroscopy

In the framework of linear MHD the study of the interaction between plasma and magnetic field leads to *large-scale complex eigenvalue problems*. With a finite element discretization in the direction normal to the magnetic flux surfaces and a Fourier decomposition in the two spatial directions that span the magnetic surfaces, the Galerkin method leads to an eigenvalue problem of the form:

$$A\mathbf{x} = \lambda B\mathbf{x}, \tag{6}$$

with λ the (complex) eigenvalue, A a non-Hermitian matrix, and B a symmetric and positive-definite matrix. Due to the use of finite elements, the matrices A and B have a *block tri-diagonal structure* with blocks of size $16\,N_F \times 16\,N_F$, where N_F is the number of Fourier modes. Many problems in physics and engineering lead to a complex eigenvalue problem of the form (6). In quantum mechanics e.g., the operators involved are Hermitian. These operators can always be diagonalized, which led to a beautiful spectral theory. In the MHD equivalent of atomic spectroscopy, called *'MHD spectroscopy'* (see [1]), however, the solution of large nonsymmetric eigenvalue problems is required, which is still by no means standard.

In MHD problems, the eigenvalues come in conjugate complex pairs and they refer to three types of modes, viz. Alfvén, fast magnetosonic, and slow magnetosonic modes. For the stability of magnetically confined plasmas one is mainly interested in the Alfvén sub-spectrum. A *complex variant* [2] of the Implicitly Updated Arnoldi Method, introduced by D. Sorensen [3], is used to determine this Alfvén spectrum. The method has been made rigorous in finding *internal* eigenvalues by the use of a complex shift and invert strategy [2]. Using a shift σ in equation (6) a new eigenvalue problem

$$\hat{A}\mathbf{x} = \mu\mathbf{x}, \tag{7}$$

is derived, with $\hat{A} \equiv (A - \sigma B)^{-1} B$, and $\mu \equiv 1/(\lambda - \sigma)$. The LU-decomposition required to invert the matrix $(A - \sigma B)$ can not be parallelised efficiently. However, the matrix inversion can be avoided (see [4]). Therefore, we here concentrate on the two sub-problems left when creating a Krylov subspace in the shift-without-invert Arnoldi algorithm [4], viz. inner products and matrix-vector multiplications.

The inner products are a potential bottle-neck for a parallel Arnoldi algorithm because of the relatively high amount of communication involved. The subroutine gbl_gen_inner_product_c1_noadd of the Connection Machine Scientific Subroutine Library (CMSSL) was used to check this on the CM-5. The results are shown in Table 1 (columns 1–4) and Figure 1. Column 1 gives the number of processors, column 2 the vector length considered, column 3 the total time for one inner product, and column 4 the performance obtained. We remark that the tests were done on different machines, running different versions of the operating system and different versions of the software, some of which are not released yet. This explains part of the 'noise' in the timing. *Note that the problem size is scaled with the number of processors*: the vector lenght is 2560×Nprocs, where Nprocs is the number of processors. Hence, the amount of work done by each processor is constant. The communication, however, increases with Nprocs and it is clear that communication indeed becomes visible for Nprocs$\geq$ 128 (even for increasing vector lengths). Note, however, the relatively high performance, 40 Mflops/s/node, and the low CPU time of only .57 ms (which will be compared with the CPU time needed for the matrix-vector multiplication below).

For the matrix-vector multiplication two CMSSL routines were tested, viz. block_sparse_matrix_vector_mult and grid_sparse_matrix_vector_mult. The block size in the tests was 80×80 and the problem size again *scales with the machine size*: 32×Nblocks were used in the tests, with Nblocks the number of diagonal blocks. In this sub-problem, communication is relatively less important (only neighbour-to-neighbour communication), and a better scaling can be expected. In Table 1 (columns 5–9) and Figure 1 it can be seen that this is indeed the case. Both routines yield a linear scaling with the number of processors. The block_sparse routine required 86 ms (54 Mflops/s/node) while the grid_sparse routine needed 110 ms (46 Mflops/s/node). However, the set-up time was much longer for the block_sparse routine (400 ms) than for the grid_sparse routine (0.017 ms). Yet, this set-up has to be done only once while a lot of matrix-vector multiplications have to be performed in each iteration step of the Arnoldi process.

3 Non-linear dynamics

For the interpretation of actual plasma dynamics in tokamaks and solar coronal loops it is crucial to understand the *non-linear phase* of the evolution of MHD phenomena in these configurations. Non-linear MHD adds two more complications: *non-linear mode coupling* involving hundreds of small-scale modes and *the discrepancy between the dynamical Alfvén time scale and the diffusion time*

Table 1. Scaling of inner products and matrix-vector multiplications

| | inner product | | | matrix-vector multiplication | | | | |
| | | | | | block_sparse | | grid_sparse | |
Nprocs	vector length	time (ms)	Mflops (/s)	Nblocks	time (ms)	Mflops (/s)	time (ms)	Mflops (/s)
1	2560	.57	36	32	88.9	54	105.8	49
4	10240	.44	186	128	85.5	229	104.3	188
16	40960	.63	524	512	89.1	882	106.3	739
32	81920	.55	1192	1024	89.0	1767	106.0	1484
64	163840	.56	2354	2048	85.7	3672	102.9	3057
128	327680	.59	4420	4096	85.7	7343	102.8	6120
256	655360	.68	7686	8192	85.7	14688	101.7	12371

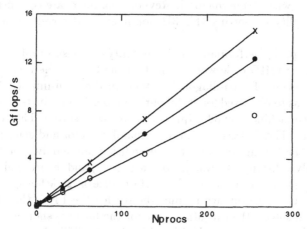

Fig. 1. Scaling of the inner products (circles) and matrix-vector multiplications with the block_sparse routine (crosses) and with the grid_sparse routine (filled circles).

scale which becomes enormous in the highly conducting plasmas of interest. The non-linear mode coupling makes implicit time stepping methods extremely complicated and CPU time consuming.

We have developed a numerical code for simulating the temporal evolution of an externally driven 3D cylindrical plasma in non-linear MHD [5]. The radial direction is discretized with finite differences on two staggered meshes and a pseudo-spectral discretization is used for the other two spatial directions. A semi-implicit predictor-corrector scheme is applied for the time stepping. In this scheme the fast magnetosonic modes, and only these, are treated implicitly in the linear start-up phase. This allows time steps up to a factor of 1000 larger than explicit methods, where the time step is limited by the CFL condition. Nevertheless, 3D non-linear time evolution simulations remain extremely computational intensive and computer memory and CPU time requirements become

Table 2. Scaling of tri-diagonal system solver and double complex FFTs

	tri-diagonal system			double FFTs		
Nprocs	Nsystems	time (ms)	Mflops (/s)	Nfft	time (s)	Mflops (/s)
1	32	61.3	23	32	.267	59
4	128	55.1	99	128	.261	241
16	512	57.5	378	512	.258	977
32	1024	54.8	797	1024	.261	1928
64	2048	53.2	1640	2048	.252	3988
128	4096	53.1	3288	4096	.253	7965
256	8192	53.3	6557	8192	.253	15911

soon prohibitive when large magnetic Reynolds numbers are considered. Therefore, the possibility of porting this 3D non-linear MHD code to a CM-5 was
investigated.

As a first step, the performance and scalability of two sub-problems arising in
the 3D non-linear MHD code were studied on the CM-5. The first sub-problem
involves the solution of a tri-diagonal system. In the semi-implicit MHD code,
such a system has to be solved for each Fourier mode. Again, the test problem was
scaled with the machine size: $32 \times$ Nprocs systems were solved. The vector length
was fixed to 512. The CMSSL routines gen_banded_factor and gen_banded_solve
were used but the timing was done for the solution phase only. The tri-diagonal
systems are solved locally (32 systems on each node) and, hence, a linear scaling
is obtained as shown in Table 2. The performance is 25 Mflops/s/node. Note
that, although the performance is much better for the FFTs than for the tri-
diagonal system solver, the execution time for the latter is shorter.

The second sub-problem studied involves double FFTs. In the pseudo-spectral or collocation method used in the MHD code, such FFTs are used to ensure
periodicity in two spatial directions (e.g. the short and the long way around
the tokamak). In principle, one computes in Fourier space, and the non-linear
terms are computed via FFTs to real space, a multiplication in real space, and
an FFT back to Fourier space. This procedure turns out to be faster than a
direct convolution sum in Fourier space when more than 50 Fourier modes are
involved. In the test, 64×64 complex FFTs were considered and the problem
size was again scaled with the number of processors: each processor performed
32 forward and backward FFTs. The CMSSL routine fft_detailed yielded a very
high performance: 59 Mflops/s/node. And as the FFTs were done locally, the
speed-up scales linearly with the number of processors, as shown in Table 2.

4 Conclusions

The tokamak plasmas studied in the context of controlled thermonuclear fusion
research and the plasmas observed in the solar corona are both characterized by

high magnetic Reynolds numbers. MHD spectroscopy and realistic simulations of time-dependent 3D non-linear MHD phenomena in such plasmas both require massive parallel computing. We have studied the performance and scalability of some sub-problems, that occur as building-blocks in MHD codes, on the CM-5.

For the large-scale complex eigenvalue problems that arise in (linear) MHD spectroscopy, we tested inner products and matrix-vector multiplications where the matrices have a block tri-diagonal structure. In the inner products, the communication shows up on large CM-5s (more than 128 nodes). However, the CPU time of 0.6 ms for one inner product has to be compared with the 86 ms required for one matrix-vector multiplication. In our application, typically 60 inner products at most are needed for each matrix-vector multiplication to build the Krylov subspace. Therefore, *the communication will not be a bottle-neck* in our application and the overall speed of the parallel part of the Arnoldi algorithm can be estimated to be larger than 40 Mflops/s/node.

The semi-implicit predictor-corrector scheme used in our 3D non-linear time-evolution code involves double FFTs and tri-diagonal systems. As both these sub-problems can be performed concurrently without communication, linear speed-ups were obtained in both cases. Therefore, the 3D non-linear MHD code will be very efficient in parallel.

The next step now is to port the complete MHD codes to the CM-5. This is non-trivial as the codes have to be (re-)written in CM-Fortran. Clearly, this means a loss of portability. The promising results reported in the present paper, however, justify this effort. As a matter of fact, our results indicate that the advent of large mpp machines will enable us to increase the spatial resolution considerably. As a result, the behaviour of plasmas with more realistic (much higher) magnetic Reynolds numbers will be simulated, which will certainly increase our insight of the interaction of plasmas and magnetic fields. Hence, *the advent of mpp systems may lead to a breakthrough in this field*.

Acknowledgements: This work was performed under the Euratom-FOM association agreement with financial support from NWO (pilot project on Massively Parallel Computing) and Euratom. This work was sponsored by the Stichting Nationale Computerfaciliteiten (National Computing Facilities Foundation, NCF) for the use of supercomputer facilities, with financial support from NWO. NCSA is acknowledged for providing CPU time on their CM-5 system.

References

1. Goedbloed, J.P.: 1991, in *Trends in Physics*, Prague, III, ed. J. Kaczér.
2. Kooper, M.N., van der Vorst, H.A., Poedts, S., and Goedbloed, J.P.: 1993, *J. Comp. Physics*, submitted.
3. Sorensen, D.C.: 1992, *SIAM J. Mat. Anal. Appl.*, **13**(1).
4. Booten, J.G.L., Meijer, P.M., te Riele, H.J.J., van der Vorst, H.A.: 1994, *this conference*.
5. Poedts, S. and Goedbloed, J.P.: 1993, Proc. Int. workshop on *Fragmented energy release in sun and stars*, Utrecht, The Netherlands, October 18-20, 1993, to appear.

First Results from the Parallelisation of CERN's NA48 Simulation Program

J. Apostolakis, C. E. Bruschini, P. Calafiura, F. Gagliardi,
M. Metcalf, A. Norton, B. Panzer-Steindel
CERN, Geneva, Switzerland

L. M. Bertolotto, K. J. Peach
Department of Physics and Astronomy, University of Edinburgh, UK

Abstract. The GP-MIMD2 project aims at demonstrating the effectiveness of using a European massively parallel supercomputer (MEIKO CS-2) in two different scientific production environments. One of its initial goals is the development of a parallel version of NMC, a specialized simulation code (developed by the CERN experiment NA48) which relies on a huge database (shower library) for maximum efficiency. NMC's memory requirements, combined with NA48's need of high statistics on a short timescale, make it a particular interesting candidate for MPP applications.

In our staged approach to NMC's parallelisation we decided to start with event level parallelisation (task farming); this was implemented using tasks that communicate via the CHIMP message passing interface. An overview of our initial experience will be given, both with and without access to the shower library. First timing tests and I/O analysis will be described, concluding with plans for future developments.

1. Introduction: The GP-MIMD2 project

The ESPRIT project P7255 *GP-MIMD2*[1] aims at acquiring experience with European parallel machines and at demonstrating the effectiveness of the massively parallel processing approach in the scientific environment [1]. Partners in this initiative include, on the users' and on the suppliers' sides:

- *CERN*, the European laboratory for Particle Physics based in Geneva, equipped with some of the largest scientific machines in the world and constantly working at the frontier of basic physics.
- *CERFACS* (Centre Européen de Recherche et Formation Avanceé en Calcul Scientifique), located in Toulouse (F), with a wide experience in the development of algorithms and tools for parallel computations.
- major *Meteorological and Climate centers* in France, Germany and the United Kingdom, with a tradition of using vector supercomputers.
- *Meiko* (GB), *Parsys* (GB) and *Telmat* (F), major European producers of parallel systems with many years' experience.

Platforms of choice are two Meiko *CS-2's* (Computing Surface 2), general purpose multi-node UNIX-based MIMD systems currently scalable up to 1024 nodes. They

---

[1] General-Purpose Multiple Instruction Multiple Data 2.

employ commodity CPUs and memory components, such as Sun's SuperSPARC ("Viking") chips, with the possible addition of Fujitsu's μVP vector processors. All nodes are interconnected by an original, scalable high-speed packet switched network using a specialized communications processor at each node and a multi-stage crossbar switch (and can have Input/Output subsystems attached to them) [2].

GP-MIMD2's major objective is to demonstrate that European parallel computing technology is mature enough to be used for high performance computing production. Basic physics applications at CERN and meteorological modelling at CERFACS have been chosen as ideal demonstrators because of their high demanding computing requirements and severe industrial production quality standards.

2. Computing in High Energy Physics

High energy physics experiments are quite often run by large international collaborations over periods of many years, using state-of-the-art equipment to:

- *simulate* the detector behaviour in order to optimize its design (and cost), and later on to reduce the uncertainty of MonteCarlo calculations.
- *collect* during the running of the experimental detectors huge volumes of *raw data*, containing for each *event*[2] the response of the single subdetectors (reducing the background in real-time as much as possible).
- *reconstruct* in detail the kinematical and physical features of single events from the raw data, or partially if the decision is going to be taken online.
- *analyze* the reconstructed events, producing distributions of functions for subsets of events.

The data itself is usually structured as a succession of events, each independent from the others. It comes, therefore, as no surprise that parallel processing at the event level ("farming") has become a reality during the last five years in the HEP world, implemented in a cost-effective way on clusters of RISC workstations.

The future generation of experiments will nevertheless exceed today's computing potential by several orders of magnitude, in terms of CPU as well as I/O capability. This makes the investigation of high performance computing of paramount importance. It will, therefore, probably be necessary to exploit parallelism within the event, considering for example the modularity of the detectors or treating particle tracks separately (since they too are independent) [3].

3. The CERN Experiment NA48

Work package 3 (WP3) of GP-MIMD2 identified a physics "demonstrator" application, i.e. a promising candidate for running on MPP platforms such as the CS-2, within the experiment *NA48* which is foreseen to take data at CERN in early 1996 [4]. Also, it was decided to start with the migration of the CERN Program Library, which contains a set of general purpose programs written and maintained by CERN for the use of the HEP community (since most HEP codes rely on it).

NA48 will use special high intensity beams of short-lived neutral kaons (K^0), comparing their relative decay rates into two neutral (π^0)[3] and two charged pions

---

[2] Which represents the "atomic" data unit in HEP and corresponds to the collision of a projectile particle with a target, not necessarily fixed, or with another projectile.
[3] Each of them decaying in turn very quickly into two photons.

(π^+,π^-). This will allow the measurement of a very important physical parameter[4] with a precision one order of magnitude better than the current value and with minimal systematic error. The results will then be compared with theoretical predictions of the Standard Model of electroweak interactions.

The high statistics, high precision character of the experiment implies that it will be necessary to cope with very high data rates due to the huge background. Potentially up to 100 Mbytes/s with several thousand events per second (after the first three trigger levels) are needed in order to be able to collect the necessary amount of "physics" events (some 10^7 per decay mode). Severe constraints are therefore being put on the data acquisition as well as on the detectors themselves. For example, the homogeneous *liquid Krypton (LKr) calorimeter* designed to detect neutral decays will be composed of as many as 13000 cells (2x2x135 cm), possessing excellent energy, space and time resolution.

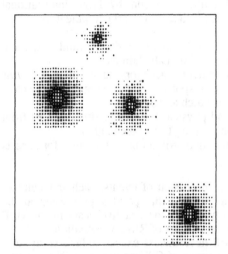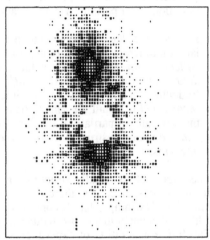

Fig. 1. Simulation of shower developments in the LKr calorimeter for a neutral (4 γ) and a charged event $(\pi^+\pi^-)$ respectively (the direction of the particles is normal to the page). Each box corresponds to a cell of the calorimeter and its size to the energy therein deposited.

In addition, it will be necessary to repeatedly simulate some 10^7 K^0 decays in the active volume of the detector, in order to estimate accurately the efficiency and acceptance (high statistics MonteCarlo).

4. The NA48 Simulation Program NMC and its Shower Library

NMC is a specialized and fast detector simulation code developed by the NA48 collaboration [5]. It does not perform directly a full event-by-event simulation of shower depositions in the LKr calorimeter (see above) because this would be excessively time consuming[5], relying instead on a separately generated, distributed *shower library*. Each entry is identified by the particle type, the energy bin to which it belongs and the coordinates of its impact point on the calorimeter surface, and

---

[4] The direct CP violation parameter ε'/ε. See also [4] and the references contained therein.

[5] For example *GEANT* [6] takes about *10 sec* per average energy photon on an HP 9000/735.

contains the energy deposited by the particle in the cells of a predefined area centered on its impact point.

The size of a single shower depends for the time being only on the particle type, amounting to about 1 Kbyte for e^+, e^- and γ and 5 Kbytes for π^+, π^-. Access time to this huge database, which will have an ultimate size of several Gbytes and contain some 10^5 entries, has obviously to be kept as small as possible so that NMC will retain its efficiency. Note in particular that the neutral events in which we are interested require access to four photons per event.

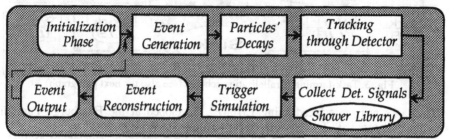

Fig. 2. Schematic NMC Flowchart

The GP-MIMD2 project became interested in NMC given not only the tight overall constraints on I/O and memory (database size, random access), but also the statistics needs described above, which could potentially be met "overnight" on MPP platforms (fast feedback). Possible future real-time applications such as online event reconstruction and calibration of the LKr calorimeter are also particularly appealing.

5. Task-Farming Parallelisation Without Shower Library

The first step in our staged approach was NMC event-level parallelisation in its simplest form, i.e. *task farming* (coarse grain parallelism). This guarantees maximum code flexibility since minimal changes between sequential and parallel version are needed, and this is particularly welcome because NMC is still in an evolution phase.

Such an implementation consists of several tasks that communicate with each other via message passing interfaces, i.e.:

- (at least) one *master program*, also called *Source*, which first initializes the working environment of the message passing interface as well as of the main code itself (setting up databases, etc.). During execution it synchronizes the slave processes (see below) and distributes the relative work loads, handing out "packets" of events to be processed. Note that the treatment of random numbers is quite important since they have to be generated and distributed correctly (i.e. in such a way that each worker will really generate different events), irrespective of the number of processors in the system.
- several identical and independent *slave programs*, or *Event Workers*, which do the actual event generation and are in fact copies of NMC with very little modification. A starting configuration could, for example, be characterized by having one Event Worker per processor.
- (at least) one program, also called *Sink*, that collects the results of the computations from the slaves (histograms for example) and deallocates resources. This part is in fact still under development.

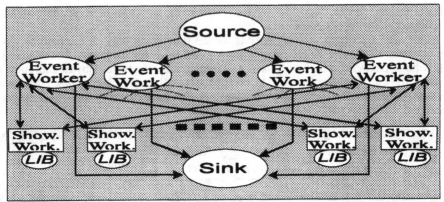

Fig. 3. Task-farming parallelisation scheme (see also the next paragraph)

The tasks were interfaced using *CHIMP*[6], developed at the Edinburgh Parallel Computer Centre (EPCC) and built on connectionless datagram services.

Scaling tests have been carried out on up to 12 processors on clusters of SGI 340 (four nodes each) or Sun IPX machines, as well as on single multiprocessor machines (SGI Challenge with eight nodes) [7]. The total number of events to be processed was kept fixed, changing the number of processors and of events per request (and consequently the number of messages) in order to estimate the message passing overhead and verify the scaling behaviour. The lowest time required for a single "ping-pong" communication between two processes was found to be 8 msec on the SGI Challenge[7], comparable to the time needed to process a single event on the same machine (remember that these tests were carried out without shower library).

Deviations from scaling appeared only using a high message passing overhead (10%), thus showing that task-farming is feasible.

6. Task-Farming Parallelisation with Shower Library

Thus encouraged we proceeded towards the second step in parallelisation of NMC, i.e. task-farming with random access to a large, distributed shower library.

6.1 Implementation and First Tests

An additional category of slave programs, the *Shower Workers*, was added to the ones described above, one of them being present on each node of the system containing a share of the library. The latter will be distributed over as many nodes as possible in order to fully exploit the advantages of MIMD architectures, and uniformly (with regard to its access pattern) in order to guarantee I/O load balancing.

During the processing of an event a worker will arrive at a point where a shower is needed; it will examine an internal database to figure where the desired information is, send a request to the corresponding task and wait. Having received the shower information it will continue until another shower is needed, and so forth.

---

[6] Common High-level Interface to Message Passing.
[7] This value is entirely due to protocol overhead and would obviously be much lower on a CHIMP version for multiprocessor machines (instead of workstation clusters).

The final version of the shower library is currently being generated; therefore we decided to work using several copies of a smaller shower library (16 Mbytes), running on the Central Simulation Facility cluster of HP workstations at CERN. This multi-user facility does not permit extensive testing nor timing analyses, but it was nevertheless possible to generate the missing code and test it with success.

6.2 I/O Analysis

In parallel to the activities previously described, we optimized also the sequential version of NMC, identifying and modifying time-critical routines, and carried out a preliminary I/O analysis on a single processor. For this purpose we created a huge file (1.2 Gbytes), whose access pattern mimics the one of the shower library itself, and measured the mean time spent in database access for neutral events (four showers each, randomly positioned in the file).

The result, about *50 msec* in total, is slightly larger than the mean time necessary to process a neutral event on a Sun SuperSPARC processor running at 50 MHz.

Ways to hide this I/O wait-time include minimizing disk access by distributing the database on as many nodes as possible (trying to exploit fully the main memory), or running several processes, in our case copies of NMC, on the same processor. The last solution, in particular, has been already tested and proven to be very effective.

7. Plans for the Future

The NA48 simulation program NMC has been parallelized at the event-level and first test have been carried out. In the near future we will generate a realistic shower library and perform more detailed analyses (timing, scaling, etc.) on dedicated MIMD platforms (a Sun SPARCenter and the CS-2) using CHIMP. First production runs will follow, in order to test on a large scale stability and results and fully assess the potentialities of MPP systems.

In the long run we wish to investigate opportunities for finer grain parallelism and real-time applications such as the calibration of NA48's LKr calorimeter.

References

[1] Project P7255 *GP-MIMD2*, described in "High Performance Computing and Networking, Summaries of Projects (Synopsis)", Jan. 1993, CEC DG-XIII

[2] "Computing Surface Documentation Guide", 1993 Meiko World Incorporated

[3] K. J. Peach et al.: "The Ongoing Investigation of High Performance Parallel Computing in HEP", CERN/DRDC 93-10, DRDC P49, January 1993

[4] G. D. Barr et al.: "Proposal for a Precision Measurement of ε/ε' in CP Violating K^0 -> 2π Decays", CERN/SPSC/90-22, SPSC/P253, July 1990

[5] F. Leber et al.: "NMC User's Guide"

[6] R. Brun et al.: "GEANT User's Guide", CERN Program Library W5103

[7] B. Panzer-Steindel: "Test of Scalability for Task-Farming with CHIMP", CN-GPM Internal Note, August 1993

SOFTWARE PACKAGE FOR REFLECTION HIGH ENERGY ELECTRON DIFFRACTION BEAM INTENSITY MEASUREMENT AND ANALYSIS SYSTEM

G.E.Cirlin, G.M.Guryanov, N.P.Korneeva, Yu.B.Samsonenko
Institute for Analytical Instrumentation
Russia Academy of Sciences,
Rizhsky 26, St.Petersburg 198103, Russia

Abstract

The three packages of software for reflection high energy electron diffraction are described. There are one window, four windows and line-like options for different applications in molecular beam epitaxial growth processes, surface phenomena and diffraction features investigations.

Reflection high energy electron diffraction (RHEED) is one of the most useful diagnostic tools in molecular beam epitaxy (MBE). The registration and analysis of the beams intensity oscillations is used widely for the growth rate determination, beam fluxes calibration, stoichiometry of compounds control etc. Moreover, the beam shape information of RHEED patterns is useful to determine such properties as anneal times, surface flatness, and for fundamental investigations of diffraction processes and surface phenomena. The inherent limitations of an optical photomultiplier [1], the most common method for RHEED measurement can be eliminated by using video interface to collect the light from the phosphorus screen where the diffracted beams are imaged. Our high sensivity recording setup for MBE processes control consists of RHEED gun (energy of electrons in a range 10 - 25 keV, incidence angle $\approx 1°$), phosphorus screen at the opposite side of the MBE growth chamber, high sensitive video camera for recording the images on the screen, specially designed interface for connection of video camera with personal computer, personal computer, video monitor, and entire software package allows us to get, to storage in files and to analyze the information obtained from the screen.

The software written in C language is divided on three independent packages: i) one window acquisition data, ii) four windows acquisition data, and iii) line-like acquisition data. All these packages consists of the programs of getting and analyzing information:

i) One window option. The main aim of this option is an operative determination of the growth rate of the compounds required. Firstly, the user have to get whole the information from the screen. Next, the part of the image of interest (approximately 10% of the whole screen) is chosen. Then, the window in which the information will be analyzed of arbitrary size is fixed. After this the time of measurement is given up and the information getting is started. When the time is finished or after operator s interruption the user can measure the time intervals on oscillation curve using special markers, calculate the growth rate, print results and save information on a disc (with or without information about diffraction patterns). If it is necessary, the user can analyze the information saved any time after using special program.

ii) Four windows option. This option can be used for measurement of the intensities of multiple diffracted beams simultaneously in real time. The difference from i) option consists of the possibility to choose up to four windows within the interesting frame of arbitrary sizes at arbitrary places of the image. Thus, this option can be applied to surface phenomena and diffraction features investigations.

iii) Line-like option. This option can be used for analysis of the beam profiles of the beam profiles investigation in real time. The main difference from two previous versions is an ability to measure the RHEED intensities in quasi line regime between two points chosen in arbitrary places within frame of interest. This quasiline is consist of a number of windows (up to 16) with arbitrary, but fixed size. The possible functions (storage, printing, control curve of RHEED oscillations observing) are the same that in i) and ii) options. But the information obtained by this option is more complex and required more complicated program of the data analysis.

First of all, the serving program allows to the user to display graphically the information (RHEED intensity vs time) in every window (up to 16) using different colors in unsmoothed and smoothed regimes. Then, it is possible to measure the intervals of time on all the curves and calculate the period of oscillations or some characteristic times (e.g., annealing times, rate of the surface reconstructions change etc.). Moreover, there is a possibility to observe the profile from the moment when the measuring of intensity is started and in multi film regime to display the profile changes. In the operator chosen moment(s) it if possible to fix the profile(s) and display it at allocated place of PC screen. More, the user can oversee the all intensities changes as a whole from left and right points of observing in three dimensional manner. All the information can be immediately printed.

We have described the software package for reflection high energy diffraction beam intensity measurement and analysis system applied to molecular beam epitaxy machine. In particular, the using this software allows us to found the effect of periodical splitting of the beams depending on the growth conditions during MBE growth of GaAs [2]. ¿From our point of view our RHEED system associated with software described here allows to precisely observe and analyze the most features which are observed during MBE growth. In addition, the presented software can easily be included in automation system for MBE growth control.

References

[1] J.M.Van Hove, P.R.Pukite, P.I.Cohen. J.Vac.Sci.Technol B., v.1, p.741 (1983).

[2] G.E.Cirlin, G.M.Guryanov, N.N.Ledentsov, Yu.B.Samsonenko. Abs.14th General Conference of Condensed Matter Division of EPS, Madrid, 1994 (accepted).

Conceiving Computationally Intensive Approaches to Vision

N. Petkov

Department of Computing Science, University of Groningen
P.O.Box 800, 9700 AV Groningen, The Netherlands

Abstract. I present some of the research activities of my group in Vision as a Grand Challenge problem whose solution is estimated to need the power of Tflop/s computers. Visual information representations which are motivated by the function of the primary visual cortex are computed. In the case of simple objects such as convex polygons, these representations allow straightforward interpretation for object recognition. Lower dimension representations which are used to simplify the problem of comparing input to prestored information have limitations. Optical flow methods applied to complete representations are studied as a possible solution to this problem. The automatic identification of persons by a face image is used as a touchstone for the proposed methods.

1 Introduction

Vision and cognition are considered to be Grand Challenge problems whose solution would require parallel computers with performance in the order of 10^{12} operations per second [1]. In contrast to other Grand Challenge problems, in vision and cognition even qualitative understanding of the underlying principles is not yet available and computationally intensive models and methods which would be able to make use of Teraflop/s parallel supercomputers have still to be developed. This paper presents two computationally intensive approaches to image pattern recognition. The problem of automatic person identification by a face image is used as a touchstone to test the usefulness and feasibility of these approaches. (For a brief summary of previous work on face recognition and references see [2, 3].)

Neurophysiological research has delivered interesting results which can inspire new image analysis and object recognition methods. For more than thirty years it is, for instance, known that a large amount of neurons, the so-called simple cells in the primary visual cortex of mammals, react strongly to short oriented lines [4]. More recent studies led to a more precise functional description of such neurons by so-called receptive field functions [5, 6]. With their help one can compute quantities which correspond to the activities induced in simple visual cortical cells by an input image and visualize the results in so-called 'cortical images' in order to get new insights into the function of the visual cortex. In Section 2 of this paper, a cortical filter model we have developed and used in previous works [2, 3, 7, 8, 9, 10] is briefly presented.

In the referred works we reduced each cortical image to a single number in order to obtain lower dimension representations of the input images and use them for object recognition. A summary of this method and the results achieved with it for identification by face image is given in Section 3.

In contrast to a lower dimension representation, the input (space domain) representation of an image is complete, in that it contains the full original information (it is the original information itself). In principle, an identification method which is based on a complete representation has a higher potential than a method based on a representation in a lower dimension space, since it excludes the possibility of projecting face images of two different persons onto one and the same point of the representation space. Exploring the possibility to use complete representations, elsewhere [11] we propose to compute a two-dimensional vector field similar to optical flow which maps optimally an image onto another image. Such a mapping is aimed at minimizing a certain dissimilarity measure between the two images, taking into account geometrical constraints such as the relative positions of image blocks. With this distance measure, one can search for a nearest neighbour of an input face image in a database of prestored face images and use the result for person identification. In Section 4 of this paper, I give a summary of this method and the results achieved with it.

Computational requirements and implementation are addressed in Section 5, and in Section 6 some conclusions are drawn and directions for future research are outlined.

2 Cortical filters and images

2.1 Modelling simple cells in the primary visual cortex

The receptive field function of a visual neuron is a two-dimensional map which describes the response of that neuron to a small spot of light as a function of position. In practice, a background stimulus, such as random noise, is used to bring a neuron to a certain excitation level and the response to the light spot is measured relative to this level. Inhibitory effects can be measured in this way. Note that, due to the use of a background stimulus, the receptive field function *cannot* be considered as an impulse response. Nevertheless, for the simple visual cortical cells, which form the majority in the primary visual cortex, this function is quite useful, since the knowledge of it allows to predict the response of a cell to composite stimuli. The response r of a simple cell characterized by a receptive field function $g(x, y)$ to a composite stimulus specified by a two-dimensional function (image) $s(x, y)$ can be computed by evaluating the integral

$$\tilde{s} = \int s(x, y)g(x, y)dxdy \tag{1}$$

(in the same way as if $g(x, y)$ were the impulse response of a linear system) and subsequently submitting the result $\tilde{s}$ to rectification (or thresholding):

$$r = \tilde{s} \quad \text{if} \quad \tilde{s} > 0, \quad r = 0 \quad \text{if} \quad \tilde{s} \leq 0 \tag{2}$$

Neurophysiological research has shown that simple visual cortical cells can be characterized by receptive field functions of the type shown in Fig.1 [5, 6]. Typically such a function has several parallel excitation and inhibition stripe zones and has non-zero values in a limited area, the so-called receptive field of the cell. It can be symmetric (even) or antisymmetric (odd) as shown in Fig.1a and Fig.1b, respectively, and is characterized by the size σ of the receptive field, the position (ξ, η) of its center, and the orientation φ of the normal to the parallel excitation and inhibition zones.

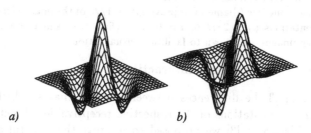

a)   *b)*

Fig. 1. Symmetric (*a*) and antisymmetric (*b*) receptive field functions.

As to the importance of these cells for the visual system, it is believed that they play an important role in the process of form perception, in that they act as detectors of oriented intensity transitions such as edges and bars. In particular, a cell with a symmetric receptive field function will react strongly to a bar which coincides in direction and width with the central (excitation) region of the cell receptive field. A cell with an antisymmetric receptive field function will react strongly to an edge of the same orientation if the excitation lobe is on the light side of the transition and the inhibition lobe on the dark side. While both symmetric and antisymmetric receptive field functions can be used to detect edges, only the antisymmetric functions can give information about the polarity of the light-to-dark transition. They also specify more precisely the position of an edge. Therefore, we use only antisymmetric receptive field functions for oriented edge detection (for more details on this topic see [3]).

For fixed size and orientation and variable center of the receptive fields, the non-negative quantities computed according to eqs.(1-2) can be grouped together in two-dimensional functions to which we refer as *cortical images*. Fig.2 shows an input image $s(x, y)$ for which Fig.3 shows a set of computed cortical images.

Fig. 2. A simple input image.

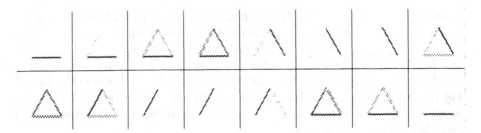

Fig. 3. A set of cortical images computed with a set of antisymmetric receptive field functions of the same size (diameter approximately 1/20 of the image size) and different preferred orientations $\varphi_i = 2\pi i/16$, $i = 0 \ldots 7$ (first row) and $i = 8 \ldots 15$ (second row). Negative images are shown to facilitate visualization.

2.2 Subsequent non-linear interactions

Note that in Fig.3 the differences between cortical images, which correspond to neighbouring orientations of the respective receptive field functions, are not really large. Elsewhere [3] we proposed to improve the orientation sensitivity of cortical filters by a pixel-wise winner-takes-all competition between cortical images computed with receptive field function convolution kernels of the same size and different preferred orientations.

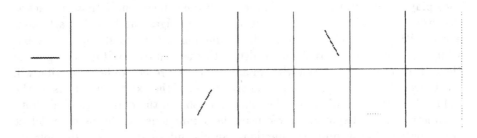

Fig. 4. Cortical images computed with the involvement of orientation competition and lateral inhibition. (Negative images are shown.)

An interesting effect is that if an edge is enhanced in a cortical image corresponding to orientation φ the same edge gives rise to a pair of weaker lines - we call them shadow lines - in the cortical image which corresponds to orientation $\varphi + \pi$. To remove this redundancy, elsewhere [8, 9] we proposed a *lateral inhibition* mechanism in which a strong line in a cortical image corresponding to receptive field parameters σ and φ suppresses the two weaker shadow lines in the cortical image which corresponds to receptive field parameters σ and $\varphi + \pi$.

The effect of orientation competition and lateral inhibition is illustrated by Fig.4. Note that each edge line of the triangle from the input image is enhanced in a different cortical image so that the effect is a decomposition of a geometrical object into oriented edge line segments. Evidently the model is doing well on simple geometrical figures, since it decomposes them into geometrical primitives (line segments) of the next lower level. With such a decomposition it is not difficult to conceive a scheme for the recognition of simple geometrical figures whereby 'recognition' means, for instance, classification according to the number of edges (see next section). However, the world we live in does not consist of simple geometrical figures and our visual system has to compute representations which facilitate the recognition of more complex objects. It is therefore interesting to look at a complex object such as a human face through the cortical filters sketched above. Fig.5 shows such an input image of a human face and Fig.6 shows a set of cortical images computed from it. Obviously, the information presented by the cortical images in this case will hardly allow an interpretation as straightforward as that in the case of a simple geometrical figure.

Fig. 5. An input face image.

Fig. 6. A set of cortical images computed from the face image shown in Fig.5 using receptive field convolver functions of one size and different orientations. (Negative images are shown.)

As to the region of the cortex where the proposed orientation competition and lateral inhibition might occur (if they actually exist), it is usually thought that nonlinear processing of this kind is carried out not at the simple cell level but rather at subsequent stages where the outputs of simple cells are combined and perceptual decisions are made (see also [3]).

3 Lower dimension representation

Although the cortical images computed according to the above model deliver usefully structured information, they themselves do not give an ultimate solution to the recognition and identification problem. The achieved structuring does not itself suggest a straightforward scheme for comparing input to prestored information for the purpose of recognising objects. Elsewhere [2, 3, 7, 8, 9, 10] we proposed to approach this problem by reducing the cortical images to single numbers which are computed by summing up all pixel values in the corresponding cortical images. Fig.7a and Fig.7b show plots of the quantities extracted in this way from the cortical image sets in Fig.4 and Fig.6, respectively.

The plot in Fig.7a exhibits three dominant maxima which are due to the three edge lines in the original input image of Fig.2. Within the class of convex polygons, this information is sufficient to classify an object whose image gives rise to such a lower dimension space representation as a triangle. For a creature which lives in a world of convex polygons, the proposed reduction scheme will solve the classification problem, one needs only add a stage which counts the number of maxima. As to the plot shown in Fig.7b, it is hardly possible to infer from its particular structure that it is due to a face input image. Plots which are produced by different face images show a certain degree of similarity (see Fig.6a and Fig.7 in [10]), but similar plots are produced also by images in which the various face parts do not occupy their proper position. This is due to the fact that this representation contains information about the strength and number of edges of particular orientation, but the information about their spatial distribution is completely lost by applying a global reduction operation.

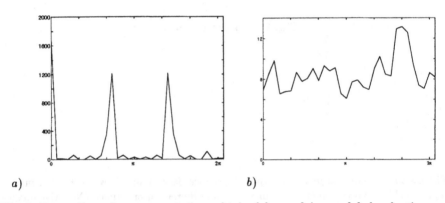

a)   b)

Fig. 7. Lower dimension representations obtained by applying a global reduction operation to the cortical images shown in Fig.4 and Fig.6.

In order to study the possibilities of the proposed lower dimension representations for identification, i.e. discrimination between objects within one class, we applied the developed method to a database of 262 different face images of 36 persons (each person is represented by six to eight face images in the database, technical details can be found in [7].) For each of the face images in the database, a lower dimension representation was computed according to the scheme sketched above. Based on this representation a nearest-neighbour was searched in the rest of the database. The search was considered to be successful if the nearest neighbour turned out to be another image of the same person and not successful if it was an image of a different person. The search was successful for 256 of the 262 images (97%).

4   Comparing complete representations

As already mentioned in the introduction, a method based on a lower dimension representation has a principle deficiency, in that it may project the face images of two different persons onto one and the same point in the lower dimension space. Comparing complete image representations such as the input images or their Fourier transforms excludes this possibility.

Exploring the possibility to use complete representations, elsewhere [11] we propose to compute a two-dimensional vector field which maps optimally an image onto another image. We make use of a multiscale algorithm to approximately solve the correspondence problem. The method we use is very similar to optical flow algorithms for motion analysis [12, 13]. It involves a number of steps (levels) in each of which one of the images is divided into blocks and for each block a best match is searched in the other image. The algorithm starts with large blocks for which large search spaces are allowed and ends with fine blocks with small search spaces. At each level, the center of the search space of a block is determined by the result of the search at the previous level. In practice, one operates with blocks and search spaces of constant size applied on the different levels of an image pyramid.

This algorithm allows to search in a relatively large space using small blocks, without large violations in the relative positions of the blocks. Multiscale resolution beginning with coarse blocks and ending with fine blocks and successive refinement of the displacement field is essential, since the direct use of small blocks - these can be chosen as small as single pixels - in combination with a large search space may yield a perfect match, i.e. each pixel of an image finds a pixel with the same grayvalue in the other image, but the mapping vector field can be completely random.

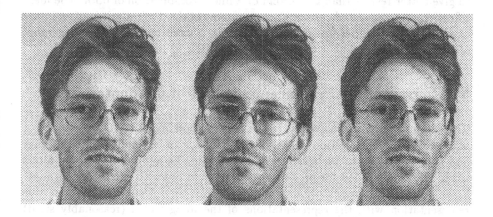

Fig. 8. Image A (left) is mapped onto image B (middle). The image on the right is obtained by replacing the finest (8×8) blocks of A by the corresponding best-matching blocks of B.

We applied the above described technique to a database of 72 face images of 36 persons, two images per person (this database is a subset of the larger database mentioned above). For each image from the database a dissimilarity measure can be calculated between this image and all other images in the database. Two measures for the dissimilarity of two images A and B were used:

Fig. 9. The same as in the previous figure but for different persons. Although the blocks used to construct the image on the right are taken from image B (middle), the result image is similar to image A (left) suggesting that geometrical relations are more important than (exact) intensity values.

(*i*) the energy of the difference image between image A and an image which is obtained by replacing the finest blocks of A by the corresponding best-matching blocks of image B and (*ii*) the energy in an image which is obtained by computing the divergence of the vector field which maps A onto B. (Fig.8 and Fig.9 illustrate the mapping process.) In practice, the first of these quantities proved to give better results than the second or a linear combination of both. The identification was considered correct if the minimum of the dissimilarities of an image of a person to all other images in the database was reached for the other image of the same person. This was the case in 66 of the 72 images (91.6%).

5   Computational requirements and implementation

The computational intensiveness of the first method is due to the large number of convolution and selection operations which have to be applied to each image and is proportional to the size of the images and the number of cortical filters used. The time needed for processing an image in order to extract an ultimate lower dimension representation prevails over the time needed to compare this representation with the representations of the images of a (reasonably sized) database.

The computational intensiveness of the second method is due to the matching of blocks and is proportional to the size of the images and the block search space. The problem here is that for each input image pair-wise image comparisons to all images in the database have to be carried out. (This explains the fact that this second method has only been applied to a subset of the database.)

Both methods were implemented on the Connection Machine CM-5 scale 3 of the University of Groningen (16 nodes, 64 vector units). A few hours vs. a few days computing time were needed to collect the identification rate statistics specified above for the first and the second method, respectively. As compared to a contemporary workstation, an acceleration by a factor ranging between a few dozen and more than hundred was observed.

6 Conclusions and future plans

Cortical images are capable of facilitating the image analysis and object recognition problem in the case of simple input images. As to natural images such as faces, the structure of the cortical images does not propose a straightforward analysis and recognition scheme. Extracting lower dimension representations directly from cortical images gives astonishingly good results, possibly due to the fact that these images encompass important characteristics of natural scenes, but the performance can easily be degraded by artificially constructed examples. The comparison of image representations which preserve the full information whereby the comparison process incorporates a means for tolerating admissible image differences seems to be the right way to go.

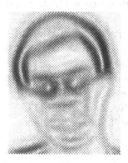

Fig. 10. Superposition of (disjoint) cortical images obtained with cortical filters of the same receptive field size and different preferred orientations.

Our future work will proceed with investigating the possibility to adapt the above sketched optical flow method to sets of cortical images. A further direction of research will be to explore the possibility to use cortical images in order to solve the classification problem, i.e. to recognize a face as a face independently of its particular form. Fig.10 illustrates our current attempts in this direction. The shown image, computed as a combination of cortical images, contains a pattern which is common for almost all face images (a large semi-circle due to the boundary between the head and the background and two smaller thick circles due to the eyes) and is simple enough to be learned by a neural network classifier with non-supervised learning. An output unit of such a network which is activated by such an input pattern may well correspond to face (broadly) tuned neural cells found in deeper cortical structures of monkeys. Further research will focus on computing and using cortical images which correspond to so-called complex cells and grating cells which do not abide to the simple cell model.

Acknowledgements

The investments in the Connection Machine CM-5 of the University of Groningen were partly supported by the Netherlands Computer Science Research Foundation (SION) and the Netherlands Organisation for Scientific Research (NWO). I also gratefully appreciate the technical support of my PhD students P. Kruizinga and T. Lourens in the preparation of the figures for this paper.

References

1. *Grand Challenges: High Performance Computing and Communications*, The FY 1992 U.S. Research and Development Program.
2. N. Petkov, T. Lourens and P. Kruizinga: "Lateral inhibition in cortical filters", Proc. of *Int. Conf. on Digital Signal Processing and Int. Conf. on Computer Applications to Engineering Systems*, July 14-16, 1993, Nicosia, Cyprus, pp.122-129.
3. N. Petkov, T. Lourens and P. Kruizinga: "Orientation competition in cortical filters - An application to face recognition", *Comp. Sci. in The Netherlands 1993*, Nov. 9-10, 1993, Utrecht (Stichting Math. Centrum: Amsterdam, 1993) pp.285-296.
4. D. Hubel and T. Wiesel: "Receptive fields, binocular interaction, and functional architecture in the cat's visual cortex", *J. Physiol.(London)*, 1962, vol. 160, pp. 106-154.
5. J.P. Jones and L.A. Palmer: "An evaluation of the two-dimensional Gabor filter model of simple receptive fields in cat striate cortex", *Journal of Neurophysiology*, Vol.58 (1987) pp. 1233-1258.
6. J.G. Daugman: "Complete discrete 2-D Gabor transforms by neural networks for image analysis and compression", *IEEE Trans. on Acoustics, Speech and Signal Processing*, Vol.36 (1988) No. 7, pp. 1169-1179.
7. N. Petkov, P. Kruizinga and T. Lourens: "Biologically Motivated Approach to Face Recognition", *Proc. International Workshop on Artificial Neural Networks*, June 9-11, 1993, Sitges (Barcelona), Spain (Berlin: Springer Verlag, 1993) pp.68-77
8. N. Petkov and T. Lourens: "Human Visual System Simulations - An Application to Face Recognition", in H. Dedieu (ed.) Proc. 1993 European Conf. on *Circuit Theory and Design*, Aug. 30 - Sept. 3, 1993, Davos, Switzerland (Amsterdam: Elsevier Sci. Publ., 1993) pp.821-826.
9. N. Petkov and T. Lourens: "Interacting cortical filters for object recognition", Proc. of *Asian Conference on Computer Vision*, Nov. 23-25, 1993, Osaka, Japan
10. T. Lourens, N. Petkov and P. Kruizinga: "Large scale natural vision simulations", Proc. *High Performance Computing and Networking 93* Conference, 17-19 May, Amsterdam (Amsterdam: Elsevier Sci. Publ., 1994, in print)
11. P. Kruizinga, N. Petkov: "Optical flow applied to person identification", in J.C. Zuidervaart and L. Dekker (eds.) *Proc. of the 1994 EUROSIM Conference on Massively Parallel Processing*, June 21-23, 1994, Delft, The Netherlands (Amsterdam: Elsevier Sci. Publ., 1994, in print).
12. D.J. Heeger: "Model for the extraction of image flow", *Journ. Opt. Soc. Am. A*, Vol.3 (1987) No.8, pp.1455-1471.
13. J.L. Barron, D.J. Fleet, S.S. Beauchemin and T.A. Burkitt: "Performance of optical flow techniques", Technical Report TR-299, University of Western Ontario, Dept. of Computer Science, 1993.

A Transputer Based Visually Guided Robot System Using Neuro-Control

S. Hagmann   H. Kihl   D. Kuhn   J.-P. Urban

Laboratoire TROP, Faculté des Sciences et Techniques
Université de Haute Alsace
F-68093 Mulhouse, France
e-mail: hagmann@univ-mulhouse.fr

Abstract. This paper presents an entirely Transputer based system conceived to investigate the performance of different types of neural networks applied to robot-control. A robot of 5 degrees of freedom is to be controlled by an unsupervised associative neural network relying on visual feedback. The modular concept of the system allows to easily upgrade processing power and to add optional extensions. Training and performance testing are supported by a Silicon Graphics Workstation.

1. Introduction

For most of the higher evolved biological organisms, *visual feedback* plays an important part for their movement control. Provided with such a feedback, their brains are able to perform an accurate sensory-motor coordination and to adapt to unanticipated changes in the environment. Recent theoretical research in the domain of neural networks proposed to apply similar, biologically oriented control mechanisms to robot control. This approach promises to obtain more adaptive robot controllers than those based on classical algorithms. Studies of [Rit 90] and [Kup 91] have demonstrated that a visually guided robot-controller based on artificial neural networks (ANN) is able to learn the association between a stereoscopic image of a target in 3D space and a robot joint angle vector. Until now, several learning algorithms for neuro-controllers have been formulated and simulated but rarely tested on real applications appropriate for industrial purposes.

In this paper we present an entirely Transputer-based system which is conceived to serve as an experimental platform for testing the performance of different neuro-controllers when applied to real applications. It consists of a robot manipulator of 5 degrees of freedoms (5 joints and a parallel jaw gripper) similar to those most currently used in industry, an image acquisition system and a modular processing unit based on Transputer technology, which contains the ANN. In a first approach, the neuro-controller should learn to make the robot perform simple grasping tasks in space by evaluating the visual feedback.

Learning has to be achieved without a teacher and must result in an adaptive control which maintains the accurate performance of the robot even if unpredictable changes in geometrical, mechanical or sensing parameters occur. A Silicon Graphics (SG) workstation is dedicated to simulate the robot and its environment in order to supply the ANN with an artificially generated training set and to test previously trained neuro-controllers.

For the design of the system, several limiting factors had to be taken into account:
• In order to perform the complex calculations of the ANN in real time, parallel processors whose number can be easily increased are indispensable.
• For industrial purposes, an optimal cost/performance ratio has to be obtained. Therefore, a relatively cheap core system had to be developed, providing the possibility to add optional modules.
• The communication between the different units should be fast and homogeneous.
• The developed code has to be processor independent and should be portable to further computer generations.

Guided by these considerations we opted for Inmos TRAnsputer Modules (TRAMs) as the base part of the entire system. They are largely available and provide the option to easily extend the system. Our first application uses T805 processors and will later be upgraded to T9000 technology.

The system is currently being developed in our laboratory and should result in a highly adaptable visually guided neuro-controller suitable for industrial purposes. Requiring a minimum of supervision by an operator, possible applications range from automation tasks to manipulations in locations with restricted access.

2. Neural Network Approach

Recently there has been a considerable growth of interest in establishing a direct connection between vision and robot action through neural networks. Backpropagation networks can effectively simulate a nonlinear function. For instance, Kuperstein trained a backpropagation network to generate an association between a visually defined target and a robot joint angle vector [Kup 91].

Ritter, et al, formed an association between a pair of position vectors representing the images of a 3D target point on the camera retinas and a joint angle vector, where individual pairs of position vectors are organized into a 3D feature map based on Kohonen's self-organizing learning [Rit 90]. The use of control loops and Self-Organization Maps (SOM) ensures both a fast learning of the algorithm and a good working precision [Wal 93].

In a Kohonen type of network [Koh 84], each neuron represents a part of the input space and associates the corresponding output vector. We are currently implementing different modified versions of Kohonen's basic algorithm in order to optimize the neighborhood during the learning phase and to obtain a continuous approximation of the desired function. The basic robotic task we address is the positioning of the end-effector of the arm relatively to a known object seen by a stereoscopic vision system (see Fig. 2.1).

For the moment, we keep the image processing simple and extract only the coordinates Im of the center of gravity of a well-contrasted object. The sensory data contains *Im* and the joint positions of the arm and the head Θr, Θe, Xh. The problem is separated into 3 independent closed-loop functions implemented with associative neural networks (AsNN).

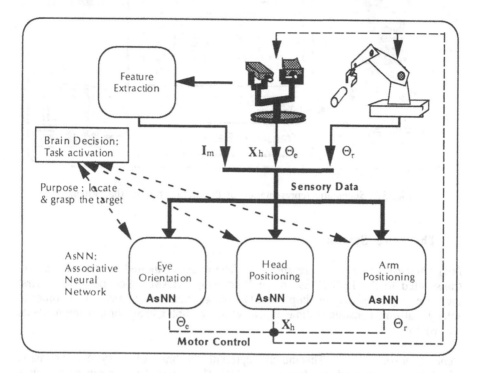

Fig. 2.1. Functional diagram of the robot-camera system

The hardware architecture is designed to allow a real-time implementation. The different AsNN and the feature extraction can be implemented separately and concurrently. Moreover, each AsNN can be efficiently parallelized if required by real-time implementation constraints [Aug 90].

3. Architecture Setup

Figure 3.1. shows a schematic presentation of the architecture of the system. Two video cameras are mounted on a robotic head, thus capturing two different 2-D images of the robot and its environment. These images are subsequently fed into the processing unit consisting of several TRAMs located on a Transputer motherboard (currently on a IMS B008) and communicating via pairs of unidirectional serial links. We first explain the modules constituting the core system and then describe any optional extensions.

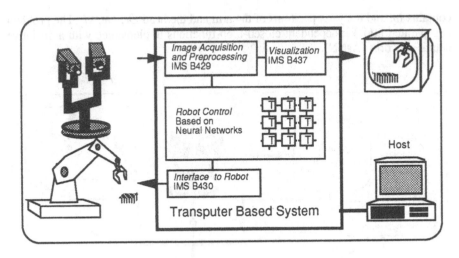

Fig. 3.1. Schematic representation of the architecture of the system

3.1 The Core System

Image Acquisition and Preprocessing.   The images captured by the cameras are transmitted to the IMS B429 Image Processing TRAM which performs a first preprocessing consisting of simple and fast image enhancement methods. In order to satisfy real-time constraints, time-expensive and complex image processing methods are avoided.

Robot Control.   This module represents the 'brain' of the system. It consists of a Transputer network and houses the ANN. The size of the Transputer network is held variable and can be adjusted to the complexity of the ANN by adding the appropriate number of Transputers such that the complex calculations of the ANN can be executed in parallel. In a first approach, the ANN is used for the robot-control, but neither for camera adjustment nor for positioning the robotic head which carries the cameras. The *Robot Control* module receives the preprocessed images, extracts their main features and passes the data to the ANN, which subsequently calculates the appropriate robot angle vector.

Interface to the Robot.   This module is responsible for positioning the robot according to the angle vector received from the *Robot Control* module. It consists of an IMS B430 Prototyping TRAM and includes a control unit which commands each of the motors used for the robot movements.

3.2. Optional Extensions

Further *Image Acquisition* modules can be added to the system, either in order to preprocess the 2 captured images in parallel or to support additional cameras.

For the future development, Interface modules controlling the camera adjustment and their position will be added to the system. The ANN, being in charge of controlling these devices, will be correspondingly upgraded by increasing the number of Transputers in the *Robot Control* module.

A *Visualization* module based on an IMS B437 Graphics Display TRAM can be linked to the *Image Acquisition* in order to visualize the preprocessed images on a monitor and to improve the quality of feedback/control for a human operator or developer.

The communication between an operator/developer and the system is realized by a connected host.

4. Simulation Procedure

During its learning phase, an ANN has to be supplied with a considerable number of training vectors. For the neuro-controller, these input-stimuli are stereoscopic images representing the robot in various positions and in a changing environment (e.g. light sources, camera positions).

In order to avoid positioning the manipulator thousands of times during the training period, we supply the ANN with artificially generated images obtained by simulations on the SG workstation, taking into account any possible factors which could influence the behavior of the robot (see Fig. 4.1). The ANN resides throughout the training phase in its final environment and benefits from the parallel power of the Transputer network.

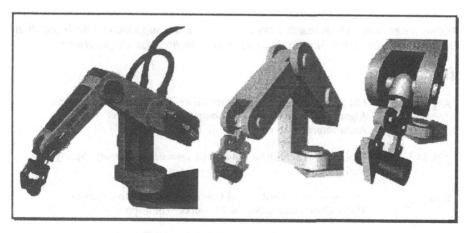

Fig. 4.1. Real photo (left) and synthesized images (middle and right) of the robot at identical angle adjustments and different camera positions.

The transfer of the images between the SG and the ANN requires a high data transfer rate and will be established by a fast SCSI link (see Fig. 4.2). Feeding back the output of the ANN to the SG and calculating the corresponding position of the robot allows to generate a sequence of images which can either be used as subsequent input stimuli or for testing the performance of a previously trained ANN.

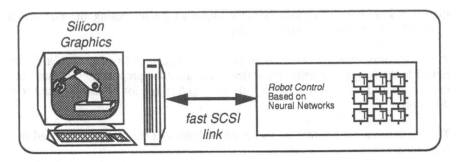

Fig 4.2. Setup for training or testing the ANN with simulation routines. The real robot and cameras have been replaced by simulation routines on the SG workstation.

5. Conclusion and Perspectives

The proper working of the individual modules is guaranteed and a first prototype of the system in T805 technology is implemented. In a first approach, the system of image acquisition is simplified to a pair of stationary cameras. A modified Kohonen ANN with the task to position the robot to an object of cylindrical shape is being examined. Further development will concentrate on the control of the robotic head performing the positioning and adjustment of the cameras. In a later version, the implementation on T9000 Transputers is planned, and these devices will, in due course, offer substantial performance improvements.

Acknowledgements. The research work of S. Hagmann is supported by the foundation *Deutscher Akademischer Austauschdienst, zweites Hochschulsonderprogramm.*

Bibliography

[Aug 90]	J.M Auger, Parallel Implementation on Transputers of Kohonen's Algorithms, Euro Courses in Computing with Parallel Architectures, September 10-14, 1990.
[Koh 84]	T. Kohonen, Self-Organization and associative Memory, Springer-Verlag 1984.
[Kup 91]	M. Kuperstein, Infant Neural Controller for Adaptive Sensory-Motor Coordination, Neural Networks, Vol 4, pp 131-145, 1991.
[Rit 90]	H.J. Ritter, T.M. Martinetz , K.J. Schulten, Three-dimensional Neural Net for Learning Visuomotor Coordination of a robot arm, IEEE Transactions on Neural Networks, Vol 1, pp 131-136, 1990.
[Wal 93]	J.A. Walter, K.J. Schulten, Implementation of Self-Organizing Neural Networks for Visuo-Motor Control of an Industrial Robot, IEEE Transactions on Neural Networks, Vol 4, pp 86-95, 1993.

A Scalable Performance Prediction Method for Parallel Neural Network Simulations

Louis Vuurpijl, Theo Schouten and Jan Vytopil

University of Nijmegen, Toernooiveld 1, 6525 ED Nijmegen, The Netherlands
phone: +31 80 652710, fax: +31 80 553450, email: louis@cs.kun.nl

Abstract. A performance prediction method is presented for indicating the performance range of MIMD parallel processor systems for neural network simulations. The total execution time of a parallel application is modeled as the sum of its calculation and communication times. The method is scalable because based on the times measured on one processor and one communication link, the performance, speedup, and efficiency can be predicted for a larger processor system. It is validated quantitatively by applying it to two popular neural networks, backpropagation and the Kohonen self-organizing feature map, decomposed on a GCel-512, a 512 transputer system. Agreement of the model with the measurements is within 9%.

1 Introduction

In this paper a method is presented for predicting the performance of large MIMD systems for parallel neural network simulations. Using the method, also predictions can be given for the speedups and efficiencies that can be achieved. The total execution time of an application is modeled as the sum of its calculation and communication times. For a neural network simulation with n neurons, w connections and p patterns running on a platform with P processors this is defined as:

$$T(P, n, w, p) = T_{calc}(P, n, w, p) + T_{comm}(P, n, w, p) \tag{1}$$

The calculation time T_{calc} can be modeled as the sum of the times required for executing a small number of *kernel* functions (e.g. compute a weight change, update a connection, update a neuron). These are executed a large number of times N_i (e.g. per connection or per neuron), where each N_i costs time t_i:

$$T_{calc}(P, n, w, p) = \frac{1}{P} \sum_i N_i(n, w, p)\, t_i \tag{2}$$

The communication time is modeled as the number of times a single information unit (e.g. a connection or activation value) must be sent over a physical communication link (modeled as $C(P, n, w, p)$), multiplied by the time required for communicating one value:

$$T_{comm}(P, n, w, p) = C(P, n, w, p)\, t_{comm} \tag{3}$$

If required by the hardware resources or communication requirements of the neural network, a more complicated model can be used. The needed benchmarks in our method are restricted to measuring the execution time of a small number of kernel functions on one processor and the time needed to communicate a single information unit between two processors. This approach can be classified as kernel benchmarking [2]. In the subsequent sections, our method is validated quantitatively by predicting the performance of the GCel-512 (a 512 multi-transputer system) for backpropagation [6] and Kohonen [3] neural networks decomposed via a technique called dataset decomposition.

2 Dataset decomposition of neural network simulations

The problem of decomposing a given neural network over a parallel processor system with given topology has often been addressed in the literature. Chu and Wah [1], Witbrock and Zagha [8] and various other authors have discussed the parallel implementation of backpropagation networks. Similar efforts have been reported implementing Kohonen networks by for example Obermayer *et al* [5]. Various techniques can be used to decompose a neural network over a number of processors. In this paper, the attention is focussed on dataset decomposition of backpropagation [6] and Kohonen [3] neural networks. Using this technique, each processor has a copy of the network, initiated with the same parameters and architecture. The parallelism that is exploited in this technique stems from the dataset. The patterns contained in this set are equally divided over the available processors and each network copy operates on its local subset. Especially for large datasets, dataset decomposition is a highly efficient parallelization technique as during the computation of the data subsets no communication is necessary.

2.1 Calculation costs of dataset decomposed neural networks

Algorithm 1 describes the heuristics for dataset decomposed neural networks. First, the dataset is distributed over the available processors (step 1). Then, a number of *epochs* are performed. During each epoch, each network copy is trained with all local patterns and computes its weight changes based on them (step 2 is performed for each pattern). After learning all local patterns, the weight changes are communicated (step 3). Finally, in step 4 each network copy updates its connections based on the accumulated weight changes.

```
step 1:    distribute_patterns();
           do_epoch:
           {   for (all patterns p)
step 2:            compute_weight_changes(p);
step 3:            communicate_weight_changes();
step 4:            update_connections();            }
```

Algorithm 1: General heuristic for dataset decomposed PNNs.

Steps 2 to 4 are repeated until the number of epochs has passed a certain value or the neural network has reached a certain error criterion. The total calculation times per epoch consist of the times for step 2 times the number of patterns and the times for step 4 (4). The equation has as parameters the number of patterns p and the network size expressed in number of neurons n and number of connections w.

$$T_{calc}(p, n, w) = p \cdot T_{step2}(n, w) + T_{step4}(n, w) \tag{4}$$

We have measured the typical routines contained in steps 2 and 4 for backpropagation and Kohonen neural networks on one GCel-512 node (respectively 4 and 3 function kernels). The GCel-512 is a 512 multi-transputer machine arranged in a 16x32 grid topology. It is controlled by the Parix operating system. Each node is a T805 transputer running on 30MHz with 4MByte RAM. All programs used for the subsequent measurements run on this machine and are compiled with the ACE expert C compiler without any optimization options. The software that was written has no specific optimization techniques such as efficient use of stack or register variables.

2.2 Communication costs for dataset decomposed neural networks

Parallel neural network simulations decomposed via dataset decomposition require all-to-all communications. In step 3 of algorithm 1, every processor needs the weight changes that are computed on every other processor. In [7], a detailed description of the different patterns of communication required for parallel neural network simulations is given. It is explained that the number of communications can be reduced enormously by using only local communications. This can be established via broadcast and gather operations. All-to-all communications are then implemented by subsequently gathering and broadcasting messages. In the case of dataset decomposition, during the gathering also the accumulation of the weight changes can take place, which can be done in parallel. For these kind of gather-accumulate and broadcast operations, a tree topology is optimal [7]. Unfortunately, the GCel does not support the physical configuration of tree topologies. We have tried to use virtual tree topologies by using the Parix MakeTree utility, but the performance of the communication was far worse than using the physical grid topology and communicating locally. Furthermore, the mapping of a tree on the GCel grid gave unpredictable results. One would expect that the larger the grid on which a tree can be mapped, the better the mapping result. However, this appeared not to be the case.

The neural network implementations used in this paper use a so called master-slave decomposition. The master process runs on processor (0,0) in the grid, the slave processes run on the other processors. The communications required in steps 1 and 3 in algorithm 1 are performed using broadcast and gather primitives. Each broadcast operation from the master to every slave requires

$width + height - 2$ communications. Each gather and accumulation operation requires the same amount. The communication benchmarks required for our model only consist of measurements over one physical communication link. The raw communication times for communicating w connections are expressed as $T_{comm}(w)$. The required accumulation benchmarks are performed on one processor and consist of the time needed to sum up two amounts of w connections, which is expressed as $T_{acc}(w)$. The total times for broadcasting (B), gathering (G) and accumulating (A) are depicted in (5).

$$GAB(P, w) = (width + height - 2) \cdot (2 \cdot T_{comm}(w) + T_{acc}(w))) \tag{5}$$

We have used the SendLink and RecvLink communication library routines of Parix. These resulted in a communication time of $T_{comm}(w) = 3.59 \cdot w + 50$ μseconds, where each connection is represented with single precision floating point. The setup time can usually be neglected, as w is relatively large. For the accumulation time, we have measured $T_{acc}(w) = 5.59 \cdot w$ μseconds. The results of experiments on different grid sizes indicate that by measuring the communication times for one transputer link and the accumulation times for one transputer enables the prediction of the times on any transputer grid, within a precision of 4%-9%.

2.3 Performance, speedup and efficiency

The performance expressed in MCUPS can be calculated by dividing the number of connections that are updated by the total time (in μseconds):

$$MCUPS(P, p, n, w) = \frac{p \cdot w}{T(P, p, n, w)} \tag{6}$$

For each of the experiments reported below, a network size of 100000 connections is used. The backpropagation architecture is a 250x200x250 network, the Kohonen map is 50x50 and has 40 inputs. Figure 1(a) plots the measured performance expressed in MCUPS for backpropagation networks, with problem sizes from 1 to 1000 patterns per processor. The performance is predicted correctly within 4%-9% (which corresponds to the deviations of the predicted values for the communication and calculation times). We have measured that even for relatively small (1 Kweights) networks, the prediction appears to be correct within 9%. Figure 1(b) depicts the measured performance expressed in MCUPS for Kohonen networks. Because the measured and expected calculation times match better compared to the backpropagation network, the performance can be predicted with even higher precision ($< 1\%$).

The expected speedup is computed as:

$$S(P, p, n, w) = T(1, p, n, w)/T(P, p, n, w)$$

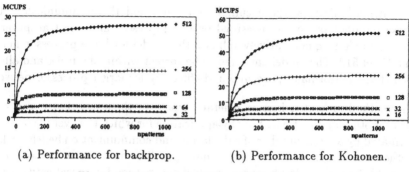

(a) Performance for backprop.　　　(b) Performance for Kohonen.

Fig. 1. Performance of different GCel grids.

The obtained speedups are depicted in the figures 2(a) and 2(b) and agree within 1%-9% with the predicted values. Note that the larger the problem size, the higher the speedups that are achieved, which is due to the communication computation trade-off. The more work each processor has to do, the less the performance is influenced by the communication overheads. Note also that only for small problems (less than 10 patterns per processor) the speedup limit is reached.

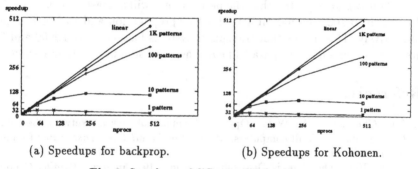

(a) Speedups for backprop.　　　(b) Speedups for Kohonen.

Fig. 2. Speedups of different GCel grids.

The efficiency of a parallel program is defined as $E(P, p, n, w) = S(P, p, n, w)/P$. Ideally, the efficiency equals 1 which corresponds to having linear speedups. As can be observed from figures 1(a) and 1(b), parallel neural network simulations decomposed via dataset decomposition can achieve high efficiencies depending on the load per processor. For example a backpropagation network running on 512 processors has efficiencies ranging from $E(512, 512, n, w) \approx 0.03$ up to $E(512, 512K, n, w) \approx 0.92$, where (n, w) corresponds to the neural networks as specified above.

3　Conclusions

We have presented a method for predicting the performance of a MIMD execution platform for parallel neural network simulations. The model used is based on only a small number of parameters that depend on the execution platform:

the calculation times, the accumulation times and the communication times. These parameters can be measured on one processor and one transputer link. We were able to quantitatively validate the model for large processor networks on a GCel-512. The model appeared to be correct within about 9% and allows to predict the performance, speedup and efficiency for larger processor networks.

The method presented here is general purpose in the sense that it can also be used for other applications. For any application for which the overall costs can be estimated by a small number of calculation and communication benchmarks, the method can be applied. For example many parallel image processing applications show this behaviour. We have also applied our method for neural networks using other decomposition techniques than dataset decomposition [7].

It is interesting to make some predictions for the T9000 transputer, extrapolating the measured parameters on the T805 by dividing them by the increased computing and communication powers of the T9000. Based on the information in [4], one could roughly say that the T9000 is about 8 times faster than the T805 and has about 6 times higher bandwidth. Furthermore, we expect that when exploiting the new C104 communication chips, it will be cheaper to use all-to-all communications, thus reducing the communication times. From equation (1) it can be expected that the performance will at least increase by a factor 6 to 8, up to 200 and 400 MCUPS for backpropagation and Kohonen networks respectively. This means that transputer systems based on the T9000 and C104, are even better suited for parallel neural network simulations than current ones.

References

1. L-C. Chu and B.W. Wah. Optimal Mapping of Neural Network Learning on Message-Passing Multicomputers. *Journal of Parallel and Distributed Computing*, 14:319–339, 1992.
2. A.J.G. Hey. The Genesis Distributed Memory Benchmarks. *Parallel Computing*, 17(2):1275–1283, 1991.
3. T. Kohonen. *Self-Organization and Associative Memory*. Springer Verlag, Berlin, second edition, 1988.
4. Inmos/SGS-Thomson Microelectronics. The T9000 Transputer Product Overview, 1991.
5. K. Obermayer, H.Heller, H. Ritter, and K. Schulten. Simulation of Self-Organizing Neural Nets: a Comparison between a Transputer Ring and a Connection Machine CM-2. In *Proceedings of the Third Conference of NATUG*, Sunnyvale, CA, 1990.
6. D.E. Rumelhart and J.L. McClelland. *Parallel Distributed Processing: Explorations in the Microstructure of Cognition*, volume 1. MIT Press, 1986.
7. L.G. Vuurpijl and Th.E. Schouten. Performance of MIMD Execution Platforms for PNNs: How many MCUPS? Technical report, Department of Real-Time Systems, Faculty of Mathematics and Informatics, University of Nijmegen, Toernooiveld 1, 6525 ED Nijmegen, The Netherlands, August 1993. In progress.
8. M. Witbrock and M. Zagha. An Implementation of Backpropagation Learning on GF11, a Large SIMD Parallel Computer. *Parallel Computing*, 14:329–346, 1990.

PREENS, a Parallel Research Execution Environment for Neural Systems

Louis Vuurpijl, Theo Schouten and Jan Vytopil

University of Nijmegen, Toernooiveld 1, 6525 ED Nijmegen, The Netherlands
phone: +31 80 652710, fax: +31 80 553450, email: louis@cs.kun.nl

Abstract. PREENS – a Parallel Research Execution Environment for Neural Systems – is a distributed neurosimulator, targeted on networks of workstations and transputer systems. As current applications of neural networks often contain large amounts of data and as the neural networks involved in tasks such as vision are very large, high requirements on memory and computational resources are imposed on the target execution platforms. PREENS can be executed in a distributed environment, i.e. tools and neural network simulation programs can be running on any machine connectable via TCP/IP. Using this approach, larger tasks and more data can be examined using an efficient coarse grained parallelism. Furthermore, the design of PREENS allows for neural networks to be running on any high performance MIMD machine such as a transputer system. In this paper, the different features and design concepts of PREENS are discussed. These can also be used for other applications, like image processing.

1 Introduction

A neurosimulator is a toolbox containing tools for monitoring, manipulating, controlling and executing neural network simulation programs. Current neurosimulators [1] such as the RCS [3], Pygmalion [1] Genesis [13], Planet [8], and others are all based on a general neural network datastructure or some neural network description language (NDL). Using a hierarchical description of its architecture, the neurosimulator is able to access the data associated with the neural network. Also, in many cases the execution of a neural network program is performed based on the data dependency between different neural network components as described in the NDL. This approach requires neural networks to be specified in a prescribed standard manner, which usually means that their implementations are not as efficient as would be the case with implementations specifically designed for a neural network and target execution platform. Furthermore, it forces neural network programmers to program their applications following the NDL syntax or using some set of neural network library routines.

PREENS is an execution environment that supports the execution, monitoring and control of neural network simulations. The construction of simulation

---

[1] For a taxonomy over neurosimulators, see [9]

programs is not supported, to develop a simulation program general programming tools have to be used. Thus unlike existing neurosimulators, in PREENS neural network programs do not have to be specified following the syntax of some general neural network description datastructure. This has the advantage that simulation programs can be efficiently coded and that the programmer has full control over his programs, so new algorithms and applications can be tailor made. Each neural network simulation can be implemented specifically targeted on a certain machine architecture or using the most appropriate datastructures and flow of control.

Based on the observations that neural network simulation programs all have a similar structure and furthermore in general are relatively easy to implement, PREENS uses a conceptual model of *programs* rather than of neural *networks*. In the conceptual model, a program is described via the actions that can be executed. Each program implements a limited number of such actions, e.g. loading of a network or patterns and training, recalling or classifying a set of patterns. Each action can have parameters for initiating it, variables and data that change during execution, and options and settings that guide the program's flow of control. For example, consider table 1 for some sample actions with corresponding parameters, variables etc. In this table, the action **load_patterns** has as parameter the filename from which to load the patterns and as data object the datastructure containing the patterns. Furthermore, it as the setting **normalize** which can be on or off for indicating whether the loaded data has to be normalized or not and it has an option **which_patterns** which can select whether either training data, recall data or data to be classified has to be loaded:

action	parameters	variables	data	settings	options
load_patterns	filename		patterns	normalize	which_patterns
recall		% correct	output		
train	learning rate	error	weights, activations	use_noise	batch_update

Table 1. Actions, parameters, etc.

By examining a program description containing the actions and corresponding objects, PREENS is able to create a user-interface *convis* that enables *control* over the program and allows manipulation and *visualization* of the objects it contains. Furthermore, it features a data communication interface via which objects can be linked with tools running on any machine connectable to the one convis is running on. Each neural network simulation program is equipped with an interface to convis that "listens" to commands of the user-interface, and examines which program objects have to receive or send information to or from tools. For an overview of PREENS and how it interacts through convis and the data communication interface with running tools and neural network simulation programs, see figure 1.

Note that PREENS fully exploits the availability of workstations in a network environment. As tools, convis and the neural network simulation can be

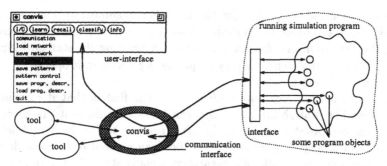

Fig. 1. The PREENS architecture

run on any machine, the environment can be executed in parallel. Therefore, it can operate faster and handle larger amounts of data than current neurosimulators. Currently, PREENS can handle tools and simulation programs running on workstations and transputer systems. It has been successfully tested on heterogeneous processor networks consisting of Dec and Sun workstations and a Parsytec transputer system.

2 Integrating PREENS with tools

As introduced above, PREENS consist of a manager and user-interface (convis), a data communication interface, a set of tools and an algorithm library. Furthermore, it features a set of interface definitions that can be used to integrate it with (new) tools and neural network algorithms. For any specific neural network application, some standard tools can be used for e.g. monitoring the evolution of weight space during training, monitoring error plots, etc. These tools are also contained in the current PREENS toolset. However in many cases also some application specific tools are used, such as a CCD-camera with framegrabber inputting data online to the running simulation program, some special weight monitoring tools (e.g. a U-matrix displayer [11] or the hyperplane animator [4]), or high quality data processing tools such as Matlab [7].

If new tools have to be added to the environment, only three interface routines have to be used, the first to setup the communication with convis, the second to find out about the data that the tool will be supplied with and the third to communicate data between a neural network simulation program and the tool. The following pseudo-code gives an idea about how this is done:

```
init_communication(host,port); /*   initiates a socket connection  */
ReceiveDataDescription(&data); /*   finds out about  the data and  */
while(...)                     /*            allocates it          */
    ReceiveData(&data);        /* receives the data sent by convis */
    HandleData(data);          /*          tool specific           */
```

The last routine is specific for the tool. For example, we have equipped PREENS with an engine for Matlab following the concept described above by storing the data in matrix format in a file and redirecting the standard input of Matlab to a pipe that sends display or processing commands operating on the data contained in the file.

This approach has two major advantages. The first is that if compute intensive tools like Matlab are used, they can be run on different machines thus reducing the computational load of the machine(s) on which the neural network simulation is running. The second is that tools can be used to examine data online. For example neural network researchers usually store their data at certain time steps during a training process, then start up a tool like Matlab, load the data and process it. Using PREENS, they can define a data object, connect it via convis to a dynamic data evaluation tool, mark the object for examination and watch its evolution online.

3 Integrating PREENS with neural network algorithms

The current PREENS algorithm library contains implementations of backpropagation [10], Kohonen [6], ART[2], Boltzmann Perceptron [5] and other neural network paradigms. If a new neural network algorithm has to be included in the PREENS algorithm library, its program description has to be specified and each action that is contained in the description has to be implemented. Furthermore, a main loop has to be installed that knows about the neural network simulation program by examining its program description. Actions contained in the description can be called via the user-interface. If an action needs to be controllable, i.e. it must be able to interrupt it and view or edit its corresponding objects, a special interface routine called action_control has to be incorporated within the code. For example, consider the following code that implements a typical action train:

```
int train (Action *train, ...)
    while (error_not_reached && niterations-- && action_control(train))
        do_train;
```

No restrictions are made about the way in which the training algorithm do_train is implemented. This involves that neural network programmers can use their own programming style and can tailor their application to their own needs. The conditional statement in the while loop contains two stopping criteria as defined by the training algorithm, and the interface routine action_control. The latter examines the program description associated with the action train and sends each corresponding object that needs to be monitored to convis. Each object can be annotated with timing information denoting the interval at which it has to be monitored. Furthermore, the routine listens for interrupts from the user-interface or for incoming data. If such events occur, the training procedure is exited and the main loop is re-entered. Any user commands can than be handled or incoming data can be received.

4 PREENS and parallel neural network simulations

As explained above, the main loop listens to update, request and control commands from convis. For each object contained in a neural network simulation program, new values received from input tools or entered by a user via the user-interface are accessed via the program description. If the neural network program is a parallel implementation running on e.g. a transputer system, new values have to be made available through the processor network. Similarly, if values have to be extracted from the simulation program, they have to be somehow gathered from the processor network. PREENS contains a distributed interface for broadcasting and gathering distributed data objects and commands between convis and a parallel simulation program. The current version supports parallel implementations decomposed via the coarse grained dataset decomposition technique [12]. As with this technique each processor hosts the same neural network, there is no problem with gathering and broadcasting distributed information. For applications which use other decomposition techniques, a set of communication routines is being supplied that support gathering and broadcasting of distributed information.

The distributed interface assumes master-slave implementations of the neural networks, where the master distributes commands and transmits data with the slaves. For distributing and gathering data that is distributed over the processor network, a set of data communication routines is provided. This set can be expanded with routines that gather or broadcast distributed data objects that are not structured following the PREENS data formats.

5 Conclusions

We have introduced PREENS, a neurosimulator for distributed environments. PREENS uses the concept of specifying neural network simulation programs via program descriptions containing actions and corresponding objects. Input and output tools for pre- or post processing of data can be bound with individual objects and started on any machine that can be connected with the user-interface convis. New (parallel) neural networks and new tools can be integrated within the PREENS environment using a small set of interface routines and the data communication interface. As neural network programmers do not have to confirm to some general neural network datastructure, the neural network code can be implemented specifically tailored for an application. Furthermore, as the user-interface, tools and neural network program are 'loosely coupled', it is possible to use neural network program code as a standalone program or to fit it in different application codes. This is an important feature for appliers of neural networks who initially want to use a toolbox for tuning and optimizing a specific neural network simulation, and later want to use its code within their own applications.

Using action-oriented program descriptions could also facilitate a means of designing toolboxes for other application areas like image processing. Similar to neural network applications, with image processing a relatively small set of actions can be identified such as loading and storing an image, filtering operations, edge detection, segmentation, etc. The possibility of incorporating these within one toolset and exploiting the resources in a distributed environment by executing them on different processors would justify the use of an approach like we have sketched for PREENS.

References

1. M. Azema-Barac, M. Hewetson, M. Recce, J. Taylor, P. Treleavan, and M. Vellasco. Pygmalion Neural Network Programming Environment. In B. Angeniol and B. Widrow, editors, *International Neural Network Conference*, pages 1237–1244, Paris, July 1990. Kluwer Academic Publishers.
2. G.A. Carpenter and S. Grossberg. A massively parallel architecture for a self-organizing neural pattern recognition machine. *Computer Vision, Graphics, and Image Processing*, 37:54–115, 1987.
3. N.H. Goddard, K.J. Lynne, T. Mintz, and L. Bukys. Rochester Connectionist Simulator. Technical Report 233 (revised), University of Rochester, Computer Science Department, Rochester, New York 14627, October 1989.
4. P. Hoeper. The Neural Network Hyperplane Animator Program V. 2.0 General Description and Applications. available via ftp: cs.rutgers.edu, May 1993.
5. B. Kappen. Using Boltzmann Machines for probability estimation. In S. Gielen and B. Kappen, editors, *ICANN '93*, pages 521–526. Springer-Verlag, September 1993.
6. T. Kohonen. *Self-Organization and Associative Memory*. Springer Verlag, Berlin, second edition, 1988.
7. Mathworks, Cochituate Place 24, Prime Pathway, Natic, Mas 01760. *Matlab, High Performance Numeric Computation and Visualization Software*, 1992. Version 4.0 User's Guide.
8. Y. Miyata. *A User's Guide to PlaNet Version 5.6, A Tool for Constructing, Running and Looking into a PDP Network*. University of Boulder, Computer Science Department, Boulder, January 1991.
9. M.L. Recce, P.V. Rocha, and P.C. Treleaven. Neural Network Programming Environments. In I. Aleksander and J. Taylor, editors, *Artificial Neural Networks 2*, pages 1237–1244. Elsevier Science Publishers, September 1992.
10. D.E. Rumelhart and J.L. McClelland. *Parallel Distributed Processing: Explorations in the Microstructure of Cognition*, volume 1. MIT Press, 1986.
11. A. Ultsch and H.P. Siemon. Exploratory Data Analysis: Using Kohonen Networks on Transputers. Technical Report Bericht Nr. 329, University of Dortmund, Fachbereich Informatik, Postfach 500500, D-4600 Dortmund 50, December 1989.
12. L.G. Vuurpijl and Th.E. Schouten. Suitability of Transputers for Neural Network Simulations. In W. Joosen and E. Milgrom, editors, *Parallel Computing: From Theory to Sound Practice*, pages 528–537. IOS Press, 1992.
13. M.A. Wilson, U.S. Bhalla, J.D. Uhley, and J.M. Bower. Genesis: A System for Simulating Neural Networks. In D.S. Touretzky, editor, *Advances in Neural and Information Processing Systems*, pages 485–492. Morgan Kaufmann, 1989.

Parallel Implementation of Control Tasks for an Automated Stereo Camera Mount.

D. A. Castelow and N. D. Gent

GEC Hirst Research Centre
Elstree Way
Borehamwood
WD6 1RX

Abstract. A system is described which makes use of a high performance mechanical camera mount and parallel processing elements to demonstrate that a surveillance system may be enhanced through automation. The mechanical system provides a controllable platform for a video camera system. The system processes video data to detect and track a moving target and to control the movements of the camera mount so that the target is held in view.

1 System Overview

Many current surveillance systems make use of multiple static cameras to cover a large area or perimeter. A security guard visually scans a bank of monitors in order to detect intruders. This task is intensive and boring and is a good candidate for automation. Some automatic detection systems are already available, but these use static cameras and suffer from high false alarm rates. The system described here uses a high performance camera mount to dynamically steer the focus of attention onto objects of interest. This offers the potential of reducing the number of cameras required, and reducing the false alarm rate by reactively observing objects prior to raising an alarm.

Automated control of the camera mount enables the system to follow an intruder once detected. This reduces the likelihood of an intruder leaving the field of view before the security guard can confirm their presence. In addition, the combined mechanical mount and vision system can stabilize the image presented to the security guard against movements induced by windshear. This is a common problem when cameras are mounted on high masts.

The dual requirements of wide area coverage and high resolution require the use and control of zoom lenses. This enables the system to zoom-back giving wide coverage and to zoom-in on objects of interest. The system can automatically direct its attention to where it is needed.

In order to perform these dynamic tasks, the camera mount needs to be capable of high accelerations and precisions. The associated processing system must also be of high performance in order to control the mount in real time.

These requirements led to the construction of a high performance mount and the development of real-time software operating on a network of parallel processors. The development was carried out as part of an ESPRIT project [1].

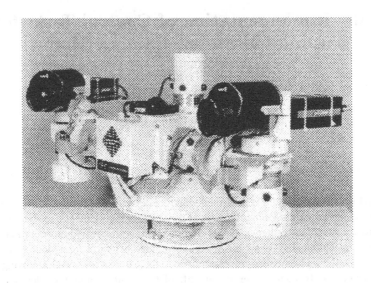

Fig. 1. The GEC High Performance Mount

2 Mount Characteristics

A High Performance Sensor Mount (figure 1) has been developed specifically for the project. The mount [2] carries two standard CCD cameras to enable future stereo imaging. The mount has four mechanical degrees of freedom - a central pan axis, a common elevation axis and two independent vergence axes. The central pan axis is driven through an 80:1 zero-backlash gearbox to give the high acceleration required for tracking moving objects. The vergence and elevation axes are driven directly by high torque DC motors. This enables very precise control to be achieved with no backlash. The lenses each have controllable focus, zoom and iris.

In order to position the mount at the desired angles, non-linear sliding mode control algorithms have been developed. These exploit the full potential of the DC motors to achieve fast, precise, and robust control.

The mount performance is summarized in table 1.

3 Processing Architecture

The processing architecture is shown schematically in figure 2. It consists of three logical blocks - the user interface, the control process and the vision process.

The user interface enables the system to be controlled and the results displayed.

Control processing consists of a hierarchy of control algorithms using a subsumption architecture:

- The behaviour generator acts as a state machine, determining the overall behaviour of the system. This enables complex sequences of behaviours to

Parameter	Vergence Axis	Elevation Axis	Azimuth Axis
Payload mass (kg)	2	–	–
Axis Inertia (kgm^2)	0.02	0.16	7.5
Axis Friction (Nm)	0.04	0.08	–
Axis Freedom ($^\circ$)	±25	$-35 \rightarrow +65$	±190
Maximum slew rate ($^\circ$s^{-1})	200	200	120
Backlash due to end float ($^\circ$)	0.04	0.03	–
Maximum acceleration ($^\circ$s^{-2})	1100	450	200
Angle readout accuracy /resolution ($^\circ$)	0.1 0.005 (16 bit)	0.1 0.005	0.1 0.005
Gear ratio	Direct	Direct	80:1

Table 1. Mount Performance

be realised such as - wait for moving object, rapidly centre object within field of view, track object. If object is lost, return to default position and wait for new object.

– The vision loop runs at video frame rate (25Hz). It determines the desired mount state from the output of the various vision processes and the current behaviour. The vision processes take of the order of 100ms (2-3 frames) to process video data. The vision loop algorithms have been designed to avoid problems associated with processing delays in feedback loops.

– The servo loop performs the most basic servo control function. Every 2ms, the process reads the mount state and calculates the new motor currents necessary to reach the desired state.

Typical digitised video images result in a data throughput of the order of 50Mb/s. In order to avoid the use of dedicated specialised hardware, vision algorithms have been developed which make use of subsampling and windowing. These algorithms, originally developed at Oxford University [3, 4], make full use of the parallelism offered by the INMOS T800 transputers.

The vision processing consists of a number of parallel vision competences such as Coarse Motion Detection, Corner Tracking etc. each with a similar architecture as shown in figure 2. Spatial and pipeline parallelism are utilised to achieve the high processing bandwidths required. The (subsampled and/or windowed) image is spatially tiled and each tile is processed by a pipeline of processors. The results of each of the vision competences are available to the vision loop controller enabling them to be used as required. This modular approach enables the system to be configured for the required behaviours or expanded for future behaviours.

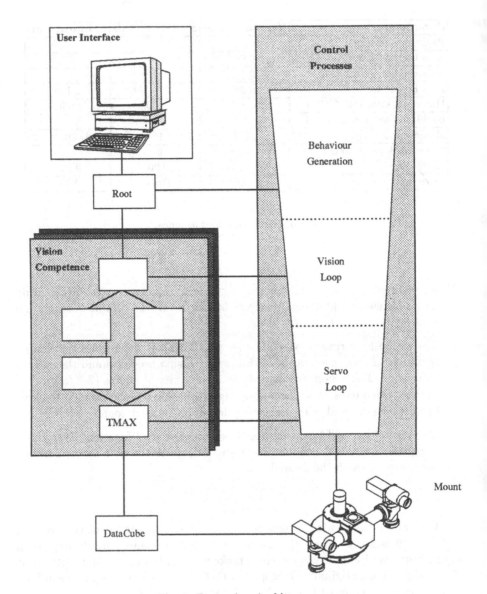

Fig. 2. Processing Architecture

Figure 3 shows a sequence of subsampled images with the results of the coarse motion detection process superimposed. The location, extent and velocity of the moving person are clearly displayed together with their uncertainties. Since the moving object is non-rigid, the coarse motion process often detects several small objects. The final frame shows the results of a simple filter applied to these detections — the object trajectory is clearly recovered. The coarse motion detection algorithm is based on optic flow techniques and, unlike existing frame difference techniques, can detect moving objects while the mount itself is moving.

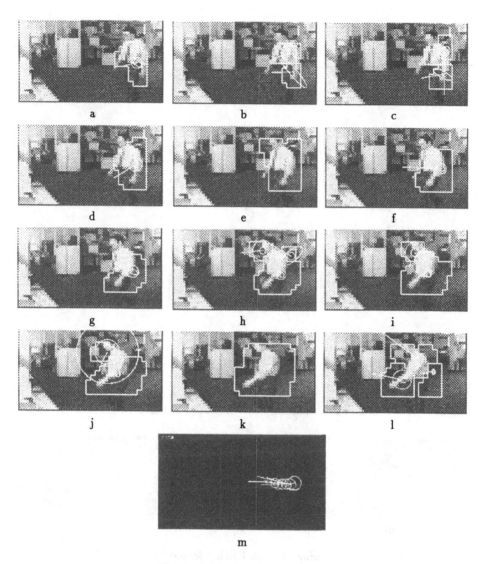

Fig. 3. Coarse Motion Detection

Figure 4 shows the results of using the corner tracker to drive the mount to follow a moving person. A sequence of windowed images with the results of the corner tracker process superimposed. The corner features (indicated by the circles) are tracked from frame to frame. A novel technique, based on affine invariant matching [4], is used to estimate motion of the underlying object (indicated by a cross) from a group of corners. This technique results in a robust object tracker. The face can be seen to remain stationary within the tracking window while the camera moves.

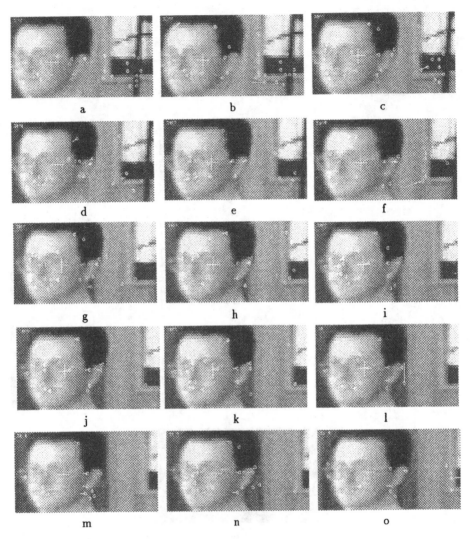

Fig. 4. Corner Tracker Driving Mount Movement

4 Hardware Architecture

The hardware used to implement the control and image processing functions described above consists of a network of transputers. For this application we use the INMOS ANSI-C toolset, a standard implementation of the C language, augmented by library functions for task creation and message passing. The software is readily mapped onto the hardware because of the support for message passing provided by transputers and the associated software.

Access to video data for the image processing sub-systems is available through a number of special purpose transputer modules known as TMAX [5]. These provide a bi-directional interface between the transputers and frame grabbers

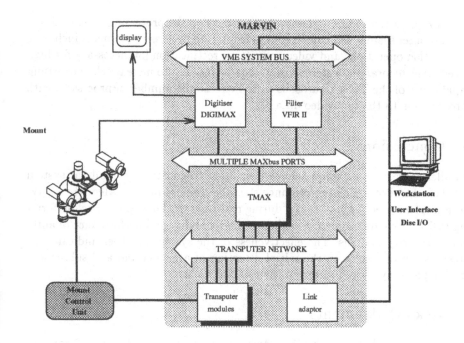

Fig. 5. Hardware Architecture

and stores, using the digital video bus MAXbus developed by DataCube [6]. In addition to the standard transputer links each TMAX card has four possible inputs or outputs. Each camera may be connected to multiple TMAX cards, allowing distribution of images to multiple processors without need to use the limited transputer link bandwidth (insufficient for full frame video at 25Hz). Use of the MAXbus standard has enabled the inclusion of commercial video stream processors, capable of carrying out, for example, convolution operations [7] or more general image manipulations [8], prior to acquisition by the transputer network. The MAXbus also provides a method for the programmer to observe graphically and at video rate data on the TMAX cards. Alternatively, output is available through the transputer links for display under the X Window System via the host workstation. An indication of the potential dataflows is shown in figure 5.

Control of the processing options, for example setting of parameters for the corner detector or coarse motion processes, is possible through use of a GUI on the host workstation.

The system implemented requires the use of 19 T800 transputers, including 6 TMAX cards. The number of TMAX cards used specifically for image processing depends on the number of distinct visual competences. For the coarse motion and corner tracking competences described above, one TMAX card is used as the data source for each competence. The coarse motion competence uses data which is pre-smoothed using 8×8 convolution hardware.

Work is currently in progress to further develop the processing capabilities of the computer system using dedicated video stream processing elements including convolution operations and video rate image rectification [8], necessary for high speed implementation of stereo vision algorithms, and to increase the processing capabilities of the TMAX cards, so as to increase the number of processors with direct access to the raw video data [9].

5 Conclusions

Parallel processing techniques have been used to construct a modular system for the control of a high performance steerable camera mount. Algorithms have been implemented for, and tested during real-time tracking operations, performing tasks which are required to enhance the reliability and performance of automated security systems. The effectiveness of the system has been indicated by presentation of results on the initial detection of a person and and subsequent tracking as they move in front of the camera mount.

6 Ackowledgements

The authors wish to thank GEC-Marconi Ltd and the ESPRIT program for funding the work described in this paper, and to their collaborators in EP 5390: SAGEM, INRIA Sophia Antipolis, and the University of Oxford (Department of Engineering Science).

References

1. Real Time Gaze Control ESPRIT Project 5390.
2. High Performance Sensor Mount - Type RTGC 400. Data Sheet APhD/8001, GEC-Marconi Ltd., Hirst Research Centre, Elstree Way, Borehanwood, Herts., WD6 1RX., 1993.
3. P. F. McLauchlin, I. D. Reid, and D. W. Murray. Coarse image motion for saccade control. In *Proc. BMVC'92, Leeds UK, Sept 1992*, 1992.
4. I. D. Reid and D. W. Murray. Tracking foveated corner clusters using affine structure. In *Proc 4th Int Conf on Computer Vision. Berlin, May 1993*, 1993.
5. B. K. Madahar and S. Cateland. Transputer Interface to MAXBus. The TMAX User Manual. Memo LRRL/63, GEC Hirst Research Centre, Elstree Way, Borehanwood, Herts., WD6 1RX, June 1992.
6. DataCube Inc. MAXBus Specification. Technical Report SPOO-3, 4, Dearborn Road, Peabody, MA., 1986.
7. A Dual Channel 8 × 8 Convolution Module for MAXbus. Technical report, GEC Hirst Research Centre, 1993.
8. A MAXbus Compatible Image Rectification Board. Technical report, GEC Hirst Research Centre, 1993.
9. T2MAX. An enhanced transputer MAXBus interface. Technical report, GEC Hirst Research Centre, 1993.

Simulating Neural Networks on Telmat T-node

Zdenek Hanzalek

Czech Technical University in Prague, Dept. of Control Engineering, Karlovo nam 13, 121 35 Prague 2, Czech Republic, HANZ@RTIME.FELK.CVUT.CZ

Abstract. Simulation programs for neural networks are notorious for being intensive in computations. This poster presents a toroidal lattice architecture used to simulate fully connected neural networks. An attempt is made to see the problem in its global complexity as the system with its own behaviour. First problem is defined, then the effective solution by virtual processors arranged in toroidal lattice architecture is proposed. Then decomposition, data distribution and mapping issues are explained for physical message passing architecture. Finally experimental results are presented.

1 The Algorithm and its Communication Requirements

The neural network (NN) under consideration is a multilayer perceptron using backpropagation learning algorithm. All layers are fully interconnected, the sigmoid activation function is used.

Given algorithm description by generalized Petri net can be done supposing that the transitions correspond to the procedures with input and output data represented by places, the initial markings are representing initial weights generated by random generator and the number of tokens is corresponding to the multiple data use.

When we assume each phase (activation → back prop. → learning →...) as OCCAM process executed in parallel with the other processes, then it is clear that they have to be done in sequence cause of synchronization between processes. If we assume a case when weights are updated in each iteration then the only possibility to make a profit of parallel processing system is to "enter" the mentioned phases.

It is evident that efficient algorithm could be realized only in a case when we minimize the amount of data communicated among processors. The solution could be found by splitting the neuron into synapses and cell body.

2 A Toroidal Lattice Architecture of Virtual Processors

Let us consider algorithm simulation in one physical node processor (NP), so we needn't worry about training data delivering to virtual processors (VP). The VPs could be divided into the three categories: synapse processor (SP), cell processor (CP) and input/output processor. All SPs and CPs are connected to their four neighbours with one way channels (up, down, left, right) that provide data transfer and the process synchronisation as well.

One important point for the above procedures is that phase learning doesn't need any communication because output from the previous neuron was already delivered as well as input error from following neuron. So each CP has two variables (input error and output) and each SP has five variables. Another important remark is that each SP is passive (firstly receiving and then sending) and each CP is active (firstly sending and then receiving). In given time all network (toroidal lattice architecture) could be seen as a set of rings.

3 Mapping Virtual Processors onto Physical Processors

To map simply group of VPs on one node processor NP is not sufficient, because each couple of NPs is connected by one channel which couldn't be shared by VPs. The solution is to create more complex process that could function as group of VPs. Then product sum operations of the SPs and CPs are integrated into one equation and partial accumulations are calculated on all NPs simultaneously. It is clear that each NP has to have VPs of both type (CP and SP) and of all layers because of workload distribution among processors in time. The mapping problem is solved by turning matrix of NPs in the 2nd layer.

The training data are available on one processor - typically on a root processor connected to host computer. The solution proposed to data distribution problem is to create communication process MP on each physical processor and to connect this MP to process performing calculation. MPs in the first row are connected with root in ring and the MPs in each column are connected in ring too. All MPs are connected by the same physical links as calculation processes but in opposite direction. Each MP is assigned as high priority process.

4 Some performance results

To get an indication of the speed-up, dependent upon the network size, a number of different NN configurations have been executed on the Telmat T-node (32 x T800). The speed-up of 4 was achieved for network of 6 processors or spee-up of 7 for network of 30 processors. The results of the varying sizes of respectively input - first - second - output layers in 4-layer network shows that speed-up is growing when a number of neurons in hidden layers grows.

References

1. Fujimoto, Y., Fukuda, N., Akabane, T.: Massively Parallel Architectures for Large Scale Neural Networks Simulations, IEEE Transactions on Neural Networks, vol. 3, No. 6, (Nov.1992), 876 – 887
2. Paugam-Moisy, H.: A Spy of Parallel Neural Networks Tech. rep. 90-27 Ecole Normale Superieure de Lyon, IMAG, (1990)

A Genetic Algorithm for Grammatical Inference[*]

Marc M. Lankhorst

University of Groningen, Dept. of Computing Science,
P.O.Box 800, 9700 AV Groningen, The Netherlands

1 Introduction

Genetic algorithms, introduced in [2], are probabilistic search and optimization techniques inspired by the "survival of the fittest" principle of natural evolution. A genetic algorithm maintains a population of candidate solutions to the objective function, represented in the form of "chromosomes". These chromosomes are strings defined over some alphabet that encode the properties of the individual. The algorithm manipulates these with operators such as "crossover" and "mutation". Because of their inherently parallel nature, genetic algorithms are ideally suited for implementation on parallel machines.

An example of such a difficult optimization task is grammatical inference, the problem of learning a grammar based on a set of example sentences [1]. Genetic algorithms have been applied to the induction of finite-state automata [5], context-free grammars [4], and push-down automata [3].

2 Fitness Evaluation

The most important issue in constructing a genetic algorithm is the choice of a particular evaluation function. To evaluate the fitness of a particular grammar with respect to the positive and negative training examples, it is not sufficient to simply count the correctly accepted (rejected) positive (negative) examples. Considering this, we have used evaluation functions that include information on correctly parsed sentences and substrings, predictive qualities and generative capacity of a grammar.

3 Implementation

We implemented the genetic algorithm on a Connection Machine CM-5 using a master-slave programming model, in which the host (the master) executed the genetic algorithm, and the CM-5 nodes (the slaves) conducted the chromosome

---

[*] Most of the computations were carried out on the Connection Machine CM-5 of the University of Groningen, the investments in which were partly supported by the Netherlands Computer Science Research Foundation (SION) and the Netherlands Organization for Scientific Research (NWO).

evaluation. At each generation, this meant parsing several hundred example sentences per chromosome. Since parsing consists mainly of symbol manipulation, we could not use the extensive floating point processing capabilities of the CM-5. Hence we only employed the Sparc processor of each of the nodes. Despite the computing power of the CM-5, the longest run of the algorithm took about two days to complete.

4 Results

The genetic algorithm has been tested with 9 different formal languages: the language of correct bracket expressions, the language of equal numbers of a's and b's, several regular languages, and a tiny natural language subset. For each experiment, we have randomly generated 100 positive and negative examples. Domain knowledge was used to determine the terminal symbols and the size of the grammars to be inferred. Populations of 50 to 100 individuals were used.

Grammars for most of the test languages were correctly inferred. Some of the languages were rather hard to analyze, but after modifying the fitness function and applying incremental learning, the genetic algorithm was able to infer more or less correct grammars.

5 Conclusions

In this paper, genetic algorithms have been shown to be a useful tool for the induction of context-free grammars from positive and negative examples of a language. Grammars for the language of correct parentheses expressions, for the language of equal numbers of a's and b's, for several regular languages, and for a small natural language subset have been inferred more or less correctly. Further experimentation will have to show whether this technique is applicable to more complex languages.

References

1. K.S. Fu and T.L. Booth. Grammatical inference: Introduction and survey. *IEEE Transactions on Pattern Analysis and Machine Intelligence*, 8:343–375, 1986.
2. J.H. Holland. *Adaptation in Natural and Artificial Systems*. University of Michigan Press, Ann Arbor, 1975.
3. S. Sen and J. Janakiraman. Learning to construct pushdown automata for accepting deterministic context-free languages. In G. Biswas, editor, *SPIE Vol. 1707: Applications of Artificial Intelligence X: Knowledge-Based Systems*, pages 207–213. 1992.
4. P. Wyard. Context free grammar induction using genetic algorithms. In R.Belew and L.B.Booker, editors, *Proceedings of the Fourth Conference on Genetic Algorithms ICGA '92*. Morgan Kaufmann, 1992.
5. H. Zhou and J.J. Grefenstette. Induction of finite automata by genetic algorithms. In *Proceedings of the 1986 IEEE International Conference on Systems, Man and Cybernetics*, pages 170–174, Atlanta, GA, 1986.

A Massively Parallel Implementation of the Full Search Vector Quantization Algorithm

Paul Lukowicz[1] and Jutta Schiffers[2] and Rudi Cober[2]

[1] Universität Karlsruhe, Fakultät für Informatik, D-76128 Karlsruhe, F.R.G.,
[2] FAW Ulm, Helmholtzstr. 16, D-89081 Ulm, F.R.G.

Abstract. We present a massively parallel version of a full search vector quantization and its application in the development of an audiovisual speech recognition system. The parallel implementation reduced the worst case runtime of (estimated) 80-100 hours on a 10 MFLOP SPARC to less then 2 hours on a 2.4 GFOLP MasPar MP2216. This demonstrates how the use of parallel computers reduces product development time and leads to a more mature design by allowing for more extensive experimentation with different data sets.

Introduction

One of the aims of the project "Landesforschungsschwerpunkt Neuroinformatik" sponsored by the state of Badenwuertemberg is the integration of lip reading information into neural speech recognition systems. The task faced by the project is that of sensor fusion of sound and image signals, in order to take advantage of the sometimes complementary information encoded in these signals. An important part of the problem is finding an appropriate reduced representation for the input data. To reduce the complexity of the classification problem the representation must be as compact as possible while preserving the relevant discriminative information. In order to obtain a very good representation we have decided to use the optimal LBG (full-search) Vector Quantization (VQ). The high computational cost of this algorithm and the necessity to experiment with different data sets lead to a parallel implementation on the MasPar.

Vector Quantization

Principles. Vector quantization (VQ) aims at representing a large number, M, of k-dimensional input vectors x_j by a small number, N, of k-dimensional of codebook vectors cv_i [1]. Using the nearest neighbor rule the positions of the codebook vectors defines a partition of the space into N Voronoi regions R_i.

$$R_i = \{x : |x - cv_i| \leq |x - cv_j| \forall i \neq j\}$$

In the codebook design phase codebook vectors are derived from a data sample consisting of n_{tv} training vectors. In the classical LBG-algorithm the position of the codebook vectors is optimized using the statistical average quantization error or distortion in an iterative procedure.

Computational Complexity The total number of operations in the codebook design phase is $O(k*N*n_{tv}*iter)$ with *iter* representing the number of iterations.

Currently we are dealing with $n_{tv} \leq 100000$, $N \leq 1200$, $k = 10$ and up to 100 iterations. On a SPARC-10 this results in a runtime of over 100 hours. In future applications further visual and acoustic information (e.g. facial expression, head movement etc.) will have to be accommodated. Thus k, n_{tv} and N will increase by up to a factor of 10 each leading to a 100 to 1000 fold increase in the amount of computing power needed.

Parallelization

The core of the sequential VQ-algorithm can be summarized as follows:

```
do { initialize new codebook_vectors with 0
    for (each training_vector) {
    i = the number of the nearest codebook vector
    i-th new_codebook_vector =+ i-th codebook_vector-training_vector}
    for (each codebook_vector) {
    codebook_vector = new_codebook_vector/
                        number of training vectors matched to it}
} while not (maximum number of iterations or minimum average change}
```

The largest chunk of work is contained in the first **for**-loop that does the full search for each training vector and has a complexity of $O(k * n_{tv} * N)$.

Parallelization The training vectors are evenly distributed over the PEs. Each PE conducts the search procedure (first **for**-loop) for all training vectors it has been assigned. This requires neither communication nor synchronization. Next new code vectors are computed by a global sum of the local new codebook vectors followed by a broadcast of the result.

Speedup The speedup of the MasPar version of the VQ compared to SPARC-10 as the function of $n_t v$ for three different ratios N/n_{tv} can bee seen in the diagram below

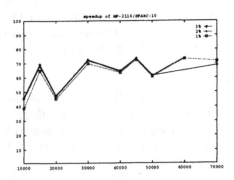

References

1. Allen Gersho, Robert M. Gray, Vector Quantization and Signal Compression Kluwer Academic Publishers, Boston, 1992

Commercial Database Applications on Parallel Systems

Iain Cramb and Colin Upstill

Parallel Applications Centre, Southampton SO16 7NP, UK

EXTENDED ABSTRACT - HPCN EUROPE 1994

In this paper, we report on commercial database and application software ports from conventional systems to Oracle with the parallel server option on Meiko and to Teradata. These have taken place in the context of our collaborations with British Gas, Rover Group, Ordnance Survey, and others, and have been motivated by the requirement that parallel database technology be investigated in detail for a range of database and application types.

We begin with a description of some of the databases and applications software that we have ported, along with some of our results and conclusions about the difficulty or otherwise of porting from conventional database systems to parallel ones. We finish with a description of some of the software tools we have developed to assist in the ports and our system evaluation activities, and some general remarks about the viability of this technology in terms of cost/performance, reliability, availability, scalability, etc.

High-performance database systems enable improved information management and improved information utilisation, offering substantial commercial benefits. But as the power and complexity of relational database systems increase, the necessity for system analysis and management tools also increases. With parallel systems, new issues affect database design, capacity planning and system configuration. System behaviour and performance become more and more dependent on the ability of database administrators and system managers to identify and remove bottle-necks as and when they occur.

We have found that MPP database systems are genuinely scalable for a wide range of application types, and that the cost performance benefits associated with such systems, when compared to conventional main frame technology, are in line with the manufacturers claims. We have also found that database ports from conventional systems can be extremely simple, but that there are some caveats associated with the transfer of software. These centre on a combination of machine configuration, RDBMS tuning issues and the design of the software itself, and are unique to parallel database systems and software.

Our experience in porting real commercial databases and applications to parallel systems has led to the development of working prototype software tools for the design, evaluation, tuning and management of parallel high-performance database systems. Taken together, these tools provide a software environment in which we can:

- drive a system to its limits in a controlled and monitored environment, using multiple transaction streams taken directly from the production environment;
- generate and display information about system resources and activity in real-time;
- predict system performance as a function of hardware and software parameters.

In the first category, Driver software has been developed to reproduce the loads placed on systems by multiple users, batch loads, and applications. The package allows exhaustive database testing using real applications software against real database structures, which would not otherwise be possible.

In the second category, software has been developed to gather, process and display system parameters (e.g. physical I/O rate, contention for data, parallel lock manager activity). This Monitor displays detailed information about system performance in histogram form at run-time, aggregating large amounts of information from many parallel processes. This package can be used to facilitate detection and removal of bottle-necks within a system - one of the most important aspects of parallel processing.

In the third category, we are developing modelling package to predict database throughput and response time, given machine characteristics, database structure, and workload profile. In principle, the package can model any platform, any RDBMS, any database and any transactions. It is being developed against controlled testing of real database systems, using the Driver software to exercise the system and the Monitor software to analyse system behaviour.

In a typical project life-cycle, the environment which these three pieces of software combine to create is used for database physical design, implementation and tuning, concentrating on performance issues such as indexing strategies, distribution of data across disks and distribution of work among CPUs. The fully-developed Model is used for database design, capacity planning, system configuration and performance prediction.

Once a prototype system is implemented, the Driver software is used to exercise the system and the Monitor software to analyse its behaviour. The results are used to refine the design and implementation of the database and the application software. Finally, with a production system exercised by a user population, the Monitor software is used to analyse system behaviour and the results used to tune the operational database.

These tools are being continually developed to extend their functionality and genericity over a range of platforms. This work is proceeding in the context of porting commercial databases and applications, to ensure that the requirements of end-users are met in providing for the design, implementation, optimisation and management of any parallel database system.

Evaluation of High Performance
Parallel Database Machines

Jon Kerridge[+], Innes Jelly[*], Chris Bates[†]
[*] School of Computing and Management Sciences, Sheffield Hallam University,
[+] Department of Computer Science, Sheffield University,
[†] National Transputer Support Centre,
all located in Sheffield, United Kingdom
J.Kerridge@dcs.shef.ac.uk, I.E.Jelly@shu.ac.uk

Abstract Many organisations are considering the use of large relational databases to implement their information needs. For large organisations this will result in the implementation of a machine dedicated to that task. In the near future, these database machines will use high performance parallel engines to provide the required computing resource. Performance evaluation is particularly important when the design is being considered for future scalability and the ability of the design to cope with unexpected data access. The paper reports on the development of a synthetic or "mimic" database which models a real application: this mimic not only forms the basis for a new benchmark for large SQL databases, but can also be used to support the design process.

1 Introduction

The ability to store and manipulate large volumes of information is a crucial requirement for the operation of most large commercial organisations. These rely upon their database systems to provide the effective implementation of tasks such as order processing, invoicing and ledger maintenance. Most current databases systems are able to support this role without providing detailed management information which could be extracted from the data if there was sufficient spare processing capacity. Projects such as IDIOMS [1,2] have demonstrated the feasibility of building a parallel relational database machine which can support both the transaction processing capability and the management information needs of an organisation at the same time on the same data. Increasingly parallel hardware will be needed to meet the demands for this enhanced functionality and to provide better performance for large data volumes. We have already seen the emergence of parallel implementations of Oracle on a number of different parallel platforms such as N-cube, Meiko and Parsys, and new parallel systems such as the recently announced database machine Goldrush from ICL. In order to evaluate the performance of this new generation of database machines, appropriate benchmarks and general performance evaluation techniques are required. These must reflect the different modes of operation of the systems and indicate how well they scale to a range of problem sizes.

The growth in application of database technology to commercial and administrative systems is leading to ever increasing need for high performance database machines It is expected that commercial and administrative use of high performance computing will outnumber scientific and engineering use by a factor of three to one in the near future [3]. Database systems differ from scientific applications in a number of respects. The data that is stored is symbolic rather than numeric and thus imposes a totally different workload upon the processing system. Such systems also require high performance disc systems that are closely integrated with the processing system. A feature of large database applications is that the supporting hardware only undertakes database processing - they are not general purpose machines. The need for processing performance improvement has been heightened by organisations' need for more extensive use of the data they maintain. This manifests itself in the need to extract information from the data, rather than just supporting the mission critical procedures of the organisation. This information is used to provide decision support systems. Increasingly, data mining techniques are being used in order to extract patterns and trends which are hidden within the data. This enhanced functionality requires much more processing power than is needed to support a transaction processing system, especially if the data mining activity is to be undertaken on the same data that is used by the transaction processing system. There is a need for database machines to be able to support varying styles of interaction with many of these being carried out concurrently. This also raises the need for higher performance database machines.

An important aspect of current developments is that parallel database machine hardware offers the opportunity to scale the system more easily than present technology once it has been installed. Prospective purchasers will therefore wish to evaluate how easily the machine can be scaled and what effect this will have on the way the data is organised. Thus any performance evaluation system has to be able to construct scaled data sets which can be related one to the other. In addition the volumes have to be realistic, and therefore it is necessary to build evaluation systems which have many millions of records in them.

Typically, database machines operate in a client-server mode, whereby a client processor makes a request upon the database server to undertake work. This interaction requires an interface which is easily specified by the use of ISO Database Language SQL [4]. Thus the client process has to be able to generate SQL queries which are then passed to the database server. The server evaluates the query and returns the resulting rows to the client where they are processed. The advantage of the client-server approach is that the client can vary in capability from a mainframe through workstation and PC to dumb terminals operating through a front-end processor. From the organisation's point of view this approach protects their investment in user application code. The actual implementation of the database server is removed from consideration when the user part of the system is modified, provided an SQL interface is used.

Performance evaluation depends upon software support for a realistic mimic of the type of applications which many organisations operate. It is unlikely that a single mimic will adequately model the entire range of commercial applications; however, we believe that the number of such mimics will not need to be very large.

2 Database Performance Evaluation and Benchmarking

The intention is to provide a new standard for evaluation of SQL databases (running on either conventional or parallel platforms) which meets the requirements of the current users of large database systems. The evaluation system models the functionality of modern commercial systems and includes both on-line transaction processing (OLTP), management information systems (MIS) and batch processing. The benchmark consists of a model or "mimic" database with sets of associated OLTP and MIS queries, and the software tools which generate the large volumes of data and transactions required to run the system. In order to support investigation of the scalability of database systems, the generated database and queries can be appropriately sized.

The development of a realistic application mimic serves not only as the vehicle for benchmarking of database systems but provides support for the design and evaluation of new systems. By the definition of default values, a standard database model can be generated to form the benchmarking systems; alternatively, the use of different parameters allows system developers to emulate different database design features and compare the high level "user's view" of performance with detailed investigations into system dependent aspects such as indexing strategies, load balancing and communication overheads.

The importance of the availability of appropriate, recognised benchmarking and evaluation systems is two fold: first, it allows potential purchasers to obtain valid comparative information on the performance of different systems, and secondly, they provide a valuable standard for system designers. In order to support users and designers, benchmark tests must model the functionality of real applications. Currently, although there are a number of recognised database benchmarks, none adequately meets this requirement for large high performance parallel systems [5,6]. These limitations can be summarised as: the simplistic nature of the database system modelled, unrealistically small record lengths, atypical mix of queries and transactions with no attempt to model realistic database functionality, and finally the use of integer data in the key and other frequently accessed fields. This use of integer data represents a failure to understand the typical characteristics of real databases where information such as "account-number" is always specified in the form of character strings. It can lead to considerable error in the timing of database functions as the duration of fundamental CPU operations on integer and character data differs widely.

The mimic database structure is based on the system used in the IDIOMS project which was built for the TSB Bank plc and is typical of any European Savings Bank. The database design developed for that project is representative of a large class of commercial systems, ranging from banking, insurance, mail order and public/private monopoly utilities. As these systems comprise some of the largest databases currently in operation, the decision to base the application mimic system on a banking model appears to be sensible. The synthetic database has been designed to include information on customers, their accounts and standing orders.

A major problem for the development of a realistic application mimic is the difficulty in generating the required data volumes. For a realistic model the typical data scaling requirements run from 100,000 to 10 million rows per table. In order to support the production of this amount of synthetic data a software tool has been developed to generate these for the mimic system. However it is not sufficient merely to generate data in volume: it must also model real data if the system is to be a marked improvement on current benchmarks.

Previous work on the IDIOMS project has already provided an analysis of the most commonly used banking transactions and the profile of their distribution by transaction type. By incorporating this information into the synthetic OLTP set, the mimic system provides a realistic test of normal database usage. In order to achieve an equivalent set of realistic MIS queries, an analysis has been carried out of the exiting MIS type benchmarks and the current (and projected) requirements of commercial users. This has resulted in a categorisation of MIS queries from which a typical mix of individual queries can be generated. Categories include such management requirements as statistical reporting, and security checking. Thus the synthetic mimic results from the analysis of a real system. It is intended that the OLTP and MIS systems should be capable of concurrent operation even though current database machines may not support this style of operation.

A further aspect of real database systems is that they generally include some aspect of auditing and security, and it is thus necessary to ensure that any application mimic contains a realistic representation of these features. By including the requirement to maintain audit information during transaction processing and query response, the database system not only mimics accepted commercial practice but provides information at completion of testing that can be used to validate that the tests have been correctly conducted.

3 Support Tools

The support environment is provided by four main tools; Data Generation, Transaction Generation, Information about the generated system and Analysis of Results. When used for benchmarking, these produce a standard mimic database; as support for design, they allow the system builder to generate a range of customised synthetic databases. By implementing the tools [7] in ANSI C, portability is assured.

3.1 Database Generation

For the purposes of benchmarking, a database with a large number of default parameters is created. However, when a database system is being designed or evaluated it may be necessary to skew the data. This can be achieved by modifying the default parameters to achieve the desired effect. The size of the database can also be set. The database definition file contains a specification of how each customer, account and standing order record is to be constructed. A *set database characteristics* function provides a machine independent means of creating a database definition file.

A *generate database* process takes as input the database definition and a number of other files which allow the parameterisation of the generated database. The *generate database* process can be configured so that it generates the database load files account, customer, customer-account and standing order in the format required by the bulk data load facility of the database system being evaluated.

3.2 Transaction Generation

A machine independent process *set transaction characteristics* provides a means of tailoring the transactions which are generated. This includes aspects such as the number of different types of transaction and the values contained in the transactions. This information is then saved in a transaction definition file. A further process *generate transactions* then takes as input both the transaction and database definition files. Transactions are generated using the database definition file to ensure that the transactions generated refer to valid accounts and customers, or in the case of new accounts and customers, that they did not previously exist. The transaction generator also creates transactions which are not valid to check the operation of the database when information is incorrectly input to the system. The transaction generator also creates further tables which are used during the auditing phase to check system operation. The transactions can be generated so that they can comply with the input format requirements of the database system under test. The generation system will also permit the creation of a number of different streams of transactions. This will allow the database system under test to be driven by any number of transaction streams.

MIS queries do not need to be generated in the same way because the aim is to run a set of queries which capture typical queries in such an environment. The same queries when executed against different size databases will naturally reflect the scaling factor which has been applied to the database generation.

3.3 Information System

The information system is intended to provide a means of determining the likely effect of a particular query. It takes as input the transaction and database definition files and, because the system has been constructed in a computable manner, allows extraction of statistics about the generated data. The information system is provided as an environment independent package which simply has to input the database and transaction definition files.

3.4 Result Analysis

In order to evaluate high performance parallel database systems, monitoring of different aspects of performance is required. During benchmarking the data must be collected and analysed to produce an end-user's view on performance, eg. number of transactions per unit time. However when the mimic database is used for design the system builder requires monitoring information on the database machine itself. This includes aspects such as processor, memory and disc usage, as well as timing information concerning the processing and residency times of transactions and MIS queries. It is likely that such analysis will be machine specific due to the monitoring information that is required. Of particular interest will be the ability to analyse what happens to performance when either the data is skewed or access to the database is skewed compared to the way in which data has been partitioned. A further use of such a performance evaluation mechanism will be to provide much more detailed information about the way in which the machine has to be scaled depending upon the change of use which naturally occurs during the life of a database.

4 Conclusions

This paper has shown how performance evaluation tools can be constructed which are applicable to any SQL database server and operational environment, and has discussed the role of application mimics as the basis for benchmarking and designing database systems within a unified and coherent structure. In particular, it has highlighted the problem of generating large volumes of realistic data which is based upon symbolic rather than numeric data. It has also shown that large numbers of transactions need to be generated for the mimic application. It has described a means of determining the likely effect of an MIS query without having to access the actual database so that output result can be checked. The system can be used to explore the effect of MIS queries which are not part of those supplied with the performance evaluation system but which better reflect the application environment. It has shown the need for a results analysis mechanism to support the system builder evaluate the performance of specific database machines under a range of different load conditions.

References

1. JM Kerridge, "The Design of the IDIOMS Parallel Database Machine", Proc. British National Conf. on Databases 9 (Wolverhampton, 1991), pub. Aspects of Databases, eds. M.S. Jackson and A.E. Robinson Oxford: Butterworth - Heinemann, 1991.
2. JM Kerridge, "The IDIOMS Parallel Database Machine: Design, Performance and Future Directions", to appear in the Proceedings of 6th Transputer/occam International Conference Tokyo June 1994.
3. H Forster, "The HPCN Programme", Invited Talk, Performance Evaluation of Parallel Systems Workshop, University of Warwick, Nov 1993.
4. International Standards Organisation, Database Language SQL, ISO 9075:1987(E), 1987.
5. JM Kerridge, IE Jelly, C Bates and Y Tsitogiannis, "Towards a Benchmark for Parallel Database Machines", Proc. Performance Evaluation of Parallel Systems Workshop, University of Warwick, Nov 1993.
6. "The Benchmark Handbook" Ed J Gray, Morgan Kaufmann, 1991
7. RJ Cook, "Performance Testing of the IDIOMS Parallel Database Machine", MSc Thesis, University of Sheffield, 1993.

A Free-Text Retrieval Index-Server on a Massively Parallel Machine

F. Richard Kroll

Aptec Computer Systems
Munich, D-81925

Abstract. Several advancements in recent years have made possible the development of products based on parallel hardware platforms suitable for the conventional commercial marketplace. Probably the single most important factor is the acceptance of client/server models by large organizations in place of traditional main-frame solutions. In the client/server world all server systems are almost by definition "open" even if they are based on exotic hardware, since they can be replaced at any time by another server with a similar software interface.

The searching for indexes in a free-text retrieval system is a perfect problem for a parallel computer in a client/server environment. Such a system has been developed for the SIMD architecture of the 4096-processor DAP system.

The paper discusses the main characteristics of index-servers in general and how such systems can benefit from implementation on massively parallel systems. Examples of performance improvements are given which show over 100 times improvements over conventional implementations. Integration with existing document and image retrieval systems is also dealt with.

1 Introduction

As a way of an introduction let us first define what we mean by free-text index-server.

Many large organizations have the need to access millions of documents created and stored in hundreds of different formats and on many media types (paper, microfilm, electronic images, electronic text, video, etc). Research bulletins, marketing information, patent applications, are all examples of documents that a company might have stored electronically in various systems. The need exists to quickly locate particular documents in this mass of information. Classical data-bank methods with keyed-fields are not suitable for searches through such unstructured documents.

As an example, consider a press agency with a document data base containing decades of newspaper articles. Such a database could easily could contain hundreds of gigabytes of information.

Journalists requiring background information can benefit greatly form such a data base. For example, a reporter writing on a the Arab-Israeli peace accords might want to check if either side has become more flexible with respect to Jerusalem. He might start by requesting to see the titles (headlines) of all articles where

[Rabin *(or)* Arafat] *(and)* Jerusalem

are mentioned.

Another reporter, researching how Japanese investment in various countries is affected by emotional political issues, might search on

(Japanese investment) *(and)* (whales)

or

(Japanese investment) *(and)* [whales *(or)* dumping *(or)* (Kurile Islands)].

Queries of this type against a data base containing millions of documents can be time consuming, particularly if hundreds of other reporters are using the search service at the same time.

Free text systems utilize two different but related data bases. The first contains the documents themselves (stored either as text or as images). The second is the dictionary data base containing all words and their locations in all the documents. Normally, unimportant words like definite articles and adverbs are eliminated from the index data base to save space and time.

In conventional systems these two data bases are on the same hardware platform and even handled by the same software. The two functions however, the management of the documents and the searching of the indexes, are vastly different in the resources they require. The document storage, although requiring enormous amounts of disk and tape storage, utilizes very little of the CPU processing power. The index search system on the other hand can bring a powerful machine to its knees through its huge drain on I/O bandwidth and CPU cycles. It makes sense therefore to separate the two functions and map them to architecture platforms optimized for the different type of requirements. In a network based system relying on client/server relationships this presents no problems.

2 High-Speed Parallel Implementation

Many fine free-text retrieval systems exist. They have been implemented on various hardware platforms ranging from desktop-systems to mainframes. By selecting the proper hardware platform they are highly scaleable. Why then is it even necessary to implement index-search algorithms on high-speed parallel architectures?

Year for year people produce more and more information. Access to this information means success and influence. A number of enabling technologies (optical disks, robotic tape robots, high-speed networks) and the acceptance of client/server concepts guarantee a dramatic increase in the size of data bases that will be covered by free text retrieval methods in the near future.

Clearly, solutions based on conventional architectures are nearing the end of their life time and will not be able to accommodate one or two order of magnitudes increases in data base size. Other architectures are required, and these architectures are of course parallel.

In addition to the obvious speed up in query response time, parallel systems offer other advantages. A fraction of the huge reserve in compute power can be diverted to other jobs: for example, the on-the-fly compression/decompression of the index data base. For small data bases of several hundred megabytes this is not so important, but for a document database of 30 GBytes, 20 GBytes of indexing disk space can be saved using compression. For large systems this can have enormous economic benefits.

3 Performance

The search/match algorithm used for index searching in free-text retrieval system maps particularly well to parallel hardware architectures. Cambridge Parallel Processing implemented these algorithms on its 4096 processor SIMD DAP computer. At the pilot installation the "typical query" was shown to have the profile:

- 2.2 terms
- 30% of the terms in phrases
- 5% of the terms truncated
- search 1 million documents out of the total 10 million (20 GigaBytes) documents stored.

The previous system, a VAX cluster, required approximately 5 seconds to process such a query. The parallel implementation on the DAP required only 22 milliseconds (equivalent to 46 queries/second). The parallel implementation is more than 100 times faster than the conventional solution. In addition, the new system was capable of inverting over 10,000 new documents a day concurrent with the on-line activities, which the old system was incapable of doing.

The table below shows, in more detail, the performance of the DAP system in queries/second as a function of the query type and the number of documents searched.

Queries/Second	Documents Searched			
	0.25 Million	0.5 Million	1 Million	2 Million
Single simple term	140	126	108	84
2 simple terms	130	112	86	60
2 term phrase	70	46	28	16
single truncated term	90	62	38	22
2 term phrase with one truncated term	28	16	8	4

Due to the use of high-speed RAID disk subsystems for index storage, the above performance levels are not dramatically affected by searches requiring heavy disk usage.

4 Integration into Existing Systems

The implementation of index-searching algorithm on massively parallel computers has shown to bring enormous speed increases, significant enough to make a parallel implementation attractive to the commercial user. However, in order to be commercially successful what form should the product have? The performance goals of such a product are clear. It should:

- allow a large increase in the number of on-line users while decreasing query response times
- provide for a rapid increase in database size
- allow for new document input at any time with instant availability for on-line use

However, since for the commercial user, environmental and operating requirements are equally important, the system must also:

- isolate the user completely from the massively parallel hardware
- allow evolutionary integration with existing document systems
- allow the user complete freedom in the selection and organization of data storage media (disk, tape, optical disk, VHS) and formats (video, text, images, graphical, audio)
- enable all document types (text, image, video) to be searched via a single query
- be network oriented
- allow organization specific user interfaces to be maintained or developed
- allow dual-redundant operation if required

Various implementation models could satisfy the performance requirements, but to satisfy the environment and operating requirements, Cambridge Parallel Processing created a index-searching and document-inversion engine based on the network client/server model. The completed product is called DAP*Text*.

By restricting the server to index-searching only, the user benefits from enormous speed improvements with minimal disruption of existing systems. Documents can remain where they are in their current form, whether text or images. New types of document storage (audio, video, graphic) can use the services of the new index server. Documents of all types regardless of their location on the network can be searched by a single query.

A key design consideration in such a system is where to create the principal user interface. The developers of DAP*Text* chose the client interface at the Berkeley socket level on the network. An interface at this level allows the user the greatest flexibility in integrating the DAP*Text* server with existing equipment and services with an interface of maximum simplicity and elegance. The API consists only of five primary service calls (invert, query, etc) with eight additional calls for rarely used functions (reboot, check status, etc).

The acceptance growth of the client/server model in the industry has simplified the creation of large systems built by integrating specialized subsystems from different vendors. Customers are no longer faced with the "all or nothing choice" in selecting new equipment. DAP*Text* is compatible with these trends, by allowing customers to create large document systems from specialized subsystems with a common user interface.

5 Summary

The implementation of the free-text retrieval system on a massively-parallel machine shows the validity of considering these architectures as the basis for products which will be sold into the commercial marketplace. In the near future one can expect more and more "shrink wrapped" commercial products based on "supercomputer technology" to be available to every-day commercial customers like banks and insurance companies.

Large Scale Data Management and Massively Parallel Architectures in Automatic Fingerprint Recognition

David Walter, Jon Kerridge

National Transputer Support Centre
5, Palmerston Road, Sheffield S10 2TE. UK
Tel: +44 742 768740

Abstract. The National Transputer Support Centre is an independent parallel processing consultancy specialising in large scale data management and parallel databases. We were approached recently by the Home Office to investigate the data management aspects of Automatic Fingerprint Recognition (AFR), and to report on design issues and technology available to support systems of varying sizes, ranging from small regional systems up to centralised national systems for large countries such as the USA. In particular, we were asked to investigate the extent to which a single design could be applied to systems of a wide range of sizes. Our conclusions pointed to a massively parallel architecture as being the only technology capable of offering a solution. In this paper we use this application to illustrate the advantages that such architectures can offer in problems of very large scale such as those found in the area of criminal justice.

1 Requirements

Initial analysis of requirements indicated that the resources required for a large AFR system are considerable. Current manual methods rely on very fine levels of classification of images in order to reduce the number of actual comparisons required to manageable levels. The emphasis with AFR on the other hand, is to provide fast matching facilities to vastly increase the number of comparisons that can be performed, thereby reducing the reliance on painstaking fine classification.

Current systems are clearly running at saturation level, and give little insight into the level of demand that could be expected of an effective automatic system. There is a high degree of pent-up demand, particularly for scene-of-crime work, and there is a feeling among operators that any given level of provision would be fully taken up.

A further complicating factor in predicting demand levels is the uncertainty over patterns of usage. The only available statistics for current systems are annual figures, yet an automatic system with a fast response (typically less than 15 minutes) will be subject to considerable peaks and troughs in demand.

We estimated that in order to provide a level of throughput comparable to UK current manual systems, an automatic system would need to run *continuously* at a rate of about 4000 comparisons per second. Current estimates suggest that a realistic target for peak throughput for an automatic system should be around 500,000 comparisons per second. As the matching process is fairly compute intensive, this represents a very large amount of processing indeed, requiring resources of the order of 600 GIPS.

The input to the matching process is in the form of encoded images. Based on predictions for the year 2000 of approximately 5 million records (each record representing one individual), this data would require 50 Gbytes of storage.

It was not possible to perform the same level of detailed analysis on the requirements for a USA centralised system, but a cursory investigation indicated a requirement approximately five times greater than the UK.

It was required that the system should be capable of being scaled up to allow for growth in both data sizes and demand levels. Ideally, the same design should be suitable for a wide range of system sizes, ranging from UK regional systems to a US national system. In addition, very high levels of availability are required.

2 Technology

Clearly, in order to meet the throughput requirements illustrated above, multiple processors will be required, as no single processor is sufficiently powerful. Similarly, the encodings will have to be distributed across multiple disk drives, as the bandwidth of any single drive falls far short of requirements.

Several different technologies were investigated as to their capability to satisfy the demands illustrated in the previous section. They can be grouped into the following categories: mainframe systems, conventional supercomputers and massively parallel architectures.

2.1 Mainframe Computers

Conceptually, it would be a simple matter to implement an AFR system as a loosely coupled collection of mainframe computers. Such a solution would, however, be prohibitively expensive, and even given unlimited funds, would probably be impractical on the grounds of sheer physical scale.

The problem stems from the fact that a Mainframe computer is a very large and highly integrated collection of hardware and software resources which provides a general purpose platform which can be put to a wide variety of uses. As such it is necessarily very expensive both to buy and to run.

Yet even the latest mainframe computers offer only a small proportion of the CPU power required for this application. By multiplying up the number of units, we multiply up the expenditure on all the unwanted aspects of the overall resource, when all we actually require is more processing power.

Mainframes can be configured for particular needs, but their fundamental design dictates that a single machine can only have a small number of processors. Mainframes are physically very large, and require specialised computer room environments and 24 hour-a-day operator manning, hence the high running costs. This places a limit on the number of machines that could practically be brought to bear on a problem. A glance at the requirements for AFR shows that it is unlikely that they could ever, in reality, be met by mainframes.

2.2 Conventional Supercomputers

The solution of problems involving massive amounts of processing has traditionally fallen to the class of machines referred to as supercomputers. There is, in fact, no single design philosophy uniting the various machines which bear this label. By referring to 'Conventional' supercomputers, we are grouping together those machines which do not use large numbers of processors. Although more powerful, these machines suffer from the same fundamental limitations as mainframes, in that they are not powerful enough individually to fulfil the requirements, and are unsuitable (and uneconomic) for combining in large numbers.

2.3 Massively Parallel Architectures

Massively parallel computers achieve performance by connecting together large numbers of inexpensive microprocessors.

As the communications bandwidth of such systems increases as the number of nodes increases, it is possible to build very large systems without inter-processor communication or input/output bandwidth becoming a bottleneck. Systems are currently installed with as many as 64K processors, but numbers of nodes in the hundreds are more common.

This approach allows full advantage to be taken of the progress which has been achieved in microprocessor technology in recent years. The performance gap between microprocessors and mainframes has been steadily narrowing since the introduction of the first microprocessors, and the current generation of devices combine high power with compactness and low energy consumption, and at a price/performance ratio which is a tiny fraction of that of current mainframes.

Massively parallel systems are not suitable for all types of problem. It must be possible to decompose the problem into a sufficient number of parallel components to be able to exploit the available processors. In addition, if the amount of inter-processor communication is large in relation to the processing done, performance will be poor because the external communications are inevitably relatively slow. In the next section we show that AFR match processing is ideally suited to a massively parallel architecture.

A wide variety of microprocessors are currently in use in massively parallel systems. Certain manufacturers, however, have produced devices which are aimed more specifically at this area of the market. The Inmos Transputer range and the Texas Instruments TMS 320C40 are examples.

A growing number of general purpose supercomputers are becoming available which exploit massively parallel technology. It is, however, possible to produce specialised architectures for particular applications. In addition to allowing the hardware configuration to be fully optimised, this approach has the advantage of minimising the amount of system software which sits between the application and the hardware. On a given problem, the performance of a dedicated machine will always be better than a general purpose machine.

The task of producing specialised parallel architectures is made considerably easier by the availability of products which are designed to act as building blocks for parallel systems. These allow processors and communication facilities to be combined with remarkably little external logic.

An example of such an optimised architecture is described in a later section.

3 AFR on a Massively Parallel Architecture

The requirements of the AFR match processing subsytem are ideally suited to a massively parallel architecture for the following reasons:

- The problem is easily parallelised. Each processor can be put to work on separate matches.

- Because the match algorithm is compute intensive, the ratio of processing to communication is high. This means that inter-processor communications will not pose a problem even in a large-scale system.

- Massively parallel machines can be scaled up to provide resources to cope with increasing demands. This applies both to performance (eg to meet increased demand for searches) and to size (eg to meet the requirements of different forces/countries).

- Parallel architectures have inherent advantages in the design of fault tolerant systems.

We believe that a massively parallel architecture is the only practical way to meet the particularly demanding requirements of this system.

4 Example Architecture

4.1 General Layout

The general layout of a suitable machine is shown in figure 1. The host computer receives requests for searches from the workstations, and passes them on to the match server. The resulting respondent lists are kept by the host computer for the lifetime of the enquiry to enable images to be fetched from the images database in response to cues from the user. The images database is keyed on Criminal Record Office number (CRO#).

The host computer also services verification requests by fetching images directly from the images database. The match server is not involved in this process.

Note that the match server encapsulates all the dedicated parts of the system. By providing it with a standard interface, it can be easily integrated into an open systems environment.

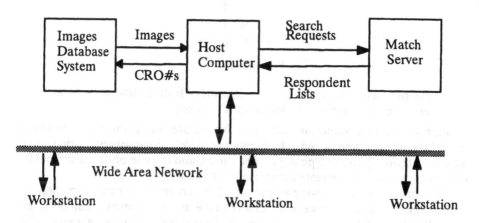

Figure 1

4.2 An Example Match Server Architecture

An example of a possible match server architecture is shown in figure 2. Note the following features of the architecture:

- The controller distributes search parameters and receives results of matches.

- The rest of the architecture comprises a collection of processor farm units, each consisting of a pair of disk drives, a pre-processor and a set of match processors.

- Paired disks give fault tolerance and increased read bandwidth.

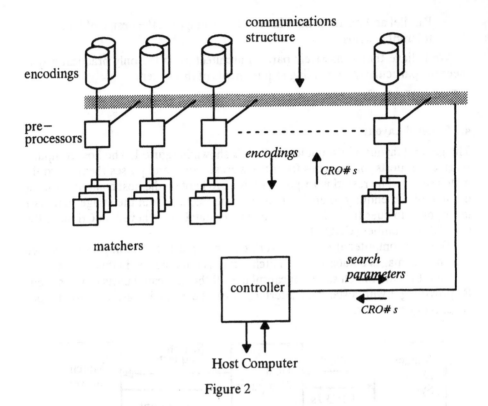

Figure 2

— Pre-processors do fast in-memory filtering of textual annotation data
to reduce the number of comparisons required.

Perhaps the most important aspect of this architecture is the extent to which
it can be optimised and scaled. The number of match processors per farm can be
adjusted according to the type of processor used, and the size of disk drive can be
chosen to provide an adequate number of data streams.

The amount of data flowing in and out of the controller is small compared to
the amount which flows between the disks and the match processors. Similarly, the
controller does little processing compared to the matchers. Thus there is no barrier
to scaling the whole system up by adding more farms.

In order to satisfy the requirements for a UK central system, the number of processors required would be in the thousands. However, as both the processors and
the disk drives are commodity products, costing hundreds rather than thousands
of dollars, the hardware for the system is extraordinarily cheap considering its
power. This illustrates the advantage of a dedicated architecture in being able to
exploit resources in a highly focussed manner.

5 Data Organisation

The effectiveness of the above architecture depends on the ability to keep its many
processors sufficiently busy. Load balancing is achieved through optimising the organisation of the data on the disks, and the strategies for searching through it.

Data can be partitioned into logical groupings according to some attribute or
attributes, then these partitions can be placed on the physical volumes in such a way

as to optimise the access strategy used. Clearly, the partitioning strategy and access strategy are closely linked.

There is, in fact, no simple way to arrive at the best strategy for a complex real system, and in the case of AFR, some experimentation and statistical analysis would be required before a decision could be made. The remainder of this section presents a brief discussion of some of the issues involved.

The workload of this system is made up of a large number of user requests, each requiring a large number of comparisons. This gives us the opportunity to exploit inter-query parallelism, intra-query parallelism, or both.

The bulk of the workload is made up of two different kinds of search, verifications, and Scene of Crime (SOC) searches. The aim of a verification is to ascertain whether or not the fingerprints of an arrested individual are already present in the collection. Typically, a set of ten good prints is available, but if the individual has no known CRO#, it is necessary to search the whole collection.

SOC searches take partial prints taken from the scene of crime and attempt to find matches within the collection. Typically, there will be partial data available on print types and finger positions. The search space is radically reduced for routine work by restricting the geographical scope of searches.

Partitioning may be based on finger position and print type, such that, for instance, a single partition may contain only left index finger tented arches. This permits inter-query parallelism for both types of search. Moreover, as verification searches are generally based on a search of one or two fingers, it is possible to select the finger with the least common combination of finger and position. This not only reduces search space, but also contributes significantly to load balancing.

Another possible strategy is to partition primarily on geographical area. As verification searches are national, these would be be performed across the partition, while SOC searches would take place within restricted areas of the database.

An important aspect of the partitioning is that whichever strategy is used, certain logical partitions will require a number of physical volumes, and those partitions should be the ones that will be more frequently accessed.

Finally, it is worth mentioning techniques for dynamically re-distributing data in such a way as to evolve a more efficient partitioning arrangement. This might involve moving records to place them together with other records which are frequently needed together. Alternatively, it might involve moving frequently accessed records onto volumes which are found, through operational experience, to be under-utilised. Once again, the strategy depends on the search strategies adopted.

Such techniques can be automatic, and may take the form of continuous small adjustments, or larger re-organisations performed periodically during quiet times.

6 Conclusion

The next generation of Criminal Justice Information Service systems will require enormous computational resources. This paper has demonstrated that massively parallel architectures can offer solutions to problems of very large scale which are inaccessible to conventional architectures. Furthermore, such solutions can be remarkably cost effective.

PARCS: Parallel Picture Archiving and Communication System

M. Fruscione, L. Marenzi,, S. Punzi, P. Stofella
A.C.S. S.r.l. - Via Rombon, 11 - 20134 MILANO

Abstract. The main justifications and technical contants of the Esprit project PARCS are described in this paper. The project addresses a major high performance application in the area of mulimedia databases, namely the development of a Picture Archiving and Communication System for radiological images. A MIMD distributed memory machine is exploited in order to build a fast and scalable archiving server, with multiple network connections to client workstations for image acquisition, visualization and (parallel) processing. The system will be integrated with an existing Radiological Information System and demonstrated in a Radiology Department.

1. The application context

The effective exploitation of large multimedia databases can, in most application areas, involve very strong requirements in terms of technological support. While small sized multimedia applications have been widely and successfully developed in many application areas, databases involving large amounts of multimedia information are still forcing the limits of current archiving and communication technologies.

The PARCS project's main idea is the exploitation of HPCN techniques in the area of Large Multimedia Archiving applications: PACS systems, as the most demanding applications in this area, are an ideal testbed to evaluate this architecture.

The term PACS (Picture Archiving and Communication System) has been created in 1982, during the conference of the Society of Photo-Optical Instrumentation Engineers, to define medical image archiving systems. The emerging capabilities of computers to deal with digitized images stimulated the idea of a Radiological Department where slides would have been substituted by images contained in digital archives and visualized on high definition monitors. Since 1982, a huge amount of work has been carried out in the area of PACS, due also to the following main expected benefits:

- digital images can be copied and exchanged without loss of information, allowing different people to consult them independently or cooperatively
- Clinical Departments can have easy access to the images
- a digital archive can reduce the research time for retrieving a given patient image
- the amount of slides can be minimized
- correlation of images from different radiological modalities can be easily used for diagnosys
- image processing techniques can be applied to the images

2. The need for a scalable architecture

Although many PACS projects have been developed, reaching good results in some important aspect of the overall complex system, none of them has been able to produce a full acceptance by the user community. In fact, a set of open problems is still slowing the diffusion of these systems. These problems belong to two kind of factors.

Technological factors

Many specific requirements of PACS systems are not currently satisfied by non-HPCN technology:

- the image retrieval time is frequently unacceptably high, due to network and I/O bandwidth saturation
- the image processing algorithms are limited to basic manipulation primitives
- the spatial and frequency definition of medical images can be in the order of 2048x2048x12bit pixels: display monitors of this size are still too expensive

This project will address mainly the first limitation: parallel computing techniques can provide support also to the second and third limitations (using multiple graphics boards with multiple monitors and eventually additional computing power, advanced parallel visualization and processing stations can be built).

Economical factors

The existing PACS systems can be classified in two main product cathegories: complete PACS covering the need of distributing images through the entire hospital and smaller sized PACS systems for (a subset of) the Radiology Department (miniPACS). The first product class is offered by large medical equipment producers; miniPACS are usually offered by smaller organizations or are emerging from cooperations between medical equipment producers, user organizations and information technology companies.

The first type of PACS systems has a very high cost, not affordable by most of the hospitals (just a few big hospitals in each European country have installed these systems). The second one, thought being affordable in terms of price, has strong limitations in terms of expansion and integration capabilities.

The PARCS system will be characterized by an affordable entry level price, in the order of a miniPACS, and a clear and seamless upgrade path towards a complete PACS. Its performance level will be potentially very high, due to the exploitation of the well known scalability properties of parallel DM architectures. Bottlenecks in I/O access and/or in network communication will be avoided by the use of multiple disks and multiple network interfaces. The new INMOS Transputer, T9000, will provide an ideal support in terms of performance and communication bandwidth, thus matching the requirements of this application area.

The project will be based on an existing prototype, developed by ACS on a T800 based machine. The prototype is currently able to drive multiple mirrored disks and communicates with a set of client stations (PCs) using a fibre optic extension of the transputer link. The level of performance shown by this prototype is already interesting for this application area. The performance in accessing the image database is not far from the specifications given by the MDIS Performance Work Statement: with the T9000 implementation planned in the project, the final product will be MDIS specifications compliant (the MDIS Performance Work Statement is a document prepared by the Medical Diagnostic Imaging Support System Technical Development Team of the US Army Engineering Division: it is a widely accepted reference document for PACS performance requirements specifications).

3. The PARCS architecture

The PARCS Architecture is based on the idea of a Multiple Disks Multiple Networks parallel machine. An overview of this architecture is schematized in figure 1.

The PARCS server can scale in the disk I/O bandwidth, in the amount of mass storage, in the network communication bandwidth and in the computing power. Client requests are processed by the multiple Network nodes accessing the disk resources through the fast internal point-to-point network. The external bandwidth can be increased using additional networks, the internal bandwidth can be increased by adding new nodes and new disks. The architecture has a very high degree of flexibility and can be finely tuned for different users, acting on the number and type of networks supported and on the number and type of disks (magnetic, WORM).

The overall system architecture is composed by the following main modules:

• Parallel Disk Server: parallel hardware/software subsystem managing a number of disks and serving file access requests

• Delivery Subsystem: Multiple network interfaces and management software

• Client Workstations

4. The PARCS application

Addressing the image database access problems is, as mentioned, the primary focus of the project. Other developments are related to medical equipment interfacing and image visualization stations.

Acquiring images from medical equipment has been sometimes difficult in the past because medical machines were not designed for an open use within an information system. Today this acquisition does not represent a problem: in the PARCS project some special development is planned in order to complain with the relevant standards, but no major activities are planned on this issue.

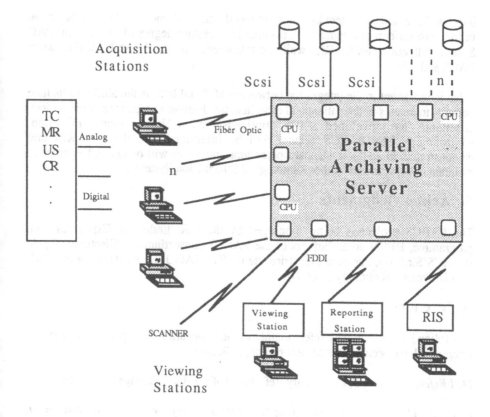

Fig. 1. PARCS Architecture

Within the project a low cost, PC based visualization station will be developed. The workstation will be based on advanced transputer based graphics boards and will provide a two-dimensional image analysis package, able to run on multiple boards inside a PC, in order to control multiple monitors (multiple monitors are usually provided by PACS vendors). The ability to connect, using transputer links, multiple graphics boards is a key point in building such stations: instead of having expensive, specially designed boards with multiple outputs, a low cost workstation can be built on the basis of single general purpose boards. In addition, parallelism can be very useful for advanced image processing algorithms.

The low cost visualization station will be one of the possible medical workstations in the PARCS architecture. The openess of the architecture, designed on industry standard networks, will allow other image analysis workstations to be integrated with the system, allowing for example the integration of 3D TC or NMR advanced software running on existing platforms.

Another area where openess is important relates to the integration with Radiological Information Systems (RIS) and Hospital Information Systems (HIS). The distinction between RIS and HIS is important because, even if a convergency of RIS and HIS into one Information System has been frequently claimed, most of the hospitals have in fact two different systems with, eventually, a certain degree of integration. PAC Systems integrate into the RIS, while no relationship is usually established between PACS and HIS.

What is important in the integration between PACS and RIS, is the ability to include pointers to images in the patient and examinations databases. A partner in the project, Gisettanta, has developed a RIS application on a Unix server - PC client environment. The PARCS system will be integrated into the G70 RIS and demonstrated: in addition, standard procedural interfaces will be defined in order to maintain openess towards other Radiological Information Systems.

5. Acknowledgments

The PARCS project is being sponsored by the EEC under the Esprit research programme, HPCN area. Partners of the PARCS consortium are Gisettanta S.p.A. (I), ACS S.r.l. (I), Parsytec Industriesysteme (G), SAGO S.p.A. (I), Intrasoft (Gr), Pisa University Radiology Dept. (I).

References

The following bibliography refers mainly to the application area: parallel technology references have been limited to very recent publications.

MPI Reference Manual, Preliminary References of standard Massage Passing Interface

Medical Diagnostic Imaging Support System: Performance Work Statement, Technical Report of Medical Diagnostic Imaging Support Development Team, US Army Engineering Division, Huntsville, 1990

The ACR-NEMA V.3.0 standard, Report of the National Electrical Manufacturers Association (NEMA) on ACR-NEMA standard, Washington, 1993

D.M. Hailey, B.L. Crowe, *Digital Radiology Systems : Some Pratical Considerations*, Hospimedica, 1991

H.U. Lemke, *Europeans begin to close PACS technology gap*, Diagnostic Imaging International, October 1990

B.B. Zobel, N. De Stefano, R. Passariello *PACS: state of the art and Perspectives*, University of Rome and University of L'Aquila, Internal Report

The Performance of a Parallel Scheme Using the Divide-and-Conquer Method

Qi Yang[1], Clement Yu[1], and Chengwen Liu[2]

[1] Department of EECS, University of Illinois at Chicago, Illinois
[2] Department of Computer Science, Depaul University, Chicago, Illinois

In a database system, relations usually have very large sizes, and it is desirable to process data in parallel to obtain high performance. A natural approach for parallel processing in data intensive applications is to employ the *divide-and-conquer* method. In [YY92], we use a linear recursive program to formalize problems to be parallized, develop a parallel scheme, PADAC Scheme, based on the divide-and-conquer method, and give a sufficient and necessary condition as to when the parallel scheme is equivalent to the sequential linear program. A parallel hybrid algorithm has been developed from our PADAC Scheme [YLY94].

Program 1
r_1 $p(\{x\}, W) : - b(x, W).$
r_2 $p(S, W)$ $:- select(x, S),$
            $difference(S, x, SS),$
            $p(SS, WS),$
            $b(x, u),$
            $m(u, WS, W).$

The following Parallel Divide-And-Conquer Scheme is developed to evaluate Program 1, assuming there are K processors.

PADAC Scheme
Phase 1 The input set S is partitioned non-decreasingly into K non-empty subsets S_i;

Phase 2 The original Program 1 (or any equivalent program) is executed at each site i with S_i as the input to produce a partial answer W_i;

Phase 3 The merging function f represented by the predicate $m(u, WS, W)$ is applied to those partial answers to form the final answer.

Theorem 1. *The PADAC Scheme is equivalent to Program 1 if and only if*
   P1   *There exists a partial order $\prec$ on any input set S such that for any $x \in S$, $select(x, S)$ is true if and only if x is a minimal element of S with respect to $\prec$.*
   P2   *The function f is associative with respect to $\prec$.*

The Performance of the PADAC Scheme
We assume a shared-nothing architecture. The input size n can be very large, while the number of processors K is limited. The main memory at a site is not

large enough to keep all data needed, even for a subproblem with a smaller input size after the partitioning. Thus, I/O time becomes the dominating factor in the response time and it is chosen as the performance metrics.

Let the time complexity of a fastest sequential algorithm be $RT_s(n) = \Theta(n^\gamma) = \Theta(n^{c_1} \log^{c_2} n)$ for some constants c_1 and c_2. Let $Div(n, K)$ be the time for the dividing phase including the I/O time in partitioning the input set and the communication time in sending the partitioned input subsets to their destination sites, $Proc(n, K)$ the I/O time for the local processing phase, and $Merge(n, K)$ the time for the merging phase including the communication time to send intermediate results across site and the I/O time at those merging sites. Then, the response time of the PADAC Scheme is

$$RT_p(n, K) = Div(n, K) + Proc(n, K) + Merge(n, K),$$

and the speedup of the PADAC Scheme is

$$Speedup = \frac{RT_s(n)}{RT_p(n,K)}.$$

When $Speedup = C \times K$ for some constant C, where $0 < C \leq 1$, we say linear speedup has been achieved. Linear speedup is the best a parallel algorithm can reach compared with a fastest sequential algorithm. We will give a necessary and sufficient condition for the PADAC Scheme to achieve linear speedup.

Lemma 2. *When $\beta > 0$, the merging phase of the PADAC Scheme has the same time complexity as the merging function, that is, $Merge(n, K) = \Theta(T_f(n))$.*

Lemma 3. *If the dividing phase has time complexity of a higher order than $\Theta(\frac{RT_s(n)}{K})$, then the PADAC Scheme can not reach linear speedup.*

Lemma 4. *Assume $RT_s(n) = \Theta(n^{c_1} \log^{c_2} n)$ and $c_1 > 1$. Then, any merging function f in the PADAC Scheme will have at least the same time complexity of $RT_s(n)$, that is, $T_f(n) = \Omega(RT_s(n))$.*

Theorem 5. *Assume the fastest sequential algorithm has time complexity $RT_s(n) = \Theta(n^{c_1} \log^{c_2} n)$ for some constants $c_1 \geq 1$ and c_2. Then the PADAC Scheme achieves linear speedup if and only if*

(1) $RT_s(n) = \Theta(n \log^{c_2} n)$, i.e., $c_1 = 1$;

(2) The dividing phase takes time at most $O(\frac{RT_s(n)}{K})$, i.e., $Div(n, K) = O(\frac{n \log^{c_2} n}{K})$; and

(3) The merging function has time complexity of a lower order of magnitude than $RT_s(n)$, i.e., $T_f(n) = o(n \log^{c_2} n)$.

References

[YY91]   Q. Yang and C. Yu, *Parallelization by the Divide-And-Conquer Method*, IEEE Systems, Man and Cybernetics Conference, Chicago, 1992, pp. 1265-1270.

[YLY94] Q. Yang, C. Liu, C. Yu, G. Wang and T. Pham, *A Hybrid Transitive Closure Algorithm for Sequential and Parallel Processing*, IEEE International Conference on Data Engineering, 1994, pp. 498-505.

Author Index

Springer-Verlag
and the Environment

We at Springer-Verlag firmly believe that an international science publisher has a special obligation to the environment, and our corporate policies consistently reflect this conviction.

We also expect our business partners – paper mills, printers, packaging manufacturers, etc. – to commit themselves to using environmentally friendly materials and production processes.

The paper in this book is made from low- or no-chlorine pulp and is acid free, in conformance with international standards for paper permanency.

Lecture Notes in Computer Science

For information about Vols. 1–719
please contact your bookseller or Springer-Verlag